CAN-AM

Pete Lyons

Motorbooks International
Publishers & Wholesalers

First published in 1995 by Motorbooks International Publishers & Wholesalers, PO Box 2, 729 Prospect Avenue, Osceola, WI 54020 USA

Motorbooks International books are also available at discounts in bulk quantity for industrial or sales-promotional use. For details write to Special Sales Manager at the Publisher's address

Library of Congress Cataloging-in-Publication Data
Lyons, Pete.
    Can-Am / Pete Lyons.
        p.   cm.
    Includes index.
    ISBN 0-7603-0017-8 (hardcover)
    1. Canadian-American Challenge Cup–History. I. Title.
    GV 1033.5.C3L95   1995
    796.7'2'097–dc20   95-6115

On the front cover: Bruce McLaren in the M8B, St. Jovite 1969. A skirmish with John Surtees provided the battle scars on the car's nose. *D.J. Markle*
On the frontispiece: Mosport: Still life with helmet, garland, and 750 horses—Denny Hulme's 21st Can-Am victory. *Pete Lyons*
On the title page: Running nearly free of rules, the "Big Banger" sports racers shook the earth; Bridgehampton 1968. *Dave Friedman*
On the back cover: Color photo: At Riverside in 1968, Hall's winged Chaparral 2G (#66) and Parsons' Lola T160 (#10) suggest the variety of designs showcased in the original Can-Am. *Pete Lyons* Black &white photo: Michigan 1969: McLaren, Hulme, and Gurney celebrate their respective 1-2-3 finishes each at the wheel of a McLaren. *Dave Friedman*

Printed in Hong Kong

ACKNOWLEDGMENTS

This book was a seed in my mind for at least twenty years. All that time I kept expecting others to bring forth Can-Am histories of their own. Now that I have done it, finally, I understand why they didn't! It has been an enormous task, well beyond anything I could have accomplished without the enthusiastic help of a great many people.

Foremost among them stands my wife, Lorna, whose assistance, encouragement, and forbearance were even more valuable than the priceless, tangible contribution she made to our book. The tables of starting grids, race results, and final points standings, exhaustively researched and painstakingly assembled for every one of the seventy-one Can-Am races from 1966 through 1974, are all her work. And it was indeed work, carried out triumphantly despite myriad frustrating and incomprehensible anomalies, contradictions, gaps, and obvious—but often unresolvable—errors in the published record and/or surviving original documentation. Lorna sometimes sputtered over all this, but she never got mad, she didn't quit, and I love her more than ever.

Both of us, in this connection, are deeply grateful to friends, as well as to strangers who became friends, for so readily sharing materials from their own collections. These certainly include Bob Brockington and Doug Waters, Canadian historians dedicated to their country's great racing heritage, as well as Harvey Hudes, whose help with points of Mosport Park's significant Can-Am history is greatly appreciated. Roger Jaynes of Road America also deserves our thanks for supplying data we could find nowhere else. Paul Joncas at Automobilia was another who generously shared his research. A very big salute goes to Steve and Debbie Earle, whose glorious Monterey Historic Races is matched only by their library of motor racing history.

Similar unselfish assistance came our way from many staff members at major motorsports publications. England's *Autosport*, to which I am eternally indebted for assigning me to cover the old Can-Am series in the first place, granted free run of its remarkable archives; particular thanks to Simon Taylor, once my editor and now my benefactor; and thumbs-up as well to Jeff Bloxham and Simon Morris. I found reports in *Autocar* a big help too, and they were made available by the man who wrote them, my friend Ray Hutton. Thanks to a stalwart colleague of many years, Quentin Spurring, and the impressively knowledgeable Alan Lis, I came away from *Racecar Engineering* with some invaluable data. I found more at Karl Ludvigsen's vast yet efficiently managed library and reference service in London. To Eoin Young, I am grateful for a helpful look through some marvelous old books in his Motor Media vaults at East Horsley.

On this side of the water, *AutoWeek*'s value to this project was enormous, and not only because of its comprehensive records of races and background events of three decades and more ago. Today's magazine, in the persons of Leon Mandel, Matt DeLorenzo, and Kevin Wilson in particular, earned my deep gratitude for bringing me into closer involvement with the burgeoning vintage racing scene, where so many fine old Can-Am cars and Can-Am people race on. Over at *Car and Driver*, both Csaba Csere and William Jeanes take a place in my roster of heros through their generosity over the years with their publication's comprehensive archives—and its red-hot photocopier! At *Road & Track* Tom Bryant opened the door of the company library, where Otis Meyer turned up information and pictures nobody else had. More excellent photos were supplied by Jane Barrett of Petersen Publishing. Ron Hussey was a great help on the photo side, too.

All these sources contributed mountains of reference material, but I can't stop short of saying a heartfelt "Great job!" to the writers and photographers who created it all to begin with.

Most of all, I want to recognize the vital roles played in this book by everyone at *Vintage Motorsport* magazine in whose pages much–but not all–of this material appeared: Art Eastman, whose vision and encouragement made it happen; John Gardner, a fountain of orderly assistance; David "Woody" Woodhouse, whose expertise saved me from many foolish blunders; Jim Sitz, whose incredible knowledge of racing history often kept me on track; our late friend Dean Batchelor, who freely offered both information and advice; and Syd Silverman, who made it all possible.

Individuals who helped are almost too numerous to thank, but I'll try. In no particular order they include Marilyn Halder, the former Mrs. Motschenbacher, who shared some wonderful old video clips and even better insights; Henry Alexander, keeper of the Can-Am flame—and a valuable list of cars and contacts; Pete Lovely, who dropped some deeply appreciated information in the mail one day; Mike Martin and Rich Robbins, generous men I've never had the luck to meet, who did the same; Lynn Larson, vintage racer and McLaren enthusiast who sent more video as well as mountains of research materials; and Bob Lee III, another in the fraternity of those who own, race, and help others understand their love for the great old cars. Then there's Fred Cziska, who went so far as to let me *drive* his! The same generosity was shown by Bud, Craig, and Kirt Bennett of R.M. Motorsports.

As a word guy, I can't agree that "image is everything," but the photographers who made their superb work available deserve particular credit. For fairness, I'll hand it out alphabetically: Tyler Alexander, Lionel Birnbom, Joe Cali, Jim Chambers, Dave Friedman, Geoff Goddard, Ray Hutton, Su Kemper, Charles Loring, D.J. Markle, David Phipps, Joe Rusz, my old Can-Am companion Jerry Schmitt, Barry Tenin, Henry Thomas, Bob Tronolone, Dale von Trebra, Bill Warner, and Cam Warren. To these I add my sister and racing buddy, Claire Lyons McHenry, and my late father, Ozzie Lyons, who set me on this road. I only wish there had been room to use more of everyone's splendid images.

Another important photographic contributor was David Hahs, whose darkroom skill brought many an old negative to sparkling life.

During the past two years it has been my good fortune and pleasure to seek out and speak with many of the drivers and mechanics and managers of the old Can-Am days. Again, I'll list them this way: Kerry Agapiou, Tyler Alexander (yes, the closet lensman), Gordon Barrett, Tracy Bird, Bob Bondurant, John Collins, Jack Deren, George Follmer, Tom Frederick, Howden Ganley, Peter Gethin, Alec Greaves, Dan Gurney, Carl Haas, Jim Hall, Hurley Haywood, Phil Hill, Skip Hudson, Leonard Janke, Karl Kainhofer, Jim Kaser, Charlie Kemp, Oscar Koveleski, Teddy Mayer, Wes McNay, John Morton, Fred Nething, Jackie Oliver, Sam Posey, Brian Redman, Troy Rogers, David Saville-Peck, and John Surtees. There were many more I hoped to include, only to run out of time and space; to those I didn't reach, or inadvertently left off this list, I offer my apologies, and my hope I can do justice to your story one day.

All of the people already mentioned richly deserve acknowledgment, but there are a few special individuals to whom I wish to dedicate this book. So:

Bruce, Carlos, Dick, François, Graham, Hawkeye, Herbert, Hiroshi, James, Jerry, Jo, Mark, Mike, Pedro, Peter, Revvie, Richie, Roger, Seppi, Stan, and Swede, and also Sherry and Spanky and Barry, and especially Denny, who made me promise to do it in the first place; this is for you.

—*Pete Lyons, Big Bear, California, June 1995*

The Grand Adventure

A great hammer struck my spine, slamming my head back. I forced it down, and stared at the long black roadway between the orange wheel bulges. It was rushing like some demonic torrent frantic to enter the gates of hell. Small markings—stains, patches, pebbles—appeared as flickers and were gone like dust on a cine film. There was no longer any sensation of speed. We were going too fast.

A bridge flashed overhead like an aircraft's shadow. The wide straight kinked to the left. Still absolutely on full bore, the McLaren bent into it. The world tilted on edge. To hold myself away from the driver's arms, I had to strain every tendon. Just ahead, the world ended in a boilerplate wall. The last time I'd seen the tachometer, it had been showing 6600. That had been 184mph, but Peter Revson's foot had been hard down ever since. I couldn't look at it now. My eyes were stuck on that wall.

I lived through that. It happened in 1971, when that year's Can-Am champion took me around Riverside International Raceway in his McLaren M8F. The experience still stands as one of the greatest of my life.

Revson's gone now; so is Riverside, and the old, original Canadian-American Challenge Cup race series came to a sad end within three years of that vivid October day. Happily, I have my memories—and a copy of the story I wrote about "Riding with Revvie" for *Autosport*, the British weekly for which I was covering the Can-Am. I was a naively enthusiastic young motorsports reporter then, living in the Ford Econoline van that toted me and my typewriter some 40,000 miles a year to race tracks all over North America.

A wretched existence, obviously, but it did afford the occasional bright spot. Like my rocket ride aboard the fastest road racer that had yet burned the face of the earth.

It's like an insane bull. There is a shattering bellow going on, which I feel as much as hear. I feel it in my chest. Everything behind me seems to be trying to push through to the front of me. The straight is nothing before such acceleration; it hurls back at us like a snapped rubber band.

They were the fastest, grandest cars in the world; that's what everyone remembers about the original, almost limitless Can-Am. Critics found things to say against the series itself, but its fans—yes, I was one—loved the cars. It's been a human generation since these wild racers last roared in rage, but you still can interject their wondrous memory into any bench-racing session and watch eyes and mouths open.

Jointly sanctioned by the Canadian Automobile Sport Clubs (CASC) and the Sports Car Club of America (SCCA), the Canadian-American Challenge Cup series of 1966 through 1974 was something more than a mere nine seasons of sports car spectacle. It was an automotive adventure, a noble experiment in virtually unrestricted technology which gave us the most powerful, fastest road course vehicles that had ever been seen. Track for track, year for year, these "Big Bangers," at their best, proved themselves quicker than contemporary Formula Ones.

Riding with Revvie: The author's 190mph jaunt around Riverside in a 1971 McLaren M8F with that year's Can-Am champion remains one of the greater experiences of his life. *Autosport*

Moving the Earth: Peter Revson, McLaren M20, powerslides the hairpin, Laguna Seca 1972. *Pete Lyons*

McLeagle Biplane: Dan Gurney tries a second wing on his much-modified McLaren M6B during practice, St. Jovite 1969. *Pete Lyons*

No, the Can-Am was not perfect *Formule Libre*—a formula free of rules. The cars were classified as International Automobile Federation (FIA) Group 7 cars, and they did have to meet certain regulations, even from the start. Those restrictions tended to multiply over time, but they remained much less constraining than in any other class. There was never a maximum engine size, nor a minimum weight. No limitations on tire size, or structural material, or turbocharger boost pressure were ever imposed. Imagination was free to roam in nearly every direction, so the boundaries of performance were being stretched in every dimension, and I had the giddy good fortune to be able to watch.

Crossing the continent to the next Can-Am, we could never be sure what we'd find. It might turn out to be simply a McLaren taken to the unimaginable next level of design elegance. But there might be an all-new Chaparral with a totally novel aerodynamic concept. Or the Ti22 "Titanium Car" that very nearly out-McLarened the McLarens. Or that first Shadow, with its startling tiny tires.

The Can-Am gave us the biggest Ferrari V-12 ever created and the turbocharged Porsche flat-12, the mightiest powerplant road racing had ever seen. Once, we found a vehicle with four small engines driving all four wheels. Sometimes we were treated to the delicious sounds of high-revving, Euro-style power. But always,

the very air trembled to the thunder of the *real* Can-Am Motor, the big-block American V-8.

They were so raw! Even at idle, the sound could send shivers from the soles of your shoes all the way up your spine. Sometimes I'd kneel behind a big Chevy being warmed up, right in close where the acrid blast from those cannon exhausts could beat on me, my body rocking to the throbbing of each of those mighty pistons, the sharp fumes crinkling my nose and watering my eyes. I could take about ten, maybe twelve seconds of it.

The Can-Am car combined rarefied aerospace science with the red-meat muscle of the dragster, the sophisticated European method with gaudy Indy showmanship. It all added up to the greatest auto racing show in the world, or so many of us thought, and for those of us who loved the Can-Am in its prime, nothing ever quite filled the void after it was gone.

Bristling with Innovation: Jim Hall's Chaparral 2E introduced hub-mounted wings and flank-mounted radiators. Las Vegas 1966. *Bob Tronolone*

Top left: Fan Car: Jackie Stewart's Chaparral 2J Ground Effects Vehicle, Watkins Glen 1970. *Dale von Trebra*

Top right: Unfair Advantage: Mark Donohue's horsepower screw could whip up almost a thousand of them; Porsche 917/10K, 1972. *Pete Lyons*

Below: Brave Try: Vic Elford struggles with the "tiny tire" AVS Shadow Mk I, Mid-Ohio 1970. *Pete Lyons*

Maybe I was a wide-eyed youth, but I used to think that cowering behind a guardrail as a Can-Am car slammed by with its dander up was one of life's great experiences. It almost did move the earth.

From the pits, the first corner is Turn 2, a 120-odd-mph right-hander entering a little valley which holds the esses. From the track you can't see all the way around 2; it vanishes between dun-colored slopes. The track is a dark gray band, and on it is a black arc. You know that arc is your lifeline. You must hit it precisely. It's all shooting back at you like falling off a mountain. It looks narrow. It's arriving very fast. Too fast, really, to think about.

The engine's throb eases. Revson's hands press the wheel. The McLaren has darted around. It was over like the lash of a whip. For one instant there was a bucket-on-a-rope sensation, then that huge engine was driving again and we were straight.

That was the only moment in the entire ride I felt any apprehension. That magnificent automobile had shrugged off that curve with such contempt that I surrendered myself completely. No twinge of doubt about the car's abilities ever formed again. I relaxed.

Though the cars commanded the attention, the Can-Am was officially a driver's championship, and a most lucrative one, thanks to Johnson Wax, the earliest major corporate sponsor in American road racing. The J-Wax Can-Am grew to be a Million-Dollar Spectacle, and attracted some of the greatest professional drivers of its epic era.

The first title winner, Briton John Surtees, was also a World Champion. So was two-time series winner Denny Hulme from New Zealand. Indianapolis victor Mark Donohue also earned himself a Can-Am trophy, as did fellow Americans Peter Revson and George Follmer. Final champion Jackie Oliver won for England again. All were F1 drivers too, as was Bruce McLaren, the New Zealander who built the cars that dominated the Can-Am for five years, and who drove them to two series triumphs of his own.

To win their titles, these men had to beat world-class talent like Amon. And Andretti. Bondurant. Bonnier. Brabham. Cevert. Elford. Foyt. Ganley. Gethin. Gregg. Gregory. Gurney. Hall. Hill. Hobbs. Hunt. Jarier. Jones. Lawrence. Merzario. Minter. Motschenbacher. Mueller. Pace. Parsons. Patrick. Posey. Redman. Rodriguez. Savage. Scheckter. Scott. Siffert. Spence. Stewart.

In the nine original Can-Am seasons there were seventy-one races on fourteen road courses across Canada and the United States. Sixteen drivers won, 115 scored points. Their best man? Denny-the-Bear Hulme, of course, whose twenty-two victories far outstripped the nine apiece of McLaren and Donohue.

The aerodynamics squash the car to the road, and it changes direction like a puma chasing a rabbit. Slashing through the esses is like being attacked on both sides at once.

The brakes are the car's most phenomenal feature. Flying down into Turn 9, aiming squarely at that boiler-plate wall at 190mph, Revvie's right leg makes one strong pumping movement, and a tremendous force, like a giant octopus, tries to suck me down into the footwell.

Pegasus: Chris Amon pops the air brakes in the winged big Ferrari 612P, Las Vegas 1968. *Bob Tronolone*

Beyond the caliber of the driving, what made the Can-Am so great were the sights and the sounds and the sensations of the cars themselves, not the on-track competition. Having attended the majority of races in the unlimited era, I must admit: most were processional. There were bright sparkling moments of tight and/or unpredictable racing, but moments were all they ever turned out to be. Each spring, hope sprang anew for better sustained competition, but the hope went forever unfulfilled. Every autumn's outcome turned out to have been decided months before, when one team best marshaled its resources and its will to tackle the job properly.

Usually, that was Bruce McLaren Motor Racing. Statistics confirm everyone's memory that the personable young driver/engineer was by far the most successful Can-Am constructor. Over the seven seasons his fac-

Chaparral, Ferrari, Lola, March, Porsche, and Shadow. Ford kept threatening to weigh in, too, and there was a remarkable number of homebuilts—some of remarkable design. Sometimes a vivid little Alfa Romeo or Matra or Porsche enduro car would enliven the show, and once the smallest machine in the field did outlast the biggest of the bruisers to win.

But the Kiwi camp seemed impregnable—until 1972, when Porsche allied itself with the Roger Penske organization and drivers Mark Donohue and George Follmer. Together they developed the most powerful road racing car ever seen, a turbocharged, twelve-cylinder device immediately named the *Panzer* for its crushing presence.

While the Porsche showed some early flaws, so that Hulme's outpowered McLaren was able to score two

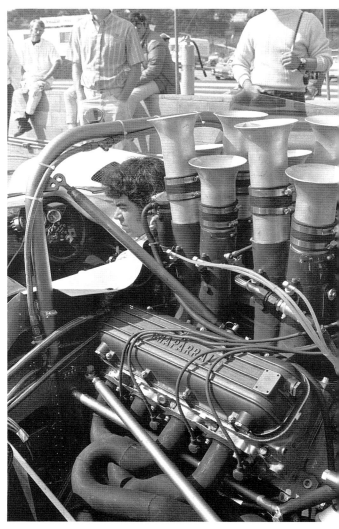

Fearsome Foursome: The four-engined, four-wheel-drive Hoare *Mac's-It Spl.* gave driver Hiroshi Fushida two more two-strokes in front; Laguna Seca 1970. *Pete Lyons*

Can-Am Thunder: Engine man Barry Crowe warms up Jackie Oliver's mighty 495 Chevy; Bryant Ti22 "Titanium Car," Laguna Seca 1970. *Pete Lyons*

tory team competed, 1966 through 1972, it entered fifty-eight events and won thirty-nine—67 percent. Privately owned McLarens won four additional Can-Ams, including the seventy-first, in 1974. That totals forty-three wins for McLaren chassis, or 60 percent.

It did take McLaren a year to come right. The inaugural Can-Am champion, John Surtees, drove a Lola to win three races. Drivers of two other Lolas and a Chaparral took the other three. McLaren's little company had to put that first season down as R&D.

But Denny Hulme drove one of Bruce's cars to victory in the first race of 1967, and that began a domination by the distinctive yellow-orange factory McLarens that lasted right through 1971. Their thirty-seven wins in the forty-three races of those five seasons come to 86 percent. They had a run of nineteen straight at one point, including all eleven races held in 1969, the Can-Am's peak year. During the same period, they strung together twenty-four consecutive pole positions. "The Kiwis," McLaren himself and Hulme, alternated the championship for three years. The Bruce and Denny Show, we called it. Bruce lost his life in a testing accident early in 1970, but Denny held the team together and won the title a second time. In 1971, his new teammate, Peter Revson, scored a McLaren driver's fifth consecutive championship.

Through these years, occasional strong assaults had been mounted by cars from BRM, Bryant (the Ti22),

more victories, by mid-season, Donohue and Follmer were in their stride. The Mark and George Show played the lead roles in six of the nine races (McLaren privateer François Cevert lucked into a win once) and Follmer became the new champion.

Overwhelmed by the Penske/Porsche budget and the factory's facilities, the McLaren team dropped out at the end of that year. So, for its own reasons, did the series' sponsor. Clearly, the Can-Am was in decline. The annual number of races was trending down, as were spectator counts, and press coverage was both declining in quantity and increasingly negative. No significant new entrants were stepping up. No replacement series sponsor ever came aboard.

Driving alone for Penske in 1973, Donohue won six of the eight races in a new, even more stunningly superior Porsche. Privately entered, year-old TurboPanzers won both of the other two. Moments after the final checkered flag, Donohue announced his retirement. Not long afterward, Porsche did too, using as an excuse SCCA's inauguration of a turbo-taming fuel-consumption formula.

That left Shadow as the only top-line Can-Am constructor for 1974, and the firm's pair of big, black, Chevy-powered cars duly overshadowed the opposition. Though a less than cordial rivalry between teammates Follmer and Oliver added some spice to the George and Ollie Show, the Englishman won all of the first four rounds to clinch the championship. Scooter Patrick, in a leftover McLaren, took race five, and that turned out to be the last-ever big-bore Can-Am. Out of lack of interest, the scheduled sixth and seventh races were canceled, and eventually so was any idea of a 1975 season.

In later years, the term "Can-Am" has been periodically revived, but it has been pasted onto a succession of lesser types of car, each shackled by more and more restrictions. Some of the racing has been reasonably intense, but the sense of technological wonder has never been rekindled. I, for one, regret the application of the great old name to these promotions.

Did the original, open-class Can-Am have to die? Debate could be as endless as it would be fruitless. Whether the noble experiment failed because of something inherently wrong in its basic concept, or whether it was killed by unwarranted meddling with that concept, or whether it simply had run its natural course, may be argued forever.

What is apparent is that, after four seasons of series growth under a virtually free formula, new rules clamped on the cars for 1970 coincided with the beginning of decline. Aerodynamic restrictions imposed by the FIA cost the series its exciting Chaparrals and focused Porsche's attention on engines, the main area remaining open to innovation. The German manufactur-

er became the first large-scale auto maker to genuinely dedicate itself to Can-Am success. It chose to do so at a time the industry at large was increasingly preoccupied with ecological and other issues, and Porsche remained unchallenged.

The long bottom gear pulls us up above 90mph. There is a pause; my spongy body recoils forward, then...slam! I can see nothing but blue California sky. My flesh is melting into every rearward cranny of the cockpit. Another pause, another slam. The acceleration feels absolutely as strong as before.

The Can-Am was a creature of the sixties, that decade of revolution both cultural and technological, that time of Flower Children and astronauts. Auto racing's sixties opened with mid-engined cars changing the very shape of the sport and continued with ever-larger engines—and ever-bolder aerodynamics and ever-wider tires—shattering all previous concepts of performance limits. In dizzying succession we saw Carroll Shelby's wild and woolly Cobras, Ford Motor Company's open, epic assault on Le Mans, and Jim Hall's clandestine collaboration with General Motors on his enthrallingly innovative Chaparrals. Motorsport, long regarded as an obscure pursuit of the borderline lawless, was achieving social respectability. At a period of intoxicatingly rapid growth, free-formula racing seemed perfectly natural, and the Can-Am gave full expression to that heady spirit of freedom.

One Kiwi who Flew: New Zealander Bruce McLaren put his personal stamp on North American racing; Riverside 1968. *Dave Friedman*

Was it too much freedom? Society lost its innocence by decade's end, and so did Can-Am rulesmakers, who began to impose ever more stringent limitations. There were many reasons, and it took many seasons, but in retrospect, it seems that the mood changed overnight, over the New Year's Eve that began the new decade. The Sport of the Seventies—that was the vision of the marketing people who were now taking racing seriously, and to maximize its commercial potential, they wanted it more businesslike, better buttoned-down.

At the same time, society was becoming more concerned with crash safety and exhaust emissions, and automotive engineers were forced to forget about flat-out performance. Then, near the end of 1973, the OPEC oil crisis struck the world, and every race sanctioning body found itself in a public relations panic.

Perhaps the Can-Am did have to go the way it went, and, in any case, we cannot go back. But we're free to look back.

While it lasted, the headlong rush of performance progress was thrilling. When the Can-Am began, its typical small-block V-8s made about 500 horsepower; six years later, the turbocars were wrinkling the raceways with more than 1,000. And the power and the speed were visible. On the supple suspensions of the day, the cars would pitch and heel and heave and wobble, and storming out of turns they would hoist their noses and cock their tails, and often they'd snake away, leaving black rubber behind with their bellow. Can-Am cars *looked* fast, and they *looked* hard to drive. You didn't need a super-sophisticate's eye to see that something big was happening.

Best of all, you could ride in them. Today's on-board TV is good, but the old Can-Am car's passenger seat was better. Believe me.

Revvie's hands are in constant twirling motion, but seldom does he need more than about one-sixth steering lock. It seems smoother than I expected.

On one lap, trundling down through 7, he held up a finger to say, "Watch this." As the turn began to open out and we had begun to pile-drive forward again, he gave the wheel a big wrench to chuck the tail out and in the next instant stamped open the throttles. The whole massive stern of the car went into a severe tremble—tire vibration. I could feel all the various sprung and unsprung masses joggling against each other rapidly. It was much the sort of feeling you'd expect should an aircraft piston engine suddenly lose a propeller blade. It was so strong a phenomenon that I could easily visualize the whole car shaking apart. As we snapped back straight and blasted away up the next piece of road, Peter turned his face to me, and I could see his eyes through his visor asking me if I understood just how serious a problem this tire vibration is. I nodded vigorously. Two other times in the ride, at other places, this started to happen spontaneously, and I could feel Peter feathering the throttle to kill it.

You deserve to know what I haven't put in this book. In nine years and seventy-one races, many things happened which I regret there has been no room to recount.

Humor, for instance. Oscar Koveleski, Can-Am racer, founder of the Polish Racing Drivers of America, and a person who liked to wear false fangs as he drove his motor home to startle passing civilians, stirred up one lunch hour by staging a Mechanics Creeper Race. Another time, Oscar awarded a special trophy, the Polish Pole Position Pole. It was a big brass, well, *pole*, about eight feet long. I know because I was just able to get it into my van to transport it for the lucky winner. Whose identity, I'm sorry to say, has vanished from my memory.

But I do remember being in a motel room one night when Oscar almost purchased the SCCA. For a dollar, I think. He made out a check using a square of toilet paper. The club officer present refused to accept it because, as he exclaimed, "You forgot the carbon paper!" Too bad. Maybe things would have turned out differently.

Then there was Spanky Smith's Rear End. I still treasure the document certifying me as number twenty-one purchaser of one share (from a total issue of 1,798,345 and 1/2) of a venture involving the hinder parts of one Edwin, a.k.a. "Spanky," Smith, who was a good friend to all, whose Winnebago served especially as McLaren's motor home-away-from-home, and whose differential lunched itself one day in 1971. At least twenty-one of us were distraught enough at the prospect of losing lunch to chip in to help get it rebuilt. Spanky thanked us with handsome, custom-printed stock certificates, suitable for framing. One of these days I'll get around to framing mine.

The Can-Am was fun. A journalist—no, not me, darn it—once enlisted the McLaren guys to help him plant a phony story about a secret "two-speed axle" in hopes of getting a rival to print it. The victim bit beautifully. The conspiring mechanics enjoyed that one so hugely that subsequently their car turned up with a mysterious little control box next to the seat. It was black, measured about two inches by three, and had a switch and a couple of colored lights. No labels, though, and I couldn't trace any wiring. I used to take great pride in trying to dope out new tweaks for myself, before asking, but finally I confessed to one of the lads that this one defeated me. "Not to wonder," came the grinning response. "It's just for . . ." and he named the gullible hero of the previous prank. Unfortunately, I believe he'd learned his lesson by this time.

Maybe the best Can-Am gag I heard of was carried out by a couple of girls who emptied a tin of J-Wax, replaced the yellow goop with butterscotch pudding, and contrived to saunter down a pit lane eating it with their fingers just as a high official of the series sponsor came by. Big success.

Yes, it was fun, but all motorsports have their fun side. Everyone who ever went Can-Am racing has cherished memories of a great time and could fill a book of their own with stories of their own. But the good times, the laughs, the strong feeling of family that developed among many regulars were not what made the Can-Am what it was.

What did was the spectacular, fascinating march of nearly unrestrained technology; the power, the speed, the noise, the wings and other "moving aerodynamic devices," the talon-toed rubber on the road. Can-Am cars from 1966 through 1974 were unique in the world. That's why I've concentrated on them, trying to express some of their color and flavor and meaning. Especially, I hope, some of their personal meaning to me.

And it's why I've stopped when they did. Later generations of "Can-Am" racing are another story.

Fans of Europe's short-lived Can-Am counterpart, the Interserie, also won't find much material here. Though there was occasional crossover of both cars and drivers, Europe's series had very little to do with North America's. I leave the Interserie book to somebody who was there. For the same reason, Japan's Group 7 activity of the late 1960s finds no place here, either.

The Bear: Master of the Big Banger. Denny Hulme won nearly 40 percent of his Can-Ams; Laguna Seca 1972. *Jim Chambers*

where I always thought the gearbox broke, but everybody else's story says a wheel fell off, or a fuel line kinked, or the team manager blew up. Maybe what really happened was the driver got distracted by a cute face at the fence. I've tried to resolve such discrepancies where I could, but I'm braced to get a lot of letters.

Similarly, in poring over my old race reports I'm embarrassed to see now that all during the Can-Am I never did get Oscar's surname spelled right, and I persisted for years in describing engine man Gary Knutson as a Knudsen. I incorrectly used to put an "apostrophe S" after Mr. Johnson's excellent company name, too. Apologies all 'round, gentlemen.

And was it "Can-Am," or "CanAm?" The series sponsor's sticker carried by all the cars left the hyphen out, and so did I at the time—it was easier to type that way—but official contemporary documents render it "Can-Am," and now, unless directly quoting old material, so do I.

McLaren Mk. IIIb, or M1C? Porsche 917/30, or 917-30? Ferrari 712P, or 712M, or just plain 712? Arabic numbers, or Roman? Every variation has appeared in print. I've tried to choose whatever seems to make sense

Captain Nice: Excellent engineer and determined racer, Mark Donohue led Porsche's drive to dominate Group 7; Donnybrooke, 1972. *Pete Lyons*

Family Affair: Lothar Motschenbacher, always backed by wife Marilyn, ran more Can-Ams than anyone else. *Pete Lyons*

To be honest, just the Can-Am is enough to overwhelm this book. At the start of the project, I drew up grandiose plans to pack in everything conceivable: full race reports, not only of the Can-Am, but of every other Big Banger event ever held, as well as detailed descriptions of every car, exhaustive team and company histories, personnel biographies, retrospective interviews with everyone living, illustrative materials like cutaway drawings, track diagrams, and engine dyno curves, plus maybe a thousand pictures . . .

Gently, the publisher suggested I was trying to bite off more than his presses could chew. He made me see that I was behaving like a novice Can-Am car designer, one whose enchantment with the myriad possibilities of a free formula had blinded him to the necessity of getting a practical, competitive vehicle to the start line by race time. So, in the end, with sorrow, I left out some of the dream stuff. Maybe one day I'll get to build a second book.

Nor are collectors and speculators going to find here any listing of the lineage of individual Can-Am cars. I've mentioned a couple I'm sure of, but compiling and authenticating a detailed history of chassis numbers is a specialized task which I am not prepared to tackle.

Frankly, I've had enough trouble getting the straight racing story straight! Research can be a humbling experience, and not only because memory is mutable. I've turned up countless instances

in such cases and is most consistent with most other materials and best keeps clay off the story's boots.

One overall impression of my ride remains: a sensation of having entered another world. A first-class racing driver allowed me to visit the place where he is home. During those few minutes we were in a capsule, a cocoon, shut away from the familiar values of action, reaction, velocity. The old world was still there all around us, but it had nothing to do with us. We were enclosed in our own world. Different laws applied. Everything was magnified. The most delicate movement on a control produced intense response. A maneuver which, from the outside, looks easy and gentle, is a maelstrom of violence from the inside. A place on the road which looks from the outside to be a disturbing bump is not even perceived from within the car; two places at Riverside which look to be shallow elevation changes become to the race car a nasty spank on the bottom and a severe drop—at 185mph, the worst bump on the circuit. The individual lap, made up of seemingly unrelated curves and straights and hummocks, becomes a single long file of problems to be solved, presenting themselves to the driver like a stream of tracer bullets. All the passenger is able to do is follow, tardily, a few of the driver's more obvious solutions. When he appreciates that in fact the driver is coping with every problem precisely and punctually, and furthermore that he is actively with his right foot trying to make them come at him even faster, then the passenger's admiration rises in his throat. He would cheer, but he knows his voice would be as nothing against the bellow of the car.

Three times we flashed around. The better of the two lap times that were taken—using a point on the back straight—was 1min 38.5sec. I was pretty impressed with that, as it was a mere 2sec off last year's best race lap.... With all the factors slowing us down that day I felt Revvie had given me a damn fine ride—and I still felt so late in the day when he went out alone to shake off the feeling of being a bus driver and went 5sec faster. I had been taken up into his world as far as it was seemly for me to go. The farther reaches are his alone.

But I most certainly was sorry to stop!

Clown Prince: Oscar Koveleski's enthusiasm, energy, and impish sense of humor helped make the Can-Am fun. *Pete Lyons*

Can-Am Cooperation: Members of rival teams often pitched in to help a fellow competitor make it to the start line. *Pete Lyons*

Racing appeals to a certain outlaw streak in human nature, and racers have a tendency to feel their only real boundaries are the laws of physics—those, and perhaps the edges of the road. Imposed limits are irksome. The notion of running free of any artificial restraint strikes a deep chord.

Hence the immortal charm of the old Can-Am car. It was the wildest of automotive animals. Relatively ungoverned, it evolved more rapidly than did its contemporary cousins, and that evolution was pure. When new features appeared, it was simply because they made the car faster—not because some fretful rulesmaker was trying to slow it down, or cram it into a conceptual cage.

Thus year to year increases in Can-Am performance were meaningful. You felt they indicated the true state of the automotive art.

For as long, anyway, as the original "unlimited" format survived. Society resists permissiveness, and throughout the long, complex history of international motorsport, genuine *Formule Libre* categories have been rare and generally short-lived. They tend to be born in obscure corners and to attract wide attention at their peril.

So it was with the Can-Am car. It was conceived more by chance than plan and grew up on the fringes of established motor racing society. In other places and eras it might well have withered, but it found rich nourishment in the America of the 1960s. Very rapidly, it grew very big. Sadly, when the once-benign climate cooled and former friends turned away, the mighty beast could not survive.

American Road Racing Specials

Bench racers could spend many a happy hour debating the origins of Big Banger sports car racing, but one clear trail leads back to the mid-1930s and an organization of northeastern U.S. sports car enthusiasts called the Automobile Racing Club of America. Rather less grand than its title, ARCA was a small creation of wealthy amateur sportsmen racing strictly for their own amusement, and the cars they drove reflected a happy-go-lucky acceptance of anything a member enjoyed. Homemade specials were welcome alongside late-model European imports.

For example, club co-founder Miles Collier had a British MG which he raced at Le Mans, as well as in ARCA events. However, his friend Briggs Cunningham, who could easily afford any factory model he fancied, created his ideal sports special in his so-called BuMerc, a crash-damaged Mercedes SSK body grafted onto a Buick chassis with its straight-8 Century powertrain. A third approach was that of John Reuter, who took parts from as many as nineteen different makes of car, including a Ford V-8, to assemble the *Old Grey Mare*. This happy mongrel became ARCA's best-known and most successful individual racer.

Such hybrids and stripped-down specials were nothing new in racing, anywhere in the world, but ARCA's homegrown road racers had a special appeal to the U.S. enthusiast. Although the organization died away with World War II, after the conflict its spirit—and many of its members—started up again with the new Sports Car Club of America.

As had ARCA, as SCCA grew and began holding races, it accepted interesting, effective mechanical mixtures along with automobiles of purer blood. In the club's first major event, held in October 1948 around a 6.6-mile loop of country roads at Watkins Glen, New York, the most powerful car entered was a Grand Prix Maserati single-seater which its owner, George Weaver, called *Poison Lil*. But Briggs Cunningham brought his BuMerc homebuilt up and beat Weaver's GP veteran for second place. However, Frank Griswold finished ahead of them both in an Alfa Romeo coupe.

So as the highborn Europeans, the Jaguars and Ferraris and Porsches, ventured across the water to race, they were met and frequently vanquished by such sassy specials as Miles Collier's *Ardent Alligator*, which was a Ford-engined Riley, and a new Cunningham toy, a Cadillac-powered Healey-Silverstone.

It was Cunningham who took the next step, when he decided that the sports car world's most famous race, Le Mans, should be won by an American sports car. Since there was no such animal, he had to breed one. He began in 1950 with a pair of Cadillac sedans, one rebodied by Grumman aircraft engineers into a huge roadster immediately dubbed *Le Monstre*. Cunningham went on to launch a line of two-seaters which bore his name, and, with Chrysler power, he ultimately finished the French endurance epic in third place on two occasions. At home, the great, growling Cunninghams all but dominated SCCA racing nationwide for a period of the early fifties, including a grand victory against international factory opposition in the Sebring, Florida, 12-hour enduro of 1953.

For federal tax reasons, Cunningham shut down his car-building operation after five years, though his race team continued to campaign alternative makes. At the same time, many other enterprising American racers devised their own competition specials with various Detroit engines, but Cunningham's torch was grasped most firmly by another wealthy sportsman named Lance Reventlow.

Built in Los Angeles in 1958, Reventlow's Scarabs were beautifully crafted, European-style sports racers powered by the relatively light, efficient small-block V-8 which Chevrolet had been offering in passenger cars since 1955. The Scarab sports racers never competed overseas as originally intended because international rules changes outlawed their "big" engines, but they readily assumed the Cunningham mantle of ownership over U.S. road racing, which remained free of displacement limits.

It was a Scarab which emerged as the hero of the late 1958 event that launched professional sports car racing in the U.S. At the time, SCCA was still determined to preserve its members' amateur standing, whether they liked it or not. No such constraints were imposed by the United States Auto Club. This decidedly professional body's main event was the Indianapolis 500, but it saw commercial potential in road racing. USAC entered into a

Revolution Complete: At Laguna Seca in October 1964, only the Cheetah (#81), many rows to the rear, retains the ancient front-engined configuration. Charging well along in the new era are pole man Jim Hall's Chaparral 2A-Chevy (#66), Dan Gurney's Lotus 19-Ford (#19), and assorted Shelby King Cobras (Coopers), Huffaker Genies, Brabhams, etc. These ground-pounding Fall Series events, as well as SCCA's contemporary United States Road Racing Championship and other Big Banger shows in Canada and England, would give birth within two years to the Can-Am. *Dave Friedman*

Big Banger Beginnings: North American sports car racing has always mixed exotic imports with imaginative homegrown specials. Here, at Watkins Glen in September 1954, Briggs Cunningham dons his helmet before taking pole position in his American team's white-and-blue, highly modified 4.5-liter Ferrari 375MM (#20). Waiting in red-painted standard examples are Bill Spear (#100) and Gentleman Jim Kimberly (#5) while the pair of brutish, big Chrysler-Hemi-powered Cunningham C-4Rs will be manhandled by Sherwood Johnston (#19) and Phil Walters, a.k.a. "Ted Tappet" (#18). Walters will win. A mammoth race car even by the heroic standards of its day, the C-4R stood on a 100in wheelbase and weighed an estimated 2500lb. The chassis was made of parallel steel tubes gussed with steel sheeting to form twin oval rails. Front suspension was independent and made of Ford parts, while the live rear axle came from Chrysler. So did the engine, a 330ci (5.4 liter) all-iron V-8 with pushrod-operated inclined valves in hemispherical combustion chambers. As specially prepared for Cunningham by Chrysler factory engineers, the massive Hemi was probably capable of as much as 400hp. It drove the rear wheels through an Italian Siata truck transmission.
Ozzie Lyons photo

sponsorship arrangement with a major Los Angeles newspaper publisher and announced the prize-paying "U.S. Grand Prix for Sports Cars" for the weekend of October 12, 1958, on a new course east of the Southern California city of Riverside. The publicity and the purse, a then-impressive $14,500, attracted a stellar field.

From Indy came Johnny Parsons, Jim Rathmann, Troy Ruttmann, and Bobby Unser. Stock car driver Ray Crawford and hot rodder Ak Miller, both of whom already had also established road racing credentials, came too. So did, of course, American "amateur" sports car stars like Max Balchowsky (creator-driver of the ugly but effective *Ol' Yeller* specials), Richie Ginther, Masten Gregory, Dan Gurney, Phil Hill, and Carroll Shelby. Europeans already used to being paid for their services included Jean Behra and Roy Salvadori.

Mechanically, the field presented a magnificent sampling of the best imported sports racers of the day—Aston Martins, Ferraris, Maseratis, Porsches—as well as a Chevy-engined Lister, Balchowsky's Buick-powered car, and all three Scarab-Chevys.

It was a great grid, and from it roared an epic race. A crowd reported at 100,000 watched Reventlow's Chuck Daigh win a tremendous battle against Phil

Hill's factory-prepared 4.1-liter Ferrari 412MI. Preston Lerner's 1991 book, "Scarab," made it live again:

Daigh and Hill were locked in a heavyweight bout so fierce that the rest of the field had dropped both out of sight and out of mind. Lap after lap, the blue Scarab and the red Ferrari passed, repassed, and repassed yet again, often swapping the lead three and four times a lap, occasionally—and incredibly—switching places twice in a single corner. They were slipping and sliding, bumping and grinding, understeering into corners and oversteering out of them, the shrieking V-12 and rumbling V-8 singing a raucous duet as the cars slipstreamed down the mile-long backstretch. It was road racing at its best...

As Dean Batchelor recalled in *Vintage Motorsport* magazine, he had "never witnessed a sports car race anywhere that had the spectators, pit personnel, and race officials so personally involved . . ."

By the midpoint of the 203 miles, the heat of the day sent the Ferrari into the pits, leaving the Scarab unopposed. Not one of the spectators went home that day doubting he or she had watched an American product beat the world's best.

Riverside 1958 was a benchmark race, and it offers benchmark performance figures. Daigh had started from pole at 2:04.3, a record average speed of 94.85mph around the then-new 3.275-mile desert road course. A prime feature of that original Riverside lap configuration was a 1.1-mile-long straightaway, along which the best timed top speed of the weekend was the 4.1 Ferrari's 163mph. The Scarab itself was capable of 161, so it must have been getting through and/or out of the nine turns just that bit better.

That Scarab speed was actually established by *Road & Track* a few weeks later, when the magazine took the winning car back to the scene of its triumph for a test. *R&T*'s John Bond rode along with Lance Reventlow to hand-time the acceleration. Although Bond explained the test subject had a tired engine and a slightly slippy clutch, and though the drag strip (the back straight of the road course, run in reverse direction) trended gently uphill, he wrote that ". . . the car's performance exceeds any and all previous data recorded by us or by anyone else for that matter." He clocked 0–60mph in 4.2 seconds, 0–100 in 9.0, and the quarter-mile in 12.2 at 120mph. The measured maximum ve-

locity on that hairy occasion, 161 at 6500rpm, was an average; in one direction, the car reached 169. Other literature says the Scarabs were ultimately capable of 174mph.

Let us keep these figures in mind as we watch the performance progress of the unlimited sports racing car.

It was indeed an era of rapid progress. In 1958 a two-car Scarab team qualified on the front row at California's Laguna Seca with identical times of 1:20.4 around the 1.92-mile lap. Five years later, one Scarab, by now an aging veteran, had been improved enough to lap Laguna at 1:17.5. That earned it twenty-seventh place on the 1963 starting grid. Fastest qualifier then was Bob Holbert's mid-engined Shelby Cooper-Ford V-8, at 1:11.8. In five years, sports racing car lap speeds had gone up 10.7 percent.

So the once-dominant Scarabs went the way of all competition machines, but as we leave those so aesthetically appealing Reventlow automobiles behind, let us note fondly that theirs was still an era when race cars had enough in common with "real" cars that young Lance was able to mildly civilize one of his Scarabs and drive it on the streets of Beverly Hills. Sigh.

Lance Reventlow picked up Briggs Cunningham's torch and strove for international honor with his all-American Scarabs. Rules changes kept these Chevy-powered specials away from Europe, but at home they were all but dominant in the year of their birth, 1958. However, the Scarab's graceful front-engined design marked the moment before a seismic change in racing technology would change the very shape of the sport. Not long after the 1959 Daytona event pictured here—where Augie Pabst (#0) and Harry Heuer (#2) join battle with Bob Carnes' BoCar Stiletto (far right)—any constructor hoping to be competitive would have to follow the mid-engined lead of that little Porsche on the third row. But, as these now-privately owned Meister Braüser Scarabs roar off into history, they do demonstrate a dawning of the concern about aerodynamics that will, in its turn, reshape the next decade: Though conceptually a descendant of the Cunningham, the Scarab had advanced to a multi-tube space frame and a de Dion rear suspension. Wheelbase was 92in, maximum overall width of the aluminum body came to 64in (by the author's measurement), and according to a contemporary *Road & Track* performance test, the overall weight less fuel and driver came out somewhat heavier than planned at 1900lb. Some running gear parts were drawn from such production cars as Ford and Morris and also from oval-track supplier Halibrand while the Corvette supplied the small-block engine and transmission. For Reventlow, Traco Engineering provided a bore and stroke of 4.00x3.38in for a swept volume of 339.8ci (5.57 liters). Speedway-type Hilborn fuel injection was used, and as raced in 1958 the Chevy produced as much as 385hp at 6000rpm, and just over 400lb-ft of torque at 4000. *Photo by Bill Warner, age 16*

The Artful Roger: Reading the thin rulebook of the day more closely than those who wrote it, Roger Penske turned a wrecked Formula One Cooper-Climax into a sports car. Sure enough, the headlights of his *Zerex Spl.* are visible inside the nose inlet. The passenger seat would be visible if a little hatch to the driver's left were opened. Not visible here at Riverside 1962 is the outrage of Penske's opponents. Their adamant pressure to ban this "cheater car" brought about the SCCA regulations which defined what became FIA Group 7. *Bob Tronolone*

Fires of Revolution

Dual-purpose sports cars faded out of racing because sports car racing's purpose had become more serious. Winning was now worth more than a tin cup. Originally, SCCA was dedicated to amateurism, but the club responded to USAC's 1958 Riverside event—and subsequent forays—by gradually countenancing commercialism. Though some officials and members continued to resist turning their sport into business, others pointed out that money had always been changing hands under the table and argued it was best to deal openly to the profit of all.

Thus there grew up a "Pro Series" of SCCA races for prize money. These races were not formally organized as a group, but Riverside, Laguna Seca, and Kent, in Washington state, cooperated every autumn to put on what the press liked to call the "Fall Series." Bridgehampton and Watkins Glen in New York state, Elkhart Lake in Wisconsin, and Mosport

and St. Jovite in Canada were other places SCCA racers drove for dollars throughout the year.

SCCA's professional races had to be set up through ACCUS (Automobile Competition Committee of the United States), an organization of the major American motorsports sanctioning bodies. ACCUS was, and is, the local affiliate of the international governing body, the FIA in Paris. This liaison was necessary to obtain the "international listing" required by the FIA for each event before famous, crowd-drawing drivers from overseas could participate.

Even as U.S. sports car racing was becoming professional and the races more worth winning, so was the increasing application of hard science making the racing sports car more specialized for the job. Technology was advancing rapidly on many fronts, but most dramatically visible was the wholesale transformation of the very shape of the racing car.

England's Cooper and Germany's Porsche had spent the 1950s proving that ever more powerful engines could safely and effectively be carried behind the cockpits. The mid-engine revolution took the Formula One fortress in 1959, when Jack Brabham drove a Cooper with a 2.5-liter, 240hp Coventry Climax four-cylinder engine behind its single seat to the first of a back-to-back pair of World Championships. Shortly, both Cooper and Lotus were offering two-seat, full-bodied versions of their F1 designs as sports racers, both powered by the Climax. Neither the Cooper Monaco nor the Lotus Monte Carlo, a.k.a. Model 19, had anything to do with the storied streets of the Mediterranean principality, but they were very popular on the road courses of North America.

So popular that Yanks raised on hot rods couldn't resist yanking the wimpy little English four-banger in favor of a real man's motor. Engine transplants were no novelty, for they'd been performed since before the turn of the century in probably every country in which motorsports were conducted. But the new generation of mid-engined chassis seemed to be particularly inviting on a continent where millions of relatively huge engines were lying around in the grass of junkyards, crying out to be put to good use. Any added weight would be carried mainly on the rear wheels, thus helping traction instead of spoiling steering. Of course, there would be problems to solve regarding structural strength, engine cooling, fuel supply, driveline durability, etc., but specials builders loved challenges of that sort.

Perhaps the first such swap in America was accomplished in 1961 by Bob McKee, a bright young Indy mechanic from Chicago. He did it to the commission of Rodger Ward, the 500 winner who had become interested in road racing. The pair chose a Cooper Monaco and installed a small, lightweight V-8,

which Buick was making for a compact passenger car. The Buick nestled neatly into the Climax's engine bay, the V-8's extra width posing no problem in that location, and thanks to having both heads and block cast in aluminum (with iron cylinder liners), it weighed approximately 350lb, reportedly some twenty less than the Climax. McKee expanded the stock 215ci displacement (3.5 liter) to 254ci (4.2 liter), which yielded more torque, if not a lot more power.

After deciding the original Cooper transaxle as used in F1 wasn't up to the bigger job, McKee and employee Pete Weismann worked out a way to assemble their own. They began with the Corvette four-speed transmission but married it to the same Halibrand quick-change gearcase used in the original Scarabs and added certain Ford and Mercedes-Benz internal parts in a McKee-made differential housing. McKee went on to manufacture and sell these hybrid gearboxes as well as a series of complete race cars bearing his own name.

With a dry weight of some 1,100lb, that original Ward Cooper-Buick was a punchy little package which showed reasonable speed against its Climax-powered sisters in the 1961 autumn races at Riverside and Laguna Seca. Overheating put it out at both tracks, but not before it fired imaginations the lengths of both pit lanes. In short order there were Coopers and Lotuses packing other Buicks; the very similar little aluminum Oldsmobile; the heavier but more powerful iron Ford as used in the Cobra; the yet-heavier but still more powerful, Chevy; and even the huge Chrysler/Dodge Hemi. There were some Ferrari- and Maserati-engined ones, too.

Simultaneously, other can-do Americans and Canadians were creating their own complete cars to the new configuration. Bill Sadler of St. Catharine's, Ontario, was one of the first. In 1961, following experience with a one-off *Formule Libre* single-seater of the year before, he built two examples of his Mark V, a twin-seater with a Chevy engine behind. To send the power to the

Dan at Home: Local lad Gurney courteously shows the visiting McLaren the quick way through the high-speed Esses into tight Turn 6. The place is Riverside, where regional partisans will always believe big-time sports car racing began. The year is 1964, but Dan's highly modified Lotus is wearing both a chin spoiler and a nose-top airfoil. *Dave Friedman*

One Decade's Difference: Cunningham won the 12-hour Sebring classic in 1953 with the C-4R (top). Twelve years later, Chaparral builders Jim Hall and Hap Sharp accomplished the same feat with their 2A. Brought back to the battered old airfield circuit in 1985, the machines offered a graphic demonstration of the astonishing pace of technological development possible in unlimited sports car racing. Both were built in the U.S., and they pack Detroit V-8s of similar displacements, but advances in aerodynamic understanding, chassis conception, suspension dynamics, powertrain efficiency, materials, etc., left them little else in common. *Autosport*

wheels, he invented his own two-speed transaxle built into the quick-change Halibrand casting. Unfortunately, Sadler soon thereafter closed his doors, so his pioneering sports racer never got the development it deserved—an all-too-common fate of many good ideas.

That same year, Californian Bill Campbell put a Chevy into an existing car to create his mid-engined Corvette Special. In 1962, Reventlow built a single, mid-engined Scarab-Buick. The next year, Texans Jim Hall and Hap Sharp uncloaked the first of their Chaparral 2-Chevys while San Franciscan Joe Huffaker offered the first of two Marks of his Genie redesigned for the bigger engines, a package which included his own beefy transaxle. In 1964, Bob McKee established himself as a manufacturer with the first of his own cars, and any number of others tried to do the same.

European constructors were consumed by the revolution, too. Ferrari and Maserati began racing their first mid-engined sports models in 1961. The latter's led to little, but Ferrari's 3.0-liter V-12 model 250P of 1963 was the sire of a significant series, some cars of which would play roles in the Can-Am.

It was also in 1963 that Cooper modified its chassis by order of Carroll Shelby to better cope with the iron-block Ford engine, thus creating the King Cobras and, later, the follow-on Lang Coopers. During 1964, Lotus introduced its type 30, also built for the Ford, and McLaren brought out three different mid-engined sports racers: a Cooper-Oldsmobile; a McLaren-Oldsmobile; and a Ford GTX, the last a roofless lightweight on the basic GT40 endurance racing coupe design.

As all these raucous, high-power if low-tech, pushrod V-8s began to overwhelm the poor old twin-cam Coventry Climax, surely it was only altruistic com-

passion that motivated a young aluminum salesman and racing driver named Roger Penske to give the gallant British battler one more hour of honor.

Since postwar road racing in the U.S. came primarily under the aegis of the Sports Car Club of America, it was only logical that most of it had been done with full-bodied, two-seater vehicles. Perhaps it was too logical, for the understanding of the term "sports car" seems to have been taken too much for granted. Penske studied the rulebook and noticed a seemingly overlooked loophole.

He bought the wreckage of an F1 Cooper crashed in the 1961 U.S. Grand Prix, had the steel tube frame rebuilt, replaced the original 1.5-liter Climax with a 2.7, then topped off the result with all-new aluminum bodywork covering the wheels. The driver's seat remained on the centerline of the car, but outside the frame, to the left, Penske added a second seat under a hatch in the bodywork. This and headlights bolted inside the radiator duct constituted a "sports car," or so he informed SCCA tech inspectors when he presented his Dupont-sponsored *Zerex Special* in the autumn of 1962.

Penske's enterprise seems to have caught club officials by surprise. At least they appeared to have no clear-cut means of disallowing his F1-car-with-fenders. After all, he did have that second seat, never mind that it was functionally absurd, so they let him race at Riverside on October 14th. He won outright. On the 21st, at Laguna Seca, he won again, this time on aggregate by finishing second in both of two heats.

Roger's competitors did not take these defeats well. Never mind that, at Riverside, Dan Gurney's Lotus 19 had been ahead until it retired, and Jim Hall's Chaparral 1 set fastest lap. Nor were they mollified at Laguna when the Zerex was outpaced by the Gurney and Lloyd Ruby 19s, winners of the two heats. Everyone thought Penske's thinly disguised Grand Prix car was unfair. They wanted it banned.

The clamor began even before its second victory. Early in the Laguna Seca weekend, one of the disgruntled parties approached SCCA governing board member Alan Tracy Bird, and made his feelings clear.

"We depended a great deal on foreign participation," Bird explains today. "To attract European drivers, the event needed to be FIA-listed and approved. I was one of the first representatives to ACCUS from the SCCA, and I was assigned as the FIA observer to this race at Laguna Seca. During practice I saw Jim Hall, and he was very upset. He asked me to come and take a look at Penske's car and tell him what I thought about it. So I went down the line and asked Roger, 'Would you please have the tarp taken off?' and I stood right behind it.

"This race was for 'sports racing cars,' which was a very loose designation. But the rules said a guy had to

have two seats, one on either side of the centerline. Roger had one seat that was really in the center, just a shade off-center to the right, and then another real small seat to the left of centerline. It was obviously a cheater car.

"I couldn't do anything about it right at that time. I told Jim that. I told him when I got back to the next ACCUS meeting I'd describe this car and recommend that it be banned.

"Roger won the race, and at the victory banquet that night Bruce McLaren, along with some other Britishers, started complaining to me about the Penske car. They said, 'Unless the rules are more clearly defined, we're not coming back to these races.' They were adamant about that."

This threatened loss of European entries was especially serious in light of SCCA's ambitions for 1963. Only recently had the club opened itself to professionalism; now, for the first time, some of what had been an unstructured collection of individual money-paying sports car races across the U.S. were to be stitched together into the United States Road Racing Championship.

USRRC, Ancestor of the Can-Am

SCCA's new series was actually a move against the rival United States Auto Club, and Tracy Bird was one of the main movers. "USAC had been making noises about a professional sports car racing series, and we were concerned that we might lose our top competitors to them. I put in for a series of races of our own to be called the United States Road Racing Championship. I was stealing part of USAC's name, but they couldn't lay claim to 'United States.' That pretty well stopped them."

That first USRRC season of eight events would begin in February. The rules problem had to be resolved right away. SCCA did order Penske to rebuild his ex-F1 car as a more recognizably legitimate two-seater for 1963 (this didn't slow it down any; it continued to win), but the club also appointed Bird chairman of its Competition Board, a position where he could tackle the regulation situation head-on.

Bird had some personal background for the task, including experience with hot rods, dirt track racers, and a long string of sports cars. Several of those could be classified as specials, especially the Cooper Monaco into which he stuffed a Ferrari V-12. But he wanted to bring in the best specials-builder mind he knew of.

"It was our policy to include one so-called professional driver on the Competition Board," Tracy says, "along with other amateurs like me. I told Jim Hall I wanted him. He said he was too busy, but finally he agreed, and we started.

"I'd call him after eight o'clock at night, to get the cheap rate, and we'd talk things over. He'd go out and

measure his car, and I'd go out and measure mine, and we'd come back to the phone and compare notes. That way we rewrote the rules, which were basically accepted verbatim by the FIA."

These regulations appeared in the International Sporting Code to define a class of race car then known as Group 9, later as Group 7. The two-seater aspect was firmly resolved, and rules established a cockpit of certain dimensions, two doors of specified minimum size, and bodywork that had to cover all four tires and remain fixed in normal position throughout an event.

It should be noted that there was no specific plan here to establish a totally unlimited formula. True, many aspects were left free, including engine size, but Bird says his goal was simply to create "a big, interesting car that would go fast. A two-seater with an envelope body, of course, not a single-seater; that was the sports car legacy. But it had to be a race car. No 'FIA suitcases,' and that sort of thing. That old idea of a race car that you could drive on the street never did work out."

One man's opinion.

The USRRC series began in 1963 and continued through six seasons to a total of fifty-two races at sixteen places. Some events were processional, but many, especially in the first years, were genuinely good, close, exciting contests. Counting only overall big-car victories (there was a separate under-2.0-liter division), races were won by a total of twenty-two drivers, including co-drivers on occasion, and five were crowned USRR Champions.

First champ was Bob Holbert, who swapped back and forth between a Porsche and a Shelby Cobra; then Jim Hall proved his new Chaparral by winning in 1964. His effort to repeat the next year was frustrated by peculiar series rules which gave equal points to drivers in the small-bore class but awarded only one trophy. With a Porsche-engined Lotus 23, George Follmer scored sixty points to Hall's fifty-eight. The Chaparral man was not amused. In 1966, Chuck Parsons was the best man, driving first a Genie and then a McLaren while Mark Donohue wrapped up both 1967 and the final year in a Lola and a McLaren, respectively.

Two-time champion Donohue scored twelve victories in all, just edging Hall's eleven. The next highest total was four, achieved by Parsons, Skip Scott, and Hap Sharp.

The title went to drivers, but it is worth noting that Chaparral and Lola were the most effective USRRC marques, each scoring thirteen wins. McLaren's total was eleven. Eleven makes of car in all were winners, and they were powered by six engine brands. By far the best of those was Chevrolet, whose thirty-seven wins come to 71 percent.

By no means was the USRRC the only pro racing for large displacement sports cars during the 1960s. Big

Giant Steps: As Chaparral and Chevrolet started working together, the state of their art advanced at a dizzying rate. Here at Riverside in October 1965, Hap Sharp is on his way to victory over Charlie Hayes' McLaren M1A (#97), the Lotus 30s of Jimmy Clark (#1) and Richie Ginther, and Graham Hill's M1A. The aerodynamically other-worldly Chaparral is still one of the original composite-chassied 2As, but it wears the driver-controlled "flip-flop" tail spoiler Jim Hall had recently unveiled on the aluminum-tub 2C model. Of course it has Chevy's aluminum engine and torque converter "automatic" transaxle, too. *Cam Warren/Autosport*

Chaparral

Statistical records alone wouldn't tell you, but if one Can-Am constructor can be considered quintessential, it has to be Chaparral Cars. To many fans, the excitingly innovative Road Runners from Texas were what Group 7 was all about.

Jim Hall and his friend and eventual partner, James "Hap" Sharp, were both fine drivers, and having made themselves wealthy in the oil exploration business, they could afford to drive the best available European machinery. But both had the restless, unsatisfied souls of hot rodders—they each built several "specials" by mixing different engines with different chassis—and Hall, in addition, had a degree in mechanical engineering. It seemed only natural to finally create an original car to suit themselves.

Hall started the process on his own, working with famed California specials builders Dick Troutman and Tom Barnes to produce a compact, lightweight but conventional front-Chevrolet-engined, space-framed design in 1961. Hall named the car "Chaparral" after the fleet "road runner" bird of the American southwest.

Sharp then joined Hall to form Chaparral Cars, and with a small staff, the pair set to work on a second model in their own facility at Rattlesnake Raceway, a private, 2.0-mile road course south of Midland, Texas. They could easily have made another conventional car, but the Chaparral 2 they presented in October, 1963, was astonishingly advanced.

Mid-engined at a time when that configuration was still daring, it had a monocoque chassis when that construction was still uncommon, and it was the first racing car (to distinguish it from Lotus' road-going Elite of 1957) to have its chassis made of composites, specifically of plastic resins reinforced with glass fiber.

The first Chaparral 2, later called the 2A, and its successors became even more astonishing as they evolved. Thanks to a friendship formed with like-minded engineers within Chevrolet Research and Development—and with Roger Penske, then both a driver and an aluminum salesman—Hall and Sharp gained use of experimental, all-aluminum Chevy engines and torque-converter "automatic" transmissions. They also enjoyed a lot of high-powered help with the engineering and fabrication of other components, as well as with testing and analysis equipment and procedures. The Chaparrals were not Chevrolets, and there would have been Chaparrals without the Chevrolet involvement, but the Chaparrals did embody a lot of Chevrolet know-how.

They also offered the company's personnel a priceless opportunity to increase their own know-how, as well as an outlet for their frustrated competitive desire. At the time, General Motors, unlike arch-rival Ford, was officially observing a "no-racing" pact between the Detroit automakers.

Thus, all parties involved strove to keep clandestine a relationship which they found of tremendous professional and personal value.

There were other significant factors in the Chaparral story. One was an arrangement to test tires with Firestone, then the major tire manufacturer in American motorsport. Another was that private test track literally outside the back gate. Perhaps most important was Jim Hall's own very rare blend of engineering and driving abilities. Even his being an enthusiastic private pilot helped, as it gave him a hands-on understanding of aerodynamic forces and how they are controlled. Chaparrals were very visibly at the forefront of automotive aerodynamics.

With their "homebuilt" race cars Hall and Sharp, and sometimes Penske as guest driver or team manager, won a large proportion of big-engined sports car races held in the U.S. and Canada in the early 1960s. These included the Sebring 12-hour in 1965, when this lightweight sprint roadster vanquished Ford's vaunted GT40 endurance coupe by four laps. The following year, the Chaparral 2 glass-fiber chassis, now refitted with coupe bodywork and renamed the 2D, won the 1,000-kilometer endurance race at Germany's Nür-

burgring. The year after that, the same design was further revised into the 2F model and won another international at Brands Hatch in England.

On the driving side, Hall himself won SCCA's United States Road Racing Championship in 1964 and came within two points of repeating as Champion in 1965 (Lotus-Porsche driver George Follmer won that year). Late in 1965, Chaparral introduced a new generation of car. Called the "2C" (the designation "2B" went unused), it was a shorter, narrower vehicle built on a lighter aluminum chassis actually crafted by Chevrolet. This model featured a "flipper" rear spoiler, an airfoil mounted between fins on the rear of the body and pivoted so as to be controllable for angle by the driver's left foot. The idea was to maximize downforce for braking and cornering and then minimize drag on the straights. It worked well—the 2C won its first race—but Hall was bothered by the deterioration in road holding caused by the much stiffer springs necessary to resist the high levels of downforce the wing was able to generate.

Over the next winter and spring, he and his engineer friends at Chevrolet worked out a way to mount the wing directly on the rear wheel hub carriers, thus bypassing the sprung chassis and permitting a return to more supple springs. It was a notion novel enough to earn a U.S. patent for Hall and three Chevrolet engineers.

The hub-mounted wing bowed before a surprised (and largely uncomprehending) world in the Can-Am of 1966 on a dramatic new model called the "2E."

Lola

As with fabled Camelot, for a couple of brief, shining seasons Eric Broadley's beautiful type T70 roadster was arguably the world's greatest road racer. During 1965, its big V-8 engine and its generally benign handling made it faster than the much more exotic but much less powerful F1 cars on the same tracks. In the following year's Can-Am it won five of six races; John Surtees won three to become the first Can-Am champion.

Broadley began, as did his fellow Brit, Lotus founder Colin Chapman, by building his own competition special. By 1958, his elegant and effective designs had stirred so much interest that he opened a small factory in Bromley, near London, to mass-produce them. As did Lotus, Lola Cars concentrated at first on small-bore models, but in 1963, Broadley dared use a Ford Cobra engine as the heart of a mid-engined coupe. This Mark 6 attracted Ford's attention at a time the Detroit giant was planning its own similar design, and Broadley spent eighteen months working for Ford in England on the early stages of the GT40 project.

After returning to his own affairs, Broadley drew up a new Lola design, calling it the T70 and announcing it early in 1965. This roadster resembled the GT40 in some respects, although it was not a copy of that coupe. Unlike the GT40's all-steel full monocoque, and unlike the traditional steel space frame of McLaren's contemporary M1A, the T70 offered a semi-monocoque (topless) chassis of mixed steel and aluminum. Also, it was engineered from the out-

set for engines based on the Ford 289 (4.7 liter) and Chevrolet 327 (5.3 liter), and in time would readily accept both companies' 427s (7.0 liter). Because Lolas had to have commercial appeal, appearance was important; the stylist for one of history's best-looking racers was John Frayling, famous for his Lotus Elite.

World Champion John Surtees, then primarily with Ferrari, had become interested in Big Banger sports car racing and formed his own organization, which acted as the de facto Lola factory team. As his schedule permitted, Surtees tested and raced the T70 through the spring and summer of 1965. He soon began winning both in England and North America, but in September suffered severe injuries in a crash at Mosport caused by a broken front suspension casting. His long recovery, his return to racing the following April, and his ultimate triumph in the 1966 Can-Am is the material of immortal legend.

McLaren

It would be hard to pencil out a better background to bring to the Can-Am than Bruce Leslie McLaren's. The New Zealander, received formal training in engineering but also demonstrated fine driving ability. He won his local racing club's innovative "Driver to Europe" scholarship program and quickly earned the respectful patronage of Australian Jack Brabham. In 1959, before his twenty-second birthday, McLaren joined Brabham on the Cooper F1 team. That December, Bruce won the inaugural F1 Grand Prix of the United States at Sebring, Florida. Subsequently

British Beauty: F1 World Champion and test driver John Surtees tells designer Eric Broadley what he thinks of the lovely new Lola T70. Though their partnership later became strained, during 1965 and '66 it produced an impressive list of victories in both Britain and North America and culminated in the first Can-Am championship. This sleek speedster hasn't yet had its roll bar installed, nor has it grown any of the spoilers later found essential. *Geoff Goddard/Dave Friedman Collection*

continued on next page

They rebuilt the middle section of the steel tube space frame to achieve greater stiffness and replaced the original 2.7-liter, four-cylinder Coventry Climax engine with Oldsmobile's F-85, a 215in (3.5 liter), all-aluminum V-8, race-tuned by California's Traco. Bruce drove this Cooper-Oldsmobile, as he called it for political reasons (it was known internally as the Jolly Green Giant), to victory in its first race, at Canada's Mosport Park, in June 1964. In August he won again at Brands Hatch in England.

That same fall, Bruce developed the basic design into the first car openly named a "McLaren," the M1A. The space frame layout was further improved, and magnesium panels were riveted and bonded to the tubing around the cockpit for added stiffness. The new car retained certain Cooper suspension and steering parts and used Cooper wheels, but it got a shapely new body by stylist Tony Hilder.

Development was greatly helped by McLaren enjoying a tire testing contract with Firestone. Powered by a larger-bore Traco Olds of 3.9 liters and 340hp, the M1A showed competitive speed right away. Bruce led the autumn 1964 races at Riverside and Laguna Seca until water hoses blew off and lasted to second place at Nassau behind Jim Hall's Chaparral. Chris Amon finally scored the first of several factory M1A victories early in 1965.

The M1A went into limited production (twenty-four examples, according to Eoin Young's book, *McLaren!*) through an arrangement with small specialty automaker Elva Cars, located in Rye. That's why all McLaren sports cars of the period, even those built in Bruce's own shop at Feltham, near London, were officially known as "McLaren Elvas." The production M1A could be ordered with iron-block Ford and Chevy engines, but the factory's own team stayed with the aluminum Olds, now hogged out to 4.5 liters.

Though the M1A was winning races by 1965, that year's new Lola T70 appeared to handle better and was designed from scratch to take the powerful Chevys and Fords. McLaren's response was to give the smaller, lighter Olds a smaller, lighter, better-balanced car to push around: the M1B.

The Resourceful Bruce: Having run against Penske's *Zerex* in 1962 and '63, McLaren bought it in '64, and swapped its Climax GP four-cylinder for a larger, but lighter, Olds V-8. The hot-rodded *Special* promptly won its first race, here at Mosport that June. This first McLaren-built sports racer was not entirely a McLaren, nor was it really "the first Can-Am car" as it is sometimes described, but it was the direct progenator of the great dynasty of Can-Am McLarens. *Pete Lyons*

First True McLaren: Even as he campaigned the revamped Penske car, McLaren was building his own first design. Bending over the new McLaren M1A-Olds at Mosport in September 1964 are key members of Bruce's tiny team of geniuses—manager and financier Teddy Mayer, left, and mechanic/fabricator/engine builder/engineer/close friend, not to mention photographer, Tyler Alexander. Note the spare wheel and headlights, then still called for in the rules. Note, too, the lack of aerodynamic downforce devices other than the radiator outlet atop the nose. *Dave Friedman*

he was first again in Argentina and Monte Carlo, and in 1960 and 1962 he scored second- and third-place points, respectively, in the World Championship. Cooper teammate Brabham, meanwhile, was World Champion in 1959 and 1960.

Bruce also enjoyed sports car racing and did a lot of it in North America and elsewhere in those years. As a Cooper factory driver, he was well placed to learn much from that firm's parallel interests in Grand Prix, sports, and Indy cars. He gained even more priceless engineering knowledge as one of Ford's primary GT40 development drivers, an assignment that would culminate in victory at Le Mans in 1966 with his compatriot and Can-Am teammate, Chris Amon.

Bruce was Cooper's number one factory driver in 1964 when he followed Brabham's footsteps to launch his own car-building enterprise on the side. He chose to begin with a sports car, and with somebody else's: the *Zerex Special*, the controversial, full-bodied vehicle Roger Penske had created out of a wrecked Cooper F1 chassis in 1962. McLaren raced against it then and in 1963, and when it came on the market in 1964, he bought it. Bruce won his second and third races in England with the car as received; then, the day after the second victory, he and his small crew tore the car apart.

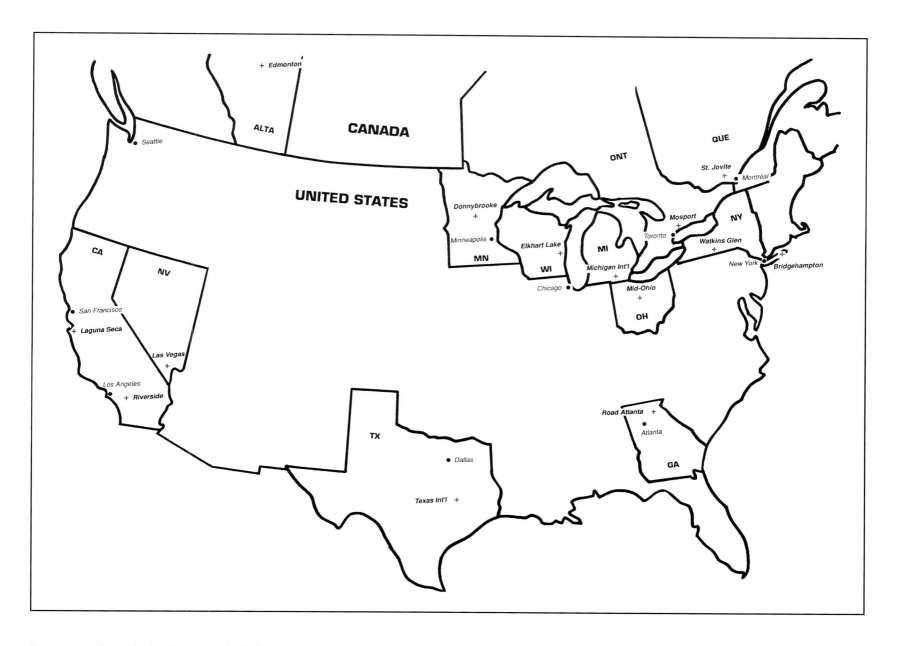

Bangers raced outside the USRRC in both the U.S. and Canada, and enjoyed a strong international following in those years, too, especially in England.

But the SCCA's formal, professional championship brought Group 9/Group 7 to maturity. It demonstrated that the unlimited sports racing car was a spectacularly popular racing instrument, and also a vi-able showcase of engineering ingenuity. One that was usually faster, wherever comparisons could be drawn, than any other form of road racing car, *not* excepting the F1 car.

These great machines, wild and free, ran at the very forefront of the automotive arts of their day.

What a charmingly simple idea was the original Canadian-American Challenge Cup series. It would comprise a small number of races, which should make it a manageable addition for people already busy with other programs. All events would be tucked into gaps near the end of the crowded calendar, thus offering likely competitors the least number of schedule conflicts. To prevent parochial politics from interfering with drivers crossing over from other sanctioning bodies, the CASC/SCCA races would be listed as international events by the FIA. The cars also would be internationally recognized as the "two-seater unrestricted sports cars" of the new FIA Group 7 (formerly called Group 9). These already existed, so they wouldn't have to be invented, and they enjoyed an established following not only in North America but elsewhere in the world, especially England. The cars were both spectacular to watch and—at that time—relatively simple to construct and campaign. Another plus: they also were easily distinguishable from cars identified with other sanctioning organizations.

They also matched the mood of the times. Big horsepower was in. This was the year Formula One had turned its back on the dinky 1.5-liter engines of the past five seasons in favor of 3.0s. It was in 1966, too, that Ford finally won Le Mans with its massive 7.0-liter GT40 Mark II. The same firm had also scored its second consecutive Indy 500 victory with its powerful DOHC V-8. Cars with super engines? Let's go!

But while the machinery demanded attention, the Can-Am championship was for drivers. It would be contested within one class only, thus simplifying things for entrants, officials, and onlookers. To attract the attention of both participants and the public, the prize moneys for both race positions and overall championship standings would set road racing records. As initially envisaged, race distances would be about 250 miles.

A simple idea, but bringing it to reality was anything but easy.

As formally announced on February 15, 1966, the inaugural Can-Am season included only five firm dates. The series would start September 11 at Canada's St. Jovite near Montreal; continue on September 24 at Mosport Park outside Toronto; swing to the southwestern U.S. for October dates at California's Laguna Seca and Riverside; and close in November at Nevada's Las Vegas. A sixth date, October 9th, was expected to be taken by Kent, near Seattle, Washington.

Talk also circulated of the series being extended to embrace additional events overseas, two in England and one in Germany. These would be outside the Can-Am's points/prize structure, but would join with the Can-Am to form something to be called the Atlantic Challenge.

That never happened. In fact, commercial support for Group 7 was waning east of the Atlantic even as it swelled in the west, and the first year of the Can-Am turned out to be the last for Big Bangers in Britain. This sad development was widely mourned by both press and public, but British motorsport at that time was largely supported through driver and team endorsements by oil and tire companies. These firms pleaded that the American-engined machines were relatively exotic and expensive in Europe, thus less cost-effective from a promotional standpoint than the small single-seaters that were the traditional bread-and-butter of the local sport.

One can speculate that there may have been political pressures applied by the traditionalists, as well. The press had been hailing the Big Bangers as faster and more entertaining than contemporary F1s. As *Autosport* had editorialized in 1965, when F1 engines still displaced only 1500cc, "Formula 1 racing is regarded as the highest form of automobile engineering, but when the products are beginning to be out-paced on the circuits by cars with modified production engines, then even 3.0 liters might not produce the answer to the ever-rising speeds of the 'hairy' big bangers!" The introduction of the 3.0-liter F1 in 1966 proved the editor right.

Whatever the reasons for the demise of Group 7 in England, it obviously strained the enthusiasm of English constructors for the class, and only Lola and McLaren-Elva stayed involved.

A few years later, a new, separate Group 7 championship called the Interserie was set up in Continental Europe, and there was some trading of entrants with the Can-Am. Also, on two occasions, selected Can-Am regulars were invited to race in Japan, where two auto makers—Nissan and Toyota—had built Group 7 sports cars of their own. But no formal transoceanic championship ever evolved.

Meanwhile, North American Can-Am preparations weren't going entirely smoothly. In March 1966, the Kent track chose not to commit the funds necessary to secure its place on the schedule. Later that summer, financial problems forced St. Jovite to the brink of cancellation. Happily, the Quebec circuit found a corporate sponsor, and Bridgehampton in New York state signed on for a September date to bring the Can-Am back to six races.

But the nascent series' greatest lift was the April 14 announcement of commercial sponsorship. Johnson Wax, maker of auto polishes, among other products, would add $25,000 to the year-end points fund to which each race promoter had contributed $5,000. There would also be a "J-Wax Can-Am" trophy, plus energetic promotion of both the series and individual events. The PR push would be pointed up by the highly recognizable and respected figure of retired driving legend Stirling Moss, who would serve as Challenge Cup Commissioner.

But who would challenge for the Cup? The famous Europeans whom CASC and SCCA had expected to come flocking to the great Can-Am were now making noises of resistance. When World Champion Graham Hill finally achieved stardom in America by winning the Indianapolis 500 that May, he startled many innocents by declaring that, while he'd had Can-Am offers, he wasn't sure he was interested.

At issue was appearance money, or, rather, the absence of it. European professionals were used to being paid by race promoters to participate, on the principle that better-known drivers brought in more spectators. The Can-Am's American and Canadian promoters preferred the principle that fat prizes would lure top drivers, who ought to earn their money by racing for it. The promoter of the U.S. Grand Prix at Watkins Glen felt the same way—that year's F1 drivers were driving for a $50,000 purse, period (except that the Glen did pick up the teams' trans-Atlantic transportation tab).

The controversy was nicely delineated in a June 11 editorial in *Competition Press & Autoweek*. It quoted from a letter sent to Can-Am promot-

Riverside: Hall took the wing extensions and "mustaches" off his 2E for this high-speed track, and gave Surtees (#7 Lola T70) one of his hardest races of the year. *Dave Friedman*

St. Jovite: From the left of the three-wide front row Amon out-drags McLaren, in the middle, and pole-starter Surtees. Two hours and 200 miles later they won't be much farther apart. *Lionel Birnbom*

ers by McLaren's Teddy Mayer: "Let's face it, gentlemen, your attendance depends on the fame of the entrants. You benefit from our appearance, not our performance.'"

CP&A took it upon itself to answer for the promoters. After duly excepting from its condemnation the McLaren team and a couple of other proven hard-chargers, the newspaper declared that, "All too often the Europeans have appeared at U.S. tracks in disgraceful and shoddy equipment. And have gone as fast as the hay truck. And have lasted far longer at the cocktail parties than in the race following." The Can-Am's prize structure, the editor pointed out, should make an appearance well worthwhile for anyone willing to perform.

The American argument must have prevailed. McLaren and other Europeans did turn up in September.

As it gelled, the Canadian-American Challenge presented six approximately 200-mile races: three each in the two most populous corners of the continent, two in Canada, and all within a span of nine weeks, starting September 11.

The timing was tight, but all race dates had to dovetail with the two major road racing series from which entrants would be drawn. Just the weekend before, the final round of the United States Road Racing Championship was scheduled for Elkhart Lake, while on the same day the Italian Grand Prix at Monza would have closed the European Formula One season. The F1 stars were then free until the

United States GP at Watkins Glen October 2, and again until their championship finale in Mexico City October 23. Everybody was expected to jump at the chance to spend their off-weekends racing fun cars for real money.

And the money was indeed eye-opening. On the eve of the first race, the 1966 Can-Am series offered a total prize value of over $358,000, made up of race purses averaging almost $30,000 plus the fixed championship fund of $55,000, plus an ever-growing total in accessory awards. Individual race purses all differed, but first place could be worth more than $12,000. The overall champion's take from the points fund was $19,250, not to mention the "floatile" trophy, a gleaming, ovoid art object which hovered mysteriously above its base.

These weren't the absolute biggest bucks in motorsport. When Graham Hill won the 1966 Indy 500, he earned approximately $175,000 out of a total purse of some $650,000. The Watkins Glen GP paid more that year than any individual Can-Am: $20,000 to win. But no other F1 event came close to that. As a series, the Can-Am was certainly the richest in American road racing and was thought to at least match F1 as a whole (the bosses of which generally kept such sordid details to themselves).

To place these numbers in the context of the times, a race-day ticket to a representative Can-Am would set you back about $5. If you wanted to make an appearance there in a new 1967 model Chevrolet Corvette roadster, its base price that fall was $4,141.

Should you take a notion to participate, Lola distributor Mecom Racing Enterprises was using *CP&A's* classifieds to offer a pre-owned T70, asking price $9,000, less engine, but "ready for Can-Am series." To fill its engine bay, you could turn to another ad in which a private party was hoping to sell a "new" 366ci/6.0-liter Chevy for less than $3,000, complete with Weber carbs and linkage. The weekly newspaper itself carried a cover price of 25¢.

St. Jovite, Quebec, September 11, 1966

First impressions are important, and the Can-Am's inaugural race got the new series off to a great start. Gathering at one of the most scenic road courses in the Americas, a crowd variously reported at 53,000 to 58,000—in any case, allegedly the largest ever to witness a sporting event in Quebec—cheered a stirring, race-long duel between John Surtees and Bruce McLaren, plus a spectacular catch-up effort by Chris Amon.

Surtees, winner of a pre-Can-Am Group 7 race at the same track the year before, set things up by driving his Lola T70-Chevy around the swoopy, 2.65-mile mini-Nürburgring to pole position with a time of 1:38.4, 96.95mph. That beat McLaren, who'd won here earlier in the summer, by a scant 0.1sec, and Amon by 0.4.

Behind the McLaren factory's M1B-Chevys, the thirty-three-car grid sheet showed some strong names: Dan Gurney, Parnelli Jones, and George Follmer (all Lola-Fords—Jones' supercharged), plus Jerry Grant, Ronnie Bucknum, and Mark Donohue (Lola-Chevys), as well as new USRRC Champ Chuck Parsons, Masten Gregory, Skip Scott, John Cannon, and newcomer Sam Posey (McLaren-Chevys). All of the above had iron-block engines displacing between 5.0 and 6.0 liters, while Canadian Champion Ludwig Heimrath brought a McLaren stuffed to the brim with 7.0 liters of iron Ford. But Lothar Motschenbacher beat them all for fourth on the grid in his McLaren with a 5.0-liter aluminum Olds.

A few strong names were missing. Though Chaparral had entered a two-car team, trouble discovered on the tow from Texas forced Jim Hall to scratch both himself and Phil Hill. Trouble in practice eliminated two good Lola drivers, first Paul Hawkins then Hugh Dibley, who independently discovered that the curvaceous T70 could be made to fly its front end over a sharp hump in St. Jovite's longest straight.

"Hawkeye," who did the deed on Friday, flipped right over backwards at 130mph and traveled 100 yards on his head, which adventure wore a hole clear through his helmet and started work on his scalp before the car stopped. The next day, Dibley, an airline

pilot, managed an even better flight over a fence into a spectator area. Nobody was badly hurt in these "blowovers," to use a boat racing term, so paddock pranksters felt free to crack jokes, and "the Can-Am Flying Club" eventually became infamous. However, the humor was papering over a sense of unease. Can-Am cars were showing a side nobody had expected to see.

In the pre-race warmup Gurney's engine spun a bearing, so he was out too, while Bucknum nearly logged the third flight of the weekend but his Lola came back down right-side-up. Then, at the last second before the standing start, Bucknum stalled, Jones couldn't find a gear, and the resulting melee took out five cars.

But nothing blocked the three-wide front row, and Amon from the outside saw he had a great shot at the diving/rising, long-right-hand first turn, and took it. Alas, he only enjoyed his lead for part of that first lap, because a few corners later he ran straight off the road. At the end of the lap he broke off into the pits to have his sticking throttles cleared and his damaged nose spoiler torn off.

That left Surtees leading from McLaren, but it was by so little that when John once missed a shift, Bruce scuttled by. Only moments later, the Lola came through lapped traffic ahead again. Surtees held on this time, but so did McLaren. This is how Don Grey described the excitement in *Sports Car Graphic*: "McLaren . . . lay glued to the Lola's exhaust pipes, ducking, weaving, and bobbing in an attempt to pass. But Surtees matched him thrust for thrust and

St. Jovite: Charter member of the Can-Am Flying Club, Hawkins flipped on Friday and launched a concern over front-end aerodynamics that would preoccupy Group 7 designers throughout the next nine years. *Lionel Birnbom*

parry for parry . . . It was a classic duel of two great masters, but behind them a younger master completely upstaged them with a solo performance that was the highlight of the entire race."

Amon's pit stop had cost one and a half laps, but he charged out as if his contract were at stake—and as if the M1B didn't need that front spoiler after all. "Amon put on the greatest display of driving that Le Circuit's fans had ever seen," declared Bob McGregor in *Autosport.* As SCG's Grey detailed it, "Tires screaming on the knife-edge of adhesion and running every lap below the previous record, Amon sliced his way through the field with ruthless precision." The young New Zealander made up forty-eight seconds in fifty-three laps, at which point he found his road full of the sister M1B and the wide red T70.

Bruce promptly waved Amon by to see if he could help with the Lola problem. Surtees was too crafty to let that happen, but the youngster was too full of fire to give up, and on the seventy-first lap, just four from the finish, Amon was clocked at a new record time of 1:37.3. That bettered Surtees' best qualifying time by over a second.

That's how they finished, the trio of Big red Bangers scratching around nose to tail, Surtees still in front, Amon in the middle ahead of McLaren on the road

but in third place in the race, still a lap back. The gap between Surtees and McLaren at the end of seventy-five laps and 2 hours, 6 minutes, 51 seconds of flat-out, high-power sports car racing was 6.5 seconds.

Cannon was fourth, two laps back, but ahead of the former 1965 and new 1966 USRRC champions, Follmer and Parsons. The top six drivers went home with Can-Am championship points awarded as in F1 of that period: nine for the winner, then six, four, three, two, and one; no additional points were given for fast laps or other achievements.

Bridgehampton, New York, September 16, 1966

Never had promoters at the sinuous, bumpy, 2.85-mile circuit in the sand hills near the eastern end of Long Island dared host such an ambitious event, but the gamble paid off. Can-Am round two also set new course records, in speed, in spectacle, and in spectators—27,000 of them.

The Chaparrals arrived this time, and what an entrance they made with their tall, suspension-mounted, "flipper" wings. And these wings worked: in his 2E, Jim Hall earned pole position at 1:32.9 (110.44mph). That was well up on his own record for the track of 103.8mph, set during a 1965 race in his old Chaparral 2A, and beat this year's second-fastest man, Dan Gurney, by 0.3sec. Behind the dark blue Lola-Ford with its Gurney-Weslake heads, both Amon and McLaren in the red factory McLarens and Surtees in the red factory Lola all tied, each turning 1:33.4.

Phil Hill, new to the Chaparral, had clocked only the sixth fastest time at 1:34.4 when a wing bracing strut failed. The tall airfoil structure leaned over to one side, a bolt cut that rear tire, and the exotic white Road Runner crashed. Hill was unhurt and soon went back out in Hall's car—but then the same thing happened. The 1961 World Champion was not only ready, this time he was warned: the late afternoon sun happened to be casting the wing's shadow on the road ahead of him when he saw it suddenly sag sideways. That car was not badly damaged, and Hall forfeited his ride to let Hill start the pole-winning 2E from fifth spot on the eye-filling grid of thirty-six remaining cars.

It was a rolling start this time. Gurney made the most of his inherited pole position to take the first-lap lead from Surtees, Hill, McLaren, and Amon. In four laps, Hill passed Surtees for second, and then at lap eight the St. Jovite winner had to pit with gearshift trouble. Two laps later he was back in with an oil line failure which retired him.

But Gurney was holding up the Lola side with a runaway pace of 108mph-plus. That was what it took

to stay just ahead of an always-sniffing Chaparral for some 150 miles. But then the 2E's wing pivoting mechanism broke, fixing it in its high-drag position, and Hill dropped behind Amon. With seventeen laps left, the young New Zealander caught a whiff of victory. As at Mosport, he rapidly closed on the leader, but this time he was on the same lap. Gurney saw Amon's red nose looming in his mirror, but held it off by a fifth of a second as the pair zoomed under the checker.

It was a magnificent success for Gurney's "little" 305ci (5.0 liter) Ford, which was equipped with his own Gurney-Weslake cylinder heads and a screaming 495hp at 7800rpm. "The redline used to be 8000rpm, but I just found out I could turn 8900," Dan said through his huge grin. Chris retorted that he'd seen 11,000.

McLaren was third while Hill hung on for fourth, both still on the winner's lap. Mark Donohue, a lap back, and Chuck Parsons, two back, took the remaining points.

There were no blowovers this weekend, but two traditional high-side rollovers occurred. In practice, Eno de Pasquale flipped his Genie-Chevrolet in the Bridgehampton sand, wrecking the car and breaking his nose. In the race, Masten Gregory did the same thing in his McLaren but crawled out from under, brushed himself off, and walked to the pits.

Anyone alert to Can-Am omens? The points lead was now jointly held by the two men from McLaren.

Mosport, Ontario, September 25, 1966

The third race in as many weekends put a strain on people and on machines. Also, peculiar event regulations contributed to a first-turn shunt that eliminated significant contenders. Unpleasant weather kept the crowd to a disappointing 20,000. But the new Can-Am series had its third winner.

As at Bridgehampton, Jim Hall's new Chaparral wing-car was fastest in qualifying around the similarly fast, dramatically hilly 2.46-mile Mosport. The Texan took 2sec off his own previous best here, with 1:22.9 (104.2mph). He set this on the second day of practice, but for some reason the Mosport grid was drawn up giving precedence to first-day times—even though it had rained then. Hall therefore found himself starting in tenth place behind several much slower cars. John Surtees, second-fastest qualifier, had to start eleventh.

The obvious potential for disaster was fulfilled. From the standing start there was a wild-looking charge into Turn 1, and several cars came together. Four were immobilized on the spot—in Surtees' case,

scarcely 50yd from the spot of his terrible accident of a year earlier. He went to the hospital again, along with George Follmer, but happily the injuries were minor.

After a restart—a rolling one this time, in single file—pole man Gurney led a few laps, but he'd been forced to change his qualifying engine for a softer one. Finally he had to give way to those two Kiwis, Amon and McLaren, plus a third. Denny Hulme had come over with the Lola he'd been racing in England to join the Can-Am fun. Gurney tucked in behind, and the four spent the first half of the eighty-five-lap race in this order. But then Hulme dropped back with apparent handling trouble (a half shaft finally failed), McLaren collided with a backmarker and retired with his suspension broken, and Amon deranged his steer-

Above and Below: Mosport: Trouble in Turn 1, thanks to peculiar qualifying rules and a standing start procedure. Getting clear are McLaren and the other front-runners—including Donohue, by the skin of his teeth—but other fast men who had to start mid-grid are tangling. Surtees goes sideways, his door popping open and his right front fender tearing apart, while the chain reaction takes out several others, and spins Hill's Chaparral right around. *Road & Track sequence*

Laguna Seca, California, October 16, 1966

Can-Ammers had a welcome R&R break now, though on October 2 some of them had to put in their F1 stint at the U.S. Grand Prix. (Surtees set fastest lap there and finished third; McLaren came fifth.) Assembled once again at Monterey, they were ready for a 201-mile event divided into two fifty-three-lap heats. Attendance was said to be 35,000, a course record.

The Chaparral team was really ready for this tight, 1.9-mile course that favored lots of downforce. The 2Es had wider rear wings with endplates, and "mustaches" at the front. Hill beat the existing lap record, set by Hap Sharp a year earlier in an older Chaparral, by 1.6sec. Then Hall beat that by a further 0.09sec for pole position at 1:05.31. (104.7mph). The 2E drivers had to hustle, because McLaren was close (1:05.48) with an experimental fuel-injected engine, and so was Gurney (1:05.83) with his little Weslake-Ford now pumped up to 520hp (torque was 415lb-ft at 6300rpm). Amon, Hulme, and Surtees got into the sixes, though Surtees was suffering from 'flu.

In addition to names already familiar, the entry list for this fourth Can-Am had Jackie Stewart joining Parnelli Jones in the pair of Mecom Lolas—but only on the entry list. Failure of his supercharged Ford engine in practice sent the "Mod Scot" to the roof of a transporter for a sunbath. Similar trouble afflicted Jones, so he only qualified for the Can-Am by winning a Sunday morning consolation race—with a Chevy borrowed from Penske to replace the Ford which a disgusted John Mecom was threatening to turn into a "boat anchor."

Hall had his hired hand, Hill, assume the lead from the start of the first heat, but inadvertently let McLaren by at the same time. Bruce took some dealing with, but by the end of the fifty-three laps, the M1B was back in third. It was almost half a minute back after a quick pit stop to change a bad spark plug; meanwhile the two Road Runners cantered around nose-to-tail, Hill still ahead of Hall. Surtees finished that heat fourth, Hulme fifth, Donohue sixth. Gurney's engine had blown after six laps, and Jones' had leaked all its oil out—apparently, the heavier Chevy had lowered the Lola's ride height enough to drag its sump.

For heat two Jim Hall decided to enjoy leading for a while, though after forty laps his paid driver took over to ensure first place overall. But it was too early for the Road Runners to be counting any chickens. Parnelli was on the track.

His leaky sump replaced and his springs jacked up, Jones started this heat from twenty-seventh and last grid place, and bulled his way up to fourth by lap thirty. Amon and Hulme had broken

ing on Phil Hill's Chaparral, which was being nursed around with low oil pressure. Hall's 2E had already dropped out with its own engine trouble.

All this put Gurney well in front again, and at ten laps to go he was cruising serenely along a full lap to the good when his battery went flat, killing his ignition. (According to official reports at the time, that is. Later information has the crankshaft breaking.)

A surprised Donohue went by to win, and to take the series lead with eleven points. Hill lasted to finish second, two laps down. Parsons scored again, another lap back, but well ahead of Earl Jones (McLaren), Paul Hawkins (in the same Lola he'd inverted at St. Jovite), and Eppie Wietzes (Ford GT40 coupe).

ings, though. So Jones just took one. As the pair dove into one of the ultra-fast left-handers that used to grace Laguna Seca, P.J. stuck his nose down the inside. Fearless John refused to give way. The two Lolas banged together. The factory one spun off, its suspension broken. The distributor one pressed on. There were thirteen laps left. The pair of Chaparrals were seven seconds ahead.

On the very next lap, Jones caught and passed them both. No knocking necessary; both Road Runners knew the score. They were winning, anyway.

Jones won that heat by some 20sec over Hill, but the Chaparral drivers were well aware that their first-heat performance secured the aggregate victory for Hill. Donohue was fourth in that heat and fourth overall, while McLaren's fifth made him third overall. Cannon

down by now, and McLaren had pitted with a stuck throttle, but Surtees was still in it, and over the next nine laps the 1963 Indy winner closed on the 1964 World Champion and started looking for a way by into third. Surtees wasn't about to offer any open-

Laguna Seca: Racing is fun when everything goes right, but what a shame the Hall and Hill Show would never again make it to victory circle. *Dave Friedman*

Left: Riverside: Car and number seem unfamiliar here, but Denny's determination would color the Can-Am for years. *Bob Tronolone*

Top left; Riverside: Coming "home" to California always swelled the Can-Am field. Here, slashing through Turn 8 onto the back straight, Graham Hill (Team Surtees Lola T70) leads Phil Hill (2E in high-downforce trim), Follmer (T70), Amon (McLaren M1B), Scott (M1B) and Hulme (T70). In the background are the M1Bs of Hayes (#10) and Cannon (#62). *Dave Friedman*

and Gregory rounded out the points. Heat winner Jones was scored twenty-first overall. Nine points for Hill made him the fourth series leader in as many races.

Riverside, California, October 30, 1966

John Surtees got a pleasant lift the intervening weekend in Mexico City, where he qualified his F1 Cooper-Maserati on pole and won the last Grand Prix of the season. Hulme was third, Gurney fifth. They then rejoined the Group 7 gang at the 3.275-mile California track where, local partisans believed, it all began. The announced crowd figure was 82,000, though said locals viewed that with suspicion.

The day was hot. So was the pace. McLaren, his M1B now equipped with a 5.9-liter fuel-injected Chevy and a body-mounted feathering rear spoiler similar to that on the prior year's Chaparral 2C, snatched pole (1:44.7, 112.60mph). From there Bruce shot off into the lead, but only ten laps along his engine started misfiring, and eventually quit. Hall, the surviving member of the Chaparral team following Hill's retirement with fuel vaporization, took over first place, but he was having the same trouble. Surtees grew in his mirrors, and at half-distance powered by.

But Hall found that by staying in top gear he could minimize the time spent at high rpm, where

the fuel delivery problem was at its worst. The price was relatively sluggish acceleration off the turns, but still the 2E was fast around the course as a whole, and three laps later Hall retook the lead. Surtees passed him back. Hall passed him back. Altogether, they swapped the lead six times. Road racing of any kind seldom puts on a show like that; let us remember this

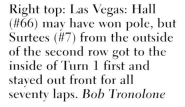

Right top: Las Vegas: Hall (#66) may have won pole, but Surtees (#7) from the outside of the second row got to the inside of Turn 1 first and stayed out front for all seventy laps. *Bob Tronolone*

Jim Hall lays the wing flat for the Riverside back straight. *Bob Tronolone*

one whenever people start prattling about monotonous Can-Am processions.

"Jim could come out a bit quicker from the corners, getting the power on the road better, but I had him at the end of the straight," Surtees reported later. He'd been pulling 6500rpm there, he added, which his gearing charts said was 179mph.

To Hall's—and most people's—enduring frustration, the Chaparral's boiling fuel problem worsened, and in the last few laps he had to watch the red Lola win by 16sec. Graham Hill, teammate to Surtees in this event, came home third. (Had Hill overcome his objections about starting money? Not according to *CP&A*, which reported that the race backer, a major newspaper, had paid extra to ensure several stars would appear. Surtees got the most, $8,000 for his two-car team, with McLaren next at $6,000.) Donohue scored fourth again, with Follmer fifth and newcomer Peter Revson (McLaren-Ford) sixth.

Other interesting additions to the Can-Am crowd at Riverside included A.J. Foyt ($1,500 appearance money), whose Lola-Ford 7.0 overheated to retirement, and Mario Andretti, who was holding seventh place in a Lola powered by another 7.0-liter Ford driving through an automatic transmission when the bigger Banger banged to oblivion. Their Indy colleague, Jones, blew his engine too, as did Amon, but Gurney's retirement was put down to clutch trouble.

The points picture? Hill and Surtees were going into the last round even at eighteen. Donohue was looking over their shoulders with seventeen. Mathematically, any of seven drivers could still take the title. Sure was boring, this Can-Am racing.

Las Vegas, Nevada, November 13, 1966

The winged-wonder Chaparrals were back at the front of the grid on this sinuous, 3.0-mile desert floor track, Hall again on pole at 1:34.5 (114.29mph). Once again his new concept clearly demonstrated its worth by beating the record lap of an earlier Chaparral model, this time by 3.5sec. Hill qualified second by 0.9sec. At 1:35.5, Amon was best of the conventional-car drivers, 0.6 better than Surtees. His and McLaren's McLarens were back on carburetors, and non-flipping rear spoilers, too.

But qualifying is one thing, racing often another. At the start, Surtees muscled by all three of the apparently faster cars and came out of the first turn in the lead. And there he stayed. All day. All 210 miles. He did rack up fastest lap, 0.4 quicker than his grid time, but then he eased off because of engine vibration. Still, at the end he was nearly a minute ahead of second-place McLaren. So, Can-Ams could be a little dull. As newspaperman Gordon Martin put it in *Autosport*, "It may have been a bit of a bore for the spectators, but Surtees could probably hear the money jingling for the full distance."

There was a lot of jangling going on behind Surtees. P. Hill and P. Jones came together, resulting in body damage to both their cars. Later on, Phil lost all hope of more championship points when his rear wing actuation system broke, and he pitted from third place to have the whole airfoil taken off its struts. The crew replaced it with a spacer bar, and took time to tack a spoiler lip on the tail, but the battered 2E was still handling atrociously. Four laps from the end, Hill had a second collision with a mid-field Lola, which caromed through a fence into a crowd area and destroyed three passenger cars as well as itself. Incredibly, only one spectator was injured, and only superficially. The driver, Norm Smith, got out with a banged knee. Hill struggled on to seventh.

Hall also had his wing mechanism break, and in this case he felt it prudent to retire. Amon went out

Data acquisition *chez* Chaparral: a reel-to-reel tape recorder rides in the 2E's passenger seat during practice. *Pete Lyons*

with a broken transmission, and so did Hulme. Stewart spun out of third place, then quit with a broken fuel line. Gurney moved up from ninth on the grid to third, but stopped with half shaft failure. USAC champion Andretti, who had made the Sunday field only through winning a Saturday "consie," went out of the "main" after one lap when the autobox behind his big Ford quit.

But Mark Donohue lasted, and finished third behind Surtees and McLaren. That was good enough to pull Mark ahead of Bruce to second in the series, twenty-one points to twenty. Phil Hill's eighteen left him fourth overall, six up on his boss, Jim Hall. Chris Amon was sixth (ten points), ahead of Dan Gurney (nine) and Chuck Parsons (six). Four drivers had earned four points apiece, but on the basis of his better finishing record, Graham Hill was awarded ninth, leaving John Cannon, George

John Surtees, 1966 Can-Am Champion

Outstanding talent, a strong mechanical background, and steely resolve characterized this quiet Englishman. Born February 11, 1934, he began racing motorcycles in 1951 and took seven World Championships on MV Agustas and another in a Formula One Ferrari before he came to the Can-Am. One of the earliest European drivers to become interested in American sports car racing, he made an exploratory foray in 1963 with a lightened Ferrari 250P endurance car. When Enzo decided against following up with a dedicated sports racer, John formed a relationship with Eric Broadley of Lola and developed the T70 into a race winner. Broken suspension at Mosport in 1965 caused severe pelvis, spine, femur and kidney injuries, but Surtees fought through months of painful rehabilitation to race and win again.

In the six-event inaugural Can-Am, he took three victories, the only man to score more than once. Here, still smeared with the grime of battle, the new 1966 champion receives his J-Wax "floatile" trophy from compatriot Stirling Moss, left, and Samuel C. Johnson, president of the series-sponsoring company. Fearless John would come back for several years but win only once more and finally decide to concentrate on his own F1, F2, and F5000 construction and racing team in Europe. Today he still maintains Team Surtees, and stays active in vintage racing and also a children's charity. *Johnson Wax/Dave Friedman collection*

Follmer, and Peter Revson sharing tenth. Earl Jones (three), Masten Gregory, Paul Hawkins, Lothar Motschenbacher (two each), and Eppie Wietzes and Jerry Titus (one each, the latter coming into the picture by his sixth place at Las Vegas) were the others immortalized on that first Can-Am Challenge Cup points table.

Surtees' points total was twenty-seven. And that jingling in his jeans? Winning Las Vegas meant some $11,000. Adding that to what he'd earned in his two earlier victories, plus over $19,000 from the J-Wax points fund, plus various accessory prizes, tiny Team Surtees flew home with a sum that dropped European jaws. England's *Autosport* put it at "a fantastic $70,000 — it was better than winning all of the Formula 1 World Championship races of 1966!"

In the same publication, Bruce McLaren noted in his "From the Cockpit" column that, despite failing to win a single race, he'd collected more prize money in the six quick Can-Ams than in three entire GP seasons.

That kind of word goes the rounds. The 1967 Can-Am was going to attract a lot of attention.

It deserved to. As Don Grey expressed it for many, "The Canadian-American Challenge Cup series is the greatest thing that has happened to sports car racing since the red-blooded days of Jaguar, Mercedes, and Aston Martin."

Cars of the Can-Am 1966
Chaparral 2E

For vehicles so stuffed with science, the 2Es were remarkably compact. Their aluminum chassis — one taken from the year-old 2C, the other all-new with slightly larger fuel capacity — rested on a 89.5in wheelbase. Track dimensions were 53.5 and 52 front and rear. Nominal overall body width was 64in, though wing extensions late in the season would have increased that measurement. Suspension was basically conventional for the day, with coil springs wrapped around tubular shocks all around, double wishbones in front, and a combination of lateral and trailing links at the rear. Geometries gave moderate anti-dive and anti-squat characteristics. Disc brakes were outboard all around, their cooling assisted by the "lace-spoke" wheels Chaparral had developed earlier.

Chaparral's engines were supplied by Chevrolet's Research and Development department. They were special versions of the company's small-block V-8, heads and block being cast in aluminum with separate iron cylinder liners, or sleeves. This construction resisted displacement increases, so the 2E continued to race at 327ci, a common iron-block production size derived from a bore and stroke of 4.00x3.25 (101.6x82.6 = 5,354cc). The carbureted engine produced a generally quoted 450hp at 6800rpm, 10 to 15 percent lower than numbers being claimed by the opposition for their larger "lumps."

The flip side was significantly less weight: at just under 400lb ready to run, the aluminum unit relieved the Chaparral of 150lb of dead iron.

The power went through Chaparral's now-familiar (if seldom seen and little understood) Chevrolet-made hydraulic torque converter to the Chevrolet-made three-speed transaxle usually cast in magnesium. As always, this "automatic" was really operated manually. Before starting the engine the driver would engage first gear and press the brake pedal with his left foot, releasing it only when ready to accelerate. Gear changes to second and top were made by easing the throttle and moving the conventional lever; downshifts were accomplished similarly, but with a blip of the throttle while passing through neutral. In fact, any race car with a conventional Hewland manual gearbox could be driven similarly (as can most motorcycles) once on the move. In the Chaparral, all braking was done with the left foot—a shield prevented the right foot getting to the brake pedal.

The left foot was free of clutch duties, but it had a third pedal to operate. This was linked to the rear wing and also to a smaller pivoting flap hidden inside what at first appeared to be conventional radiator ducting. (The radiators were in the flanks, another Chaparral innovation.)

When the third pedal was depressed, the pair of "flippers" would move to their low-drag, low-downforce settings; the rear wing would pivot to a nearly flat angle, and the front flap would close off the nose ducting in the manner of a butterfly throttle valve. When the driver released the wing pedal to go for the brakes, the flipper would default to its high-downforce, high-drag angle, and the front flap, itself an airfoil, would open its duct to allow downforce-producing vertical airflow.

All in all, the 1966 Chaparral 2E was one of the most beautifully integrated automotive performance *systems* in history. Everything worked together: the fluid-clutch transmission allowed two-foot control of accelerator and brake; it also allowed the driver-controllable aerodynamic package; that package gave rise to the hip-mounted radiators, which improved both weight distribution and the cockpit environment.

That first winged car-light, handy and supple-forever remained Jim Hall's personal favorite of all his Chaparrals. For those watching from outside, a be-winged Chaparral on a fast lap was a spectacular vision. The compact white roadster with its fantastic rear appendage would hurtle into sight at startling velocity, riding the bumps smoothly on its soft springs but tilting obviously in the turns, with the tall wing struts leaning right over. That wing would be flippering vigorously from level to canted and back again as the driver balanced drag to downforce for the best possible speed on every section of the lap. Seldom has a race car been so visibly an artist's instrument.

Had the *Road Runner* not suffered some flipper system teething problems, as well as a few others of more conventional nature, it might well have rewritten that first year's Can-Am history. As fast as it was fabulous, the 2E set best qualifying time for its debut event and three subsequent ones, set quickest race lap during another, and scored an outright one-two in one of the five Can-Ams the team contested.

By sad irony, that single success in 1966 would stand as Chaparral's only Can-Am victory despite four

more seasons of effort. But the wild, winged white *Road Runner* forever fixed every race fan's image of "The Chaparral" and, by extension, that of the archetypal American race car. Bristling with innovation, the 2E was indeed the quintessential Can-Am car.

Lola T70

Eric Broadley's 1965 design won races, but before that season was over he introduced a significantly revised version. Whereas the first, mainly steel semi-monocoque chassis had been assembled with spot welding (as on the Ford GT40 Broadly had helped design), the new, largely aluminum structure used rivets and adhesives for a claimed 70lb weight saving with no loss of stiffness or torsional strength. At the same time he deleted the spare wheel from the

Lola T70: At Las Vegas, Gurney countersteers a turn ahead of Amon's McLaren. *Dave Friedman*

McLaren M1B: A cheery
Bruce McLaren takes his
ease behind the Mosport pits
as Tyler Alexander (far left)
and the other guys do all the
work; Chris Amon keeps an
eye on the back of his own
car (#5). *Dave Friedman*

nose as regulations no longer required it and improved numerous other details. This Mark II was offered in 1966 and driven by Surtees and others to five of six victories in the inaugural Can-Am series.

All T70s rolled on a 95in wheelbase; track of the Mark II was up slightly over the Mark I to 58in front and rear. Wheel diameters were all 15in, with 8in and 10in rims at first, wider later. Coil-over suspension was conventional at each corner, with double wishbones at the front, and two trailing rods locating a single top transverse link and a reversed lower A-arm at the rear. Because the full-length monocoque extended either side of the engine, the lower trailing rod's forward pickup point was inside the structure, coincident with the engine mount at the side of the cylinder block. A more visibly distinctive T70 point was how the cast magnesium uprights exposed all four

12.5in vented brake discs to the airstrip inboard of the wheels—the discs at the rear were actually inboard of the uprights.

Lola gave the Mark II roadster's empty weight as 1600lb with Chevy engine and standard Hewland LG 500 transaxle. This was a 4-speed, although a 5-speed LG 600 was also available; cases for both were magnesium castings, and dry weights were 125 and 136lb, respectively. Total fuel capacity was 60gal (370lb), held in two rubber-bagged cells. At that period headlights were still provided for, though Can-Am regulations did not call for them—later, in fact, front-end glass would be outlawed.

Chevrolet's small-block was the typical T70 engine of 1966, and those offered by well-respected Traco Engineering in Los Angeles can be considered definitive. The bore remained standard at 4.0in (101.6mm),

but a stroker crank of 3.625 (92.1) gave a displacement of 364.4ci (5.97 liter). Breathing through a quartet of two-barrel, 58mm Weber side-draft carburetors on a "cross-over" manifold, such a package was rated at about 490hp at 6800rpm, and 465lb-ft of torque at 4500. With block as well as heads cast in iron, and "dressed" with carbs, manifolds and clutch, it weighed about 540–560lb. Price was just under $5,000.

The T70 could also carry Ford's small-block, the same one that powered the first-generation Shelby Cobra and the Mark I GT40. The advantage was a weight saving of about 100lb compared to the Chevy, thanks to slightly smaller package dimensions and a more modern "thin-wall" casting design. The disadvantage was less potential for increased displacement. Although the Ford block accepted the same 4.0in bore as its GM rival, a lower deck height limited stroke to 3.25. Most Ford cranks of the period in fact were no larger than 3.0 (76.2 mm), which gave a capacity of 305ci (5.0 liter). Ford's one and only Can-Am victory was scored by Gurney with such a high-winding package, its standard iron block topped by his own Harry Weslake-designed big-port aluminum cylinder heads. The ultimate horsepower claim was 520 at 7800rpm.

According to chassis records compiled by John Starkey for his book, "Lola T70," there were fifteen Mark Is and thirty-three Mark IIs. With two additional Marks, III and IIIb, introduced in 1967, plus two subsequent coupe versions for endurance racing, total T70 production appears to have reached 104. In all its guises the Lola T70 was very popular for several years with sports car racers all over the world.

McLaren M1B

Presented in September, 1965, this improvement of the M1A retained the simple, familiar space frame rather than adopting the Lola's monocoque. However, McLaren's new designer, Robin Herd, had added, subtracted, and rearranged steel tubes to gain a measured 20 percent in torsional strength for no penalty in weight. More parts were McLaren's own now, including the four-spoke wheels.

At 91in, the M1B's wheelbase was 4in shorter than the Lola T70's, and track dimensions were both 51, 6in narrower. Suspension layout was generally conventional for the day and similar to the Lola's—except that the rearward link of the McLaren's front upper wishbone was virtually a leading radius rod. No-fuel weight was supposedly 1300lb, 300 lighter than claimed for the Lola-Chevy, although the alu-

minum Oldsmobile which Bruce still preferred allegedly accounted for about 200lb of the difference.

The most significant feature of the M1B was a new body shape originally penned by motorsports artist Michael Turner, who also had designed the McLaren company logo featuring New Zealand's flightless Kiwi bird. The B's blunt, pragmatic shape—not unlike Penske's *Zerex*—was intended to eliminate the aerodynamic lift that had been apparent with the more wing-shaped A.

Light, handy and stable, the M1B was the first really successful McLaren. It won numerous Group 7 races for both factory drivers and private owners in both England and North America (where the M1B was marketed as the "McLaren Elva Mark 2"). There were twenty-eight of these in all.

As with the M1A, customers could choose various powerplant sizes, but McLaren was still convinced of the virtues of the little Olds. Eventually Traco made use of special blocks with greater internal strength to take the displacement to 5.0 liters for McLaren.

The basic 1965 design was so good that McLaren retained it for his 1966 Can-Am program, although the team further stiffened the frame with additional tubes in the front and rear bays, went to wider wheels—a then-remarkable 12in at the rear—and developed slightly revised bodywork that eventually incorporated a separate rear airfoil-spoiler to replace the former air-dam. Bruce was also persuaded to finally abandon the weight advantage of the Olds for the power and torque advantage of the iron-block Chevrolet displacing 330ci/5.4 liters. To shed some of the weight gain that caused, he switched from a Hewland gearbox to the ZF used in F1.

McLaren and Amon were strong contenders with their special M1Bs in the first Can-Am season, achieving several fastest laps in both qualifying and racing, leading some races, and finishing second in three of them. But even taking the Chevy to 364ci/6.0 liters and over 500hp, trying Hilborn fuel injection in two races, and a manually-adjustable "flipper" rear wing in one never quite made the M1Bs winners in that series.

In the same year's USRRC, however, a production M1B ("Mark 2") was one of Chuck Parsons' championship-winning mounts. Another would take John Cannon to a surprising Can-Am victory in 1968.

While McLaren decided to build an all-new monocoque car for his team to race in 1967, Elva incorporated the revisions made to the 1966 factory cars into a further series of twenty-five tube-frame customer models designated M1C ("Mark 3").

"The Can-Am series was a solid success in 1966. There were record crowds at four of the six circuits, and fastest times were established at all of them. Champion John Surtees earned around $78,000 and for the first time road racing received exposure comparable to Indianapolis. This year is better."

That's the upbeat intro Al Bochroch gave to the second Can-Am year in *Road & Track*. In some respects, he would prove to be right.

Already very rich racing, the Can-Am offered some 40 percent more money for 1967. The added ante apparently forced St. Jovite's organizers out, but Elkhart Lake's Road America promoter stepped up to keep the rounds at six. On the technical front, the series administrators had resisted pressure to impose a ban on Chaparral-type wings, but they were now requiring impact-resistant fuel tanks and shoulder harnesses. On a more political front, SCCA was moving to implement the strongly expressed wish of a number of drivers, car owners, their sponsors, and some manufacturers that the formerly amateur club form a professional racing division.

Big Bangers were indeed going big-time. Anticipation for the new season was intense; the months counting down to the series opener were full of rumors of new cars, and, one by one, new cars were indeed unveiled.

However, not all the promised cars appeared, and too many of the ones that did proved uncompetitive. That was partly because, as would become evident, too many teams were preparing to re-run 1966. By stark contrast, one team was about to raise Can-Am to a whole new level.

Bruce McLaren and Chris Amon had been very strong contenders the first year, but the team saw its record as a humiliating failure. That provided the spark to ignite a powerful synergy, a perfect mixture of the team's great talent, wide experience, efficiently managed resources, and intense enthusiasm. With an ultimately fortuitous problem in another area, it all came together in the most sharply focused assault American road racing had ever known.

McLaren's problem was a holdup on its parallel F1 program. The team had contracted with BRM for a new V-12 engine, but when this ran into repeated delays, it was only natural for the ambitious, energetic little team to focus most of its attention on the Chevy-powered Can-Am car.

Everything Bruce and his boys had learned went into the M6A. From the Ford GT experience, in particular, came wedge-shaped bodywork reminiscent of Ford's experimental 1966 J-car. That had produced too much drag for Le Mans, but McLaren realized its high inherent downforce was just the thing for the short, twisty Can-Am courses.

His time with Ford also had taught Bruce the value of thorough testing, and now another American company saw his efficient, methodical little team as ideal for its own purposes. Goodyear signed McLaren for a race tire development program, supplanting Firestone, and the M6A's suspension was designed around a new generation of wide-tread rubber.

McLaren also launched an engine development program, which featured the team's own fuel injection system for more power and snappier response.

In the cockpit department, when Chris Amon signed for Ferrari, Bruce replaced him with another Kiwi, one who just happened to be on his way to the World Championship: Brabham F1 driver Denis Hulme.

All during the summer of 1967, while McLaren's new F1 chassis lay powerless back in the shop near London, the new Can-Am car was spending day upon exhaustive day flogging around Goodwood, a southern English circuit that just happened to be very similar to the significant North American ones. The prototype M6A logged a couple of thousand hard test miles there long before it was time to go racing.

When the pair of fresh new McLarens in their fresh, high-visibility caramel or papaya paint scheme turned up at the first Can-Am, they were ready to race. In that, they were just about alone.

Elkhart Lake, Wisconsin, September 3, 1967

A pair of bright, yellow-orange cars sparkling at the head of the grid: color the Can-Am all-new. Anyone claiming prescience at Road America 1967 would have said they were seeing the next five years of North American sports car racing.

The story of that opening event of an era can be told simply. Bruce won qualifying with a lap 10sec better than the previous circuit best and a tenth better than that of his teammate, Hulme. Denny went on to set fastest race lap at another new record and won the 200-miler at an average speed above any previous single-lap mark. True, McLaren's car failed to finish because of an oil leak, but Hulme's margin of victory was a daunting 93sec. The man he beat was the new USRRC champion, Mark Donohue. The defending Can-Am champion, John Surtees, was an even more distant third.

It's not that nobody was trying. Eighteen of McLaren's would-be rivals also beat the existing track record during practice. There were several advanced new cars, and several drivers of great repute. The Can-Am's big money and international notoriety had lifted Group 7 racing to a much higher pitch. As Donohue was quoted in *Road & Track*, "The USRRC was fine, but it was like playing tennis with your wife."

McLaren's pole position time was 2:12.6. The record he beat was 2:22.8, which Chuck Parsons set that July while qualifying a McLaren M1C-Chevy for the USRRC. For September's Can-Am, Parsons raised his game to 2:16.6.

Dan Gurney emerged as the fastest of McLaren's opposition. He put his dark blue Lola T70 Mk. IIIb-Ford third on the grid and briefly held that position in the race until dropping back with throttle and gearshift problems. (Gurney's engine this year was based on Ford's new mid-size "351" block which AAR had stroked to 377ci). Fourth fastest qualifier was George Follmer, who had joined Penske Racing as Donohue's teammate for the Can-Am. His T70, Donohue's older USRRC car, practiced with an aluminum small-block Chevrolet but started the race with a conventional iron one. After a spin, Follmer fell out of contention during a stop to change a punctured radiator.

But Donohue, who had qualified fifth in his big-block Mk. IIIb and then changed back to a small-block for the race, passed his teammate at

Riverside: Their Penske partnership only results in a third and a sixth here, but one day Donohue (#6 Lola T70) and Follmer (#16) will come back to dominate the series. *Bob Tronolone*

Elkhart Lake: He is going to become World Champion later this fall and will go on to be the all-time dominant Can-Am driver, but Hulme is always happy to help with the little backstage chores. *Pete Lyons*

Elkhart Lake: Gurney (left) and Donohue were race winners the year before and certainly expect to do even better this time. They have no idea what McLaren is about to unleash on them. *Pete Lyons*

the start for fourth, and soon inherited second when Gurney stopped and McLaren retired. He then was passed by Surtees, whose IIIb had been held back to seventh on the grid with handling and engine problems. Donohue held on, though, and late in the race repassed to second when Surtees spun on oil.

Finishing fourth, after a disappointing fifth-row start and an ignominious mid-race collision with Chuck Parsons' third-row McLaren, was Jim Hall in his Chaparral 2G. This was actually one of the previous year's winged 2Es repowered by an aluminum-block 427 Chevy. Though the big-bore 2G was clocked fastest through the Elkhart speed trap at 182mph, its lap time deficit of more than 4sec to the new McLarens—which were only reaching 172mph—indicated Hall had work to do elsewhere in the performance envelope.

Nobody else showed at all well in that first Can-Am of the new season. Ford Motor Company was supposed to have a three-team, six-car program, but only one entry turned up. And it turned up late—its transporter hitting a phone pole as it did so, knocking out the track's communications—and went home early.

Elkhart Lake: Heimrath's McLaren demonstrates why some officials, even this early, are uneasy about the power of aerodynamics. *Pete Lyons*

This unfortunate was the Holman-Moody *Honker II*. Unlike its namesake, John Holman, who was famous for his prowess on the horn buttons of the big-rig trucks he loved, the Alan Mann-built racer was a sleek-looking design. It also boasted a fuel injected Ford 351 engine and Mario Andretti as the designated driver. But it all too obviously was not ready to race, and it didn't.

The only thing the Ford debacle did do at Elkhart was spotlight McLaren's ultra-professionalism. The short second Can-Am season looked like a long haul for a lot of people.

Bridgehampton, New York, September 17, 1967

Denny beat Bruce for pole this time, and both M6As had stronger brakes, but not a lot else was different about the lineup for round two. Gurney's Lola-Ford was third quickest again, Hall's Chaparral Chevy was going better to start fourth, and Follmer again out-qualified Donohue—but so did Parsons, whose McLaren split the Penske entries. Surtees, grumbling that his Lola IIIb needed a suspension redesign, was eighth; all the euphoria of his September

10th victory for Honda in the Italian GP had quite melted away.

Andretti did persevere with the *Honker II* this time, qualifying twenty-third, but as this writer was unkind enough to record in *Autosport*, "[Mario's] description of the handling, complete with Italianate gestures, sent the crew off into gales of laughter." The Honker's lavender body was now adorned with the name of actor Paul Newman, who was becoming interested in the sport through work on his movie, *Winning*. The racing friendship formed then would see much success during the next twenty-eight years, but at the time Mario was less than sold. "Why don't you put my name on the car and let Paul Newman drive?" he plaintively asked his appreciative audience.

Bridgehampton was the first of 1967's tracks to have a Can-Am history, so we could take a direct measure of Group 7 progress. Hulme's best qualifying lap in the M6A was 1:29.85, which was an improvement of just over 3sec on Jim Hall's 1966 time of 1:32.9 with the Chaparral 2E. With this year's 2G, Hall improved by less than 2sec.

Once again Hulme stormed off to the early lead, and once again the race as such was effectively over. Even a mid-race spin didn't prevent The Bear staying out front all the way. Boss Bruce lasted this time, and the Bruce and Denny Show duly took its first Can-Am bows. Or, to use Don Grey's metaphor in *Motoring News*: "Once again it was a McLaren ball game and no one else was even dressed for the game."

Gurney ran into trouble with his new fuel injection system. Hall retired with the big alloy Chevy streaming oil from every orifice and the right rear suspension pulling away from the aluminum tub. Donohue quickly charged up to third, but his small-block blew; teammate Follmer, close behind, spun off on the oil, though he recovered for an eventual third, a lap behind the winner. George just managed to fight off John Surtees, who came within 2sec by the end. Andretti struggled home eighth.

Mosport, Ontario, September 23, 1967

This third round was on a Saturday, leaving the key Bridgehampton contenders—minus Hall, who hauled the Chaparral straight back to Texas for alterations—a scant five days for travel, prep, and practice. Perhaps that played some role in a number of prerace crashes. Donohue had his left rear stub axle shear as he approached the right-hand Moss Corner. Hitting the bank bent Mark's IIIb chassis. Just minutes later, the other Penske Lola made Follmer a member of the Can-Am Flying Club when it took off at the crest of the rising back straight. George later became a fine private pilot, but this time he flubbed his landing and spun into a pole. Penske

Bridgehampton: On the pace lap, Gurney (#36 Lola T70) signals his intentions, but Hulme (#5 McLaren M6A) and McLaren (#4) are planning something different. *Dave Friedman*

Bridgehampton: The Bear in his lair. Cockpit design, seat belts, fire protection and eyewear are all due for major upgrades in the years to come, but the racer's hard-eyed intensity will never change. *Pete Lyons*

Racing now had two tubs to fix, but they managed it, and both cars made the race.

Charlie Hayes also had suspension failure, also near Moss Corner, but the result this time was heavy damage to the McKee Mark 7. Posey had a shunt in the Autodynamics-built Caldwell D7A, but this was in Turn 1. In Turn 3, Patrick crashed the Mirage. Sam was able to make the race; Scooter was out.

So was Andretti, this time because he had engine problems on top of the *Honker's* terrible handling. After qualifying dead last, 19sec behind pole, and hearing from officials concerned about it, Mario announced he wouldn't race the car until it had passed a thorough testing program. The right approach to the Can-Am, but some months late.

Team McLaren, meanwhile, having done its testing in good time, once again set fastest times. Hulme earned pole again, with Bruce second. At 1:20.8, Hulme beat the 1966 best (Hall's, again) by 2.1sec. He also was well ahead of Jim Clark's 1:22.4 pole for Canada's first Formula One GP held a month earlier.

Gurney, back on carburetors after his injection trouble, took his third grid place for the third time. The Lola-Ford man's performance was better than it sounds, though, for Dan actually equaled Bruce's time, only 0.3sec behind Denny's. But it took an all-out effort—the AAR T70 was spinning as it crossed the line on that lap!

Another great job was Mike Spence's, who qualified the ex-Amon 1966 factory McLaren M1B fourth, ahead of Surtees. The would-be defending series champion had altered his Lola Mk IIIb's suspension, but was still so unhappy with the handling he was now talking of an all-new car. At least he was one of five Group 7 drivers to beat the best of the F1 times.

Any rival looking for a chink in the McLaren armor must have thought they saw it just before the race, in the form of a leak in one of Bruce's fuel cells. But there was nothing wrong with the Kiwi defenses. The team plunged into a bag-change that normally took ninety minutes, and did the job in a reliably reported forty-five. By then, the remainder of the field had started the pace lap, and Bruce charged off after them to take the flag three quarters of a minute late.

Left alone at the front, Hulme once again simply drove away. At the end of the first lap he was 3sec up on Gurney, and presently "The Bear" chewed 0.1sec off his own qualifying time. He spun then, but recovered safely, and by lap twenty Denny had built a 27sec cushion on Dan. By lap forty, half-distance, the cushion was more like a whole mattress: 40sec-plus.

By this point, McLaren had made it up through the field to overtake Spence for third place. He still had

Gurney to go, but was catching him at a second a lap. "McLaren, a favourite of the Mosport fans, was cheered on at every corner," wrote Bob MacGregor in *Autosport*. "As McLaren nosed his way forward through many of the back markers he seemed to be handling the big car as though it were a Formula 1 machine, taking almost any line he chose . . . Gurney's car was obviously no match for the new McLaren as he was consistently out-handled, outbraked, and out-accelerated everywhere on the course."

At lap sixty-four, the yellow-orange McLaren was right on the blue-black Lola's tail, and at lap sixty-six it was on the grass at the apex of Turn 3 and squeezing ahead. At lap sixty-nine it was alone—Gurney rolled down the pit lane with his clutch exploded and water and oil streaming from his engine.

Surtees had long since retired with a misfire, and so had Donohue, with a blown head gasket. Spence was back in third but back a full lap. Hulme, over a minute ahead of McLaren, was signaled to "cool it."

He already had. In the last quarter of the race, his steering rack had worked itself loose. But he didn't ease back quite enough. "With only a lap and a half to go, and apparently sailing to an easy victory," MacGregor reported, "Hulme went off the course at Moss Corner and into the banking. He paused only momentarily to see if the car was burning, then got back onto the track and limped slowly toward the start-finish line, where he seemed to pause for a while

Mosport: His M6A is in slightly less than optimum condition, but Hulme refuses to let it lie down and die. *Lionel Birnbom/Road & Track*

to consider whether it would be better to await his teammate and be assured of second place, but then accelerated down the straight trailing smoke . . ."

Its left front tire flat, the fender ripped apart, the fiberglass rubbing on the tire and finally jamming the wheel to a stop, the M6A did make it around that last 2.46 miles. Denny didn't risk a cooldown lap, though. He parked at the end of the pits guardrail and strolled back to collect his third trophy in a row. With twenty-seven points to McLaren's twelve and Surtees' seven, the man who was on his way to the 1967 F1 World Championship also seemed to all but have the Can-Am wrapped up by the series' halfway point.

Well, we had wanted big-league teams in our Can-Am. But we'd wanted more than one! As *Sports Car Graphic* headlined its story, "Oh, come on Denny . . . come on Bruce . . . You don't have to rub their noses in it!"

Laguna Seca, California, October 15, 1967

But was it indeed all but over? The grid for round four gave another impression. Hulme's M6A didn't start from pole. Not even from the front row. Denny experienced trouble with ignition and fuel injection, plus a broken brake pedal, *plus* cracking wheels. Gurney, driving very hard, beat him by 0.1sec to earn the photogenic place alongside the untroubled McLaren.

Another Lola-Ford was fourth fastest. This was a new entry to the series, with a four-cam Indy engine in back and Indy star Parnelli Jones up front. Hall had the strengthened Chaparral running well enough for fifth, just ahead of Spence in the year-old McLaren. The big-block 2G proved capable of taking 1.38sec off the 2E's 1:05.31 pole position time of the year before, but it fell 1.24 short of this year's fastest small-engined, non-winged McLaren (1:02.69).

This year Laguna abandoned its earlier two-heat format, and the Can-Am ran as a single 201-mile race. Gurney capitalized on his front-row start and snatched the lead from McLaren, while Jones muscled ahead of Hulme for fourth. Similarly, Spence beat Hall.

The Can-Am had a whole new look!

Not for long. After eight laps in the lead, Gurney's Ford gave up. Jones' followed soon after. Spence dropped back with several different troubles. Guess what that left: Bruce McLaren Motor Racing, a.k.a. Bruce and Denny, cruising one-two. Chaparral Cars was holding third, but losing a second a lap.

Then McLaren was slowing! He coasted around the final hairpin, hugged the pit wall, and dropped his speed to a crawl . . . so he could have a *bath*!

By prearrangement, a crewman was ready with a bucket of water to give the boss a nice refreshing drench as he went by. Well, it was hot, and those were the days before coupes with coolsuits. In fact, Bruce was in extreme discomfort. His cockpit was like an oven and his lips, which he'd bared trying to gulp air, were getting badly sunburned.

The pair of orange M6As went on steadily for eighty-two laps, twenty-four from the end, when only one appeared. Hulme's engine had blown.

Half the field of thirty-two starters was gone by half-distance, and all but nine by the end. Those out included a very unhappy Surtees, who had resurrected his 1966 championship-winning T70, qualified only mid-pack, worked his way to sixth, but finally retired after hitting Lothar Motschenbacher at the hairpin while trying to pass into fifth. Donohue, another who didn't shine in practice, blew another engine. Follmer, who'd qualified even slower, kept going and wound up third.

For once the Chaparral kept going too, and with second place secure but the fuel supply less so, Hall was content to let McLaren lap him before the end.

Winning his first Can-Am hoisted Bruce much closer to Denny, twenty-one points to twenty-seven. ("Maybe when the blisters go down I'll feel happier about it," he said in his next column.) Hall and Follmer were equal third, but their nine points apiece gave them no chance of catching the McLaren men, no matter what strange things might happen in the two races remaining.

But one other little matter was settled the very next weekend. By finishing third in the Mexican GP, Denny Hulme clinched the World Championship.

Riverside, California, October 29, 1967

His Majesty Dan, King of Riverside, really put the spurs to his Gurney-Weslake Ford and set a Friday time that stood for pole position by 0.3sec from Bruce McLaren. Denny Hulme, another full second slower, qualified third again. Jim Hall was fourth.

So far, so familiar, but Mario Andretti had come back with the *Honker*-Ford and put it fifth on the grid, just alongside the Lola-Ford DOHC of Parnelli Jones. Peter Revson and Lothar Motschenbacher, both in Lola-Chevys, out-qualified the similar cars of Surtees and Donohue. Another Ford project, Shelby American's King-Cobra, finally made its Can-Am debut in the hands of Jerry Titus. He was thirteenth on the grid, just behind Spence and Follmer but ahead of such notables as Chuck Parsons (McLaren), Chris Amon (Ferrari P4 Spyder), Charlie Hayes (McKee-Olds), Frank Matich (Matich-Repco), and Sam Posey (Caldwell D7B). This last car had a new magnesium chassis to replace the original aluminum one, which crashed in testing at Lime Rock when a suspension bolt broke. The first car's chassis-mounted, hand-controlled flipper wing had been abandoned. Altogether, the Riverside grid extended to an impressive thirty-nine Group 7 cars.

As at Laguna, Gurney beat McLaren into the first turn, and Jones again charged up to take third. Hulme dropped back behind Andretti and Hall. Unfortunately, that placed him just right to hit a buried-tire apex marker Jones had torn loose in Turn 8. The impact shattered another McLaren left front fender. Denny pitted for surgery, but as he tried to rejoin the race, the official at the pits exit stopped him. In the official's opinion there wasn't enough of the fender left to comply with the Can-Am rule about bodywork integrity. The Bear backed up at what looked like 100mph to discuss the matter with the officials at the start-finish line, but they saw it the same way. Hulme climbed out.

That was lap two. On lap three, Gurney was forced out of another lead when another engine blew. Surtees understeered off Turn 2 on the oil. But that didn't put McLaren up front—Jones had passed him. An Indy man with an Indy engine was leading a Can-Am.

Only for a lap, though. Jones seemed to have used up his tires and was sliding all over the road. McLaren soon repassed and went ahead. So did Hall. And then Hall started closing on McLaren.

That set up the best Can-Am of the season, and one of the best ever. Never mind that every other potential contender fell back or out with the standard litany of Group 7 disasters; never mind a mid-race

gale that blew up a desert sandstorm: the two leaders were running a Grand Prix. And that's how they kept on running, the Chaparral hounding the McLaren, until a little over half-distance, when Bruce, twice in as many laps, had to avoid spinning backmarkers. Jim pounced the second time, and his tall, white 2G, its wing waggling triumphantly, was at last at the head of a Can-Am.

He held it until McLaren out-braked him at the end of the long back straight. But then Bruce ran afoul of more traffic, and the Chaparral whipped by again. Hall, his flipper wing visibly giving the big-block better traction off the turns, was able to stave off McLaren for a few more laps, but then the orange car squeezed back in front. This time McLaren kept it there, though he had to callously over-rev his little Chevy to do it. The gap at the checkered flag was 3sec.

"The other chaps are catching up!" Bruce breathlessly noted.

Las Vegas, Nevada, November 12, 1967

So Bruce was leading Denny, thirty points to twenty-seven. Bear could still beat Boss, but he'd need better luck at Las Vegas than he'd been having.

At first, he seemed to be having it. At the end of the first practice day Hulme was quickest. On Satur-

day, however, a broken valve rocker sidelined him at the critical moment and four drivers passed him. The grid shaped up with McLaren on pole, Hall alongside, then Gurney and Jones sharing row two. Hulme had Peter Revson's Lola next to him on row three

Riverside: Flat out to the flag, Hall (#66 Chaparral 2G) and McLaren give the fans one of the best Can-Ams of all time. *Bob Tronolone*

Las Vegas: The glamorous backside of the sport. During practice, Surtees uses a mirror to check his own Hewland gear selector forks. *Pete Lyons*

Las Vegas: Going backwards gets Surtees to the front. Unhappy with the latest T70's handling, Surtees drives his resurrected 1966 car to a repeat victory at Stardust. *Bob Tronolone*

when time came for Sunday's rolling start. Donohue and Spence were right behind, then Surtees and Motschenbacher. Andretti and Titus would have been next, the *Honker* and King-Cobra sharing the fifth row, but engine trouble and suspension failure, respectively, forced both the Ford efforts out. Posey, in the Caldwell, also non-started after another suspension bolt failure.

"It is hard to say," wrote Gordon Martin for *Autosport*, "what the race officials would have done had Parnelli Jones continued to lead the race for longer than four laps, as they were in deep conference on his somewhat unorthodox start . . ."

Though he'd driven the pace lap in his proper place on the outside of the second row, P.J. stuck his

him the title because he'd won one more race. It took him to lap fifty-one, but he did it, clocking fastest lap, passing the leaders to take back the lap he'd lost in the pits, then catching and passing fourth-man Hayes. He was all set for his second international championship of the year.

Then his luck ran out. The second of McLaren's normally reliable Chevys exploded. Right in front of the pits and everybody. At that instant, Bruce Leslie McLaren of New Zealand was the second Can-Am champion. But after five straight victories, the Bruce and Denny Show was blacked out in Las Vegas.

By this time Jones was also offstage, a failure in his gearshift mechanism on lap five letting him avoid

boot in the Indy Ford a lot sooner than anyone else, and passed the green flag first. Halfway around that first lap, he had a 3sec lead.

Meanwhile, back in the first turn, a bunch of mid-fielders had disappeared in a great plume of desert dust and flying rocks. Eight of them emerged in various states of damage.

Though Hulme wasn't directly involved, the scattered debris may have been the cause of the flat tire that forced him into the pits at the end of lap two. At the same time, McLaren had started the race knowing his engine was mixing its oil with its water. Pouring in gasket "goo" and crossing fingers didn't do the job. He had to park in only a few laps.

Denny knew what he had to do: finish fourth. That would tie him with Bruce on points and give

a likely confrontation with outraged officialdom. That left Hall leading from Gurney, but shortly both of them ran into trouble, and Donohue inherited first place. Surtees was right behind him until lap fifty, twenty from the end, when he lost some gears and dropped away.

But halfway around the final lap, with 21sec in hand on Surtees, Donohue felt his engine die. He was out of gas! As the blue Lola spluttered helplessly toward the flag, the red one roared by in the last 200 yards and snatched it away.

Surtees was driving the same car that had won for him the year before. The only difference was its wider Firestones—"and the extra heavy coat of Johnson's Wax I had on the car," as the defeated 1966 champion happily quipped. A thorough pro.

However, it was the overwhelming professionalism of Bruce McLaren Motor Racing that had shaped the history of Can-Am 1967—and that would continue to do so for many Can-Ams to come. "Trying to learn how to go motor racing properly over the last couple of years has worn us down nearly to our knees," Bruce said in his season-ending *Autosport* column, "but the 1967 Can-Am series stood us back on our feet again, and now we're going to try even harder to walk tall."

Cars of the Can-Am 1967
McLaren M6A

The car that would found McLaren's dynasty of definitive Can-Am designs was simple, light, and practical, but most importantly it was ready. The M6A began as lines on paper in April 1967, and emerged from McLaren's new Colnbrook factory as a running prototype a mere eleven weeks later—on Monday, June 19, two and a half months before the first race.

Nominally in charge was Robin Herd, a young British engineer who had come from the aircraft industry, but there was plenty of input from design assistant Gordon Coppuck (British); mechanics/fabricators Tyler Alexander (American), Wally Willmott (New Zealander), and Don Beresford (British); McLaren business partner Teddy Mayer (American); and, of course, Head Kiwi Bruce himself. In fact, this turned out to be a rare, truly successful committee effort.

It was only natural to agree to use the same monocoque chassis technology just adopted for that year's M5A McLaren F1 car. The M6A two-seater tub comprised bulkheads made of square-section steel tubing weldments linked by riveted and bonded box-structures of magnesium and aluminum sheet. As was conventional at the time, the twin-pontoon tub ran the full length of the car's wheelbase, thus being the primary load bearer, but some extra strength was contributed by solid-mounting the engine block between the rear chassis "forks."

Fuel was carried in three rubber cells, one each inside the chassis on either side of the cockpit, the third under the driver's knees. The tanks were linked through one-way valves which could be arranged to keep the fuel weight on the best side for a given road course. Total capacity was 65gal (U.S.).

Suspension was similar to that of the preceding M1-series cars, and had no "anti-features," but was laid out in consultation with Goodyear to keep a new, wider tire more nearly flat on the road. As on Lola's T70, the

Engineer Robin Herd frequently rode with McLaren to assess first hand various aspects of the car's behavior forwards and, in some cases, backwards. *Tyler Alexander*

Top left: McLaren and Herd compare notes concerning the prototype wing. *Tyler Alexander*

Top: McLaren testing the M6A sans bodywork, 1967.
Tyler Alexander

Matich SR3: Neatly laid out and nicely made but underpowered, this car came from Australia, where Frank Matich was a champion. He used both Oldsmobile's small aluminum V-8 and the derivative engine built up by Repco with single-cam heads. This Repco, in 2.5-liter form, powered Jack Brabham and Denny Hulme to the 1966 and 1967 world championships. Matich ran it at about 4.0 liters, which wasn't enough for the Can-Am. He planned to come back with a bigger Repco in 1968, but didn't. *Pete Lyons*

M6A's lower rear suspension radius rod disappeared into the chassis "fork" to the mid-block engine mount. Wheels were the now-familiar McLaren four-spoke, four-stud type cast in magnesium. They all measured 15in in diameter, and the rear rims were 13.5 wide—an impressive dimension for the day. Track measurements were 53in front and rear; overall width, 68.

The wheelbase of the first car, Bruce's M6A-1, was 91in, the same as the M1B's. (Some contemporary accounts give the figure as 89, but this appears to have been a misunderstanding. The author has measured the surviving vehicle's wheelbase at slightly more than 91.) When the taller Denny Hulme joined the team he found he could only drive the prototype with his shoes off, so he asked for his chassis to be built 2in longer through the center of the monocoque. (A tape measure quickly shows M6A-1's doors are 2in shorter than those on any of its sisters.) With other adjustments, this resulted in 3in more leg room. The 93in wheelbase was carried forward to the team's third, spare chassis and the following year's line of M8B production models.

As was his practice, McLaren first tested the M6A in bare-chassis form, to balance the basic handling to his liking before adding aerodynamic loads. Engineer Herd, one of the field's numerous frustrated drivers, often cadged rides in the passenger seat to study first-hand one aspect of behavior or another. On one memorable occasion he was riding backwards, his knees in the seat, watching the rear suspension, when his butt sagged over in a turn, fouled Bruce's arm, and Robin got to watch a spinout from the inside.

He told Eoin Young, author of "McLaren!" about it. "It was fascinating to see the combination of throttle bursts, steering movements, and brake applications that sent us spinning harmlessly down the center of the track." When the car stopped, he added, "We both looked at each other and started hooting with laughter." Data acquisition in the heroic age.

Once installed, the fiberglass body displayed the then-new "wedge" profile at the front for aerodynamic downforce. The shape basically was McLaren's own, although Bruce admitted it reflected his experience with Ford's experimental J-car. Development was undertaken in a full-size wind tunnel using Bruce's 1966 M1B chassis as an armature. To balance the front-end downforce, and no doubt urged on by the aeronautically-minded Herd, McLaren tested a variety of tail appendages, including a separate airfoil body-mounted on struts. The wing yielded no significant lap time advantage, and anyway, "Never copy something unless you understand it," was a favorite motto of this pragmatic conservative. In the end, he chose to race with a simple, molded-in ducktail rear spoiler trimmable with a height-adjustable blade.

For the sake of simplicity and practicality, again, Bruce vetoed the urgings of some on his team to adopt the hip-mounted radiators pioneered by Chaparral.

For power, McLaren stayed with the small-block Chevy he'd learned to love the year before. However, his determination to have the best Chevrolet led him to the Los Angeles hot rod industry and such specialists as Al Bartz, Fred Carillo, Ed Iskenderian, and Mickey Thompson. Their products were assembled in England by McLaren's Gary Knutson, an American previously employed by Chaparral. His package used a bore of 4.04in with a stroke of 3.50 to displace 358.9ci (102.6x88.9mm = 5,882cc).

Knutson developed his own fuel injection system based on a Lucas mechanical metering unit, as used in F1, combined with a Thompson "crossover" intake manifold intended for side-draft carburetors. One of his system's features that drew much notice at the time was his routing the fuel through specially-formed passages within the manifold so that it would

Bruce McLaren, 1967 Can-Am Champion

Tiny, far-off New Zealand has sent an amazing number of great people into the sport, and this man led them. Born August 30, 1937, Bruce repaid his enthusiastic nation's annual racing scholarship by winning his first F1 Grand Prix at the age of twenty-two. That GP happened to be the first in the U.S., at Sebring in 1959, and North America was to became a happy hunting ground for McLaren and the organization he founded in 1964. A cheerful, universally well-liked young man, Bruce never claimed to be the world's fastest driver, and he often smilingly discounted his own engineering ability—"Make it simple enough even I can understand it," he'd tell his team. But his own work at the drawing board, on the shop floor, and in the cockpit resulted in racing machines that vanquished all comers in Group 7 for five years; were top contenders at Indianapolis; and won many F1 championships. Sadly, Bruce McLaren wouldn't see all that he wrought. He died in a testing accident June 2, 1970. *Bob Tronolone*

be cooled on its way to the metering unit. Power output was as much as 525 at 7000rpm, though in races the drivers generally held the shift point to 6500 or less. A cutout in the Scintilla magneto ignition operated at 7500. The oil sump remained "wet." Borg and Beck supplied the three-plate clutch and Hewland the LG 600 transaxle in 5-speed form.

At least one of Chevy's rare, 400lb aluminum engines came McLaren's way, but this failed to retain the team's confidence, and for the most part, the M6As raced with iron blocks. All-up weight of these, including exhaust system, was a claimed 560lb.

To show the Yanks the Kiwis were in synch with the Psychedelic Sixties, some of these engines appeared with little plaques affixed to the valve covers proclaiming they were full of "Flower Power."

Apart from occasional engine failures of various sorts, all of which were considered normal with highly stressed Chevys, the M6As gave little mechanical trouble during the six-race 1967 series. Need was encountered for heavier-duty brakes, halfshafts, wheels, and radiators, and Hulme's Mosport shunt caused by a loosened steering rack led to some chassis buckling discovered later.

Late in the season, though, Bruce was pleased to note that the M6A chassis had been so nicely set up at Goodwood that he reached the last race in the States before he felt any need to change anti-roll bars. Both he and Hulme reveled in handling that was at once stable and responsive. Envious outsiders spoke of the M6As behaving like F1 cars—or "sophisticated go-karts," as one driver put it.

Hulme described his impressions in a column then published by England's *Motor Racing* magazine. "I like the basic simplicity of the M6A, and also the way it was possible to drive it quickly without it appearing to be quick. It seems to go round corners like a slot-racing car, and the engines we are using are very sweet with little vibration . . .

"I think we have a big advantage with the new McLarens—they will change direction quickly and are far more maneuverable. This means that you can even change your line in the middle of a corner, whereas I could never do that when I was driving last year's Lola."

On its unveiling, the new McLaren was said to weigh 1,354lb. If accurate, this must have described the original, short-wheelbase car and presumably as fitted with the early all-aluminum engine. In its championship-winning trim, the M6A probably scaled closer to 1500lb. That first chassis, M6A-1, was considerably lighter than successive ones and has been called "flimsy." It lacked certain internal bulkhead stiffening members applied to later chassis, and the junction between side tanks and footwell box had some gusseting added as an apparent afterthought. This and several other details were improved on later cars.

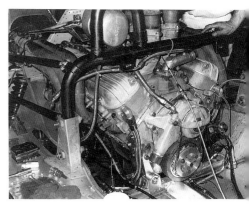

Same tub, new lump: The small-block of the 2E (top) gave way to the big 427 to create the 2G. *Bob Tronolone, Pete Lyons*

As a Can-Am design the M6A was dominant in 1967. Of the six races, it started from pole in five, won five, finished one-two twice, and set fastest lap in six. Between them, its two drivers scored more than three times the points taken by anyone else. (Certain information courtesy of Lynn Larson, present owner of M6A-1.)

Chaparral 2G

Having lost one of the 2Es in Hap Sharp's crash at Nassau, after the 1966 Can-Am season, Jim Hall chose to soldier on solo for 1967. He did so with the sole remaining tub, once again making such extensive alterations that he renumbered it 2G. The primary change was to Chevrolet's much more powerful, 427ci/7.0-liter big-block engine.

Chevy's 427 first appeared in prototype form at the Daytona NASCAR stock car race early in 1963. It

Ferrari 330P4-350 Can-Am: In 1966, as back in 1963, Ferrari managed to field nothing but a cut-down endurance coupe, and this year's Group 7 model was only a little more of the same thing. Ex-McLaren man Amon (#23, shown here at Laguna Seca) and teammate Williams were given a pair of now-obsolete P4s with the roofs removed, their nosepieces reprofiled, and their three-valve, twin-plug V-12s enlarged to 4.2 liters. Power rating was 480 at 8500rpm. Entering the series only at round four, their best qualifying position was 13th and their best finish a 5th. *Dave Friedman*

Neither Mario Andretti behind the wheel nor Paul Newman's name on the nose could overcome the *Honker II* 's inadequacies. *Pete Lyons*

However, the prototype of the first great McLaren was strong enough to carry its creator to the 1967 Can-Am championship and then to make Mark Donohue the 1968 USRRC champion. Two major wars won with this single weapon within a twelve-month period. No other Group 7 chassis can claim a similar distinction.

was very fast, but it dropped out of the 500-miler and vanished from the scene, leaving behind only its nickname, "Mystery Engine." Two years later Chevrolet put a much-revised version into production. Its primary job was hauling the huge, "full-size" passenger sedans of the day, as well as light trucks, but it was an

option for the Corvette as well. It came at first in a displacement of 396ci, but in 1966 was taken out to a bore and stroke of 4.25x3.76in. for a displacement of 426.7ci. (107.95x95.5mm = 6,993cc).

It was primarily a street engine, but racers of every stripe drooled over the new Chevy's magnificent cylinder heads, which took advantage of stud-mounting (as opposed to shaft-mounting) of its valve rockers to splay the intake and exhaust valves at different angles. This array permitted large valve heads, big, free-breathing ports and an efficient, high-turbulence "semi-hemispherical" combustion chamber. The bristling appearance of the valves fostered a new nickname: "Porcupine." All this muscle and modern science made the familiar, faithful 1955-era "mouse motor" look suddenly small and old.

The 427's one problem, especially for road racers, was its great weight. As cast in conventional iron and equipped with normally installed accessories, it scaled some 680lb.

Chevrolet R&D tackled that as it had with the small-block, by developing an aluminum version,

again with iron cylinder sleeves. Though company personnel still were not supposed to be involved in racing, letting someone else race-test new hardware could be passed off as a legitimate part of the development process. The first such test was in a pair of Chaparral enduro coupes in the Daytona 24-hour in February 1967. One car led at the beginning, but both retired for reasons other than engine failure. During the rest of the international season, when tuned for longevity with about 525hp, the big-block generally continued to run well. An inadequate transmission bearing was the main problem, and with that finally fixed a Chaparral 2F won at Brands Hatch in England in July.

Meanwhile, back at Rattlesnake Raceway, Hall was getting the 2G with the same basic power package ready for the Can-Am. Even when made of light alloy, the bigger, more powerful engine demanded a lot of chassis changes.

The new 427's weight was about 460lb, only some 65lb more than Chaparral's aluminum 327, but it was a bulkier lump to install. The basic small-block had been 20in long and 18.5 wide; the big one formed a cube about 24in on a side. As tuned for its first Can-Am season, it produced approximately 570–580hp, or 120–130 more than the 2E had packed the year before. Obviously, the same car had to be re-engineered in many areas: fuel system, cooling systems, brakes, wheels and tires, wheel hubs and hub carriers, even bodywork. The 2G came out of it about 100lb heavier.

"You could feel it, you could tell it was heavier," Jim remembers with clear distaste. "It felt more ponderous. It was not quite as nice to drive as the lighter one. The torque reaction was certainly greater, the feel was more 'butch,' if you will. There was this deep rumble, and it would go like hell. But there was not as much finesse involved in it."

That wouldn't rankle so much had the car been successful. It wasn't. The 2G was fast. But it would seldom last.

Left: *Honker II* source of motivation was based on Ford's new 351 engine series. *Pete Lyons*

Shelby King Cobra/Terry T10: Hitting the ground even later than the *Honker II*, this other Ford-powered project managed to race only at Riverside. Commissioned by Carroll Shelby, it was drawn by former Lotus and Eagle designer Len Terry, who started with an aluminum monocoque but then departed from convention. His suspension, both front and rear, utilized single coil springs. These were mounted transversely, with each end clamped by the opposing suspension arms to take bump loads, chassis lean being resisted only by anti-roll bars. After one of these coils popped right out of the car during testing, they were replaced with more traditional arrangements. Also, at first the radiator laid down horizontally in the long "needle" nose, but when it proved not to cool the engine it was relocated to the tail. That didn't work either, so it was moved back up front. The handling was visibly dreadful, and there were structural failures. On its debut the contraption lasted three laps. It never made it to the grid for the season finale. *Bob Tronolone*

Posey steers the Caldwell D7 out to its debut at Road America. *Pete Lyons*

"We took that good car, put the big-block engine in it, and we had all kinds of engine problems in 1967. I had eleven engine failures in '67 trying to run the big block. So that particular design, which I think was probably the height of our car development, failed to fulfill its promise because of poor engine durability."

Although the 1967 Chaparral 2G was a disappointment, its performance did improve during the short Can-Am season. Of the five races it ran, it qualified four times in the top four, once started from the front row, was taken by Hall into the lead of two races, and finished second twice.

Honker II

Ford won Le Mans for the second time in the summer of 1967, but the automaker's great motorsports juggernaut was already losing steam, so its Can-Am program was always sporadic and plagued by politics. Still, some individual race-minded employees and vendors tried their best. Following assorted experiments with Ford-engined Lolas in 1966, the first dedicated Ford Group 7 car was built the following year. With funding channeled through Holman Moody, the stock car specialists who would campaign this road racer, Ford of England designer Len Bailey—previously assigned to the GT40 project—and fabricators at Britain's Alan Mann Racing produced a car initially called the "Project 77." Later it received a formal nickname in honor of John Holman, known for making good use of the air horns in the big-rig trucks he loved to drive. In many respects the car was conventional, with a full-length aluminum monocoque said to be particularly stiff, and generally contemporary suspension geometries. However, in hopes of better brake cooling all four discs were located inboard of the upright castings, and at the front this layout required rocker-arm suspension with inboard springs. At the rear, as on early GT40s, the inboard U-joints were rubber donuts and the transaxle was a ZF. The engine was based on Ford's new mid-size block, a tall-deck version of the familiar Cobra/GT40 unit which allowed longer strokes; the car first raced at 351ci, later a 3.75in stroke yielded 377ci. (Gurney was using this engine that year in his Lolas). The *Honker* installation featured a GT40-style crossover exhaust system and used England's Tecalamit-Jackson fuel injection to produce horsepower which probably reached the mid-500s. Dry weight was allegedly 1,520lb. Wind tunnel testing evolved a particularly sleek, low-drag body shape, but track testing revealed that the unusually long tail was not providing the anticipated stability, and spoilers had to be tacked on. Another early problem was inadequate fuel capacity, the original tanks only giving 54gal (U.S.). At first, too, the shift lever was between the seats, but driver Andretti immediately asked for it to be moved under his right hand. That was only the first of his complaints, for the handling and braking never earned his confidence. Sadly, this was another of those all-too-common Can-Am efforts which stepped off on the wrong foot and never recovered. Nor did a later trio of coupe-bodied Group 6 enduro versions with Ford Cosworth F1 engines (P68) achieve success.

Caldwell D7

Hoping to make the best use of the newest tires, 15in wide in back, Ray Caldwell readopted the oldest suspension idea—beam axles. Not beams, in truth, but trusses of tubing, which followed the de Dion principle at the rear. The front "axle" was simpler, with two lateral members between the steering uprights braced by a single diagonal. Lateral location at both ends was by Watt linkage, and there were leading and trailing rods at front and rear, respectively. At first the steering was by drag links to a VW box mounted just ahead of the aluminum monocoque's cockpit, but a redesign for 1968 had a rack-and-pinion system bolted to the front "axle." The car first raced with a "flipper" wing atop the roll bar. Unlike the Chaparral system, which fed its loads directly into the wheel hubs,

this was chassis-mounted and was "power operated," at first by engine oil pressure, later by compressed air. The driver controlled the action with a hand knob—as the transmission was a ZF manual, his left foot had other duties. Reluctantly, the team abandoned the wing because it seemed to cause straight-line instability, and there was too much else needing attention to concentrate on that. In fact Group 7 was an ambitious step up for the manufacturer of Autodynamics Formula Vee racers, and this was an ambitious Group 7. Though the cornering speed was high, the handling was erratic. There were various breakages, too, one of which destroyed the first car during mid-season 1967 testing. A replacement tub was crafted of magnesium, which saved 60lb but didn't fix the problems. During 1968 encouraging speed was shown in some 1968 US-RRC events, the car leading for a time in Mexico, finishing third at Riverside, and qualifying second at Watkins Glen. Its Can-Am record was another story. Finally original driver Sam Posey (seen here steering the first car in the Elkhart Lake paddock on its debut), who also financed the project, admitted disillusionment. But he still owns the survivor.

Mirage

Though it didn't appear in the Can-Am until 1967, the Mirage dated from 1965, when small dimensions, light weight, and low drag were still widely esteemed. Built for Jack Nethercutt, who had been racing a Lotus 19, the Mirage was designed by aerospace engineer and racing consultant Ted Depew. He assured low weight by specifying the aluminum Oldsmobile, which in '65 was still Bruce McLaren's weapon of choice, and sought to reduce body frontal area by developing special 13in-diameter wheels, 2in smaller than usual. "Special," because he wanted powerful brakes, and conventional discs and calipers wouldn't fit inside 13in cast-magnesium wheels because of their thick wall sections. But he could reach his goal by, 1) using Frank Airheart's unusually small brakes with vented rotors, and, 2) fabricating the wheels of relatively thin sheet aluminum barrels, with bolt-on rims to eliminate the need of dropped centers for tire mounting. The rest of the wheel was made similarly, as a riveted assembly. This was a labor-intensive method, but it resulted in a light, strong piece of the necessary dimensions. After that, it was child's play to make the chassis the same way. Unfortunately, by the time Scooter Patrick drove the car at Bridgehampton 1967, the wheels and tires had grown to 15in, the extremely sleek body designed by Peter Brock had grown a draggy rear airfoil, and the feathery little Olds had been ousted for a weighty iron Chevy.

Fabricated 15in wheels used by the Mirage. *Pete Lyons*

Born out of SCCA's Big Bang Theory of race promotion, the Canadian-American Challenge Cup began to achieve real maturity in its third season. Although for 1968 the number of events remained at six, not including an invitational extra race in Japan at the end of the year, prize funding once again swelled impressively. The race purse total was up by $10,000 to $225,000; the championship prize fund, which paid down to tenth place, had been increased by 40 percent to $126,000; possible contingency awards came to another $175,000. That made the Can-Am a half-million-dollar series. Cubic money indeed to the wallets of 1968, and most of the serious Can-Am contenders saw more cubic inches as the way to go after it.

By then, of course, biggest-block Detroit power was no longer really new in road racing. Ford had won Le Mans in 1966 and again the next year with its own 427ci (7.0 liter) cast-iron V-8, and Chaparral's 1967 long-distance and Can-Am models, the 2F and 2G, were competitive using special aluminum Chevrolets of the same displacement. Other Group 7 teams had been experimenting with similar installations of their own, most notably Penske Racing, winner with Mark Donohue of the '67 and '68 United States Road Racing Championships.

In its all-iron form, Chevrolet's big engine had its roots in stock car racing and was now a regular, mass-production item. Drag racers had come to love the angle-valve "semi-hemi" or "porcupine" (hence "rat") for its efficiency and tuning potential, but Can-Am builders found its weight daunting. However, GM engineers had an aluminum version about ready for public sale as 1969 Corvette option "ZL-1," so some early units were to be made available to road racers in 1968.

In the 1967 Can-Am, however, the only winning powerplant had been the small-block, all-iron Chevy displacing no more than 6.0 liters. It was a bold move on the part of Bruce McLaren Motor Racing, whose success was built nearly as much on staying power as on the other kind, to cut its dependence on the tried and trusty, 1955-era "mouse motor."

"Cut" is the operative image. McLaren literally chopped the back off a 1967 M6A chassis—Hulme's—to create the 1968 prototype of its big-block "rat motor" racer.

As with so many automotive advances, the use of the engine as a stressed frame member was established in racing by Lotus founder Colin Chapman. He did not originate the basic principle, but his elegant employment of it on the Formula One Lotus-Ford 49 was eye-opening and convincing. The seminal design qualified fastest, set best race lap, and went on to win its very first event, the Dutch Grand Prix in June 1967. Bruce McLaren was an unhappy backmarker that day, but he did not miss the brilliance of Chapman's design.

"That new Lotus is a little sparkler," he reported in "From the Cockpit," his periodic *Autosport* column, "built right down to weight and right up on power . . . [It's] a fireball." By unifying both major elements, noted this trained engineer, "you have a complete car and engine designed as a racing combination."

McLaren's 1967 Can-Am program was too far along at that stage to think of a redesign, but when the happy band of Kiwis launched their 1968 assault on the Americas, they had armed themselves with a Grand Prix-style gunship.

"We started running a prototype car in March," Bruce was quoted as saying in a *Road & Track* story by Eoin Young, the fellow New Zealander who also typed up McLaren's tape-recorded columns. "It was really one of last year's cars with lower profile tires and the body cut down. Then we tried a cast-iron 427 engine in it, a liter bigger than the engine we ran last year . . . The old chassis was cut in half and the engine became the rear of the car with the rear suspension hanging off a subframe. With this mobile test rig we tried a dry-sump setup, wings, new brakes, and all the while the new M8A was taking shape on the drawing board."

One of McLaren's engine men, Lee Muir, recently told journalist Alan Lis about Bruce's first taste of big Chevy power. "The first engine was a 427 with iron block and aluminum heads. It made 560lb-ft. of torque and 624bhp at 6500rpm. Bruce took it for the first drive, and he came back with a grin from ear to ear. 'Jesus Christ, there's never been anything like this! There's no way we can use all this horsepower.' But within three weeks he was asking what we could do to get more."

As with all previous McLarens, the M8A resulted from collaboration among widely experienced racers who were also like-minded friends. "Hanging the engine off the back of the monocoque was pretty much my idea," Bruce told Young for *R&T*. "Gordon Coppuck and I worked out the rear bulkhead, the suspension detail was a group effort, the front half of the chassis was largely Jo's work, and I worked out the body shape and general layout with Jim Clark of Specialized Mouldings."

"Jo's" surname was Marquart. He came to McLaren's drafting department from Lotus to replace Robin Herd, who had moved on to Cosworth (and who would later co-found March). "Of Swiss birth, [Marquart] was immediately christened 'The Foreigner' by a bunch of Americans and New Zealanders working in England," Young dryly recorded. The Americans on that year's team were Teddy Mayer (team manager), Tyler Alexander (crew chief for McLaren's car), Gary Knutson and Lee Muir (engine development), Haig Alltounian (mechanic), and Frank Zimmerman ("gopher"). Other key figures included designer Coppuck, engine man Colin Beanland, and master fabricators Don Beresford and Bill Eaton. As in '67, World Champion Denny Hulme was the team's formal lead driver.

Bruce, the reigning Can-Am champion, was no lightweight in the cockpit himself, but neither was he about to weigh his team down with a rival ego. As Young put it, "The pair get on well together, Hulme respecting McLaren's urge to design and build his own cars while reckoning himself to be a better driver than Bruce, and Bruce happy to acknowledge the point if it makes for a smooth running operation and lets him concentrate on new ideas."

When finally unveiled to the press, McLaren claimed the M8A weighed about 1,450lb, and stated that its 427 engine made 620hp at 7000rpm. That was a boost of about 100hp, or nearly 20 percent, over the

Laguna Seca: Six hundred horsepower in the wet; this was the second race in four to run in the rain. As the rest start the pace lap, Hayes and Hall are already out of it, parked far left. Cannon is already looking for clear air between Parsons (#10 Lola T160) and Donohue (#6). *Bob Tronolone*

Elkhart Lake: Brute force tactics. In racing, as in life, there's a time for finesse and a time to make things happen. For 1968 McLaren turned to Chevrolet's giant 427. To make it fit, Lee Muir returned to basics. *Pete Lyons*

old 5.9 car, for no gain in overall weight. Team insiders say the true power number was closer to 640, but even the public figure prompted Britain's *Motoring News* to note with awe that the new Can-Am machine presented "a power to weight ratio . . . better even than the fabulous Mercedes and Auto-Union prewar grand prix cars which remain legendary."

Bruce McLaren had now built himself a racer "right down to weight and right up on power . . . a fireball."

The new M8A was ready for its first test on July 16, six weeks before the first Can-Am. So far, so good, but if the defending champion intended—and he must have—to develop his all-new '68 mount as thoroughly as his '67, he was thwarted by two new factors. One was the hectic pace on the F1 side of his shop. Giving up on the laggardly BRM V-12 of the previous year in favor of Cosworth's superb Ford V-8 had made the team a genuine contender in Europe, but that meant there was less time for the North American sports car program.

Second problem was the English climate. That summer turned out to be especially dismal, and in addition to the normal frustrations of wet test days, Bruce found the limits of Goodyear's fat new slicks during one sudden rain shower at Goodwood and

crunched his prototype. Five days before the pair of brand new M8As was due to fly to America, visitors to McLaren's Colnbrook factory near Heathrow airport found both Bruce and Denny helping the mechanics fit big orange fiberglass body sections.

"The workmanship throughout is superb," complimented *Autosport's* Simon Taylor, "with all the complex piping for the fuel injection and dry sumping neatly thought out and displaying no sign of being rushed, although the McLaren boys have been at it day and night to get the cars ready for a couple of days' testing before they leave the country."

Deftly, the journalist had put his finger on the problem. At that late stage, a mere 500 developmental miles had been logged, a quarter of the previous year's total. The all-conquering Kiwis of '67 could not have felt themselves on solid footing this time. True, while testing at Silverstone, Hulme took better than a second off an F1 pole-position time which he himself had set earlier that summer—yes, in dry conditions, it was a fair comparison—so at least Group 7 cars were still the fastest. Maybe that's why England no longer offered races for them.

But what really counted was the new McLaren's speed against other Can-Am cars, and so far Bruce's

fastest lap with the big M8A around Goodwood, his team's 2.4-mile baseline circuit, had been 1:13.1, a mere 0.3sec quicker than the best Hulme had managed in the small-block M6A. Bruce had been reckoning he'd need a performance jump of about three percent—call it 2sec. Decent weather did grace the subsequent, last-minute test there, and Bruce did get into the 12s, but that still fell short of proving the new, bigger Banger would be enough weapon for the new war.

McLaren wasn't even sure it would stand up to battle. We know now that engine reliability throughout testing had been anything but confidence-inspiring.

Bruce and his boys must have been nursing just a little apprehension as they boarded the plane for Road America, not only about their own cars, but about everyone else's. The press was full of stories about how difficult the dominant 1967 team would find it this time.

Autosport gleefully predicted that "The Can-Am opposition is going to be pretty tough: most people will be using the same 7-liter alloy Chevrolet . . . but there is no capacity limit (apart from a minimum one of 2500cc), and Jim Hall's latest Chaparral is rumoured to have a new 8-liter Chevy lump." Other reports gave the mysterious Texan's mystery car a "magnesium" engine, a new automatic transmission, possible four-wheel drive and/or tires an astounding 18in wide. Whatever Hall unveiled, as the British weekly put it, "is sure to be light, potent, and out of the ordinary, as have been all of his previous projects."

Autosport and other magazines also looked for great things from 1966 Can-Am champion John Surtees, in a new-design Lola with special Weslake cylinder heads on its big-block Chevy, and 1968 USRRC champ Mark Donohue in a fresh McLaren with big-Chevy power. Other GM runners considered likely to be strong were Chuck Parsons, USRRC champion of 1966, and Skip Scott, both in Carl Haas Lolas; Sam Posey in the de Dion Caldwell ("sort of a poor man's Chaparral," *Autosport* called it); Charlie Hayes, in a new McKee-Oldsmobile; and Swedish star Jo Bonnier in his own McLaren M6B-Chevy. Formidable Ford-powered entrants were expected to include Dan Gurney (for himself and Swede Savage with medium-block Gurney-Weslake motors), Lothar Motschenbacher (ditto), Carroll Shelby (Peter Revson, aluminum 427), and George Bignotti (Mario Andretti and Al Unser, DOHC Indy engines). There was also talk of a pair of 700hp Ferrari V-12s (Chris Amon and Jacky Ickx), as well as some ultra-lightweight (800lb) Porsches. *Autoweek* added Australian Frank Matich's new SR-4 and ran a photo of its engine, describing it as a 5.0-liter, 32-valve, 600hp Repco-Brabham V-8.

Motoring News' Mike Cotton could not contain his wistful enthusiasm for a wonder he'd have to travel to America to see. "Now in their third year, the Can-Am Series have taken the 'free formula' breed of Group 7 cars to an intensely exciting pitch for sheer power, spectacle, and competitiveness which is sadly missing from British circuits."

Concluded *Autosport's* Taylor, "Group 7 racing may not be as subtle as Formula 1, but it's as fast, and it looks like being a very spectacular Can-Am this year—especially if the Ferraris turn up to sort out the American V-8s on their home ground."

Elkhart Lake: The new McLaren M8A (#5 Hulme) derived from the previous year's design (#9 Bonnier's M6B) but departed in almost every detail. *Pete Lyons*

Elkhart Lake, Wisconsin, September 1, 1968

Kiwi confidence must have begun to recover even as Brucie's boys rolled through the Road America gate. For one thing, they had arrived in wooded Wisconsin a day ahead of almost everybody else, giving that much extra time to get themselves over six hours' worth of jet lag—and, more importantly, to get their cars properly race-prepared with fresh engines trucked in from Knutson and Muir's Los Angeles shop.

Secondly, the pair of new McLarens proved to be the sensation of the paddock. As this reporter told *Autosport*, "The impression made on onlookers was tremendous—if last year's M6As were advanced, the M8As are fantastic. The whole concept and construction is ultra-modern and the massive motors, topped by huge curved intake horns, are stunning—you can *feel* the power."

They were so impressive because of the third encouraging finding: surprisingly limited opposition.

Though the defending champions had been running late, several of their projected rivals weren't even on the way.

Supply delays forced John Surtees to miss the opening round. Dan Gurney would skip this one too, while the vaunted Ferrari project was even farther behind. As for Porsche's, it would never materialize at all. Nor would the Matich-Repco.

The Chaparral team did make it to Elkhart, but without its much-rumored mystery bird. During final testing at Rattlesnake Raceway on the Monday before the race, the super-secret new 2H model experienced, as Jim Hall put it, "a suspension failure that looks as if it was a design mistake." Naturally, the tight-lipped Texan revealed no more, though we know now that violent axle tramp had destroyed the de Dion rear suspension beam of a radically low, narrow quasi-coupe with two-wheel drive and—yes—very wide tires. Redesigning the 2H would wind up taking another year.

Luckily, Hall still had 1967's 2G, which he'd development-raced in a couple of rounds of the 1968 USRRC. The old winged monster arrived for its third Can-Am season (its aluminum chassis had first raced as a 2E in 1966) looking a trifle tatty, but at least it was a known quantity. Various early troubles with the big lightweight Chevy which Chaparral had run in pro-

totype form had been solved, and it was now inhaling through a high-pressure fuel-injection system. The torque converter transmission now had a power-saving lockup feature, and there were much wider rear Firestone tires covered by add-on "truck fenders." Hall would still be a contender to reckon with.

To anyone who had watched the USRRC, it was no surprise to see that another strong runner was Mark Donohue. And his was a better McLaren than the one in which he had dominated the summer series. Penske Racing had sold the frankly weary ex-Bruce McLaren M6A-1 to Jerry Hansen, Donohue's co-driver in July's Road America 500, and put all its big-block technology into a brand-new chassis. This was actually a third, unfinished McLaren team tub which Penske had purchased along with M6A-1 at the end of 1967. It could therefore be regarded either as the last M6A or the first M6B; production B chassis numbers began with "-2," leaving room for the latter interpretation.

But Donohue and his ambitious little crew under Karl Kainhofer created an M6B like no other. Its suspension had been redeveloped for the bigger engine and wider tires, its body had been reprofiled and remanufactured out of lighter materials, and its all-aluminum 427 Chevy was Traco-tuned to numbers equivalent to McLaren's (and Chaparral's) own. Like Chaparral's, but not McLaren's, Penske's tall engine injector stacks sported a big air scoop to boost high-speed performance. Donohue also had been working on another aerodynamic "unfair advantage" in the form of a hinged section of the rear air dam which he could hand-operate to increase straight-line speed.

Mark didn't have time to try this trick spoiler at Elkhart, but his beautifully prepared, boldly pinstriped, dark-blue McLaren made him the envy of paddock privateers even before he qualified fourth fastest to the pair of papaya-colored factory cars and Hall's winged white Chaparral.

With forty entries vying for thirty-five grid places, Can-Am '68 looked healthy. But that was more on paper than on the track. Only the first four drivers beat the existing qualifying record, Bruce McLaren's 2:12.6 of 1967. Bruce beat it by 2.8sec (2.1 percent—ah-hah!) to take pole again at 2:09.8, or 110.94mph. As the year before, he was a single tenth of a second faster than Hulme. Hall finally lapped precisely 1sec slower than the pole winner, with Donohue 0.2 behind him.

Though a distant 2:13.4, Lothar Motschenbacher's 377ci Ford-Gurney-Weslake-engined M6B was best of the rest, with Chuck Parsons (Haas Lola T160-aluminum Chevy 427), Peter Revson (Shelby McLaren M6B-aluminum Ford 427), and Mario Andretti (Bignotti Lola T70-Ford 305 DOHC, the same car raced

by Parnelli Jones the year before) also in the thirteens. Charlie Hayes, in the McKee with "wedgie" bodywork and big-block Oldsmobile, took the fifth row, along with Pedro Rodriguez in a N.A.R.T.-entered, 4.2-liter Ferrari Spyder cut down from an endurance coupe, both with times in the fifteens. The rest of the lineup trailed off at ever slower speeds, some so slow that finally the organizers only permitted twenty-nine cars to form up on the 2x2 grid.

The front of the grid was colored a bright "McLorange" for the second year running. The Bruce and Denny Show was back—and it was an even better show than it looked, because both men had been struggling.

"Vanished was the accustomed McLaren air of effortless grace," *Autosport* noted about Friday's practice, when the weather was sunny and bright, but moods were not. "On Bruce's car the last-minute tail spoiler fouled the latest tires, the handling seemed wrong, a damper was leaking, a throttle bracket was cracking, and then the great aluminum engine began drooling oil from every pore [that night a holed piston was discovered; it was not the first]. Hulme's couldn't even move for hours; first a supplier error prohibited the fitting of the new wheels, and then there had to be some work with chisels where the front brake discs were fouling the calipers. Once Denny started lapping, he found the differential wasn't locking properly. All these are fiddling little details common to all new machines; it was unfortunate that they had to be worked out under the public eye."

On Saturday morning the McLaren men looked tired, but their cars were looking much fresher. It was soon clear that their problems today were no longer those of the test track but of the race track—tuning and trimming, not rebuilding. Though at one point they let the Boss run out of gas, Bruce soon had his car right for the conditions and snatched pole from Denny, who'd lost time after flat-spotting his tires.

So the comfortable Kiwis took the night off, right? No way, as Denny used to say. On race morning their faces looked as gray as the clouded-over skies. "It's tough at the top," Bruce had said in his column, and his mechanics had spent the wee hours going over their sophisticated new machines with a meticulously detailed, eight-page checklist—three longer than for the previous model.

After a relatively injury-free two years, 1968 opened with a sobering accident. During practice, Tom Swindell put his McLaren into the trees along Road America's fast, curving back straight and suffered nasty burns around the face, neck, and hands.

On Sunday, rain and the pace lap started together. Most drivers had guessed right and were starting on treaded tires, but one could imagine them clutching their little leather steering wheels and mumbling, "I have 600hp and it's wet, I have 600hp and it's wet . . . " As the flag dropped, Hulme powerboated right away into the murky forest, followed in plumes of spray by McLaren, Hall, and Andretti, and leaving Donohue spinning in the grass at Turn 2—debris of some sort had come into his airbox and jammed the throttles open. In a lap, Andretti cut past Hall and set off after McLaren; Parsons was fifth ahead of Revson. Everyone seemed to be going absurdly slowly on the streaming wet surface, but little twitches showed how near the limit they were pushing. Hall was leaving the Chaparral's wing in the downforce position all the time, but the 2G looked unhappy on its narrow rain tires and soon spun off twice.

So McLaren's two strongest competitors in practice were no factors in the race. Hulme, the reigning World Champion seasoned in the rains of Europe, was choosing his own lines through turns and accelerating savagely between them. That was pulling him rapidly away from McLaren, who was running just hard enough to fend off an eager and very sharp Andretti. This was Mario at his brilliant best, a USAC champion unpracticed in the wet but well used to the dirt ovals, keeping his obsolete Lola T70 with its peaky little Indy engine tamed down to vicious little twitches and short bursts of wheelspin.

It wasn't quite the Can-Am spectacle everyone had hoped for during the past year, but it was keen enough.

For a while, anyway. It didn't last. The rain tapered off, and as the track dried, Andretti's 5.0 Lola lost ground to the 7.0 McLarens. That included Donohue's, whose first-lap spin had dropped him to eighteenth, but who was driving very hard and had worked his way back up to fourth and finally had Andretti in his sights with five laps to go.

That's when Hulme, still far ahead of everybody, thundered by with his engine making a terrible clatter. He'd lost a valve rocker, the Detroit V-8's Achilles heel. That wasn't enough to stop the Chevy, but losing a connecting rod did stop Andretti's Indy Ford with less than two laps to go. As Don Grey described the incident for *Motoring News*, "Donohue, sitting right on the Lola's tail, had the traumatic experience of clearly seeing a connecting rod flying right at his car. It sliced into the McLaren's radiator, which then dumped its contents on his feet. As he remarked later, though, he couldn't really tell what the damage was since the temperature gauge was broken anyway!"

As he started the very last lap, seven-cylinder Hulme saw his oil pressure go to zero. He knew he

still had more than 40sec in hand on his teammate, so he motored around the last four miles very gently in top gear, and took the flag amidst great jubilation pit-side. Very hard work it had been to get the complex new McLarens to the start line, and with a day's less time, the team wouldn't have made it, but it paid off—over $24,000 worth for their one-two finish and their nine and six championship points, respectively.

Donohue made it home in third place (four points), Revson lasted to fourth (three), and, after a pit stop to check over his injectors, Hall brought the Chaparral in fifth (two). Sixth place (one) went to Motschenbacher—along with honors for setting fastest lap (2:16.0) after an early spin; he was one of the few who chose to start on slick tires.

Five McLarens in the first six, and the first two were factory orange. An omen?

Bridgehampton, New York, September 15, 1968

If the third Can-Am season had looked like McLaren's second after round one, the picture after the New York race was a little different.

First of all, opposition had strengthened by two. Dan Gurney, winner of this race two years earlier in a Lola, arrived with a new McLaren, but it was no standard M6B. Reckoning that lightness and dash could beat thunder and mass, All American Racers had installed one of their Eagle (Gurney-Weslake-headed) 325ci Fords. That in turn permitted use of Hewland's smaller, lighter DG300 transmission. The track dimensions were narrower, the body was reconstructed with a longer, lower nosepiece, and suspension arms, exhaust system, gear linkage and bracketry were remade out of titanium. Altogether, Gurney's guys said they had managed to take some 100lb out of the original car; they were so proud of their work they were calling it a "McLeagle."

John Surtees had made it to "The Bridge" early enough for some private testing. In this case, too, the car was a unique piece of equipment. Having become estranged from Lola, but having been denied a new McLaren (so McLaren's team manager told *Road & Track*), the inaugural Can-Am champion bought one of Lola's new T160s, but so extensively rebuilt it in his own Team Surtees shop that he entered it as a "TS-Chevrolet." Its "-Chevrolet" part was one of the aluminum GM big blocks with new cylinder heads made by England's renowned Harry Weslake. Similar in pattern to those he'd designed for Gurney's small Fords, they allegedly improved gas flow by seven percent. "On the bench, that is," John admitted. "Not in the car as yet."

There were many other modifications, but the most noticeable was a rear airfoil mounted directly to the suspension uprights on tall struts. Unlike Chaparral's innovation of 1966, unveiled at this same circuit, Surtees' wing was not a "flipper," being fixed at one angle of attack.

Donohue's flipper was fixed, too. He'd apparently abandoned the idea of laying down the hinged panel in the ducktail spoiler. Why? "I'm not going to tell you!" said Mark, smiling pleasantly. Happily, years later he used his book, *The Unfair Advantage*, co-authored by Paul VanValkenburgh, to tell all:

I was going to trim it out on the straightaway, and that car would take off like a rocket. So, about halfway down the pits straight, going well over 170 mph, I released that beauty—and I damn near lost it! On the *straightaway!* It happened so suddenly that it was like being hit with a brick. Naturally I backed off immediately and kept it in a straight line, but that scared me *so* bad that I could never bring myself to use it again.

Not surprisingly, the two M8A McLarens qualified fastest again. However, both were still giving trouble throughout practice. Hulme's engine cracked one of its heads; more ominously, both big-blocks began leaking oil. Gasket replacement seemed to work for Denny's, but after the race-morning warm-up, Bruce's big orange spaceship went up on jack stands to have epoxy glue slathered over every joint in sight.

Hulme, fresh from his McLaren-Ford victory at the Italian GP, was starting his McLaren-Chevy from pole in America. His 1:27.69 (117.47mph around the rough, swooping 2.85 miles) was an improvement of 2.16sec (2.4 percent) on his best qualifying lap of '67. But Denny had no fat cushion. McLaren was just 0.08sec behind, Revson was within two-thirds of a second of Hulme at 1:28.33, and Donohue was a mere 0.2 off that. Hall flippered the Chaparral around at 1:28.85, and Gurney's McLeagle also beat the old record with a stimulating 1:29.27.

Motschenbacher beat Andretti this time—Mario's Indy Ford had also been leaking oil—while Skip Scott had finally received the second Haas T160 Lola and proceeded to out-qualify every other one in the field despite using an old iron small-block. Surtees, held back by various new-car problems, including a dropped cylinder during his final run, qualified tenth. In all, twenty-five cars made it through practice to the start line.

It was a great race! A magnificent white Aston Martin allowed Stirling Moss to set a cracking pace lap. Under the green flag, McLaren dashed ahead of Hulme, and within a couple of laps the two M8s had paired off a little ahead of the rest. On the third lap, Bruce was clocked at 1:28.88 (115.93), which would remain as the race record. This early, apparently, the track was becoming slick with oil.

Back in the pack, the usual Can-Am calamities were taking out car after car. Andretti saw his oil pressure dropping and shut off. Gurney—whose morning warm-up had been enlivened by a flash fire—came into the pits to check out a sudden flutter in his steering. Surtees retired with another valvetrain failure, Parsons and Scott both lost their motors too, Rodriguez (Ferrari) and Posey (Lola T160) collided, and so on. As the afternoon wore on, the attrition rate mounted to levels *Autosport* termed "scandalous."

But this would not be another McLaren runaway. After nineteen laps of ever-harder work on the increasingly slick surface, Bruce let Denny take over the lead, and dropped back, as if to protect him from the third-place man. This was Donohue, who'd taken the position when Revson's brakes began to fade. But closing up behind now was Hall, who'd spent the first few laps scuffing in a set of fresh Firestones, and who was now finding them working very well on the oil. In

a dozen more laps, Jim had caught Mark and passed. Two laps after that he swept by Bruce—yes, Can-Am fans, a factory McLaren had been set down by a Chaparral.

These two left Donohue a little behind as McLaren chased Hall toward Hulme. For one instant, the orange-white-orange sandwich closed right up and it looked like three cars in the lead at once, and then there came a white wing flying over the Long Island sand hills to complete lap thirty-seven first.

Three, four, five laps, and the Texas moment of glory was over. On lap forty-two, the Chaparral lost power. McLaren, who had followed Hall past Hulme, retook his original lead, and this time he was alone. Hulme, his engine puffing white smoke, and Hall, his suffering a stuck injector check valve, dropped back into Donohue's clutches. Mark passed the Chaparral first, then, as he stormed uphill around the last turn

Bridgehampton: McLarens lead lap 1 through Echo Valley, Bruce (#4) from Denny, then Revson (#52), Donohue (#6), and Gurney (#48) in their M6Bs. Hall's and Surtees' winged cars stand tall in the back.
Pete Lyons

Bridgehampton: Donohue chose more-is-more, and his big-block M6B proves out the principle. Here, anyway. *Dave Friedman*

of lap fifty-four, he watched delightedly as the McLaren scattered its engine violently and laid down yet more oil as it veered off into the pit. The Grand Prix was over.

No, not quite. Eight laps later, only eight from the end, with Donohue looming 2sec behind, McLaren's engine died. He caught it, but lowered his goggles and trundled around to retire at the pits, his main bearings gone. Mark eased off, his face one great smile. Second place would have been fine; to win was . . . well, it was the lead of the Can-Am series, with thirteen points to Hulme's nine!

The Chaparral's engine had cleared, but too late to recatch the Penske McLaren, and Hall had to settle for second, half a minute back. Motschenbacher took third, two laps down. David "Swede" Savage, Gurney's young protégé, drove AAR's Lola T160 to fourth, a further three laps behind—a decent reward for a weekend that had begun with a transporter crash in Oklahoma. Swede was four laps up on his Boss; Dan's crew hadn't been able to find anything wrong with the McLeagle's steering, so he had come back out in fourteenth place. Vividly slinging the lightweight dasher around the course like a GP car brought him up to sixth, behind Dick Brown's M6B.

Writing in *R&T*, Al Bochroch expressed the Bridgehampton experience for many fascinated onlookers: "This was the most interesting of all Can-Ams to date. The McLarens are not invincible. Jim Hall, a man not given to brag, said, 'I think I'm faster . . . I had them from 150mph up. My advantage is in aerodynamics—I think the wing makes the difference.'" Donohue, no doubt thinking of flipper spoilers, agreed. "He went by me in the straight like I was in reverse."

As for the new McLarens, Mark added, "'The difference . . . is in their maneuverability—they have more in traffic.'"

While they were running, anyway. Obviously, the Kiwis had a serious reliability problem.

Edmonton, Alberta, September 29, 1968

Thus it was with understandable anticipation that the circus towed the great distance up to Edmonton, the one Canadian venue of this year's Can-Am.

And it was a great distance—the McLaren, Chaparral, and Caldwell transporters, among others, suffered dropped prop shafts, burned wheel bearings, failed brakes, and what not, and the poor old 2G got dropped off the trailer and had its nose battered.

Two regulars didn't even come; Andretti had a clashing USAC date on the dirt at Sacramento, and Rodriguez was busy helping to win Le Mans for Ford. However, Hayes, who had missed race two, was back with the McKee-Olds, and Jerry Titus joined the series in a small-Chevy M6B.

Anybody who thought they'd scented McLaren blood at Bridgehampton arrived here knowing Denny and Bruce had just finished one-two in the Canadian GP at St. Jovite—it raised Hulme to joint first in the World Championship standings with Graham Hill—and Edmonton practice offered no more encouragement. Once again, the pair of M8As qualified one-two, and this time at identical times: 1:26.0, an average of 105.78 around this brand-new, still dusty 2.527-mile course. Hulme did it first, so he'd start from pole.

There was still the specter of engine failure, but Gary Knutson was confident he'd traced the Bridgehampton blowups to a combination of pre-ignition, piston blow-by and oil loss, and he hoped a different piston ring package would cure it all. That, and an auxiliary oil tank in Hulme's car.

Knutson, who had worked on this same engine's problems the year before when at Chaparral, later told *Autosport* that he never did harbor any suspicion that using the engine as a stressed member of the chassis was making it warp under load. "We run our bearings pretty close, and they would have shown any distortion right away," he said. The trouble was high crankcase pressure. With eight huge cylinders above a very small sump, which wrapped tightly around the crank, a little piston ring blow-by meant a lot. The scavenge pump was designed to handle a reasonable amount, but the rings were obviously passing far too much.

Suddenly, he recalled that his earliest 427s, running in the cut-up M6A hack, hadn't shown the problem. In a flash of reverse-development insight, the special racing rings he'd since adopted, but which weren't seating properly, were replaced by a set from a GM parts shelf. End of problem.

Concurrently, a head gasket leakage tendency was cured, and some evidence exists that a different type of oil was adopted. Eventually, engines that McLaren had detuned in futile search of reliability, to well below 600hp in some cases, were allowed back up to their full strength, and then some.

Just to preserve the McLaren lads from complacency at Edmonton, though, their M8As found little ways throughout practice to keep them on their toes: one cold morning, one of their Lucas mechanical metering units seized, a wheel nut jammed on a hub and resisted everything but the most brute force, a couple of throttle butterflies loosened....

Hall, having given the Chaparral a wider wing and more prominent "mustaches" for greater downforce, wound up third-fastest qualifier by 0.4, a tenth up on Donohue. Revson, in his big-engined, generally standard M6B, qualified fifth at 1:27.1, 0.4 better than Gurney in his small-engined, highly nonstandard one. Altogether, this grid had twenty-four starters.

Hulme seemed keen on the idea of winning his fourth international race in five weeks, and when the green flag released him, he simply thundered away. McLaren spent several laps fighting off Hall, then several more chasing him. Both were pulling away from the remainder of the pack, and during this early stage they both clocked 1:25.3, seven-tenths quicker than the front-row grid times. What resolved their duel was not speed but a cracked rear brake caliper fitting which forced the Chaparral into the pits for a frustrating fifteen laps.

Donohue also made a stop to have leaves cleared from his radiator, though the job was done quickly enough to keep him on the leader's lap. Both Revson and Gurney dropped out entirely with dropping oil pressure. Surtees, who'd had engine trouble all during practice, retired with a head gasket gone. Motschenbacher, who'd started seventh and worked up to fourth,

had a radius rod ball joint pull apart at maximum speed on the main straight and his M6B was heavily damaged. In all, half the field finally fell out. This Can-Am had degenerated into just the sort of Denny and Bruce procession everyone else had feared after Elkhart.

Ah, but what of McLaren's engine fears? Around half-distance, Hulme's began smoking, and he saw his oil pressure flickering. Dumping in his reserve supply brought the pressure back up, but not far from the end the needle dropped again. Just as at Elkhart, he went into nursemaid mode, and again it worked. He took the checker at the end of the eighty laps still ten seconds up on his teammate. Donohue was a further half-minute back, his engine having been hurt by the early overheating incident, but at least he was third. On points, he was now second by one from Hulme.

On this day of rampant attrition the fourth place driver was four laps back; it was Posey, who'd started eighth with the Lola (he'd decided the de Dion Caldwell needed a redesign). Parsons scored fifth-place points this time, despite a spin. Sixth was Hayes; not a bad result after a start on the last row at a time over 17sec slower than the front row's because of engine problems, and after a race with a transmission that had jammed itself in fifth—*and* after a last-lap pit stop taken because one of the "Wedgie's" modular wheels had disintegrated. It's tough at the bottom, too, McKee's men might have murmured to McLaren.

Biggest hero, though, was Hall. After getting his brakes fixed and coming back out dead last, he plunged into one of the drives of his life. His 2G caught both the McLarens and passed them, taking back one of the lost laps, and while doing so it recorded the absolute fastest lap of the race: 1:25.3, or 108.55mph on an increasingly oily track. "Well, I didn't have anything else to do!" he grinned at the end. What might have been...but the flying Road

Edmonton: A new venue, a new engine package, and renewed confidence put Denny and Bruce back up front. *Pete Lyons*

Runner was classified a mere eleventh, fourteen laps behind.

Laguna Seca, California, October 13, 1968

Moving to the west coast usually pumped some life into Group 7 entry lists, and there were indeed some series newcomers at Laguna, but several teams once seen as key Can-Am contenders were not. Surtees had decided he'd need more time to sort out his TS-Chevrolet's many problems. Andretti and Rodriguez were once again busy elsewhere, and the struggling Bonnier took a miss too. Nor did the much-anticipated Ferrari effort show, although one car had been entered.

Of the faithful who were there, Bruce McLaren took his second pole position in four races. However, he didn't do it until the second day of practice, and the man he had just beaten was in a car of another color. Jim Hall, taking 1.36 seconds off his own USR-

hue, who had been having rare engine trouble, was on the fifth row alongside Parsons. Engine problems also afflicted Gurney, who could qualify no better than twenty-third. In all, the Laguna Seca grid extended to thirty, the highest number for the series so far this year.

At least, that would have been true had they all started. Hayes, lined up with the McKee in twelfth place, couldn't get the big Olds fired. Hall, up there at the front in second place, got his big Chevy fired, but for only an instant; then it backfired and jammed the starter. Both cars had to be pushed to the side.

Race drivers don't look at things this way, but really, both men were better off missing this one. For the second race in four, it was raining.

This was the Can-Am that, in 1967, had been so hot that Bruce McLaren had arranged to be showered with a bucket of water. The weather gods must've gotten the message this time, because they laid on a full

RC pole time of a few months before, winged the 2G around to 1:01.53 on Friday, and that looked like standing up for pole until the last few moments of Saturday, when McLaren shaved less than a tenth off. Bruce's 1:01.44 (111.33mph around the 1.9-mile circuit) was just shy of a 2% improvement over his own 1:02.69 pole of 1967.

But behind the bare numbers lurked a lot of drama. McLaren lost most of Friday with oil pump problems while Hulme put his car away early with gearbox trouble. On Saturday, Denny's last-minute attempt to put himself on the front row with Bruce was thwarted when something lodged in a combustion chamber, locking the engine.

That meant the second M8A would start from the second row, alongside Revson's M6B-Ford. Dono-

shower from dawn to dark. After the warm-up, Bruce reported, "We're having to feather-foot everywhere." Denny opined, "A stock motor would be bloody fantastic today." Young Swede Savage, gridded tenth in his Gurney Lola, was rolling his eyes. "I've never even *seen* a wet race before!"

Meanwhile, something else was going on in a corner of the paddock that would decide the race. John Cannon, an English-born driver better than the old tube-frame McLaren-Chevy he'd qualified fifteenth, asked Firestone technician Bruce Harré what he'd recommend for the conditions. Harré pointed to a single set of "intermediate" tires originally designed for F1, which he'd brought along at the request of an FA (F5000) competitor in one of

the weekend's supporting events. It hadn't rained for that, so the tires hadn't been used. Cannon tried them for a few laps in the warm-up, and found they were ideal.

"He promptly parked the McLaren," wrote Don Grey in *Motoring News*, "and then spent the next 2-1/2 hours calling on the rain gods to keep up their good work."

They did. It was still raining steadily when the green flag waved. Revson took advantage of the Chaparral's removal to out-drag Hulme into second place behind McLaren. Donohue tucked into fourth, and the race vanished in a comet cloud of spray. Conditions were such that poor Savage spun off into hay bales on his second lap.

But for happy Cannon, the conditions were such that he was whisking around more powerful and modern cars on all sides. By lap five he had buried Donohue in his spume. Next lap he was by both Hulme and Revson, and on lap seven the bulbous little red McLaren threw water all over Bruce's big sharkish orange one and went into the lead of the Monterey Grand Prix.

Lapping as fast as 1:14.4 (92mph), some two seconds better than McLaren could manage, Cannon simply drove around through the entire field again, and once again caught and passed McLaren.

By this point, Bruce had taken off his fogged-up goggles. He and everybody else was having a miserable time. There were innumerable incidents, spins, crashes, breakdowns, and pit stops, so there was a lot of activity all along the lap chart, but none of it mattered to John Cannon. All alone, he took the checkered flag at the end of the eighty laps and 152 sodden, slippery miles, in 1 hour 46:24.6—85.6mph. It was fast enough to win just short of $20,000, or enough to buy the three-year-old car about four times!

Second place might well have gone to George Follmer, who had taken over a Lola T70-Ford for-

merly driven by Ronnie Bucknum and whose Firestone rain tires gave him almost the same spectacular grip as Cannon's, but not far from the end, a deep puddle caught them out and Follmer crashed near the finish line. It was Hulme who finally trundled in second, a lap back but not far ahead of George Eaton, a young Canadian in another old McLaren on Firestones. Motschenbacher, whose hastily rebuilt newer McLaren had been running poorly all weekend, at least scored another decent points finish. Fifth was McLaren himself after a pit stop for new goggles. Jerry Titus was sixth. These five and the next two, Scott and Donohue, all completed seventy-nine laps, so without Cannon and his trick Firestones it might have looked like a pretty good race on paper.

If only your rain-drenched paperwork had been legible.

Riverside, California, October 27, 1968

Had the Can-Am series been a movie, John Cannon would have found work at the wheel of an up-to-date, competitive car. It wasn't, and he didn't. He drove the same M1B-Chevy again, and qualified it fifteenth again.

Of course, it was too much to hope for rain.

Some of his fellows did upgrade their equipment, or tried to. Riverside, possibly the ancestral home of Big Banger American sports car racing, always loomed large in the racer's imagination, and the racer always tried to bring something special for its long straights. Gurney, a man with a lot of reputation at Riverside to uphold, abandoned his less-is-more

Laguna Seca: The right tires and the right don't-quit attitude carry quiet Canadian John Cannon to a famous victory. *Pete Lyons*

Left: Riverside: Flood of power, with McLaren at the point. The reigning champion will finally score his first win of the year. *Dale von Trebra*

Las Vegas: Revson's big Ford-engined Shelby M6B won't last here, but two weeks later, at the post-season invitational World Challenge Cup at Fuji in Japan, it will carry Revvie to victory over Donohue and nine other Can-Ammers (not including team McLaren) and ten local entries led by a five-car factory Toyota effort. *Bob Tronolone*

theory and swapped cars with Savage and swapped engines too—into the dark-blue AAR Lola T160 was stuffed a big aluminum-block Ford 427 prepped by Holman Moody. Announced power was "580-plus." Andretti rejoined the series with a very similar package. Motschenbacher gave up on his mid-size Ford in favor of a full-size Chevy for his McLaren M6B.

Of those who had begun the season with Big Bangers, Bruce McLaren once again was fastest of them all, at 1:38.51, 119.68mph over a course which that year still measured its original 3.275 miles. That did beat Gurney's 1967 Can-Am pole time of 1:39.3, but by less than one percent. Apparently, the track surface had deteriorated, and the weather was hot. Hulme lined up second at 1:38.72. Apart from a Fri-

day transmission failure for Denny—a contingency for which the Boy Scout team proved well prepared, with stronger shafts ready to install in both cars' boxes—the M8As were trouble-free for once.

Not so the rest. Here, near the end of a hectic, stressful series, the true value of McLaren's preseason work emerged. Andretti's big engine missed all of Friday's practice, coughed all its oil out in two laps of Saturday's, and never made the grid. Gurney's did make it and onto sixth place at that, but it was overheating and rattling ominously as it did so. Motschenbacher's was simply overheating, but that robbed him of chassis sorting time, and he could only manage twenty-first starting spot. Donohue's similar package was running hot too, but he was able to install a larg-

SHELBY RACING CO.
Driver: PETER REVSON

GOOD YEAR · 76 · Autolite · STP

er radiator, and finally qualified third (1:39.2). Mark had his lay-down tail spoiler hooked up again, but again he didn't have time to experiment with it, and disconnected it for the race. Hall, after changing engines because of a cracked head, took fourth slot at 1:39.31.

Nobody else beat the 1:40 mark. Revson was fifth, but it was a distant fifth at 1:41.30. Revvie couldn't seem to get a healthy engine, and would go through three before the weekend was over — on race morning, Carroll Shelby clapped him on the shoulder and apologized. Behind Gurney, Parsons outqualified Surtees, who was back to renew the struggle with his Weslake.

As usual, Riverside brought out a big entry. Thirty-five cars appeared on the grid, plus another four as reserves. They did make an impressive sight, but at second glance the quantity merely pointed up the low quality. The thirty-fifth starter had been able to lap no faster than 1:54.5, his average speed more than 16mph off the pace of the front row.

It was just the kind of race the Kiwis had spent so long preparing for. Finally confident of their engines, they hammered them as hard as they pleased and simply drove away, Bruce leading Denny, leaving others to continue what should have been their preseason development.

Hall, making a mighty out-braking effort at the end of the long back straight, took third place from Donohue, but then had the same brake problem crop up as at Edmonton — the identical hose fitting had cracked. This time he elected to keep his pit stop short and struggle around with front-wheel braking only. Revson, Gurney, Parsons, Surtees, Posey, Follmer, and many others all dropped back or out with various ailments. Even Hulme finally had a problem: late in the day, he had to veer off course to avoid a skidding backmarker, which damaged one of his front fenders, and he pitted twice for repairs.

At the end of what was an uninspiring race for everyone else, but which he thought had been great fun, McLaren came home first for the first time this season, followed at a respectful 37 seconds by Donohue. Hall brought the Chaparral in third, a lap behind. A further lap back was Motschenbacher, then came Hulme. Taking one point for sixth was the redoubtable Cannon. Only fourteen cars were still running. Unfortunately, it was one of those Can-Ams that gave the Can-Am a bad name.

On the good side, the points picture was more interesting going into the last race. Hulme, at twenty-six, only just led McLaren and Donohue, with twenty-three each. For the third time in the three-year Can-Am history, the last round would decide the championship.

Las Vegas, Nevada, November 10, 1968

At last! Chris Amon and the long-rumored big Ferrari type 612 had come to the Can-Am, blood-red and supplying a welcome transfusion of technical interest. Not to mention emotional interest. At a raceway throbbing with big-bore V-8s, the Ferrari's sound was soul-satisfying: not particularly loud, nor that eerie liquid scream of the old Testa Rossa engines, but rather a heavy mechanical rasp overlaying a frantic animal moan.

Amon's compatriot and 1966 Can-Am teammate, Bruce McLaren, made it his business to follow the Ferrari around the track during practice and reported that the heavy newcomer had all the acceleration of his own car. Which had to mean the big V-12 had even more steam than the even-bigger Chevy V-8.

The rest of the competition had changed only minimally, if at all. Two non-entries were Surtees, who was out of engines and patience (though the two-time Las Vegas winner did turn up in person), and Scott, whose car had been sold out from under him. Still the grid extended to thirty-two, with thirty-seven cars and thirty-nine drivers, in all, competing.

For the fourth time this season Bruce McLaren come out on top of the time sheets, and once again he beat the previous year's record, though not by much. In 1967, Bruce had been best qualifier on the fast, sinuous 3.0-mile Stardust International Raceway at 1:30.8; now he turned 1:29.63. It was a scant improvement of 1.3 percent on a track that seemed oily, but at least it was an average speed of 120.495mph. Bear backed up Boss with a 1:29.98 (120.027); actually, he did it first, so Denny Hulme was the first man ever to lap a Can-Am course at the magic 120.

Hall qualified third at 1:30.80, and Donohue was next at 1:30.91. So far, it was a familiar Can-Am pattern, but fifth-best man was Sam Posey, who cut a 1:31.47 with his Lola T160-Chevy. That was a mere 0.13 up on Mario Andretti, with his T160-Ford, and 0.2 up on Dan Gurney with his. Gurney was a scant 0.02 quicker than Peter Revson's 1:31.69 in his McLaren M6B-Ford, so things looked promising for a keen mid-field scrap. And right behind them was the new unknown, Amon's Ferrari, ninth fastest at 1:32.20 after practicing on Saturday only.

Saturday evening practice at Las Vegas offered one of those experiences that don't make it into the statistics, but which do make it all worthwhile. As this writer described it in his *Autosport* story:

The last 15 minutes were in fact a rare delight, with all the top people out and trying. The sun dropped into the mountains, and suddenly it was a three-ring circus to stand in the infield: should we watch Sam violently assaulting the esses, Dan knifing

through Turn 7, Chris and his air brakes into 2, Peter hanging it out in 6, Mark's incredible aplomb and Mario's intense savagery in 1, Jim's artistry with the wing through the full-bore S-swerve, plus his shocking upshifts which seem to hurl the Chaparral bodily forward; or should we enjoy the twin McLarens quietly circulating to be ready for a reply if anyone threatened their time? It was a treat, that last 1968 qualifying.

The McLaren long suit was preparation, and, on Sunday afternoon at Las Vegas, it reached a new high. A spare motor hung from a crane, ready to drop into either car in any last-moment panic, and a complete set of new body panels stood ready for any possible repetition of Hulme's problem at Riverside. McLaren's car—but not Hulme's—also wore a big mesh bin over its intake stacks to filter out stones. In

the hindsight of what was about to happen, the Kiwis seemed positively in touch with the occult.

Or had they simply read their Stardust history? In the prior three years of this event, the pole sitter had never won, and indeed had always been involved in some kind of incident.

Poor Mark Donohue had an incident even before the start. His big Chevy refused to fire, and the immaculate blue M6B was pushed aside. That meant Andretti was free to fill up the empty second-row-outside slot ahead of him at the end of the rolling pace lap, and as the pack bellowed under the starting flag, he followed Hulme as McLaren lagged just a bit. This brought Andretti, McLaren, and Hall into the very fast right-hand first turn more or less side by side.

There were a number of views of the next microsecond, but however it was, Mario felt a bump on his right rear and Bruce on his left flank. The M8A's tail swung to the right, off the inside of the curve. The on-rushing pack broke in all directions. For a few heartstopping moments; then, nothing was visible.

One of the better contemporary magazine accounts of this event featured a full-page photo of the spectacular explosion of dust and flying rocks, and nothing else, under the headline, "The Desert War!"

Gradually, the scene cleared enough to see strewn race cars gathering themselves up and setting off once more; all but two. Both Hayes' and Amon's engines were choked dead with Nevada dirt; after missing five Can-Ams, the ill-fated Ferrari 612 had ventured 6,000 miles to contest one turn of one lap.

Meanwhile, the race was going on, and Hulme led it, with Andretti right on his tail, Revson third, and Gurney closing fast. Titus and Follmer, who had started tenth and thirteenth, were fifth and sixth. Hall appeared next, but he went straight into his pit, where his left front bodywork was taped up. McLaren followed him in to have his men check for fuel tank damage, but he was unaware that an entire chunk of his nose was missing, and he shot back out before they could communicate the fact.

As the leaders got into their second lap, Andretti slowed. His right rear tire was going flat, and before he got the 3.0 miles around to the pits, a metal fuel line wore through on the pavement. Fixing that dropped him to last. During his second lap, McLaren realized how badly his nosepiece was damaged and pitted again for the standby replacement to be slapped on. But Gurney passed Revson and set out after Hulme, throwing the big blue T160 around the course like one of his little F1 Eagles.

Whew. Did anyone ever try to tell you the Can-Am was dull?

Gurney's magnificent effort ended after fifteen laps, when one of his half shafts broke; he recalled

feeling a blow on that wheel amidst the first-turn madness. By this point, Revson had dropped back, first to change a flat tire and later to retire with suspension breakage, and Lothar Motschenbacher had come from his eleventh grid place into second.

There was a lot more going on all around the track, both good and bad, but the historically significant incident turned out to involve three men.

A little past half-distance, Hall had made his way from something like fifteenth place up to fourth, but smoke was coming from the tire where the 2G's front wheel arch was disintegrating again, and he stopped for some more plastic surgery and a fresh wheel. The Chaparral charged out of the pits just as McLaren came by.

After a third pit stop because officials wanted him to have a mirror (although they didn't make him take time to adjust it), Bruce had finally rejoined the race with a complete car—though one looking oddly virginal with no number or advertising on its replacement prow. Much as at Mosport the year before, when he'd had to start from the back, he'd been hurling his racer around Stardust with joyous abandon and already had set the best lap of the race (1:30.95). Now, with Hall tucked into his slipstream, McLaren had charged his way up to sixth place when they both came upon Motschenbacher.

Lothar, well ahead of both men on the lap chart, was still holding second place in the race. But he was not holding it comfortably. He had become aware of a painful burning sensation in his lap. The fuel pressure gauge had sprung a leak. Then he felt something go wrong with his front suspension. A bolt had come out of an upright and was machining that wheel into two halves. He backed out of the throttle.

The three cars were now into the fast, already disastrous first turn. McLaren was safely by, but to this day Hall says he does not understand why he failed to miss the slowing M6B. The 2G rammed it, and was launched into a horrifying tumble. With both legs severely broken, his jaw fractured, and his suit soaked in fuel, Hall was pulled from the inverted wreckage just as flames burst out. Motschenbacher's car also caught fire, and he suffered leg burns.

Hulme, all alone and untroubled at the front, only had a dozen more laps to reel off, and he duly did so to take his third Can-Am victory of the season and his first Can-Am championship. It was Follmer who came second, thus giving Ford its highest placing of the year. Titus was third, Parsons fourth a lap down, and Posey dropped to fifth with a failing engine after holding third mid-race. McLaren took the flag for sixth—with his brakes completely out of fluid from a failed seal. As Denny at one end of the pits was al-

ready being wreathed and kissed and interviewed, Bruce's boys at the other end had to pile bodily onto his battered car to drag it to a stop.

At least his one point resolved what would have been a tie for Donohue for second place in the series. Hall ranked fourth on points, Motschenbacher fifth, and Cannon sixth.

So for the second season in a row, the Kiwis from Colnbrook had raided the Colonies for well over $160,000. In the *Road & Track* seasonal summary mentioned earlier, Bruce and Eoin Young explained how McLaren's Can-Am offensive had been planned like a military campaign. The overall cost had been around $180,000, and the overall winnings had come to nearly the same amount. But salable leftover assets—cars, engines—were reckoned to amount to about $100,000. Of course, sponsorship moneys had poured in; no figures were revealed for that, but sales of production race cars with McLaren's name on them were booming, too. Obviously, the smiling young driver-engineer from New Zealand was doing a tidy little racing business in North America.

But the greatest reward had to be the satisfaction of watching his team's superb job performance. Bruce told his friend Eoin of a moment during the year when Shelby American had come by to borrow an engine hoist. "I was reminded that it used to be us who did the borrowing and it used to be us who ran the little setup with one car. This time we had five chassis men, five engine men, three spare engines, two cars, three trucks, 4500 lb. of spares and even a radio telephone!"

Overkill? Perhaps it seemed so in hindsight, but once again McLaren could not be faulted for having

Las Vegas: Hall soldiers on for a while, but his race will end badly. McLaren, minus numbers and mirrors, will make it to the finish.
Pete Lyons

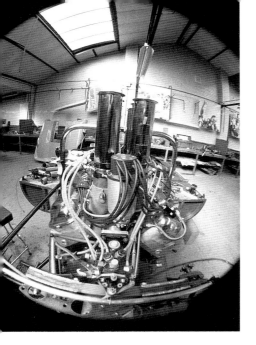

Above: The M6A-based test hack. Note rounded chassis sides and M6A tailpiece #5 in background. *Tyler Alexander*

Right top: Note how the M8A engine serves as the rear one-third of the chassis. *Tyler Alexander*

Bottom: Goodwood: A rainy English summer, fat slicks, and a rueful smile; Bruce starts work on tonight's job-list. *Tyler Alexander*

accepted at face value the preseason posturing of all his would-be rivals. As Denny Hulme remarked while accepting his Johnson Wax trophy, "We were expecting to have a harder time of it this year, but to our surprise many of the efforts turned to you-know-what."

And, given the long litany of problems that struck during the rugged ten-week season, there were moments when even the mighty McLarens only *just* escaped disaster.

Did the sanctioning bodies, SCCA and its Canadian counterpart, CASC, fear that two years' worth of McLaren domination had lessened overall interest in the series?

"Yes and no," Jim Kaser, Director of SCCA's new Professional Division, told *Autoweek.* "Everybody roots for the underdog and everybody likes a winner. The depth in the Can-Am fields is without question something we're concerned about and looking at. The McLaren team had an edge going in, which is not a big edge, but in a series like the Can-Am if you start off with a disadvantage it's almost impossible to make it up when you have to run a race every two weeks. I think we're going to see a lot better preparation on the part of some other teams for the 1969 series."

Teams that would be tackling a lot more races for a lot more money in the Can-Am's biggest-ever fourth year.

Cars of the Can-Am 1968
McLaren M8A

Though a logical development of the M6A-based test hack, the M8A was an all-new design in almost every respect. Jo Marquart's bathtub-type monocoque was a generally simpler structure, with fewer and lighter bulkheads made of square steel tubing united by the aluminum and magnesium paneling. A few inches were added to the tub's width, because the latest Goodyears were wider, and also because the bigger Chevy required more fuel—74gal (U.S.) after

the modification. The M8 carried its fuel in a pair of side tanks alone, without the M6's third, under-knee reservoir. In contrast to the more graceful-looking M6, the 1968 model was slab-sided like the previous year's Fords and Chaparrals. McLaren's own experiments with extra panels pop-riveted onto the prototype had shown that this did improve aerodynamics around and under the sides of the car.

McLaren was not too proud to learn from anyone. In an interview with Eric Dahlquist for *Motor Trend,* development engineer Gary Knutson explained why the new chassis retained steel bulkheads despite the obvious weight handicap compared to the all-aluminum structures used by such builders as Lotus and Lola. "[W]e've noticed that the Lotuses are continually poking holes in their fuel cells. We'd rather have the dependability."

It cannot be an insignificant factor in Bruce McLaren's success that he was racing simultaneously in several arenas, where he could see a broad variety of engineering problems and solutions. Many of his

would-be Can-Am competitors suffered relatively narrow vision.

Although to the outside eye the M8A monocoque continued behind the midship fuel tanks to the rear wheel wells, this last section of the tub merely housed auxiliary equipment on either side of the engine. No heavily-stressed structure existed behind the steel seatback bulkhead and magnesium-plate front engine mount other than the stout, aluminum engine-block casting, plus a pair of triangular steel-tube bracing structures leading from the seatback bulkhead to the rear of the engine block. Behind the engine was no chassis but the bell housing, which contained a three-plate Borg and Beck clutch, and the Hewland LG500 gearbox. This was a 4-speed, for three reasons: it saved 12lb over the LG600 5-speed; all Can-Ams now had rolling starts so a low bottom gear wasn't necessary; and the shorter shafts of the 4-speed were thought less likely to suffer under the brutal torque of the big engine.

Wheelbase was 94in, one up on all the M6-series cars except the shorter (91in) M6A-1. Track dimensions were wider too, but thanks to its new dry sump system, the big new Chevy sat lower than had the "little" old one. In fact, despite the towering, new, stainless steel intake horns, the whole car had a lower appearance, especially to the driver peering over the front fenders. Though add-on airfoils had been considered, McLaren finalized the M8A with just a low fiberglass dam riveted across the stern.

Published poundages of racing cars are always to be swallowed warily, and contemporary accounts offer a wide scale of claims for both the M8A and its engine. But it seems safe to believe that the alloy 427 weighed a mere 460lb, 100 less than McLaren's old iron 359 of 100 less horsepower. Without fuel, the complete 1968 car probably scaled close to or even under the weight of the 1967 series-winner, perhaps 1450–1475lb.

Ferrari 612P

Rather than continue modifying enduro models for sprint racing, Maranello finally designed a car from scratch for the Can-Am. Especially its engine. During an unveiling ceremony, Enzo Ferrari jested that his other V-12 engines had cylinders the size of wine glasses, whereas these were like whole bottles. The actual dimensions were 92mm bore by 78mm stroke (3.62x3.07in), making a total displacement of 6,222cc (380ci). Each cylinder head had two camshafts, and each cylinder breathed through four valves. There was Lucas fuel injection, the working rev limit was 7500, and power output was said to be 620.

Denny Hulme, Can-Am Champ

He was wary of people and could indeed be irascible, even brutally rude, with those who rubbed him wrong, but to get on the right side of the Bear was to find bubbling humor, warm generosity, and deep intelligence. "Denny? A lovely man," attests Tyler Alexander, who worked closely with him for years. Hulme was a New Zealander, born June 18, 1936, and grew up in his father's construction company trucks. Friends recall that he liked to drive without shoes, because it gave him a better feel of the pedals, and when he took up racing he was known as "the barefoot boy from Te Puke."

In 1960, Hulme followed fellow Kiwi Bruce McLaren in winning a local association's Driver to Europe award. In five years he was partner to Jack Brabham in F1 and backed up Black Jack's third world championship in 1966 with his own title in '67. That was the year Indianapolis named him Rookie of the Year, after he finished fourth, and also when

McLaren asked him to join his Can-Am team. Denny got results with any kind of car, but it was the big, heavy Group 7 cars that he seemed born to. Both his burly physique, built through years of filling his dad's dump trucks with a shovel, and his keen mechanical sympathy—he was fascinated by mechanisms of every kind—helped him get the best out of the musclebound Big Bangers. Hulme didn't always seem to be working very hard, in fact he sometimes looked to be a lazy old bear, and never missed a chance to take a nap atop a toolbox or a stack of tires. Often, when all about him were chicken-littling about some car-preparation crisis or other, he'd settle nerves by calmly declaring, "She'll be right." And if she wasn't, he'd *make* her right, seizing a recalcitrant vehicle by the scruff of its neck and hurling it bodily toward the finish line. Watching Denny drive could drop your jaw. Though he retired from the big leagues in 1974, he wouldn't give up the sport and was at the wheel of a race car when he died of heart failure on October 4, 1992. *Dale von Trebra photo*

Ferrari 612P with Amon at the wheel. *Pete Lyons*

Awe-inspiring 6.2-liter Ferrari V-12. *Pete Lyons*

All this cylindrical splendor was embraced by a steel multi-tube space frame stiffened in the cockpit area by riveted aluminum sheeting. Wheelbase was a not-unusual 96.5in, and suspension design was conventional, but the hand-formed aluminum bodywork showed some independent aerodynamic thought. It was very wide (85in, according to *Motoring News*, 88.5 in other sources, but in any case the Ferrari was a good foot fatter than a McLaren M8A), but rather than adopting the "racer's wedge" shape of the successful McLarens, the Ferrari was more rounded for lower drag. Even the windshield wrapped tightly around the driver's head. The aerodynamic highlight was a wing mounted to the chassis above the seatback bulkhead. This wing, similar to one previously tried by Ferrari in F1, was pivoted and had an engine-driven hydraulic system so the driver, pushing a thumb button on the steering wheel, could feather it for low drag on the straights. To add air drag for braking, a secondary hydraulic circuit linked to the foot brake system raised two trim tabs on the wing, as well as a perforated panel atop the nose. This panel did not indicate any air outlet; the front-mounted radiator exhausted laterally into the front wheel wells.

The team admitted the 612P weighed some 1750lb, which was about 300 too much, and it was obvious to anyone's eye that both handling and braking still needed work. As for the original aerodynamic theory, ungainly aluminum tabs appearing front and rear during practice told their own tale. But the "wine bottle" engine was intoxicating.

Lola T160

Eric Broadley's business was selling cars to privateers, not running a race team like McLaren's, and the distinction was evident throughout his new model. He himself described the T160 as a "cleaned-up" version of the T70, a basic concept now three years old, and said his main goals were to reduce weight, increase stiffness and strength, and improve ease of manufacture, maintenance, and repair. The aluminum monocoque was designed with the now widely available big-block Chevy in mind, but unlike McLaren's M8A half-tub, the Lola's chassis remained full-length and did not rely on a stress-bearing engine. Although the structure did not incorporate steel bulkheads, and indeed had a magnesium rear crossmember, the car apparently came out heavier than the McLaren; weights of between 1470 and 1600lb were published at the time. Suspension was similar in general to the T70's, but wheelbase was down 1in to 94, same as the M8A's.

Broadley's earlier friendship with John Surtees had soured, and, when the 1966 Can-Am champion's

attempt to buy a new McLaren was rebuffed, he took a T160 to his own Team Surtees shops, extensively rebuilt it, and relabled it a "TS" (see color photo section). This project turned out to be a sad disappointment, but the factory's cars failed to go well also. Numerous revisions to suspension geometry, chassis structure, and body profile were carried out that first year and on through 1969, when both a T162 and a T163 appeared; "161" was skipped, and so was "164," but a further evolution called the T165 raced in 1970. Quite a few T160-series Lolas were sold, and though they never challenged the factory McLarens, their drivers often enjoyed tussles with racers in customer-model McLarens.

Burnett Specials

Stan Burnett was a machinist from the Seattle area who had studied mechanical engineering, and to whom it seemed perfectly natural to take up racing by first building his own car. Rolled out in 1959, the Burnett Mk 1 had a Chevy engine in the front of a tube frame chassis inside one of Bill Devin's commercially available bodies. Five years later Burnett was ready to join the mid-engine revolution. His Mk 2 had another tubular chassis with his own suspension, and the engine was again a Chevy, but this time the bodywork came from Huffaker's Genie factory. Rather than buy anyone else's transaxle, Burnett made his own using Halibrand and Corvette components. The car was finally ready to

race in 1965, and soon local driver Don Jensen asked for a duplicate. The pair raced their Burnett Mk 2s in western events of all levels for several years.

Meanwhile, Burnett completed a single new Mk 3, retaining the cockpit structure of his old car with a new rear half to accept a big-block Chevy and a revised suspension to suit wider wheels and tires. He also built a new body along McLaren M6B lines. In the following year's Elkhart Lake Can-Am, front suspension failure destroyed the car and injured the driver's neck and back. Undaunted, he set to work on a new model for the 1970 season. Still space-framed

and 427-powered, the Burnett Mk 4 featured a distinctive tail-mounted radiator and an innovative longitudinal torsion bar which resisted pitch, rather than roll. Burnett qualified the new car for its debut event, the Donnybrooke Can-Am of 1970, only to have a blown oil filter keep him out of the race. He didn't make another Can-Am that year, but was preparing for 1971 when, during testing at Seattle International Raceway (Kent) on July 4, the car veered into a guardrail along the main straight and Burnett suffered fatal injuries.

Riverside 1968: Chuck Parsons (#10) in a T160 entered by Lola importer Carl Haas defends his line through Turn 9 against an aggressive Jerry Titus (M6B). *Petersen Publishing*

During the first Can-Am year, 1966, the McLaren marque was competitive, but failed to win. In 1967, the factory's pair of drivers won five races out of six. In 1968, their record was four of six.

Eighteen races, nine victories—plus two more achieved by privately owned McLarens. It was a success ratio high enough to stop some people raving about McLaren magic and start griping about McLaren's monopoly.

They hadn't seen anything yet.

With the end of SCCA's USRRC series in 1968, the American club and its Canadian counterpart, CASC, expanded the Can-Am from six events to eleven. The increase in race purses, plus a boosted contribution by series sponsor Johnson Wax to the year-end points fund, confronted the world with a million-dollar sports car championship. A Big Bang, indeed.

As before, in each of the three past seasons, all this Can-Am gold captured imaginations in race shops around the world, and bold announcements, or at least rumors, poured in, describing all manner of new contenders.

Just as in every season past, only a few of these ever reached the stage of making noise at a race track. And as in the two most recent seasons, only one team proved capable of fielding everything needed to win.

Mosport, Ontario, June 1, 1969

Bruce McLaren launched his fourth Can-Am season in the manner to which he—and everyone—had become accustomed. His superb team's new, purpose-built, thoroughly tested M8B cars dominated the front row of the Mosport grid. Bruce once again took pole from his reputedly faster teammate, Denny Hulme, who on Friday had been busy at the Indianapolis 500 (he retired a Gurney Eagle-Ford there while running second). McLaren, undistracted by Indy, spent Friday testing tires on the bumpy, undulating Canadian road course, and in Saturday qualifying he lapped at 1:18.2 (113.2mph). That represented an improvement of 3.7 percent over Hulme's 1:20.8 pole of 1967, the last time the Can-Am had run here.

Once again, the pair of glistening, caramel-colored machines proved dismayingly superior to everything else. The closest car, and it wasn't very close at 1:20.0, was another McLaren powered by another aluminum Chevrolet displacing 7.0-liters (427ci). This was a new customer-model M12, one Chaparral Cars had purchased for new hired hand John Surtees to race while modifications he'd demanded on the long-awaited Chaparral 2H were carried out. Unfortunately, a wheel supply problem handicapped Surtees with undersized tires. Fourth fastest at 1:21.0 was a lightweight Lola T163 with a Chaparral-built big Chevy entered by importer Carl Haas for Chuck Parsons. Starting fifth with the same time was Lothar Motschenbacher, now the official U.S. McLaren distributor, who was driving an M12 with a similar engine tuned by his own organization.

A much smaller V-8 of another make powered the sixth-best qualifier. Long-time Ford man Dan Gurney, another who had been preoccupied in Indiana until after Friday (he finished second there with his own Eagle-Ford), only managed 1:23.9 in Ontario on Saturday. Having abandoned F1, Gurney's All American Racers had been planning a much stronger Can-Am campaign but did not receive anticipated Ford factory support. In the end, Dan could only bring out his year-old, McLaren M6B-based McLeagle with a 5.6-liter (344ci), 540hp Gurney-Weslake engine.

Another Ford-powered car appeared for practice only, a G7A built two years before by Ford's Kar Kraft on a GT40 Mark IV aluminum honeycomb Le Mans chassis. It was now entered by privateers Charlie and Kerry Agapiou on Ford's behalf. Peter Revson was the driver (he'd finished sixth at Indy), but after Saturday's practice, the car had nothing but trouble with its aluminum-block 7.0-liter motor and Revson withdrew. So did Joe Leonard (fifth in the 500), when a new, turbocharged Oldsmobile in the old McKee Mark 7 "wedge" showed no signs of being race-ready.

One other entrant had a new car, but George Eaton's McLaren M12 was so new it never ran until Sunday morning, and the young Canadian had to start from the back. Each of the remainder were two- and three-year-old Lolas and McLarens, and there weren't that many of them. In the end, only twenty-one starters lined up for the opening round of this, the greatest Can-Am season yet. They brought out a crowd reported at a little over 30,000, far short of the biggest ever here, but presumably the dull, sometimes damp race day weather had something to do with that.

The Kiwis may have felt comfortable in practice, but the green flag signaled a harder time. As the stream of bright, bellowing big sports racers poured down into Mosport's plunging first turn, McLaren's winged yellow-orange M8B was still in front, but Surtees' white M12 was shouldering by Hulme on the inside, and Parsons' orange Lola and Gurney's dark-blue McLeagle were crowding up close behind. Farther around the course, Parsons followed Surtees past Hulme, and for two grand laps Chuck enjoyed watching the defending Can-Am champion in his mirrors. But unlike most others, the 1966 USRRC champ had started on rain tires, and as soon as they got hot on the dry surface, the Lola started sliding wildly and dropped back.

Meanwhile, the 1966 Can-Am champ was pressing the 1967 one, and on the fourth lap, Surtees passed McLaren for the lead. Bruce repassed immediately, but on lap six John again thrust the customer McLaren ahead of the works model. "This was a really exciting show," this writer recorded with some relief in *Autosport*. "Hulme and Gurney were moving up to join in, with Motschenbacher in their mirrors. All the big-bodied sports cars were jumping and darting about, lifting their flat noses under acceleration, blowing up dust from the verges and shaking the air almost physically; it was precisely what Can-Am racing is all about."

Unfortunately, the Can-Am was also about attrition. After eight or ten laps, Surtees saw his temperature gauges rising, and let McLaren go. He then had to let Gurney go, too. On the eighth lap Dan had forced his nim-

Mosport: Bruce and Denny are back, and watch out—they've brought faster cars, more reliable engines, and better luck. *Dale von Trebra*

Mosport: If style earned points Gurney would be champion, but his McLeagle's rear suspension can't take it this time. Dan's Ford engine dramas continue; this year he's got a special 344ci aluminum block—but only one of them. *Pete Lyons*

ble little McLeagle past a seemingly lackadaisical Hulme into third place, and on lap fourteen made his way past the slowing Surtees into second, and started closing on McLaren. Bruce responded with a new lap record, 1:20.6, but by lap twenty, quarter-distance, the new factory McLaren was only inches ahead of the highly modified old one.

Maybe that's what woke up the Bear. On lap twenty-five, Hulme took a breath and launched himself past Surtees; on lap twenty-seven he shot by Gurney and his momentum carried him right up to McLaren and into the lead on lap thirty.

"For Gurney things were now twice as grim," enthused the *Autosport* account. "Driving very hard indeed, he was able to lap as fast as 1:21.1 [beating his own qualifying lap by nearly 3sec], forcing the underpowered machine by sheer willpower around the curves and using full throttle sooner and longer than seemed possible. The big, winged orange cars ahead seemed to hang back to tantalize him . . ."

The pressure encouraged McLaren to another best lap, 1:19.5, and that's where the pace on this bumpy surface got too hot for Gurney's older chassis. A rear upright casting broke, and at forty-nine laps, Dan pulled out of the great drive that, with Surtees', had made the opening 1969 race a race.

Now the McLaren boys settled down to enjoy their prowess, swapping positions again and again, playing with each other at 160mph on the long, rising back straight. After eighty laps, 197 miles covered in just less than two hours, the Kiwis staged a nose-to-tail finish, Bruce first by 0.9sec to take the twenty points now being awarded for Can-Am victories. Hulme got fifteen. It turned out Denny had been roasting alive in his brand-new car. Drivers of the new M12s reported the same problem. Undeveloped cockpit aerodynamics were blamed.

Surtees nursed the overheating Chaparral McLaren home nearly a minute later for the twelve

third-place points. Parsons had been due next, but on his final time through Moss hairpin at the far end of the circuit, his well-worn left rear rain tire, which he had been feeling going soft for five laps, blew out and chucked the Lola into the grass. Trailing clouds of rubber smoke, Parsons struggled on to the checker, but he had to watch John Cordts, a Swedish-born Canadian of impressive ability, pass into fourth (ten points) with his old tube-frame McLaren M1C. Both had lost four laps to the winners. Another Canadian, Jacques Couture, in another M1C, completed seventy-three laps to finish sixth (six points). Thirteen cars were still running, but only eleven did enough laps to be counted as official finishers. (The remaining points for the top ten were distributed four, three, two, one.)

St. Jovite, Quebec, June 15, 1969

Can-Am apologists breathed a little easier at round two. Though the entry wasn't significantly bigger, many of those teams that did come on to the lovely Le Circuit-Mt. Tremblant-St. Jovite looked better prepared. And a few more drivers managed to mount a more convincing challenge to the McLarens.

Strongest of them in qualifying was Lothar Motschenbacher. He'd faded away at Mosport with engine trouble, but his big Chevy was in better voice here, and he put his bright red M12 third on the grid at 1:34.6. That was 0.6sec faster than John Surtees in Chaparral's similar McLaren—the 2H was still unready. The white M12 was still struggling on inferior rubber, but it now had a low-profile, crossover fuel-injection rig which we later learned was a Chaparral 2H part. Chuck Parsons qualified his Lola T163 fifth at 1:36.4, and George Eaton's M12 was next at 1:37.9.

Farther back, people of note included the racer/writer Jerry Titus, making a return to the Can-Am in an old McLaren M1C-Ford (eighth at 1:39.1), Joe

St. Jovite: Le Circuit in the Laurentians is a lovely place to race, but it does make the Big Bangers look bigger. The Camaro paces another B&D Show. *Claire Lyons McHenry*

Leonard, whose twin-turbo, iron-block 389ci Olds kept running this time (ninth, 1:39.3), and John Cordts, who'd been upgraded to a monocoque McLaren M6B chassis but downgraded to a 5.0-liter engine out of a Formula A car (tenth; 1:39.8).

Dan Gurney should have been well up among them, but early in practice his only Ford broke a piston, so AAR packed up for the long, cross-continent drive home. The Ford in the G7A was running even worse than at Mosport, and this week's driver, John Cannon, pulled out too. In the end, the grid officially extended to twenty-three cars, but three more dropouts meant only twenty actually started.

And heading them all? The Bruce and Denny Show, of course. Again, Bruce was the real showman, winning pole at 1:31.7 (104.035mph). It had been two years since the Can-Am last ran at the twisty, hilly, 2.65-mile Quebec track. The fastest qualifier then, Surtees, did 1:38.7, and the fastest race lap was Chris Amon's inspired 1:37.3. A better perspective of Group 7 technical progress was gained by looking back to the 1968 F1 race here, when the quickest time was 1:33.8. So McLaren's Big Banger sports car was more than 2sec faster than the old F1 time—and about 4sec better than Bruce's own best in his own F1 single-seater.

As two weeks before, the crowd count was down, about 20,000 braving a dull and chilly race day. But again the rain held off.

And once again the Kiwis amused themselves by toying with the opposition.

McLaren led off from Hulme, but then both Motschenbacher and Surtees passed Denny—and then they both passed Bruce. It was very hard to recall the last time *two* cars had been in front of the factory McLarens.

Surtees passed Motschenbacher into the lead, and then McLaren scratched by his U.S. representative to give chase to his customer. He actually nosed ahead on lap five, but "Texas John" took the lead back just a corner later. This was like their epic duel in the first-ever Can-Am race at this same circuit three years before, only better. McLaren went in front again. Surtees passed him back. McLaren passed *him* back.

By this time, Hulme, who had let himself fall to sixth behind both Parsons and Eaton, had decided he'd better help his employer, and powered back up toward the front. For a glorious several laps, then, the trio put on a splendid Can-Am spectacle, Bruce and Denny and John swapping places, the M8Bs looking relatively smooth, the M12 very ragged, but its driver demonstrating all the grit that had won him multiple championships on two wheels and four.

Hulme was in front, Surtees second, and McLaren a tight third when an older Lola brought

out waving yellows at the right-hand Namerow hairpin just before the pits. John saw the flags and shied toward the right. Bruce didn't see them, and carried out his plan to out-brake Surtees into the apex. The orange McLaren's chisel nose axed into the white one's flank just ahead of the rear wheel.

The damage was not severe, but both men had to pit for tape jobs. McLaren was soon back up into second place. Surtees probably would have made it back to third, at least, but the repair gave way, and the whole right rear corner of the body tore off. That brought out the black flag, because of the Can-Am rule about coachwork integrity. Chaparral Cars had ordered spare panels but hadn't yet received them, so one of the few men ever to make the factory McLaren drivers look like they were working had to stand in the pits and watch them cruise on to another one-two win.

To *Autoweek's* Jack Brady this race had been run to "a script vaguely reminiscent of television wrestling," but as soon as he stopped, McLaren apol-

St. Jovite: McLaren and Mascot. Bruce found a spectator crossing the track, invited him (?) to join the team, and "Rick McTurtle" wound up starring in his own Gulf magazine ad. (No animals were harmed during the course of this photo opportunity.)
Dale von Trebra

Watkins Glen: New blood; the Ferrari is back, and it's fast. Amon discusses the next step with mechanics Roger Bailey (left) and Doane Spencer. *Pete Lyons*

Watkins Glen: Surtees' bewinged McLaren M12 (#7) shows well for a while, but soon he has to wave the factory boys by. *Pete Lyons*

ogized to Surtees for hitting him. He and Hulme admitted they'd been indulging in showmanship—running alone, they'd each set the race's fastest lap at 1:33.8, whereas Surtees' best was 1:35.9—but Bruce had never intended that kind of show.

Parsons, all but brakeless at the end, finished third ahead of Motschenbacher, who'd had to stop to fix his throttle linkage. Cordts was fifth. Sixth was Fred Baker, who was in the M6B driven by Donohue the year before and which was now owned by the Smothers Brothers of television fame. Eaton came in next, after several mechanical failures robbed him of fourth, and Leonard brought the Can-Am's first turbocharged engine home eighth, three laps behind the winner's sixty. The whistling Olds wasn't running right, but it was running. Titus' Ford wasn't, though. After only eighteen laps, Titus had abandoned sixth place with his engine bearings rattling. He was one of eight of the twenty starters not to finish the 159 miles.

Watkins Glen, New York, July 18, 1969

After a month to regroup, the Can-Am circus looked more impressive for its first stateside date of the season. Part of that came from appearing for the first time at the glamorous, high-speed home of the U.S. Grand Prix. Another part was the addition to the grid of several 3.0-liter Group 6 and 5.0-liter Group 4 long-distance cars that had survived the Glen's annual six-hour on Saturday. Nice weather and a healthy 50,000 at the fences helped, too.

But the biggest boost was a new car. A Ferrari. And it proved to be a genuine challenger.

Chris Amon's pet project had only made the last round of 1968 and hadn't made it past the first turn. The same chassis and 6.2-liter V-12 was back for '69 with more power, less weight, revised suspension, and all-new bodywork. Though air freight delays allowed only a few, last-minute laps of practice, Chris qualified a strong third to his fellow Kiwis.

Bruce and Denny seemed delighted to have to get back to work for a living. They let it be known they'd brought stronger engines to Watkins Glen with horsepower "in the mid-600s." They'd also brought a complete spare car and left it lurking menacingly under a cover but in full view. Some of their would-be competition couldn't manage to scrape up a spare *engine*.

McLaren took his M8B around at 1:02.21, a stirring 133.1mph. Hulme backed him up with a 1:02.54. The fastest qualifier for the previous October's Grand Prix, Mario Andretti, making his F1 debut in a Lotus, had lapped the 2.3 miles at 1:04.20, or 128.97mph. Looking ahead a few months to the 1969 GP, Jochen Rindt's best F1 effort would still fall short of the Can-Am front row by more than a second. Go Group 7!

Amon clocked 1:03.73. Surtees—still in the M12, though now it was wearing an old Chaparral 2G wing at a fixed angle—was fourth at 1:04.40. Fellow M12 drivers Motschenbacher and Eaton were next, then Parsons with a new, heavier but stiffer tub under his graceful Lola T163 bodywork, and Baker's M6B. Qualifying ninth was Jo Bonnier, who was making a temporary Can-Am comeback in his Saturday car, a Lola T70 coupe which he'd treated to a 5.9-liter engine overnight. His 1:08.08, set on Saturday morning with a 5.0-liter engine, forced six-hour co-winners Jo Siffert and Brian Redman to start tenth (1:08.54) and eleventh (1:08.74) with a pair of 3.0-liter Porsche 908 Spyders. A total of six of these enduro interlopers brought the Group 7 starting field to twenty-five. Gurney, Cannon, and Leonard were missing, but gridded fourteenth was Can-Am newcomer Ronnie Bucknum in a T163—a good job for a man with a typically troublesome new race car and broken ribs after a highway accident.

The big red Ferrari skulking on the grid behind them spurred the orange McLarens on like nothing had for a long time, and they spurted right away from the flag. Surtees latched onto Amon, and presently passed him into third, and for a while these two stayed close enough to the first two that the crowd once roared in joy as backmarker traffic on this narrow track forced both the McLaren men to back off. But the next lap, the rampaging M8Bs were pulling away again. No more playing around for the McLarens; the Can-Am had turned serious, and a brand-new Ferrari and a winged Chaparral-substitute were making them hustle.

Not for long, alas. Surtees dropped back with overheating and finally lost a cylinder. Amon too had to ease off, driving on his temperature gauges, but the Ferrari stayed on the McLarens' lap, and within about 30sec.

Meanwhile, the front-running machinery remained sound. Hulme kept as close to McLaren as traffic allowed, and late in the day set fastest lap (1:02.6), but never made a move to unseat the Boss. That's how they finished, less than a second apart after eighty-seven laps and 200.1 miles covered at 125.99mph, by far the fastest Can-Am to date. The Ferrari screamed under the checker 29.6sec behind the second McLaren. Eaton's McLaren was fourth, three laps down, then came Parsons' Lola at eighty-three laps after running a dismally long time on seven cylinders and also having to pit to remove a loose sway bar. Siffert finished sixth at eighty-two laps; his little Porsche was entirely healthy, but he'd had to stop for fuel. All but one of the six-hour cars (Redman's, which started misfiring) ran to the end, but most of the sprint cars broke down as usual, so there were only fourteen finishers.

Edmonton, Alberta, July 27, 1969

It was a very long haul from the Finger Lakes Region up across the Canadian prairies to this oil city in the lee of the Rockies, but the promise shown by

Edmonton: How even champions traveled in the Sixties. This is one of McLaren's simple Chevy pickup-cum-trailer transporters, caught somewhere along the long, long haul to Alberta. *Pete Lyons*

Edmonton: Worth the wait for novelty, if not results; Surtees finally debuts the, um, unconventional Chaparral 2H. *Pete Lyons*

Both of them. For the second year in a row at Edmonton, the McLarens qualified at identical times. Hulme did it first, thereby gaining his first pole position of the season. At 1:22.9 (109.74mph) the M8B was 3.1sec faster than 1968's wingless M8A, an improvement of 3.7 percent.

Chaparral's new 2H did join the show at Edmonton, and at first sight appeared to be a real addition to an "unlimited" race series. The sleek-looking semi-coupe turned out to be at least as innovative as a year of rumors had forecast. Unfortunately, it didn't seem to work. Surtees was disappointed with handling that he appeared to consider both sluggish and unpredictable and which onlookers considered wallowy. Cruel ridicule started almost immediately; "White Whale" was one of the kinder sobriquets. Lapping at 1:28.1, the 2H qualified a relatively poor fifth behind Eaton (M12, 1:27.8) and alongside Motschenbacher (M12; 1:30.2). After Parsons (T163) came Cannon, back with the Agapious' Ford G7A. Ron Grable (Lola T70) and homebuilder Stan Burnett (Burnett-Chevy Mk. 3) had joined the series too, but in all, only sev-

Edmonton: This early, the relationship between Hall (left) and Surtees has unraveled; that's Chaparral mechanic Franz Weis in the middle, wondering if he shouldn't be. *Pete Lyons*

the Ferrari, and the promise of seeing the new Chaparral at last made the trip worthwhile.

Amon had a stronger, new 6.2-liter engine—strong enough to break his gearbox in practice—and once again qualified third to the pair of McLarens. But the other two New Zealanders were up for the challenge, and were precisely 2sec faster.

enteen drivers made the starting grid. It was the thinnest Can-Am field so far.

But the crowd was a decent 35,000 or so, and it saw one of the keener Can-Ams. On the first lap, Amon shoved the big red Ferrari into second place behind McLaren, and that set off a pass-and-repass, three-way duel that went all the way to the moment the pace proved too much for one of their pistons.

No, not that one's. McLaren's. Perhaps it was a moment of cost-conscious complacency that led the team to re-install slugs already used at Watkins Glen in both their rev-happy 430ci Chevys. In fifteen cases, it was not a mistake. But on lap thirty-six, four short of half-distance, the top came off one of Bruce's. He stumbled into the pits with oil spraying from the breathers to post the team's first retirement. The difference in prize money between McLaren's fourteenth place and a theoretical second was $6,700. New pistons would have been cheaper.

Hulme, who happened to be ahead of Amon at that moment, realized the time for fun was over. Revealing what he'd been holding back, he immediately began leaving the Ferrari behind at a second a lap. When the gap got to about ten seconds, he relaxed a little, but Amon could still see him and kept pushing. As late as lap sixty-eight, Hulme still felt the pressure, and pulled out the fastest tour of the day: 1:23.7. Amon only strained harder and replied with a 1:24.1, according to official watches, or 1:23.9, according to his own team's—which, if true, was a full second quicker than his grid time. At the flag, the Ferrari was a scant 5.1sec behind. A stout performance with a car that had been overheating and losing power and whose gearchange had become very heavy.

Eaton wound up third, ahead of Surtees, but it was close. They'd been racing hard together early in the race until Surtees apparently knocked his ignition switch off, then had to make two pit stops to service sticking throttles. He was also having some trouble with the torque converter transmission's hand-operated shift mechanism, but he did manage to improve on his qualifying time. Eaton's M12 was no longer at its best, and in the remaining laps, the wallowy white 2H made up ground. Then, just past the start of the very last lap, Eaton had a rear tire go flat. As the Hulme-Amon race for first hurtled past the checker, all eyes were looking for the race for third. The red McLaren roared into sight first, snaking and trailing smoke and rubber shreds.

Only seven of the seventeen starters were still running at the end.

Mid-Ohio, Mansfield, Ohio, August 17, 1969

Like Watkins Glen, Mid-Ohio had hosted the old USRRC, but this was its first Can-Am. After Edmonton, the entry list looked spectacular: the grid was up to twenty-four cars. All of them were proper Group 7 cars, so in that respect it was a seasonal high so far. Once again, however, the number of actual starters was a less impressive twenty-one.

Jo Siffert reappeared, this time in the cockpit of a Group 7 roadster based on Porsche's Group 4 type 917 endurance coupe. The 4.5-liter, opposed-12 917PA was a solid piece of work with plenty of top-end power—about 620—but it seemed to be down on torque, up on weight, and lacking in handling. The Swiss GP star qualified seventh on the tight, twisty track, exactly 5sec back of the pole.

Showing better was Mark Donohue in Roger Penske's new Lola-Chevy. Painted its sponsor's dark blue, the T163 looked beautifully prepared, but it did give some trouble. First, a half shaft sheared in private testing, and in official practice it happened again, this time damaging the suspension and chassis. Later, an engine valve rocker mounting stud broke, a typical pushrod Chevy problem. Besides that, Mark himself

Left: Edmonton: Hulme or McLaren may win every race this year, but runners-up can still offer excitement, as Eaton shows by two-wheeling his McLaren M12 to third place. Fellow Canadian McCaig's M6B (#55) stopped short. *Pete Lyons*

Right: Mid-Ohio: Mark Donohue and Karl Kainhofer (behind car) turned out a beautiful Lola, but after just this one race Roger Penske's cold eye saw it wasn't going to do the job. *Barry Tenin*

Bottom left: Mid-Ohio: Porsche would persevere; team manager Richie Ginther (right) proposes a program to Jo Siffert (left) and the factory's Rico Steinemann (in sunglasses). *Pete Lyons*

Bottom right: Mid-Ohio: The Kiwis have nothing to worry about here and now, but one day Donohue (#6 Lola T163) and Porsche (Siffert's #0) will get together. *Pete Lyons*

was feeling unwell. Given all that, his third-fastest starting spot was remarkable, even though it was 3.6sec back.

In fact, the effective qualifying period was shortened by rain, and most people's poor times couldn't be held against them. Parsons qualified his T163 fourth. Surtees was having his second run in the Chaparral 2H, which now had a hydraulic ride-leveling system to counteract the downforce of the body-mounted rear flipper, but it qualified fifth again. Eaton was sixth-fastest in his M12.

Alongside new-boy Siffert on the fourth row was Peter Revson, winner of a recent USAC road race

near Indianapolis, who had taken over the T163 run by Bucknum at the Glen. Motschenbacher's M12 was ninth. He would have been next to the G7A, whose driver this time was George Follmer, but once again the big alloy Ford was useless, so the entry was pulled. That let Cannon up to the fifth row in the Ford-engined M6B he'd driven at Mosport. Inside the sixth row was Tony Dean, an Englishman who'd made enough money from finishing ninth in his 3.0-liter Porsche at Watkins Glen that he decided to become a Can-Ammer. Next to him was Amon in the 6.2-liter Ferrari, which was having troubles with its engine, its handling, and the mounts of a new, tall, hub-mount-

ed wing. That aero aid was finally removed. Parsons made the same decision for the same reason.

First and second? Who do you suppose? Oh, Denny was on pole for this one, having managed a 1:25.9 (100.38mph). Bruce, admitting that the Edmonton piston failure was on his mind, said he'd held his revs to 6600 and was 0.3sec slower. But he was trying something new on his M8B, a complete front suspension from his F1 car. This offered longer wishbones and wheels with less offset for lighter steering.

Imagine being able to borrow from your Grand Prix racer to fine-tune your Can-Am. Imagine your mood if you couldn't.

The weekend's damp weather carried over to race time, although most people, and all the fast people, gambled on dry tires. From the rolling start, McLaren on the outside out-dragged Hulme into the fast first turn and led on around the lap. Part-way around lap two, Denny took over and began to pull away. At half-distance, he was 30sec ahead of his teammate. Bruce had a similar cushion on the third-place man.

What kept this from being as dull a race as it sounds was the fact that the third man was now Amon. The Ferrari's poor practice had put it behind a lot of slower cars, but it was going strong now, and Amon was going through them like a wolf through sheep. After six laps he was going after the trio of drivers who were practically falling all over each other on the narrow, bumpy track in dispute of third place. At the moment Amon came up to them, Parsons was leading the little subgroup, ahead of Donohue and Surtees.

It shaped up to be a great fight, but suddenly it was all too easy for the Italian machine. Surtees had the strap of his goggles break, of all things. Holding them on with one hand, he slowed and headed for the pits. That let Amon nibble at Donohue's heels, who with that as a goad scrambled around Parsons into third for a portion of lap eight. In the final turn of that lap, however, another half shaft broke (post-event diagnosis held the Penske team had lowered the engine/transmission too far, thus subjecting the shaft joints to excess flexing), and the blue Lola shot off onto the grass. The red Ferrari made short work of the orange Lola, then, and owned third place free and clear. After a while, Parsons faded with engine trouble, and Siffert's Porsche settled into fourth. Surtees was heading for fifth, Eaton for sixth.

Hulme presently came up behind Amon and lapped him, but then let his compatriot go back by. Easing off still more (as he said later, the circuit was hard work, and he was getting hot), he let McLaren come up behind, and on the seventy-second lap of

the eighty Denny let him go by into the lead. Well, everyone nodded to themselves, it was Bruce's turn.

No, it wasn't. The very next time around, McLaren broke away into the pits to shout that his oil pressure gauge was registering zero. There were only seven laps left, so crew chief Tyler Alexander thumped Bruce on the helmet and told him to go back out and see if he could keep another second-place purse out of Amon's greedy hands. Hulme did his part and lapped the Ferrari, so that when McLaren eased around to complete eighty laps, Amon had already been flagged off at seventy-nine, and another McLaren payday was secure.

Bruce pulled off course right after the finish line. There was plenty of oil in the tank, but the pump had seized. The big aluminum racing Chevrolet ZL-1 had run at least 16.8 miles with absolutely no oil feed.

"Hey!" the incredulously grinning driver yelled from his cockpit to a man wearing the jacket of one of his prime sponsors. "It'll run fine *without* your Gulf!"

Siffert, Surtees, and Eaton rounded out the top six of a total of sixteen finishers. It was a higher relia-

Mid-Ohio: The 917PA Spyder is short of power, but long on durability, and Siffert will take fourth both here and in the championship. *Pete Lyons*

Elkhart Lake: To wing, or not to wing; maybe the grid suggests the answer. Behind the M8Bs, the Revson (#31) and Parsons T163s, the Amon 612P (#16) and the Eaton M12 are all converts to the faith. *Pete Lyons*

Elkhart Lake: Built by former Chaparral aerodynamicist Paul Lamar, a new wing finally nails the Ferrari's tail to the road at Road America. *Pete Lyons*

bility record than usual, and most teams were naturally in a relatively self-congratulatory mood. But just why McLaren was beating them so badly became evident in the next few moments. After a Can-Am like that, you'd have opened a beer and started trading war stories, right?

You wouldn't have made Bruce's team. As the rain grew heavier, his boys set to, right in the pit lane, and yanked his engine. They had to have the car back in service by morning. McLaren had the circuit booked for... more testing!

For scoring, the eleven-round 1969 series was split in two. After this first segment of five races, defending champion Hulme had actually earned ninety points, but discarding one result, per the new rules, brought him down to an official seventy-five.

McLaren was close at seventy, while third with thirty-nine points after only three events was Amon. Of the twenty-one other drivers in the points so far, only Eaton had been consistent enough to have to subtract any, and he was fourth, with thirty-two.

Elkhart Lake, Wisconsin, August 31, 1969

In years past, the sixth Can-Am round would have been the finale of the series. In 1969, it merely marked the midpoint. But by now, it was perfectly clear which way the rest of the season would go.

That said, crouching behind the Road America guardrails was a relatively upbeat experience after the weak fields of the previous races. Thirty-five cars established qualifying times, and thirty-three of them actually raced.

So far, Can-Am '69 had been something of a Car-of-the-Week Club, and for Elkhart, we got two more new ones to enjoy—in practice, anyway. The first real Ford entry of the year finally appeared, one of the ex-Shelby McLarens driven in '68 by Revson, now prepared by Holman Moody for 1969 Indy winner Mario Andretti. The M6B was greatly modified and now called the "429'er," but the hemi-head mon-

ster stuffed into the back actually displaced 494ci (8.1 liters).

This was one of several engines Ford had under development at the time. It was based on a new, bulkier engine block family which would be sold to the public in both 429 and 460ci forms. One version, called the Boss 429, had aluminum cylinder heads with pushrod-operated inclined valves in hemispherical combustion chambers, and these heads, on a specially cast aluminum block with iron cylinder liners, formed the basis of the experimental 1969 Can-Am powerplant. Bore and stroke was 4.52x3.85, for a displacement of 494.2ci. A horsepower number of 720 was issued, and Mario complained that full acceleration made it hard to get his hand forward to the shift lever! He could get wheelspin any time, he added, anywhere, in any gear.

During pre-event tests at Elkhart, Andretti allegedly cut a lap that would have taken pole, but when it counted he couldn't repeat it. His official 2:08.4 made him third on the grid, 2.1sec behind the fastest starter. Andretti's problems were a wide variety of teething troubles, which culminated in an undetected CV joint failure that broke an upright in Sunday morning warm-up, then stopped the hastily repaired 429'er in its tracks as Mario attempted to start the race from the pit lane.

Also a nonstarter was the long-awaited four-wheel drive McKee with automatic transmission and twin-turbocharged, 455ci (7.5 liter), all-aluminum Oldsmobile. What was finally discovered to be a clogged fuel filter held Joe Leonard to a total of eight laps of practice and a twenty-fourth grid place. Once the fuel feed problem was licked, the engine proved to be too strong for the brakes, so Bob McKee reluctantly took the car home early. He never did manage to bring it back.

A third entrant not to make the race was Mark Donohue. He didn't even try. According to a press release, Penske had decided a Can-Am program was "too ambitious for our present organization." A pity, but Roger's was precisely the kind of coldly realistic thinking the Can-Am required. It is unknown if anyone at McLaren felt a cold shudder of premonition.

The McLaren team, of course, was busy being fastest again. It so happened that Saturday, August 30, was Bruce's thirty-second birthday ("I think John Holman is sending all these people around to give me a cramp in my gearchange hand," he cracked), but it was not in Denny's mind to give him a present. In the last moments of qualifying, he turned a lap at 2:06.3 (114.01mph). That, for those keeping score, bettered the 1968 best, set by Bruce in an M8A, by 3.5sec, or 2.7 percent. Birthday boy only managed 2:07.4.

Bridgehampton: Psych Job. Another Hulme victory came after the whole team missed final qualifying in favor of . . . water skiing. *Barry Tenin*

Bridgehampton: They're two-passenger sports cars, honest; Motschenbacher gives Eaton a lift home in—ok, on—his M12. *Pete Lyons*

Top left: Michigan: Roaring the "wrong way" along the banking, Hulme leads McLaren, Revson, Siffert and the rest down onto the road course. Gurney is flying under one of the wings way in back. *Pete Lyons*

Top right: Bridgehampton: Tony Dean traveled in style, toting his dollar-earning Porsche 908 in the back of a converted British bus. *Pete Lyons*

Bottom: Michigan: Denny displays three generations of McLaren evolution, passing both Hobbs' M6B (#99) and Apel's M1C (#37) at once. *Pete Lyons*

Come to think of it, there had been quite a party for him Friday night . . .

As the waving green flag under the old Road America pagoda unleashed the frightening flood of horsepower, 55,000 fans watched the two winged orange machines once again spurt away. Amidst all those left to sort themselves out in their wake, Amon emerged first. His now-winged Ferrari had only managed a fourth-row qualifying time (2:13.0), just inside Siffert's Porsche (2:13.2), but now he quickly slipped by Eaton, Parsons, and Revson to third and found he was able to keep his fellow Kiwis in sight.

Obviously, they were letting him do this, but if they wanted to play he was willing to take them on, and he came right up in their mirrors. After four laps of leading, Hulme dropped back into third. Lazily, it seemed, Denny sat watching the Ferrari ahead for ten laps.

Then, on lap twenty, still with thirty to go, perhaps more to keep himself awake than anything, the

Bear stretched and went Zoom! In two laps he was back up to Bruce's tail and, as if to say, "Come on, let's go, I'm bored," he passed back into the lead. McLaren took the hint, and with obvious ease the pair forged away by themselves. Amon soon found himself abandoned a quarter-minute behind. Hulme finally made the race's best lap at 2:08.4, but McLaren led across the finish line by inches. All this time Amon could get the Ferrari around no better than 2:11.7—1.3sec faster than in qualifying, but far too slow to pretend to be a threat in the race. And with seven laps to go, the Ferrari's fuel pump failed.

For the record, Parsons came in third and Revson fourth, both a lap back, Revson with his Hewland only giving him fourth gear. Then came Tony Dean, enjoying himself hugely in his flingable little Porsche 8-cylinder, and an unhappy Motschenbacher, both at forty-seven laps. Siffert missed a shift and blew his Porsche 12. Surtees suffered a cut tire—there were

reports of bottle-throwing from the spectator areas—and since that caused an ultra-low front suspension member to drag the ground, he abandoned the Chaparral where it was. Eaton shut off his dying engine. Follmer lost the G7A's gearbox. Stan Burnett rolled violently, destroying his homebuilt and sustaining neck and back injuries. Only thirteen of the thirty-three starters made the finishers' list.

Bridgehampton, New York, September 14, 1969

Six races, six M8B walkovers. Sensitive to the muttering he was hearing about the McLaren monopoly, Bruce expressed his own views in his next "From the Cockpit" column:

We were beginning to think that our domination of the series might have kept people away from the Can-Am races—the only person it seems to have kept away is Roger Penske!—but seriously, it seems to be reaching the Moss/Clark stage where we are getting so much publicity that people are coming along just to see us win. It's like elephants at a circus—there might be only one or two there, but you don't feel like going to a circus or a zoo and going home without seeing the elephants, no matter how many monkeys there might happen to be . . .

Talk about a circus. Orange elephant drivers McLaren and Hulme did put in some serious business on Saturday morning in the first of two scheduled qualifying sessions, when they both clipped off laps in the 1:24 bracket. Bruce was fractionally quicker than Denny at 1:24.62 (121.76mph), better than 3sec up on Hulme's 1968 pole of 1:27.69. Both were about 4sec up on anything anyone else had managed to that stage.

So the Kiwis went water-skiing. At noon, the McLaren team packed up and left the circuit. Hulme grumbled a bit, saying he figured it was all a plot to keep another pole out of his hands, but he readily enough went along with this ultimate of psych jobs. Teddy Mayer drew the duty of staying to keep an eye on the opposition, and late in the day, Bruce checked back on his minibike, but nobody was mounting any kind of threat.

However, the "monkeys" left to their toil at the track must have thought they were witnesses to divine retribution the next morning. Halfway through the prerace warm-up session, Bruce came slithering into the pits with wheels locked. Most un-Brucelike. Leaping out, he yelled, "One cylinder's gone!" It was only a broken valve rocker stud, and it was soon changed, but memories brimmed up of how both the team's big Chevys had failed in this race last year.

No such luck this year. This race was just about a replay of the one two weeks before. Again, the two McLarens charged away right from the start; once again, Hulme then amused himself by dropping back to study other cars from vantage points just behind them; once again, he eventually tired of this and zoomed back up to swap the lead back and forth with Bruce. The only real difference this time was that it was Denny's turn to cross the finish line a few inches ahead. Both engines ran perfectly.

Amon's didn't. The Ferrari started third again at 1:26.31, but it threw a rod. Surtees' engine didn't last, either. He was back in the McLaren M12 this time and happy about it. He started a much more competitive fourth at 1:26.53, and for a while, Hulme let him race along in second place. But when the Chaparral-built Chevy started overheating again, then steaming, then smoking, then misfiring, Surtees followed what he said were specific Jim Hall orders: "I'm not to stop, the car is to stop." The wretched thing finally did so twelve laps short of the scheduled seventy.

Eaton's blew, too. Revson's didn't blow, but broke a hub. Parsons' car managed to finish, but way down, the orange car wearing Revson's white nosepiece because its own was wrecked by debris on the track.

Siffert's Porsche did go the full distance, and was third after starting seventh, but it was stuttering and Seppi was yanking it back and forth to slosh up the last of the fuel. Then came Motschenbacher, three laps down with transaxle trouble. Another lap behind were a pair of 3.0-liter cars. The fifth place one was this weekend's newcomer, a gorgeous Ferrari 312P Le Mans racer, a coupe complete with headlights, driven inspiringly by Pedro Rodriguez. Tony Dean's open-topped Porsche flat-8 908 was a fighting sixth.

The big Ford? The 4WD McKee? No sign of them. Nor of a lot of others. Twenty starters, thirteen finishers. The spectator number was 26,000.

Michigan International Speedway, Brooklyn, Michigan, September 28, 1969

The fun in Michigan was in the politics. What could be seen of them, anyway. Exactly what was going on behind the scenes has never become entirely clear, but here's what happened in public.

This was the first Can-Am—and it would be the last—at this brand-new facility in the Irish Hills west of Detroit. Although primarily a tri-oval superspeedway, it had some auxiliary loops of pavement making up a three-mile road course. Most of the Can-Am regulars came, so the starting grid extended to a better-than-average twenty-seven. Fastest of them, of course, was the trio of factory McLarens.

Trio?

Yes. That's where the fun entered. McLaren's spare M8B, which had only been used for testing up to this point, even though any number of outsiders had been lobbying and cajoling and begging and waving fistfuls of dollars to be allowed to race it, finally was prepared for a third driver at Michigan.

What third driver? Well, which day do you want to know about?

On Saturday, it was Jack Brabham. Yes, that Jack Brabham, Australia's "Black Jack" who was the F1 World Champion in 1959 and 1960 (when he headed the Cooper team alongside a young New Zealander named Bruce McLaren) and again in 1966. In 1969, his Brabham F1 cars were using Ford Cosworth engines for the first time. The weekend after Michigan's Can-Am, he'd be racing them at Watkins Glen's USGP. So it wasn't too hard to understand why Brabham was the designated driver of the week in the Ford-backed Agapiou Brothers' G7A.

But when he arrived for his first Can-Am, he was somewhat less than thrilled with the aged vehicle, which Ford seemed to be using just to test engines. This weekend's engine was a stone, and the best efforts of a three-time World Champion managed to qualify it tenth, not quite 10sec off the pace of pole.

One of the perks of being a World Champion is not having to worry too much about what people think, so at one point Black Jack turned his back on the Ford pit and sauntered down to visit his old buddy Bruce. The spare McLaren-Chevrolet was parked there, of course, but curiously enough, it already was wearing number 15, the same as on his Ford-Ford. Brabham proceeded to set a time about 4sec off those being turned by the factory drivers in the sister cars, but it would have been good enough to start him from the second row. Three rows up on his "own" car's place.

However, Sunday brought another act to the Bruce and Denny Show. Another Ford driver—a formerly Ford driver, that is.

Dan Gurney, winner of one Can-Am in 1966 and a fast, if unlucky, contender the few times he ran subsequently, posted entries for several 1969 races, but had only appeared twice so far. Part of his problem had been some conflicting USAC open-wheel events— he'd won at Donnybrooke, near Brainerd, Minnesota, on the same day as the Bridgehampton Can-Am—but a bigger problem was in his engine bay.

Having realized his small-block, Ford-based engines just weren't competitive against the big-bore Chevys, Dan had been planning a new program involving the 8.1-liter supermotor that Andretti introduced at Road America and that Ford had been promising to all its long-time campaigners. When it became apparent that the 8.1 was not going to be released to him, Gurney turned to a backup project of his own: new, three-valve heads atop 6.5-liter Ford blocks specially cast in aluminum. All that summer of '69 this new AAR powerplant had been under intensive development, but various problems had kept it off the tracks.

It wasn't for lack of ambition that one of America's greatest drivers and teams had been largely absent from North America's premier road race series.

Finally, Dan's own desire and his commitment to other sponsors forced him to take the Big Step. He acquired a used 7.0-liter Chevy, crammed it into the little McLeagle, and had time to test it for twelve laps at Riverside on the way to Michigan. There, he qualified it ninth, but his runs kept being interrupted; a weld in the sump split twice, and a rocker stud broke once. ("Welcome to the Chevy Owners Club," murmured someone.)

Every time Dan looked up from his troubles, his eye would fall on that third factory McLaren. Bruce had been a good friend for years. Maybe . . .

Hulme started from pole (1:32.5; 116.76mph), and when he took the green flag, running the "wrong" (clockwise) way along the 12-degree banking of the tri-oval's front "straight," he didn't fool around at all. He took the low-line swoop into the right-hand first turn

Laguna Seca: Now that everyone's gone to wings, Denny, we've come up with something new. *Dale von Trebra*

into the infield and vanished into the countryside beyond the speedway's back straight. McLaren followed a bit more conservatively. Revson's big Chevy boosted his Lola from the outside of the second row into third ahead of Siffert's "little" Porsche. Eaton preserved his McLaren M12's fifth starting place from the sixth-fastest Chaparral team entry. This was the white McLaren M12 this time, but Surtees had bronchitis and had invited a member of his own F5000 team, young Italian Andrea de Adamich, to sit in.

Gurney, starting the third M8B from the back, wearing number 1, passed twelve cars on the first lap. The writing was on the wall, or the banking, if you will. Each lap, Tall Dan passed fewer cars, but he passed them relentlessly. He gave the impression of being careful, of feeling the car out, not risking breaking it, yet the big orange gun shot his black helmet along like a cannonball. When he caught Brabham, he went by so fast the two could hardly exchange glances. By the sixteenth lap, he split de Adamich from Eaton. The only thing that saved the young Canadian from being passed in turn was a flat tire that forced him into the pits instead.

Laguna Seca: Winged White Whale. Didn't work. *Pete Lyons*

Riverside: Manx-tailed newcomers, Oliver's new Bryant Ti22 chases Parson's new, lighter Lola. *Pete Lyons*

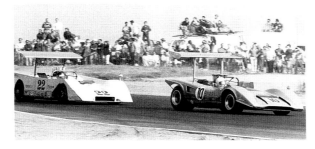

So Gurney was fourth, now, because Revson had already pitted when a half shaft snapped, and there was only the white number 0 Porsche to slice off. Siffert was trying his hardest—which was very, very hard—but somewhere around lap twenty the air-cooled engine's mechanical fan drive broke. Though the rasping flat-12 kept going, it lost its edge, and at the end of the thirtieth lap, its driver pulled wide in the turn back onto the grandstand straight to let the orange McLaren thunder by.

There it was: three mighty McLaren M8Bs running 1-2-3 like the parading pachyderms Bruce had written of in his column. Take that, world.

It was Bruce's turn to win, so toward the end, Denny eased back and let him. At the same time the crowd of 22,000 was on its feet yelling GO DAN! But the Show's junior partner knew his place: third.

Though the Porsche was smoking by the end and fell a lap behind, Siffert preserved his fourth place. De

Adamich's highly professional Can-Am debut earned fifth, though he was a further lap back. Parsons came home sixth, having had to hold his shift lever in fourth gear all day. Brabham was forced out by a wheel falling off the G7A. Amon never started, his sole available Ferrari engine having welded its bearings to its crankshaft in practice. The time he'd turned at that point would have held up for third on the grid. So only twenty-seven cars raced; eighteen finished.

Laguna Seca, California, October 12, 1969

The end was in sight, now. Good thing, as round nine didn't offer much new and nothing new at the front. McLaren's team had the series clinched, and either Bruce or Denny was going to be champion again, although it wasn't yet evident which it would be. McLaren started from pole this time and won his second race in a row. Hulme was second and second. Though neither was really pushing in practice, both broke the magic minute over the old 1.9-mile Laguna lap. Bruce's pole time was 59.53sec (114.898mph), which bettered the 1:01.44 he'd done the year before by 3.2 percent.

Let's see, what else was going on. Oh, yes, Amon once again qualified fast enough (1:01.8) to start third, but on Sunday morning his only Ferrari V-12 had another oiling system failure, so Chris went to see his old buddy Bruce about a job and was given the spare M8B to start from the back of the grid. This time, it wore number 3.

It was available because Gurney was concentrating on his Chevy-engined McLeagle (the team had stopped calling it that, but nobody else ever did) and qualified fourth, alongside Revson's Lola-Chevy.

Still a member of the Ford camp was Mario Andretti. There was no conflicting USAC date, for once, and Holman Moody had done a lot of work on the 494in 429'er. Prerace testing at Laguna resulted in some strong lap times, but, as at Elkhart, Mario couldn't repeat them when it mattered, so he had to start eighth behind Eaton, Siffert, and Parsons.

Lining up right behind the big blue Ford was a tall white Chaparral. Surtees had been ordered back into his hated 2H, which was carrying out an experiment in downforce. Although Jim Hall had designed this car for ultra-low drag for the tight, 1.9-mile Monterey circuit, he created absolutely the biggest airfoil ever seen in road racing and bolted it high atop the middle of the car on massive, body-mounted struts. Surtees did say it made the car better, but his tenth-best qualifying lap was 5.6sec off the pole pace. It was even a third of a second slower than the McLaren M12, which Motschenbacher qualified ninth; this was only the second time all season John had qualified slower than Lothar, no matter which of Chaparral's cars he drove. Worst of all, the 2H failed by 3sec

to match a time Hall had done here with the old 2G in 1968.

In every race so far this year there had been either a new car or a new car-driver combination, and this time we had a brand-new vehicle with a fresh face inside. The new man was Jackie Oliver, Grand Prix driver with BRM and recent co-winner of Le Mans for Ford. The car was called the "Ti22." This is the chemical symbol for, and the atomic weight of, titanium, which was used extensively in the chassis and suspension. Builder Peter Bryant was an English racing mechanic who'd come to America in 1963 to work on the Ferrari 250P with which John Surtees was feeling out American sports car racing and stayed on. The Ti22 was Bryant's first complete design, but it was a sensibly simple, compact, practical one. It was also a very new one, and it arrived at Laguna in time for only a few shakedown laps on Saturday, so Oliver had to start from the back with Amon.

A total of thirty-one cars rumbled off on the pace laps, a refreshing sight, and at 35,000 to 40,000, depending on report, the spectator count was supposedly a track record.

But there was an immediate hitch. The Chaparral engine died partway around the first pace lap, and at the end of it, a red flag brought everyone to a stop so the 2H could be towed to safety. That let the AAR crew attack Gurney's engine, which had just broken a rocker stud. The race countdown resumed before they finished; Dan had to hustle to catch the field on the pace lap, and as he cut across the nose of Siffert's third-row Porsche, the M6B knocked one of the 917PA's add-on dive planes awry.

Finally unleashed, Hulme immediately tore loose from McLaren and set the fastest lap of the day (1:02.19) before finally waving the Boss by. It was McLaren Racing's ninth Can-Am victory of the year, and its eighth with a 1-2 finish.

Not another 1-2-3 finish? No. Kiwi number 3 was doing his part; Amon passed eight cars on the first lap, and another five next time around. Before long, he was up to Siffert, who was running seventh. Both men, of course, were seasoned Grand Prix competitors, and it was no surprise to hear Chris say later, "Seppi wasn't really helping me get by." During the struggle, the McLaren driver hit a half-buried tire marker—familiar Can-Am story—and had to pit for a new nosepiece. That cost Amon a lap, but he spent the rest of the race regaining ground, and was close to once again coming to grips with Siffert, who was on his way to a fifth place finish, when the M8B's differential broke.

Nine races so far, twenty starts by three factory McLarens, and this was only the second DNF. But it was probably just as well that Amon stopped when he did. Postrace inspection turned up a crack in one of the rear wing struts.

Riverside: Cramming Ford's hemi-head 494—and Mario—into an old M6B almost makes a match for Denny's 430ci M8B.
Petersen Publishing

Texas: Honest, Bruce, I just *tapped* this rubber cone. Flamin' thing must've been filled with concrete!
Pete Lyons

Texts: The joy of victory; Bruce, Frank, (left) and Tyler exhibit an unusual—and never explained—reaction to the winner's second championship and the team's third. *Pete Lyons*

Not a lot of good was happening elsewhere. Gurney, after getting black-flagged for a tongue-lashing for biffing Siffert on the pace lap, lost more rocker studs, and finally quit. Revson stopped too, giving up third place because his engine was overheating. Motschenbacher slowed with fuel system trouble. Eaton, struggling for many laps without clutch or brakes, finally missed a downshift going into the Corkscrew and found the escape road full of spectators. He spun to avoid them, rumpled the M12 on some fences, and became a spectator there himself.

Sixth was John Cordts. The Swedish-Canadian had put up some impressive drives early in the season, only to have his cars taken away. He found another one for Laguna, although it was an M6B so problem-plagued it had already broken such stout hearts as John Cannon's and David Hobbs'—and Jo Bonnier's, the year before. But look at his result with it. This quiet man was good.

So was Siffert, of course, who kept the ill-handling Porsche from losing more than a lap to the leaders, and finished fifth. Andretti was saddled with an ill-running 8.1-liter Ford, but he didn't lose any laps, and was fourth. Parsons, who was not happy either, at least finally got a third-place finish with his Lola.

Oliver, treating the race as a test session, finished the Ti22 thirteenth. In all, eighteen cars were

running at the flag, but only sixteen did enough laps to be classified as finishers.

Riverside, California, October 26, 1969

Because Denny had never won here, it was understood this race was his from the start. Ten events into the season and McLaren Racing still had that much of a grip on the 1969 Can-Am. The happy Hulme, who'd just come from victory at the Mexican GP the weekend before, wanted Riverside and he took it. He started by winning pole at 1:34.03 (126.34mph on a repaved and lengthened track). At the green, he waited around for nobody, played no games, set fastest lap (1:35.23), and at the checker was one lap up on every other driver.

But the Kiwi control wasn't as absolute as it looked. Just to keep the team on its toes, the hubris police got into Bruce's engine on Friday and blew it up. They repeated the deed on Saturday. Then on Sunday, in the middle of the race, they snapped the lower left rear suspension wishbone and sent him crashing off Turn 1 at 150mph. A stout chassis and strong seatbelts preserved the driver from any injury at all, but a corner worker had both legs broken.

Not many others came away from Riverside with warm smiles, either. On race morning, some mechanics discovered evidence of overnight tampering. One of Motschenbacher's brake lines appeared to have been pinched with pliers while Amon's Ferrari was missing a locking pin the mechanics were sure had been in place the night before.

Sabotage of a different sort cut Amon down in the race. Once again he had put his Ferrari third on the grid. It was a good third this time, barely more than a second off Hulme's pole, because the Ferrari factory had finally released a longer-stroke, 6.9-liter engine.

Which wouldn't self-start on the grid. The crew, believing an official had gestured his permission, pushed it into life. A few laps into the race, Amon was black-flagged out of a close third place behind McLaren, and told to switch the engine off and restart it on the button. The incident ended with Amon climbing out and stalking away, and 80,000 paying customers were robbed of their only real hope of seeing a good race.

That left Gurney, up from fifth starting place, disputing third with Parsons, who'd come all the way from ninth. Chuck, who was driving a brand-new T163 with a stiffer tub, revised suspension and short-tailed bodywork, finally outmaneuvered Dan in traffic, and his new third place turned into second when McLaren went off. But the Lola was feeling odd now, and thinking the McLaren crash debris had punctured a tire, Parsons came in to check. The real problem was in the differential, about which the crew

could take no action, so the stop was brief, and Parsons shot back out before losing third place. However, now he was right in front of Andretti.

The big-bore McLaren-Ford had started sixth, only to fade back with a sick engine, but now Andretti had something to chase. Meanwhile, Gurney was losing cylinders and also suffering fumes in the cockpit, so in the last few laps the Parsons-Andretti duel overwhelmed him. On the last lap, Mario made his best bid for second around the long, steeply banked Turn 9, but Chuck held him off by half a second at the flag.

Fifth, several laps back, was a brakeless Revson Lola while a similar car driven by Gary Wilson was sixth. Surtees wound up his unhappy Chaparral season—and his Can-Am career—by starting fourteenth and stopping early with a bad engine. Siffert's Porsche was black-flagged and retired because of an oil leak.

But Oliver qualified Bryant's exciting new Ti22 fourth fastest and was in the thick of the early battle for third until the differential broke. This week's new car, an "Open Sports Ford" from Alan Mann in England, builder of 1967's *Honker II*, started tenth, and Australian Frank Gardner moved it to seventh before suspension failure stopped him. Of an impressive, thirty-five-strong lineup, sixteen were counted as finishers.

Texas International Speedway, College Station, Texas, November 9, 1969

Originally, the Can-Am's grand finale was once again to be at Las Vegas, but when the Stardust track was damaged by a desert rainstorm and changed hands, an alternate, brand-new site was found near the university town of Bryan in east Texas. Owned by the same group that had built the Michigan facility, this was another tri-oval with an auxiliary road course of 3.0 miles. This one used more of the speedway's fast banking, though, and for the first time Can-Am cars were able to stretch their legs to 200mph and beyond.

The plot was for Bruce to win this last race while Denny would finish second and thereby scoop up his second J-Wax "Floatile" Can-Am trophy.

Never count your egg-shaped trophies before they're safely in your hatch. McLaren did win, driving the team's spare M8B. But he had to accept the championship too, because, after a ten-for-ten finishing record in 1969, Hulme's car failed to last through round eleven.

That unexpected development followed another: Andretti displaced McLaren from the front row of the grid. From there, Mario used his 494 engine to out-drag Hulme's 430 (they were going the "correct" way along the tri-oval this time) and lead the first lap by a fat second. Perhaps the Bear was up to his old toy-with-'em tricks; perhaps he was waiting for The Boss

to assert himself as planned; but after letting this Ford driver show up well for four laps, he gave his Chevy the boot, passed, and motored right away. The M8B was reportedly clocked as fast as 208mph on the banking. Not long afterward, Andretti's 429'er blew up. So did Amon's Ferrari, which had started fourth and had been holding fourth right behind McLaren. It was the unhappy little Ferrari team's second blowup of the weekend; the 6.9 had done the deed in practice, leaving Amon nothing but the 6.2 for the race.

So here it was again, the old Kiwi two-step. Nothing for 24,000 grandstanders to do but watch the twin Orange Elephants stampede around and around. Denny let Bruce catch up and pass—the Boss finally clocked 210mph—and The Bear was settled into a loyal second place with eleven laps to go when his engine died.

Most of the pack had run into trouble by now. Revson's Lola, fifth fastest in practice, lost more and more ground and finally retired with a sick engine. Oliver's Ti22, from the outside of the third row, ran third for a while until the engine began to leak oil and finally quit. Jack Brabham, back to run his second Can-Am but this time in the Mann-made "Open Sports Ford," moved from his seventh grid place to take over third when the "titanium car" dropped back. Brabham stayed there to the finish despite oil system problems, which, however, allowed George Eaton to overtake into second and score his best day of the year with his M12. Fourth was Siffert, whose Porsche had again lost its cooling fan but again kept soldiering on. Then came Parsons and Motschenbacher, both struggling with multiple problems of their own. Exactly half the twenty-four starters lasted.

Neither Gurney nor Surtees participated this time. The Chaparral was entered here in its home state, but stand-in driver Tom Dutton, who'd campaigned his own Lola T70 earlier in the series before joining Chaparral as a test engineer, lost the difficult 2H in the first hour of practice and cracked its plastic monocoque against a wall. Cannon also left early when the G7A's only engine blew.

McLaren's points score was 165 to Hulme's 160, and he'd won six times to five. Out of twenty-four starts with three cars, they'd only had four DNFs. *Autoweek* tallied their combined series winnings at nearly $305,000, which brought Bruce McLaren Motor Racing's four-year Can-Am take to over half a million. Tough campaigner Parsons had earned eighty-one points, good for third in the series and a total of $71,000. Siffert was fourth, Eaton fifth, and Amon sixth.

Looking back over the eleven races, it was not hard to pick out what Bruce McLaren had done to achieve his third successive success—nor how so

Right: Testing the M8B, sans bodywork, at Goodwood. Note the chassis taper behind the front wheel—and also how resolutely Jim Stone, Teddy Mayer and Cary Taylor are ignoring that friendly little pub on the horizon. *Tyler Alexander*

Top left: McLaren used a baby van to carefully road-test the airfoil concept before trying it full-scale. *Tyler Alexander*

Top right: Bear's favorite: Hulme loved the M8B. *Pete Lyons*

many other would-be contenders had contrived to lose every race. The lessons were clear. Why couldn't anybody but McLaren learn them?

Cars of the Can-Am 1969
McLaren M8B

Bruce McLaren had advanced his grasp of Group 7 technology by two giant steps with 1967's monocoque M6A and the following year's big-block M8A. For the 1969 campaign, his team contented itself with refining the 1968 model. Both M8A chassis tubs, in fact, were rebuilt with fresh sheet aluminum on the same fabricated steel bulkheads. One of these was used as a test hack and then served as the race team's first spare car—a precaution which would pay off during the series. The Colnbrook, England, factory assembled a third, all-new chassis and assigned it to Denny Hulme.

Differences inside the M8B from the older model were subtle, and mainly the results of a season's hard experience. A triangular, unstressed portion of the chassis behind either front wheel well was deleted during the rebuild to create tapered cutaways. This change was widely attributed to concerns about brake cooling, but the mechanics said its real value lay in forestalling damage from hitting curbs and grounding on the track. Other changes included a more elaborate fuel system to ensure using more of the available 75gal, refined suspension geometry with increased travel, and overall attention to weight reduction. But the M8B's most distinctive signature became a high-mounted rear airfoil.

That aerodynamic aid seems to have been adopted late—almost too late, given subsequent rules restrictions. Though McLaren was a trained engineer with a sharp eye and a lively mind, his approach to racing was relatively conservative. Relative to Jim Hall, anyway. Bruce's frequent wheel-to-wheel battles with the Chaparrals certainly kept him well aware of Jim's aerodynamic innovations, but the New Zealander's nature was to try such things out for himself. In 1966 he installed a driver-operated "flipper" tail spoiler on his M1B for one race, but then abandoned it. In 1967, while developing his M6A, he secretly tested a fixed-angle rear wing on chassis-mounted struts. That didn't make the car's final specification, nor was neither device adopted during 1968.

That year's success speaks for itself, of course, but it does seem strange that McLaren—along with almost everyone else—waited more than two years before realizing the worth of Hall's idea of feeding downforce directly into the wheel hubs. "I don't know," Denny Hulme tried to explain years later, "we just thought it was a crazy idea. We thought, well, *that* can't work. We finally did try it, and it worked a *cracker!*" However, McLaren never extracted the most out of the idea by incorporating a feathering mechanism.

Ironically, following a series of accidents in F1, the FIA banned unsprung "moving aerodynamic devices" in May 1969, just before the first Can-Am race. The ban was meant to apply here too, but series administrators decided to allow their local retention through the end of the season.

After all the trouble with Chevrolet's aluminum 427 during 1968, McLaren moved his engine shop from California to Colnbrook. Though Lee Muir went along, Gary Knutson returned to Chaparral, and was replaced by another American, George Bolthoff, who had been with Traco. Though some 427s were used early in the 1969 series, the team's main effort went into a new package, a special Chevrolet block with a larger bore of 4.438. With a shorter stroke of 3.475 this yielded a slightly bigger displacement of 429.9ci, but the real benefit was a wider rev range and more torque and power throughout the range. The "430" allegedly was safe to above 8000rpm, but McLaren fixed 7500 as the redline and arranged a magneto cutout at 7600.

At the M8B's unveiling in England, the press was given a peak power figure of 635 at 7000rpm—"an immense speed for an engine with pistons like bloody great flower pots and valves like small umbrellas," stammered *Autosport's* technical editor, John Bolster. He found the torque output, 560lb-ft, "unbelievable." But he apparently had no problem with the theoretical top speed: 215mph.

And those impressive numbers appear to have been for the 427. The higher-revving 430 would give similar power at 7000, but the curve continued to rise from there, and if spun to redline the 430 could show 680–690hp. Subsequently, according to Lee Muir as quoted by journalist Alan Lis, cam and port development yielded such figures down at the more conservative 7000. That was enough that year—most times. Chevrolet's new block could take longer-stroke cranks, and though McLaren consistently denied racing any during 1969, Muir has been quoted as stating both primary cars had 465ci engines at Michigan (the spare car finished third there with an old 427).

In later years, Denny Hulme would look back on the "little," rev-happy 430 as his favorite motor, and on the supple, stable, reliable M8B, undefeated star of the Can-Am's longest season, as "the best car McLarens ever built."

Ferrari 612P

This was Amon's third Can-Am quasi-campaign with Ferrari, and he must have been really frustrated at how the Prancing Horse was dragging its feet in its supposedly most important market. The 1969 car didn't get to America until the series was three races old. That was better than the year before, but still short of what it took to succeed.

The new 612P was built on the same chassis (number 0866) as the one that so-briefly appeared in 1968, but substantial weight was removed, the suspension was revised, and the reshaped, simplified bodywork lacked the pivoting wing and pop-up air brake flaps featured the year before. Power in the 6.22-liter V-12 was up a little, to a claimed 640–660. For Can-Am fans, this four-cam, 48-valve "proper racing engine" was a great addition to the scene. It didn't scream like smaller Ferraris, but its heavy, raspy drone bristled with aural excitement.

Once it appeared, at Watkins Glen, the red threat proved fast enough to put the McLaren team on its toes. During the rest of the series Amon often

Amon wonders how all those horses keep escaping from the Ferrari's monster V-12. *Pete Lyons*

First turbo: At the St. Jovite round Joe Leonard made Can-Am history by taking the start with this twin-turbocharged Oldsmobile engine in the wedge-bodied McKee. He finished eighth.
Pete Lyons

qualified well, sometimes led a few laps, and enjoyed some second- and third-place finishes. Far more often, though, the engine let him down, usually because of oiling system problems which remained elusive despite every inventive experiment tried by mechanics Roger Bailey and Doane Spencer. They even installed Chevrolet bearings at one stage. For his part, the disgusted Amon once installed himself in front of the Chevrolet engine in the spare McLaren chassis. During the season downforce tabs were added to the Ferrari's blunt front, indicating an understeer problem typical of Group 7 cars, but after a hub-mounted Paul Lamar wing was added Chris reported he could comfortably fling the car around for the first time. Steering remained heavy, however, and the close-coupled cockpit was hot.

Amon's small, underfinanced team received very little help from the factory and only two 6.2 engines, one of which was a little more powerful but far less reliable. Late in the season a longer-stroke 6.9-liter finally appeared—technically transforming the car into a 712P—but it proved no more dependable. At the end of the year Amon left Ferrari to join March, and thus faded one of the

Top and left: Second step: An all-new Oldsmobile turbo installation by Gene Crowe appeared for practice at Elkhart Lake in an all-new McKee featuring a two-speed automatic transmission, four-wheel-drive, and a flip-up air brake flap atop the engine's induction plenum. Trouble with the wheel brakes and other systems caused premature withdrawal, and trouble with finances prevented a reappearance. *Pete Lyons photos*

new Chaparral he'd been developing. Though he'd suffered savage leg and knee injuries, and endured months of painful rehabilitation, he'd proven the 2H was the fastest car yet around his private Texas test track, Rattlesnake Raceway. He wasn't up to racing it, but he replaced himself with inaugural Can-Am Champion (and former World Champion on both four and two wheels) John Surtees. Although the 2H, which had missed all of 1968, was still not ready for the first races of '69, Hall provided Surtees the best available alternative, a new McLaren M12.

The new Chaparral took so long to develop because it embodied several extremely radical concepts. Most unusual-looking of an always unique tribe, the 2H was very narrow (67.25in by the author's tape), had a long nose projecting ahead of a very short wheelbase (85.5in), and had peculiar windowed hatches in its body sides. The highly cambered, low-drag body shape appeared to reject all the work Hall had done to establish the value of downforce; moreover, at a point in Can-Am history when almost every other significant contender had finally adopted the tall, suspension-mounted rear airfoil pioneered on Chaparrals, this new Chaparral reverted to a flipper perched low on the bodywork much like that on 1965's 2C. Even more curiously, the new model's rear suspension revived the ancient de Dion beam-axle idea—but here the beam was split into halves linked by a big U-joint.

Above, bottom left and right: Quasi coupe: Hall intended the Chaparral 2H to have a fully-enclosed cockpit, but Surtees complained about visibility and demanded to have his seat raised into open air. That introduced such a degree of asymmetry that, during tech inspection at the car's debut, mechanic Franz Weis was asked to assume the passenger position to prove the vehicle was still a sports car. From there, he could peer through the original side windows that doubled as the required doors. Through them, outsiders could see the oddly-located auxiliary gauge panel, the unusually elevated steering wheel, and the "automatic's" gated manual shift lever. *Pete Lyons photos*

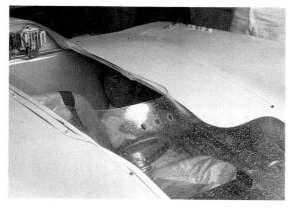

most golden of the Can-Am's many missed opportunities.

Chaparral 2H

Despite his accident at Las Vegas in 1968, Jim Hall was determined to persevere with the secret

What everyone noticed first, though, was that while the 2H met Can-Am regulations by being a legitimate two-seater, any passenger would sit beneath a roof. Yet on the driver's side the finished car was an open roadster.

All this startling innovation came about because

Complexity within: Its sleek engine cover removed, the 2H reveals more unique features. At the extreme rear is the steeply slanted radiator. Arching over the transmission is the de Dion "jointed beam." Controlling its motion is an array of links, including a "steering link" attached to the center on the rear side. The suspension springs and shock absorbers pick up on the cylinder heads, but the sway bar is mounted on a rear subframe and so are the hydraulic "load leveler" cylinders, extending down to the bottom ends of the de Dion arch. The rear suspension's bulk has led to a coiled, side-exit exhaust; concern for low drag has led to a low-profile, crossover induction manifold. Stout aluminum struts link the bottom rear of the engine to the "shoulders" of the fiberglass monocoque chassis. Also visible are the struts of the parasol wing used at Laguna Seca, which was still on the car when this photo was made early in practice for Riverside. *Pete Lyons*

Hall once again had gone right back to first principles. In the years since this strange-looking "White Whale" appeared, people unconnected with the project have published their own speculations as to Jim's thinking, but this is the way he himself explained it to the author for *Autosport* magazine in 1971:

"The idea behind it was that the rubber has gotten to the point where, with independent suspension, the way you have to run it for cornering on the outside you don't use the inside wheels much, you decamber them. They run on the shoulder and you're really carrying around a lot of extra tire, as far as cornering is concerned.

"So I figured that a de Dion axle would give me increased cornering power. And then I said that if I'm going to have increased cornering power I'm going to make the car narrower. That way I'll have a wider road to go around in, and I'll cut the drag down at the same time; but I'm not going to sacrifice anything in cornering because I'll use the tires more. In fact I thought I was going to pick up something in cornering. I thought the compromise was such that I was really going to corner faster with a narrower car and be able to go faster on the straight at the same time."

As originally designed, the de Dion beam was just that, a one-piece fabrication of aluminum sheet arching over the differential housing to unite the rear wheels. Those wheels were huge—the rims were 20in wide. But in tests just before the opening 1968 Can-

Am race, wheelspin induced by the big Chevy's terrible torque set up an unforseen gyroscopic precession, an "axle tramp" so violent that it literally tore the beam apart. The solution proved to be a pivot in the center, but the redesign took time. That's why Hall had to shelve the 2H for that year, and press the aging 2G into another season of service.

Just before the '69 series opened, a second problem cropped up. To optimize its straight-line capabilities, Hall originally built the 2H as a fully-enclosed coupe. One extremely low; both driver and theoretical passenger were covered by a flat, full-width roof arcing no more than 29in from the bottom of the floor pan.

That put the driver's eye-point well below the tops of the front wheel housings. He could see straight ahead through a very steeply slanted windshield which formed the top of the nose, and to either side through transparent hatches (one of Can-Am's few rules at the time called for "doors" of certain minimum dimensions), but obviously vision was blanked to the forward quarters.

Recently, during interviews for *Vintage Motorsport* magazine, Hall made the point that he researched contemporary F1 cars before designing the original 2H seating position. His car's seatback angle was the same, and the driver's eyepoint was in a similar relationship to the front wheels. He does acknowledge that the coupe's wheel arches blocked some vision, but he researched

that too. By test driving one of his leftover 2F coupes with its windshield taped up, Hall decided this was not a significant handicap, and he proved it again to his satisfaction with the 2H. In any case he demonstrated that a system of large mirrors arranged in the manner of horizontal periscopes in the door windows could effectively eliminate the blind spots.

But Fearless John Surtees rebelled. He flatly refused to race the 2H until the roof was cut open and his seat raised so he could see over the fenders. Hall complied, although he felt this compromised airflow over the top of the car to the rear-mounted radiator and body-mounted flipper wing. It also robbed time.

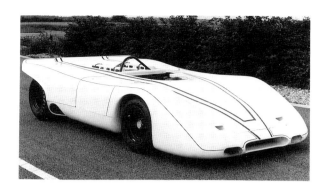

Three Can-Ams of the eleven-race '69 season had passed before the new Road Runner finally came out for the July 24 round at Edmonton.

Chaparral's latest Supercar certainly was the sensation of the series. Only in general terms could it have been described as conventional: it was mid-engined and two-wheel-drive, had a control-arm front suspension (albeit of unique detail design), and of course it featured Chaparral's well known (if usually well hidden) "automatic" three-speed transmission.

However, the chassis of this low-drag, de Dion-rear-axled quasi-coupe was constructed of "pre-preg" fiberglass, rather than the aluminum of which recent Chaparral tubs had been made. In returning to his composite roots, Hall and his engineer of the period, Mike Pocobello, designed the 2H as a true monocoque, with the chassis also serving as most of the outer body shape. Even the upper door frames were part of the load-bearing structure. Various small ports offered access where needed while, of course, the large, removable engine cover was unstressed.

The car's integral belly pan continued on to the tail, where it swelled out in an array of panels and tubes to tie certain suspension links and the wing mounts to the transaxle. The 465ci, 680hp aluminum Chevy block served as part of the structure, braced by stout, taper-ended aluminum struts between its bell housing and the shoulders of the cockpit. Because of the bulky rear suspension, the exhaust pipes curled around themselves like ram's horns and exited the body ahead of the rear wheels.

In quest of rearward weight distribution and minimal drag, Hall put the engine radiator right in the tail, mounted at a steep slant and fed by a ramp-shaped inlet atop the engine cover. Vortex generators sprouting from the floor of the ramp helped bring air in without the need for drag-inducing scoops—except for those in either side of the driver's head fairing, a later addition to the once-ultra-low topside shape necessitated by the new seating position.

Such importance did Hall place on clean aerodynamics that he fed the Chevy engine through a special set of low-line, crossover injector stacks. Outsiders have criticized this arrangement because it restricted the air inlet diameters, and therefore cut potential maximum power. But Hall recalls the penalty as a mere 7hp, and he considered the tradeoff for reduced drag worthwhile.

Snapshots taken during early testing and reproduced by Richard Falconer and Doug Nye in their book *Chaparral* show an incredibly simple and pure streamlined body without any fins or wings. These appear to show the 2H was intended to be devoid of any add-on aero aids.

Not so, Hall told *Vintage Motorsport*. In fact, any impression that he had abandoned aerodynamic downforce is false.

"We did build the first body real long in back, without any spoiler, but that was just to get it out and running. We knew we were going to chop it off later, but we wanted to try it like a streamliner first, because we wanted to try everything. Who knows, we might have wanted to go back to Le Mans someday.

"But right from the start, the 2H was intended to have a considerable amount of download on it. The front end was shaped to make downforce, and we always planned to put a flipper on the back."

Why had he reverted to a body-mounted rear airfoil? It was not because the articulated de Dion rear suspension was somehow unsuitable for a 2E-type strutted wing. "No, that would have worked fine. It's just that we thought we had come up with a better way to do it. Less weight, less drag."

That way involved a load leveling mechanism. Whenever the rear flipper put increased load on the rear suspension, hydraulic cylinders would automatically resist, thus keeping the chassis attitude unchanged. "Active suspension" in 1969.

This system was not quite ready by the time the car made its debut at Edmonton, so it raced there with the tail flipper fixed in the downforce position. That meant a related flap atop the nose was also left inoperative at first. In familiar Chaparral fashion, this front flap closed a duct which, when opened in concert with the rear flipper actuation, would relieve front-end downforce at speed.

Unhappily, no matter what configurations were tried, performance never matched plan. Surtees was never competitive in the 2H. He blamed the car. Hall blamed him. Both men agreed there were certain fundamental flaws in the design—that its handling was too unpredictable to inspire confidence, and that it was mysteriously deficient in straightaway speed—and they also agreed that the design had certain promising features. But they were utterly opposed about persevering with it.

Ford G7A

Fans saw more of this vehicle in the enthusiast press of 1967 than when it finally raced two years later. Originally it was known as the *Calliope*, a nickname owed to the elaborate appearance of a huge experimental three-valve V-8 Ford engineers were trying to prepare for the Can-Am. They tested other powerplants, however, including the four-cam Indy unit. Another distinctive feature, featured especially on many magazine covers, was a "dihedral" rear wing, an airfoil split into two hinged halves and mounted on three tall struts. The outer struts rode the rear hubs as on contemporary Chaparrals, but the center one was bolted to the chassis. The wing was pivoted, too, and the driver—primarily Mario Andretti—could control

Previous page top and bottom: Porsche progress: The roadster-bodied 917PA had a very smooth, simple shape when first photographed at home in Germany. By season's end in Texas, downforce arrangements had been grafted on front and rear. But the aero experimentation had only begun. Same applied to power. Nestled in the aluminum-tube space frame was the normally-aspirated flat-12 engine Porsche had just introduced for its endurance-racing 917 coupes. Very much an enlargement of its 8-cylinder 3.0-liter 908 powerplant, at this stage it displaced 4,494cc with a bore and stroke of 85x66mm. It offered a power output of 580 at 8400rpm, and torque of 376lb-ft at 6800. These weren't big enough numbers to do the job against the big-block Chevys, especially considering its weight. The opposed-cylinder, 4-cam engine was bulky and, despite its magnesium cases, weighed about 550lb, some 90 up on the 7.0-liter Chevy. Empty weight of the complete 917PA was a little over 1700lb. *Porsche factory and Pete Lyons photos*

Ford G7A with Brabham "hitting" the banking at Michigan. *Pete Lyons*

angle of incidence with a hand lever. Also, there were experiments with a two-speed "power-shift" transmission coupled to a torque converter.

All that had been scrapped by the time Ford sold the chassis, plus a spare, for one dollar to veteran mechanics Charlie and Kerry Agapiou, who had been running a Lola for George Follmer. They installed a conventional Hewland 5-speed and relatively conventional Ford engines of various descriptions and displacements (427, 429, and 494ci), as well as a conventional two-strut wing on occasion (as seen at

Michigan in the photo). With some Ford help—not much—they campaigned it with various drivers for two years. That included the Can-Am's second venture to Fuji in Japan that November, where the G7A outlasted other Can-Am entrants (again, minus the McLaren factory) and carried Cannon to second place behind Minoru Kawai's winning 5.0-liter Toyota.

Under the G7A's Group 7 roadster bodywork was one of the bonded aluminum honeycomb chassis Ford had built for its so-called J-car, the GT40 suc-

cessor known as the Mk IV when it won Sebring and Le Mans in 1967. Other revisions for short-distance racing included lighter suspension parts. The Agapiou brothers held back the actual *Calliope* development chassis, J-9, and only raced J-10. Although some outsiders wrote of a G7B and then a G7C, Kerry Agapiou affirms that only one car raced, and that he and his brother never referred to it as other than a G7A. It was heavily damaged in an accident at Riverside in 1970, and the brothers moved to F5000. A subsequent owner has rebuilt J-10 (reports of it being stolen are inaccurate says Kerry) as a Mk IV coupe while Kerry retains J-9 and plans to restore it as the *Calliope*.

Left top and bottom: Titanium Car: Briton Peter Bryant (standing) came to America as John Surtees' mechanic for Ferrari's fact-finding foray into Big Banger racing in 1963. Bryant stayed on and in 1969 designed and built his own Group 7 car. Though generally conventional, it was distinguished externally by its forthrightly wedge-shaped bodywork incorporating full-length "fences" to help make downforce. Inside, titanium was used lavishly, especially in the full-length chassis tub. The lightweight metal's chemical symbol and atomic weight resulted in the car's name, Ti22. Bryant built the car simple and strong and pragmatically sourced wheels and suspension uprights from Gurney's Eagle factory. Wheelbase was 94in, track dimensions 61 and 59, and overall width 74. Of course the engine was the big, aluminum Chevy, the transmission Hewland's LG600 5-speed. Jackie Oliver put up some spectacular performances in this car late in 1969, including pole position for the post-season invitational race in Japan (details of this event in Ford G7A description), and again early in 1970 before the first Ti22 flipped and was destroyed at St. Jovite. *Pete Lyons photos*

June 2nd was a balmy, somewhat breezy early summer's Tuesday in southern England, and Bruce McLaren was making the most of it. He had come to his favorite test site, Goodwood, a circuit now closed to racing but popular as a rudimentary proving ground, and spent the forenoon shaking down the second example of his company's brand-new M8D Group 7 sports racer. It was the car he himself was going to drive in the fifth Can-Am season, practice for which would open in ten days at Mosport. That morning, he'd also done a few laps in one of his Formula Ones, and between times had been discussing some of his bubbling ideas for a new Indianapolis car.

Three months short of his thirty-third birthday, the engineer-driver from New Zealand had climbed, if not yet to the top of the international motor racing mountain, at least well up its slopes. He was reigning Can-Am champion, having earned the title for the second time in the series' four years. As a team, McLaren had taken it the last three years—most recently, by a crushing record of eleven victories in eleven races.

Bruce hadn't yet put such a stamp on F1, but as a driver he'd finished third in the previous season's World Championship, the third time he'd been ranked in the top three. His career total of Grand Prix victories stood at four. As an F1 constructor, Bruce McLaren Motor Racing had been fourth in 1969, with one victory, after having been second overall the year before. The team had begun 1970 with a couple of second places in the first three Grands Prix.

McLaren's first run at the Indy 500 had not been so encouraging. Bruce himself wasn't driving there, but his team leader and friend, fellow Kiwi Denis Hulme, suffered severe burns on his hands when a fuel cap opened during a practice lap. That incident convinced teammate Chris Amon, who had never become comfortable at the Speedway, to withdraw. Called in as replacements, Peter Revson retired after running seventh and Carl Williams finished ninth. But Bruce came back from America with a much more competitive McLaren Indy car already taking shape in his mind.

At a quarter past noon, having been in and out of the pits for adjustments for the past hour and a half, he took the M8D out for one more test before lunch. At twenty-two minutes past the hour, as the 700hp car accelerated to probably 170mph through a flat-out, left-hand kink in the track's longest straight, a bodywork fastener somehow failed. The entire rear section lifted into the airstream, throwing the car into an uncontrollable spin off the road toward a concrete flag station platform left over from Goodwood's days as a public race track. It was the only obstruction for hundreds of yards. The car hit nose-first, ripped apart, and burst into flames. Bruce was thrown clear, but he had been killed instantly.

Every Can-Am season had its own flavor. This one began bitter, and did not improve.

There had been crashes and injuries in the Can-Am, some of them very nasty, but no one had died before. In fact, in an era when death seemed to lurk around every corner in other branches of the sport, the full-bodied Big Bangers had seemed almost safe by comparison. Now it was no longer possible to see this as a bright, carefree game.

Nor was Group 7 what it had been, a formula free of fetters, an invitation for the most innovative engineering minds to explore their wildest fan-

cies. Can-Am rules were still less restrictive than most, but aerodynamic clamps had been applied at the insistence of the FIA. These were intended to outlaw such "moving aerodynamic devices" as spoilers and/or wings that pivoted or were attached to the wheel hubs.

In return, the FIA, beginning in 1971, would formally list the Can-Am as a recognized international championship.

Essentially, the significant 1970 Can-Am rules required any part of the car's exterior body located *above the wheel centerlines* and which had "an aerodynamic influence on the stability of the vehicle" to be unconnected to the wheel suspension and to remain fixed in position relative to the body. Any "forward facing gap located in the airstream" could have the upper edge of its opening no higher than 80cm (32in) above the bottom of the chassis. This latter prohibition applied to any engine intake scoops, but not to the gap formed by the roll-over hoop, which, however, could not have an aerodynamic effect.

As before, the body had to fully cover the wheels when seen from above, and major body parts had to remain intact during the race. A rule refinement required the cockpit opening to be symmetrical in plain view about the centerline, and windscreen protection to be equal for both driver and (theoretical) passenger. This, of course, outlawed not only such "quasi-coupes" as 1969's Chaparral 2H, but also the tonneau-style of cockpit openings like that on the Ferrari 612P. To answer complaints about flying stones, rear fenders now had to extend down behind the tires. Body width was limited to four inches outside of the tires on either side. Underbody shape was not controlled.

As before, engines had to displace at least 2500cc (152ci), but there was no upper limit, nor any restriction on numbers of cylinders, camshafts, superchargers, fuel consumption, etc. However, gas turbines were specifically banned.

One rule which had caused distress in the past would continue to do so, despite an alteration. For 1970, the mandatory on-board engine starting system had to be used exclusively *once the green flag had been displayed*. Chris Amon would have welcomed that interpretation at Riverside in 1969.

Increasing limitations on the cars seemed to have a parallel in the series itself. Economic times had turned tight, and though the initial calendar showed eleven Can-Ams again, some of the venues were known to be questionable. Finally, Bridgehampton and Sears Point (which would have replaced Texas) canceled, and only one new course, Road Atlanta, stepped up.

Though the championship ran shorter, Johnson Wax kept the faith by maintaining its year-end points fund at the previously announced record level of $200,000. As was the case the year before, points were awarded on a twenty-fifteen-twelve-etc. basis, down to tenth place. The split-season/drop-one-result points structure also carried over.

Encouragingly, several new cars and teams came out for 1970, including new models from Bryant, Chaparral, and Lola, and all-new efforts from BRM, March, and Shadow. There was said to be a Lotus in preparation, too, but this never appeared. Nor did Porsche come back—but as early as the spring of 1970, reports were circulating that the Stuttgart auto maker had a turbocharging program underway.

McLaren's bold white nemesis, the Chaparral "sucker," qualified fastest three times out of four, including here at Laguna Seca—where, however, it didn't make the race. *Pete Lyons*

Mosport Park, Ontario, June 14, 1970

Saddened, shaken, but refusing to sink, Bruce McLaren's teammates and friends came back to the Americas determined to keep the great Can-Am organization he built powering ahead at full throttle. They built a third new M8D, and to drive it alongside Denny Hulme they asked the best man they knew, old friend Dan Gurney. As always, the pair of bright orange McLarens were the best presented, the best prepared, and the fastest cars on the grid.

Although Gurney had never driven the befinned Batmobile before, and though an engine problem wasted most of Friday practice and even though he was just too tall to get comfortable in the car, he put it on pole. At 1:16.8, 115.31mph, his effort upheld Group 7's tradition of beating not only its own previous record (by 1.4sec, in this case, or 1.8 percent), but contemporary F1's best speed as well (by 0.6sec). "I wasn't conscious of holding anything back," Dan said, but he reckoned more experience with the car might be worth another second.

Hulme, his hands still bandaged, stiff, and desperately tender after his fire at Indianapolis, never tried to reach his potential in practice.

The new Lola went pretty well for Peter Revson, as did Lothar Motschenbacher's McLaren M8B, the spare factory car from 1969. The new BRM was running and handling very badly, so Eaton pulled out of practice early.

To judge by its sixth grid place, the startlingly innovative AVS Shadow was showing promise, but a lot of that was George Follmer. Whenever the tiny-tired "go-kart" exploded to 7.0-liter life, the effect was attention-getting, to say the least. Fearless George was obviously working very hard in the bumpy Mosport corners, and he admitted the term "go-kart" was not wildly inappropriate. Segment-timing indicated the cornering power was not especially high, and on the straights, a quaver in the exhaust note suggested the small-diameter rear wheels were bouncing off the road. "They find all the holes," Follmer agreed. The car's low-drag design principle was said to be working, to the tune of 190mph-plus, where the McLarens were only doing 170-something, but the wheel-bouncing meant a lot more time

Right: Mosport: Dick Brown (#28) proudly debuts his M6B with the gleaming new aluminum body he crafted himself. Sadly, this is to be his last race weekend. *Pete Lyons*

Mosport: A somber hour, but Gurney (left, his cheek bandaged) will do his best to give the team something to work for. Alexander (right) waits to fit a mirror on the new, extra-tall windscreen. *Pete Lyons*

had to be spent on the brakes. There also was an over-heating problem. Interesting, but not yet convincing.

Late on Saturday afternoon, tragedy struck. Dick Brown, a well-liked privateer from Birmingham, Michigan, who had prepared for his third Can-Am season by putting his own new, wedge-shaped aluminum body on his M6B, reportedly hit oil at maximum speed at the crest of the longest straight and veered into a gully unprotected by guardrails. It was the Can-Am's first fatality at an event.

Though Hulme hadn't stretched himself in practice, he charged ahead at the start of the race from his outside-front place to take the lead. His new teammate tucked into a faithful supporting position, and McLaren's marauders set off toward yet another Can-Am finish flag.

But this time the familiar sight had something different about it. It was the Peter Bryant-built "Titanium Car," the tidy Ti22 that Jackie Oliver had driven so well at the end of the previous season. Ollie had qualified it third here, and at the start, he'd fastened its fangs to the rumps of the Orange Elephants and would not be thrown off.

Hulme was trying to build a cushion, and twice gained some 6sec on Gurney, but both times heavy traffic cut him back. Presently, Oliver grabbed the initiative and popped into view as a white wedge splitting them. It was a very enthusiastic performance from this interloper in only his third Can-Am, and the Establishment didn't seem to be able to do much about it. Gurney, watching the cheeky chap ahead, might have had time to recall himself being in the same position while driving his own little McLeagle here just a year before.

At the forty-lap point, half-distance, the three were covered by a blanket 3sec long. Hulme was still trying to thrust ahead but was still being frustrated. One could only guess at the pain in his hands. Then, coming up to lap one of the slowest of the old cars at the tight Moss corner, Denny was forced to put a wheel on the curb. The steering kicked back sharply. Immediately he was off his pace, and Oliver passed him for the lead. His hands bleeding inside his bandages, and his engine running hot anyway, Denny waved Dan by too.

The sense of purpose at the front sharpened. Nose to tail, threading through the backmarkers as if they were so many pylons on a 175mph gymkhana course, Oliver and Gurney were visibly no longer having fun and games, they were racing. On lap fifty they got a clear track, and each set his fastest time of the day. Gurney's was 0.4sec quicker than Oliver's, but still it took another nine hectic trips around the swooping, plunging 2.46 miles before the big M8D finally nosed ahead of the fleet little Ti22.

Oliver had passed Gurney once, and obviously would try again, but now they came up to lap Lothar Motschenbacher in his year-old McLaren M8B. The new factory car made it by the distributor's. The rival brand didn't. Oliver's waving fist was matched by waving blue flags at every station, but over the next three laps he could see Gurney going from 2sec ahead to 12. At last, Oliver pulled alongside and slightly ahead of Motschenbacher as they hurtled up the rising, curving Andretti straight. Going by, the Ti22's right rear wheel contacted the M8B's left front. The white car continued on, but the red one veered off the road and crashed heavily.

The accident was frighteningly near the site of Brown's the day before. Luckily, Motschenbacher walked away from this one, but he was very upset.

There were only fourteen laps left, so every sense of a race was lost. Oliver did what he could, and closed to about 9sec behind Gurney, but at the end, the gap had increased to 16. Hulme soldiered on to finish a lonely third, having been forced to let Gurney lap him twice, but when it was all over and he was on his cool-off tour, the Bear saw the crowd pouring over the fences and lining the curbs to give him a huge ovation. Of the rest of the field, the new cars were suffering various new-car problems; none figured, and most quit.

Motschenbacher entered a protest against Oliver, who countered with a like charge. The stewards found them both culpable, reprimanded each, and fined Oliver $50 under the FIA International Sporting Code.

St. Jovite, Quebec, June 28, 1970

McLaren's boys were pushing ahead with his F1 program, too, and the weekend after Mosport, Gurney joined them in Holland for his first GP drive in two seasons. It did not go well. Dan started an M14 from the back of the grid but the engine lasted just three laps. Hulme was there too, but decided he'd better give his hands a race off, so Peter Gethin, who'd won the 1969 British F5000 championship driving a McLaren M10, stood in. His and a third factory car driven by Andrea de Adamich also broke down.

Other familiar Can-Am names there at Zandvoort, incidentally, were Amon and Siffert, in Marches, and Oliver and Eaton in BRMs; all retired. Surtees, however, who had retired from the Can-Am and was using a McLaren pending completion of his own Surtees F1 chassis, finished the GP sixth.

Back in Canada, the Group 7 drivers found lovely little Le Circuit had badly deteriorated over the past

Mosport: Everything is different but the result. Rules have changed, and Bruce McLaren is gone, but his M8Ds with Gurney (#48) and Hulme are still the class of the "conventional car" field. On the pace lap, coming down into Moss hairpin, Oliver (#22 Ti22) and Revson (#26 Lola T220) are next best, followed by Motschenbacher (#11 M8B), Follmer (#16 Shadow Mk 1), and Eaton (#98 BRM P154). Then it's Brown, McCaig, Wilson, Koveleski, Dean, and Titus.
Pete Lyons

Above: Mosport: Hulme's hands, still so raw after his Indianapolis fire that they'll bleed at the slightest jar, are a constant torment. But he'll race. *Pete Lyons*

Bottom left: St. Jovite: It's Gurney leading the team again, with Hulme fending off the ferocious Oliver—for half a lap. *Pete Lyons*

Bottom right: St. Jovite: Bigger ones are better, they keep telling me. Me, I want my sweet old 430 back. *Pete Lyons*

winter. His long arms whirling furiously behind the Batmobile's deep, transparent windscreen, Gurney worked very hard to earn his second pole at 1:33.0, 1.3sec off Bruce McLaren's of the year before. (However, three months later, the quickest F1 driver would get down to 1:31.5.) Though Hulme's hands were much better after their rest, he could only do 1:33.3, but that was enough, by 0.5, to hold Oliver to another third grid place after the Ti22 snapped a titanium suspension link. As he lined up, Ollie had Motschenbacher's repaired M8B to his left. In ten days, Lothar and his tireless mechanics had rebuilt or replaced "nearly everything but the instrument panel."

Of the new cars, both the Revson Lola and the Eaton BRM were going better, though not really well — and not as well as John Cordts' and Bobby Brown's older McLarens — but Follmer's Shadow was in serious trouble. At Mosport, tech inspectors had let the radical little car run despite their view that its wing-top radiator system violated the rule about the height of "forward-facing air gaps." For St. Jovite, the AVS team lowered the radiator by installing it *inside* a new wing split like a sandwich. The Shadow had run hot at Mosport; now, it quickly boiled. More coolers were added, but before the value of these could be established, the transmission packed up. Follmer's fifth-row grid place was remarkable, considering the circumstances.

St. Jovite was the site from which a couple of drivers had launched brief flying careers back in 1966. This year, on the much bumpier surface, the much more forceful 7.6- and 8.1-liter cars were taking the notorious hump in the back straight in such an alarming fashion that at one point in practice a plaintive request came over the paddock PA. Would any drivers experiencing front-end lightness please fit tabs to the nose, or something, because they were frightening the flagmen.

Sound advice. A brave sight the twenty-two big sports cars made, their bright colors reflected in the tents and bright clothing of the spectators under the trees. At the green there was a noise like an air strike, and two orange shapes, with a white one glued to them, hurtled away into what everyone hoped would be another great race. They whipped 'round the hairpin at the far end of the track and accelerated hard toward the hump, into fourth gear: 130, 140, 150mph. The two orange machines lifted over the crest and dropped back heavily. The white one, tucked tight into their draft, lifted—and kept lifting. Its flat belly riding on air, the Ti22 climbed a ramp of wind, its wedge-shaped nose rearing to the vertical, past vertical, tilting backwards, flying finally stern-first. It slammed down on its titanium roll bar, dissolving in a chaos of shattering bodywork and splattering earth. The onrushing torrent of following cars was braking, swerving, scraping. Two shunted heavily and spun to rest.

Jackie Oliver walked away. He was unhurt physically, but in his eyes was a long, deep, hollow look.

So our great race had lasted three-quarters of one lap. The rest of it was a procession. Gurney let Hulme pass, but Denny's engine was running hot again. After a pit stop for water he did the day's fast lap, a good thing to watch, but the engine was smoking now and when it started making unusual noises he shut it off and coasted in. To anyone who dared come near him, the disappointed Bear wondered aloud what had been wrong with last year's nice little 430 engines. Why did people think these new 465s were so great? Every time Dan came by his sounded rough, too. It could all be over any minute.

Gurney did nurse it all the way to the end, driving

with one eye on his temperatures and the other on his mirrors, but Motschenbacher was still 11sec back at the end, and he was the only man on the same lap.

Watkins Glen, New York, July 12, 1970

Gurney scored a World Championship point for finishing sixth in the French GP on July 5. Hulme settled back into his F1 saddle with a fourth. Back across the Atlantic, the Dan and Denny Show took up the Can-Am campaign with another one-two qualifying performance and another McLaren victory.

But in both cases, this time, it was Hulme first. Denny had talked the engine shop into making up more of his beloved old 430s. Dan started out with one too, but it failed to earn his affection. After a persistent misfire resulted in second-fastest qualifying time, Gurney went to the grid with the only available spare Chevy, one of the suspect 465s. Though this was a fast course, both M8Ds were lacking aerodynamic structures that originally filled the tapered gaps behind the front wheels. The reason given was that these had turned out too easy to damage.

Hulme's pole was his first of the Can-Am year, but for the second race in a row the M8D wasn't able to match times set by the M8B the year before. Whether the cause was the lack of the older car's more direct-acting rear wing, or another inferior track surface—fresh patches were breaking up, here—was impossible to say. Some other drivers did better their 1969 times, but they were driving much different cars.

Most different of them all was the shiny white Chaparral 2J, Jim Hall's and Chevrolet's astonishing Ground Effect Vehicle, striking a welcome (in some quarters) blow for Group 7 innovation. Various problems with the auxiliary fan motor and its belt drive system, as well as with the wheel brakes, kept the complex machine from showing its true potential. However, an increasingly enthusiastic Jackie Stewart—who'd won his first World Championship since his brief Can-Am appearances in 1966—was able to put every conventional car but the factory McLarens behind the Chaparral on the grid.

Stewart called the road adhesion "fantastic," saying the difference compared to conventional cars was like that between a street car and an F1. "It requires a new type of sensitivity from the driver," he remarked to *Autoweek*, adding that the ground effect technology heralded "the beginning of a new era in motor racing." He was enjoying being a pioneer of a new concept. "[T]here aren't many race cars you can get high on now days."

Unfortunately, two interesting cars from the Canadian rounds were missing. No replacement Ti22 was yet available, and the Shadow team had also suffered a crash—a crash involving its trailer on the highway after St. Jovite. Revson's Lola was showing well, fourth on the grid, and Motschenbacher's McLaren was sixth, with Brown's McLeagle next, but the rest of the Can-Am crowd was obscured by interlopers. As always

at the Glen, some world-class driving talent in Group 5 endurance cars from Saturday's six-hour race were joining in. (One of which, a Porsche 917 coupe, Hulme had co-driven with Vic Elford to fourth place Saturday, so the Bear's burned paws were healing nicely. Elford went on to drive another 917 in the first of what would be many Can-Ams for him with many mounts.)

At the start, Hulme powered straight into the lead, with Gurney taking up guard station behind. Guarding looked like it was becoming necessary, for Revson was enjoying his first good run with his new Lola, and from his fourth-place start, he accelerated past Stewart's heavy Chaparral.

Because of vapor-locking carburetors on the fan motor, the 2J was not developing full suck, but it was still noticeably more able to make sharper swerves in traffic than Revson's conventional T220 and soon moved back up to third. Stewart kept pressing and set best lap of the day. But again the Chaparral was faster

than its brakes, and a dozen or so laps into the race, Gurney's mirrors were free of the white brick. A pit stop for work on brakes and blowers didn't help in either department, so after a few more laps, Stewart parked it.

Watkins Glen: If anybody thought the new decade's cars would be boring, Chaparral, Chevrolet, and Stewart had another think for 'em. *Pete Lyons*

Watkins Glen: Sing hallelujah! The ardent young spectator jumped the fence just at flagfall, and a cop will hustle him away before this first lap is over, but he does succeed in letting Denny, Dan, Peter, and Jackie know how he feels about Can-Am racing. *Pete Lyons*

Top right: Mid-Ohio: The
Shadow is back, and Elford
shows its startling new shape to
the mid-field pack, including
Parsons (hidden), Koveleski
(#54), Dutton (#79), Wilson, and
Causey. *Jim Chambers*

Above and top left: Edmonton:
F5000 champ Gethin (left)
spends his first weekend learning
all about Group 7 from the
master. *Pete Lyons photos*

Right bottom: Mid-Ohio: Hulme
is long gone, but a great fight
shapes up between
Motschenbacher, Revson, and
Gethin; Rodriguez watches for a
while from his Ferrari (#20).
Pete Lyons

Meanwhile, Revson applied himself to the job of filling Gurney's mirrors. The McLaren's 465 was helping because it was getting hot again and Dan was losing ground to Hulme. At the same time, spectacular Seppi Siffert had filtered his Porsche 917 coupe through to the front of the mid-pack and was smelling second place.

It was an enthralling battle, but it broke up at half-distance, when all three came into the pits at once. Gurney was answering a black flag for passing under a yellow. Revson was concerned about dropping oil pressure. Siffert was making a planned refuelling stop. The Porsche left first, Seppi making one of his notorious screaming, wheelspinning departures. Right behind roared Gurney, every one of those 465 red hot cubes working to melt his hapless Goodyears.

Pity it didn't go on from there. Only four laps later, Gurney was back in for water, having realized a low-place finish was better than a long walk. But maybe a finish could get too low. After a second water stop, Gurney's eventual ninth was behind Brown in Dan's old McLeagle.

Hulme, too, was nursing high temperatures. This was no fault of the 430, it seemed, but of the new sections of the track surface, which were breaking up into showers of tarry gravel that clogged cooling ducts. It was so bad, Denny said, that the reduction of radiator air-flow caused serious understeer. Also, the stones were sandblasting his visor, and the sticky asphalt had about glued him into his seat. Toward the end, the M8D slowed so much that the 917 came sniffing up to within 7sec, but then Siffert slid off the atrocious road at the

high-speed summit of Graham Hill. He got back on, but the Bear's grip on a twelve-grand paycheck was secure.

Still, the $9,000 for second place was good money in those days. In fact, the big bucks for paypoints three through seven also flew away to Europe with drivers of underpowered, overweight, but fully developed Group 5 coupes built to reel off an entire Can-Am season's mileage nonstop.

Edmonton, Alberta, July 26, 1970

In the intervening British GP, Hulme qualified fifth and finished third. Gurney was eleventh on the grid and in retirement at the end—in more ways than one. His agreement with McLaren involved clashing oil company sponsorships, and as time went on, his own backer was developing second thoughts. That was the official reason for his leaving the team.

But there had been some disaffection growing on a personal level. As Dan freely admitted later in an *Autosport* interview, his well-known, not to say notorious, urge to constantly "tweak" his cars, searching for the ultimate setup, ran very much counter to the culture at

Colnbrook. He said the McLaren team flatly forbade him to make any changes, and it was obvious he found this both frustrating and demeaning. In any case, he was looking toward his own retirement at the end of the year, and keen to concentrate on his Eagle Indy car business.

McLaren hired Peter Gethin to take his seat, and the British F5000 champion turned in a workmanlike weekend, qualifying second to Hulme by 0.4, running a disciplined second throughout the race, and finishing second after only a little last minute trouble.

There was frankly nothing to worry the McLarens at Edmonton, which again had one of the thinnest entry lists of the season. One might have expected the top team to take it easy. Maybe it's just that there was no place to go water skiing, but both drivers put in a lot of track time during practice, and much of it was for just the kind of experimenting Gurney hadn't been allowed to do. Hulme tried out different fences and dams, wing angles, ride heights, camber settings, spring rates, tire pressures, tires, even valve lash variations (to alter cam timing). Then he demanded a different engine.

Both M8Ds had started with 465s, and practice had proved, to the engine men's satisfaction, that the persistent overheating trouble had nothing to do with their work after all but with chassis installation. Thicker radiator cores and area-pinching bowed panels riveted into the duct outlets to speed up airflow seemed to work. But Denny still wanted a 430 like the one that had taken him to victory here the year before. He trusted it more and preferred its power characteristics.

It was with a 430 that he set his pole time now—set it three times, in fact, putting in three identical laps, back to back. That those laps were 0.7 slower than his and Bruce McLaren's identical front row times of the year before with identical engines, he said, was due in small part to a bumpier surface but in greater part to the loss of the hub-mounted wings, which required stiffer springs. He said this with authority. It was clear we'd seen the best back-to-back comparison Can-Am 1970 was going to give us.

Newcomer Gethin's first impressions were that the Can-Am sports car seemed big and heavy after his F5000 single-seater—he did look lost in a cockpit tailored for the much bigger Gurney. He also discovered that the M8B didn't invite a hang-it-out style. He pointed out that, if the car were allowed to get very far sideways at high speed, the body sidepieces supporting the rear wing would block the airflow and cut adhesion quite suddenly. Peter felt that the car as delivered to him had too much understeer, and he calmly, professionally, set about tuning that out with tire pressures and bars.

Not to be unkind, but another team was pointing up McLaren's vast experience by contrast. The BRM, which

had shown itself a handful in the three races before, was handling abysmally here. Young Eaton seemed unable to say more than "it's lurching." To get at what he meant, crew chief Roger Bailey, who'd been with Amon the year before, got official permission to go along for a ride. He came back a bit shaken, saying that by comparison the Ferrari 612P had been "like taking a bus to church." The P154 never seemed to do the same thing twice. But now Roger had some ideas to work with. Data acquisition circa 1970.

Oh, yes, the race. An Orange Elephant parade, Hulme showing Gethin the way around, the newcomer staying close so he could absorb all the tricks. Until, that is, the add-on panel suddenly blew out of Gethin's radiator duct. Shortly his gauges showed that it had, indeed, been doing its job, so he eased his foot. Hulme

Elkhart Lake: It's supposed to be just another romp in the woods for the Bear. Peter means only to trail respectfully. Really. *Pete Lyons*

Elkhart Lake: Revvie makes the most of his front-row start to treat the world to the sight of a Lola leading McLarens through tight Turn 5. *Pete Lyons*

Above: Elkhart Lake: Revson's rear tire goes and so does the rest of the car by the end of the long Road America lap. *Pete Lyons*

Top right: Road Atlanta: Elford likes the Chaparral and drives it brilliantly, and Hall smiles for what seems the first time in years. *Pete Lyons*

Bottom: Road Atlanta: The "Martian Brassiere" on its stern is only one of the many changes that have transformed the Ground Effect Vehicle's performance. *Pete Lyons*

pulled off alone, going ever faster, and just out of pure delight at the way things were going at long last, he did his fastest time and the race's, of course, seven laps from the end.

Motschenbacher, third on the grid, had been tagging along to make it a McLaren threesome until he spun. Lothar recovered before losing his place, but drove on more conservatively, and was a lap down by the end. What with handling, mechanical and/or driving troubles, nobody else came into the picture.

Mid-Ohio, Lexington, Ohio, August 23, 1970

The Lola lasted and was second. That was the big news from round five. His engine dead-reliable at last, Peter Revson thrust the big T220 into the middle of a fierce struggle with Motschenbacher and Gethin. Motschenbacher's ex-works M8B finally dropped back from an overall second place with failing brakes, leaving McLaren's Peter to chase Lolas until the engine in the works M8D, evidently wiping a cam lobe flat, finally lost a cylinder, trailed smoke, and stopped a few laps short of the finish. The Lola pit crew, one solid mass of crossed fingers and chewed fingernails, kept counting laps until, incredulously, they had reached eighty and saw the checkered flag.

In the month's break after Edmonton, some competitors—though not all—were able to carry out the development they no doubt had intended to do before the season started. Significantly, the Haas-entered factory Lola team switched engine builders, and a new George Foltz 465 lasted through a solid test session at Elkhart Lake. The BRM boys carried out some suspension geometry changes in hopes of eliminating bump-steer and also received their first BRM-built Chevy 465 to replace the hack 427s used until now, but there had been no time to run the new combination.

The AVS Shadow people did test and spent a lot of time here at Mid-Ohio. Their original super-low machine, damaged in a transporter accident, was tied up in litigation, but they had a second one. Painted black instead of red, it also showed some mechanical rethinking.

Originally, this second chassis had been built for a turbocharged 5.0-liter Toyota engine, but it came to Ohio with a big-block Chevy sticking tall out the top. As a first solution to the overheating problem, all concern over frontal area went by the board, and a pair of bulky radiators was installed atop the tail, but independent of the wing. The wing itself was mounted at a steep angle on four slabs of 5/16in aluminum honeycomb. The inner pair of these also supported hydraulic dampers to replace the friction devices on the original design. Friction discs remained at the front, but the brake extractor fans on the front wheels now were protected from direct wind blast by molded lips in the body, ahead of the wheels.

In the middle of the long, low, black wedge was a new driver. Though George Follmer participated in the test, he didn't want to race the car any more, so Vic Elford was called in. Versatile Vic, the English driver who'd come to racing from rallying and had just won a Trans-Am in Chaparral's Chevy Camaro, settled into the innovative Shadow with interest. In several days of testing he learned much, and altered much, to the point where he said the vehicle began to behave like an automobile. In corners it turned out to be not bad at all, on speed if not stability, though in a straight line it was nearly unmanageable. One problem was ultra-quick steering; a change from a 9in to a 12in wheel helped. He also suggested that narrower front tires would improve the response and be less disturbed by bumps. He felt an inherent disadvantage was the pure parallelogram suspension geometry, which required stiff spring rates if the tires weren't to tilt in the turns, but the 4in total travel didn't strike him as a big problem—many older cars of the day had as little.

Whether this particular car would ever come good was one question, Elford summed up, but he could see no reason why the small-diameter Firestone tires themselves should be faulted. He was able to qualify seventh, within 4sec of fastest.

Fastest, of course, was Hulme. Once again, however, he was not as fast as the year before. The deficit this time was 1.7sec. He attributed that partly to 1970's inferior aerodynamics and partly to the hot, humid weather during the practice days that seemed to bring oil out of the surface. Perhaps the lack of anybody pushing him played a role, too.

Gethin, who'd never seen the tight, narrow course before and found he didn't much like it, at least not when having to herd such a massive car around it, looked puzzled all through practice. Every time he just touched the throttle, he said, the *front* end went sideways. His best qualifying lap put him fourth, alongside Revson and right behind Motschenbacher.

Hulme's race was untroubled. He was using a 465 this time, one with a different cam and shorter intake stacks to suit. It ran cool. He won by well over a minute. Only Revson's Lola ran the same distance.

Elford retired the Shadow after nine laps. The team said it was because a wheel weight had spun off and vibration made it impossible to hold the steering wheel, but it was too time-consuming to fit a new wheel. In fact, Elford had told his crew before the start that he'd pull in if the car's straightway instability threatened any other driver's safety, and he'd decided this was the case. Afterward, the discouraged team announced its withdrawal from the series pending construction of a new, more orthodox Shadow.

Elkhart Lake, Wisconsin, August 30, 1970

Peter Gethin clearly understood his role with McLaren. He was to finish second to Denny Hulme. In his third Can-Am, he did exactly that. But he won it anyway.

During practice in Wisconsin, several mechanics wanted it known that they considered it unsafe to schedule Can-Ams on successive weekends. These muscle-bound Group 7 cars demonstrated their fragility every time they were exercised, and every part demanded a complete checkover after each race. McLaren had the dedicated personnel and cooperative subcontractors and stocks of spares to get the job done. Lesser teams had to let certain things go, and that must have been a major reason for a very high failure rate at Road America this time.

Because rain was forecast for Saturday, Hulme made sure he set a grid time on Friday. It was a good enough time for pole, and although Denny said he

Road Atlanta: A real threat at last! It's like sail against steam, and the suddenly old-tech M8Ds cannot match the 2J's speed.
Pete Lyons

Road Atlanta: But the Chaparral loses its "suck," and Hulme comes through for another win, right? Nope. *Pete Lyons*

could probably have taken another two seconds off if necessary, that still would have been two seconds short of his 1969 time. The circuit hadn't changed at all, he said; it was all in the car.

Rain did come, heavy rain, and though it stopped by qualifying time on Saturday, the track remained streaming wet. Denny never suited up. He appeared in the pits in civvies and a minute, mischievous smile to play the part of the older uncle watching how junior got on. Two years before, he well remembered, the Elkhart surface had been *extremely* slick in the rain. But he refrained from offering any advice.

Gethin had claimed he enjoyed driving in the wet, but he'd never tried so much horsepower in so much wet. He came back in almost immediately. There was a vacant stare in his eyes. "There's no connection at either end! On the straights at twenty miles an hour I'm using *this much* lock! In the corners I can't get the front to come round, but when the engine just *ticks* over the back is gone! Just *gone!*

"Can we take some plug leads off?"

Sunday's skies were a joyous blue. Revson basked in an interesting position—his big red and white Lola was up front, alongside Hulme. Obviously benefiting from his test here three weeks earlier, Revvie too had qualified on Friday. Not because of the weather forecast, but because on Saturday he was due in California at Ontario Motor Speedway to qualify a USAC car for McLaren. He was the fastest McLaren driver there, but only tenth overall. (Gurney qualified second in his new Eagle.) Then Revson bounced back to Wisconsin to try to beat McLaren on behalf of Lola.

At the drop of the flag he made the most of his chance, crossing the line a nose ahead of Hulme and leading through the first two turns and down the speed trap straight behind the pits. The Bear was snarling at Peter's heels, feinting at the braking points, and at the long, sweeping Carousel, he snatched the lead. But Revson took it back on heavy braking into Canada Corner and roared up by the pits to lead the first lap. Gethin, who had started sixth, was already third.

Partway around the second four miles, Hulme made a determined braking effort and just scraped through on the inside. Gethin followed him through a moment later, and the pair of M8Ds romped right off. No denying it, McLaren was still tops.

Having established that, Denny let up on the gas a little, let his teammate by to see what leading a Can-Am was like, and let himself fall back to taunt Revson. At the same time, Motschenbacher's McLaren was hassling the Lola from behind. Left alone up front, Gethin was gaining whole seconds a lap.

Revson only had to endure the sandwich treatment for fourteen laps. Then, just past the pits, a rear

tire went flat. Over the next four long miles a half shaft broke, the tire tore completely off, the fuel tank started scraping on the road, and when the metal was gone, the road started in on the rubber cell; it was worn halfway through by the time Revvie dragged the smoking debris into the pits.

Next time around Motschenbacher was second, leading Hulme. Hulme was slowing further. A couple of seconds developed between them. Trouble?

Playfulness. Four laps for Lothar's pride, then Denny snatched it all away. Gethin was nearly half a minute ahead now after twenty laps, but Hulme was shooting across the gap. Eleven laps after leaving third place, he was back up to his teammate, and then he was back in the lead. If he meant to demoralize anybody, he must have succeeded.

But before he completed the lesson, poor Motschenbacher was gone from the classroom. On Friday his crankshaft vibration damper had exploded, bashing awesome dents in the surrounding chassis and cracking Lothar's left shoulder blade. Now, at the Carousel just after half-distance, he went violently off through the woods and slammed into an embankment. He got out without injury, as at Mosport, but he must have had trouble believing it because this time the red M8B was a write-off. Investigation showed the left rear wheel spindle had snapped.

Then Hulme spun.

Never scorn the backmarkers. They might gang up on you. Or maybe it was oil on the track. Whatever; thirteen laps from the end of the race, Denny caught a group of three slower cars going into Turn 5, and from a point somewhere amongst them he very uncharacteristically looped and stalled the engine. He couldn't seem to restart it. The D was in a place the nearby workers considered dangerous, so they ran out and pushed. They were sure the driver dropped the clutch to refire

the engine. Not allowed. He drove away. They got on the phone.

Hulme had lost half a lap, but Gethin had eased right off by signaled order of his team manager. For one thing, no one had ever won four Can-Ams in a row, and Denny had that chance today, but Teddy Mayer was thinking more of points and prize money. On one lap Gethin practically crawled past the pits, waiting for the flash of orange in his mirrors. Eight laps after his spin Hulme was there, and next time he was ahead. He was still in front as the twin Batmobiles thundered under the flag. Bobby Brown was shaping up to be a rewarding third with the McLeagle, but he too fell afoul of slower traffic, so Bob Bondurant's Lola was flagged off third.

Which became second. After a lot of talking, and after the winner's engine failed two chances to demonstrate it could start itself solely with the small on-board battery, the stewards decided to discount all laps Denny had done after his spin. That made him fifteenth, an official retirement.

That's how Peter Gethin reluctantly scored his only Can-Am victory. It was Bruce McLaren Motor Racing's twenty-fourth, and its nineteenth in a row.

Peter Revson returned to Ontario, where he drove the McLaren to fifth. Hulme went to the Italian GP, where he was just a few meters behind Jochen Rindt's Lotus when it slewed into its fatal accident. Hulme finished that race fourth. Gethin was ninth.

Road Atlanta, Georgia, September 13, 1970

We'd lost the wild little Shadow, but we got the wild big Chaparral back. And after the wildest Can-Am ever, we had a winner never included in our wildest dreams.

After a spectacular but short debut at Watkins Glen, Chaparral nearly sent the 2J to storage. Apparently Vic Elford's Trans-Am victory at the same course a few weeks later in the Chaparral-prepared Camaro helped persuade General Electric, manufacturer of the Lexan used in the Ground Effect Vehicle's skirts, to write another check. Not a big enough check to bring Stewart back, though, so Elford was asked if he was interested. He was so interested that he went to Texas first, to get in some of the testing the busy Stewart hadn't managed. As a result, the whole Chaparral team arrived in Georgia feeling like a cohesive unit.

About his new driver, Jim Hall enthused, "He looks at the gauges more than anybody I've ever known. If I ask him the oil pressure, he's able to tell me what it is at every point around the track." About the car, Elford was equally impressed, saying like Stewart before him that it was a whole new order of driving experience.

In the nine weeks since the Glen, the 2J had been modified in several areas. The brakes were larger and the driver was given more pedal leverage on them. Chaparral's engine man, Gary Knutson, had converted the two-stroke "little motor" to fuel injection to prevent the trouble with vapor-locking carburetors experienced before. The drive system to the two stern-mounted extractor fans was redesigned, too, with the belts moved to the outside of the engine compartment because loose stones thrown up by the rear wheels had sometimes jammed the belts. The new pulley package was neatly covered by a molded housing featuring a trio of bullet-shaped bumps, which Chaparral's master fabricator

Road Atlanta: Nor does Revson make it to his first victory flag (ouch). Nor does Brown. Nor Eaton. Who, then? *Barry Tenin*

Road Atlanta: So Gethin backs up his teammate for McLaren's 20th consecutive score, right? Nope. *Pete Lyons*

Donnybrooke: With a new, longer-wheelbase Lola, Revson is the second man in two races to deny the McLarens the pole. Hulme has to resort to racecraft to snatch the lead. *Pete Lyons*

Right: Road Atlanta: Tony Who??? Dean's the name, Mr. Moss. From Yorkshire. And it's a Porsche. P-O-R-. . .*Pete Lyons*

Donnybrooke: Amon's brand new March is fast too, and once they get the fragile worked out of it, who knows what the Can-Am could look like? *Pete Lyons*

Troy Rogers enjoyed calling "the Martian brassiere."

As expected, the Chaparral was fast. It was very fast. During Friday practice, Elford was lapping 3sec quicker than Hulme to the moment the Road Runners packed up to go home early. Some people remembered times the Kiwis had done that to *their* struggling opposition. Denny stayed on, and by the end of a sweltering hot Southern afternoon had scraped off all but half a second of the disadvantage. And that was the way to look at it: *Denny* was doing the job, not his McLaren.

Watching Group 7 cars driven hard was always exciting, but the Denny Hulme versus The Chaparral Show at Road Atlanta in 1970 deserves to live in the annals of motorsport for all time.

The 2J would herald its coming with the familiar, deep, big-bore Can-Am roar, but there was also a faint chain-saw drone audible above it. Then an ugly white box would shoot into view. You knew the thing was squashed down tight on the road, and that its cornering velocity was uniquely high. Like a normal car, it would be weaving a little, maybe even fishtailing slightly, but everything was happening faster. As it whisked over a patch of red Georgia dried clay there would be a half-second lag, then a jet of pink dust out the back. The last thing you were aware of was the nasty buzz of the two-stroke hanging at a steady note amid the varying rumble of the Chevy.

But you didn't quite realize what you had seen until a conventional car came by. Hulme's, especially, when he was trying his damnedest. His brilliant yellow-orange M8D was lean and sleek. It was just about the best-looking race car you'd ever seen. It was doing everything a World Champion driver could make it do. Its nose would dip low under ferocious braking, the car would slither as it heeled into the turn, and then that ax blade prow would lift to the monstrous urge from that huge engine. The whole machine would writhe, teetering on the edge of adhesion.

But you could tell it was slower. It was scrabbling to get around the turn like a dog on ice.

Someone remarked that the new Chaparral bore the same relationship to familiar racing technology as the first steamships had to sail-driven clippers. Yes.

Elford was not trying to psych anyone when he said he hadn't yet reached the limits of the 2J's cornering power. That was so far above his experience that he would be quite a while feeling his way up there. Still, the magnitude of the forces on his body was almost more than he could stand. His seat had to be modified a couple of times as the weekend went on, and the Chaparral engineers were trying to think of practical ways to help him hold his head up. He found it impossible to change gears in a corner because the steering effort was so high he dared not take a hand off the wheel.

His mightiest push on the brake pedal failed to make the wheels lock.

Jim Hall and his guys were enjoying themselves. After so many months of calculating and building and testing, it was all proving out. The car worked. Nothing could take away from that essential fact.

Not that their weekend was trouble-free. Early on Saturday afternoon a front tire went flat, and when the car drove into the pits, a thin wedge had been ground away from a Lexan side skirt. That was estimated to kill about ten percent of the "suck." A patch was bolted on, but then the fan motor started cutting out. It was simply running out of gas.

Vic reported that when the suction faltered the 2J began to "feel more like a racing car," by which he meant that the steering would go light and the car would drift away from the line, but quite progressively and without drama.

Then he went back out and, with all eyes and watches on him, really put his head down. He knew, he said later, that he was into a quick one. He was braking later than ever, and as he got into the turns the car began to break away, hang its tail out. But in that attitude it did not require, as did conventional cars, constant minute corrections. It merely settled into its slide, and when he was finished sliding Vic straightened up in one motion and drove away.

He pitted then, and an oil leak was discovered, so the J-car was finished for the day. It had been clocked at 1:17.42, 117.35mph, and it was still an hour before the end of the session. Hulme's best to this point was only 1:18.73, so as the Texans packed up to leave they were prepared to accept that the McLaren man might take the pole from them. But they didn't really believe it would happen. The effort of everyone connected with the Chaparral team to keep a steady expression, to keep from breaking out into wild grins, was a very heart-warming sight.

Hulme was confronted with something Team McLaren had not faced for nearly three years—a faster car. It was Riverside 1967 when they were last robbed of a pole, by Dan Gurney in a Lola. Denny cracked all the jokes he could think of, but he knew there was only one thing he could really do. So the people in the pits and the handful of spectators had a chance to see a sight that not many had ever seen—the Bear on the limit. In 1967, his World Championship year, he put his F1 Brabham on the front row for the Canadian GP with a heartstopping, grass-clipping lap far above his usual level of lazy ferocity. At Road Atlanta in 1970 he pulled his Can-Am McLaren around him like a space capsule and set off with the same purpose.

That grand racing machine weaved and it wiggled, it twitched, it shivered. It did a whole series of laps in the 18s. But it never went any faster. As the last minutes of the afternoon drained away there were other drivers on the course, trying to go fast but usually making a mess of it, getting in the way, throwing clouds of dust and clots of clay. Denny could get no clear laps, and finally quit. There was no point in beating himself against a wall.

And so to race day, with the big ugly white stranger crouching on pole position. The McLaren men knew it was a race in earnest this time, and they both gathered themselves up at the fall of the flag and beat the Chaparral into Turn One. Revson also went through in his Lola, so Elford was, surprisingly, fourth.

As quickly as that it began to look like the same old story, for Hulme and Gethin moved away in first and second places, though Elford passed Revson for third. But the two-stroke buzz sounded odd, and the Chaparral was visibly not cornering as quickly as it had been in practice.

Hulme didn't know about that, of course, and was really motoring, determined to put as much road as possible between himself and the monster. On lap ten, he came up to lap a bunch of mid-field cars busy with their own race. He was going a lot quicker than they were, and the McLaren squarely hit the back of Gary Wilson's Lola. Hulme, the M8D's nosepiece wrinkled up in front of his face, was able to limp back to the pits, but his crew told him to climb out; he'd bent more than the bodywork.

So now it was Gethin, Elford, and Revson. The Lola T220 was going very well—Revvie turned a 1:18.0 on the same lap that Hulme crashed, and only Gethin would later match it—and was closing back up on the Chaparral. Elford could only reply by diving for the pits. The trouble was in the "little motor's" ignition, and the 2J was stationary a long time while the team tried to fix it.

Now it was Gethin's turn for trouble. Somebody's oil sent him slithering off into the weeds, and he retraced Hulme's path to the pits with his bodywork looking almost as bad. But there was still enough car left to put a new nosepiece on. He rejoined sixth.

Revson had been left up front, with Brown's McLeagle coming along nicely in second, but in this amazing race nothing lasted for long. As the new leader thundered over the blind brow before the pits entrance to complete his thirtieth lap, his right rear tire went flat for the second time in two races. This time, the Lola plunged straight into the dirt bank under the bridge. Revson was shaken, bruised, and cut, but he staggered away in one piece. Not a second too soon.

Twenty seconds later Bobby Brown arrived. He saw the yellow flags too late through the dust cloud as he crested the brow, tried to stay out of trouble, but failed on the littered surface and slammed straight into

Laguna Seca: Oliver (foreground) will have to get by Causey's Lola before he can catch Hulme, who is having his own struggle with Bondurant (Lola). As they all explode out of the old ultra-fast Turn 2 probably nobody's taking time to appreciate the California coastal scenery. *Pete Lyons*

Riverside: There's that pesky Chaparral again, and on pole again. And—alas—it's about to drop out early again. *Pete Lyons*

Riverside: As the Fan Car's "little motor" dies, so does the race. But the controversy will go all the way to Paris. *Pete Lyons*

Above right: Laguna Seca: By winning, Denny has clinched his championship; Revvie's and Ollie's (far left) times will come. *Pete Lyons*

the Lola, reducing an already badly damaged racer to a pile of junk and making the poor old McLeagle look very secondhand.

All this was what it took to put the BRM into the lead. After several dismal weekends Eaton was finally rather happy with the handling, and the engine had been going fairly well, too. But George already had noticed his oil pressure gauge flickering, and near the end of lap forty-eight there was a big bang at his back. Eaton veered toward the pit entry but spun. Fortunately, he avoided adding a third heap to the Revson-Brown wreckage.

So it was Gethin again, but his drive was not going easily. The replacement nose didn't have the same downforce fence package he'd developed in practice, so the car was pushing. It also lacked cockpit cooling ducts, so he was getting very hot. Then the nosepiece started to come loose, and he pitted again to have some more tape applied. As he roared back out, he apparently misinterpreted a flagman's signal. The officials put out the black flag to bring him in for "consultation," but Gethin, who, as a works McLaren driver, must have been pretty used to seeing other drivers get the blue flag, thought this one was blue as well (he said) and pressed on. He pressed on hard enough to equal Revson's earlier best time.

But then Teddy Mayer's chance of banking McLaren's twentieth consecutive Can-Am victory check disappeared as Gethin came by the pits fishing for gears. Probably strained by his two restarts, the input shaft had sheared. Peter parked it at the end of the pit rail and sauntered back up the grade on foot. Nobody recorded whether he stopped for a friendly chat with the officials.

So who does all this put in the lead? Who? Tony Dean? Sure enough! There came the little Porsche 908 popping down the hill, plugging cheerfully on as usual, busy making money for its owner-driver, only this time it was looking like making winner's money. There were only nine laps left. But of course this had been no usual race. Why should it settle down now? Tony's mechanic, Graham Everett, was hanging out the signals and trying to look unconcerned about it all, but not quite succeeding. As it turned out, there were no more trick cards up fate's sleeve, and Dean took the flag with a comfortable margin of 72sec over veteran Dave Causey's ex-Revson Lola T163.

Motschenbacher, who'd hastily resurrected his last-year's McLaren M12—luckily, nobody had answered his classified ads for it—was third from Oscar Koveleski's ex-factory, rebuilt M8B and Canadian Roger McCaig's M8C customer car. Those three were three laps behind the first two, but three ahead of Elford, who'd come back out to finish the day in a subdued manner with the Chaparral's fan motor running on one cylinder because an ignition wire had broken; so had a skirt cable. Gethin had done enough laps to be classified seventh.

Well, we'd been asking for something to break up the elephants' parade . . .

Donnybrooke, Brainerd, Minnesota, September 27, 1970

"At this point in the season one might glance back and notice how rugged it's been," suggested the author in his *Autosport* report.

We've written off Hulme's and Revson's and Oliver's and Motschenbacher's cars (the last twice), heavily damaged Wilson's and Dutton's and Goldleaf's and Dini's. Cordts and [Bobby] Brown had to give up their cars for financial reasons, and we have lost two drivers [Bruce McLaren and Richard Brown]. Porsche did not come at all, Ferrari toyed fitfully with the series, BRM's attention was elsewhere, March couldn't find enough money, and Chaparral had trouble finding enough. The Shadow didn't work. The traditional winners seemed to be disintegrating. Two race circuits [Bridgehampton, Sears Point] were forced to close down completely before their races, only one of those races finding a replacement venue [Road Atlanta] . . .

But up in the birchwoods at Donnybrooke something of a revival happened. There were suddenly *two* BRMs. A March appeared. Lola had replaced their destroyed car with a better one. There were sparkles of hope from Ferrari and Ford, there was a workmanlike home-built car, and both Brown and Cordts had rides. And if you want to look at it that way, there was no Chaparral to upset things . . .

In all, more than forty cars were entered!

That Ford sparkle never panned out. Much to the Agapiou brothers' disappointment, they never saw any of the aluminum engines a top executive said he would try to release to them, so their aging G7A raced on with an iron one they'd bored out themselves to 8.0 liters. But at least they had the multifaceted Vic Elford guesting for them this week. For practice, anyway. When the Ford blew again, Quick Vic found another ride—his sixth in five Can-Ams!

The Ferrari sparkle glittered only to the extent of some refurbishing at the factory for the new owners of Amon's 1968–69 612/712P, which made its 1970 debut at Donnybrooke with Jim Adams in the seat. It only had a 5.0-liter engine now, so it was a 512P, but Adams qualified an impressive sixth.

The homebuilt car, Seattle machinist Stan Burnett's interesting and neatly crafted Mark 4, didn't make the start.

Both BRMs did, and reasonably well up, despite nagging problems. Smiling out of the new second P154 was Pedro Rodriguez. The brilliant Mexican F1 and long-distance driver went way back with Group 7, ever since he scored the very first win by a big-bore car, a Ge-

nie-Chevrolet, in the old USRRC series in 1963. His Can-Am participation had been sporadic and in cars too small to contend overall, but now he had a nice, muscular 465 under his nice, heavy foot.

Another former Can-Ammer, Chris Amon, had been testing the long-awaited March 707 in England and had come to Minnesota early enough for a private midweek session. The new car, therefore, should have been pretty well sorted, but twice its practice was cut short with suspension failure.

Peter Revson's brand new Lola was another T220 but not a duplicate. The destroyed original's short, 88in wheelbase concept had been abandoned, and the replacement had its front wheels ten inches farther forward. Revvie's first impression was of improved stability under braking.

Also starting over was McLaren, in two senses: on a new winning streak and with a new car for Hulme. His needed another tub after Atlanta, and characteristically the Kiwis had one ready—in fact, they had it already running in the guise of a prototype M8E, the planned 1971 customer model. Would-be competitors were still trying to get their 1970 models working. Refitted with the Batmobile's wider suspension and bodywork, the first E became the fourth D, and casual onlookers would never have known there'd been any drama.

Drama was still Denny's lot at Donnybrooke. The only qualifying sessions were both scheduled for Saturday afternoon, and just a few minutes into the first one, Hulme came into the pits unexpectedly to report a bad noise in the 465 engine (later revealed to be the first of a new generation of all-aluminum, sleeveless blocks). A rocker had broken, and both the associated lifter and its cam lobe were damaged. There was no time to make a complete repair. He'd done a timed lap at 1:30.9. Would it be quick enough?

Then Gethin stopped, with his transaxle smoking. Again, changing it would take more time than remained. Great. Both McLarens out of action early, with at least two rivals showing serious speed.

Amon was one of them, but he'd had some drama of his own. During Friday's untimed practice, a lower front suspension arm had pulled loose from the March chassis. Overnight, a patch job was done on both sides, and the car was back at the track for the last qualification session. But Chris had no confidence in it. He drove around for a few slow laps, half certain his suspension was going to split again, and when everything felt warm and ready he bit his lip and stood on the gas. One hot lap, and the broad red 707 came skittering around the last turn: 1:31.2 was what the watch showed.

Riverside: Teamwork at the top; how many other World Champions have you seen helping with a hasty engine change? *Pete Lyons*

Another three miles, another 90sec, here he comes, roaring toward the finish line, and SNAP! The thing started to wriggle. Only yards to go, so Chrissy kept his foot down: 1:30.9. Exactly equal to Hulme.

He shut off immediately, turned into the pit lane the wrong way, parked, climbed out. "That," he said, "was one of the hardest things I've ever done, going that fast expecting to break." Everyone bent down to see where the front end was broken. But it wasn't. The *back* end was broken—casting flaw in an upright.

Hulme was still on the bubble. His pole had survived the Amon assault, just, but there was still Revson to watch. The brand-new Lola hadn't been finished on Friday, so this was its first-ever day of life, but Pete had been making quiet, steady progress with it. Now he was ready. The Donnybrooke pit straight doubled as a drag strip and was 4,000ft long, with a flat-out, banked bend at the end. Hulme's M8D had been clocked at 185 there. The T220 reached 190. The watches showed 1:30.8. There it was! The second time in two races some other team had beaten the McLarens out of pole!

Denny came to the track the next morning with a brand-new engine, and his favorite—a 430. For the morning warm-up, he loaded 55gal of fuel into the tanks and went out with studied casualness to do a lap at 1:29.5. If he was trying to psych Revson, admitted Pete, "He's succeeding!" The Lola did a mere 1:32.

While he was at it, Hulme took an opportunity to tuck in behind Amon for a lap. Chris didn't see him—he relocated his mirrors before the race—and so Denny was able to observe that the March seemed to get through the turns as well as the McLaren and was at least as fast in a straight line, but it didn't brake as well. Informed of that by a troublemaking tattletale, Chris nodded and went off to find a better set of front tires.

And people called the Can-Am boring.

It wasn't the worst race we'd seen, either. Taking the flag at the launch end of the long, long drag strip, Hulme kept the corner of his eye on the Lola alongside, and when Revson made his shifts, Denny wound another 500rpm out of his rev-happy 430 before making his own. The added momentum accumulated with each shift, and when they arrived at a frightful speed at the flat-out first turn, the McLaren was a couple of lengths ahead. It chopped in across the Lola's bow and was away.

That was the story in terms of who was going to win, and all Denny did was drive around for 209 more miles; en route, he casually duplicated his warm-up time for fastest race lap. Behind, Revson was fending off Gethin for second place, but then the Lola veered off into the pits. Its throttles had jammed wide open. About two minutes went down the drain while a new spring was fitted. By the time he got going again, Revvie was two laps behind, in seventeenth place.

Gethin couldn't breathe free, though, for Amon, having taken the first few laps to scrub in his new tires, had moved up behind. In a dice that went on for a good 100 miles, Amon once got ahead in traffic, but then Gethin repassed in the same circumstances at the same place. This was going to be good in the last few laps!

No it wasn't. The March started stuttering. It wasn't getting all its fuel because an internal pipe had broken. Three painful laps from the end, Amon had to park on the grass. As he sat there, Revson drove by to take over third, and Adams' Ferrari, itself just about out of gas, took fourth.

Laguna Seca, California, October 18, 1970

The Chaparral team was back. So was Elford. They qualified on pole. By a big margin.

But they never raced.

As always, coming "home" to California seemed to perk up the Can-Am. The entry was strong, and so were many of the cars. Of the conventional ones, the McLarens were back on top. Once again, the 1970 model wasn't able to match times set in 1969, but neither was any other (conventional) design. For once, the M8Ds appeared to be equal—both Hulme and Gethin turned identical lap times at just a tick over a minute. The numbers, however, hid the fact that Gethin's chassis had a persistent, unsettling twitch in the corners, while Hulme had been unsettled by a failed wheel bearing and also a seized water pump.

The engine he was using was an outwardly familiar 465, but its block was made of a Reynolds Aluminum high-silicon alloy which eliminated the need for iron cylinder liners. Though the material was already in production for Chevrolet's Vega, Reynolds—a key McLaren sponsor—was keen to show it off on the race track. Removing eight liners saved about 15lb, it was said, but the improved heat dissipation through the naked aluminum, while probably beneficial overall, reportedly cost a little power.

At some times and places during the season, that might have been no worry, but the competition was gaining. The next three cars all had 495s, conventional ones, and they were all running strong. Revson qualified the Lola only 0.6sec behind the McLarens, and Amon's March was 0.6 behind that. But an even more familiar threat was splitting them: Jackie Oliver in a new, improved "Titanium Car."

After months of dogged toil, Peter Bryant had managed to put together the sponsorship package, the parts, and the driving talent to produce the Mark II version he'd been intending for 1971. The same design in principle to the one that flipped at St. Jovite, the new model was 2in longer in the wheelbase, 4in wider in the track, and a bit lower and lighter. The suspension geom-

etry was refined, and the chassis stiffened. The 0.032in titanium sheet monocoque now ended behind the cockpit, as in the McLarens, with a titanium tube structure bracing the stressed, big-Chevy aluminum engine. As on the first car, the wedge-shaped body featured prominent integral fences running the entire length to trap high-pressure air for added downforce. These functioned in conjunction with a dam across the rear instead of a wing.

Another new design concept joined the fray at Laguna, albeit for practice only. This was Jack Hoare's "Mac's-It Special," a device featuring four-wheel drive—by four engines. A quartet of 800cc, air-cooled Rotax two-strokes pooled their power through a belt drive system. Small, light, and quite neatly made, the vehicle carried its creator's stated hope of reversing the trend to bigger, heavier cars with ever bigger engines. The driver was a young Japanese named Hiroshi Fushida.

A bold effort, but not successful. The little car made a lot of slow, very smoky laps, between which a lot of plugs were changed. It all sounded rather like a barroom brawl with chain saws, and the car's best lap of 1:24 left the officials doubting the experiment was ready for prime time. But without the "unlimited" old Can-Am, where could such an experiment have been tried?

After that, an experiment with only two engines didn't look quite so odd. Especially as it was working very successfully. Elford had been doing more testing back at Rattlesnake Raceway and had taken another second off the Ground Effect Vehicle's best time there. The big white box was really ready for Laguna Seca, a course that responded to lots of downforce.

Conventional cars depended on speed to make their downforce, but the 2J stuck nearly as tight in slow corners as in fast ones, and Laguna's hairpin offered proof. A stopwatch showed cars like Hulme's getting through in about 7.5sec. The Chaparral was making it between the same reference points in 6.9, an advantage that worked out to ten percent. Elford's advantage over the lap as a whole was a slightly less sensational three percent, or 1.8sec, but at 58.8 he was the only man to beat Bruce McLaren's 1969 time of 59.5, and of course he would start from pole again.

Sorry. After all the niggling troubles through the summer with the innovative auxiliary systems, it was the familiar old "big motor" that blew. Blew in a big way, scattering shrapnel and greasy fluids all over Turn 2 during the morning warm-up. Changing it would take more hours than remained before show time. Abruptly, this Can-Am was just another conventional sports car race.

A pretty good one, though. In the past, the McLarens had usually been in a class by themselves, but this time three other teams had made up most of the gap. Hulme and Gethin set off smartly, and very

gradually pulled out a short lead from Revson, Oliver, and Amon. But it remained a short lead. Denny and Peter would have to watch their mirrors and their step.

First to offer them relief was fifth-place Amon, when the March's brakes started going spongy, and he couldn't hang onto Oliver. A while later, Revson began to have trouble with both his brakes and his dampers, and the Lola fell back behind the Ti22. This was at nearly half-distance, but the gap up to the leaders was still only a few seconds.

It's been toned down a lot from its first configuration, but the "tiny tire" Shadow is still an eye popper on its debut at Mosport.
Pete Lyons

OK, one hand on the shifter, one hand on the clutch, and one. . . Uh, let me take that again: One hand on the . . .*Pete Lyons*

Below right and left: At St. Jovite, the rulebook has forced relocation of the shadow's radiators from atop the wing to inside it. The team is steamed (Follmer is holding his helmet, crew chief Jim Mederer wears the black hat). *Pete Lyons*

Hustling, the two McLaren drivers were running close together. That's why, when Hulme spotted oil going into Turn 2 and shied away from it, Gethin, with his vision full of teammate, ran right over it. In an instant the big orange D was backwards up a bank. The dam-

age was negligible, but the engine had stalled. As was usual with Can-Am cars, the battery was inadequate to restart it.

During the ensuing several laps of confusion, Hulme suddenly found the Titanium Car square in his

mirrors. Oliver was offering battle, and battle they did. For the next forty laps, the second half of the race, they were nose to tail, separating only once in traffic when Oliver lost 3sec in a wild slide up a sloping curb to avoid a balking backmarker. It must have sent a flash of St. Jovite through his mind, but he bore in again, and presently Hulme in his turn lost time in traffic, and the gap was less than a second.

This was such earnest stuff that it began to be frightening. They were going so fast, slicing through so many slow cars. One slip . . . But they were Grand Prix drivers, and both were showing all their stuff now. Denny was smooth, incredibly smooth, under the pressure. Toward the end, Ollie seemed just the tiniest bit ragged by comparison. That's when he set fastest lap.

Then, in the last few minutes, with one of Can-Am's best-ever battles looking like going all the way, the Ti22's 495 began to stumble at peak rpm. The fuel pressure was too high, making the mixture rich. Oliver kept his foot in it anyway, and as he pursued Hulme into their last lap, Parsons and Rodriguez, having their own race for position, were just ahead. The crowd roared as the white Bryant closed to within a second of the orange McLaren, but the gap at the line was 1.2sec, and the crowd settled back in an audible collapse of tension. They'd seen a Can-Am *race*.

Such a one, evidently, that the official with the checker couldn't stand to let it end. Everybody raced around an extra, uncounted lap.

Though the Chaparral had disappeared even before the race, it still weighed on all minds. Asked if he expected such cars to be common in the future, winner Hulme had a sharp retort. "Not if we can help it."

Riverside, California, November 1, 1970

The Bear's win at Laguna, his fifth of the year, clinched his second Can-Am title, but that didn't diminish his desire for another honey pot from Riverside.

But Can-Ams were not necessarily his for the taking these days. There was Oliver and the Ti22, for one thing. And The Chaparral, for another.

There are still people who were in the pit lane that weekend whose eyes will come alive and their voices go loud when they recall the moment when, in the words of veteran mechanic Fred Nething, "the Chaparral went around Denny in Nine *and destroyed his mind!*"

Jim Hall and his team had so refined the 2J by now that, they said, Jackie Stewart would not have recognized it. At Riverside it was generating so much downforce going through the long, dramatically banked Turn 9 just before the pits that Elford said he was "running out of muscle" trying to keep it on line. Its superior speed through that bend, easily seen from the pits, had everyone agog. The stopwatch defined the superiority as about five percent, the 2J consis-

tently covering an arc in 10.8 seconds that occupied other cars for 11.4 or so. But the visual superiority was much greater. The others were twitching and slithering and slipping and sliding. The Chaparral simply tracked around smoothly.

Of course, Elford had no need to push to any ragged edge that might exist. He was quite quick enough keeping it neat.

His lap time advantage over Hulme, as established on Friday before the track surface became oily, was on the order of 2.4 percent: 1:32.49 versus 1:34.69. Again, the Chaparral was the only car to beat the 1969 McLaren best of 1:34.03.

Never mind that, between fast laps, the fan motor kept giving trouble, and so did its replacement, and so did *its* replacement, and obviously the Ground Effect Vehicle's chances of lasting the race were questionable. The main question was the very principle of the thing, and that hung like a dark cloud over the whole weekend.

In public, no one talked about anything else. In private, there were long meetings. It was the last Can-Am of the year, everybody was there, and it all came to a head. One side talked about the letter of the rules, the other side talked about the spirit of the rules. The night before the race, meetings behind closed doors went on until late hours, all parties having been invited to present their views to the SCCA Competition Board.

At the same time, back in the real world, Riverside's pair of steel garage buildings were thick with almost the intensity of prerace atmosphere normally felt in Formula One. It was the final race; the world was watching; it was vital to do one's best. But gradually the gangs of weary workers melted away, until at the Witching Hour there were just three left: those worrying over the twin McLarens; the lone Ti22; and the very lone Chaparral.

Worlds may end in whimpers, but race meetings tend to do it in bangs. Bangs like the ones during the morning warm-up that came from the Chaparral *and* from the Hulme McLaren. In the 2J's case, the two-cylinder little motor had snapped its crank this time. Whew. *That* was changeable in time. In the M8D's case, there was only the one engine to blow, but the McLaren sweathogs—including Hulme, hands-on—were able to get it replaced too. With a fat fifteen minutes to spare.

What a great race it was—for about ten seconds. There came a river of glinting racers pouring around Nine, and a shattering explosion of noise and dust and haze and fumes. From the right side of the front row Hulme sprinted around the outside of the heavy Chaparral and through the first turn to take the point, but as the flood reached the narrows of the Esses, Elford was still holding off Oliver and Revson and Amon and Gethin.

Tiny tires, tiny brakes, and tiny springs. But the overgrown kart had big problems. *Pete Lyons*

Right top: McLaren evolution is efficiently shown at Mosport as Hulme's M8D passes Janke's M1C, a design that dates to 1965. *Pete Lyons*

Bottom: The D undressed. Behind the front wheels are seen the separate fiberglass fairings used in the first two races. These were abandoned because, it was said, they were too vulnerable to damage. *Pete Lyons*

Next page top, middle, and bottom: Chevrolet's big engine enjoyed good breathing and high combustion efficiency by virtue of its "staggered" valves, in which the intake and exhaust stems were at different angles. It was the bristling appearance of this arrangement that earned the nickname "porcupine." A quirk of the design was unequal-length intake ports, which some tuners blame for this engine's characteristic two-hump torque/power curves. But thanks to its single camshaft and aluminum construction, this was a remarkably compact and lightweight package of pure performance and remained the definitive Can-Am engine. Photos made in 1970 at McLaren Engines in Detroit. *Pete Lyons*

Three miles later, at the end of the lap, the 2J had dropped to sixth. The damned two-stroke was four-stroking. When it lost power, right in the middle of Turn 9, the car canted sideways just like any conventional machine, giving the closely following drivers a fright.

Sag. However anyone lined up on "the Question," they wanted to see the Chaparral play out its fate on the track, not the pit lane. But there it was, inevitably, pulling in at the end of the second lap, and as the first excited frenzy died away into methodical troubleshooting, so did the excitement of the race.

Hulme was doing his appointed thing as Can-Am champion, ripping away from Oliver at a good second per lap. The Ti22 was a rocket on the straights, but not doing so well in the corners, and its brakes were tender. Oliver seemed safe enough from anybody else, though. Revson stopped with a water hose popped loose. Gethin and Amon were dropping back. Peter simply wanted to guard his second-place points position in the championship and wasn't having to drive very hard to do it because the March in his mirrors was not handling or running well. For a while, Tony Adamowicz, the 1969 SCCA F5000 champion now driving Motschenbacher's M12, was a strong threat until stuck throttles spoiled an eye-opening run.

But Gethin's plan blew up anyway. Because the engine did. After a mere twenty-one laps, using a very conservative 6200rpm rev limit and going so cautiously that "If I'd gone any slower I'd have overtaken myself," Gethin felt the fourth McLaren engine of the week blow its own brains out. The team said it wasn't using any Reynolds blocks this time, incidentally.

From the back of the circuit towered a black column of smoke. It marked a chain reaction involving several cars, the end result of which was John Cannon, back in the Agapiou G7A, slamming nose-first into the side of Dick Smith's modified McLaren M12. The T-bone impact badly crumpled the honeycomb Ford chassis and destroyed the McLaren in a huge fireball. Both drivers escaped unharmed, but Smith's friends embraced him with real feeling. The week before, his *house* had burned down.

So it was going to be Hulme, Oliver, Amon . . . nope, sorry, Chrissy. Just before the end, the 707 spluttered, and he brought it in for fuel. These cars weren't designed for quick refuelling. Asked later how many gallons had been added, a March man grinned, "Five. Four in the car, and one on Chris." The stop dragged on long enough for Amon to drop behind Rodriguez.

The BRM man was right at the edge of his enormous ability in a very evil-handling car. Eaton's sister P154 had already crashed, for the second weekend in a row, when during practice a cast rear suspension

mounting broke. But on a day like this, Pedro's perseverance was worth third place.

Motschenbacher's fifth in his M8C—his third mount of the season—was worth second place in the series, and bravo to him after such an up-and-down year.

Hulme's first place in the championship was worth $50,000, which brought his season's personal winnings to some $161,000. Even more important, probably, he'd maintained the momentum of his friend Bruce McLaren's team. At the end of a tragic, difficult summer, the Kiwi stamp was still on the Can-Am.

Cars of the Can-Am 1970
McLaren M8D

Having settled on a winning formula with 1968's M8A, and now busy with Indianapolis as well as F1 and F5000, McLaren once again was content with evolutionary changes for Group 7. The first of the 1970 factory cars was in fact built out of the M8B raced in 1969 by Hulme (the other two were sold, McLaren's regular M8B crashed at Riverside to Oscar Koveleski and the M8A-based spare to Lothar Motschenbacher). As the designation M8C had been assigned to a Trojan-manu-

factured customer model derived from the older M6B-based M12, the new factory racer was called the M8D.

A third tube was added to the bracing structure either side of the engine, turning triangles into pyramids. Wheelbase remained at 94in, but the "D-type's" track was widened by 4in. Equivalently broader bodywork bulged over the existing chassis tub. Compared to the B, the leading edge of the nose was a little sharper, and the radiator ducting noticeably wider. Because the new regulations outlawed high, hub-mounted rear wings, but because McLaren had accepted the value of high downforce, a foil of the same size was mounted some 18in lower between two sturdy fins. These fins instantly earned the car the nickname "Batmobile."

Originally, the downforce and drag generated by this wing were carried only by the fins. Bruce McLaren's fatal accident occurred when a locking pin at the lower front of the rear body section came loose—it was found on the track—and the large panel pivoted sharply upward into the airstream, throwing the car into an uncontrollable spin. Before the M8D raced, a pair of stout steel struts were added near the middle of the wing to carry its load directly to a chassis subframe.

It was in the M8D that McLaren first raced the Reynolds-block version of the Chevrolet engine. The casting used the aluminum company's "390" alloy, which contained silicon to create a hard-wearing surface and thus eliminate the need for pressed-in iron cylinder liners, or sleeves. The pistons, however, were iron plated. Otherwise identical to the previous ZL-1 Chevrolet aluminum block, the Reynolds did allow a little more cylinder bore diameter, though it wouldn't be until 1971 that McLaren took advantage of it.

BRM P154

The work of Tony Southgate, former Gurney Eagle designer and subsequently responsible for the Shad-ows that would win the Can-Am in 1974, the 1970 BRM P154 was a basically good concept which failed for lack of support by a firm preoccupied with F1. Southgate spent much time evolving a compact, efficient, stable shape in the wind tunnel. Notable was the broad, flat nose, the pronounced extra width of the rear bodywork, which swelled to 83in, and the careful shaping of the front wheel wells to extract air laterally, because more conventional topside vents had been found to disturb pressure distributions farther aft. No rear wing was fitted.

Contemporary critics believed the rest of the car was done in more of a hurry, although BRM, which thought of itself as the British equivalent to Ferrari, manufactured as much in-house as possible. The company did buy transaxles from Hewland, rather than make its own as in F1, but it ambitiously set up its own engine shop to develop its aluminum Chevy engines. The P154's aluminum monocoque extended behind the cockpit, although it tapered down to nearly a point where it met the lower rear corners of the engine block. Elaborate aluminum castings featured prominently as suspension pickups. Geometry appeared reasonably conventional, and the 93in wheelbase wasn't unusual, but the handling was often visibly terrifying, and there were some serious structural failures. Nor were the engines reliable. The team in the field was unable to carry out a meaningful development program. Despite its enthusiastic beginning, by the end of the season the factory gave every indication of indifference.

Not until a significantly revised version called the P167 came along in 1971 did the BRM Group 7 car come good, good enough to win two Interserie races in Europe. Unfortunately, it didn't come to the Can-Am until the end of the season.

Shadow Mk 1:

"We're playing it strong. We'll either win big, or lose big." That's the attitude Don Nichols presented as he launched his startling Advanced Vehicle Systems Shadow Can-Am project.

It had a conventional big Chevy in the back. That's where conventionality ended.

The designer was Trevor Harris, a bold free thinker who has produced some very successful race cars since. For the Shadow, which originally was scheduled to race in 1969, the fundamental design goal was reduced aerodynamic drag achieved through minimal frontal area. This became possible—or so it seemed—when Firestone agreed to develop special tires some 30–35 percent smaller in diameter than normal ones of the day and to do so without giving up sidewall height or tread width. At the front, the tires stood 17in tall, compared to 24 for conventional rubber, and were mounted on two-piece spun rims 10in

Top left: BRM P154 in action at Edmonton. *Pete Lyons*

Top left: The 2J's "big motor" used the crossover induction made for the 2H. Its "little motor," perched atop the transmission, drove twin extractor fans through a shrouded belt system. Low pressure thus created was "sealed" in by the articulated Lexan skirts hanging from cables linked to the suspension. *Pete Lyons*

Top right: Flexible but tough, the skirts were normally set at a road gap of 1/2in. Less increased downforce, but raised wear rate. *Pete Lyons*

Right: Behind the pair of simple flaps under the front (left) was the more important transverse hinged skirt (right) behind the front wheels. Discernible here is the plenum spring arrangement which pressed this skirt to the road when the car was moving. *Pete Lyons*

"It looks like the box it came in," was a common first impression of the Chaparral 2J. To which sentiment a famous Denny Hulme dictum might well apply: "Yeah, but if she wins the race on Sunday, she'll look effin' *beyoouuutiful!*" *Pete Lyons*

in diameter by 11 wide. The outside diameter at the rear was 19in, versus 26 while the rims measured 12x17. The Shadow's original bodyshell came out 14in lower at the front fenders than a contemporary McLaren and 10.5 lower at the rear. With a (planned) narrow, single-file engine induction system and no spoilers (yet) considered necessary, the resulting frontal area was calculated to be 13sq-ft, compared to 19 for the 1969 McLaren M8B. Projected horsepower of 700 was supposed to send the low, flat, "two-dimensional car," as Nichols called it, down the back straight at Riverside at 250mph. But Firestone promised its "tiny tires" were good for 300.

Such a radical departure in tires had a cascade effect on every other design element. To fit the front brakes within the 10in wheels, Harris machined standard vented discs down to an 8in diameter. Reduced swept area called for more cooling, so he fitted magnesium centrifugal fans to the outsides of the rims—in the grand tradition of hot rodding, he simply took these from Chevrolet's air-cooled Corvair engine. He added a third Corvair fan to help the rear brakes, which remained of nearly standard diameter (they actually came from Ford's Mustang) but were mounted inboard, next to the hot transaxle. The transaxle was a Hewland, but Harris

chose the Indianapolis version because of its extended shaft for the external starter used at the Speedway. He used the shaft to drive his rear brake cooling fan.

Although some outsiders thought there might be some kind of torque converter or automatic gearchange involved and there was at one stage a microswitch installed on the gear shift lever, the transmission remained conventional except for a welded-on bulge to fit larger gears required by the smaller tires. However, the case was trimmed a little at the bottom, to let it ride lower in the chassis and thereby match the relatively low engine position permitted by an ultratight dry sump and small flywheel.

The clutch was operated by hand lever. To preserve the low body height at the front, the driver's feet were splayed out nearly horizontally, and that left room for only two pedals.

The cramped quarters at the front led Harris to employ very small coil springs. They looked like large engine valve springs, though they actually came from the tool and die industry, and there were four at each side. Fine-tuning of spring rate was to be achieved by replacing one or more of these coils with ones of slightly different stiffness. At first there were more conventionally-sized coils in the rear, mounted horizontally and operated by crank-extensions of the suspension arms; later these were replaced by the "valve" springs used at the front.

Suspension damping at both ends of the car was not by means of hydraulic shock absorbers but lever-actuated friction discs of the sort not seen on automobiles for decades. "Friction material technology has come a long way since then," was Harris' smiling response to incredulous questioners.

His thinking also ran free when he laid out the Shadow's suspension geometry. Having calculated his ultra-low car would only roll half a degree per g-unit in corners, he drew a perfect parallelogram for each front suspension, with two arms of identical, 10in lengths

both laid parallel. The rear suspension arms were also parallel, although a bit of camber-change was induced here by having the lower ones a little longer than the top ones, 14.5in to 12.5. At both ends fore-aft loads were taken by the arms alone; there were no trailing links. Nor was there any anti-dive or anti-squat geometry, despite the stubby, 86in wheelbase. There was, however, an anti-roll bar at each end.

The Shadow's aluminum monocoque tub also bore some relationship to contemporary practice, although the aluminum sheet was anodized black (for hardness, durability, and appearance, it was said), the structure's torsional stiffness of 6,000lb-ft/deg was nearly twice that considered adequate at the time, and the fuel tanks were incorporated as far back as possible, either side of the engine bay. The car's weight distribution was an extreme 25/75.

Wait, there's more. There were originally going to be air brakes on the car: one rising up from across the tail, and two more from the front fenders. Calculations indicated that these alone would give an eyeball-popping braking force of over 4g at 250 mph.

Besides that, Harris intended a further air brake effect from swiveling vanes mounted in the radiator ducts. There were to be two radiators, you see, carried in the very long tail of the body and fed by scoops projecting from either side behind the rear wheels. The duct vanes would adjust as necessary to cool the engine, add air braking, and/or direct air into the disturbed flow behind the car to reduce straightaway drag.

Perhaps it was a real relief to the team members tasked with making it all trackworthy when the 1970 ban on "moving aerodynamic devices" came along.

In fact, although Americans love this sort of wild-and-free race-think, and while many fans thought the surprising Shadow was exactly what the Can-Am was all about, and the ambitious adventure got a lot of press, this was a lot of innovation to bite off in one project. The team ran into problems of practicality.

The wide rear scoops kept getting knocked off. The engine would not run cool without bulky additional radiators. The car just could not be made aerodynamically stable without rear-end downforce. The air brakes, of course, became illegal. So did a wing-top radiator package that looked odd but was, finally, effective. The single-file induction system never made it off the dyno. Thankfully, the "tiny tires" did seem to work as theorized, but they were very sensitive to real-world track surface imperfections, and the stiffly suspended car was extremely hard work to drive—but if the springs were softened, tire performance suffered because of chassis lean. The Shadow never even approached competitive lap times, no matter what major changes of configuration were tried.

Element by element, Harris saw his original concept compromised. Month by month, Nichols saw his

original schedule slip—and his dollars drain away. Toward the end, there were legal problems leading to an injunction on tangible assets. According to an exposé published in *Road & Track* after it was all over, the first car made it to its first race in Canada only through bold evasive tactics in California. The driver made it only after Nichols drove overnight from Mosport to Akron to get the tire company to demand Follmer's release from a team owner in Indianapolis.

Racing rewards audacity while punishing excesses of it. What a shame the original Can-Am Shadow didn't strike the right balance. Happily, four seasons later the ultimate one did.

Chaparral 2J

After his bold leap forward with the 2J "White Whale" had earned him nothing but painfully barked shins, Jim Hall might have been expected to follow up with something more conventional. After all, the FIA's mid-1969 ban on suspension-mounted wings and other "moving aerodynamic devices" had been accepted by CASC and SCCA for the 1970 Can-Am. Surely this closed the door on what historically had been Chaparral's primary realm of innovation.

If a pair of SCCA officials harbored any such notion as they traveled to Texas in February, 1970, what

Top right and bottom: Lola T220: A fresh conception owing little to the previous T70-T160 design family (which continued for 1970 in a commercial model designated T165), Lola's T220 did exhibit the evident Lola preference for relatively rounded shapes and did seem fast in a straight line. Contrary to at least one published description the chassis was again a full-length design, and there was nothing especially experimental in the suspension layout. However, wheelbase was a relatively short 88in on the first car (shown in chassis form at Mosport). After that was destroyed at Road Atlanta, its replacement appeared with a wheelbase of 98in, the added length inserted at the front of the chassis (shown in action at Laguna Seca). The first benefit Revson reported was improved braking stability. Lola put this design in production for 1971 as the T222. *Pete Lyons*

March 707 at Laguna with Amon at the wheel. *Pete Lyons*

Bottom: Herd designed the 707's engine, 5-speed Hewland LG 600 transaxle and rear suspension as a self-contained unit, which could be unbolted from the tub and rolled away on its own rear wheels for rapid replacement. *Pete Lyons*

they found in the unprepossessing steel-sided race shops on the rolling scrub lands six miles south of Midland must have dropped their jaws to their shoes. Taking shape there was a novel new Road Runner—one so novel that, given the new wing ban, Hall felt an official ruling was in order.

Chaparral had gone from one edge of the envelope to the other: the 2J was a wide, blocky, decidedly non-streamlined full roadster in which everything was dedicated to the production of aerodynamic downforce. Huge levels of it.

But how? The FIA ban supposedly eliminated suspension-mounted and/or articulated aerodynamics. The English-language version of the French body's final rule was, "Any specific part of the car which has an aerodynamic influence on the stability of the vehicle must be mounted on the entirely

sprung part of the car and shall be firmly fixed whilst the car is in motion."

However, some wording in SCCA's own Can-Am regulations was subtly different. To more clearly embrace such things as Porsche cooling fans and also to integrate the new restriction into existing rules covering brake cooling ducts and exhaust systems, the SCCA language focused on "coachwork." Specifically exempted as "coachwork" were any elements either hidden from external view or located externally but below the wheel center lines.

The club's representatives looked the 2J over and didn't see anything that looked like unfixed coachwork to them. "Go ahead," they told Hall.

Sighs of relief sounded in Michigan as well as Midland. In fact, what was now called a Chaparral had been born as an experiment of Chevrolet's Research and Development department. It was originally constructed in Detroit, and Chaparral Cars' role was "simply" to turn a heavy, awkward test vehicle into something raceworthy.

Jim Hall has long acknowledged the 2J's mixed parentage. He and his fellow engineers at Chevrolet certainly knew of the skirted-fan "ground effects" principle used for seaborne hover-craft and also an experimental French train. Perhaps some of them had heard of an American dragster built with such a blower system working in reverse, to generate increased tire traction. Jim does remember a sketch of a car with a suction-fan coming to him through the mail from an apparently young admirer. He may have passed this on, he says, but did not follow up the idea himself.

It was a Chevy R&D team under Don Gates that carried out functional tests at its own proving ground,

first with chain saw motors and a crude skirting system bolted to the department's Suspension Test Vehicle. That worked well enough to encourage the construction of a dedicated developmental platform.

Hall didn't come into the picture until, facing the 1970 season without a suitable car, he agreed to enthusiastic entreaties by his long-time friends at R&D that he adopt their project as his own.

The Chaparral 2J "Ground Effect Vehicle," or "Vacuum Traction Vehicle" as it was sometimes called, bore no apparent relationship to the 2H. The 2J was a box-shaped, open-cockpit car with its rear wheels enclosed and its radiator in the front. There was a distinctive chisel-shaped prow that appeared to force nearly as much air sideways as over the top. The front wheel wells were also vented laterally. The only evident concession to what had become conventional downforce aerodynamics was the radiator air exhausting over the cockpit, and a dam across the square tail.

Unlike the 2H's, the 2J's fiberglass front bodywork was not stressed as part of the chassis. Though the central part of the visible structure was made of aluminum, it did bear some resemblance to the 2H, as it was also part of the monocoque chassis and was of full depth enclosing hatch-type doors meeting the letter of the rules. The rear bodywork was quickly detachable, as was common, but it incorporated aluminum honeycomb slabs to resist exterior air pressure.

Overall length was 145in, width 76, and wheelbase was just under 96. Suspension, fully independent at the rear as well as the front, was essentially conventional for the period. The power package too was familiar: a big-block aluminum Chevy, now sized at 495ci

Bryant Ti22 Mk II: After months of dogged toil following Oliver's St. Jovite crash, Peter Bryant had finally pulled together the sponsorship package, the driving talent, and the pieces to produce the new, improved "Titanium Car" he'd been intending for 1971. The same design in principle, the new model was 2in longer in the wheelbase (to 96), 4in wider in the track (65 front, 63 rear), and 4in wider overall (to 78). It was also a bit lower and lighter, although the builder was coy about its true weight. He'd refined the suspension geometry to suit the latest wide tires, and stiffened the chassis. This time, the 0.032 titanium sheet monocoque ended behind the cockpit, as in the McLarens and the March, with a titanium tube structure bracing the stressed big Chevy aluminum engine. More Ti was used in the roll hoop, steering and suspension parts, and all three foot pedals.

As on the first car, the wedge-nosed body had prominent fences running the entire length. These functioned in conjunction with a dam across the rear, instead of a wing, to trap high pressure air atop the car for added downforce. *Pete Lyons*

No boredom in the Mac's-it Special cockpit—there are four tachometers and four cylinder-head temperature gauges to watch. *Pete Lyons*

and producing more than 700hp, driving through a lock-up-type torque converter to the Chevy-made, manually-controlled three-speed transaxle.

But there was a second engine. It was an air-cooled, 2-stroke twin of 274cc made by Rockwell-JLO (pronounced "HEE-lo") for snowmobiles. Running at constant full throttle, it produced from 55 to 70hp. Mounted above the transaxle, it had a system of belts driving a pair of 17in ducted fans bolted to the car's flat, vertical stern. Commercially-available units designed for cooling the Army's M1 battle tank, their purpose on the Chaparral was to extract air from inside the engine compartment. Because the compartment was all but completely sealed, the result was to "suck" the whole car down on its springs, thus creating a traction-enhancing downforce for the tires. In simple words, the 2J was a giant mechanical suction cup.

It was those air-sealing arrangements that Hall had asked the SCCA to approve. The seals took the form of skirts made of sponsor General Electric's tough new Lexan plastic. Along both sides and across the rear, the skirts were more or less simple vertical curtains which hung on an arrangement of bell-cranks and cables linked to the suspension. This system maintained the all-important minimal air gap of about half an inch with

the road surface no matter how the car itself bounced, rolled or pitched.

The fourth skirt, necessary to complete the enclosure of the "vacuum box," ran transversely just behind the front wheels. Because of the driver's legs it had to take a more compact form, and this was accomplished by letting it trail at about 45 degrees on a hinge. To press it against the road there was a clever air spring, a plenum behind the upper part of the trailing skirt which was energized by ram air through orifices in the upper part of the lateral skirt. But underbody flow was discouraged both by the shape of the lower lip of the radiator inlet and flexible flaps attached transversely under the nose.

Weren't all these fans and skirts and flaps "moving aerodynamic devices?" Rival teams immediately protested that they were, but Jim Hall didn't see it that way. "Aerodynamics implies relative motion of the atmosphere to the car. This device works just as good sitting on the grid as it does anywhere," he asserted in a 1971 interview with *Autosport*. "It's not an aerodynamic device, it's a static pressure device." In any case, as he maintains today, the Can-Am was organized under SCCA rules, and in the SCCA's view the system elements were either not externally visible (the fans inside their vaned ducts), or visible only below the wheel center lines.

What was not in question was the system's effectiveness. And the effect was visible. When the 2J was ready to go the white-overalled Chaparral crewmen would fire up the raucous, smoky JLO, air would start blasting from the fan enclosures, and after a moment the big white box would settle about an inch closer to the ground.

On the track, the car's speed advantage through any corner was plain to both the eye and the stopwatch, but was most marked in slower turns. According to official claims, the ground effect Chaparral could corner at upwards of 1.75 g, which was about half again what contemporary racing tires could manage by themselves without aerodynamic download. Their airfoils might have let conventional cars chase the Chaparral through very high-speed turns, but the Can-Am offered few such turns. In any case, the relatively low, fixed-angle, chassis-mounted airfoils now permitted had to be set at the best compromise angle for all corners plus the straights. Spring selection was a compromise, too, because the downforce varied so greatly with speed.

The 2J was subject to no such compromises. It enjoyed the same downforce, and the same suspension behavior, everywhere around the race track.

How much downforce did the 2J generate? No figure was officially released, but one can be calculated. When running properly in racing trim, the fan/skirt system could maintain a negative pressure differential of 0.2lb/in-sq, or 5.25in of water according the gauge in the cockpit. That's not a high number, but given the large plan area enclosed by the skirts, approximately 100 inches by 75, total downforce must typically have been about 1500lb.

Much more downforce would have been possible, Hall says today. "The ground effect varied substantially with the air gap under the skirts. You could make the downforce almost anything you wanted by closing the gap right down to nothing. But half an inch was about all we could manage to hold it at. If we tried to run it at, say, a quarter of an inch, we'd get double the downforce, but the skirts would keep wearing away on the road."

Theoretically, the 2J could have been configured to clamp itself upside down to a ceiling. Unfortunately, plans to prove it in a TV commercial were never realized.

And at something over 1800lb empty, the 2J was no lightweight. It hadn't been intended in the first place as a race car, and in any case its extra systems and heavy-duty supporting structures meant it was substantially heavier than preceding Can-Am Chaparrals, and all of its rivals.

But it turned out to be measurably the fastest Can-Am car ever created to its day—and arguably the most controversial race car ever to this day.

March 707

Robin Herd had been part of the design team on McLaren's first successful Can-Am car, the M6A of 1967. Three years later, a certain similar simplicity was evident in his own new company's Group 7 model. First of all, there was nothing really unusual or experimental about the design. Secondly, Herd remembered the long summer of hard work that went into developing even as simple a car as the M6A into a race winner and had no illusions about beating McLaren at its own well-practiced game right away. He regarded 1970 as a warmup for a major effort the next year.

The first thing everyone noticed about the 707 were the separate, adjustable canards which recalled the company's contemporary 701 F1 "hammerhead" model. Everyone next remarked about how wide the car looked. The low-slung March did appear to take up a lot of track, and an overall width figure of 93in was published. However, by the author's measurements the span across the nose fins was no wider than 83.5in while the rear wheel arches swelled only to 83.75. That year's McLaren M8D taped out at 79.5 at the latter point. The tub was indeed wider than the McLaren's but carried a little less fuel, 70gal (U.S.). No doubt the thirst of the big 502ci (4.47x4.00), 730hp, Chaparral-built Chevy helped account for the sad fact that, in one of its three 1970 races, the 707 ran out of gas (a broken pickup pipe stopped it another time).

Dry of fuel, according to some literature, the 707 supposedly weighed a competitive 1460lb. However, for an end-of-season story in *Motor Trend*, Chris

Hoare (right) checks the head temperature of one of the four 800cc Rotax engines that powered the Mac's-it Special.
Pete Lyons

The Mac's-it Special was compact, light, and unfortunately, non-competitive. *Pete Lyons*

Amon told Karl Ludvigsen that the car had never been on reliable scales, and that he personally reckoned the true figure was higher than 1600, maybe as high as 1800.

Wheelbase was 96in nominally, 96.75 as recently measured (wheelbase dimensions can vary on cars with highly adjustable suspensions). Suspension was familiar practice, and brakes were outboard all around. The 707's aluminum semi-monocoque chassis was similar to that of the McLaren M8-series, as it

ended behind the cockpit and used the engine as a structural member with the assistance of tubular steel braces. However, instead of steel front and rear tub bulkheads, Herd speced magnesium castings.

Former McLaren and Ferrari factory driver Amon proved the 707 was nearly fast enough right from the start, but it arrived late in its first season and ran out of races before it ran out of bugs. There was no second season for March, though the 1970 car itself continued in private hands. An improved

717 model with side radiators ran in Europe the next year, but the factory never brought it to America.

Hoare Mac's-it Special

After a couple seasons of struggling, with little success, to keep an aging McLaren M6B (originally Jo Bonnier's) running with a big iron Ford engine under a variety of drivers, veteran crew chief Jack Hoare felt sure there must be a better way. "I think we're about to see the end of the trend to bigger and bigger V-8s in the Can-Am," he said bravely when unveiling his alternative vehicle under the banner of a company called Innovation Racing. "By going the other direction—and being first out of the gate with this new kind of car—we expect to gain a good bit of ground on the competition."

Hoare certainly went another direction with his Special. It had two motors in the front. And two more in the rear. Each was a twin-cylinder, air-cooled, 800-cc Rotax two-cycle snowmobile engine making a stated 110hp. Their power was pooled through centrifugal clutches, automatic variable-ratio belt pulleys, and a longitudinal shaft to drive all four wheels through a pair of cut-down Volkswagen differential cases. There was no clutch pedal to operate and no shifting to do; full throttle immediately brought the engines up to raucous speed, and the car accelerated until it caught up. The theoretical beauty of the power-pooling system was that the engines didn't need to be synchronized and matched, and if one cut out, there was no effect except a drop in overall thrust.

Theoretically. After a memorable plug-cut drama, it was realized that some form of freewheel device should have been incorporated between front and rear, and for the Special's debut the longitudinal connection was deleted so the two ends could run independently.

This nicely made and rather cute little "push-me-pull-you" was quite compact, but if the 1200lb. and 440hp figures mentioned at Laguna Seca were accurate, the power-to-weight ratio did not come to that of front-line Can-Am cars. More importantly, the full quartet of two-strokes never ran well, and the vehicle showed no signs of gaining any ground on the competition. It never actually raced in a Can-Am.

The Chaparral "sweeper" question went all the way to the FIA in Paris, where SCCA's favorable view was argued by ACCUS, but in the end the vote went against Jim Hall's (and Chevrolet's) 2J. This really did mark the end of an era. As put so finely by L.J.K. Setright in his book, *The Designers*, published in 1976, "Thereupon Hall, recognizing that the regulation of motor racing was now governed by alien considerations to impose a mindless egalitarianism upon a sport that had once been a cradle of innovation and a harbour of genius, announced that he would take no further part in it."

In fact, Jim Hall would go on to have a long and successful subsequent career in other forms of racing, but it is true the original Can-Am held nothing more for him.

Whether it still held anything for its fans remained to be seen. Would the "conventional" cars now called for by the rules be exciting—or at least adequately interesting? Would their drivers be able to make up, in wheel-to-wheel action, for the inevitable decline in technical spectacle? Would the new-think, buttoned-down, less-*libre* Group 7 work?

Early indications were mixed. Horsepower was still totally unlimited, of course, and competitive engines were going to be pumping out well over 700 this year, a figure half again as high as in F1. Nor was there any restriction as yet on weights, widths, materials, tires, decibels; plenty of paths for innovative thought still existed, and the cars certainly would be loud, hairy, and fast.

As for contenders, McLaren was coming back with its accustomed pair of "elephants," and the increasingly impressive American driver "Champagne Peter" Revson was teamed with Denny "the Bear" Hulme. Lola was taking the Can-Am more seriously than ever and would have an all-new car pedaled by World Champion Jackie "The Mod Scot" Stewart. The other Jackie, Oliver, who had given the McLarens some good, stiff runs in Peter Bryant's Ti22, would be back in a new Bryant-designed car built by Don Nichols' Shadow team.

Who else? March? No, despite the promise of speed shown by Chris Amon with the 707, the company abandoned its ambitious two-year Can-Am program announced in 1970. The follow-on March 717 would appear only in Europe's Interserie.

BRM? This factory was now showing even less interest than it had the previous year. One of the admittedly poor P154s had been improved into a P167, but again, it wouldn't be coming to America, at least not in time to be a championship contender.

Ferrari? Maybe. There were rumors, but then there always were. Same applied to Lotus. And Toyota and Nissan.

Porsche? Yes. After a year away from Can-Am to concentrate on the Manufacturer's Championship, Porsche would field a new, improved Spyder and the ever-enthusiastic Seppi Siffert. This new 917/10 car still wouldn't have the power to beat the McLarens, but it did represent another step in a serious factory plan to do so. Whispers of turbochargers were still being heard.

Whispers were also linking Roger Penske and Mark Donohue to the Porsche plan. That turned out to be true, but at the time Roger was denying it, and anyway, there had been competing rumors connecting John Wyer's great JW Automotive team to the same Can-Am project. Not to mention the rumors that Penske had been offered cars by, count them, McLaren, Lola, Chaparral, and Ferrari, too, but had turned them all down.

Hoping to attract all of the above and to encourage the rank and file of privateers who did in fact make up the bulk of the show—and who had been complaining—Can-Am organizers made some alterations for 1971.

Sentiment had been voiced the year before in favor of restricting starting grids to the twenty fastest cars, on the theory that this would force the slowest entrants either to raise their game or to clear out. This idea was folded into the new prize system to the extent that purse moneys—increased to a uniform $55,000 per event, now—would be paid out only to the top twenty finishers, rather than down to the end of the field, as before. Grids were still open to all comers, provided, as always, they were fast enough not to be a major hazard.

Also, the previous year-end points payout was reduced in favor of a new bonus qualifying fund of $20,000 distributed to the top ten qualifiers at each race. Earning pole was worth $2,600. To capitalize on this new emphasis on grid positions, the organizers hoped to raise crowd and media interest by adopting single-car qualifying.

The cut in the overall championship prize fund amounted to 75 percent, from the previous year's $200,000 to $50,000. It would be paid out only to the top three points scorers, instead of ten, the champion's take being $25,000, a cut of 50 percent.

At the other end of the equation, entry fees doubled, to $100.

The intent of all these changes was to discourage points-hunting in favor of more intense racing. It would also help the marginally financed teams—there were a lot of them—by distributing more of their winnings during the year, rather than making them wait until the season-ending banquet.

From the start, only ten races were scheduled this time. Although some dates were rearranged, all of the venues were familiar, and all the organizers had been battle-tested.

Another sign of a series striving for maturity was the Can-Am's incorporation into the international calendar as an officially recognized FIA championship for the first time. This meant no Can-Am dates would clash with Grands Prix, nor with SCCA Trans-Am or F5000 events. Sports car dates such as Le Mans were not covered by the agreement, however, and neither were USAC, nor the aggressive new IMSA organization, subject to it.

Working against these encouragements were a malaise in the international economy and advancing negativism about the Can-Am. The series was into its sixth season. Even its ardent apologists were growing skeptical about perennial projections that this, finally, would be The Year.

What could not be foreseen was that this would be a tragic year for some special Can-Am friends. Early in July, Stan Burnett was killed while testing his self-built Mark 4 at Seattle. Days later, Pedro Rodriguez died in the flaming wreckage of a Ferrari 512 coupe at the Norisring in Germany. Just before the Riverside Can-Am, Jo Siffert lost his life in an F1 BRM at Brands Hatch in England.

Edmonton: Stewart and his Lola, seen here at Edmonton, were McLaren's sole opposition in this sixth Can-Am season. *Autosport*

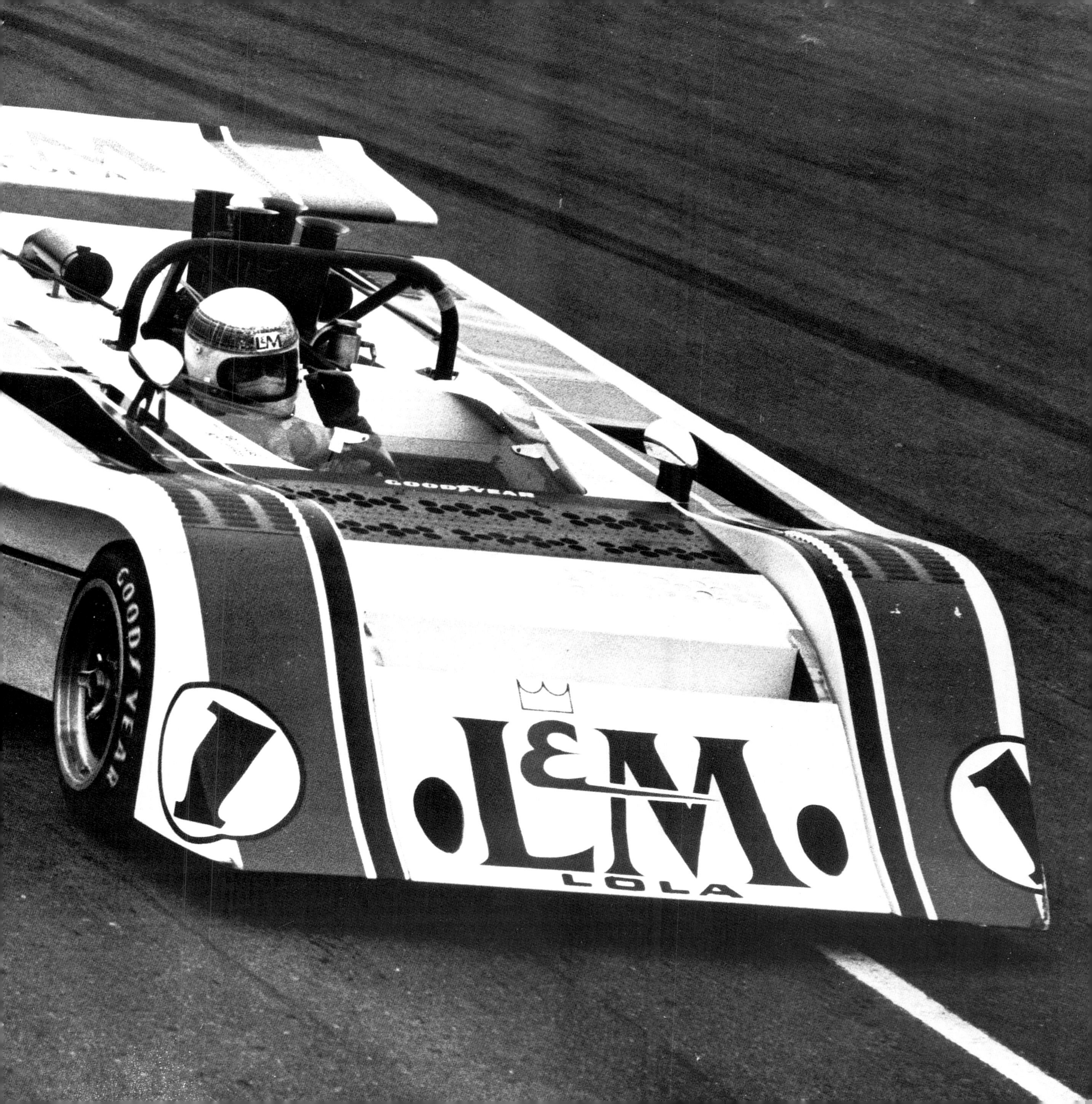
GOODYEAR
L&M
LOLA
1

Mosport: Denny tells Revvie how he wants the Show to go; could Tyler and Lee be trying to stifle laughter? *Pete Lyons*

Mosport Park, Ontario, June 13, 1971

Give thanks for Jackie Stewart; that was the enduring sentiment from the opening round. Without his own talent for drawing the eye, backed up by an intriguingly different and competitive new Lola, Mosport would have presented nothing but another Parade of the Orange Elephants.

The entry list offered a good supporting cast, surprisingly good, considering the desultory economy. But only two other men beside Stewart, reigning champion Denny Hulme and new McLaren teammate Peter Revson, honestly enjoyed the combination of all the factors—car, team, backing, and prerace testing—that made them unquestioned contenders.

Stewart actually had done the least testing. It was Aussie veteran Frank Gardner who'd put the early miles on the blunt-nosed new Lola, with the busy Scot only stepping aboard at the last minute for a single, rain-soaked shakedown at Silverstone. At Mosport on Thursday, Stewart had a second private test in slightly better weather and discovered that, though the times were good, the handling wasn't. The front end was understeering badly, and the rear wheels were wayward on the bumps.

Once the Batmobiles got going, too, it turned out they weren't quite as quick as the Blunt Box. The two M8Fs looked steadier and were faster through the corners, as proven by segment timing, but the T260 was reaching higher straightaway speeds. It also seemed to be charging out of the turns a little more smoothly, likely because of different engine characteristics.

Lola was using 495 Chevys tuned by former McLaren engine man George Foltz, whose preference was for a wide, flat, easy-to-drive torque curve which he said peaked at, in this instance, 618lb-ft. Gary Knutson, back at McLaren now that Chaparral was out, had gone for a stronger but sharper torque curve on his engines of the same displacement. The high number was said to be 700lb-ft , but that was at the peak of a shorter, steeper slope. Both Hulme and Revson said these engines came on more brutally than the previous year's 465s, so they couldn't hold a nice, smooth slide. Once again, Hulme was heard to wax wistful on the subject of the sweet old 430.

All this complaining was despite Knutson having brought to McLaren the staggered-length intakes he (and Chevrolet) had pioneered for other teams, the function of which was to fill in a "hole" in the

middle of the big Chevy's torque curve. Though McLaren was moving toward regular use of the all-aluminum Reynolds motors, at Mosport both cars were still using iron-sleeved blocks.

Partly because the new, one-at-a-time qualifying procedure wasted a lot of vital setup time, and partly because Saturday's surface was spoiled first by light rain and then by oil, the grid lineup was not entirely representative. But Stewart's pole did represent the first time in what seemed like ages that the McLaren team had been beaten on ostensibly level terms. In addition to his $2,600—and it was his birthday—Jackie collected an award named for Bruce McLaren.

At 1:17.3, though, the Lola failed by 0.9 to match 1970's best qualifying time, set by Dan Gurney for McLaren. And on race morning this year, Hulme restored his confidence with a pair of 1:17.2s; Stewart, at the same moment, was in the pits with maladjusted throttle linkage after an overnight engine swap.

In the absence of the new Shadow, missing because Jack Oliver was running Le Mans that weekend, the prominent fourth-best grid place went to the always impressive John Cordts, who was still driving a year-old, customer-model McLaren M8C.

Side by side on the third row at identical times were two all but identical cars running in the same team. Lothar Motschenbacher, the faithful McLaren campaigner who finished second in the 1970 championship, took over and rebuilt the M8D which Hulme crashed at Road Atlanta. He also bought a new 1971 M8E production model but converted it to wider D-type suspension and bodywork—as McLaren itself had done in replacing Hulme's shunted D the previous season. Driving this "E/D" was Bob Bondurant. Both cars looked just like M8Ds, but the bodywork, painted Lothar's trademark brilliant red, had actually been re-manufactured in Los Angeles, of lighter materials.

Seventh best was Bobby Brown, still driving the ex-Gurney McLeagle which he'd been unable to sell over the winter. Alongside was Jim Adams, back in the ex-Amon Ferrari 612P which, because of its 5.0-liter engine, was now properly called a 512P. It wasn't precisely the same car, however. Over the winter, crew chief Doane Spencer had attacked a growing problem with cracked welds in the steel space frame by sawing off the whole rear half of the structure and replacing it with many fewer, stouter tubes running in many fewer directions.

Farther down the grid after an engine blowup was a second genuine ex-works M8D, the one Hulme finished the season with. Its new owner was former Porsche-pedaler Tony Dean, but Chuck Parsons was standing in until the surprise 1970 Road Atlanta winner recovered from a broken neck suffered in a F5000 accident in England. This M8D was painted blue.

Another car of note was the ex-Siffert Porsche 917PA of 1969, which sat unused for a year until Vasek Polak bought it. Ambitiously, his team shortened and stiffened the frame and reprofiled the front bodywork. Then they installed both "the only 5.0 liter in private hands" and Milt Minter. Unhappily, engine trouble forced both Chuck and Milt out before the start.

The rolling grid got three pace laps to allow a slow starter to catch up, which gave Stewart a better feel for his car since its engine change and throttle problem. The throttle still wasn't right, sticking half-open when he lifted off, and on one of the pace laps he nearly spun. He decided to take it easy at the start.

Hulme, though, made just the right sort of start for a reigning Can-Am champion and proceeded to open about a 5sec advantage on Stewart in as many laps. But by the time Denny began to come around into the first of the slower traffic, Jackie had come to terms with his sticky throttle and was closing in. On lap ten, the McLaren was badly balked, and the Lola

Mosport: And then there were three; at least the McLaren twins have a single Lola to worry them this year. *Pete Lyons*

came right up under its befinned tail. A few corners along on the same lap, Jackie delightedly watched Denny get himself "snookered" again and darted the other way to take the lead. The Canadian crowd cheered lustily.

But Hulme knew something they didn't. Oil was splattering onto his visor. Oil from Stewart's car. Denny felt he could have gotten back in front, but decided to drop back and await an easier solution. He did his best to communicate this to his pit by pointing to the Lola and making a thumbs-down signal.

He was right. On only the nineteenth lap there was a big puff of blue smoke, and the Lola coasted to the side. The leak had been from the transaxle, and, having run completely dry, the gears finally seized.

The crowd deflated almost audibly. There was some good racing going on downfield, but the orange McLarens were first and second again, and it was obvious no one else on the course that day was going to interfere with them. A lot of spectators climbed into their cars right then. It was clear: watching elephants might be all very well, but having seen one of another color, finally, people weren't going to be satisfied with the same old show.

St. Jovite, Quebec, June 27, 1971

A black elephant came to join the circus at Le Circuit. Having completed his Le Mans assignment, Oliver settled into a test program on the new Shadow, and the team set off for Quebec in good time and ready to run.

Luckily, there was a race to set off for. On June 16th, three days after Mosport, SCCA announced cancellation of round two. The release was terse: "CASC withdrew its sanction for the St. Jovite event when negotiations with the race course management reached an impasse. The action was taken after consultation with the SCCA, administrator of the Can-Am series." Within two days the problem was sorted out, and the race went on as scheduled. No complex human enterprise is free of internal strife, and that this dispute roiled the series' surface was no condem-

nation of the Can-Am, but it did suggest much turmoil below.

The Shadow was using Chaparral-built engines, so on the way from California the team stopped off in Texas for several days of testing at Jim Hall's now largely disused Rattlesnake Raceway. That went well at first, and much useful development was accomplished, but the session ended prematurely. When the story went around the St. Jovite paddock, former Chaparral test driver Tom Dutton laughed and said, "Guess nobody told them about the Rabbit Procedure."

He explained that one normally tested very early in the morning there to avoid the heat of the West Texas day, and the drill was to start with several slow laps in bottom gear, making a lot of noise to scare away the local jack rabbits. A West Texas jack is a substantial beast, and on his second lap one morning Oliver hit one at some 140mph. The damage done to the Shadow almost matched that suffered by the unfortunate animal.

The Can-Am press corps took a solemn vow not to say the Shadow's season had gotten off to a "jack rabbit" start.

In welcome contrast to the first event, St. Jovite offered ample practice time, plus a more workable qualifying procedure whereby drivers went out in groups of four. Also, Saturday's weather was fine, so the grid lineup was reasonably representative. Exceptions to that included Revson, who was spending half the weekend at Pocono qualifying seventh for a USAC event so he never got his Can-Am car fine-tuned to St. Jovite, and Bondurant, one of whose practice laps would have been good for third on the grid but he spoiled it by spinning in formal qualifying.

Jackie Stewart raised a laugh in practice by exclaiming that Can-Am cars were like "pregnant elephants" to drive around this tight track. Neither was he pleased when the bumps cracked a rear suspension mount during untimed practice. But when the times counted, he kept his foot in it and put up a front-row performance.

Yes, Denny Hulme won pole this time, but once again Group 7 had not come back up to its pace of 1969. His M8F's 1:32.9 was still over a second short of the 1:31.7 Bruce McLaren turned in the old winged M8B. Even worse, the sports car was slower than the existing F1 record, Stewart's 1:31.5 pole of 1970.

Drivers experienced with both car types said the disparity was the fault of the Hump. This sharp rise in the return straight was scarcely noticed in an open-wheeler, but for wide-bodies it dominated the whole lap. Not only were aerodynamics trimmed in hopes of preventing a "blowover," but drivers said they eased the throttle every time anyway.

Still, the Hump seemed scarier than ever this year. During final qualifying, Chuck Parsons got Dean's M8D's blue nose right up to what must have felt like the point of no return. It thumped back down the right way, but Oliver had been hustling along behind, and watching this near rerun of his own flight to destruction in the Ti22 did his Shadow's lap times no good at all.

A few minutes later, Stewart's Lola performed the same trick. The blunt-nosed T260 wasn't supposed to do that. "Oh, dear," said everybody.

Next morning, many people were saying something worse. For some reason, those staying at one particular resort were feeling very ill. They included most of the McLaren personnel, and poor Lothar Motschenbacher, who had qualified a fine fourth, was feeling so rocky he asked permission to start from the back of the grid. He was determined to start, because in the entire history of the Can-Am to date he was the one driver who had competed in every race. But he didn't expect to last the distance.

As the bulky, heavy machines rumbled around for two pace laps, one had a fleeting impression that it was a case of gallon-sized cars in a pint-sized circuit. Then they were off. Everyone's tense anticipation was on the first lap over the Hump. It was just like the first time into Turn 1 at Indy.

But nothing went wrong.

The field settled down to racing, with Hulme charging away from Stewart, who was leaving Revson behind, who in turn was holding off Oliver. But Oliver was not shaking off Parsons. The day before, the two had had words about "blocking a faster car," and now Parsons' whole mind was filled with the desire to get by Oliver. The low-line Shadow's handling was getting looser as its small tires heated up, and before long, the

McLaren scrambled by. Oliver was visibly keen to answer the insult, but his engine wasn't up to it—the fuel pressure relief valve was stuck—and, after a pit stop, he finally retired.

Up ahead of Parsons, Revson was holding a lonely third, unable, with his underdeveloped McLaren, to help his teammate. And Hulme could have used help, because Stewart was piling on. Anyone putting serious pressure on Denny Hulme for any length of time was a rare sight in a Can-Am, and the Quebec crowd was vocally appreciative of Jackie's untiring efforts with the unruly Lola. But the gap was holding pretty steady at about 5sec, and the McLaren's lead seemed secure enough until the pair came upon a particularly dense knot of traffic. Suddenly, Hulme had the bluff, white Lola's nose in his mirrors. As if startled, he put on a spurt, and set the fastest race lap: 1:33.6. For a moment, Denny seemed to have the situation in hand.

Only a moment, though. The gap was closing again. The M8F was in some kind of trouble. Right up on its tail came Stewart, and he began feinting to get by. For a few laps it was the kind of Can-Am racing all the promise-makers had been making every spring for years. Then, on the fifty-second lap, the T260 bulled its way ahead. The crowd perched on the hillsides sent up a cheer that nearly drowned out the engines.

Jackie now pulled out his own best lap of the race, 1:35 flat. But he had to try no harder. His mirrors were empty of orange McLaren. Hulme obviously had been forced to give up the chase.

Why? asked everyone of his neighbor. The engine sounded OK, there was no smoke, nothing was dripping or dangling. But Denny's pace was obviously off in the corners, and on the straights he was lifting his visor to scoop in air.

Hulme lasted to the checker, but he pulled right over and stopped without making a cooldown lap. He was so exhausted he couldn't take his own gloves off. He'd obviously succumbed to the same "bug" that had laid Motschenbacher low.

And what of Lothar? Well, far from stopping after a few token laps, he'd driven from the back of the grid right up through most of the field like a man at the peak of fitness, and finished fifth, 20sec behind Parsons in the other M8D. Yet once it was all over, the rangy German-American looked right on the edge of consciousness.

During a race that had gone on half a minute short of two hours–holding their heavy, awkward, bouncing machines on a heaving, twisting, plunging track; bathed in hot radiator air–neither Motschenbacher nor Hulme had so much as put a wheel over the edge, nor the tachometer over redline.

So, like the Martians in the H.G. Wells novel, the mighty McLarens were finally laid low by microbes. But as the defending four-time series champions loaded their cars, they'd already decided to get to the next track early for some extra testing. The Lola wasn't yet right, but it was close, and the Kiwis knew only one way to respond to genuine competition.

Road Atlanta, Georgia, July 11, 1971

Watching Stewart drive the Lola was worth the trip to Georgia. Fresh from a convincing victory in the French GP with a Tyrrell, appearing determined to convince his "pregnant elephant" it too might become a Formula One car if it simply thought positive thoughts, he seized it by the scruff of its neck and literally hurled it around Road Atlanta. To overcome the 260's tendency to power-understeer, he was using all the power the 8.1-liter Chevy could make to break the rear tires loose, so that both ends of the big, boxy vehicle were wiping across the road in the most electrifying manner imaginable.

Stewart only qualified third fastest, a full second off the pole, but early in the race, he passed both

McLarens to lead. Later in the day, he set a lap time that not only beat this year's pole position, but precisely equaled the previous year's best speed, by the "sucker" Chaparral.

This was not a spectacular Can-Am, and no, Jackie didn't win, but his was one of the best drives in Can-Am history.

For the rest of it, this was a work-intensive weekend in enervatingly hot and humid weather. The Lola had some front suspension geometry alterations, and during practice, its wing was moved a little farther aft, and some extra tabs appeared on the nose. Between adjustments, Stewart got two spins under his belt.

The Shadow team too tried a suspension change, a matter of decreased anti-squat characteristics at the rear, but it didn't work as hoped, so they reverted. The July 4th holiday was blamed for another disappointment, when a shipment of supposedly improved, low-profile Goodyear tires didn't arrive. A visible change to the formerly all-black car was white paint on its topside surfaces, an attempt to reduce underbody temperatures. Still, more and more air ducting was installed as time went on. Oliver qualified at a decent-looking fourth best, though the Shadow was three full seconds slower than Hulme's McLaren.

As for the M8Fs, apart from a retuning of power curves to make them more drivable and Revson running an all-aluminum Reynolds for the first time this season, which this time displaced 479ci (7.87 l), there were no major alterations. But neither were the McLaren men untroubled, for vibration of the inside rear tire, caused by Revvie's enthusiastic power-sliding, cracked a rear suspension subframe, and Hulme had two engines go bad before the race. Then, during prerace warm-up, binding throttle linkages robbed Denny of his chance to bed-in new brake pads.

Among the rest, Vic Elford rejoined the series—not with "his" ultra-quick Chaparral, unfortunately, but with a potentially more reliable McLaren M8E. David Hobbs replaced Parsons in the Dean team's M8D, while Oscar Koveleski handed his M8B over to his Polish Racing Drivers of America co-founder, Tony Adamowicz. In the latter two cases, the deals involved supplies of fresh aluminum-block engines, which were running short that summer because of a problem in Chevy's foundry.

SCCA's restless tinkering with qualifying procedure finally produced a good system at Road Atlanta. The field was divided into three groups according to proven potential speed, and after open practice, each group had a pair of half-hour timed sessions to do their best on a relatively clear track. This basic idea would be the norm in Indy car road racing two decades later.

At flagfall, the two M8Fs powered away side by side, with the T260 trying to get by into the first turn but not quite making it. At this point, Hulme, mindful of his unbedded brakes, volunteered to baby-sit Stewart, so Revson swept around the outside into his first lead of the season.

The McLaren boys might have thought that settled it, but the Lola boy had another thought. On the third lap, going into the double-90 at the far end of the track, Jackie pressured Denny into braking a little too late, which carried the McLaren a little too wide, and ZAP! The Lola was through into second. In four more laps Stewart was hounding Revson, nose to tail, and as they came down the hill and past the pits to start lap eight, Revvie abruptly found a much slower car in his face and had to ease his foot. It was for only an instant, but Stewart was close enough for it to be a deciding instant. Slowly, slowly, the Lola pulled alongside as they plunged into Turn 1 and . . . ZAP! again.

Well, now. Who'd expected this? Far from being an honorable also-ran, as suggested by the grid sheet, Stewart was blowing the mighty McLarens into the north Georgia weeds!

Of course, Can-Am races lasted more than one lap. At the end of thirteen, this particular one slipped down a notch to ordinary. The white Lola popped into view under the bridge on schedule, but it darted off into the pits road, its left rear corner sagging over a punctured tire. The Carl Haas crew got the wheel changed, but when they tried to restart the engine, their single external plug-in battery wouldn't do the job. By the time they'd borrowed a double-battery setup from a neighboring crew, Revson and Hulme had roared by three times, and Stewart was twenty-first.

Even backmarkers can put on a show, though, and the Stewart Show was terrific. By lap twenty-seven, Jackie had carried the Lola up to thirteenth place. That's when he broke off to the pits with two more problems: his red-hot brakes were starting to feel peculiar, and at certain places on the track the right front wheel was popping up through the bodywork in clouds of smoke. His crewmen attacked the second problem by slapping on strips of racertape, the first by patting him on the back, and waved him out again.

On his very next lap, the timekeepers caught the spectacular Stewart at the race's best lap, a fantastic 1:17.42, 1.3 faster than his own qualifying time, 0.3 quicker than Hulme's pole, and exactly equal to the all-conquering performance of the ground-effect Chaparral the year before.

The T260 took it for sixty-two laps in all. Then it came back down that hill into the pits again, leaning over again, to the right this time. That side's rear shock absorber shaft had snapped off at the eye, so it was finally all over. As

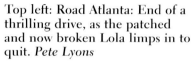

Top left: Road Atlanta: End of a thrilling drive, as the patched and now broken Lola limps in to quit. *Pete Lyons*

Top right: Road Atlanta: Revson climbs out after winning with a loose wheel. *Pete Lyons*

Stewart bounced out of the poor beat-up, smoking car, looking as fresh and energetic and enthusiastic as two hours before, he was asked why he'd driven so incredibly hard when there was absolutely nothing to be gained by it.

"Ooch," he piped in his irrepressible Scottish tones. "Ye must never let y'self fall into the habit o' drivin' at anythin' less than yer maximum!"

Revson had spent the entire race nursing fade-prone brakes, then, with about five laps to go, felt his car "doin' a worm" under him. He kept going, but as he took the checker he was slowing and pulling onto the grass opposite the pits. He trotted across to say the left rear tire was flat. But in fact the big central wheel nut had unscrewed itself, only stopping when it backed out against the safety pin. All four drive pegs were sheared off that hub, too.

Hulme, whose brakes never had come right, was still 20sec behind.

Watkins Glen, New York, July 25, 1971

Take nothing for granted. Here was the Lola back up front in qualifying: Stewart won pole at 1:05.11, 134.24mph. Revson's McLaren lapped a mere 0.12 slower; Hulme's, just a quarter-second farther back.

These times could not be related to previous years (nor to the subsequent GP), because of track layout differences, but what a tight lineup for a Can-Am.

And what a track full of contenders. First of all, two brand-new machines finally arrived, and both were interesting and quick. Mario Andretti's Ferrari 712M Spyder displayed plenty of power, though its

handling was only good enough for fifth grid place, 2.5sec off the Lola-Chevy's pace. With a standard 5.0-liter, 630hp Porsche 12, Jo Siffert's second-generation Spyder 917/10 wasn't fast in a straight line, but it lapped within a second of the big-bore Ferrari to make the fifth row.

Then there was the annual invasion of the Saturday six-hour cars, most of whom fronted up for Sunday's 199-mile sprint. Fastest of these was the Penske Ferrari 512M. Mark Donohue's grid time in this 5.0 coupe was scarcely half a second slower than Andretti's with the big 7.0 roadster—and in the separate qualifying period for the Saturday event, Mark had lapped within 0.1sec of Mario's Can-Am time. On the long uphill straightaway, the smaller but more slippery coupe was 2mph faster, 188.5 to 186.5mph.

To make sure they stayed on top of their own series, the Group 7 teams were working hard. The Lola mechanics had to beef up a rear suspension radius rod mounting point after a practice failure. They'd already switched to shocks with stronger shafts, and also massaged the T260's brake system. McLaren addressed Revson's Atlanta brake fade with additional air ducting—but then gave the brakes more work by cramming in a bigger engine. Pete was again using a Reynolds sleeveless block, but this time a longer-throw crank brought the displacement to 509ci (8.36 liter).

Hulme stayed with the normal, iron-sleeve 495 (8.1 liter), and his car lacked the revamped rear sub-frame put on his teammate's to withstand "powerslide

vibration." Denny's hadn't cracked, which was a matter of driving style, according to a team member's droll observation: "The only similarity between those two is they both hold licenses."

Unhappily, the mood in the Shadow camp wasn't so light because Oliver was starting from a very disappointing eighteenth place. The handling remained way off, and the new tires still hadn't come.

From the thunderous rolling start, Stewart held off Revson into the first turn, but David Hobbs, still sitting in for Tony Dean, capitalized on his excellent fourth grid place to thrust the blue M8D ahead of Hulme going up the hill. David hadn't had a good chance to try the car on full tanks, though, so at the far end of the straight he played his braking point conservatively and watched Denny nip by. Next time he did the same thing, and Andretti got ahead. By the next lap, Hobbs said later, he'd figured out that the D's braking was just as good on full tanks as empty. Unfortunately, the engine wasn't up to the brakes, and it died after just ten laps.

There was a fabulous variety of shapes and colors and engine types forming a long, snarling, rasping, bellowing dragon of race cars with three Groups snaking around the track, but its head was all Group 7. Stewart was leading Revson, the Lola looking right on the edge through the turns but the McLaren losing ground on the straights, both lapping in the 1:06s and the gap between them varying between 3sec and 7sec, according to the luck of traffic. They were running so closely and regularly, and there was such an absorbing dragon-fight going on everywhere else that anyone not paying perfect attention missed Stewart's pit stop. It was only a flat tire, and the wheel was quickly changed. He was gone exactly one lap, and rejoined in his familiar position just ahead of Revson.

But Revvie's position was completely different. He was leading the race, and comfortably so, because his teammate, Denny, was just driving around listlessly, pressured by nobody.

Nobody but Jackie, that is, who now decided to see if "never driving less than maximum" might salvage second place, anyway.

That set up an interesting direct comparison. On lap fifty-one, Revson cut his personal best lap of the race, 1:06.7. This exactly duplicated a time Stewart had done earlier; now, on lap fifty-four, Jackie did it again. At the same time, a speed trap at the crest of the straightaway was clocking Revson's Bigger-Banger McLaren at 184.6mph. Stewart's Lola was bulleting along at a scintillating 194.6.

Whether Stewart could have caught Hulme would never be settled. Two laps later, Jackie felt "very, very strong vibrations" and instantly reached for

the switch. The Lola coasted to its third halt in four starts.

Tension now focused on a battle for what had become third place. Andretti had settled there with the droning big Ferrari, but Siffert's humming big Porsche was looming up behind, coming ever closer. "Plus 3 s" was flashed to Mario, and then he overdid the new "90" past the pits and spun. Porsche finished third, Ferrari fourth.

Earlier, another dramatic incident at the same place affected the outcome between teammates. Lothar Motschenbacher had qualified well, but at the last minute had trouble getting his engine going, so, as at St. Jovite, he started from the back of the pack. His big red Batmobile made up ground rapidly, so that in seven laps he was closing on Bob Bondurant's identical-looking M8E/D. Bondurant, admitting he wasn't feeling on form here at the scene of his massive accident four years earlier, said later that he offered no opposition. But the two cars went into the "90" side by side, Motschenbacher's on the inside, and in the middle of the turn, Lothar lost the front end and plowed across Bob's nose and crunched into the catch fence on the outside. The damage didn't go as deep as the tub, but the partnership was destroyed.

Through all this, Hulme had never turned a hair. Convinced his engine was soft, and understanding that his teammate was running the engine that was supposed to win anyway, he seemed content—if not happy—to trundle around way behind, all the way to the flag. But on lap sixty-eight, something happened to wake the Bear. The big orange Batmobile came storming in a cloud of dust down the pit lane; in seconds, the

Watkins Glen: This time, the No. 1 car was in No. 1 position in the longest lineup yet this year. Behind Revson, Hulme, and Hobbs (#8 M8D) are Andretti in the new Ferrari G7 car (#50) and Donohue in the fastest of the Saturday 6-Hour coupes (#6).
Pete Lyons

Watkins Glen: How to wake up a Bear—stop him with a broken wheel, then run like hell. *Pete Lyons*

Mid-Ohio: Example of a bad guess on photo location. They look nice and tidy here, just before taking the green. Seconds later, up at Turn 1. . . *Pete Lyons*

crew hoisted the front, swapped the left front wheel, and sent the car wheelspinning and fishtailing on its way.

A puncture? No, all four spokes of the cast magnesium wheel had cracked.

While he was stopped, Denny had seen Revvie roar by, and this alone of all events this day seemed to switch him on. From a standing start in the pit lane, leaning on a cold outside front tire, Denis Hulme went through the speed trap at 185.6mph and completed his first lap in 1:06.083. The race record! *That's* the Bear we knew. With seven laps to go, he unlapped himself, but kept driving as hard as he could; two laps from the end, his crew thought he went faster yet.

So there was a little life at the end, but it ended as a Can-Am like most Can-Ams before: McLaren-McLaren-nobody. Nobody, though, knew better than the Kiwis how much of it had been luck recently. They were in a real fight.

Mid-Ohio, Lexington, Ohio, August 22, 1971

Stewart's first impression of Mid-Ohio was negative. More precisely, he was appalled. The track surface, he stated, was so bumpy it should be torn up and relaid. When he saw trees and telephone poles standing in areas he considered dangerous, he said he was worried. Worried "that *somebody* had sanctioned this race track."

Europeans were used to the safety-minded World Champion's activism, but his implication that Americans had no appreciation of modern motor racing and no understanding of its modern problems did not go down well in heartland Ohio. Stewart didn't care. He supposed he'd have to live with the car-killing surface, but if the obstructions weren't removed before the race, he declared, he would put the Lola back on its ramp-back truck.

More than one opinion about his stand went around the paddock. "If *he* doesn't want to drive it, *I'll* drive it!" groused Chuck Parsons, former official Lola driver, who had spent the past year and a half picking up lesser rides here and there. "Hell, saw the damn *suspension* in half and I'll drive it!"

But the promoter had already seen Tony Dean write off his McLaren M8D by crashing it into trees (no injuries) and agreed to do what could be done. All through the night before the race, working amid a tumultuous thunderstorm, crews sawed down poles and trees and stacked hay bales and bulldozed grassy dirt into protective embankments.

The rough surface remained, and though it wasn't exactly shattering cars left and right, some of the faster ones suffered quite a few breakages throughout practice. Both Stewart's Lola and Revson's McLaren repeatedly bent or broke suspension members at the

rear. On the M8F, the problem was concentrated in the subframe atop the gearbox, while the T260 came in three times with failures involving the right upper suspension link. First the outer bolt snapped, then its replacement bent, then the *inner* bolt snapped. The third breakage gave Stewart a high-speed ride across the grass. He didn't care for that at all, but what he found really disturbing about all these failures was that this rear suspension assembly was the only element of the T260 that had been carried over from the previous year's T220, which meant the design had gone an entire season without trouble.

Both Lola and McLaren informally requested that the race distance be shortened. The officials, after interviewing several other drivers, decided to make no change. Thereupon, Stewart made a decision. He would drive, but he wouldn't race.

It had been a month since Watkins Glen, ample time for anticipation to build, but the entry for Mid-Ohio was disappointing. Missing were the big Ferrari, which was back in Italy looking for more power, better handling, and some sponsorship; and the Shadow, which was at Riverside, testing some hopefully better tires. Also out were the Adams Ferrari, the Cordts McLaren and, unhappily, the Bondurant McLaren. The Watkins Glen incident, as well as tight finances, led Motschenbacher to run solo this time.

No new front-rank cars turned up, and none of those which did displayed anything really new. It was interesting, however, to see how even identical cars on the same team can diverge in detail as a season progresses. Hulme's had new bodywork from the same molds, but with increased air ducting noticeable at the nose. Hulme seemed to use his brakes harder than Revson, so some of this extra air went to the front discs. He also had rigged an air feed to a thin plenum behind his seatback, which was pierced with holes.

Revson's solution to driver-cooling was higher-tech: at the press of a thumb button, an electric pump shot ice water down his neck! His car also now had thicker front brake discs, thanks to the personal enterprise of one of his mechanics, who'd grabbed a set off the shelf during a flying visit to Colnbrook.

In one respect, the two M8Fs were the same. The team announced that from now on they'd be using the sleeveless blocks exclusively. However, at this race, their displacements differed; Hulme was using a 495, Revson a 479. It was probably a combination of other factors that determined their grid positions. Once again, lap times fell short of the 1969 standard, by not quite 0.2sec in Hulme's case. There was nothing mechanical wrong with his car, he said, it just wouldn't "point."

Stewart's Lola looked the same as before, except for higher arches over the front wheels, but under the

boxy bodywork there were rear suspension geometry and subframe changes. The Haas mechanics let on that they'd spent the month in utter slavery, determined to make the troublesome new vehicle worthy of its driver's talent. After Saturday's suspension dramas, they went totally sleepless to strengthen the area and to install a fresh engine.

Pacing the field under a bright sun, Hulme outdragged Revson up past the pits, arced under the bridge into the fast first turn, and spun in the face of the onrushing pack. Everyone managed to scrape by except Dave Causey, who'd qualified on the third row ahead of all his fellow privateers. His Lola T222 T-boned the M8F, badly crumpling itself and bashing the McLaren's side, but neither man was hurt. Several following cars spun wildly, and several ran over debris.

As the survivors came around to finish the first lap, Revson was leading Stewart by a few feet and Siffert's pink Porsche by a lot of feet. A longer way behind, in fourth place, came Roger McCaig, who was now ahead of eight still-running drivers who'd started ahead of his fourteenth grid place. Way back in fourteenth place now was Adamowicz, who'd started seventh. Motschenbacher, who'd started fifth, was eighteenth.

It was some kind of first turn! All that time-consuming qualifying; they might as well have drawn numbers from a hat.

Hulme spun because his outside right U-joint "cross" broke as he got on the brakes for the first turn,

Mid-Ohio: Denny went out on the first lap. Revvie almost made it to the last one. Almost.
Pete Lyons

Mid-Ohio: Slow and steady won *this* one, anyway. Stewart takes his second race by refusing to race. Note domed front fenders installed after Road Atlanta's bottoming problems. *Pete Lyons*

Mid-Ohio: Following his third-place finish at the Glen with the new Porsche 917/10, Siffert comes second here. Will the trend continue? *Pete Lyons*

which meant all the rear-end braking effort was going into the left-side wheel, and the spin was inevitable.

As early as the second lap, the decision Stewart made the day before became apparent. He was making no effort to stay with Revson. The McLaren went on alone, Peter driving briskly, using every inch of road and occasionally more, lapping steadily in the 29s. Jackie was hanging back, leaving plenty of margin at the roughest edges, avoiding the apex-mounds particularly, and falling back by half seconds and even whole seconds every lap. Occasionally the Lola's blunt tail would step out as the power came on, but it was rather dull driving to watch. Stewart was determined to treat this 192-miler as an endurance contest. He hated to drive like that, and one could almost hear him talking to himself. For the fans, it was no fun at all.

Among the rest of the runners there was plenty of mid-pack and even back-pack action, as always, but

the Can-Am was supposed to be world-class, big-time professional racing, and McLaren's lone surviving factory car was running away with this one. Revson was still driving briskly, still raising the odd puff of dust from the verges, and on the forty-ninth lap he did the fastest race lap—though at 1:28, nearly 1.5 slower than his grid time, it wasn't very fast. He effortlessly overtook Siffert, who was cruising around a lonely third, and then lapped him again; with twenty laps to go, the Porsche was only firing on eleven cylinders. By lap seventy, with only ten more to go, Revson's lead over Stewart was more than 20sec. The race was such a foregone conclusion it was hard to keep watching. Naturally, that's when the McLaren broke.

Going around for the seventy-second time, Revson's right outer U-joint cross snapped, exactly as it had on Hulme's. The flailing shaft made a mighty wreckage of the entire corner of the car, but Pete kept it all on the road, and staggered on, with the body down on the tire and smoking. He reached the pits before Stewart came in sight, but Jackie caught the excitement from the crowd and knew immediately that his strategy, this late in the game, had in fact paid off.

Speaking on the PA system later, Stewart all but apologized to the crowd for his lusterless performance. But he'd made up his mind it was the only way to make the car last.

So we had arrived at the seasonal midpoint. The results of round five made no difference to the McLaren team, for everyone had to throw away a result anyway, and Revson still led Hulme sixty-seven points to sixty-five. Stewart, however, moved into third with forty, ahead of Motschenbacher's thirty-two.

Elkhart Lake, Wisconsin, August 29, 1971

With only four days of repair-and-travel time available, Hulme's crew had reskinned his tub on the left side, which involved straightening a steel bulkhead. They also remounted this arch-conservative driver's rear brakes outboard; they said they'd planned to do that anyway for Road America, because the course demanded such heavy brake use, but the rear discs remained inboard on Revson's M8F. Both engine bays were stuffed with Reynolds-block 495s.

Making a welcome return was the Shadow, and it was even more welcome to find five weeks of tire testing in California had done a lot of good. The chief change was at the front, where Goodyear had asked the team to go up an inch to 13in wheels. That was no repudiation of the theory behind the smaller dimension, it was said, but simply that the manufacturer found it more expedient to test construction and compound ideas in a size for which a variety of molds already existed—13-inchers were common in F1 and

F5000. The larger tires required the front body line to be elevated slightly but noticeably. At the rear, the wing now rode a little farther forward in search of better aerodynamic balance without adding downforce to the front. For the first time, the unleaded fuel of prime sponsor Universal Oil Products was actually in the tanks.

Both McLaren drivers spent Friday in California preparing for an upcoming USAC event at Ontario. In their absence, Stewart was the fastest first-day qualifier, which caused not the slightest tremor of astonishment, but then the other Jackie's time with the Shadow came in. It was a matter of 2:09.969 vs. 2:09.973—Oliver was only 0.004sec slower! What a shot of life for the grid. It looked like we had a genuine, new, front-rank car.

That was Friday. On Saturday, Hulme appeared from the west coast, engine trouble there having induced him to withdraw his entry, and settled into tuning his rebuilt Can-Am car to one of his favorite courses. A few warm-up/practice laps and—SLAM! A lap at 2:06.662. Never mind that it was *still* 0.36 off his 1969 pole. It was 2.3sec better than second-best man this year.

Who was—wait for it—one Keith Jack Oliver. He'd been a contender with the old Ti22, and he was getting the Shadow there too. Handling and aerodynamics still weren't right, but Ollie took more than a second off to get down to 2:08.952.

What of Stewart? Engine trouble. He was still using the Ohio race engine, and now it was reaching the end of its life. His Saturday time was an improvement but not enough to put him on the front row.

Several drivers didn't make the grid at all. Milt Minter's description of how the engine was going in the old Porsche 917PA prompted the Vasek Polak crew to load up and head straight home. (There they found that the very long, very expensive crankshaft had broken.) McLaren owner Roger McCaig's only Chevy blew. Dick Durant's Lola T163 went into a guardrail when "something broke;" went *over* the guardrail, went *over* a courseworker's parked car, and clipped a phone pole on its way to destruction. Durant escaped with loosened and cracked ribs. Then, on race morning, Bobby Brown's M8E had a U-joint let go, causing too much damage to repair safely before the race.

Even Stewart had a morning scare. During the warm-up, the fresh engine, installed overnight, pegged its temperature gauges. A worried George Foltz pored over the cooling system, finally concluding, hopefully, that it was nothing but a vapor lock.

But none of this drama drew as much attention as Peter Revson. He'd stayed at Ontario to qualify on

Elkhart Lake: Another Corvette pace car, and another odd-looking front row; Oliver starts the Shadow from second spot.
Pete Lyons

the outside of the front row, accepting that he'd have to start Road America from the back row. Sunday morning was the first time he drove his M8F, though Hulme had spent some of Saturday bedding everything in for him. Revvie's first flying lap was in the 11s, his next in the 9s, and his *third* lap was 2:07.9. A front-row time. He stopped for adjustments, then took off another 0.2—all this on a full load of fuel. At one race the year before, he'd spoken of Denny psyching him on race morning. This year Peter was in the psych seat.

It was a good sight the Shadow made on the front row, alongside one McLaren, but all eyes were on the other one charging up from the back. By the fifth turn of the first lap, Revvie had passed six cars, and by the end of the 4.0-mile lap he was eleventh overall. Next lap, he was seventh, then sixth, fifth, and by lap seven, he'd overtaken Elford for fourth.

Up at the front, it was no contest. Hulme was simply, instantly gone. Stewart shot by Oliver, but never got to grips with the fast-dwindling McLaren. The Shadow, running on older tires with more erratic handling characteristics (because the best of those tried in practice wouldn't have lasted the distance), soon had the storming Revson McLaren in its mirrors and lost third place to it on lap eight.

Revson still had about 9sec to make up on Stewart, who by that point had lost almost 20 to Hulme, but now the Lola driver began giving thumbs-down signals to his pit. After ten laps, when white smoke started coming from the pipes on the overrun into corners, Jackie parked it. (Teardown revealed a sleeve had "sunk," a Chevrolet bugbear of 1970 that a detail

Elkhart Lake: Overheating its little tires, the Shadow drops back; meanwhile, Revson is coming up from the rear. They meet powering out of Turn 5.
Pete Lyons

redesign had supposedly fixed for 1971.) Five laps after that, one of the Shadow's rear tires went flat. Stopping in the pits, preceded by three miles of slow driving to get there, dropped Oliver to eleventh. Later he suffered the same experience, and fell to dead last.

Once again, that was it: race over, McLarens one-two, all the rest in one vague lump somewhere behind. Right?

Only for a couple of laps. Hulme, growling down into a turn, suddenly veered into the escape road and stopped behind a barrier. The crankshaft had broken. So there was Peter Revson, who, upon reaching second place, had settled down for the cruise to the flag, leading a Can-Am he didn't expect to. This time, nothing interfered with his winning it.

The rest had their usual adventures and misadventures, but only one of the latter was serious. While being lapped by the second-place Jo Siffert Porsche, the Stan Szarkowiz McLaren was brushed. It did a wild gyration across the road into a spectator fence, slightly injuring a child and cutting a woman's leg.

But on the bright side, Tom Dutton's McLaren finished its sixth race in a row, a unique feat so far this season.

Donnybrooke, Minnesota, September 12, 1971

At this race in 1970, the author's *Autosport* report had been quite upbeat. This time, it was gloomy:

The official entry list promised us a works BRM, but this went to Imola instead. Thus for the seventh event of our Million Dollar Road Racing Series we had to fall back to watching the Same Old Stuff struggling unequally around, trying to put on a show. It is obviously *very* difficult to build a McLaren-beating Can-Am car. As the season progresses (if that's the word) the gap between the M8F and the T260 is getting larger, not smaller. The entire Lola team is working as hard as they know how, but they are not closing on the Kiwis. The McLaren team have an advantage in numbers, in experience, and probably in budget; they still have as well the incredible Bruce McLaren spirit to which steady success is merely a goad to harder efforts. The reasons for their domination are as old, and as maddeningly simple, as they have always been. The plan is there for anyone to follow, but no one is following. The other teams have plenty of sound reasons for not following, but in racing there are no excuses. There is only winning and losing.

Lola design engineer Bob Marston expressed his own feelings with a rueful smile. "This is a great life for giving you an inferiority complex!" He'd carried out yet another revision to the T260's rear suspension, explaining that the huge torque of the engine, coupled with its sheer mass and height, magnified problems he'd thought he'd learned to deal with in smaller cars.

Despite the change, Stewart was not happy with the handling, which he said was too oversteery, nor with the straightaway speed, which, at about 187, was some 10mph off expectations. That was even after the Mid-Ohio front fender "domes" were scrapped—they proved to be very draggy.

That the World Champion (he'd now clinched his second F1 title) was giving his best was never in doubt; indeed, at one point, he absolutely amazed his crew with his sensitivity. He came in to say he'd felt something break in the rear. It turned out to be a tiny crack in one small suspension mounting bracket. The presumed cause was the violent shaking that powersliding could set up in that era's rear tires. "The tire vibration is really quite incredible," Jackie remarked.

The Shadow was still making do on inferior tires, ones borrowed from F5000 this time. Oliver reckoned he was losing 1.5sec per lap, but expected it would be another month before the next generation of purpose-built Goodyears came along. He had an odd additional problem during practice: the adjustable shock absorbers were "unclicking themselves," so they were wrapped with tape. Siffert, though, was happier; after several races struggling with incorrect suspension springs, his Porsche finally had ones of suitable rate and height.

Meanwhile, the McLaren steamroller was rolling along, steam well up. The crankshaft that broke at Elkhart had logged just over 400 miles, so that fixed the 495's life limit, and every weekend from then on each car would automatically get a fresh engine with a new crank. There were still teams struggling along with a single engine. The McLarens were both using Reynolds-block Chevy 495s again, and they were both reaching nearly 190 on the long Donnybrooke drag strip straightaway. A few other drivers were seeing like speeds, but nobody other than the M8F men kept seeing them as they dove, throttles wide open, into the long, banked first turn. Revson wound up quickest qualifier, 3sec faster than Hulme's best speed of the year before (a race day time) and almost half a second faster than Hulme this time. Stewart's third place was very distant, more than 2sec off the pace, and not much better than Motschenbacher's fourth-place time.

The Lola may have had its problems elsewhere on the circuit, but it was strong at the start line, and

from his grid position directly behind Revson, Stewart kept his foot in it all the way up to the peeloff point for Turn 1, then veered down low over the yellow stutterbumps and shouldered by into first place. Oliver, right behind on the grid, followed his lead and nearly got by Hulme for third, but Denny just staved him off. Then he turned to seeing what he could do about helping his teammate's counterattack on the Lola.

Stewart stayed out front for two grand laps. Finally, as they braked down from high speed into the tight Turn 3, Revson scrambled by. Immediately he pulled away, leaving Stewart's mirrors full of what must have looked like the same broad orange nose. Hulme made that image as large as physically possible, but he couldn't get by. From all accounts, that year's Lola cut a very rough hole in the air while the McLaren's high-downforce body shape was ultra-sensitive to turbulence. Denny was clearly able to get into the turns faster than Jackie, but then, as he tried to apply power, the front wheels, deprived of most of their aero load, would push wide of the line. Once, balked in traffic, Hulme lost ground. He caught up again immediately, only to run into the same barrier of churning air.

Jackie, afterwards, said he was delighted to learn he had been upsetting Denny's stability.

This went on until the twenty-second of the seventy laps, when Stewart felt a change in his car's behavior. He'd been driving just a little under maximum to keep the tire vibration down, but after so many races when the car had broken so often, he was extremely sensitive to feelings of this sort and immediately stopped at the pits. His mechanics gave everything a thorough checkover, but found nothing wrong and sent him back out, down in tenth place with one and a half laps lost. He hoisted himself back up to fourth, but then a rear tire went flat. Stewart's second charge out of the pits left tremendous black stripes of rubber which displayed extreme vibration patterns, and halfway along he only just caught a wild fishtail. He seemed a trifle annoyed. There was no longer any chance of his winning this championship.

With clear air in his face, Hulme turned the wick up and set fastest lap, but that brought his temperature gauges up, so he eased off to finish not quite a minute behind Revson.

Edmonton, Alberta, September 26, 1971

Rain: Racing's great equalizer. That's what it took for the Lola to pull away from the McLarens and lead nearly an entire race. That, and a new aerodynamic package.

Plus a little outside help from somebody—apparently—who tossed a stray bolt down one of the McLaren intake stacks.

About that rain. It was a very cold rain. After two years of July dates, the Edmonton event went back to its original scheduling in late September, and that was getting pretty late in the season up there above the fiftieth parallel. Wintry showers kept sweeping the track, and though they never quite turned to snow, the safety margin above freezing was a matter of very few degrees. At one point, snow was reported falling twenty miles away. Everybody came up with jokes about studded race tires.

The Lola's aerodynamic changes consisted of a new front end with a stubby, slightly recurved chisel shape, on the outside edges of which were low fences, and inside of which was ducting intended to create a ground-effect suction. This was balanced at the rear by relocating the wing to an overhung position behind the tail. Lola head Eric Broadley was on the scene, and F. David Stone, reporting this race for *Autosport*, approached him to ask whether the changes represented "an abandonment of the previous theories or a modification." Broadley's reply was a thoughtful "Yes."

The two McLarens were using iron-sleeve 495s. The Shadow had been painted all-white. Jim Adams was back with the ex-Amon Ferrari, which now had a pair of airfoils on the tail, one on either side. Chuck Parsons was Motschenbacher's teammate this time, and Dave Causey was back, too.

John Cordts also rejoined, driving an M8C wearing a pair of Indy-style AirResearch turbochargers on either side of its transaxle, with a single wastegate behind. According to builder Dave Billes, the Chevy displaced 465ci and made 750hp, 110 up on its normally aspirated output. Cracks in the intake manifolding forced removal of the system before the race.

Stewart, just back to Group 7 after winning his sixth GP of the year at Mosport, put his safety hat on at Edmonton and demanded that some concrete barriers be replaced by catch fencing. He missed having some buried-tire corner markers removed as well, but his car didn't miss them; his Lola was one of several cars, including Revson's McLaren, Oliver's Shadow, and Siffert's Porsche, to suffer shredded bodywork on them.

The pair of McLarens was fastest all through practice; no surprise there, but for once they managed to break a Can-Am track record. Two years before, the Bruce and Denny Show qualified at an identical 1:22.9; now Revvie and Denny turned 1:20.3 and 1:21.4 respectively. Jackie too beat the old record, though by less than a second.

When engines were fired just before the race, the mechanics hovering over Revson's felt the throttle

Donnybrooke: It's going Revvie's way nicely, now. This is his fourth win in seven starts with the splendid big Batmobile.
Pete Lyons

Donnybrooke: It decidedly is *not* going Jackie's way; there's no longer any chance of the championship. Is that a little frustration showing on the pit road there? *Pete Lyons*

mechanism jam and then heard a bad noise. They shut down, and Lee Muir traced the problem to one cylinder. Looking into the spark plug hole he could see a 3/8in bolt, but he couldn't fish it out until he had removed the exhaust header. The race didn't wait for him. It wasn't until eleven racing laps were·on the chart that the second M8F launched into the fray from the pit lane.

Light rain was dampening the circuit, but most cars wore dry tires. From his starting position behind Revson's vacant pole, Stewart repeated his Donnybrooke trick and snatched away the lead from Hulme into the first corner. Oliver followed him through, forcing Hulme back to third.

Stewart's lap times were nearly a full minute off dry-weather times, but the Lola seemed totally at home on the wet track, and by the five-lap mark had an 8sec advantage on Oliver's Shadow. That in turn was 4sec up on the poor, lonely, factory McLaren, which had the aggressive factory Porsche sniffing its tailfins.

By lap forty, half-distance, with weather conditions having gone from bad to better to worse, Hulme had left Siffert behind, closed on Oliver, and passed into second. Stewart, however, was a long three-quarters of a minute ahead.

Three laps later, the gap was only one quarter of a minute. Stewart had gone onto the grass while lapping Motschenbacher. This excursion may well have damaged something, but whatever the reason, the Lola was no longer handling well and was losing ground to both Hulme and Oliver. At the three-quarter mark, with twenty laps left, Stewart only had 10sec

in hand. Hulme was doing his best, slithering around the slick track like a man with a mission, cutting fastest time of the day (1:26.3) on lap sixty-three, and whittling those seconds down. Was he carving them off quickly enough? In the next seven laps he gained only 3sec. Let's see, that works out to . . .

Stewart was missing. With thirteen laps to go, Hulme came around into sight first. And all alone. Oliver's Shadow had dropped away, having clipped one of the tire markers and received the black flag to repair the nosepiece. And Stewart's Lola?

Jackie had spun. Just lost it. By the time he got going again, his nice, 7sec cushion was a 7sec lead weight. And it got no lighter. His car handling abysmally now and with the nearest threat—Oliver— two laps behind, Stewart just endured to the end. He crossed the line 60.4sec after a very pleased Hulme. This was Denny's first victory since Mosport.

After pitting with a flat tire, Revson was twelfth. At least it never actually snowed.

Laguna Seca, California, October 17, 1971

As always, a fresh breeze seemed to blow in off the Pacific here and bring a more upbeat atmosphere to the Can-Am. Two important new entries joined the show, though they weren't so much new as revamped.

David Hobbs, who'd been running occasional Can-Ams as a break from his more successful F5000 career, appeared with the ex-Oliver Ti22 Mk II. Builder Peter Bryant had lost control of his "Titanium Car," and its subsequent owners had failed to make good on grandiose plans, but now the project was in new hands. The chief change was to larger front brakes, which reduced a handicap apparent at this race a year earlier, though a change in kingpin axis, necessary to fit the new discs, resulted in heavier, stiffer steering. In contrast to its previous appearances, the Ti22 wasn't wearing a rear wing, which seemed odd at a track that rewarded downforce. But Hobbs qualified a resounding third fastest, ahead of Stewart—and of Oliver—at a time 1.55sec faster than the Ti22 had gone here the year before. Such seasonal improvements for individual cars were extremely rare in the Can-Am.

The other returnee was one of 1970's P154 BRMs, actually the car driven late that year by Rodriguez, which had been heavily modified and given a new "project" number, P167. The aluminum monocoque chassis was 4in longer, a new segment having been inserted at the center of gravity behind the seat to preserve weight balance. The rear brakes were remounted inboard. A rear airfoil replaced the upturned rear bodywork, which in fact had been cut away between the wheelwells to improve airflow to

St. Jovite 1966: The first-ever Canadian-American Challenge Cup race got the new series off to a great start. John Surtees (#3 Lola T70) and Bruce McLaren (#4 McLaren M1B) dueled flat out for more than two hours, and once McLaren scratched into the lead, but Surtees finally won by 6.5sec. His victory here in Quebec and two more later in that year's six-race series made the former World Champion on both two wheels and four the inaugural Can-Am king as well. Between them, these cars set the contemporary Group 7 technical norm, with carbureted, cast iron Chevrolet small-block engines displacing 5.4 to 6.0 liters and making some 450–500hp. *Lionel Birnbom*

Above: Bridgehampton 1966: Phil Hill, America's first F1 World Champion, posted the race debut of Chaparral's spectacular 2E. Its suspension-mounted "flipper" airfoil controlled by the driver's left foot was only the most visible element of a radical design package that also featured an aluminum Chevrolet engine, a torque converter transmission, and hip-mounted radiators. Team boss Jim Hall was fastest qualifier overall, but after airfoil-related problems damaged both 2Es in practice he turned his own mount over to his teammate for the race. Hill pressured winner Gurney for most of the distance, but more wing trouble finally dropped him to fourth. *Autosport*

Left: Bridgehampton 1966: Stirling Moss (Iso Grifo) paces New York's round two, which wound up with an even tighter finish. Starting from pole, Dan Gurney (#30 Lola T70) just managed by a fifth of a second to stave off a late-race charge by Chris Amon (#5 McLaren M1B). At a mere 5.0 liters, Big Dan's Ford-based engine with his own Gurney-Weslake heads was the next-smallest Big Banger ever to score in the nine-season original Can-Am and the only Ford. Behind Surtees, McLaren, and Amon on the grid here, other contenders included Phil Hill (#65 Chaparral 2E), Mark Donohue (#6 Lola T70), Mike Goth (#86 McLaren-Goth Spl.), and George Follmer (#16 Lola T70). *Autosport*

Top: Laguna Seca 1966: Third time was the charm for the "wing things," Hill (#65) and Hall (#66) scoring an apparently effortless one-two at this twisty track that responded to the 2E's light weight and efficiently variable aerodynamic downforce. So convincing was the advanced design's victory over more conventional machinery that it would have seemed foolish on that California afternoon to predict this would remain Chaparral Cars' only Can-Am success. *Cam Warren*

Bottom: Elkhart Lake 1967: Color the Can-Am Kiwi. At the first race of the new year New Zealanders Bruce McLaren (#4, McLaren M6A) and Denny Hulme (#5) put a stamp on the North American championship that would remain indelible for five full seasons. Bruce's distinctive caramel cars were never the most imaginative technically, but they always had ample power and handled well; more importantly, they were practical and reliable, and came to the races ready to race. It was a remarkably simple approach, all the more remarkable because so few rivals ever managed to follow it. Following the all-new McLaren-Chevrolets and the Chevy Camaro pace car through Road America's Thunder Valley, here in wooded Wisconsin, are the older-tech Lola T70s of Dan Gurney (#36), Penske teammates George Follmer and Mark Donohue, and the McLaren M1C of Chuck Parsons; John Surtees and Peter Revson (T70s), Jim Hall (Chaparral 2G) and Lothar Motschenbacher (#11 T70) come next. *Pete Lyons*

Top right: Elkhart Lake 1967: It may have been the Psychedelic Sixties, but the McLaren boys put those "Flower Power" badges on just for fun. Inside the M6A's stout little 5.9-liter Chevy it was all business; broad-based business, with the best in cranks, conrods, and camshafts developed through years of hot rod industry experience on dragstrip and speedway as well as road course. Topping it all off was a Lucas fuel injection system, modified by McLaren from its F1 experience to make 525 smooth, ultra-responsive horsepower. *Pete Lyons*

Top left: Elkhart Lake 1967: Second-most innovative design of the early Can-Am era was the Caldwell D7 with its de Dion suspension geometry front and rear. As seen here, initially there was also a chassis-mounted "flipper" controlled by hand. Designed by Ray Caldwell, builder of the successful Autodynamics Formula Vee cars, and both financed and driven by Sam Posey, this bold project showed promise in national-level USRRC racing, but the pace of Can-Am competition seemed to bring out severe handling and reliability defects. At Elkhart it qualified mid-pack and lasted only two laps. *Pete Lyons*

Bottom: Laguna Seca 1967: Gasping for air on a sweltering hot day, suffering sunburn on his lips, and having to slow mid-race for a bucket-bath, Bruce had a hard ride to his first Can-Am victory. Critics who were beginning, even that early, to carp about McLaren's seemingly effortless domination of the series ought to have ridden along to see how much work it really was. *Cam Warren*

Riverside 1967: Defending his home turf, Californian Dan Gurney (#36, Lola T70) stole pole away from the foreigners and led until his high-winding pushrod Ford scattered itself. Parnelli Jones (Lola T70), sixth-fastest qualifier already running fourth here, put his quad-cam Indianapolis Ford up front too, but it blew as well. Ford-man Mario Andretti (#17 *Honker II*), fifth on the grid, lost his transmission. That left Chevy-faithful McLaren and Hall, trailing Gurney here through Turn 8 at the head of Riverside's long, long back straight, to embroil themselves in one of the Can-Am's most heated battles.
Cam Warren

Top right: Las Vegas 1967: John Surtees (#7 Lola T70) may have qualified way back on the fifth row, but his mid-season gamble in resurrecting his year-old, but better-handling 1966 championship chassis finally paid off on the Nevada desert floor within sight of the infamous Strip. However, though both the McLaren team's Chevys failed here at last, Bruce (#4 M6A) wrested the Johnson Wax "floatile" trophy away from John.
Claire Lyons McHenry

Previous page bottom: Bridgehampton 1968 `Watch out! Ron Courtney's old McLaren is overwhelmed by a great race for the lead, even as the Road Runner from Texas is pouncing on the flightless birds from New Zealand. Jim (#66 Chaparral 2G), up from the third row, has already passed Denny (#5 M8A) and is about to flipper ahead of Bruce (#4) to lead another Can-Am. Alas, the glory will only last five laps before fuel injection trouble. However, a rare double breakdown will stop the mighty McLarens cold. *Pete Lyons*

Top left: Bridgehampton 1968: Characteristically conservative about engines, McLaren didn't step up to the big-block Chevy until other teams had been test-racing it for two years. But even 1968 proved to be too soon, as the team inherited oil leakage problems with the aluminum version which Chaparral had suffered all through 1967. Here, reigning World Champion Denny Hulme (left) may be trying to coax insight from veteran Indy crew chief—and Can-Am rival with Ford—George Bignotti. *Pete Lyons*

Left: Bridgehampton 1968: Mark Donohue won his first Can-Am in 1966 because others broke down; here at the Bridge he does it again (#6 McLaren M6B). Enroute, the immaculately pinstriped Penske entry drafts Brett Lunger in the revised, wingless but still hapless Caldwell. *Pete Lyons*

Top right: Laguna Seca 1968: Can-Am surprises rarely came as big as this one, when English-born Canadian John Cannon craftily chose the right rain tires for his ancient, underpowered McLaren and simply splashed around everyone else at the decidedly non-seca laguna to win by a clear lap. *Barry Tenin*

Above: Riverside 1968: One of the hardest of hard triers, German-born Lothar Motschenbacher never won a Can-Am, but one year his always immaculately prepared car did carry him to second in the championship, and he did establish the record for the longest run of consecutive race starts, fifty-three. Here, he arcs his beautiful McLaren M6B-Ford from Riverside's mile-long back straight into the original, tighter Turn 9 banking on his way to a fourth place. *Pete Lyons*

Right: Riverside 1968: John Surtees (#7) hoped to repeat his 1966 triumph with his highly personalized Lola T160, but its special big-block Chevy with Weslake cylinder heads was a severe disappointment. The car started only three races and finished none. George Follmer (#16) did much better that year in an aging Lola T70-Ford, finishing second here at Riverside and winding up the season seventh on points. *Pete Lyons*

Bottom: Las Vegas 1968: Possibly the worst-ever Can-Am debacle was achieved by Ferrari with its first-generation 612P. The aerodynamically ambitious machine arrived only for the final race of the season and raced only to the first turn of the first lap. But the power from this then-huge, 6.2-liter V-12 encouraged driver Chris Amon to press Maranello to continue for 1969, when the same, simplified car would demonstrate far brighter promise. *Pete Lyons*

Top: :Las Vegas 1968: No cars better epitomized for many fans the original meaning of the Can-Am than Jim Hall's wild and wondrous Chaparrals. Sadly, this was the superb driver-engineer's last race in one. A collision with another car which abruptly slowed destroyed the 2G and caused leg injuries, eventually ending Hall's driving career. *Pete Lyons*

Bottom: Mosport 1969: Three years after Chaparral introduced the hub-mounted rear airfoil, and the same year Chaparral abandoned it, conservative old team McLaren finally adopted it—and proceeded to wing its conservative Kiwi way to victory in all eleven races of the longest-ever Can-Am season. Here, at Ontario's opening round, the Bruce and Denny Show (McLaren M8Bs) play to a foilless field which includes John Surtees (#7 Chaparral-entered McLaren M12), Chuck Parsons (#10 Lola T163), and Dan Gurney (#48 All American Racers-modified McLaren M6B "McLeagle"). *D.J. Markle*

Above: Mosport 1969: One of the truly happiest people in motorsport, boyish, buoyant Bruce McLaren was so well liked that most people forgave the way he seized the Can-Am and made it his own. His victory here at race one was the first of six and the prelude to his second championship. *Cam Warren*

Top left: St. Jovite 1969: Just to prove the show doesn't always play out according to the script, McLaren misjudged a pass while playing with John Surtees and had to pit for a tape job. Somehow, the scars failed to spoil the graceful lines of the M8B, the agile, high-revving racer that Denny Hulme always recalled as "the best car McLarens ever built." *D.J. Markle*

Top right: St. Jovite 1969: First flame of the future, the turbocharger made its Can-Am debut here in the McKee-Oldsmobile "wedgie" driven by Joe Leonard. It didn't finish high up, but it did finish. One day, some would say, the turbo would finish off the Can-Am. *Barry Tenin*

Middle left: Elkhart Lake 1969: Though it never raced, the four-wheel-drive McKee-Olds deserves attention as one the most intriguing of Can-Am projects. In practice, here, Leonard displays the air brake mounted atop the twin-turbo engine. Even with this aid, the wheel brakes were overmatched; so was the little team's budget, and the innovative, ambitious machine was taken home, never to appear again. *Cam Warren*

Laguna Seca 1969: The only Chaparral never to earn respect, the peculiar-looking, narrow-track 2H quasi-coupe never performed as Jim Hall thought it should, and the failure ultimately destroyed his personal relationship with driver John Surtees. Not even the huge parasol airfoil installed for this twisty circuit brought the "white whale" up to competitive lap speeds; perhaps mercifully, engine trouble kept it from competing here. *Bob Tronolone*

Elkhart Lake 1969: Ford Motor Company's assault on Chevrolet's Can-Am domination was always fitful, and this half-hearted hybrid was the strongest salvo Dearborn ever fired. A McLaren M6B reworked by Holman Moody, it was called the "429'er" after its supposed engine size. The actual displacement was 494ci (8.1 liters), which at that stage was the mightiest motor road racing had seen. Mario Andretti was unable to join the race. *Su Kemper*

Top: Riverside 1969: By round ten, everybody was wearing wings. But the McLarens were still dominating the grids, as seen here during the pace lap on the approach to tight Turn 6 at the end of Riverside's multiple Esses. Their big Chevys now debugged and throbbing out some 650hp, the works M8Bs were winning all the races, too. This one will go to pole man Denny's (#5), after Bruce's (#4) crashes with a rare suspension breakage. Chris Amon (#16 Ferrari 712P) has a 7.0-liter at his back this one time and will give hearty chase until taken out by petty officialdom. *Dale von Trebra*

Middle: Riverside 1969: Many Can-Am cars offered promise, but few came as close to fulfilling it as the Ti22 "Titanium Car." British-born Peter Bryant built it simple and strong, and British F1 driver Jackie Oliver pedaled it hard and fast. In its second-ever race, here, Ollie started fourth and was contesting third when his transmission wilted. *Bob Tronolone*

Bottom: Texas 1969: Right at the end of the year, the big Ford "429'er" finally came on strong— for a few minutes, anyway. Andretti (#1) started from the front row on the superspeedway banking and led four stimulating laps. Just think what might have been . . . *Dale von Trebra*

Top left: Texas 1969: McLaren and Hulme owned the Can-Am that year, but two other men from the antipodes could well have disputed the situation had they received better factory support. Three-time World Champion Jack Brabham (#2 Open Sports Ford) brought the car home third here in only its second race—but it never raced again. Chris Amon (#16 Ferrari 612P) didn't finish at all—once again. *Dale von Trebra*

Top right: Mosport 1970: Initially a cradle of free-form innovation, in its fifth season the Can-Am outlawed "moving aerodynamic devices." But even shorn of its originally planned air brakes, the radical little Shadow on its tiny tires was startlingly unconventional. Unfortunately, as George Follmer proved, it was innovation that didn't work as well on the track as on the drawing board. At least they tried. *Pete Lyons*

Middle: Mosport 1970: A far more orthodox approach than Shadow's was BRM's, but it wasn't right either. In the sad case of the tidy-looking but ill-handling and unreliable P154, driven here by Canada's George Eaton, failure could be blamed on an F1 constructor which talked a good Can-Am game before the season, but which then found itself too busy in Europe to support the American adventure. *Pete Lyons*

Bottom: Watkins Glen 1970: Denny Hulme's hands were burned, then Bruce McLaren was killed, but Dan Gurney helped the team back to its feet with two lead-off victories in the M8D "Batmobile." By the season's third race Denny was back up to speed and Dan, struggling here in New York to a troubled ninth place, decided to return to his own business. *Pete Lyons*

Top: Laguna Seca 1970: Although the big, broad March 707, shown here powering out of the Laguna Seca hairpin came late, Chris Amon quickly showed it was a strong challenger. Perseverance might have moved March to the front the next year, but the firm never came back. *Henry Thomas/ Petersen Publishing*

Middle: Donnybrooke 1970: Peter Gethin (#7 M8D) stepped into Gurney's cockpit and served as a loyal No. 2. Hulme needed the help, because Peter Revson (#26 Lola T220) was one driver increasingly able to mount a challenge—as seen here in the Minnesota woodlands, where he started from pole. *Pete Lyons*

Bottom left: Riverside 1970: Fastest by a wide margin in qualifying— 2.2sec, here—the bold white box of the "fan car" (#66 Chaparral 2J Ground Effect Vehicle) threatened to give the Can-Am a whole new shape. But rivals with much invested in their "conventional cars" succeeded in having the concept banned. Thus when Vic Elford paced the pack down through Riverside's Turn 7, it was for the last time. *Lionel Birnbom*

Bottom right: Elkhart Lake 1971: Many would-be Can-Am contenders arrived with great fanfare, only to fade away quietly. Porsche played it differently. This 917/10, underpowered but driven enthusiastically by Switzerland's great Jo Siffert, was the German automaker's second cautious foray into unexplored Group 7 technical terrain. Meanwhile, back in the Black Forest, a third-generation vehicle turbocharged to overwhelming power levels was already underway toward 1972. *Pete Lyons*

Top: Laguna Seca 1971: McLaren was not blissfully unaware of the rumors from Stuttgart, but this year Jackie Stewart (#1 Lola T260) was offering plenty to worry about. During the season the "Mod Scot" clinched his second World Championship in F1, and he never stopped trying his spectacular best to wrest the Can-Am title away from "The Bear" (#5, McLaren M8F) as well. *Pete Lyons*

Bottom: Riverside 1971: After four straight years of watching Can-Am gold go to New Zealand, "Champagne Peter" Revson (#7 M8F) patriotically stepped in to help America's balance-of-payments situation. As he clinched his title, McLaren's fifth, Revvie briefly posed here at Turn 8 with Tony Adamowicz in one of Bruce McLaren's own chassis of two years before (#54 M8B). *Pete Lyons*

Top: Mosport 1972: After five years, McLaren's run was over. The Kiwis were finally overtaken by an organization that brought everything to the track they had, only more so. Mark Donohue (#6 Porsche 917/10K) didn't win this first time out, but he started from pole and showed enough race speed that it was clearly only a matter of time. McLaren's Revson (#4 M20) and Hulme (#5), and Shadow's Jackie Oliver (#101 Mark III) all tried their hardest, but their normally aspirated Chevys weren't in the same class with the TurboPanzer. Only luck let Denny into the winner's circle this time. *Dale von Trebra*

Middle: Road Atlanta 1972: One month later, at round two, three things had changed. Donohue, injured, had been replaced by George Follmer. The Porsche didn't win the pole. But it ran trouble-free, and won its first race. Hulme flipped into the red Georgia clay, Revson and Oliver retired, and the privateers had a rare good day at the pay window. *Dale von Trebra*

Bottom left: Watkins Glen 1972: Twelve fan-cooled cylinders, four camshafts, twenty-four spark plugs, and an ultra-complicated twin-turbo system; it all added up to—well, to whatever power the driver cared to ask for. During 1972, usually, the 5.0-liter 917/10K *Kompressor* motor's boost screw was set for less than 900hp. Usually, it was enough. *Pete Lyons*

Bottom right: Watkins Glen 1972: Huge, staggered-length injector horns atop massive Reynolds-block Chevys hogged out to 8.1 and 8.3 liters—and once even to 9.26; the McLaren M20 bulged with power. At upwards of 750hp, it was enough to make the pitlane tremble. Here, it powered a McLaren to one more factory victory. But it was a lucky one, and it was the last. *Pete Lyons*

Top left: Donnybrooke 1972: Race fans love the unexpected, and despite all the critics who called the Can-Am too predictable, it did offer its moments of surprise. Here at race six, on a day when the Porsches and factory McLarens battled themselves to oblivion, French star François Cevert was surprised to drive his ex-Revson M8F under the checker first. *Pete Lyons*

Top right: Edmonton 1972: At the beginning, Lola was the dominant Can-Am manufacturer. Six years later, just one new Lola tried to compete. David Hobbs (#1 T310) did the best job possible, but the car began late and never caught up. Here in chilly Alberta, it could only split the troubled Shadows. *Ozzie Lyons*

Middle left: Laguna Seca 1972: After years of also-ran rides, he'd given up on the Can-Am. Then he was summoned to stand in for the injured Mark Donohue, and forceful George Follmer became the series' fifth champion. *Pete Lyons*

Right: Anywhere 1973: Enlarged to 5.4 liters, the second-generation Porsche turbomotor was reportedly good for 1100hp in normal race circumstances—and possibly as much as 1500 in abnormal ones. Such circumstances seldom arose, because the 917/30 was more than a motor. It was a total weapons system, finely honed by Penske and Porsche engineers to achieve a balance of performance so perfect that Donohue called it "a monument to my career." *Dale von Trebra*

Top: Riverside 1973: America's Chevy-faithful, left badly behind by the turbocharged Teutonic terrors, strove to catch up by bolting blowers on their big-blocks. These 1200hp V-8s never worked very well, but they did put on a show, as Mario Andretti demonstrates with a firebreathing old McLaren M20 dragon. *Dale von Trebra*

Bottom: Laguna Seca 1973: Donohue took a second deep breath over the winter, and in his second summer with Porsche brought out the greatest, grandest Can-Am car ever. This time there were no injuries, no teammates, and no opposition, and his big blue 917/30 (#6) carried him to six victories in eight races. With the works McLarens gone, and the black Shadows still not right, only drivers of older 917/10Ks such as Brian Redman (#3) and Follmer (#16; note widened rear bodywork) could hope to pose any threat. *Dale von Trebra*

Previous page bottom right Laguna Seca 1973: They called him "Captain Nice," but Mark Donohue was a complex, driven individual who competed with himself at least as hard as with his rivals. One of the world's foremost engineers, he greatly advanced the state of the automotive arts in his time; as a driver, he won the Indy 500 and several hard-fought Trans-Am titles along with his long-awaited Can-Am championship. *Dale von Trebra*

Watkins Glen 1974: Color the Can-Am black at last. After four years of trying everything else, the Shadow team finally went back to basics and followed the McLaren prescription for success. Specially built around smaller tanks to minimize the effect of new fuel restrictions, the DN4 with its normally aspirated big Chevy was a simple and practical design, it was tested on time, and it was fielded by a sound organization. Best of all, it was well driven by a pair of accomplished drivers—drivers so determined to beat each other that the George and Ollie Show almost made the tired old Can-Am stand upright again. Almost. Jackie Oliver won all four of the first races to clinch his crown, promoters of scheduled late-season events opted out, and the series died. *Dave Friedman*

the wing. The nose section was little more than a sloping plate, without much of either sides or bottom.

Brian Redman had recently driven this car to victory in two Interserie races in Europe. The team could not have expected as much success from its venture to America, and it was a little disturbing to see a rear chassis subframe break during practice, a repetition of incidents at this track and at Riverside the previous year. However, Brian's best lap took 2.27sec off the old P154 time, and his third-row grid place also improved on 1970's.

Speeds were much higher at the front, too. When Peter Revson snatched pole with a couple of brilliant laps, he looked like he was breaking records, and he was. In 1969, McLaren's high-winged M8B was capable of lapping Laguna at 59.53. The 1970 Batmobile couldn't match that pace, its best time being 60.6, although Chaparral's fan-car turned a 58.8. Few records had been broken during 1971, but Rev-

son now turned a 58.78—0.02 quicker than even the Chaparral. Granted, timing this year was taken to an additional decimal place, so the comparison wasn't perfect, but it *was* official.

A great performance, but one or two enthusiastic observers of the Group 7 scene found themselves a little wistful that they would never see what a second-generation "sucker" Chaparral might have been able to do.

Hulme, though not happy with the way his engine was pulling, did at least beat the 1969 McLaren time. A clue to the higher speeds was suggested by Goodyear engineers when they revealed that the two factory McLarens, and also the factory Lola, were on new rear tires this weekend. The tires had a normal compound, but the carcasses had a different—and highly secret—construction which all but completely eliminated the dreaded tire vibes. That meant the drivers could plant their throttle feet sooner coming out

Laguna Seca: The Cowcatcher; clear proof that Lola would go to any lengths to give Stewart the front-end stick he wanted.
Pete Lyons

Laguna Seca: The Incident; smokey proof that you can never count on a last lap to go the way you want. *Bob Tronolone*

of corners, without the whole back ends of their cars shaking apart.

And all this time the tire guys had been saying it was a chassis problem.

The Orange Elephants were the same as before, except that Revson's was wearing a set of the cross-drilled front brake discs that were coming into vogue.

The White Elephant, however, was something to behold. Lola had already abandoned the sucker-nose tried at Edmonton. Stewart said the attempt at aerodynamic ground effects hadn't worked very well, but obviously he did like the idea of added front-end downforce. So his mechanics added some for him. The T260 appeared with its original blunt fron-tispiece, but propped out ahead of it was a huge sep-arate airfoil, the most ungainly looking aero aid seen since Chaparral tried its parasol wing here in 1969. It did seem to work, for it let Stewart turn the rear wing up to a high-downforce angle. Still, he was saying the car didn't have enough grip, and he failed to follow Hobbs past the 1969 McLaren lap time barrier.

Fifth fastest, Oliver was running the Shadow on new, U.S.-made F1 tires. These, and some extra fenc-ing atop the body, were its only changes. He just beat the best 1970 McLaren time.

Among the rest of the healthy entry, one point of in-terest was what Vic Elford learned by taking over the Tony Dean McLaren M8D. Vic had been driving an M8E for Roy Woods, who was building one of the better privateer teams. They had missed Edmonton to fit the car with Cal-ifornia-made, D-type Batmobile bodywork, although they

left the track dimensions narrow, and had arrived at La-guna as early as Tuesday to begin testing. That went well, but on Thursday, Elford put a wheel wrong and backed into a bridge abutment. He got out of it with a headache and a cut forearm, but the chassis was totally destroyed.

Within hours, Woods had approached Dean. Following his Mid-Ohio crash, the Yorkshireman had rebuilt his M8D with a new M8E tub, complete with wide suspension, and planned to resume his Can-Am career at Laguna. But "the price was right," as he said cheerfully. Elford took to this E/D immediately, saying the 4in-wider track made it much more stable. "The E always felt like it was going to fall off the edge." He added that the more efficiently located D-type rear wing seemed to plant the car more firmly on the road.

A peek into insights McLaren had been gaining at Goodwood all those spring test days.

Laguna's was one of the tightest grid lineups ever seen in the Can-Am, and Revson wasted no time try-ing to get away from it. Hulme nosed in close behind while Hobbs held off Stewart into and through the fast second turn. Up at the Corkscrew, though, the Lola sneaked by going in and took away third. At the end of that lap, Oliver pulled the new Shadow ahead of "his" old Ti22 under braking into the hairpin.

But Ollie couldn't latch onto the leaders. The first three, Revson-Hulme-Stewart, blasted away, once again showing themselves to be in a Can-Am class of their own. Class Two was at least as good to watch, though, with Oliver-Hobbs-Redman-Siffert-Motschen-bacher-Elford forming themselves into as grand a

"dragon" as we'd seen back at Watkins Glen: bold, bright sports cars bulking big between the rails and bales, all wheelspinning viciously out of the slow corners and hurling themselves over the hills like strafing fighter jets. Other multi-car battles took shape behind. It was all good stuff, and the sheer volume of noise was stunning.

The Shadow suddenly slowed and pitted, its brake hydraulics gone wrong. That left Hobbs watching Redman in his mirrors, and as the laps went by, the view got better. Brian was really into the spirit of his first Can-Am in a Group 7 car, throwing the BRM's tail out. He later described this as the most frightening race of his life! Hobbs was bracing himself for an attack.

Then, on the twenty-seventh lap at the Corkscrew, Dave Causey's Lola T222 came across in front of the Ti22. They collided, and both went weaving and spinning off the road in clouds of dust. Hobbs collected himself and drove away quickly, but the Lola had gone into a spectator area, struck a parked car, and injured some people. Causey climbed out unharmed. Moments later, the wreckage burst into flames.

Hobbs drove around to the pits to get a new right front wheel. But it wouldn't go onto the hot hub. After a few frustrated minutes, David shut off the engine. The wheel was finally affixed, but then the starter motor wouldn't turn over. Push starts were forbidden. There was nothing more to do.

Other things happened: Redman tapped Motschenbacher into a spin, breaking up Lothar's struggle with Elford, but then Elford pulled wide to let the leaders go by at the hairpin, and his engine died. Typically, it wouldn't restart. One by one, the other dices died away, and there was nothing to distract from the real race going on up front.

Revson held his advantage over the other two, gaining about half a second per lap. After about ten laps, Hulme's engine soured, refusing to run over 6000rpm because of broken valve springs, so he had to watch Stewart's bewinged nose thrust on by. Then Denny had a minor brush with Tony Adamowicz, and dropped completely from the picture. But even with the one McLaren out of his way, Stewart could do nothing about Revson's. The gap between first and second kept growing until it was 25sec and more.

Until Revson came up to lap the Lola of Hiroshi Kazato. Once again there was a Can-Am collision, and the young Japanese went off the road, lost fire in the engine, and had to sit out the race there. The McLaren came away still running, but the right-side door was hanging down on its hinges. Revson drove straight into the pits to have it refastened. He was stationary about 12sec; when he got back onto the track and up to speed, Stewart had closed to 9sec.

There was a big flurry of onlooker interest for a while, but the gap gradually began to widen. Obviously, all Revvie had to do was drive to the finish.

It wasn't that obvious to Revvie. With about twenty laps to go, he felt his engine lose power. He began to nurse it. The gap to Stewart was 16sec. Revson held it there as best he could through the heavy traffic. The laps reeled away. Maybe it would be all right.

Lap eighty-eight completed. Two to go. Smoke. The big orange M8F was in trouble. A huge, blue-

Riverside: On the road again. Denny and Revvie qualify one-two, run one-two, finish one-two, no troubles, no opposition, no problem. Nice day, too. Was there anything else you wanted out of your Can-Ams? *Pete Lyons*

Peter Revson, Can-Am Champion

His family's wealth and social standing might have held him back, or his looks, but he never let *anything* hold him back. In a tough-hearted fraternity where nothing matters but results, Peter Revson made his own way on his own merit. "I really feel he was one of the top six drivers in F-1," Teddy Mayer once told *Autoweek*; yes, the two were long-time personal friends, but when it came to professional evaluation, Mayer was as coldly clinical as they come.

"Revvie," as his teammates and competitors all called him with genuine warmth, was born February 27, 1939, to one of the founders of a major cosmetics company. Determinedly athletic, Peter played several sports before taking up racing in 1960 with a Morgan. After his third race—the second of which he won—his small, local club dismissed him for being "too aggressive." Proving they had it at least partly right, he kept right on racing, first with the SCCA on a national level, and then by moving to Europe in 1963 to pursue a serious professional career. Traveling and often sleeping in a converted bread van he called "Gilbert," and helping his mechanic with building and rebuilding chores

on his Formula Junior Cooper, the dashing young Yank soon drew the right kind of notice on the track. By the end of the year he'd been invited to show his ability in a Formula One car. More paying rides followed, on both sides of the Atlantic, in all sorts of equipment. Ford hired him for its international GT40 and also its U.S. Trans-Am teams, and he started in the Can-Am as early as 1966—as did his younger brother, Doug, who tragically was lost in a racing accident the following year. After Peter made several strong Can-Am showings for Carroll Shelby and Carl Haas, Mayer brought him into McLaren in 1971 and promptly had another champion. But perhaps Revson's widest recognition came at Indianapolis that same year, when this "rich kid from New York" was fastest qualifier; it was one of three poles and one outright victory on this versatile young man's Indy car resume. In 1973, still driving for McLaren, he added a pair of F1 Grand Prix trophies. On March 22 of the next year he was killed while testing a Shadow in South Africa. *Jim Chambers photo*

---

white plume was coming from the right exhaust pipe. A valve head had snapped off. It was the eighty-ninth lap. As Peter rumbled up under the flagman's bridge to start the last one, the official whipped out the black flag. This was the McLaren's first time past the man while smoking, and he had not then seen the back of the car to check for oil. There had been reports of oil from other stations, but reportedly none thought it worth displaying an oil flag. For the man on the bridge it was a spur-of-the-moment decision; he said later that had he realized it was the last lap, he wouldn't have shown the black flag.

Revson said later that he didn't see it anyway—he was, indeed, staring into the afternoon sun. He drove carefully around the last lap to receive the checkered flag. But there was no checkered flag waiting. Just the black flag. He drove one more lap. This time the official was holding the checker, but it was still furled, and he did not actually wave it until Stewart hove into view about 10sec later.

Revson drove around yet again, and entered the winner's circle. Stewart finished his cooloff lap, but instead of taking the pit road, he parked his car under

the starter's bridge. A big discussion took shape around it. Lola entrant Carl Haas emerged to formally protest Revson's disregard of the black flag. The results were held up for more than two hours while the officials considered the matter. Their decision was to let the order of finish stand as of the scheduled ninety laps, instead of the ninety-one, but to fine the winner $250.

Riverside, California, October 31, 1971

Mr. Johnson's trophy was going to go either to Mr. Revson or to Mr. Hulme. And evidently it was still open as to which. Any number of bystanders had been sure since the beginning of the season that McLaren's many American sponsors—Gulf, Goodyear, Chevrolet, Reynolds, Coca-Cola—would smile on the idea of feting the series' first American champion, but there was another smile to consider.

That of the Bear.

While Revvie certainly wanted to win it, and was on pins and needles all weekend, Denny gave no sign he was going to make it easy. He seemed in rare form, and in the car he *flew*. The drivers' two—quite separate—teams of

mechanics were in serious competition with each other. This late in the series, there may have been only two parties still in contention, and they may have been in contention in different ways, but they *were* in contention.

The American who would be Can-Am king had nothing on his mind all weekend but making it to the end of it in sixth place, at least, to out-point his teammate if he won.

The Kiwi who had twice been king had nothing in his head but foot-to-the-floor fun. He really liked Riverside's wide-open spaces and fast, smooth bends. He'd won here the past two years; winning again would wrap up an unprecedented hat-trick, and besides, there was something of a score to settle.

This was where the Chaparral 2J had made him look bad. Where he'd been blown off by 2.2sec. Where the great ground-effect controversy had come to a head, and where he and his team had taken a firm stand on principle. They'd succeeded (along with others) in getting the fan-car banned from the Can-Am, but somehow it had been there anyway, hovering like a phantom just ahead of them all year, mocking their best speeds by giving everyone a chance to say, Yes, but you haven't beaten the Chaparral's records.

The Chaparral had set three. At Atlanta, Stewart—Stewart!—had merely equaled it. At Laguna, Revvie had *just* been faster, but there had been a bothersome difference in timing precision between the two years; not totally convincing.

Last chance coming up.

The McLarens came loaded with 509-inch engines. They also had stronger rear outer U-joints, and heavier front stub axles. They started running at Riverside as early as Tuesday. When official practice opened on Friday morning, in unusually chilly weather, they both quite easily lapped at 1:34.3. That soon, they'd beaten the best McLaren time of the year before, which had been Hulme's 1:34.69. That afternoon, Denny left his teammate behind. He ripped off a sparkling 1:32.32. There it was! Seventeen-hundredths of a second better than the old Chaparral benchmark. The McLaren-Reynolds/Chevrolet M8F was the fastest Group 7 car in history.

Wait, Denny wasn't done. Saturday was warmer, so the track was slower, but he wasn't. He wrote about it in his column which appeared in *Autosport* as "Behind the Wheel" and as "Denny's Column" in *Autoweek*:

This season we've been running under the shadow of the Chaparral 'super-sucker' lap times . . . On the morning of the final qualifying day I was down into the high 32s fairly quickly, and in the afternoon official session with a light fuel load I started

to chisel at the morning time. I came in and had the front spoiler lowered perhaps an eighth of an inch, fitted a set of scrubbed tires and with about 15 gallons of fuel aboard the thing seemed to sprout wings. It was hard to believe that such a small alteration could make such a difference. I saw a board at 32.1 and then a 31.9, and it was downhill from there on. The light fuel load doesn't make any difference to your top speed, the main difference is how much sooner you have to get into another gear—it makes the world of difference to acceleration.

The clock read 1:31.96, defeating the old Chaparral bogey by 0.53 percent.

After that, it would be teddy bear stuff. Laguna's close grid times had allowed hope to sprout for Riverside, but Hulme was long gone. Revson was a second slower. Stewart was 1.2 slower. The next man was 2.2 slower than Hulme. And so on.

One problem might have involved tires. The new ones that had worked so well at Laguna, cutting vibration, had been mass-produced and widely distributed for Riverside. Where they *increased* vibration. A black art, indeed.

The Lola was still wearing its "cowcatcher" bow wing and now had end-plates fitted to increase the efficiency of the rear wing, but Stewart was not happy with the handling. The blocky white car looked unsteady going into the faster turns while the driver described slow turns as a matter of increasing understeer suddenly turning into snap-oversteer. Despite that, segment-timing showed the T260 to be at least equal to the faster M8F in the fast Esses, and, if anything, slightly quicker through some of the slow U-bends. But the McLaren was making a lot of ground down the long back straight and through the long, long, banked Turn 9.

Nor, predictably, was Stewart happy with the circuit, at least until he'd seen some trackside phone poles cut down. As they carried PA speakers, their removal could be seen as a double blessing.

The man alongside Stewart on the second row was making a Can-Am comeback. George Follmer, busy with other things since early the year before, had been invited to take over the Woods M8E/D from Elford, who was busy in Europe. George settled into the McLaren with impressive rapidity. The team also had repaired its M8E and installed Sam Posey. Apart from a Ferrari coupe drive at the recent Watkins Glen, this F5000 star hadn't been part of a Group 7 event for years. He qualified seventh in a car still crawling with bugs after its rebuild.

Another new face belonged to Howden Ganley, a New Zealander who'd been a mechanic with McLaren and was now an F1 driver for BRM. He was

The champion's McLaren M8F at Watkins Glen. *Pete Lyons*

Next page: M8F undressed: Note inboard rear brakes, "staggered" inlet trumpets, molded-in bodyside "fences," and generally very stout construction. *Pete Lyons*

assigned to the P167 this time and qualified it ninth.

Hobbs now enjoyed a rear wing on his Ti22 but did not enjoy having a titanium cross member break on Friday, which prevented his qualifying then. On Saturday he had another failure, in a front subframe—and *another*, in the rear suspension. David had to line up on the back without a time.

Fifth place on the grid went to Oliver. The lowline Shadow's engine was now breathing through the conventional, upright style of injector stacks, but the car was otherwise unchanged. As usual, its performance appeared to depend on its relatively small tires, and this week there was ample drama in that department. The same F1 designs that stuck well on the Laguna surface were disappointing here. Eventually, a suitable compromise between European-made fronts and American rears was settled on, and Oliver seemed reasonably content with the handling, but spectators were being treated to a real spectacle. The white Shadow was sweeping through every turn with the tail hung way out. Wonderful to watch, but . . .

But worse, the driver revealed that during his Riverside tests some months earlier he had the interesting experience of his front tires deflating at high speed on the straight. It happened again now, on Friday, and again on Saturday, and *again* on Sunday

morning. Each time, Ollie managed to stop without any damage or even spinning, but having his front end let him down repeatedly at about 197mph was becoming a bit of a bore.

His team had already figured out the problem, a mismatch between the tires and the rims which wouldn't let the beads maintain their seat under extreme centrifugal force. On Sunday morning they decided to try literally bolting the tires to the rims. This operation took every minute available before the race; the last wheel was going on the car as the pack began the pace laps.

"Before the start Pete and I got together and agreed our race strategy," wrote Denny. "He said he would let me clear into the first corner and cool it while I did my thing out front."

Which is precisely what everyone saw happen. Hulme roared right away, showing the same second-a-lap advantage as in qualifying, going faster and faster until he did 1:34.33. That was the third lap; he saw he was 3sec in the lead, and he never bothered to go any faster. But he did keep on pulling away from anybody and everybody else.

"I could have pressed on quicker. . . but I wasn't pressing my luck. I had been winding a lot of revs out of the engine in the early stages, but it never faltered and never even ran hot. I headed Peter home . . ." By over three quarters of a minute.

Revson held off Stewart—though Jackie later said there was no balking going on—until a traffic situation gave the Lola driver a better run out of one corner into the next. The McLaren driver with so much at stake was satisfied to settle into third, running a steady 3sec behind, out of the Lola's turbulence. Obviously, the only tension in this race was going to be of a cross-your-fingers kind, like the last two hours of a dull Le Mans. It was one of those times when a race is sacrificed to a series.

Hobbs was some kind of star, though. From dead last he'd passed ten cars through the tight part of the track before the head of the straight, and by the end of the first lap he was fifteenth. He went on to get as high as fifth before making a mistake—his own admission—and ripping off a fender on—you've heard this before—a buried-tire marker. With no spare bodywork available, the Ti22 had to retire.

Oliver, who had started from the pit lane, drove as hard as he could, but didn't make any ground on the leaders. After thirteen laps he felt his tires going flat again. He retired voluntarily.

Follmer made a pit stop to have his mixture richened. Later, he ran out of fuel.

Stewart lost a secure second place when a piston blew.

The second McLaren ran to the finish, and Champagne Peter was Can-Am champion. He'd won

five races this year. Hulme had taken only three, but Riverside '71 was his twentieth Can-Am victory, and Bruce McLaren Motor Racing's thirty-fifth. The Kiwis had now dominated the series for five years straight.

Had the 1971 season brought us any answer to the big question of conventional car competitiveness?

Stewart suggested an answer two days after Riverside, when he announced he was joining McLaren for 1972.

Cars of the Can-Am 1971
McLaren M8F

Though designer Gordon Coppuck based the F-type very closely on its M8 predecessors, he lengthened the chassis by 3in through the cockpit area, and increased wheelbase to 98in. The extra tub length actually housed a little less fuel, because now there was a total of four foam-filled rubber cells, instead of two, with a combined capacity of 72gal (U.S.). For better impact resistance as well as increased structural stiffness, the exterior panels of the tub were of heavier-gauge aluminum—enough heavier to accept flush-rivets, an elegant touch. The tub's footwell section was more robust, too. In the stressed-engine end, the tubular pyramid structure was broader-based for even better bracing.

Track dimensions were slightly narrower so that wider rims (17in in back) could fit within the same overall body width. This led to slightly different suspension geometry, and since the rear brakes were now inboard, the former lower rear reversed wishbone had to be replaced by two parallel links to clear the disc. At the front, the hub casting was a stronger and also more adjustable item based on that of McLaren's contemporary Indy car. The transaxle was Hewland's new LG500 Mark II, still a 4-speed but with beefier case and sideplate castings. All this beef evidently added some 100lb, because the officially announced dry weight was now 1520.

M8F bodywork was an evolution of the D-type "Batmobile's," with its nose somewhat reshaped for increased downforce. There was also a greater drop behind the engine and rear wheel arches to encourage more airflow under the fin-and-strut-mounted rear wing. The fins were a little less prominent but leading forward from them were full-length body fences to keep high-pressure air atop the body and channel it to the wing. To the same end, NACA inlets on the body sides replaced topside ducts to the flank-mounted oil coolers.

With Chaparral out of racing, Gary Knutson returned to McLaren. Working out of a new McLaren Engines shop near Detroit, Michigan, he and Lee Muir had two slightly different engine programs underway. One was based on Chevrolet's own aluminum-block/iron-sleeve big-bore design introduced

in 1969 as the 430. Longer strokes gave still larger displacements, and Knutson preferred the largest. A bore of 4.438in. (112.7 mm) with a stroke of 4.0 (101.6) gave an engine called either a "494" or a "495;" the precise displacement was 494.9ci (8109.9cc).

He also brought to McLaren the two-length, or "staggered," inlet configuration, which gave much smoother power characteristics. When breathing through conventional, equal-length tuned intakes, the big Chevy developed a sinuous torque curve with two peaks separated by a pronounced mid-range dip. The forces involved were great enough to make the cars handle erratically when accelerating out of corners. The "staggered" intakes in effect split the engine into two in a tuning sense, each "half" making a torque curve of the same shape but peaking and dipping at different rpm. The net result of these combined curves was to "take a little off the tops to fill in the hole" for a nearly linear, much more driveable power band.

For this engine McLaren released power and torque figures of 740hp at 6400rpm, and 655lb-ft at 5600. According to this information, the performance curves were fat, torque running above 600lb-ft all the way from 4000 to 6000 rpm, while the power was more than 600, between 5200 and 6800. The drivers said they were supposed to use 7000 as a rev limit, even though on the dyno the engine continued to give good power all the way to 7800. They also stated

that, even with the staggered intakes, the power came on very strongly and very suddenly. At the tight St. Jovite circuit, Hulme asked for his engine to be detuned because of excess wheelspin. Later in the season, the engine shop smoothed the powerflow.

Meanwhile, sponsor Reynolds Aluminum was in modest production of its own high-silicon, sleeveless block which first raced (and won) late in 1970. Lack of liners permitted even larger pistons, but Knutson began the season with a relatively conservative 4.5in (114.3mm) bore. The 3.76 (95.5) stroke he used first created a "480" (actually 478.4ci, 7.84 liter). Later, the 4.0 crank raised swept volume to "510" (508.9, 8.34). Chevy Can-Am engines had gone from "mouse motors" to "rat motors," and now we had "moose motors."

Now that McLaren had taken a modest step forward with the M8F, it finally released the original stressed-engine M8A/B/D chassis design for production by Trojan. Called the M8E, this 1971 customer car wore a sharp-nosed body and low-mounted rear wing extremely similar to the previous year's M8C, but the E was readily distinguished by its slab-sided chassis rocker panels. Wheelbase was 95in. Two teams modified two of these chassis with the wider-track suspension and "Batmobile" body shape of the M8D, resulting in a hybrid commonly called the M8E/D.

Lola T260

Anyone expecting 1971 Can-Am cars to be conventional lookalikes found the new Lola as refreshing as it was startling. In contrast to the slinky McLarens, and Lola's own voluptuous T220 of the year before, the brutish T260 was almost as appealingly *ugly* as Chaparral's sadly defunct 2J.

Mainly the work of chief design engineer Bob Marston under the direction of company founder and head Eric Broadley, it was built to an aerodynamic theory already embodied in a few small-bore sports cars of the day. The intent was a shape that would bullet through the air on the straights, and also remain stable as the car's pitch attitude, ride height, and positioning behind other cars changed everywhere else. In particular, as Broadley remarked at Mosport, a more conventional downforce-producing wedge nose, such as McLaren's or, even more to the point, the old Ti22's, could abruptly change from downforce to lift under certain conditions. Conditions such as those sometimes found at the Hump at St. Jovite, where the Ti22 (not to mention two of Broadley's old T70s) had reared up and flipped over backwards.

The T70, of course, had not been a wedge, but it had flipped. Unfortunately, during practice at St.

Not Jackie Stewart as advertised, but Frank Gardner shaking down the new Lola in England. Note the smooth line of the front wheel arch while the car still wears its original 13in front wheels. *Phipps Photographic/ Autosport*

Jovite only two weeks after its debut, the non-wedge T260 very nearly did too.

A more subtle feature of the T260's nose was a multitude of small, screened holes located across an area of low pressure. These, and presumably the extreme cutaway behind the front wheels, extracted underbody air to create some downforce. There was no other evident downforce generator on the nose at first except a very small "splitter" on the leading edge. The original location of the rear airfoil well forward of the car's tail, suggesting there was nothing up front to balance its effect, was another indication that the priority was low drag. Speed traps did prove the car was getting along the straights very well. Perhaps the designers, knowing that Jackie Stewart was to be the driver, were confident of his ability to get the car through the turns.

As the season progressed, however, so did a downforce-inducing program. The splitter grew, tabs were added, the wing moved aft, a different nose shape was tried once, and during the last two races a huge second wing hung out in front of the nose.

The full-length aluminum monocoque chassis had conventional elements, but some were arranged differently. The weight of the 65gal of fuel was carried well aft. Both water and oil radiators were flank-mount-

ed, which moved weight to the rear and also created a cooler cockpit, simplified (and lightened) the plumbing, and permitted the desired nose shape. Radiator air came in through NACA ducts atop the doors and was sucked out through openings in the afterbody beneath the wing. Suspension was conventional, with two exceptions. At the rear, only two longitudinal locating arms linked the upper end of the hub carriers to the

By the time it got to America— Road Atlanta, here—the T260 had 15in front wheels and a more aft-mounted wing. The spiffy ramp-back truck was the rage in transporters. *Pete Lyons*

Among many other bold strokes, the Lola's designer had specified inboard front brakes and horizontal springs. The springs survived. *Pete Lyons*

Above and bottom: The Shadow's inboard front brakes proved generally reliable, but required forced-air cooling help after hot laps. *Pete Lyons photos*

seatback bulkhead. A wide lower control arm structure on either side kept the bottoms in line.

The other suspension exception was at the front, where the upper control arms were three-dimensional trusses to operate horizontally-mounted coil springs and dampers. This was to permit inboard-mounted brakes, although as the car appeared for racing all its discs were outboard. It is believed Stewart vetoed the inboard brakes because of close friend Jochen Rindt's fatal accident the year before, caused by a failed front brake drive shaft on his F1 Lotus.

Wheelbase was 98in, overall length a stubby 139in width only 76. Stated weight was a somewhat porky 1575lb.

Lola did plan to sell copies of the T260 once it was proven, but to start the season massaged its 1970 design, the T220, for production as the T222.

Shadow Mk II

Two men who felt they had something to prove came together on this one. Don Nichols, the American prime mover of the unsuccessful "tiny-tire" first generation Shadow, still wanted to demonstrate that "a top flight sports racing car—one that reflects the tremendous technological capabilities of this coun-

try—can be built in the U.S." For his part, British-born Peter Bryant was smarting from "business" maneuvers that had taken away his control of his very competitive Ti22 "Titanium Car." Their collaboration produced a blend of the two essential elements of their prior projects: the second-generation AVS Shadow rolled on relatively small tires, but everything else was hard-headed, practical Bryant.

Not as tiny as the 1970 Firestones, 1971's Goodyears were still unconventional in the Group 7 context, though they were similar to F1 and F5000 wear. The fronts measured 18.8in in overall diameter, with a tread width of 10in, and were mounted on 12in rims 11in wide (later the rim diameter increased to 13). At the rear, the dimensions were 22.3 diameter by 14 tread, 15x16 rims. Thirteen-inch rims were planned for later introduction at the rear.

Bryant's chassis was compact and neat. Standard suspension front and rear was united by a conventional, full-length aluminum semi-monocoque. Virtually the only use of titanium was at the rear, in a pair of struts uniting the back of the tub with the engine. The rear suspension was carried on a subframe attached to the gearbox, which was a four-speed Weismann. Another subframe at the front carried the front

suspension, steering rack, and inboard-mounted brakes. Bryant was reluctant to adopt this controversial brake location, but the size of the front wheels left him no choice—he didn't choose to use the trimmed-down discs of the previous car. In fine specials-building tradition the brake shafts and joints were made up of Porsche and Audi components, but the front upright castings were custom-made. The rear brakes were mounted outboard on the same Gurney Eagle uprights used on the old Ti22.

Wheelbase was 96in, and width came out to 72. Track measurements front and rear were 60 and 56. At a static ride height of 3in, the body rose less than 23in from the road at the front fenders, and 25.5 at the rear. The overall shape resembled the low wedge of the old Shadow, with fences added. Fiberglass honeycomb under the surface added strength. The radiator was front-mounted, and there was a small, pits-adjustable airfoil forming the top of its inlet duct—the driver reported that it was extremely sensitive to adjustment. A wing from the old Shadow stood on struts at the rear. It was hoped the wing would be especially efficient because of superior airflow afforded by the low body profile, as well as the low-line, crossover engine induction system borrowed from Chaparral, tuner of the Chevy engine.

Ferrari 712M

Abandoning both the 612P of 1968–69 and the principle of building a Can-Am car from the ground up, for 1971 the factory started with a steel space frame left over from a 512S/512M coupe experiment with somewhat different front and rear suspension geometry. The cab structure was removed, and the rest of the bodywork reprofiled to generate more downforce. At first a slim airfoil perched above the tail on stalks, but it collapsed during testing and then Mario Andretti said the car handled better without it—though it never handled very well. An oil cooler occupied a nose duct while twin water radiators were flank-mounted, fed by sloping inlets atop the doors.

The four-cam, 48-valve V-12 engine also was closely related to the 5.0-liter endurance unit, prototypes of which had been enlarged to 6.2 and 6.9 liters for the 1968–69 Can-Am car. But the 1971 Can-Am engine made use of entirely new head castings and a block casting altered for more bore and stroke. Just what bore and stroke? "Oh, there are four different combinations, I don't quite know which this is," the author was told by a frazzled engineer on the car's debut. So the precise displacement of this "7.0-liter" is uncertain. The power output of 680 cited in some literature is at least believable. Obviously it was a strong

Ferrari 712M. *Pete Lyons*

engine, and beyond that Andretti said it had broad shoulders, pulling nicely from under 4000rpm to 7500. All this was said to be a rough-and-ready test bed, pending an all-new, smaller, lighter car which was supposed to appear later that season, but which never did.

We have been able to learn little more about this Ferrari, and even its model designation has been rendered in different ways by different reporters. We have chosen to adopt the 712M used by *Autosport* late in the car's life, which distinguishes it from the 712P of 1969 and also references the 512M origin of its chassis.

Porsche 917/10

Taking an opposite approach to Ferrari's, Porsche created its second new Can-Am contender by putting another perfectly standard air-cooled, four-cam, 24-valve (and 24-plug), Boxer-12 endurance racing engine into a virtually new space frame. This was an absolute symphony of aluminum tubing running in all possible directions, more complex in appearance than even the 917 coupe's. The frame was wider, to match wider wheels and tires. This brought overall width to 83.4in, according to Karl Ludvigsen's

At Watkins Glen the new 917/10 bears little resemblance to its direct ancestor, the 917 coupe in the background. *Pete Lyons*

Porsche, Excellence was Expected (other sources give a narrower figure). The frame was stiffer, too, thanks in part to the aluminum rocker panels between the wheels being welded to the frame tubes. However, these panels did not indicate closed torque boxes. They served as mere troughs to carry the fuel cells, and metal did not enclose the cells on top—the rubber bags were exposed to any inquisitive poking finger. Fuel capacity was an impressive 80gal.

Wheelbase remained at the normal 917 dimension of 90.6in, but the sketchy spyder fiberglass body was shorter than that of the old 917PA. Rakish tail fins appeared on the upswept, sharply cut off tail, as on some 917 coupes, but there was no airfoil. At the front, a close look under the wedge-shaped nosepieces either side of the massive oil cooler showed they were open to the road, without underside panels parallel to the ground. This configuration was thought to generate some extra downforce through aerodynamic ground effect.

The 917/10 made lavish—and expensive—use of magnesium and titanium components, and Ludvigsen states the car weighed 1638lb empty of fuel, 70lb less than the 1969 Group 7 car. That was still some 100lb heavier than the latest McLarens, and though the 5.0 engine's power was not far off at 630, its torque of 425lb-ft fell short by a third. Late in the 1971 season a 5.4 engine came along. This was rated at 660hp, but torque only came up to 470. Back at its Weissach skunk works, though, Porsche's dynos were already whistling up an answer to the power problem.

BRM P167: At Laguna Seca, Redman revels in the much greater competitiveness of the greatly revised 1970 car.
Pete Lyons

The 1972 Can-Am season began, appropriately, in November of 1971. Appropriately, because the climate of that next summer of racing would be cold.

It was November 2nd, two days after the Riverside finale, when Jackie Stewart announced he was leaving Carl Haas and Lola in favor of driving a McLaren alongside Denis Hulme. On the 16th, Roger Penske announced what he had been denying and everyone else had been predicting: Penske Racing was coming back to the Can-Am as the Porsche factory team.

Which meant Roger and Mark Donohue were coming back in a big, big way.

Two days after that—soon enough after the other two items of news that there could have been no connection—six-year series sponsor Johnson Wax announced it was redeploying its resources elsewhere.

There certainly had been a connection between the first two items. "The main reason we signed Jackie for the Can-Am series is to have someone on our team to lead us against the Porsche opposition," McLaren's Teddy Mayer explained to Eoin Young in an article syndicated to several publications. "With Jackie on our team, Denny and our whole crew will respond to Stewart's ability to rise to a situation. This will help Denny to perform to his maximum which may become very important if Porsche comes up with the type of car we feel they are very much capable of."

In other words, Mayer had made a straightforward, cold-blooded business move. Anyone in his position would have. He knew Penske well; he had raced against him in opposing teams, had raced alongside him in parallel teams, and had dealt with him over the sale of cars. Teddy knew what a threat Roger would mount. Signing Stewart was simply a matter of protecting one's interests. He was honestly surprised to hear a torrent of criticism.

The Can-Am was in so much trouble, it was loudly suggested, that McLaren ought to show more altruism. Mayer was "castrating the Can-Am" (as Young expressed other people's protestations) by stealing away from his only proven opposition the one driver who had been successful against his. Not only that, he had dumped the first American series champion! And how could he be so mean to the poor man from Lola?

Stewart, too, drew criticism, a sentiment implicit in the number of times and places he was quoted as saying unrepentantly, "Show me a gracious loser, and I'll show you a loser."

In the expressions of dismay can be sensed a fundamental handicap embedded in the Can-Am. Though nominally a professional auto racing championship, it was still seen by many people, even by many of its participants, as good old SCCA sports car racing—emphasis on "sport." Despite the gaudy prize structure, despite the world-class competitors attracted by all that money, despite the international repute they conferred upon the series, despite the deep involvement of major corporations, some of which deployed their highest technologies and most valued personnel, and despite the thorough professionalism displayed by the one organization that had truly done the job right—despite all the evidence to the contrary, somehow, to many people, the Can-Am was still the happy old Bruce and Denny Show. Just down-home, good-time weekend road racing among friends.

Putting Stewart in a McLaren was overkill; darn it, it was just *greedy*. No, said Teddy Mayer. It was just business. His business.

Can-Am '72 would be serious.

As it turned out, Stewart didn't drive for McLaren. Just days before the first round, a doctor prescribed a month's complete rest to treat a duodenal ulcer. Mayer called back Peter Revson—who had not been "dumped" at all, but promoted to F1 at his request. The Revvie and Denny Show would go on the road again with a pair of all-new McLaren M20-Chevrolets, more aerodynamic, more agile, and more powerful.

But not as powerful as Mark Donohue's new twin-turbocharged, Penske-prepared, lavishly sponsored Porsche 917/10K.

Was this to be a repeat of 1971's two-make contest? Wasn't any other team preparing a strong assault on fortress Can-Am? Hopefully. Shadow was coming back, with the same key personnel and basically the same sound car now running on conventional wheel sizes and with new bodywork featuring hip-mounted radiators. BRM was said to be bringing back two P167s. Lola was building an all-new T310, one emphatically not embodying the T260's design precepts, and was looking for the best available replacement for Stewart. Of course, both Lola and McLaren had sold cars to privateers, as always, and so had Porsche, although these didn't have the turbo engine.

It remained to be seen what the lack of a series sponsor would mean. Though officials uttered brave statements about eager replacements hovering in the wings, none ever stepped on stage. Thus, there would no longer be a year-end points fund. At least the competitors had been somewhat weaned from that—entirely by chance?—the previous year. CASC and SCCA did guarantee the same race prize moneys this year, including the qualifying bonuses. Distributions were a little different, however; of the $75,000 per event, $10,000 (instead of $20,000) would go to only the top five qualifiers (rather than ten), and the rest would be paid out to the first twenty-five finishers (an addition of five).

Beyond dollars, though, Johnson Wax had pumped in a lot of valuable promotion. Stirling Moss had been a credible, visible, and energetic series spokesman. The sponsor also had assumed a burden many road race promoters of that primitive day apparently found beyond them, that of making the media feel welcome and ensuring they could do their jobs. Perhaps only itinerant journalists, tap-tapping out their race reports in the barren but hospitable "J-Wax trailer" very late on Sunday nights, knew of the baggy-eyed toil of PR man Brad Niemcek to distribute results, news, and tape-recorded quotes to papers and stations across the continent. This fine sponsor would be missed.

As originally announced, the 1972 schedule carried the same ten rounds as before, but St. Jovite dropped out and was not replaced.

Mosport Park, Ontario, June 11, 1972

This was the Golden Anniversary Can-Am, the fiftieth, and we got the nicest possible present: a Porsche. A brand new, big, factory-backed, complicated, expensive, problematical, puzzling, powerful Porsche. And it *worked*. In fair, open competition for grid positions it was *fastest*. It beat the

Mosport: "That thing cut in like a JATO unit!" Revson thinks his M20 (#4) is getting into Turn 1 first. But Donohue's 900hp TurboPanzer is just now coming on-boost. *Pete Lyons*

The Penske-Porsche Partnership

Had you just met Mark Donohue for the first time, you'd have understood immediately why the early 1970s press called him "Captain Nice." It was that smile, so ready, so sunny, so boyish. Mark was such a genial, approachable fellow, so unobtrusively intelligent, so quietly capable at his profession. A university graduate with degrees in both engineering and business and always well-groomed, he was a highly successful race driver who made the oft-maligned sport of speed look so . . . well, so *nice*.

But behind that cherubic Mark Donohue smile lurked a devilish streak. He was a notorious prankster, yes, but it went deeper. As a master of the unlimited-horsepower Can-Am car, he used to have a special term for that form of racing: as he once said, the Can-Am was a "knife fight." He loved it.

Mark and his team, Penske Racing, were in at the beginning of the Canadian-American Challenge Cup series in 1966, and some say they brought it to an end in 1974. That's not strictly accurate, but anyway it's less an indictment than a compliment in the fiercely competitive motorsports arena. "Captain Nice," Roger "The Captain" Penske, and the determinedly competitive auto maker behind them, Porsche, simply fought a better fight than anyone else. And they started by bringing a bigger, sharper knife.

Mark certainly did not go into any racing series intending to shut it down, but it's equally safe to presume he tried his best to dominate it. A mechanical engineer by trade, he began racing on the amateur level in 1957 with various sports and small-bore formula cars. Three SCCA national championships in the early 1960s, as well as an intelligent approach to preparation, notable discipline behind the wheel, and an appealing personality, gradually attracted attention in the professional world. In 1966, at the age of twenty-nine, the club racer suddenly found himself a paid member of Ford's huge GT40 Le Mans program, as well as a key figure in retired driver Penske's new organization.

Donohue and the Penske team ran the last three seasons of the United States Road Racing Championship and the first three of the Can-Am as a privateer operation, with purchased Lola and McLaren chassis and purchased Chevy V-8s. These cars were superbly prepared and driven and carried Donohue to a position of dominance in the USRRC.

But the Can-Am was another matter. Apart from two lucky Can-Am victories in 1966 and 1968, Penske's privateers seldom managed to more than threaten the McLaren factory team. McLaren, enjoying its own chassis- and engine-building facilities, and able to muster the talent and will to exploit the advantage fully, utterly dominated the series from 1967 through 1971. Having been carved up too often, the last time in a single skirmish in 1969, Penske had long since pulled out of the Group 7 fight in favor of other ones, when Porsche called.

The Stuttgart auto maker also bore scars from Bruce's blades. Two fact-finding Can-Am campaigns, in 1969 and 1971, established the fact that good handling, fine driving, and impressive reliability might earn points, but victories called for more horsepower. More than Porsche could get by putting "fat" cylinder barrels on the basic 917 endurance racing motor to achieve 5.4 liters.

By this stage in Can-Am history, many of the original design freedoms had been lost to new rules which restricted aerodynamic downforce—Chaparral-style wings and, later, mechanical ground-effects devices had been banned outright. The startlingly tiny tires of the original Shadow of 1970 turned out to be technological dead ends, so no gains were to be found in reduced frontal area. By 1971, the only freedoms a would-be competitor had left to exploit were a lack of any limitations on engine power and car weight.

Getting the raw power was not the problem. Turbocharged 5.0 test engines were soon blasting out some 950hp and 690lb-ft; impressive numbers but actually fairly modest increases of about 50 percent, a factor anyone else

McLarens in pure over-the-road performance. What a lift.

Innovation is, of course, a very hard road, and there had been a moment only just before the first race when Donohue was doubtful of making it. But at the last minute, he and Porsche engineers solved a fuel calibration problem, and the team went to Mosport in time for several days of solid pre-event testing.

Testing had been underway for a long time, and the team claimed to have racked up 6,000 miles. Quality miles. As far back as January, reportedly, Mark had driven an early, normally aspirated development car around Road Atlanta at record times: 1:16.6, versus the 1:17.42 done officially by both Elford in the 1970 Chaparral and Stewart in 1971's Lola. At Mosport, the best official Group 7 time was still Gurney's 1:16.4

could have been expected to achieve with almost any engine. What came harder was making the test engine drivable on a twisty course, where crisp, timely throttle response at mid-range rpm was vital.

Enter Mark Donohue. While at Le Mans in 1971, where Penske Racing was running a Group 4 Ferrari 512M coupe against the Porsche 917s, Mark and Roger were quietly approached by representatives of the nominally rival factory. In that period, Porsche did not campaign its own cars directly, preferring to contract the job to specialist racing organizations. In Group 4, its primary team was John Wyer's, and it was logical to suppose—the British press certainly supposed—that the British company would go on to handle the upcoming, full-scale Group 7 effort. But working with a team born and based in the U.S. made some logistical sense, and anyway, during early talks between Penske's and Porsche's people, everyone found to their great delight that they spoke the same engineering language.

Donohue was blessed with a very rare racing gift: he was brilliant, both at developing cars to their peak performance and at driving them to that peak. It was not magic; it was talent, brains, experience, competitive fire, and sheer hard, relentless work. Mark started work at once, virtually moving to Stuttgart as he immersed himself totally in developing what he probably already realized would be the most challenging, and ultimately most satisfying, race car he'd ever driven.

Of course, as usual, it was a human challenge that proved toughest. The proud Europeans, perhaps a trifle set in their class-conscious ways, were not used to a mere driver trying to direct engineers. Particular difficulty arose over the engine drivability problem. For some time, the screaming horsepower they were getting at high rpm deafened the test bed personnel to Donohue's complaints about poor idle, mediocre low-speed performance, and bad throttle response on the test track. Time dwindled—Mark was just a little

busy with such extraneous chores as winning the 1972 Indy 500 that May—and after one particularly disappointing test day, Roger announced to the shocked factory men that they'd better brace themselves to skip the first Can-Am race in June.

This, and hands-on work by an exasperated Donohue, finally brought about revisions to the fuel and induction system to make the engine drivable throughout its rpm band. Mark proved it by setting a new lap record on the factory's test track.

Honing the handling to a competitive edge was no simple task, either. Consider that the 1,000-horse turbocar had evolved directly from the 350hp, eight-cylinder type 908 sports cars of the mid-1960s. When Porsche added four cylinders to make the 917 engine, it crammed the 600hp twelve into a very similar, ultra-light chassis with the same stubby, 90.6in wheelbase. The original 917 coupes had been notoriously evil-handling at high speed, and it took a great deal of work before they were tamed by aerodynamic and suspension development. Now, another gross boost in power was revealing further flaws. Donohue again had to brave enemy territory to win the suspension geometry and aerodynamic revisions he knew he needed.

It would be wrong to discount the Porsche factory's enormous contributions to the 917/10K in terms of ability, resources and enthusiasm. Project engineer Helmut Flegl and engine specialist Valentin Schaeffer, in particular, were vital figures. And, of course, it was Porsche's idea in the first place. But the car as a whole probably would not have been a success without the proficiency, experience, and determination of the personnel of Penske Racing. Especially Mark Donohue, who could stop being nice when he had to.

pole of 1970, though in September 1971, Stewart turned a 1:15.1 while qualifying for the F1 Grand Prix. Now, in June 1972, in private practice, Donohue—who had just triumphed at the Indianapolis 500—reportedly lapped Mosport with the turbocar at 1:13.4.

Outsiders who had witnessed this believed the engine was detuned for formal practice the following week. The Porsche just wasn't steaming away from the

corners as hard, they said, nor was it such an obvious handful. Meaning, everyone thought, there must have been a lot more power available at the turn of a screw.

They were right, of course, but they didn't know the whole story. More boost meant less reliability. In fact, that prerace test had ended prematurely with the failure of a gear on the internal shaft which took power from the center of the flat-12's long crankshaft.

There were actually two glistening white-and-red-and-black cars; their standard of preparation was spectacular, and Roger Penske took care to let everyone know it all represented a *lot* of money. That word would be sure to get to Teddy Mayer. But the most effective element of the whole huge psych job was the calm and confident air surrounding the team; of the entire entry, Penske's seemed most ready to race at the first race. For years we'd been wondering why others had been unable to learn the McLaren lessons. Finally someone had. The McLaren team, this time, gave the impression of having been very busy on other projects.

The Shadow team had been busy, too, and in their case they'd been able to concentrate on their revamped Can-Am car. Jackie Oliver had reached some very encouraging speeds at Laguna Seca, and the team made it to Mosport in time for more private testing. But they still looked just a little breathless.

McLaren's first really new design since 1968 was a compact race car, lithe-looking by comparison to the previous year's M8F, but it was not giving its best this week. Both drivers were complaining of understeer, and the story soon circulated that Donohue had been responsible for developing the new tires all the top cars were given, but only the Porsche worked on them. It went beyond tires, though, because Hulme described his M20 as "leaping about from pillar to post" over the Mosport bumps. Neither man was impressed with his brakes, either, while Revson's car—which had logged a grand total of six running-in laps at Goodwood before shipment to Canada—seemed to have something amiss in the fuel injection.

Jackie Oliver, too, was unhappy with the Shadow's handling over the bumps, and his best shot at a qualifying time was spoiled by a speck of dirt in the fuel system. There was also a lubrication problem in a new version of the Weismann gearbox, which the year before had been bulletproof.

As for any Penske Porsche problems, there was a good deal of fiddling going on with valves and linkages in the elaborate turbo system, and one embarrassing moment when a stone-cold transmission cooler burst on startup, spraying red oil into the cockpit.

What it's all about, however, is getting around the race track, and a hike out to the embankment overlooking Mosport's fast, bumpy, plunging first turn revealed what was really happening. Stopwatch-timed, all three Chevy-cars showed themselves capable of getting through the bend in 6.0sec. All three looked more than somewhat ragged doing it, both Revson's and Oliver's doing especially heartstopping things. Both drivers seemed to be actually hurling their bounding cars into the turn; there was lots of

lock-to-lock action, and when the raucous bellow from the engines hardened nearing the exit, the back wheels jumped whole feet towards the edge, so that the cars took up angles that would be almost indecent on a dirt track. Hulme was tidier, but on his quickest lap, his tail too stepped out smartly as he powered out of the corner, so he lifted his foot for an instant.

All this while Donohue's ungainly looking white Porsche seemed to be cruising around smoothly, not bouncing very much, the driver holding a nice, steady, positive lock and quite a steady throttle pedal. The segment times? Consistently 5.8sec. The Porche's rivals would have been well advised not to proceed on any theory that the turbocar was making all its time on the straightaways.

Everyone sensed they were watching history. It was the sound, mainly. Turbo engines were now common in USAC racing, and this had the same "muffled" quality, in that the familiar, smooth Porsche 917 hum seemed to be coming through a restriction. Amid that was an additional soft whistle from the blowers. Although the turbo-12 wasn't as loud as the open-pipe V-8 Chevys, it was very heavy and strong, with an irritating timbre. It *sounded* like 900hp.

Donohue's official best lap was 1:14.2, an average of 119.3mph. Looking back to the first Can-Am held at Mosport, this was a six-year Group 7 gain of 8.7sec and 12.5mph, or 11.7 percent.

More importantly, the Porsche beat the best of the rest by 0.8, the three of them clustered within 0.6. The next closest car was a further 3.0sec away, so for most people, observers as well as participants, it was "*deja-vu.*" For the McLaren boys, it was an experience they'd often visited upon their rivals, but which they themselves had suffered only in the year of the Sucker Chaparral. Teddy Mayer's worst nightmare had come true.

There remained the mere matter of covering eighty more laps. Everybody was keen to see the rolling-start drag race between normal Chevy versus blown Porsche. Donohue admitted to a slight throttle lag, and pointed out that the first corner wouldn't decide the whole race, but he did say, "I hope to be able to mold the start into the kind of start *I* want, rather than the kind *they* want."

Apparently, he did. Even though Revson on the outside jumped the flag a little, and had enough time to form an image of himself getting through the first turn first, by the time he got to the starter's bridge, the Porsche was alongside. From that point, it was no contest. Donohue just drove away.

On the first lap, Oliver took the Shadow ahead of Hulme, but after the transmission trouble he had been ordered not to use bottom gear, and he had to

watch the McLaren accelerate by out of the tight Moss corner. Even so, after just six laps, the box broke again. That left the Orange Elephants alone on the track as so often before, except that this time the picture included the Porsche Panzer contentedly humming and whistling along well in front and going away. By the sixth-lap point, when the Shadow coasted onto the grass, Donohue had a 5sec advantage on Revson. He was getting through the first turn in 5.9sec; the McLaren drivers were taking 6.2.

But what looked effortless wasn't. The Porsche was in trouble. It was an intermittent thing at first, a temporary loss of horsepower-cum-throttle response, and it seemed to cure itself. Mark had time to think he was going to be OK. Then, just before finishing the eighteenth lap, too late to take the pit lane, he felt the engine go seriously sluggish. The car became "undrivable," he said later. He had to go on around the entire nineteenth lap with Revson gaining dramatically. The gap was down to 2sec as Donohue peeled off for the pits.

As the Elephants trumpeted by, one-two, the Panzer guys attacked the enormous, elaborate, heat-reeking 12-cylinder engine with its maze of ducts and valves. Both turbos were sucking air, so they were all right; a process of elimination finally focused attention on a linkage in the throttle system that operated a valve in the inlet manifold, apparently to let outside air in under certain conditions. It had jammed closed. A quick squirt with an oil can freed that up, but then Donohue had to be strapped in again. He'd started to climb out in despair. By the time he whistled back into the fray, the fray was three laps ahead, and the mighty turbocar had sunk to ninth.

For a while, Mark fought back, driving as hard as he could and step by step climbed back up the chart. Eventually, he overtook Milt Minter's non-turbo Porsche, and was third. He also caught Revson, still the leader, and took back one of his lost laps. But Donohue's pace was off a bit, now. Penske had signaled him to cool it, and anyway the Porsche's ungainly, snow-shovel nose section had started to flap, scraping the road until much of it tore off.

The second-place McLaren wasn't having a good day, either. Hulme's oil pressure was down, his throttle was sticking open, and he was worried about a vibration from somewhere—maybe those awful tires. When his leading teammate made up a whole lap and loomed in his mirrors, Denny waved him by. Then the Porsche appeared behind, and easily went by too. That put Donohue on the same lap as Hulme.

Coming around to finish lap seventy-eight, his race all but won, Revson started into the last corner—

and clank-grind-rattle. He lifted his foot, pulled over to the pit wall, and drove slowly along the end of it. He let the engine die, as if intending to park there, but then decided to see if he could make it on around the next lap. He let the clutch out; the engine fired, made maybe two revolutions, and locked up solid, spinning the M20 off the road to the inside, into the chicken wire.

Hulme, driving more cautiously than ever, made it around all eighty laps and trundled under the flag 55.5sec ahead of Donohue. Though he was standing watching, Revson was classified third.

History hadn't been made, but clearly it was just a matter of time.

Road Atlanta, Georgia, July 9, 1972

Racing itself is a matter of time and the management of it. The original second round had been canceled, but nobody took this as an excuse for a holiday. All three of the top teams went to Road Atlanta early for testing.

Two of them wished they hadn't.

On a day late in June, Oliver had his throttles jam wide open approaching the uphill, left-hand second turn at about 160mph. Its front tires smoking but its rears driving hard, the Shadow shot off the track into an embankment. No injuries to the driver, but his side of the tub was crumpled. Luckily, there was still time to truck it back to the California base for a rebuild before the race.

Giant Killer: George Follmer's success with Porsche power went back to 1965, when he and former Shelby mechanic Bruce Burness installed an under-2.0-liter type 904 Carrera engine in this Lotus 23 and snatched the U.S. Road Racing Championship away from Chaparral's Jim Hall. Seven years later, George himself would graduate to giant status as designated driver of the Penske Panzer. *Pete Lyons*

Road Atlanta: Technically, the big news of the weekend is the super-wide, lowline Lola. It's not front-page news. *Pete Lyons*

Then, on the Monday before the race, Donohue crashed. In an accident disturbingly similar to the one that took the life of Bruce McLaren, the Porsche was accelerating along the very fast return straight when its entire rear body lifted off. The car spun and cartwheeled and disintegrated, the whole front of the magnesium chassis ripping off. Mark was left strapped to the engine, his legs sticking out onto the ground.

He remained conscious, and actually didn't think he was too badly hurt, though his left knee was particularly painful. There was some thought of his being able to race the spare car (which under its current bodywork was the same aluminum chassis he'd used for testing here months before). Just in case, Penske summoned George Follmer, who'd driven the Can-Am of 1967 alongside Donohue. Mark, his face wan, accompanied George around the course in a rental car on Thursday. But when a specialist in injured knees for the Atlanta Falcons football team saw Donohue's, he ordered surgery. This was carried out on Saturday. The prognosis for driving again that year was doubtful.

So some of the shine had gone off another of those Greatest-Can-Am-Years-Evers we'd been hearing about for, well, six years.

Fortunately, in the real world we still had some solid pros determined to win this race and well worth watching as they tried. McLaren's testing had resulted in improved aerodynamics, better brakes, different springs, and wider track dimensions, and with another new type of Goodyear fitted, the M20s were going very much better than at Mosport.

There was still a spot of engine bother, though. On Saturday afternoon, Revson was hurtling flat out past the pits, going for a time, when a rod bolt broke. The rod ran for it straight through the Reynolds block, and the crank locked up solid. Peter went for a wild sleigh ride down into Turn 1, absolutely unable to see for smoke in the cockpit, but there was no further harm done.

Unless it was to the composure of McLaren's mechanics. One of them came back from inspecting the huge smear of emulsified oil and yellow coolant on the track with his hand cupped. It was full of little metal fragments, among which could be discerned a neatly chopped-off chunk of camshaft. The lad was giggling. He had the Right Stuff.

Another driver to put on a great show that day was David Hobbs, the reigning SCCA F5000 champion. Lola's new Group 7 car was finally ready for him, or almost; with all of 100 miles of testing in England behind it, the long, broad T310 arrived at Atlanta airport late Friday night as essentially a kit of parts. These were together in time for Saturday practice, during which Hobbs, never having driven the car before, was taching some 180mph along the straight when a rear suspension joint snapped. There ensued a long period of violent spinning, but nothing worse. "It didn't hit anything, so when it stopped I climbed out, did a bow, and collapsed." Three weeks earlier his F5000 Lola had done a similar thing at Watkins Glen, writing itself off between the pale blue steel rails at 170.

The rebuilt Shadow, too, was disappointing, Oliver experiencing one problem after another: the rear radiators were overheating in the hot, muggy climate, a fuel pump failure delayed finding out if new scoops worked, then a half shaft broke, and on Sunday morning so did a transmission gear. "We're four seconds quicker than last year and we're still in trouble," Peter Bryant grinned to *Autoweek*'s Leon Mandel. "It's like trying to chase a kangaroo uphill."

Several newcomers came to Atlanta. One was Stewart's F1 teammate François Cevert, who was driving the ex-Revson M8F. Never having driven anything remotely similar, he qualified it fourth, 2.74sec faster than it had gone the year before.

Follmer settled into his surprise assignment with impressive professionalism, driving the powerful Porsche hard enough to spin it a couple of times while evaluating different tires. He said he thoroughly understood there were two conditions to his renewed employment with Penske: he was not to break the car, and he was to win.

Denis Hulme had his own idea about that. All the changes to his McLaren had worked, and it was running well, and it was as fast as the Porsche. Faster, in fact, by twenty-nine–one-thousandths of a second. Their effectively joint 1:14.1 was well over 3sec faster than the old 1970/71 record. What a promising Can-Am it appeared.

But it would be hard to single out a more disappointing Can-Am. Oh, it started out great. From the outside Follmer powered ahead of Hulme into the first turn, but he didn't get away. Both McLarens

Road Atlanta: Penske, leaning over the driver's side of the cockpit, has summoned Follmer. Donohue can only stand by on crutches in case somebody wants his advice. *Bill Warner*

Road Atlanta: The McLarens can run with the Porsche in practice, but the race makes history. *Pete Lyons*

tucked right up under the twin white rudders and stayed there for the whole first lap, and the whole second lap, and half of the third lap. That's when Revson's engine shut itself off on the long straight.

Peter knew what to look for. Earlier that day the magneto rotor had broken, so before the race he'd tucked a spare in his pocket. He was busy replacing it there at the side of the track when his teammate went airborne right in front of him.

Hulme was staying with Follmer, the McLaren losing a little on the straight—only reaching 188mph, whereas the Porsche was touching 198—but making it back elsewhere. Sliding out of the tight double-ninety onto the straight for the fifth time, Denny settled into his pursuit mode, knowing he wasn't going to gain anything there. As the pair neared a crest in the road, accelerating through about 175mph, he prudently moved to the right, as always, to keep the M20's wedge-shaped prow out of any turbulence trou-

ble. It was exactly what he'd done the previous four times, and the car had sailed over the rise flat and steady.

This time it flew. The front wheels lifted, the belly climbed the wind, and the McLaren flipped straight over backwards and crashed to earth upside down. The roll bar bent forward about 45 degrees but didn't snap off.

Revson was there as quickly as the courseworkers and helped turn the car over. There was a flash fire then, but it was quickly powdered out. Denny was awake, able to talk, able to wiggle his toes, unable to explain what had happened. Revvie saw him off in the ambulance, then turned back to get his own car running. By the time he did, he'd lost twenty-three laps, and was dead last. He called in at the pits for a talk, then set fastest lap, a new race record. Soon after that, the oil pressure dropped off, so he called it a day.

Oliver had the cockpit fire extinguisher pipe come loose and jam his gas pedal wide open for the second time in two weeks. No crash this time, and a pit stop freed the pedal, but then the Shadow's engine failed.

Hobbs, freely admitting he was unsettled by the sight of Hulme's McLaren inverted at the same place his own Lola had spun, treated the rest of the race as a test session.

Cevert was holding second and closing on Follmer at one stage, but his engine gave up. That put Peter Gregg into second place in his non-turbo 917/10, but he ran out of fuel. So Gregg Young, owner of the Cevert car and driving its ex-Hulme sister, inherited the position in turn. Nobody who was left was going fast. Several drivers came in to have pails of water thrown over them. It was hot and sticky and dull.

The Panzer kept running, so Follmer kept his job, but that was about the best thing to be said for one of the most anticlimactic moments of history in Can-Am, uh, history.

Watkins Glen, New York, July 23, 1972

There was still time for hope. McLaren had lost a Road Atlanta Can-Am to a Porsche once before, yet had bounced back. In the nine days before unloading at Watkins Glen, the team pulled a replacement car together for Hulme. It was actually the original chassis, the prototype used for testing. By the time it got to the Glen, it looked absolutely state-of-the-M20-art, with all the latest modifications. This was one of those occasions when McLaren class really showed. Anyone who'd missed Atlanta would never have known anything had gone wrong.

Hulme's class was showing, too. The Bear still had a sore head, actually a sense of disconnection be-

tween brain and body which he experienced in the high-speed, high-g swerves up "Graham Hill" onto the long straight. Denny dealt with that most times by easing his foot, but reckoned he could keep it down for one banzai lap, and he did. His grid time of 1:40.472 meant nothing in relation to previous Group 7 times, because once again the track had been changed, but it beat the previous October's F1 pole on the same new track by 2.2sec. It would stand up the following October, too, by eight-thousands of a second.

But Revson was even quicker, well over a second quicker, and we had an all-McLaren front row. First time this year.

What of the Porsche? That's what everybody else wanted to know. Especially the crowd of Continental correspondents the factory had flown over to watch its Can-Am Panzer crush the Kiwis. How do you say egg-

on-the-face in German? The turbocar just wasn't working this weekend. Follmer came within 0.1sec of Hulme, but a second-row grid place was nowhere under the circumstances.

What was wrong? Who can say. The Penske style of press relations was cold-eyed unresponsiveness to serious inquiry. Reports did circulate that the engine wasn't up to snuff, being the unrefreshed Atlanta unit, and also that the chassis was responding badly to tire vibration.

As at Atlanta, Cevert was fourth fastest in the year-old M8F. Hobbs was much happier with the new Lola after Carl Haas' mechanics had worked hard to exorcise its various demons. That included exorcising its brake servo mechanism over the back fence, as well as changing the twin-radiator cooling flow from "parallel-connected" to "series-connected," adding aero fences to the nose, and raising the low-slung rear wing into cleaner airflow. The Shadow mechanics, too, were working on their cooling problems, finally adding a third radiator, while they short-cut their unaccustomed transaxle troubles by changing brands to Hewland. Oliver joined Hobbs on the third row.

For the first time, only a couple of Saturday's enduro cars stayed on to play Can-Am racer. Restricted to 3.0 liters, now, they were just too slow—their best time, recorded during the Saturday race by co-winner Jacky Ickx, was a Ferrari 312P's 1:47.2.

A couple of the little-car drivers were interested in trying out Group 7 power, though. Reine Wisell stood in for Tom Heyser, a schoolteacher who owned 1971's unraced, spare Lola T260 (known as "The White House Car" for its only public appearance that year) but who had sprained his wrist. Another, Jean-Pierre Jarier, was standing around when Sam Posey decided he'd rather not drive NART's big Ferrari 712M.

This was the same monster-motor car Andretti had debuted here last year, but all too obviously nothing had been done to it since. About its handling, Sam said, "It feels like a combination of chassis flex and bump-steer." Perhaps Mario heard that. He was here—he was co-winner of Saturday's race—but he graciously allowed the fearless Jarier to beat him to Sam's seat and a back-row start.

There's no reason to dwell on the race. Hulme got ahead of Revson into the first turn, and stayed there the rest of the day. Revvie set fastest lap, and clearly felt no compunction about beating Denny out of his "Can-Am Comeback," but his rear brakes were running hot, and anyway, every time he got close behind, his car lost aerodynamic balance, so he couldn't pull off a pass. Finally, his manager signaled him to settle for second.

If a dull race had a bright star, it was David Hobbs. Driving the Lola hard enough to make it wob-

ble and puff up dirt from the roadsides, he scrambled past car after previously faster car, and finally outbraked Follmer's not-so-mighty turbo Porsche in a startling inside-at-the-apex move that made him third. So fiery was Hobbo's driving that it must have overheated him. Late in the race he had to stop for the ever-popular water bucket treatment, which dropped him to fourth at the end.

That was behind Cevert's private McLaren, now. Follmer, obviously struggling, had finally come in to report a bad front-end vibration and also a serious loss of power. A new set of tires was applied to the one problem while the other required a new return spring on one of the same manifold valves that had given trouble at Mosport. Porsche's guests had 2min, 50sec to study the supercar while it was stationary. It wound up fifth, two laps down.

The Shadow had another dismal race. It started with a brake pad installed backwards, and after a pit stop to put that right, the brakes were spongy. Oliver finally hit a guardrail.

So the Orange Elephants were back on top of the Can-Am. Hulme had scored his twenty-second victory and his factory's thirty-ninth and was well in the lead of the points race toward his third championship.

Happily, it was impossible to foresee that Watkins Glen 1972 would mark the end of the era.

Mid-Ohio, Lexington, Ohio, August 6, 1972

Mark Donohue came to Mid-Ohio with cast, crutches, and icy determination to get the Porsche working again. He succeeded. Follmer put it on pole. He led into the first turn. He led the first lap by 2sec. He kept increasing his lead until increasing rain turned the newly resurfaced track into a skating rink. Then he spun twice. But he never lost the lead, and he won.

A great many other things happened during a really interesting weekend, but none of them wound up mattering. Hulme's M20, displaying further aero tweaking on its nose, was second-fastest qualifier by a very narrow margin. Revson was only a little off that pace. The new, smoother surface let both McLarens finally beat previous Group 7 speeds here, and let them do so without hammering themselves to bits.

Unfortunately, none of that mattered. Revson beat Hulme into the first turn to chase Follmer, but soon dropped back with ever-worsening handling, and finally clanked to a stop when something broke in the transmission. Hulme kept the Porsche in sight for a while and glimpsed it again when the rains came on but got tangled up with

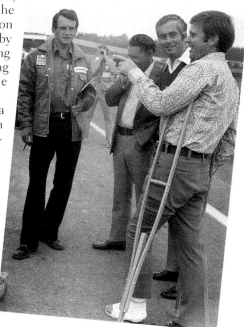

Mid-Ohio: They need him after all; Donohue accelerates his rehabilitation by talking the Panzer back up to speed. Roger Penske appreciates his mood, but the factory's Helmut Flegl doesn't seem sure what to make of this amazing American.
Pete Lyons

Mid-Ohio: At the start, Follmer just whistles into the distance (far, far left), leaving the McLarens and the Shadow in their own dust. *Pete Lyons*

Mid-Ohio: Sudden rain almost changes everything; Follmer finds the Porsche (#6) a major handful, but Oliver's Shadow (#101) is in its element. Everybody else gets out of the way—or out entirely. *Jim Chambers*

another car, bent his nosepiece, and decided it was time to stop for rain tires. It was the first of *five* tire stops he was going to make, one because of a flat, the rest because of constantly changing conditions, drier-to-wetter-to-drier-again. He did manage the fastest race lap, on his last lap, but that didn't matter to the outcome. Having dropped four laps, he finished fourth. Later, with a sort of me-mum-told-me-there'd-be-days-like-this smile, Denny quipped, "After the first stop I decided we might as well go tire-testing, you get five bucks a mile for it."

There was a good early-going battle between Oliver, fourth-best qualifier in the Shadow (actually a

new, second Shadow), and fifth-fastest Hobbs in the Lola. But the rain broke that up, when the Lola became so unmanageable on the wet road that Hobbs brought it in for tires—three times, eventually. Oliver, however, found the rain brought out the best in the Shadow. He never stopped, and his driving on slick tires was magnificent to watch. Though he'd gone a lap down to the Porsche, in the worst of the wet he caught it again.

Follmer was now struggling. Though the engine had been fitted with smaller-diameter turbos, which improved its low-end throttle response for this tight course,

one could see from trackside that it was coming on too strongly too suddenly for the conditions. Compounding that problem was a set of new rear tires larger in every dimension: 28in tall, they were mounted on rims 19in wide and measured 16in across the tread. That Follmer only spun twice was a testimonial to tremendous skill.

Oliver finally passed back onto the same lap and went on to score a most impressive second place in the Shadow's first finish of the season.

Elkhart Lake, Wisconsin, August 27, 1972

Shadow's second car had been devoted to the team's turbocharged-Chevrolet development program. That engine wasn't yet ready to try in public, but now that the second car was in the East and race-blooded, it seemed worthwhile to run both. Joining Oliver was rising Brazilian driver Carlos Pace. He took over the older chassis, which remained in its Atlanta configuration while Oliver worked out some aerodynamic experiments with the new one. But both black cars proved mechanically malevolent, and neither driver managed many laps.

Mid-Ohio's grid sheet had been intriguing, but Elkhart's was next to meaningless. As commonly happened here, a conflicting USAC date kept some significant cars idle on Friday, and a real frog-strangler of a rainstorm did the same on Saturday. Hulme, though, was on duty Friday, when he clipped more than 2sec from his M8F pole time of the previous year. He did nearly as well while setting up his absent teammate's M20.

Like Revson, Follmer didn't start practice until Saturday, when both found Road America as slick in the wet as ever. So the grid sheet showed two of the proven top three men starting from the seventh and the thirteenth rows. It was going to be an interesting first lap.

Interesting points among the rest of the pack included front suspension modifications to Hobbs' Lola T310 to lighten its steering and a further elevation of its rear wing plus added front-fender louvers to increase its downforce. Also, two older cars made reappearances. Jean-Pierre Jarier and NART brought the Ferrari 712M back, having discovered a cracked steering part which may have explained some of its evil behavior at Watkins Glen. They'd added full-length downforce fencing to the body. An even more familiar sight was the old ex-Gurney, ex-Brown McLeagle, now driven by Dave Causey. Altogether, the grid extended to a startling thirty-four drivers.

Missing from amongst them, unhappily, was Lothar Motschenbacher. A nasty F5000 accident the week before had left him with a burned arm and a dizzy head, so reluctantly Lothar was ending his un-

Elkhart Lake: After his two spins in the rain in Ohio, Follmer is happy to sit out the Saturday showers in Wisconsin. No matter; Sunday's weather is just what Dr. Porsche ordered. *Pete Lyons*

equalled Can-Am starting streak at fifty-three. But his car was there, driven by F5000 rival (and former de Dion Caldwell driver) Brett Lunger.

Throughout the weekend, rumors buzzed of a much larger, super-powerful—"1,200hp!"—Porsche engine with its cooling fan running backwards to "suck" air from under the car to create ground effects. Such a monster may have existed in Germany, but it didn't appear at Road America, and it certainly wasn't missed.

It took Follmer the first four-mile lap to get to tenth, and Revson to thirteenth. Lap two, and they were sixth and tenth. The main thing to watch, of course, was the gap from Hulme to Follmer. Denny was on a clear track and flying, while George had to carve through the second-class citizens to get at him. By four laps the Porsche was fourth, and by seven laps, he had disposed of Oliver and finally Cevert and was running free, too. Next time around, he did the fastest race lap. The turbocar was into wobbly fishtails out of the right-angled corners and emitting its heavy, whistling, powerful sound up the long straights, and the gap was indeed narrowing: 8.4sec on that lap; 6.2 on the next; opening a bit to 7.4 on the next.

Revson by this point had come through to fifth, but he was 28sec behind Hulme, so he was obviously not able to match Follmer's speed, and the weight was all on Denny's big shoulders. The Bear wasn't going to go down without a fight. But neither was Follmer going to go easy on him. He matched his eighth-lap record. What a battle this was going to be when they came to grips!

Lap eleven, and the gap was just 2.4sec! Lap twelve . . .

No gap at all. Just a big, white, whistling Porsche. No orange car in sight. None. Still none. Where . . .

Parked on the grass. Dead engine. Something in the mag. Damn.

Revson also retired: something in the clutch. Both Shadows quit. So did Hobbs' Lola. Cevert's McLaren

didn't quit, but it slowed; François finished where he started, second but he was stumbling with a sick Chevy. Follmer's thrice-triumphant Porsche was a whole lap ahead.

"So the McLarens were vanquished again," read *Autosport's* report card from Road America:

It's now happened twice in a row, and it's the third time out of the five races so far this year. Even having double the number of cars doesn't seem to overcome the superior Porsche reliability, which must be a bitter pill indeed at Colnbrook, for it was their superb finishing record that helped get the job done five years in a row. Now, at this midpoint in this season, George Follmer with the Porsche has more points. The McLarens have shown better speed on some tracks, but of the four remaining venues only Laguna Seca is a 'handling course' . . .

The McLaren problem was real, and the Kiwi mood after Elkhart was tense.

Donnybrooke, Minnesota, September 17, 1972

Business. Just protecting his interests. That must have been the only reason Roger Penske turned up with *two* 917/10Ks. Two big, white, immaculate, super-powerful Porsche Panzers. Which dominated the grid. And led the race.

And besides, Donohue wanted to drive again. Confounding medical opinion that held he wouldn't be ready to race again this season, Mark was ready in ten weeks. Sooner, in fact. He'd already been testing. In moments of repose, his face still showed pain, but it was time to drive.

Driving a brand-new car—though it was wearing the number 6 Follmer had been using—Mark started practicing on Thursday. That ended with a fuel leak. On Friday he had severe oversteer. On Saturday the balance was better, but it still wasn't as good as Follmer's. This puzzled Donohue the engineer. "The two cars are set up perfectly identically and perfect should be perfect, but mine just isn't handling."

That afternoon, he took the pole.

Donnybrooke: Happy day; driving again takes the pain away.
Pete Lyons

Bruce McLaren Motor Racing fought its hardest to be fastest. The M20s had drilled brake discs, instead of grooved, on all four wheels, and the rear discs were mounted outboard on both cars to get them away from the heat and, possibly, the mechanical distortions of the gearbox. Both rear wings were set back 6in to work in cleaner airflow. Both drivers adopted Porsche-sized rear Goodyears.

In final qualifying, Revson scattered his engine. At absolute maximum speed, near 7000 in top and about 195mph, there was a colossal bang and bits flew everywhere: bits of crank, of rod, of crankcase, of camshaft, and every bit of oil. The track was closed for a good hour while some attempt was made to mop it all up.

After that there was no hope of winning through to the front, but Hulme tried his hardest anyway. It was no good. He came back in growling bearishly about turbocharger screws and people who merely had to turn a spanner to dial up hundreds of horsepower.

The unusual sight presented by the grid, with two identical white cars blocking our view of two identical orange ones, gave rise to much speculation. It was a long race, 210 miles, and the Porsches had been given some 6gal more fuel capacity. One could assume, too, that their screws would be turned back a bit for the same consideration. Would that make the difference? Under race conditions, could Denny and Peter stay with Mark and George? Or, would Donohue just possibly have his screw turned tight and would he go like a rabbit in the early stages, mindful that his knee might give out later on?

And how about Revson's speed in the morning warm-up: his pit hand-timed him at 1:25.6—just the same as Follmer in qualifying.

The green flag waved, and the white front row burst away, chased by the orange second row. Up, up the long, long straight they toiled, reaching up toward 200mph, dwindling rapidly into little blobs of color until abruptly they veered across the banked turn at the end. It was a single white blob, then two orange ones, and a white. Wait for them to come back through the woods . . . There they are! Donohue. Hulme. Follmer. Revson. All absolutely nose to tail, bellowing and scrambling around the last turn like mad-drunk bison. It was the long-awaited race of the year, with nobody holding back and nobody gaining, and it was going on for lap after lap, enthralling and frightening at the same time. How could it last?

Finishing the tenth lap, Hulme tried a run at Donohue, coming out of the last turn low and pulling up side-by-side; up, up the long straight, the Porsche pulled away a length or two, but Denny said later he was satisfied he was going to be able to make all that up and more in the curves coming back. Mark was on the very edge, his Porsche wobbling raggedly—an odd sight for Donohue-watchers. The McLaren was handling like a dream, said Denny, and the engine was strong and clean. On the eleventh lap he settled back in behind Donohue, content to hang there and wait. That's when, partway around the lap, the big 509-inch Reynolds block split, spewed out oil and water, and the bright orange M20 was the head of a long, sad comet of blue smoke and white steam.

Revson remained to pursue the assault, and he hung on closely behind the Porsches. For lap after lap, the spread between the three was 2 or 3sec. It was two against one, and it was a long distance to go yet, but if anyone could get through and past the Penske pair, it was Peter.

Around the back somewhere on the twenty-fifth lap, the second McLaren went missing. Revvie hitched a ride home in an Austin Healey to report, drearily, that it felt like a valve had dropped.

So. The Mark and George Show. Droning around happy as clowns, occasionally swapping places, the pair of them playing at all the old McLaren tricks, rubbing in all the salt they could think of. Both cars were looking much steadier through the turns, now that the pressure was off. They only displayed haste when they came up to traffic, both making a point of slicing past with a lunge before the next corner. Turbo engines don't respond well when balked.

Donohue's left rear tire burst on his forty-fourth lap, while he was ahead of Follmer and diving into the banked first turn at maximum speed. The 917 spun down to the inside; Follmer headed down there, too, but scrambled by in the inside, untouched, as the other car continued spin-

Donnybrooke: The Mark and George Show. *Pete Lyons*

Donnybrooke: French accent. Francois of the flashing eyes is an accomplished pianist, Jackie Stewart's F1 teammate at Tyrrell, and now a Can-Am winner. *Dale von Trebra*

ning on up the banking and over the lip and across the rough ground beyond. Mark was unhurt in his second high-speed misadventure in as many meetings.

From that point it was all over, all over until the last lap, when everyone stood gazing up the track for a white Porsche—but here came a blue McLaren popping into view! Cevert!

The second Porsche was coasting to a silent halt. Out of fuel.

To be sure, there'd been a lot of other people in this race, and now they had to be noted. Cevert's crew, Greg Young's Young American team, having seen the boss' car retire some time before, had long been resigned to another good second place. Now they turned to each other and the world at large with ear-to-ear grins and fingers jabbing "Number ONE!" at each other in frantic delight. In the champagne-drenched winner's circle they heard an insouciant young Frenchman asking them why they'd given him such a bad car. One responded like a shot: "Well, we only do things to it you tell us to do!" The mood was warming. Like Tony Dean's win at Atlanta and John Cannon's at Laguna Seca, this was going to be a famous victory.

The McLaren factory found little comfort in it, but this private McLaren victory happened to represent only the second one for a given car in the same Can-Am: Cevert's M8F was Revson's 1971 Donnybrooke winner. (Previous instance: Surtees' Lola at Las Vegas in 1966 and '67.)

Edmonton, Alberta, October 1, 1972

In the Canadian GP at Mosport, Revson salvaged some of his pride by qualifying on pole (1:13.6; a lot faster than Donohue's official time in the Group 7 Panzer) and finishing second to Stewart. Hulme started third and finished second. Then it was out to Alberta to see about salvaging something of the Can-Am.

On paper, the beginning of round seven looked a lot like number six. Two white cars up front on the

starting lineup, then two in that curious color that used to convey Can-Am domination. Then all the rest, hopeless spear carriers.

But now everyone had it firmly in mind that racing brings the unexpected.

McLaren, fed up with unexpected fragmentation of its engines, had reduced their power levels for Edmonton. They said so. In what quite possibly was an auto racing first—and last?—the team put out a press release about it. The unexpected document wasn't specific, however, so *Autoweek* reporter Leon Mandel went around until he found a team member willing to expand. "Why, they've taken out all those little things they worked so hard to get over the winter to give them that extra 35 horsepower they reckoned they'd need.'"

Even so, Mandel noted, three laps into the first qualifying session, Hulme's engine exploded. Hmmm.

Warmed up now, Leon gleefully logged another unexpected happening:

Gregg Young sailed down the long main straight, got rolling about 180mph and his motor popped. He got sideways, then sideways the other way around, and turned around completely and came up the track backwards still going enormously fast. That, of course, caused a little problem in aerodynamics. The air caught under the big rear wing and lifted the car right up in the sky. George Follmer, who was streaking by underneath him at the very moment he took off said, 'I could see right into the cab and everything was hanging right out, I could see his belts, everything.'

Young flipped end for end four times, came to rest, staggered out of the car and collapsed on the grass. The car was utterly and completely destroyed, not even a souvenir piece of fiberglass was left. Young was rushed to the hospital where his injuries were diagnosed as a bruised right elbow. He entertained twenty at dinner that evening.

The second immortal Can-Am memory in two consecutive race weekends, and both thanks to the Young American team. That had been Denny Hulme's 1971 M8F, by the way.

Hulme's and Revson's M20s did indeed look less competitive this time. Their disadvantage to the Porsche pair during qualifying was a fat second. However, they'd been to Edmonton before, and they managed to avoid a little unexpected embarrassment that befell newcomers Follmer and Donohue. Both Penske cars came back to their pits looking ragged about the nosepieces, thanks to Edmonton's notorious buried-tire corner markers.

It was Follmer on pole this time, but the front of the pack looked just like Donnybrooke's as it shook

the earth at the start line. Up at the end of the long, long drag strip straight, though, something was just slightly different. Something orange was going into the first turn first. It was Hulme's McLaren. He'd beaten Follmer. And Revson had beaten Donohue. Detuned engines, huh?

Denny's detuned M20 rather rapidly built up a lead on George's 917. After three laps, the gap was 5sec. Revson was still third, holding off Donohue.

But on lap four, Revson dropped out of it. His left front fender was scraping the road. There ensued a comedy of miscommunication, because the roar of his blipping engine drowned out what he was trying to shout, and it took an unwanted change of a front wheel and a second stop before he went back to racing, a long way back and very discouraged. How very unexpected to see McLaren pitwork go wrong.

So it was one McLaren against two Porsches, but soon the odds were even again. Follmer dropped back, let Donohue by, and came into the Penske pit. He thought the left front tire was flat, but it turned out to be the left rear. (He'd experienced this once before with the 917, he said. "It's a funny car.") The confusion cost him more than a minute, and dropped him to sixth.

Time for the Mark versus Denny Show. After letting Hulme lead—it would seem—for thirty laps, Donohue picked the far end of the main straight to slip by, and from there just motored into the distance. Only something unexpected could prevent him staying in front all the way, but—it would seem—there were no more dirty tricks left in Fate's funny bag. At the end there was a little confusion with Follmer, who'd done fastest race lap after his pit stop and come up to pass Donohue. Mark actually had missed the fact that Follmer had stopped, and thought he was letting his championship-leading teammate by to win. So Mark's first victory with the Can-Am turbocar to which he had devoted so much of himself came as something quite unexpected to him.

Feeling the need to drop anchor in reality, Mandel hunted up a slide-rule type from Stuttgart. How about it? Were you slow at the start because you were carrying extra fuel? Were you running with the boost turned down? Saving fuel? Conserving tires? Sandbagging? Psyching the Kiwis? What was going on?

"It was all under quite good control," came the reassuring answer. "We were, as planned, running a technical race."

As expected.

Laguna Seca, California, October 15, 1972

Hulme started third in the U.S. Grand Prix at Watkins Glen, and finished in the same position after holding second for a long while. Revson qualified second this time, but dropped out. At least nobody beat his Can-Am pole time. On to California.

Let's make it mercifully quick. We'll quote *Autosport*:

Just before the end Mark Donohue, who had started from pole and led the whole way, slowed down to allow team-mate George Follmer to win the race. That act did not clinch the championship, for it would have been enough to finish second, but the fact is the Penske team are now in the position the McLarens were in during years past. They can decide that, for appearance's sake, the champion can take the race. The race itself was over just after half distance when both McLarens had retired. Together with Jackie Oliver's Shadow, which went electrifyingly well and split the orange cars until springing an oil leak, the three "conventional cars" made a very good show, but it was the exotic, tricky, expensive ones that made it to the finish line trouble-free. It was left to François Cevert, who very nearly didn't make the grid, and started from the back with very little practice, to come in with another excellent finish, in third place.

Laguna Seca: Panzer payoff. Even as they set off on the pace lap, the Porsche team knows there is no one behind to worry them. Follmer (#7) qualified second and only has to finish second to clinch his title. *Gerald Schmitt*

Laguna Seca: Hobbs qualified poorly after bending a spoiler, but the interesting Lola T310 gives a better account of itself in the race. *Pete Lyons*

Laguna Seca: Grumpy Bear. Denny can only wait for the wide-open spaces of the next venue. *Pete Lyons*

What stands in memory from that weekend was the display of talent and skill and artistry by some of the greatest drivers. Can-Am cars were not the delicate, refined instruments of Formula One, but their combination of enormous power with considerable mass, relatively soft springing, and giant, rather pillowy tires, coupled with a diversity of design that was still quite wide, made their open cockpits showcases for driving styles. Especially in qualifying.

Follmer: noticeably smooth, the big Porsche hardly ever getting out of shape but getting along the straight sections with a tremendous rush. He came in saying he thought he should have gone faster, but he didn't understand how; nothing seemed wrong.

Donohue: distinctly wobbly by contrast, teetering through the faster corners with lots of lock-to-lock. In the hairpin he would frequently seem to pitch the car so that around the second half he had some countersteer going, then the car would straighten out and arrive at the exit all nice and tidy before Mark planted his foot and shot away like a rocket. As at Mid-Ohio, both Porsches had smaller blowers which gave audibly less throttle lag for this on-off-on circuit. Their bottom gears were very low for the same reason. The Panzers were looking controllable in the corners, but in the very tight hairpin beginning the pits straight, it was distinctly obvious that both drivers were waiting until the cars were lined up absolutely straight before getting hard on the boost. Then, with a stunning rush, they would just about quadruple their velocity in a few car lengths.

Revson: driving quite hard with several spectacular powerslides out of the hairpin.

Hulme: again by contrast, he almost never let the car get out of shape, yet was getting the very maximum from it. His final few laps at the close of the session were an education. The big orange M20 would come piling down into the hairpin with its huge brakes working to their fullest; Denny would bend the car in to brush the apex in one fluid motion, then apply what sounded like full throttle immediately. His hands never moved the wheel as the car drifted across to the exit, front wheels pointing straight ahead although all four were slipping sideways and the rears were leaving 16in-wide tracks of gray rubber. The McLaren was on much taller gearing than the Porsches, but Denny was still grabbing all four in succession before he got away from the short pits straight. His changes were lightning fast, absolutely without pause in the heavy exhaust blast. You weren't supposed to be able to do that with those big boxes....

Denny never cut a time that pleased him, because he was still running his now-weary Edmonton race engine on Friday, and Saturday was rained out. But, surprisingly, he still didn't think the M20s had much of a chance against the 917s on this "handling course." No, he said, a course like Donnybrooke, wide and flat, was their sort of place. The McLarens liked to maintain momentum. Any Can-Am car was a handful on a tight track, especially when trying to get through traffic, and although one might expect a normally aspirated engine to be better at cutting-and-thrusting, the Porsches had so much more torque they could "lift" themselves back to speed more quickly.

But Riverside was coming up. Wide, flat, and fast. The Bear liked Riverside.

Riverside, California, October 29, 1972

It was very closely held information at the time—even Peter Revson didn't know about it—but Denis Hulme's McLaren went out to qualify at Riverside packing 565ci of Reynolds-block Chevrolet. Yes, that comes to 9.26 liters.

The speed trap showed something was up. Nearing the end of the long, down-trending back straight, George Follmer's turboPorsche was clocked at 210.76mph (in the race he would reach 212.76). Mark Donohue's terminal velocity was 207. These were the highest figures ever seen here, by 10 or 15mph, but what was really intriguing was Hulme's 204.54. Not that much slower at all for a machine that was supposed to be giving away 200hp.

And lap speeds as a whole? There was a general failure to improve on previous times, and the best evidence indicated the track surface this year was from 3 to 4sec "slower" than in 1971. Follmer was finally the only man to beat the existing pole time, and it was by only a quarter of a second. But Hulme was a scant 0.3 behind Follmer. Which put him not behind, but alongside on the grid. Denny hadn't been able to do *that* for months. The second row told a similar story: Revson was very close to Donohue. A tarpaulin less than 3/4 of a second square could have covered the four.

Riverside's barren terrain made segment-timing easy, and the stopwatch showed that the McLarens were getting through the corners as fast as the Porsches, whether the corner in question was the long, banked Turn 9 or the tight, off-camber, double-apex hook of Turn 6. The McLarens seemed to be going deeper by several car lengths into the turns before the brake lights flashed. The drivers reported that the major advantage enjoyed by their turbocharged colleagues seemed to be in the initial acceleration out of the slower corners, and that almost everywhere else on the lap there was no difference.

And what of the reliability factor? Well, Donohue's transmission locked up in Friday practice and spun his mighty Porsche smartly off the track. McLaren didn't have any trouble to speak of during practice this time. However, we know now that Hulme's mega-motor was replaced with something more likely to last for the race.

We know because Denny told us, a week later in his "Behind the Wheel" column:

"Big Bertha" arrived in from Detroit the night before the last day of practice, stroked out to a full NINE liters with a special crankshaft and giving 800 horsepower. It must be the ultimate Chevy. It had the extra 50 horsepower all the way through the range and compared with our 'little' 8.1 liter motors, this one had torque like a traction engine. And the delightful thing was that nobody knew we had it, least of all Roger Penske's Porsche crew. It gave the sort of extra lift off the turns that the Porsches must have been enjoying all summer, and towards the end of the session I started to stand on it, whittling my times down so suddenly that I had eased Mark's Porsche off the front row and

looked like toppling George off the pole before the Panzer brigade had worked out what was happening.

Unfortunately for me the engine had been little more than a morale booster with the life expectancy of a butterfly. We knew it was only going to last out the afternoon and that we'd have to go back to the regular engine for the race. I had strict instructions not to rev over six-five (we run the others to six-eight) and my target was Follmer's pole time of 1 m 31.7 s. With about five minutes to go my pit signal showed 1 m 31.9 s and I knew I was "hot." The track was clearer than it had been but I realized that the engine was starting to lose its crispness. Next time round I edged it to 6500 rpm but still the pit signal showed 31.9 s and the guy was getting ready with the chequered flag to end the session. I tried all I knew to put together the perfect lap round Riverside on that final run but

First cut: Porsche's huge experimental flat-16, displayed here by designer Hans Mezger, offered the power but not the challenge. *Autosport*

Above and next page top and bottom: Final solution: Though it could boast only twelve cylinders, the chosen alternative offered four camshafts, twenty-four spark plugs, two turbos, and the most complex array of ducts, valves, linkages, pipes, and popoffs ever to enchant a Group 7 technofreak. Big power, too—more than 1000, if needed. *Pete Lyons photos*

according to Teddy Mayer's watches it was my third identical lap and the official timers gave me 1.32 flat. It was fun while it lasted.

The last rampage of Can-Am's beloved Bear.

Though they'd lost their first Can-Am championship in five years, and hadn't won a Can-Am race in the previous five tries, for some reason the mood in the Kiwi camp was up. Speculation had been rampant that this would be McLaren's last appearance in the series it had so dominated for so long, but team members said the decision was not yet made. In any case, they all seemed determined to put a 100 percent effort into contesting this last race of the season. This was an improvement in spirit from recent events, and from the grid times it wasn't a far-fetched ambition.

Somewhat lost in the spotlit glare of the David-and-Goliath Show were the efforts of Don Nichols' Shadow team to finish their bitterly disappointing season with positive momentum for the next. Jackie Oliver's fifth-best grid position, while it didn't threaten the front four on time, did best some strong contenders, including four Porsche entrants who now all had turbo engines tucked away in their 917s.

But Shadow now had a turbo of its own. No, not in Oliver's race car, but in the second chassis. Early in the year the team had openly announced it was developing such an engine, and throughout the season its debut had been said to be imminent. Obviously, judging from its performance in practice, it still wasn't race-ready, but this was the last race, the track was close to home, and the sponsor had been very patient.

First, in what was supposed to be secrecy, the turbocharged car was taken to the nearby Ontario Motor Speedway late Friday afternoon for its first shakedown run. That was delayed—Shadow's huge semitrailer got itself ignominiously stuck in the access tunnel. Not until the sun was actually below the hazy western horizon did Oliver drive out onto the huge 2.5-mile oval to run in the engine at a careful 145mph or so.

The engine poured out a fascinating sound, a mixture of a nice, crisp rasp from the crossover exhaust and a whistle from the blowers, all heavy and muted. It sounded extraordinarily like a WWII vintage four-engined bomber cruising around and around the deserted speedway. There were no lights on the jet-black vehicle, of course, and it was running without its engine cover, so as the dusk deepened and Ollie persisted in his task, guided by the white-painted concrete walls, the most visible part of it became the entire turbo system glowing bright cherry red. Misty blue flames poppled from the pipes. That tiny meteor streaking through the gray-blue gloaming was a sight both eerie and portentous. Surely all their ef-

fort and inspiration and devotion would one day bring this relentless team to success.

Unveiled at the track on Saturday, the TurboShadow was the instant center of attention for technology enthusiasts who'd found the latter part of this season rather dry. Mainly the work of Lee Muir, with input from Indy specialists Danny Jones and George Bignotti, it was a formidable-looking package with a lot of shiny, heat-reflective swaddling. To southern stock car star Bobby Allison it looked like "putting antlers on a canary."

But the numbers being quoted were seriously impressive. Apparently the engine was never taken above 5000rpm on the dyno, at which point the horsepower figure was 800 and the torque curve had swelled to 985. Yes, nine hundred and eighty-five pound-feet of torque. The test stopped there because the dyno's capacity was only 1,000.

Allison was on hand to drive the normally aspirated car if the turbo worked—he was well known to be interested in road racing, and Oliver had been doing some stock car racing, so this was not as unnatural a liaison as it might sound. Bobby was disappointed, along with everyone else, when the engine ate one of its own pistons on Saturday and found that so tasty it chewed up most of the rest of itself in the Sunday warm-up. Oliver went back to the conventional car.

Here's how the author called that last race for *Autosport:*

It would be cruel to bring the readership up to the same pitch of anticipation that onlookers felt as the thirty-three starters rumbled and whistled off on their own two pace laps. The let down was too great. From the start, already at a very good speed under the starter's box, Follmer flew like a released arrow up into the flat-out first turn, Hulme tucked in close behind with Donohue and Revson in tow. For several laps it went on like that, a one-two-three-four display of the four fastest road machines on the face of the earth; they resembled a flight of some military aerobatic team hurtling low over the brown desert and arcing into the long shadowy banking. Gradually, gradually, the lead Porsche pulled away from the rest, so that at five laps gone Follmer was some 4 s ahead of Hulme. Gradually, gradually, Donohue was pulling up, and it seemed the McLaren's engine note was off. On the eighth lap Donohue passed into second, and now it was obvious, Hulme was in trouble. Revson was not keeping up with Donohue, for his engine too was not up to snuff, but within two laps he'd caught his teammate and gone by as well. Denny's exhaust beat was rough now, and dirty black smoke was

pouring from the pipes. That was it, then, it wasn't going to be the grand final showdown fight after all. A hard pill, latest in a long series.

Hulme struggled along until he'd seen the leaders lap him twice. Finally, having tumbled down the lap chart to ninth, he drove the dying Elephant into the pits and climbed out. A mechanic was able to drive it on into the garages, but just barely, and Denny actually laughed as his poor engine struggled away to the graveyard. In his column, he said it had started to miss on the third lap, and then described how he was "driving on the oil pressure gauge and getting depressingly slower and slower and being passed by people I hadn't even seen during the season, until finally the engine ate the top off a valve which chewed its way through the piston, dropped into the oil system, the pumps gagged and it was all over."

It wasn't all over for the twin turboPorsches, they still had a race to run out, but they were settled so securely in the lead of it that Follmer was able to return the favor of Laguna Seca and let Donohue go ahead (he let him do it in front of the pits, which some people—including Mark—thought unkind). But just five laps later, Mark swerved off into the pits. Something felt strange, he said. The car was trying to veer to the left, and when Follmer came up alongside on the back straight, weaving to get his attention and gesturing, Donohue decided he'd better not risk another Donnybrooke incident. The Penske crewmen swapped his left rear tire—such a *huge* chunk of rubber—and sent him on his wild, wheelspinning, people-scattering way, then bent to see what was wrong with the tire. Nothing. Whatever was wrong was still on the car.

Mark had rejoined third, behind Revson, but during the remaining ten laps he made very little impression on him. The squadron of low-flying fighters was shaping up to finish that way, Porsche-McLaren-Porsche, but on the checkered-flag lap, as new Can-Am King Follmer hummed by to win and deposed King Revson roared by to take second, Donohue coasted silently past the pits wall, with just enough momentum to cross the finish line. He was out of gas.

Denny Hulme finished a distant second in that year's championship—his points score exactly equaled Milt Minter's, but the McLaren man had at least won two races. Donohue, who Follmer freely acknowledged had been responsible for making the Porsches winners, was a narrow fourth. So badly had the season gone for the factory McLarens that previous champion Revson was sixth, behind Cevert in Revvie's old car.

Jackie Stewart would have needed lots better luck to do any better than Peter.

Top left: Command Center: Mark's office is simple, spare, and straightforward. Space frame tubes seem anachronistic in the monocoque age, but those in this Mosport race car are magnesium. That's a helmet on the floor. *Pete Lyons*

Top right and bottom: Nose know-how: Throughout the evolution of the Can-Am car, a prime problem was keeping the front end nailed down. During early testing, Penske's first Porsche wore a relatively simple fascia with a shallow concave profile, and a relatively modest rear wing. Donohue and the factory aerodynamicists tried several other configurations, including the "venetian blind" array, but it wasn't until the ungainly slats and their channels were cut away that enough downforce was generated to balance the finalized 917/10K's enormous rear wing. *Joseph H. MacGregor/Penske Enterprises/ Dave Friedman Collection.*

That winter, Teddy Mayer tallied the bottom line of this least satisfactory of Can-Am seasons and made a decision: McLaren was pulling out. Just good business.

Cars of the Can-Am 1972
Porsche 917/10K

The only mainstream automaker ever to commit itself to a serious Can-Am program, Porsche made preliminary forays in 1969 and 1971 with two topless versions of its 917 endurance racing coupe. Helped by strong mechanical reliability—only two retirements in thirteen starts—Switzerland's Jo Siffert wound up both seasons fourth in the points standings.

However, Seppi never managed to finish a race higher than second, and then only by outlasting faster machines. Lap times made it painfully obvious that, no matter how impressive the ultimately 5.4-liter 660hp, reportedly 1638lb supercar may have looked on the shop floor in Germany, on the tracks of North America the 917/10 of 1971 was no competition for the even lighter, more powerful McLaren M8Fs. The torque gap yawned even wider—at about 450lb-ft, the Porsche fell some 200lb-ft short of the 8.3-liter Chevys.

To match the McLaren torque-to-weight ratio by dieting, the Porsche's already sketchy fiberglass bodywork, diaphanous aluminum-tube chassis, and inherently massive quad-cam, opposed-12 engine would have to sweat off something like another 35 percent; obviously impossible. The only option was a whole new engine concept.

Ever thorough, the German firm explored two concepts. One was a physically bigger unit: an experimental flat-16 with a displacement of 7166cc and an output of 880hp. This mother of a motor probably would have done the job, but there was a more technically intriguing line of investigation: turbocharging. The notion was not new, not even in road racing, but so far nobody had made an exhaust-boosted engine

work really well on a road course. The challenge was irresistible.

As finally unveiled at Mosport in 1972, the 917/10K (K for "*Kompressor*") had a 5.0 engine with two Eberspächer truck turbos. There was one common wastegate, and a balance pipe between the two inlet manifold "logs." A high pressure Bosch fuel-injection pump fed fuel to the twelve downdraft inlets above the throttle butterflies.

Can-Am regulations imposed no boost limit, but Porsche fixed maximum operating pressure at 1.5 bar on the common European scale. At this level the dyno would show close to 1000hp at 7800rpm, and 725lb-ft at 6400. Normally, though, a reduced boost of 1.3 was preferred, which yielded a little less than 900hp and not quite 700lb-ft. There was no intercooler, and the single wastegate's adjusting screw was not yet under the driver's control.

An elaborate array of air valves to reduce throttle lag was the most complex part of the system. Some were connected to the throttle linkage in such a way as to dump excess manifold pressure when the throttles were closed, thus reducing back pressure on the turbine wheels. Other valves operated independently, but were spring loaded to admit atmosphere when the

George Follmer, Can-Am Champion

Forceful and effective in any kind of car he tried, and a winner in most, this Californian didn't show his talent until a little later in life than do many drivers. He was twenty-five when he took up autocrossing with a Volkswagen in 1959 and didn't turn pro until he was thirty-one. But that year, 1965, he won the United States Road Racing Championship by outpointing Jim Hall. Coincidentally, he did it in a Porsche-powered car—one he created by installing the German engine in a tiny English Lotus 23. Moving on to the Can-Am in an unusually wide variety of bigger iron didn't bring any immediate success, but in 1969 he celebrated his first wins in both SCCA Trans-Am sedans and USAC Indy cars. Several more Trans-Am victories for several factory teams culminated in the series championship in 1972; he clinched that title only days before he stepped into Mark Donohue's Porsche at the Road Atlanta Can-Am. Follmer's future would include an impressive rookie showing in Formula 1 in 1973, when he finished his first two Grands Prix in the points and a second Trans-Am title in 1976. Today he remains busy with vintage racing, flying, and business ventures. *Dave Friedman photo*

Subtle but significant, the open underside worked with the topside extractor vents to create a ground effects "suction." *Pete Lyons*

Coke bottle: Wooden model of the McLaren M20 chassis shows the shaping to bring air into the hip-mounted radiators. *Pete Lyons*

inlet manifold pressure dropped below a certain level as the driver's foot went down.

All this plumbing and valving and linkage added 75lb to the massive opposed-12's package weight, bringing it to about 625. Not a high price for 50 percent more power. (The big sleeveless aluminum Chevy of the time scaled about 450lb.)

The existing three-plate 917 clutch turned out to be adequate for the K-model, but a completely new transaxle carried only four forward speeds, rather than five. A larger final drive crownwheel pushed the axle centerline back a little, resulting in a slight wheelbase increase from 90.6 to 91.2in. Initially, fuel tank capacity was just under 80gal (U.S.), but after a race was lost by running out of gas, an auxiliary tank of 6gal was added in front of the right rear wheel.

As always, Porsche employed its familiar space frame construction, making most chassis of aluminum tubing. However, one 917/10K used magnesium (in a playful mood with outsiders, Mark Donohue enjoyed claiming the material was "unobtanium") which saved 39lb at the cost of some stiffness. According to figures freely released by the factory afterward, the car with the mag frame weighed about 1760lb empty of fuel—considerably more than outsiders were told at the time, and still a good 200lb heftier than contemporary McLarens. The two aluminum-framed cars that replaced the crash-destroyed mag car scaled more than 1800.

So the Porsche was still on the porky side, but the twin turbos made all the difference. Their great power was used less to get the car up the straights than around the turns. The original 917 coupes had been designed for Le Mans' long straights, primarily, but in the Can-Am the important factor was cornering speed. After exhaustive trials of various frontal configurations, Donohue helped evolve the /10K's distinctive "snow shovel" nose. This incorporated fender-top louvers and an open bottom to generate ground effect "suction," and was able to balance the downforce of a huge rear wing cantilevered behind the tail. On Porsche's "steering pad," where the car could be driven around in circles 623ft (190m) in diameter, a best lateral cornering force of 1.61g was recorded at about 85mph. Of course, at higher airspeeds the downforce and hence the cornering power would increase exponentially. Testing indicated the body could generate downforce equal to the car's weight—presumably about 2500lb with driver and full fuel—at 200mph.

Journalist Doug Nye has told of taking an earlier g-number of 1.54 to McLaren designer Gordon Coppuck for comment. "[H]is jaw dropped."

According to Porsche's computer—and who would dare doubt it—the 917/10K could go up 0 to 60 in 2.1sec, 0-100 in 3.9, and 0-200 in 13.4.

Road & Track listed the Porsche at $124,000. Thus in six years, a top Group 7 car had gone up about twice in power and about eight times in price.

McLaren M20

McLaren had dominated Can-Am racing for five years by establishing a method of operation that nobody

Works in progress: The last Can-Am McLarens never reached their power potential, but their performance was almost strong enough. *Pete Lyons*

Sucker nose: Like Porsche, McLaren cut away the bottom of its front bodywork in hopes of creating ground effects. Carbon-fiber "ropes" form a reinforcing network on the underside of the hinged fiberglass panel. *Pete Lyons*

Next page: McLaren's mega motor: Though the factory never raced its turbo-Chevy, the team did turn up at Riverside with a normally-aspirated one stroked to 9.26 liters, nearly one liter larger than usual. According to official team documents made available by this M20's present owner, Bob Lee, the mammoth showed 787hp at 6400rpm and 740lb-ft at 4400. It only lasted a few laps of qualifying, but while it lived it boosted the Bear past Donohue's TurboPanzer to the front row of the grid.. *Pete Lyons*

else seemed able to copy. Finally, 1972 brought the Kiwis an opponent they were unable to match. Porsche could manufacture its own engines and transmissions, not just its chassis. It also had its own state-of-the-art proving grounds at Weissach. The number of specialized personnel available far outstripped McLaren's staff. So did financial resources; Porsche/Penske were thought to have spent some $2,000,000 on their first-year TurboPanzer effort, while Teddy Mayer has stated that McLaren's annual Can-Am budget never much exceeded $500,000.

Faced with all that, the boys at Bruce McLaren Motor Racing did the only thing possible. They put up a great fight.

First, they launched a turbocharger program of their own. That was not successful, but they went ahead with the all-new chassis built for it. The M20's most immediately noticeable points were twin hip-mounted radiators and an airfoil in the place where its predecessor had a single front radiator. Stripped of its bodywork, the aluminum monocoque chassis revealed a pronounced "coke bottle" shape in plan view, to bring air into the radiators.

The half-length tub was fabricated as before of riveted and bonded aluminum sheet but did without a separate front bulkhead made of steel, was about an inch shallower, and had a fifth fuel cell behind the seats. As before, the big Reynolds 390-alloy sleeveless

Chevrolet block was part of the chassis, braced laterally by tubular struts. Suspension parts front and rear were basically carried over from 1971's M8F, but the brakes were bigger, and a longer bell housing increased the wheelbase by 2in to 100.

Bodywork repeated McLaren's Batmobile theme—in fact, a 1971 M8F body had been cut apart, draped over the first M20 chassis, and the gaps filled in to make the new mold. The M20 came out about 25lb lighter than the previous model, it was said, and more efficient aerodynamics gave a trap speed of 194mph at Watkins Glen, ten better, with essentially the same engine power. Drivers Hulme and Revson reported better handling, reduced understeer letting them use more power sooner out of corners. Denny, always a fan of powerful brakes, called the M20's "mighty." For McLaren customers, Trojan put together about ten production versions of 1971's M8F called the M8FP.

Shadow Mk III

For its third Can-Am season, Don Nichols' Shadow team took an almost entirely conventional approach. Shelved were the previous small-diameter tires in favor of Goodyears in normal sizes: 23.5in OD on 15x11 rims at the front, 26.8 on 15x17 at the rear. However, they supported the same actual car as in 1971. Designer Peter Bryant was able to fit the new tires and their appropriate suspension geometries to his existing aluminum monocoque chassis. He even retained the inboard brake location at the front, since there had been very little halfshaft trouble during the previous season, and relocated the rear brakes inboard as well.

A total of fifty-five detail changes justified the new "mark" number. Apart from the larger wheels and consequently higher body profile, the biggest visual difference was at the front. Like McLaren's Coppuck, Bryant moved his radiators to the sides of the car and filled the vacated nose space with an adjustable wing, one much larger than that which had formed the top of the 1971 car's radiator duct. Because of the bigger wheels, wheelbase increased by 2in to 98. Track dimensions, however, remained the same at the front, 60in, and increased by only 1in at the rear, to 57. Overall body width went up by 5in, to 77 (author's measurement). Weight went down by a massive 160lb. Distribution was a conventional 40/60.

The team began testing in ample time, and at Laguna Seca Jackie Oliver took 0.8sec off the best time of the previous year's McLaren M8F, which indicated that after all the modifications the Shadow itself was 2.5sec better. He was pleased to note the handling stayed more consistent with changing fuel loads, too. In the background Shadow's new engine man, Lee Muir, was developing a turbocharged ver-

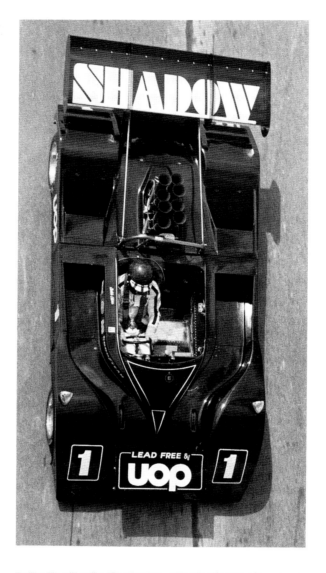

Spy shot: Captured at Mosport, the Shadow Mk III reveals its separate nose wing, the channels ducting air to the flank-mounted radiators, and the inboard front brake discs. *Pete Lyons*

Ontario Motor Speedway: Can-Am transporters have come a long way—too long, in this case. The Shadowmen are here to try out their turbocar on the high-speed oval, but first they have to unstick their truck. Already suited up, Oliver watches with team owner Don Nichols (in sport coat). *Pete Lyons*

sion of the Chevrolet, and a second car was built to test it. This had greater fuel capacity—up from 76 to 84gal—and stronger driveline parts to stand up to a projected output of 1200hp.

Unfortunately, a promising beginning faded away to nothing. The turbo engine never did become race-ready, and there were unforseen problems with the previously reliable Weismann transmission, which prompted a time-consuming change to a Hewland. There was also some unexpected cooling trouble, causing mid-season delays to revamp the bodywork and radiator ducting. The front wing theory didn't pan out either, not even when a big Lola T260-style "cowcatcher" was tried in practice at Elkhart Lake. Finally, the front wing idea itself was discarded, leaving just the central channel between the front fenders to produce downforce.

Lola T310

From narrow and blunt to broad and sharp; Lola's new Can-Am car showed a reversal of aerodynamic thinking only seen before between certain successive Chaparral models. Developed through wind tunnel testing by bodymaker Specialized Mouldings, the T310's startlingly longer, lower, and wider shape gave a better ratio of downforce to drag than any previous Lola body. The nosepiece was, in effect, a huge shovel, designed to scoop up a load of air. The rear wing was well back and well down to minimize overall drag. As on the T260 of the year before, the radiators were in the flanks and fed by body-top inlets either side of the cockpit. Scoops inboard of the front fenders cooled the brakes.

The full-length tub was a conventional structure of aluminum alloy, except that it was so wide the 78gal of fuel didn't need all the volume available; under the visible tops of the monocoque sills there were air-gaps of about 4in to the upper sides of the actual tanks. Further lowering the center of gravity was the installation of the engine at a 2-degree rake angle. Much of the chassis running gear, including the brakes—inboard at the rear—were straight off the previous year's T222 production model. Unlike the inboard-spring T260, the T310 had a conventional front suspension layout. Wheel diameters were all 15in, with 11in rims in the front, 17 in the rear.

At 105.5in, the new Lola had the longest wheelbase ever seen in the Can-Am; at 85.5, it had one of the greatest overall widths, 10.5in up on the T260; track dimensions at both ends were 66in, eight more; at 180in overall, it was 41in longer than the original T260. Official empty weight was 1550 lb.

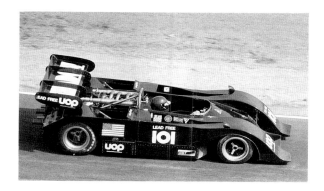

Top left and right: Turbo tryout: By Riverside, Shadow has given up on the wing in front, but is still trying to make its twin-turbocharged Chevy work in the back. After one look at the bristling installation, stock car racer Bobby Allison is said to have said, "It's like puttin' antlers on a canary!" *Pete Lyons*

Unfortunately, the T310 was one more of the Can-Am's all-too-common too-little/too-late efforts. The decision to proceed was tardy, there was little pre-season testing, the car missed the first race, and never came really right. Mid-season mods to its front suspension and nose aerodynamics finally cured most of its original strong understeer. Hobbs said the handling balance remained constant as the fuel burned away, and braking was excellent. But the car was not a success, and there was no successor. Thus came to an end the once-great line of Lola Can-Am cars.

Broadley debriefs Hobbs in the shovel-nosed Lola T310 at Donnybrooke. *Pete Lyons*

With McLaren gone from the Can-Am and no other team able to show a track record indicating they could take their place in 1973, Porsche and Penske really could have rested on their 1972 accomplishments. But racers aren't like that. Working as hard through the off-season as if they still had something to prove, Mark Donohue and his colleagues painstakingly honed every remaining rough edge from the mighty Porsche. They gave it a new chassis, a new body, and a bigger, more powerful engine. An engine that could race comfortably at the 1,100hp level, and which could show readings over 1,500 on the dyno.

The Porsche people asked Mark if that was enough. Was he finally satisfied with their engine now? No, he retorted. He wouldn't be satisfied until he could spin the wheels all the way down the longest straightaway.

He probably said it with a smile, but he was serious. He had a deep affinity for Group 7. "Racing runs by rules sometimes so restrictive that it's sometimes hard to tell where the book ends and the sport begins," he was quoted as saying in a Penske press release later that year. "Can-Am racing is a relief from the iron band of the rule book."

Bravo to that, but there's no point in pretending the eighth Canadian-American Challenge Cup championship series was a great competitive spectacle. Yes, there were moments of great racing action. But not many. Certainly, there were some great drivers. But not enough. Absolutely, there was one great car. But just one.

All these positive things together were not adequate to defend the beleaguered old Can-Am against the carping of its critics. That year, they were right.

Mosport Park, Ontario, June 10, 1973

Round one came up just a little too soon for the big blue Porsche 917/30 Panzer. It wasn't perfect. Donohue wasn't perfectly confident of it, because a snapped suspension arm had almost turned him over during final testing at Atlanta. At Mosport it took him most of the first day of practice to fine-tune its handling with small, add-on aerodynamic lips, and finally to qualify it fastest.

"The Porsche seemed to be rolling into a gentle understeer condition," wrote Gordon Kirby for *Autosport*. "Late on Friday a change was made to softer front rubber and this, in addition to a few secrecy-shrouded tweaks, allowed Donohue to do a tidy [1:14.1] which was almost 2 sec. quicker than he had gone throughout most of the day and one tenth quicker than his pole time of last year." The reporter explained the track had been extensively repaved, so it was much smoother in critical areas, but wind-blown sand was making it slick.

About the 917/30, he added, though it looked "incredibly long and cumbersome" at rest, in motion it was a marvel of fluid grace. "[T]he car seems to be extremely precise and Donohue is able to simply drive it through the very worst plunging, downhill turns with virtually no change at all in the car's attitude. It is deceptive motoring at its best, and the muffled whine of the enlarged 5.4-liter flat 12 completes the illusion of an easily controllable and entirely driveable motor car that you or I might be able to handle."

One who did make Panzer driving look difficult was Jody Scheckter, the up-and-coming, very aggressive and athletic South African. He had come to America to race F5000, where he was so impressive that Vasek Polak couldn't resist putting the turbo-power of a 917/10K under his foot. Jody "provided an enjoyable contrast to Donohue's efficient display," noted Kirby. He took the outside front row alongside the Penske car, a position which made him seem like more of a threat than did his time—over a second and a half slower.

Later in the season, after he was thoroughly used to the car, Jody still said, "It's like riding a bicycle with an afterburner on the back. It's too fast on the straights, and too slow in the corners. If it's wet tomorrow, they can get someone else to crash it!"

Right in Mark's mirrors at Mosport, only a tenth off Scheckter's pace, loomed the reigning Can-Am Champion, George Follmer, driving one of the championship-winning, ex-Penske 917/10Ks now owned by Bobby Rinzler. (Follmer, member with Jackie Oliver of the new Shadow F1 team, had recently earned World Championship points by finishing sixth and third in his first-ever Grands Prix, South Africa and Spain.) The sister Porsche was just to the left, although from the time he'd managed to do with it (1.3 slower than Follmer), Charlie Kemp did not appear to be a contender on pure speed. Even slower was a straggle of assorted 917/10s and Chevrolet-powered McLarens and Lolas of various vintages, all now in privateer hands.

The one factory entry among them was Jackie Oliver's new, Tony Southgate-designed, Don Nichols-owned Shadow DN2. Unfortunately, it was too new. Expansion into F1 had usurped most of the AVS team's time. The Can-Am car was still unfinished when it arrived at Mosport, and its initial debugging laps had to serve as its qualification trials. Though Shadow was still working on an all-new version of its own turbo-Chevy, it was no nearer being race-ready now than the original had been eight months earlier, so Oliver had the familiar staggered stacks of a normally aspirated 495 behind his shoulders.

One car expected to be a well-sorted and strong contender never made the grid. The ex-Revson McLaren M20 was now owned by Roy Woods, who trucked it up from Los Angeles for David Hobbs. On the way, the truck broke down, then, on the black-painted McLaren's very first warm-up lap on Saturday, it broke a half shaft. That caused enough damage that Hobbs didn't get out again until late in the day. Halfway around his third lap, something else broke, and the car punted a guardrail. The team trucked back home.

For the second year running, Donohue "molded" the start to suit himself, and was first down the hill beyond the starter's bridge. As he came rocketing back over the crest of the return straight, though, Scheckter whipped out of his draft and aggressively dove in front, going into the very fast righthand bend at the end. "Scheckter was literally chucking his Porsche down the road," wrote Kirby. Donohue, possibly as amused as he may have been amazed, sat watching this display for two laps, then retook the lead in the same way at the same place. One more lap and, again at the same place, the blue Porsche swooping over the crest with the white one a few lengths behind, Mark was presented with the first backmarker of his day, a car that had

Riverside: A goodbye lap for "the most perfect combination of man and machine ever seen." *Petersen Publishing*

Mosport: At the start, it looks like a good tussle between Donohue's new 917/30 (#6), and the year-old 917/10Ks of Scheckter (#0) and Follmer. *Joe Rusz/Road & Track*

qualified at more than 22mph slower. The man did see him coming and tried to get out of the way, but he and Donohue, traveling in different worlds of speed, kept making the same decisions at the same instant. Mark finally left the road on the outside and rode through another frightening near-inversion. Scheckter drove on to lead again, while Donohue drove into the pits, his nosepiece bent upwards.

The race, as such, was over. Scheckter, unpressed by anybody, drove around comfortably, building up a lead of over half a minute, until a tire went soft and finally blew, pitching the Porsche into a rail. Follmer had already pitted with tire trouble, so his Rinzler teammate, Kemp, inherited the lead now. Follmer tried his best to disinherit him, but the transmission let him down. No other challengers came forward. Kemp won by two laps.

Donohue wanted to quit because, despite the hasty pitwork, his beat-up front end was still trying to fly, but his owner prevailed on him to show the corporate colors to the finish. Which came out to be seventh place, seven laps behind.

The Shadow went two laps before its gearbox broke.

Denny Hulme won the Swedish Grand Prix for McLaren seven days later.

Road Atlanta, Georgia, July 7, 1973

In a couple of senses, as things turned out, the previous race at Mosport had been the last traditional Can-Am. For one thing, it had presented a race for the lead, if only for four laps. For another, so desultory and failure-plagued had been the remaining seventy-six laps that series administrators decided to split remaining events into two heats.

At the very beginning of the Can-Am, the Laguna Seca race had been run in two parts, with final positions decided by totaling times. At Atlanta now, the race was treated simply as one continuous event, with a compulsory, overnight pit stop in the middle. The ninety total laps were divided into a run of forty on Saturday, fifty on Sunday.

The theory seemed to be that drivers would benefit from enhanced safety and better handling stemming from reduced fuel loads. Besides, the public would at least have two occasions to see the cars bunched and charging forward from the start line, and also dead and dying cars would be granted a second chance to make it to the finish line.

On the other hand, this wiped out any faint hope harbored by drivers with normally aspirated engines of outlasting fuel-thirsty turbos. And, as it turned out, it gave rise to some odd official finishing positions, wherein drivers who were lapped in the first heat couldn't make it up in the second.

With all the testing work he'd carried out at this circuit, Donohue was much more comfortable at Atlanta. Using the second of his two '30s, he earned pole again with evident ease. Again it was a new course record: nearly 1.2sec quicker than Hulme's McLaren had managed the year before. This year, though, there wasn't a margin of less than three one-hundredths over the second qualifier

Follmer was the other man on the front row again, as in 1972, but this time the gap was more than 1.77sec. He was unable, by more than 0.5sec, to match his own previous time in essentially the same car. But nobody else was able to come close to matching Follmer's time of this year. Teammate Kemp's hour of stardom at Mosport was succeeded by a high-speed Group 7 "blowover" during testing at Atlanta, which he survived with a broken back, so he missed this round.

Donohue simply drove around to win the first heat—and it was hot, some 90 degrees. Next day, in the same sauna-like weather, the methodical operation resumed, but even on the pace lap, a spray of gasoline started erupting from a coupling in the cockpit. Mark took it for five race laps before pitting for a slosh from a water bucket, then again to stanch the leak. His suit soaked with fuel and his skin extremely sore, he set fastest time and unlapped himself from Follmer in a gritty but fruitless charge to make up

enough ground to take the win. Follmer was still 51sec ahead at the end.

Behind Scheckter, who was troubled by chunking tires, Hobbs' normally aspirated McLaren finished fourth, "first in class" as David wearily quipped. Another ex-factory M20, Hulme's second car, had taken over Hobbs' Mosport role of retiring without racing. This one's Chevy had been turbocharged by Gene Crowe, who'd been involved in McKee's turbo-Olds Can-Am program a few years earlier. The driver was Mario Andretti. He qualified on the third row. So far so good, but the car was on tires 3in narrower and of another brand than it had been designed to wear, and in any case the entire machine proved desperately unprepared. Mario said, "*Ciao.*"

The Shadow was going better, Oliver earning fifth-best grid place for the first heat, but he went out early with front suspension failure.

The weekend after Atlanta, McLaren's Peter Revson won his first Grand Prix, the British.

Watkins Glen, New York, July 22, 1973

Mark Donohue had already molded this Can-Am season to suit himself. All that was left before he could profit from his work was to get his luck turned around. He did it now.

Though it took more work. During practice, one of the very costly 1,100hp motors went sick and had to be exchanged. Then a rear suspension link snapped and pitched the car into the guardrails on both sides of the track at 150mph at the same place Mark had suffered burns in a USRRC event seven years before. He walked away with his face pale, but he walked straight to the Mosport car. This lacked the right gearing for Watkins Glen, but Mark clocked his pole time with it in three laps.

"For once we had seen Donohue the racing driver rather than Donohue the restrained engineer," noted Gordon Kirby, with approval. "There were hints of locking brakes, of bursts of power and slashes of lock. It was really a very fine effort."

There were many fine efforts elsewhere in the field, too, as there always were, but none of them achieved historical significance this time. This time Mark steered clear of trouble, as did the Sunoco Porsche, and he and it won both thirty-lap heats (each held on Sunday in deference to Saturday's traditional Six-Hour) with apparent ease. On each first lap, he gained 3sec on the next man.

Let's let Kirby summarize the wearisome rest of it for us:

The scrambling behind Donohue was resolved by a broken turbocharger in George Follmer's RC

Mosport: By the middle, Mark is not looking so good. *Joe Rusz/Road & Track*

Mosport: In the end, it's Kemp on top. *Autosport*

Cola Porsche and the wrong tire selection for Jody Scheckter's Vasek Polak Porsche, all of which let David Hobbs take an isolated second place with a neat drive in the Black Label McLaren M20. Scheckter was third after struggling with a barely controllable Porsche in the first heat and using softer Goodyears to restore his confidence and pizzazz as he drove on to second in the second heat. After Follmer's first heat demise, the other RC Cola Porsche of Charlie Kemp

Road Atlanta: Mark's magnificent supercar once again sets off in front. But, once again, it can't stay there. *Autosport*

finished fourth. ["Ironman" Kemp was driving with his broken back encased in a body brace.]

Otherwise it was all too much of the typical Can-Am non-action with the occasional After-You-Claude train in the midfield hinting vaguely at what could be. Perhaps Peter Gregg put all this hoo-ha into perspective by driving his Porsche Carrera prototype [a 3.0-liter 911 left over from the enduro] into ninth place and entertaining the masses by gobbling up the tarmac between him and many of the G7 cars as they trundled through the braking zones and those bothersome corners.

Watkins Glen: Try, try again; after using up one car in practice, Donohue finally launches his real Can-Am career. *Dave Friedman*

At least Oliver's UOP Shadow managed to finish the second heat. Its water pump broke in the first.

Oh, yes: Group 7 was still faster than F1 at Watkins Glen. Donohue's record qualifying time of 1:38.848 (nearly 123mph) was 1.632 faster than the previous year's GP pole. It remained 0.827 faster than the following October's best F1 time and even stood up the following year by 0.122.

Mid-Ohio, Lexington, Ohio, August 12, 1973

Donohue's qualifying advantage here over the second man was 2.5sec. His improvement over the previous year's pole was 3.7sec. Last year's honoree, Follmer, only managed to clip a quarter of a second off his old time with the 917/10.

To the *Autosport* reporter's eye, the difference was mainly in the 917/30, which "seems to show a greater sophistication with every new appearance. This time it was a display of tractability and pointability through slow corners—corners that were normally the painful-to-watch Achilles heel of a Can-Am car—which the Penske Porsche showed its control of. Donohue was quick and very neat, and the car answered all of his demands with the precision of a Grand Prix machine. 'The car just does everything you want it to do,' remarked a refreshingly relaxed and happy Donohue....

"'There is no doubt that this is the finest racing car that I have ever driven.'"

Racing drivers being the type of people they are, however, neither Follmer, third fastest on the grid behind Donohue, nor Scheckter, from second grid place alongside, accorded the Panzer on the pole the respect it deserved. Both "molded" the start to suit themselves, Follmer actually tapping Donohue as he blasted by on the left, and Scheckter swooping across from the outside in front of Donohue's startled face to tuck in behind Follmer.

The second real race of the season! It took Mark two laps to find a way back ahead of Jody, and another four before he outbraked George to assume his rightful place at the front. Rightful, because he thereupon drove away at nearly 2sec per lap. The pair he left so decisively behind busied themselves with their own race for second place, and with Follmer's brakes fading, Scheckter was about to pounce, when they both overwhelmed a backmarker so suddenly that the man's startled reaction forced Jody to find an escape route across a field. That bent a suspension arm, which led to a couple of spins and eventual retirement from the heat. Scheckter decided not to bother with the second heat, because the engine was going off color anyway.

At the start of heat two, Follmer, starting alongside Donohue this time, out-dragged him again to take the lead. With the first heat experience under his belts, George did a much better job of preserving his position this time. "Follmer was driving hard and crisply, slicing across the slow corners and late-apexing the faster stuff—all in an effort at keeping Donohue foiled in his efforts at finding a hole," said the delighted Kirby. "For lap after lap it went on like that, and despite Follmer's brakes fading away yet again he remained composed and kept his door-shutting efforts in order."

Donohue, too, retained his composure. "Mark appeared to be just sitting there, watching and waiting for the right time. There were no wasted efforts, no tense feints and twitches. We waited for Donohue to strike."

Donohue waited until lap thirty-seven. Then, as he later told writer and lifelong friend Burge Hulett, he turned up the boost knob and launched onto the longest straight with an extra 450hp at the rear wheels. He didn't tell Hulett whether it was enough

Mid-Ohio: Haywood (#59) runs a smooth race for third, but Kemp (#23) is totally out of luck.
Autosport

Mid-Ohio: Shadow's DN2 is way off the pace, but at least it gets Oliver to the finish this time.
Autosport

to make them spin all the way, but it did thrust him ahead of Follmer by the braking point. In the remaining four and a half laps, Donohue built a 10sec cushion. On aggregate, his winning margin was more than a minute and a half.

Gary Wilson rejoined the series at this race, and he posted what available records indicate to be the first Can-Am start by a turbocharged Chevy (another Gene Crowe installation). He finished ninth. Shadow's own turbo-Chevy was on the scene, but it went unused. Oliver was having quite enough problems with truly evil handling to bother with extra power. However, the DN2 posted its first finish, eighth, with the same total laps as Wilson.

Elkhart Lake, Wisconsin, August 26, 1973

More tinkering with the format, but no change in the outcome. The two heats were run as separate races paying their own prize money. However, the first race, called the "Can-Am Sprint," had nothing to do with the overall result beyond qualifying twenty-four cars to start the second. This was the "Can-Am Cup," and it alone counted for points.

None of that had any effect on Donohue's domination. He still qualified faster than anyone else—by 3sec this time, thus becoming the first to lap Road America in less than 2min. He still won the heat and, of course, dominated the final.

Scheckter did mount a little opposition in the Sprint, jumping the start and leading through a couple of corners before Donohue overwhelmed him to cross the line at the end of the first lap 3sec ahead. Follmer then tried to engage Scheckter, but faded away as his brakes did.

Donohue didn't let Scheckter get away with the same trick in the Cup, and cruised to a half-minute win. Scheckter stayed well clear of Follmer to the end. There was an entertaining mid-field scrap among Hurley Haywood, Charlie Kemp, Scooter Patrick, and Bobby Brown. F1 driver James Hunt guest-drove the normal Shadow while Jackie Oliver debuted the turbo model; neither had a pleasant time. It was another douse-me-with-a-bucket-hot day.

Edmonton, Alberta, September 16, 1973

Two weeks later and many degrees of latitude farther north, the weather was icy cold. Donohue coped with that by mounting up a set of older, narrower tires to get more heat in the rubber. But his grid position advantage was less than a second this time.

In the Sprint, after three slow pace laps to satisfy the starter, both Donohue's and front-row partner Follmer's plugs were fouling, so Scheckter was able to squirt between them both to lead. Follmer beat Donohue too, but halfway around the second lap he slid wide, beginning a series of misadventures that dropped him way back with damaged bodywork. Two laps later, Donohue, his plugs now nice and hot and clean, pulled past Scheckter. Jody tried so hard to pursue he went off the road and later tapped another car, damaging his shovel nose. Oliver, back in the normally aspirated Shadow, found its handling much improved, and finished the Sprint third, still on the winner's lap.

Only fifteen cars fronted up for the next day's Cup race. A clean start let Donohue drive away as he pleased. Starting from the back, Follmer quickly zoomed up into Scheckter's mirrors and engaged him in an entertaining squabble over second, which Jody was winning until his engine blew. Kemp and Oliver

had a similar tussle, and it was resolved in a similar way, the gearbox of the famously reliable import breaking and letting the cheap domestic product through to an encouraging third. OK, OK, this Shadow had been built in England, but the team was making progress at last.

Laguna Seca, California, October 14, 1973

In Italy the week before Edmonton, Jackie Stewart had clinched his third World Championship title. The week after Edmonton, Peter Revson drove his McLaren to his second Grand Prix win at Mosport; Oliver held his Shadow in the lead there for eight laps. Two weeks after that, François Cevert was killed in practice at Watkins Glen. His Tyrrell teammate, Stewart, immediately retired. Roger Penske revealed he was setting up a race shop in England.

At Laguna Seca, Mark Donohue failed to win the Can-Am Sprint.

He started it well enough. A pole position time more than 2sec faster than your nearest opposition is doing well enough, don't you think? As a matter of fact, he took out both his pretty blue toys and qualified them. "For a while, it was thought Mark might drive both in the race, standing up and wearing them like roller skates," joked Jim MacQueen in *Autoweek*.

Mark settled on one car and set off for another Donohue drive-away, building up his lead at an unassuming second per lap, until the engine started trailing smoke, and expired with an oil leak.

Well, now, here was a thing. A Penske-prepared Porsche had broken down!

No problem. We'll just roll out the other one for the Cup race later on this afternoon.

No you won't. Rules say you can't.

Normally, it was said, the crew reckoned it was a five-hour job to swap the massive turbomotors. With Roger himself helping—MacQueen swears The Cap-

Road America: Rising F1 star "Lord Jim" Hunt has a taste of Group 7 in the Shadow. He doesn't much care for it. "I had expected 750bhp to be rather exciting," he will write for his *Motor* column, "but the car seemed rather gutless . . . not being a racing engine, it's not very lively and thus the only hint I had of any power was that every time I put my foot down the back wheels let go and I got violent wheelspin." When a fuel leak keeps him out of the final, he is "secretly relieved," because "driving that car was like doing press-ups in a steam sauna for an hour!" *Autosport*

oil pressure and tire traction problems (wheelspin everywhere) induced him to withdraw from the final, and John Cannon took over.

Riverside, California, October 28, 1973

While developing the 917/30, Mark Donohue saw over 240mph on the long straight of the Paul Ricard circuit in France. He had been looking forward to trying for 250 at Riverside. But those in charge figured he'd had enough fun, and specified that this year's Can-Am would use a shortened version of the course, which cut out half the back straight.

If the idea was to foster competition, it failed miserably. This round was the least competitive, and frankly the most boring, of a desperately dull season.

For everybody but Mark. He was having a great time. Much of his weekend was taken up with the first three rounds of the inaugural International Race of Champions (IROC), a Penske promotion featuring a dozen of the world's best drivers in identical Porsche 911s. Mark won two of those rounds, defeating the likes of Emerson Fittipaldi, George Follmer (who won the other round and emerged as points leader),

Edmonton: Mark the masterful. No one has ever won four Can-Ams in a row before. And he's not done with the record book yet. *Charles Loring/Autosport*

Right: Laguna Seca: A flaw surfaces! Trouble in the first heat forces the Penske Panzer to start the final mid-pack. *Dale von Trebra*

tain soiled his Gucci loafers—John "Woody" Woodard, Greg Syfert and Heinz Hofer did it in three hours. It was time enough to get Mark to his sixteenth grid position for the second race.

All he had to do was make his way to eighth by the finish to clinch the Can-Am title. He was fourth by the third lap. A moment later, there was a little kerfluffle involving six other cars, which brought out the pace car—first time ever in a Can-Am, it was believed—for six laps. The incident resulted in Scheckter dropping out. The cleanup done, Donohue set about passing Oliver, who was running third, then addressed Kemp in order to get finally to Follmer, winner of the Sprint. The job was a little harder than it looked, because the Penske Porsche now had broken a valve spring and also its rear antiroll bar. But the other two Porsches made the job a little easier when first Charlie's disappeared from in front of Mark, with a broken suspension, and then George's disappeared from in front of him in a cloud of smoke, apparently because of debris sucked into a turbo. Donohue's margin over Oliver at the end was more than a lap.

Oliver was driving the unblown Shadow again, but the turbocharged car was having another run in the hands of Mr. Versatility, Vic Elford. The brakes, not Lee Muir's engine, put him out. Mario Andretti was also back with the turbocharged McLaren M20, the engine of which was now built by Barry Crowe (no relation to Gene). This time he ran the heat, but

A.J. Foyt, Denny Hulme, David Pearson, Peter Revson, and Bobby Unser. This was such a good show that the assembled press members billed it as better than the weary old Can-Am, though at least one reporter shed a tear as he agreed.

When he had a few spare moments, Donohue turned to the task of tuning his big Porsche for the feature event. *Autosport's* Kirby watched with deep satisfaction the last exhibition of this perfect melding of man with machine. "There was simply not a patch of California pavement where any other car could approach the 917/30. Donohue was the quickest and most precisely adventurous of all as he pressed the squatting blue car around with remarkably tidy vigor. For lap after lap he would flick and squirt his way along the tarmac in unerringly clear designs, holding the car in easy, tire-chirping slips, building the revs and letting the throttle catch up with things just in time to settle the car into a powerfully graceful arc as it shot away down the straight."

Mark's margin of superiority in qualifying was 1.3sec. The man he humiliated was Follmer this time.

In the race, everybody humiliated themselves. "The race that we had hoped would develop behind Donohue was a desolate event," mourned Kirby. "Both Scheckter and Follmer clipped some of Riverside's old, tire turn markers, crumpling their Porsches' fronts and packing up with unmanageable machines. Jackie Oliver was another to clout the tire markers, losing all of his Shadow's nose as he did so, while David Hobbs pulled in with yet another cracked head. . . For most of the final, Brian Redman worked hard to hold second place with Vasek Polak's updated 917 Porsche [the old 917 PA], but a ball joint snapped giving Brian a nasty fright and Hurley Haywood and his 917/10 an easy second. . ." Elford's turbocharged Shadow let him down on the first lap of the final, and once again Andretti refused to start the final, so teammate John Cannon forsook his own M8F for Mario's turbocharged M20.

Kirby: "As car after aged Can-Am car broke under their own stress the final forty-nine laps of Riverside degenerated into a dismal procession. Only eight men cruised their ways carefully to the chequered flag. . . The sun was sinking, casting deep shadows from its harsh orange mass, aggravating the tired tone of this final Can-Am."

The one happy man was Mark Donohue. After Laguna Seca, he'd replaced the broken rear antiroll bar with one he could adjust from the cockpit. In his book, *The Unfair Advantage*, he described the benefit. "After I got way out in front, I began playing with the bar, turning it up to oversteer, and broadsliding

the car around the tighter turns. I really had a good time sliding all over the place—knowing that I could rebalance the car at any time—and more importantly, knowing that it was my last Can-Am race."

He won the race, his sixth in a row and his eighth Can-Am in all, parked, and announced his retirement.

There didn't seem to be much more to say than what an anonymous *Autoweek* editor tried to express about the experience of watching that last 1973 Can-Am:

When one reaches a certain sophistication in the sport of motor racing, such performances have a tendency to seem boring and blasé. But there is a smoothness to the Donohue driving technique, a spectacularness to the 917/30 that seems to hold the interest. Perhaps this is what brings in the crowds— the desire to say, I saw Mark Donohue drive that invincible Porsche. I was there and saw it and knew that it was the best combination of man and machine that had ever appeared on a race track.

Cars of the Can-Am 1973
Porsche 917/30

What Mark Donohue wanted for his new Can-Am fighting knife was easy to put into words: more of everything. Putting it into hardware was just a little harder.

By having a chassis cut in half and bolting it back together with different spacer sections, Mark settled on a new wheelbase of 98.4in. Along with juggled track dimensions, this improved stability, but also allowed an increase in fuel capacity from the former 86gal to 106—just think about that. The finalized 917/30's aluminum space frame was now so long the tank area was boxed-in with sheet aluminum for stiffness.

Meanwhile, Porsche contracted with a French aeronautical company named SERA to see if some of the drag could be trimmed off the body shape without losing any downforce. The resulting "Paris body" retained the basic idea of the 917/10K front end, with its scoop-shaped, heavily-louvered fenders, but the fender line was higher to let air circulate more freely around the wheels. The body's leading edge was re-profiled, too.

SERA also came up with its own new tailpiece and rear wing, but Donohue felt it had too much drag and badgered Porsche into trying an afterbody profile developed earlier for Le Mans. According to Mark's book, *The Unfair Advantage*, in back-to-back tests on

Laguna Seca: More trouble! Cuddy (#4 McLaren M8E), Felter, and Settember (both hidden) tangle, and neither Dutton (#34 M8E) nor Saville-Peck (Costello SP7) can escape.
Dale von Trebra

Mark Donohue, Champion

As do most road racers, he started on the amateur level, but he would reach summits few professionals ever attain. Born on March 18, 1937, Mark was still a university student in 1958 when he entered his first competitive event, a hill climb, with his street car, a totally stock Corvette. He won. Characteristically, he considered that a bit of a fluke, but, again characteristically, he resolved that flukes would never play any role in his racing. Perhaps there were areas of this incredibly complex pursuit where he lacked outstanding talent, but the combination of his abilities was unique. Some drivers are clever with machinery; Donohue was not only brilliant, he took formal training and then built vast and varied experience. Some have an innate knack at the wheel; he strove to understand the engineering dynamics behind performance, and relentlessly honed his skills in extracting it. Where others prepared their cars well, he was obsessive about preparation. Some racers had dedication; Donohue was driven. And he never stopped thinking, thinking, thinking. The results: three national championships as an amateur, two as a professional in the USRRC, three more—and the still-standing record for race victories—for factory Trans-Am teams, one triumph in the Indianapolis 500 as well as two other Indy car wins, and near-total domination of the 1973 Can-Am. Oh, and in 1975 he established a closed-circuit lap speed record. Exactly ten days later, on August 19, he died of injuries suffered in the crash of an F1 car in Austria. *Petersen Publishing photo*

Riverside: Last time in Nine. Donohue's SuperPorsche brings the pack around the banking for the start of the final heat of the last Big Banger event to be held at the historic circuit. *Petersen Publishing*

the long straight at France's Paul Ricard circuit, the new bodywork finally proved responsible for an increase in top speed from 212 to 240mph.

The longer, stronger 1973 chassis frame—still aluminum—was 75lb heavier. Now displacing 5.4 liters and wearing larger turbochargers, the engine weighed a little more, too, and of course there was more body material. But the suspension was back to aluminum arms. As it finished that season, the empty 917/30 car weighed 1872lb, only 64 more than the lighter of the two '72 models. Fully laden, the /30 could scale almost 2700lb.

With the normal 1.3-bar boost setting, torque was 810lb-ft at 6400rpm, and power reached 1100 at 7800. More boost, of course, gave even more power; readings above 1500 were seen on the dyno. During 1973, the driver was given a cockpit control to adjust the wastegate. (For the last race of that year, he also got an adjuster for the stiffness of the rear sway bar.)

To cope with the extra power, the clutch asked for and received a fourth plate. The brakes complained, too but were mollified by better air ducting at the rear and centrifugal fans on the front wheels.

During the brake-cooling work, Porsche tried reversing the direction of the airflow past the engine, pulling air out the top rather than cramming it down underneath. Ever since the FIA banned the Chaparral "fan car" at the end of 1970, everyone had been on the lookout for alternative means of inducing negative underbody pressure. The overheating rear brake problem is what led Porsche to actually try it, but the experiment didn't last long because the engine soon overheated. During the time it ran in sucker mode, the car demonstrated no improvement in track adhesion.

Pity. It would have been fun at tech inspection.

Not that the Penske Panzer needed any further Unfair Advantage. It was the uncontested master of its domain in 1973. As Mark Donohue used to say, the Porsche 917/30 was "a monument to my career as an engineer and driver."

Shadow DN2

With both McLaren and Lola out of the Can-Am, this was the only new car to go up against the

Riverside: Ollie (#101 Shadow DN2) will be interested to hear how easy it's been for Donohue; himself, he's having quite a workout with Mr. Kemp (#23)at turn 7. *Jim Chambers*

By Riverside Donohue had installed a driver-adjustable rear sway bar in the Porsche 917/30 and spent an otherwise boring race playing with it. *Pete Lyons*

Rinzler Porsche 917/10K: Follmer drove one of the ex-Penske cars, which during the season received a longer, wider tailpiece and a cockpit knob to control turbo boost but seldom was able to match his performances of the year before. *Pete Lyons*

Oliver's bulky Shadow DN2 was built for a turbocharged Chevy that didn't work. *Petersen Publishing photo*

(for a 1970 track debut) with the idea of showcasing American technology, but now he'd set up shop in England. That was because he, driver/manager Jackie Oliver, and sponsor Universal Oil Products were expanding into F1, and a European base made more logistical sense. To replace former designer Peter Bryant they engaged Tony Southgate. His first car for the team was an F1 called the DN1; alongside that he drew up the DN2 Group 7 car.

Shadow was still working on its turbocharged Chevy, and the DN2 was designed from the outset to take its projected 1200hp. Dry weight was given as a hefty 1650lb. Southgate put the wheelbase up to 103in, an increase of 5in over Bryant's 1972 model, and widened the track dimensions to 62in front, 61 rear. Overall body width rose to 82.5. His suspension was generally orthodox, with unequal-length A-frames at the front and a lower frame plus single top link and single radius rod at the rear. Brakes remained inboard at the rear but moved out into the 15in wheels at the front. Hewland supplied the LG500 4-speed transaxle from the outset. The chassis was a full-length aluminum monocoque to which the rigidly-mounted engine added stiffness. After much tunnel testing, a long, wide "shovel" nose was evolved that recalled the 1972 Lola. However, the pair of rectangular front-end inlets led air to radiators located low in the body sides just behind the front wheels, and a pronounced upsweep of the rear fender line contributed some downforce at the same time it delivered air to the rear wing. The cockpit enclosure swelled relatively high over the low mid-car bodywork.

Had the turbo project been successful, this car's story might have been happier. In fact, despite periodic promises of an imminent debut, the supermotor only raced three times late in the season, and never went well. With nothing but a normally aspirated, 735hp Reynolds-block Chevy, the heavy, bulky DN2 would have been no threat to the Porsches even had it handled well. It didn't. Oliver complained all season of heavy steering and gross understeer. He also suffered numerous mechanical breakdowns, and well before the end of a disappointing season onlookers felt the team was focused almost entirely on its F1 program.

Costello SP7, SP8

After racing several small-bore cars of his own design in England, engineer David Saville-Peck built his SP7 there specifically so he could continue his career once he emigrated to Canada. Begun in 1971, the design was primarily his own, but he named it after a friend, Brian Costello, who helped with financing. For reasons of both expense and preference Sav-

overwhelming Penske Porsche. It was indeed an all-new car and, in fact, an almost completely new operation. Don Nichols had launched his team in 1969

Previous page top and bottom: In its second generation, the Shadow Chevy's two turbochargers were relocated from the extreme tail of the car to either side of the engine bay. The plumbing was somewhat simpler, but the performance was no better. *Pete Lyons, Dale von Trebra photos*

Left: Another turbocharged Chevrolet project was installed by Barry Crowe in a McLaren M20 ahead of a Weismann transaxle. Nominally the driver was Mario Andretti (seen at far left, talking with cowboy-hatted Bobby Unser at Riverside), although he was contracted to Firestone and that company's rubber seemed unable to hook the tremendous power to the road. Better results were obtained when John Cannon drove the car on Goodyears, but this was never a competitive package. Its fiery exhaust was a real crowd-pleaser, though. *Pete Lyons*

ille-Peck chose the veteran small-block aluminum Oldsmobile V-8 and laid out the smallest, lightest possible car around it. In McLaren fashion the engine was a semi-stressed element of a half-length aluminum monocoque. Transmission was the Hewland DG300 commonly used in F1, and there were some other F1 parts incorporated, including a bell housing from a Matra V12 and front uprights from a BRM. Rubber fuel cells came surplus from a French Mirage jet fighter—hot rodding Euro-style. Suspension was conventional Group 7 practice, but the wheelbase was a mere 88in, and the car's dry weight came to a scant 1230lb. Twin water radiators were flank-mounted, fed by door-top inlets. After a lot of engine trouble the first year, the owner-driver-and-finally-engine-builder settled on a relatively conservative 4.4-liter (271ci) package which gave him about 430hp. He retained this through a more reliable second season, al-

though then he called the engine a Leyland for commercial reasons. Although it had been test-driven in England, the SP7's first-ever race was the Mosport Can-Am of 1973. Later, at Laguna Seca, a multi-car shunt heavily damaged it—and broke three of the driver's ribs—but within two weeks a new chassis with more rectangular sides came from England, and a new SP8 was ready for Riverside (where it is shown in the photo). Unfortunately, a steering part salvaged from the wrecked SP7 broke in practice, and the car didn't make the race. Results (and prize moneys) were much more satisfactory during the 1974 season, short though it was. In 1975, Saville Peck set a British Columbia hill climb record, but later in the year, having qualified on the front row for a race at Elkhart Lake, he crashed heavily in warmup and suffered severe burns. David did not race again until recently, when he enthusiastically took up karting.

Costello SP8 at Riverside. *Pete Lyons*

Rules. As the cars in the Can-Am dwindled, the rules governing them multiplied. All during 1973—as often in earlier years—one interest group after another had advanced pet packages of prescriptions to save an obviously dying series.

SCCA's idea was to adopt the engine limits already established in its F5000 open-wheel series, where 3.0-liter "racing engines" (those with more than one camshaft) would race alongside 5.0-liter "stock blocks."

Certain European factories and teams who were already running the 3.0s in sports car enduros said they'd be interested in a Can-Am that let them get extra value out of the same cars after their primary season was over.

When that was first proposed, in mid-season 1973, the Can-Am race promoters all said no. They were still seeing good crowds and didn't want to risk a change. By the end of that desultory year, though, the engine size limit and its implicit promise of bigger, higher-quality starting fields looked more attractive.

But some of the established entrants still resisted, especially Porsche/Penske and Shadow, both of whom had a lot invested in big turbocharged engines and the relatively big cars designed and developed to carry them. They did not hesitate to remind SCCA of its oft-emphasized policy against changing rules without at least a year's notice.

Yes, but this is an emergency, came the countervailing reply. We have a dying patient to save here.

During a mass meeting of all interested parties the day after Riverside in 1973, a time when the first OPEC oil crisis was a major new consideration for every racing organization, a compromise idea was proposed: let the big-blocks and turbos continue for 1974, but introduce a fuel consumption formula of, say, three miles per gallon. To meet it, the most powerful engines would have to be detuned to, say, the 800hp attainable with garden-variety big-block Chevys. That, it was said, would level the playing field for a closer game without making existing equipment obsolete, yet still allow those teams mounting the best efforts to rise to the top in the end.

In essence, this describes the scheme adopted for 1974. The fuel limits were presented as "Energy Measures." Eight race dates were announced, along with the information that this would be an "interim" year, with the 3.0/5.0 formula coming in for 1975.

But the Panzer people saw nothing in any of this for them. Porsche let Penske out of the third year of his original contract. Into the void did not step McLaren, nor Lola, nor anyone else able to make a challenge to the Shadows.

Did that leave the Can-Am a corpse? Did the black cars of the sole remaining constructor represent the hearse?

If the Can-Am was dead, you wouldn't have known it by watching the Don Nichols Shadow team prepare for its fifth season. Peter Revson was signed for both Can-Am and F1. New team manager Mike Hillman, hired away from Ford of England's competition department, completely reorganized the Shadow operation. The operation laid down a new car, smaller and lighter to take fair advantage of the new rules. Jackie Oliver began testing this DN4 in early March, and logged some 1,800 miles before the first race. It was all strongly reminiscent of the old McLaren (and Penske) approach.

Tragedy struck when Revson was killed by suspension failure during F1 testing at Kyalami, South Africa. The team maintained momentum by bringing in George Follmer.

They almost lost him, too. Ten days before the opening event at Mosport, he was testing there when the throttle stuck open at high speed on the steep plunge down toward Moss hairpin. So badly destroyed was the chassis, it was said, that nothing but the left rear wheel and radiator were salvageable. George got out of it without major injury, and there was already a third chassis well along, so the team still was able to present two cars for the race.

Mosport Park, Ontario, June 16, 1974

When this ninth Can-Am tour opened at Mosport, it was joining SCCA's F5000 circus, already in progress. Though the Sunday Group 7 race was nominally the featured event, Saturday's smaller-engined single-seaters proved a tough act to follow.

Connoisseurs of pure-blooded motorsport could not help but feel that the highly restricted 5.0-liter formula put on a more artistic show. It offered a reasonable variety of competitive chassis, and the driver lineup included the likes of Mario Andretti, who started from pole (1:14.8) and led the early going, David Hobbs, who won, Brian Redman, Sam Posey, Brett Lunger, Eppie Wietzes, and Elliott Forbes-Robinson.

Can-Ammers knew and missed some of those names. Also, those whose memories reached back to the legendary Chaparral days must have had a little trouble taking in the sight of tall Jim Hall, team manager and engineer for Redman, leaning over a fixed-formula open-wheeler with an iron engine and—gasp—a *manual* transmission!

Luckily, the Can-Am had one thing going for it: two Shadows. "Thank God for the persistence of Jackie Oliver, Don Nichols, and Universal Oil Products," declared Gordon Kirby in *Autosport*. "Without them the 1974 Can-Am would be little more than a tenth-rate sideshow. Those days of thunder and glory and innovation have slipped into the murky past, and other than the Shadows and precious few hard triers, the 1974 Can-Am consists of a motley collection of barely competent amateurs in old and thoughtlessly prepared cars."

Perhaps it sounded as if the reporter was trying not to get invited back, but a craftsman can only work with the materials in hand. Apart from the pair of glistening black DN4s, Kirby found one car and team worthy of special praise: the 1972 McLaren M20 originally raced by Peter Revson, then by David Hobbs, and now by Scooter Patrick. "Patrick and crew chief Herb Kaplan have put in an almost equal amount of energy to that of UOP," Kirby wrote, "and their immaculately prepared car was as deserving of its placing [third] as the winners were of theirs."

Compared to its original configuration, the Kaplan M20 wore its central nose wing farther forward and free of the full-width skirting McLaren had developed. The brake-duct inlets were relocated from the front fenders, too. At the rear, the wing was carried farther aft on extended fins. Another paint job made it a blue elephant now. Patrick's best time of 1:17.8

Road Atlanta: George (#1 Shadow DN4) tries again to take one from teammate Jackie, but . . . *Bill Warner*

Follmer's Shadow as he crested the hill, looking already for room inside the leading black wedge.

It went on like that for three laps, then Oliver was balked by a backmarker halfway around the fourth lap—already!—and Follmer out-dragged him up the long, rising straight. Once in front, Follmer kept the hammer down and pulled away at almost a second a lap until Oliver suddenly disappeared from his mirrors. A broken washer had fouled his fuel system.

When the two came together back in the garage after the heat, they had heated words. Oliver reminded Follmer that team policy forbade the trailing driver to force the pace unnecessarily. Follmer replied physically. Rather than respond in kind, the shorter Oliver chose to disengage. Rapidly.

It must have been with some relief that the rest of the team saw the George and Jackie Show line up far apart for the fifty-lap final. From pole, Follmer easily hurtled away from Patrick, gaining 2sec in the first lap. From the eighth row (of nine), Oliver made it through the midfield to fourth place in the same first lap. It took him another lap to pass Bob Nagle's two-year-old Lola T260 (apparently the actual ex-Stewart car, not the "White House" one) and one more to pass Patrick's two-year-old M20, but as he started lap four, Ollie was less than 8sec behind his teammate.

Then he eased off. Team policy, of course, and also some prudence in traffic, but most of all a growing sense that something was wrong. At high rpm he started feeling a vibration in the engine or driveline. He stopped using high rpm. Then he noticed the oil pressure was iffy. So at half-distance, the gap between the hulking black Shadows was more than half a minute.

That's when a slower car scattered its engine all over the track, and Follmer ran over the fragments. He ended his twenty-seventh lap in the pit lane, where the wheel change went badly and he lost almost 90sec. Finally up to speed again, he had Oliver more than 50sec ahead, and there were only twenty laps to go.

Team policy be damned.

"Oliver was driving carefully and as quick as he dared, keeping a watchful eye on the fluctuating oil pressure gauge," wrote Kirby. He continued:

George was soon back into his rhythm and braking and flicking the Shadow as if it were an F1 car. He started lopping three and four seconds a lap off Ollie's lead. By the 40th lap George had forced his way to within 32 seconds of his teammate. Five laps later there was only 21 seconds in it and George was cracking away at the lap record with every new circuit.

The gap came down dramatically in those final laps. Sixteen seconds, then 13, then with just two laps

---

Mosport: New-look Can-Am; there are no Porsches, the only Lolas and McLarens are old ones, and the Shadows are up front. Oliver (#101 DN4) and Follmer (#1) pace the pack, which features Patrick's M20 (hidden behind Oliver), the M8Fs of Cordts (#6) and Motschenbacher (#11), and Nagle's T260 (#17). The last indicates the prohibition on tall airscoops is no longer operative. *Joe Cali*

failed by 2.8sec to match that of Revson two years before, though this year it was good enough for third on the grid. Nobody else was fast, either.

Except the Shadowmen, as they were dubbed by writers obviously frantic for fizz. Oliver, having done ample testing here, was economical with his laps this time, and after trying a few suspension and wing variations, he settled for 1:14.5. This was only 0.4 behind Donohue's 1973 pole time with the big, turbocharged Porsche 917/30 and well up on any other G7 car no matter the engine or year. Follmer only received his brand-new replacement car in time for twenty laps of running-in-cum-qualifying but managed a 1:15.1. That did beat the 1:15.9 he'd clocked with the 917/10K here the year before.

The thirty-lap preliminary heat was effectively reduced to twenty-nine at speed because of an extra pace lap, but once unleashed, the pair of Shadows instantly seemed to belong to rival teams. Kirby called it:

Oliver and Follmer barreled away from the flag side by side, with George going deep into the first corner and almost leaning on his teammate as Ollie slid through on the inside line. Follmer flicked his chisel nose right in beneath Oliver's gearbox as the two black cars accelerated off that first apex and shot up the rise into Turn 2. There was a hint of locking brakes from

need more work. But the team did learn something about the latest rain tires: they needed more work, too.

At the end of the qualifying runs, Follmer had won the pole. He wasn't all that pleased. He'd been really keen to beat Donohue's year-old record, but the intermittent periods of wet cut his track time, and he missed by nearly 2sec. He did get within 0.2sec of his own 917/10K time of '73 (but not of his time of '72).

George still had another mark to shoot for: his third Road Atlanta Can-Am trophy in a row. Starting from the inside for the first heat helped, and he led Oliver up and over the hill and down through the Esses, but then, at the twin right-handers at the far end of the track, he dropped a stitch. Oliver snatched it up, and lead along the ultra-fast straightaway.

But he wasn't leading Follmer. Follmer was sagging toward the side of the track, out of the traffic stream. His gearshifter wasn't shifting. He made it on around to the pits, where the crew was able to join together that which had come asunder, but the cost was falling a complete lap plus 40sec behind Oliver and dropping to dead last. He made it back through the backmarkers to fifth by the end of the heat.

Since that sprint race did no more than establish grid places for the final, the fact that Follmer had lost a lap then had no relevance now. The only thing that mattered was that he took the flag for the rolling start with only three other cars separating him from Oliver. As he thundered into Turn 1, there were no cars separating them. The two black machines popped into view at the end of the first lap nose to tail, and seven long seconds went by before any other appeared. That, it would appear, was the shape of Can-Am '74.

There remained the matter of Follmer's ambitions for the finish, but the team presumably had had one of those closed-door discussions in the motorhome about Team Policy. At any rate, George was being a good boy for now, following Jackie like a loyal, er, Shadow. Maybe later.

Maybe not. About halfway along toward the end, just after the pair had lapped the two cars disputing third place, Follmer began to lose touch. An exhaust pipe was broken. Lap by lap, the fumes began to get to him, and by the end he was lagging Oliver by half a minute. Groggy and disgruntled, he shut himself away in the motorhome.

Patrick had disappeared from heat one with transmission failure.

Atlanta's declared crowd was 15,000.

left Follmer was less than ten seconds down. Settling the car hard under braking, its nose snapping up under power and George just riding his fat Goodyears to the top of the curbs, he pushed his way around well into the 1 min 14 sec bracket. With one lap left he had hauled Oliver in to within four seconds, but Jackie was well aware of his teammate's charge and he held George off by just less than two seconds.

Whew. The old Can-Am may have lost some of its friendly, but it sure had a lot of fierce left!

A week later, Edmonton canceled its Can-Am, citing loss of its event sponsor. Earlier, Laguna Seca had decided to switch its spring F5000 show to its October date, ousting the Group 7s. So now the old Can-Am was down to the six races it had boasted in its youth. At this stage, it didn't seem like a boast.

Mosport announced a crowd figure of 60,000.

Road Atlanta, Georgia, July 7, 1974

Acting just like the old McLaren team used to, as if they had some opposition, Shadow went to Atlanta early for more testing.

E for effort. Summer rain showers robbed most of the time, and once sent Oliver backwards into a guardrail. The next day a dog sacrificed itself to test the structural integrity of Ollie's front end. It turned out to

Watkins Glen, New York, July 14, 1974

This was a busy weekend. Not only were the Can-Am guys competing for attention with those F5000 people again, there were all those Six-Hour

types about. At least with the turbos gone from the scene, there ought to be some screaming little 3.0-liters tempted by all that legendary Can-Am gold, right?

Nope. Just one of them bothered. Busy man Mario Andretti, who was there for the F5000 event (he won), posted a Can-Am entry for the Alfa Romeo he was co-driving on Saturday (fifth under the flag, but disqualified for outside assistance during a trackside broken wire incident).

One other Six-Hour driver did present himself. Sam Posey had been invited to drive NART's aging, but still brutally powerful, 712M Ferrari that was making something of a career of racing at Watkins Glen and Watkins Glen only. Something went wrong with the brakes during practice, however, and when Sam stood on the pedal, the pedal went to the floor so sharply that it literally broke a bone in his foot. He threw it into a spin to get it stopped. A change of fluid fixed the brakes, and NART turned to the ever-game Brian Redman, who agreed to start from the back.

Sideshows were all very entertaining, but the main action should be at the Shadow team transporter. But where was it? A day late—it had thrown a rod on the dash from Atlanta. By pulling an all-nighter, the mechanics got both cars prepared for practice. That went all right, except that Oliver had a left front tire explode at maximum speed on the long straight. A very nasty experience, but he kept it off those endless Glen guardrails, and the only damage was a shattered fender. A leaking fuel pump the next day kept him from a last-minute challenge of Follmer's pole.

Once again, George had his mind on records, and he threw the DN4 around the course on the very edge. He came close to his old TurboPorsche time, but not Donohue's, nor was he able to defend the last generation of Group 7 from contemporary F1 speeds. Many drivers thought the track was slippery this year, and in any case George was driving in considerable discomfort in his back and wrists, likely a legacy of his testing crash at Mosport in June.

Scooter Patrick received good reviews for his inspired driving of the M20 into third grid place.

Follmer was still in a flat-out mood at the start of Saturday's twenty-lap preliminary race, and rapidly ripped free of Oliver, who was taking things much more easily. But Follmer lost all that lead because a shock absorber broke, forcing him into the pits. Patrick and fourth-starter John Cordts had their engines fail, but Redman brought the big 7.0 Ferrari all the way from the back to second place a minute behind Oliver.

Watkins Glen: Redman takes over the ex-Andretti Ferrari 712M, now befenced, befinned, and bewinged, after fading brakes break Posey's foot. *Charles Loring/Autosport*

After the Can-Am sprint, Follmer raced a BMW CSL in the Six-Hour, and at the end of it his back was seriously painful. He was ordered to stay in bed until 2:00 PM Sunday, and his team asked David Hobbs to stand by. There were some other overnight lineup changes: Andretti turned the Alfa over to teammate Arturo Merzario, and Milt Minter turned up with Otto Zipper's Alfa to start from the back, too. Neither car had run the Sprint. The Can-Am was getting confusing in its declining days.

George Follmer was no man to give up his seat, and he was in it when the time came. Starting from the fifth row, he was fourth into the first turn, and third out of it. Before the end of the first lap he was by Redman's red Ferrari and, just like that, color this Can-Am black too.

The two Shadows flitted around the track together for a while, but Oliver kept a sharp eye out for any moves contrary to protocol. After a further while he could let his guard down, because Follmer was dropping away. Visibly fatigued, his head lolling over in the corners, George lost 26sec by the end.

Redman too was having to watch his back, because Patrick was there, but then the blue McLaren's new Chevy went off color. Left alone, Brian started tossing the Ferrari around with enthusiasm. That happy game ended with rear suspension failure. Patrick was third now and had Merzario's Alfa's lights in his mirrors (apparently, the old rule about no glass up front in a Can-Am was no longer operative), but the Six-Hour car turned out not to have a seven-hour engine.

Minter's Alfa had gotten itself pinched into the guardrail on the first lap.

The official crowd was 73,500 this time, although that was an admitted two-day figure.

Mid-Ohio, Lexington, Ohio, August 11, 1974

Life! New blood! Well, not exactly new, but the Penske Porsche Panzer came back to the Can-Am for Mid-Ohio, and suddenly it all had meaning again.

The official story was that the 1973 turbocar had given its best gas mileage at this twisty track, and there was a chance that metering unit mods and backing the boost screw out a bit might let it meet the new consumption limit. Another story was that the promoter and the sanctioning body, desperate to get some action going, might not enforce that limit too rigidly. Just a story, of course.

Mark Donohue showed Brian Redman all the complex ropes he'd rigged over two years of intense development, and the team went to Mid-Ohio for private tests on Wednesday before the race. Brian was soon lapping in the 1:23 bracket and getting just under three miles per gallon while doing it, and these numbers indicated promise.

The rest of the Can-Am contenders arrived for Saturday, the only day of practice offered. However, there were no supporting events, either. Another Porsche swelled the ranks, Hurley Haywood's 917/10, but it wasn't wearing its turbochargers. To meet the challenge, Shadow had lightened its front bodywork by ten pounds, adopted a new, stiffer front tire to replace the ones that had given trouble at the Glen, and Follmer's engine was trying relocated fuel injectors. Gosh, it was almost like a Can-Am.

There was even a new car. Gary Wilson, a veteran campaigner whose Lolas and McLarens had always been particularly immaculate, had finally built a Can-Am car of his own. The Sting GW-1 was a generally conventional Chevy-powered design with a body resembling that of the Porsche 917/30. He qualified it thirteenth.

Qualifying was a real race within itself. *Autosport* told it this way:

The day of practice quickly became a match race between the two, flat Shadow wedges and the bulbous, whirring Penske Porsche. Redman didn't go out at all until the beginning of the second session and then he only did four laps before being called in. Brian had got down to the mid-1 m 22 s bracket in those few laps and that was enough for team manager Mark Donohue. For the rest of the session Brian lounged on the grass behind the pitlane, while at the other end of the pits the Shadows worked and worked hard.

Despite his disaffection for the tight, busy nature of Mid-Ohio ("I like big balls places far better"), Oliver was trying very hard . . .

Follmer lost a lot of time when a rear shock absorber broke (this is the second time this has happened to George's Shadow this year) but when he was on the track he was charging as hard as ever. George's strained back is still bothering him and by the end of the day he was looking very pained and stiff. But to watch him [drive] gave no hint of any such pains. He was hurling and flicking the Shadow around with volumes of energy, smoothing out the brisk lurches of the Shadow with every new lap and going faster and faster. Whenever Oliver managed a quicker time, Follmer would stiffen his face, slip on his helmet and storm out to prove *he* was the faster of the two. It was quite a needle match.

Before the final session, Oliver's car was pushed away with a cracked rear subframe, so he had to stand and watch Follmer carve his final qualifying time down to 1:22.285, 0.487 quicker than Ollie's own.

"But it was all to no avail," continued Kirby.

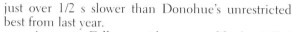

At the very outset of that final session the blue and yellow Penske Porsche whirred and popped down the pitlane. Redman pressed his way around for five unobtrusive laps. It was beginning to look like last summer all over again. The only difference was the white helmet with its band of Union Jacks rather than the yellow helmet of Donohue. It was that old, familiar display of total understatement which marks out the 917/30K as the finest racing car ever. "It's an incredible car," said Brian, "it tends to oversteer but it's *very* predictable and as soon as the turbo boost comes on it just straightens out and shoots away. I'm using second gear in all the corners where Mark used first, so that we can conserve fuel, yet I'm still getting wheelspin!" His final flying lap was in 1 m 21.093 s,

just over 1/2 s slower than Donohue's unrestricted best from last year.

A sweaty Follmer said, matter-of-factly, "All I need is 400 more horsepower," while Oliver, kicking his heels in the paddock, thought aloud, "I could have got into the 21s if I had got out in this session."

Gordo then joined his colleagues in trying to find out how much boost and fuel the Porsche had been using, to gain some sense of what to expect on the morrow, but secrecy *chez* Penske hadn't changed either.

Sunday's preliminary heat was a letdown. The sky was dark, but it didn't look like it would actually rain until just before the start. The Shadow team had gambled on slicks, and the officials wouldn't let them change at the last minute. The Penske team had gambled on wet tires, so Redman simply drove around unchallenged. "Simply" wasn't a fair word, of course. The enormous power lurking under his foot, every one of those horses poised to stampede wildly at the least twitch of his toe because of the turbochargers' self-energizing effect, was very fatiguing, mentally.

But just as two years before, when he'd had to drive a Shadow around Mid-Ohio in the rain on slicks, Oliver was brilliant. He and Follmer dropped back sharply at the start and were quickly surrounded by cars they'd never seen pass them before. One of them forced Follmer to spin, so he stopped for rain tires. But Oliver pressed on, "pitching and slithering around the circuit, his eyes peering intently through his yellow visor," as Kirby put it. He moved up to

third, behind everyone but Patrick in his rain-tire-equipped M20. Redman came around and lapped him. Then Follmer, fighting back from his stop, came up and passed his teammate too. Still Oliver stayed out and got his reward when the rain eased and the track began to dry. Shadow repassed Shadow, so the starting lineup for the final would be Redman-Patrick-Oliver-Follmer, ahead of Mueller's open-topped Ferrari 512M, with a 5.7 engine, and Nagel's Lola. Haywood had suffered wet electrics, so his Porsche was way back. Wilson's Sting wasn't there at all, as he'd shunted it.

For the forty-seven-lap final the track was practically dry, but the weather looked like it could go either way. The Penske management decided on slicks this time, but hedged its bet by hand-cutting rain grooves in them. Even if it didn't rain, the thinking went, the reduced rubber surface area would run a little hotter on this cool day, thus reducing the wheelspin factor and keeping fuel consumption more in line with the precise Penske calculations.

The Shadow management's approach was more direct. Both drivers would start on slicks again, and try to get by Patrick as fast as possible so they could push Redman as hard as possible in hopes he'd have to pit for his seven-gallon reserve.

Kirby was in his element:

Redman leapt away from the start, easily pulling clear of Patrick as he swept into the first turn, while Follmer came barreling through inside the McLaren, forcing Scooter to give way and leaving black marks all along the side of the sky-blue car. As George charged across the road, he also shut the door on Oliver. . . As they flicked out of the Keyhole and accelerated down the straight towards the esses the Shadows were able to close up in the Porsche's slipstream and as they braked for the esses Follmer ducked to the inside and snatched the lead! Oliver tried to follow his twin through but had to give way and as they tore past the pits after one lap it was still Shadow-Porsche-Shadow and Patrick all alone in fourth, some 3 s behind.

They raced on, nose-to-tail like this, for three tense, terrific laps, until the trio came up on the first slow car at the Keyhole, and Follmer lost just enough momentum that on the following straight, Redman was able to thrust the Porsche's nose in front. Next time along the straight, Oliver slipstreamed his fellow Shadowman and darted into second. Ollie wasn't able to repeat Follmer's pass on Redman, though. They were in the thick of the traffic, now, and the Porsche was getting through easier. But whenever they got clear, both Shadows closed right back up

again. On lap seven, Follmer did the fastest race lap, less than 0.2 over his grid time. The Brian-and-Ollie-and-George Show was still hooked up like a train as it started the eighteenth lap. Halfway around it, Redman made a mistake.

One of Mid-Ohio's many "vertical curves" coincided with a right-hand one, and Brian had been very conscious of the need to wait until the Porsche was over the crest and well planted on the road again before he unleashed its mighty engine. This time, he was an instant too anxious, and the big, long car snapped violently sideways. He saved it, but both Shadowmen seized the opportunity and blasted by.

Half a dozen laps later, the pair of black rockets and the blue spaceship close behind were plunging down the long straight and catching another slow car as they neared the tight, downhill right-hander at the end. Follmer read this as his chance. Kirby was watching:

He waited until the last minute then, with his nose inside Jackie's, he stomped on the brakes, bobbled for an instant, tapped the side of Oliver's car and in a scuffling moment, each Shadow refusing to give way to the other, each banging against each other before they

Elkhart Lake: Best in class becomes best overall; Patrick's 1972 model lasts when the 1974 cars can't. *Charles Loring/Autosport*

Elkhart Lake: Cordts in the other Kaplan McLaren (#6 M8F) picks up second and Gunn guns the Lola T260 (#39) to third, but Haywood's non-turbo 917/10 won't make it home. *Charles Loring/Autosport*

separated and Follmer spun into the grass. George was able to keep the engine going but for a long while he sat there, the top bodywork hanging free of its mounting points. Finally, he snatched a gear and set off again, now hopelessly out of the chase. . . Mike Hillman waved at him to come in and next time around in came the Shadow to have its bodywork fastened into place. But instead, George climbed from the car, his spirit broken, and after a few curt words he stalked away from the pits, took off his helmet and drove out of the circuit.

Oliver might still have had an assault from Redman to worry about, but the Porsche's grooved front tires were overheating badly now and Brian was dropping back. On the thirty-seventh lap he understeered right off the road in the loop before the pits and only just avoided the guardrail. The Shadow was 15sec ahead at the flag. Haywood came through the rest of the field for a decent third.

This event's spectator count was said to be 40,500.

Elkhart Lake, Wisconsin, August 25, 1974

Could the Panzer, having crushed the Can-Am to near extinction, have come back at the last moment and saved its life? Had SCCA followed the lead of some U.S. sanctioning bodies and relieved some of its "ener-gy measures"—offered more fuel—might that have encouraged Penske's further participation at Elkhart Lake? Could the spark kindled in that magic Mid-Ohio race somehow have been nursed into a self-sustaining flame?

We'll never know. There was no turbocar at Elkhart. The pair of UOP Shadow drivers qualified long seconds faster than anyone else. They ran one-two throughout the heat race, totally unopposed. In the main race, they were opposed only by things out of their control—both their cars broke. Scooter Patrick won. Good for him, but the Can-Am was a long way past being saved by two-year-old cars run by privateers, no matter how well they ran them.

Up to the point the second Shadow fell out, the team did its usual, solidly professional job. There was a spare DN4 available, a new car built on the repaired tub crashed at Mosport. It wasn't required, because both regular cars were performing beautifully. They didn't need the special, new, finned front wheels the team made up in case more brake cooling was called for on this track. Follmer did lose an engine on Friday, but on Saturday he won himself another pole. Once again his time (2:01.460) was well short of the Donohue '73 bogy (1:57.518), and this time it was about a second and a half short of his own '73 time. He said the Shadow was at least 20mph slower on the

straights than his Porsche had been, but its brakes were stronger.

As in Ohio, Oliver missed his chance to contest the pole. He spent Friday complaining of poor handling. "I've just fishtailed for the first time since I left school!" he told his team manager. (It was safe to tell him that. Hillman hadn't been in America to witness Ollie's driving style in the older Can-Am Shadows!) The problem turned out to be real, a broken differential locker. Saturday ended early, too, with a slipping clutch.

But there was no problem in Sunday's sprint race. By the end of the first four-mile lap, the pair of Shadows had a 4sec lead over Patrick's McLaren. Follmer led for a few laps, very likely enjoying the way Oliver was twitching about in his mirrors and throwing up dust from the edges. Jackie set fastest lap doing that. By pre-arrangement, then, Follmer let him by, and they cruised on to the finish. On the way, Follmer's car somehow lost its right-side door, but that presented no reason to stop.

Poor Patrick stopped, though, the blue McLaren losing a lonely third place when the left front wheel locked up under braking into Turn 5 and went straight off into the escape area. A brake disc had shattered. Herb Kaplan's crew replaced that whole suspension corner but didn't have time to line it up before the main race.

The first half of the first lap was almost a replay of the first heat. The first difference was Oliver being in the lead.

The second difference was Follmer spurting off the road halfway around. He brought it back, but could only limp around to the pits to retire. A half shaft had sheared.

So by the end of lap one, Oliver had nothing in his mirrors. He was already whole seconds ahead of the second place John Cordts driving Kaplan's sec-

ond car, a McLaren M8F. Ollie settled into a comfortable cruise-and-collect mode, going only fast enough to keep inflating his cushion at a casual second per lap.

For racing, there was still Scooter Patrick to watch coming up from the back of the grid. He got through cleanly, and was third by the third lap. All he had to do now was pull in his teammate's older car, and he did so on the seventh lap. Cordts made plenty of room for him in a braking zone, and that was all over, too.

Gordon Kirby strolled back to the pit lane to take in the finish, while "Oliver drove serenely on in his Shadow, lapping at least 6 s slower than his practice best and looking very comfortable. As the last half-dozen laps came up, the Shadow crew put on their Nomex tops in preparation for a possible fuel stop. But just as they did so Oliver went missing and their anxious eyes collapsed loosely as someone brought the news that the engine had blown up mightily. It hadn't given the slightest hint of failure. One second it had been booming along perfectly, the next second it had blown itself to bits along 100 yards of Road America tarmac.

"Patrick came by at the end of the 24th lap to see the surprise of his life. There, waving ecstatically from his pit was a sign reading P 1 1 1 1!"

Scooter drove safely through the last four laps, and Cordts followed him across the line about half a minute later. Behind the two McLarens came "the world's only two Lola T260s," driven by John Gunn and Bob Nagel—it was Nagel's fourth fourth place of the year. Gary Wilson's Sting finished its second-ever Can-Am with an encouraging fifth place.

Road America said 32,844 people had been watching.

The next day, at a promoter's meeting with SCCA officials in Chicago, the sixth Can-Am round,

Elkhart Lake: Wilson's second outing with his Sting GW1 (#2) results in a fine fifth just behind Nagle (#17 T260) and ahead of Mueller's chop-topped Ferrari 512M (#7). *Dale von Trebra*

Jackie Oliver, Can-Am Champion

Fast hands, heavy feet and the dogged mindset of a street fighter finally brought success in his sixth season of trying. As were the six series champs who preceded him, Ollie was an F1 driver. He was born in England August 14, 1942, and was racing a Mini while still a teenager. Next came small-bore sports cars—including a wooden-chassied Marcos, which on one occasion provided spectators a legendary memory of flying flinders. From there it was an orderly climb up the F3 and F2 ladder until, in 1968, he was with Lotus as F1 partner to that year's World Champion, Graham Hill. Neither that seat nor subsequent ones in BRMs, McLarens, or Shadows brought any victories, but he co-drove winning Ford GT40s and Porsche 917s at LeMans, Sebring, and Daytona. He also tried his hand at NASCAR. Almost from the moment he came into Can-Am he was a contender with countryman Peter Bryant's Ti22, and he never let up despite his horrifying "blowover" at St. Jovite in 1970. Three subsequent seasons in Don Nichols' Shadows were frustrating but also educational, as Oliver took on a role in the team's organization. After his retirement from driving—and an acrimonious split from Nichols—he co-founded the Arrows F1 team, which he still heads. His Can-Am title remains his only personal championship; here he savors his Road Atlanta trophy with wife Lynn. *Bill Warner photo*

Sting GW1: Gary Wilson, a rancher from Kansas, had been driving purchased equipment in the Can-Am almost from the beginning. Just in time for what turned out to be the series' finale, he produced his own car. Designed by John Collins, originally a mechanic from England who had been with Shelby and Motschenbacher, the GW1 resembled a blend of McLaren M8F chassis elements clad in Porsche-like bodywork. As in the McLarens, the stressed part of the aluminum monocoque ended behind the seats, and the big Chevy, braced by A-frames, was part of the load-bearing structure. Wheelbase was 100in. There were two radiators mounted in the body sides and fed by NACA inlets atop the doors. The Sting first raced at Mid-Ohio (shown in photo), where Wilson qualified mid-pack but crashed after fifteen laps of the first heat. At Elkhart Lake he started 11th and lasted to finish 5th, a satisfying—if ultimately fruitless—result for a "homebuilt" car in a class of racing that began with them. *Dale von Trebra*

scheduled at Riverside, was canceled. The announcement was leavened with much promising talk of the 1975 series, but the talk led to nothing. As it turned out, 1974 wasn't an interim year. It was the end.

Car of the Can-Am 1974
Shadow DN4

At the beginning of the Can-Am, a designer's mind was free to roam almost anywhere. By the end, his pencil

was nearly as tamed as in any conventional formula. Both mind and pencil still could be kept sharp to get the best performance within the rules, of course, and the significant new design factor in 1974 was limited fuel capacity. Up through 1973, Can-Am cars could carry as much gasoline as the engine might require to cover race distances up to 210 miles. The superpowerful Porsche 917/30 was built as a veritable fuel tanker. For 1974, however, SCCA took "energy measures" which, in final analysis, gave the cars a maximum fuel allowance of 37gal.

Thus was established a much smaller tank around which the designers might shrink their cars, and Shadow took advantage of it. Compared with the bulky, unsuccessful DN2 of 1973, the DN4 was a more compact, lighter vehicle built around tanks displacing a total of 45gal. Wheelbase was increased by 2in to 105, but track dimensions and overall width were narrowed.

Otherwise the DN4 was basically conventional in layout and similar to the previous Group 7 model both inside and out. The easiest way to distinguish the two visually was the shape of the front inlets, which changed from rectangular to circular on the new car. Radiators were now carried farther aft in the flanks, and air came to them through troughs either side of the swelling cockpit. Also, the front fender profiles were smoother and wrapped more tightly around the 13in wheels that replaced the 15s of 1973. Fifteens remained at the rear, but plans to mount tires with an outside diameter of 26.5in fell through when Goodyear could only supply the older 28s. That was enough of a discrepancy to require a late geometry redesign.

Under its glossy black skin, the 1974 car adopted some suspension parts from Shadow's new DN3 F1 design. The rear suspension had a total of four trailing radius rods with parallel lower transverse links, instead of single top rods and a lower wishbone. Brakes were still outboard at the front, inboard in back, and the transaxle was still a four-speed Hewland.

Perhaps unexpectedly, given the fuel limitations, the Chevrolet-based engine remained at 495ci. However, Lee Muir found that assembling the fuel metering system with greater precision not only yielded the necessary mileage increase, but an additional 35hp as well. Though PR materials quoted 735hp, the same number given the year before, the real 1974 output is thought to have been closer to 800.

"There's no substitute for horsepower," George Follmer recently told writer Preston Lerner for *Sports*

Car International, "but chassis-wise, the DN4 pointed in well and was very predictable. And because frontal area was so small, it was fast in a straight line. It was an extremely good race car."

It was, in fact, the last great Can-Am car.

Shadow's more compact, lighter DN4. *Bill Warner*

"It's rather like the death of a Chinese prime minister that gets announced to the outside world some weeks after it has happened. The Sports Car Club of America has finally stopped propping the cadaver of the Can-Am series in their window and have admitted that the series is finally dead."

Eoin Young may have been a little short on compassion when he put that in his *Autocar* column in the waning weeks of 1974, but his appraisal could not be faulted. The lingering misery of the once-mighty Big Bangers was over.

The official death blow came November 19. In a press release from SCCA's Denver headquarters, the club's executive director and director of professional racing, Cameron Argetsinger, blamed high costs and a depressed economy. "Notwithstanding a reduction in investment through implementation of the 5-liter stock block and 3-liter racing engine specification for the 1975 Can-Am, constructors and entrants find today's economic climate again rapidly escalating costs and therefore felt unable to offer race promoters and the SCCA firm commitments for participation in 1975.

"On the other hand, constructors and entrants felt they needed guarantees of a minimum number of series events in order to amortize their investments."

The director went on to say that the sanctioning organization had been trying to bring both sides together with "a step-by-step program of reciprocal assurances and guarantees." The process had gone as far as "the fifth phase." Unfortunately, at that point "several highly-regarded constructors and entrants . . . were forced to withdraw their planned participation due to the uncertainty of the world's economy."

An uncertainty which did not seem to be dampening enthusiasm for SCCA's open-wheel cars with the same engine formula. "Several circuit promoters have acknowledged an interest in staging a second Formula 5000 race to replace the open date created by the loss of the Can-Am event," the announcement concluded.

So it was done. The noble experiment had been shut down.

At that stage, very likely, no juggling of rules could have saved the old, original Can-Am car. Once it was a grand and glorious celebration of unbridled technology and unlimited power. It stood tall, its own unique magnificence its very reason for being. By its last season it was a pathetic anachronism, trembling from cuts in its hamstrings, trussed by endless regulations, bowed low under the weight of good intentions.

The great cars died hard. Don Nichols brought the Shadows out a couple of more times late in 1974 for exhibition races, once against each other, once against their F1 teammates. In 1975, Roger Penske got Mark Donohue to dust off one of the Porsches and prepare it for an assault on the world's closed course speed record. After a lot more work than just dusting, and after an abortive attempt at Daytona, Mark finally succeeded at Talladega, lapping the NASCAR superspeedway at 221.12mph.

The year after that, Mosport invited owners of leftover Group 7 cars to try their speed against the latest generation of Le Mans Mirages, Porsches, and Renaults. The big old iron easily beat off the new kid-stuff, Jackie Oliver winning overall in a Shadow DN4 after a battle with George

Follmer in a McLaren M20. But there was no follow-up to this one-off, spur-of-the-moment *Formule Libre* spectacle.

SCCA finally got its way on the 5.0-liter matter in 1977, when it ordered F5000 owners to drape their single seaters with full-coverage bodywork and call them "Can-Am" cars. That lasted until 1986. There was also a "Can-Am" category limited to 2.0 liters. More recently, the name has been granted to a Dodge V-6-powered, "spec-car" series created by Carroll Shelby for low-cost amateur motorsport. Each formula has been more restrictive than the last.

Some of the original unlimited cars did live on in club racing for a while, and a few were grandfathered into the subsequent generation of 5.0-liter "Can-Am." Recently, veteran Can-Ammers of the golden age have achieved great popularity in vintage racing.

But the course of professional racing had veered out from under the Big Bangers. As years passed, ever heavier rulebooks were piled on every kind of racing automobile. The motivations were multifarious: concerns about speeds and safety, about expense, about filling TV screens. None of these are unworthy considerations, but ruleswriting feeds on itself. Partly because of the law of unintended consequences, every new rule seems to create a need for another. Rules are stacked atop regulations, and regulations atop restrictions and one innovative notion after another is banned, until the cars are designed less by designers than by politicians. It becomes increasingly hard to find any area where creativity is permitted, and more and more time and money has to be spent achieving smaller and smaller technical advantages.

To be sure, the resultant racing is close. CART and USAC Indy cars, NASCAR stock cars, SCCA's Trans-Am sedans, IMSA's World Sports Cars, even FIA Formula One cars on a good day, all put on good, tight, competitive shows. What's wrong with that?

Just this: to me, it seems too stage-managed. It seems unreal. The pressure to put on a show has crushed the sense that I, for one, used to en-

Laguna Seca 1974: Shadow Showdown! To keep faith with Shadow's sponsors—and their public—after the premature termination of the Can-Am season, Don Nichols staged two intra-squad match races later in the year. The first, a quick fifteen-lapper squeezed in ahead of a Saturday morning F1 practice session at the Watkins Glen U.S. Grand Prix, pitted Oliver, Follmer, and Jean-Pierre Jarier in a trio of DN4s. Oliver qualified fastest, matching the 1:39.9 pole time that Follmer had done earlier in the year, but valve and clutch trouble left him unable to prevent his aggressive teammate scoring his first win of the season. Jarier was a cautious third, but a week later at Laguna Seca, where the original Can-Am date had been given to F5000, the Frenchman seized his honor back. This time he was driving an F1 Shadow DN3 (#17) and easily outqualified the two big black bangers. So did teammate James Hunt, who took pole at 58.731. At the start of the twenty-seven-lap race the pair of nimble single-seaters simply drove away from the heavier iron, both of which compounded their ignominy by spinning. Oliver finally stopped— more clutch trouble—but Follmer stayed out and soon saw the F1s looming in his mirrors. Trying to prevent their lapping him he succeeded in blocking Hunt, but Jarier slipped by them both to win by 6sec. *Autosport photo*

Below and next page: Talladega 1975: World Record! Reluctantly taking time from his first F1 campaign in Europe, which he was finding heavy going, Mark Donohue acceded to Roger Penske's demand that he refurbish the Porsche 917/30 and break something called the World's Closed Course Speed record. That stood to A.J. Foyt, who had recently gone some 217mph at NASCAR'S Talladega Speedway in Alabama with his Coyote Indy car. Mark made an attempt at Daytona, but the long periods of full power overheated the engine. Porsche made up a pair of intercoolers (seen at the extreme rear of the vast, 1190hp 5.0 engine, on which Earl MacMullin is working), a set of "Moon disc" wheel covers were added, and the red-painted machine was taken to Talladega. There on Saturday, August 9, in threatening weather conditions and with the long-tailed streamliner worming uneasily on the steep bankings because its wing was flattened for minimal drag, Mark made a brave, four-lap timed run. His last-lap average was 221.120mph. Calculations showed he'd finally seen 250 on the straights. It was the concluding triumph of his life. *Dave Friedman photos*

Writer Plays Racer

Shadow Mk 3

I stall it on my first attempt. I punch the button again, bite my lip, and gave it a little more gas this time. The huge rear tires spin free. As I lurch away, I picture the owner shaking his head with misgivings.

Actually, as I discovered later, the owner's reaction had been very different. Lorna, my wife, told me that, as I hazed his expensive slicks and lurched incompetently away around Sears Point raceway in his priceless, 800-plus-horsepower 1972 Shadow Mark 3, one of only two in the world, vintage racer Fred Cziska turned to her with a smile of approval and said, "You can't baby this car." What a guy.

This is where these grand machines live on, now, in historic racing. It's something like heaven, in that they only run for fun. Their time in the real world has passed.

But yeah! After all those years of watching, in 1994 I finally got to do! I wrote about sweating up Jackie Oliver's old seat in my "Fast Lines" column for *Vintage Motorsport*.

Surprise: this is a car. Just a car. I'm not sure what I'd expected, perhaps some kind of titanium alloy-cum-composite carbonfilament space-timecraft coursing a metaphysical continuum inaccessible to mere protoplasm such as myself, but—ha!—it's a car! Turn the steering wheel, and the car responds by changing direction. Press the brake pedal, and it obediently slows. Press the accelerator . . .

WOOAAAHHH! Not so much. Not so soon. Let's take this a single dizzying plateau at a time.

Of course, most of us writers who think they're racers lack the skill to critique such a car. Of course, that doesn't stop us. So, to me—go ahead, laugh, I did when I heard the thought in my head—the Can-Am car feels like a giant go-kart. There's the same sense of sitting up between the fat front wheels, the same impression of vivid response to the least movement of the plump little steering wheel, the same sensation of total lack of lean while cornering.

I said giant go-kart. I feel immersed in boxy black bodywork. There's a lot more car behind me than in front. Most of what's back there is engine. Lots of engine. Engine enough to put a backspin on the earth and launch us into high orbit. Or at least to fire me like a 12-gauge slug through the nearest steel guardrail.

So I gas it. Not right away, and not everywhere, but presently I identify a couple of places around the lap where I think I can get away with experiencing full power.
S-SHAZZAAAMMMM!
Good Golly Miss Molly!
Wow!

By the end of my drive, I'd figured out it was the mind-bending acceleration of these great cars from the Psychedelic Age that so endear them to their present owners. In my column I said I wouldn't reveal the secret if they'd continue slipping me the occasional power fix. It worked. That same summer another vintage racer let my foot find its way to his loud pedal.

Lola T163

To duplicate the acceleration sensation of an 8.0-liter Lola, you might try ramming yourself into the breech of a 16in battleship rifle, waiting while the gun crew stuffs eight big bags of powder in behind you, then yanking your own lanyard.

Sixteen inches happens to be precisely the amount of space for hip-bones in the Lola T163 I drove while doing a story for *Car and Driver*. Originally raced in 1969 by Ronnie Bucknum and Peter Revson, the car was restored and prepared by Bud Bennett and his sons, Craig and Kirt, "The Big Noise Boys" of RM Motorsports in Wixom, Michigan. Chrysler generously let us do our instrumented testing on its proving grounds at nearby Chelsea.

On the two-mile straightaway there, with regular racer Kirt driving, *Car and Driver's* data acquisition system recorded 0–60 acceleration in 2.6sec, 0-100 in 4.7, and the standing quarter-mile in 9.7 at 152mph. Top speed, limited that day by gearing and aerodynamics, was only 188 in road racing trim. We got another 7mph or so by taking the wing off. Minus the driver, but with the 16gal of gasoline typically on board for vintage races, the car weighed 1910lb, distributed 34.3/65.7. The engine, built by Bill King with Chevrolet heads on a Keith Black aluminum block, displaced 482ci, made 723lb-ft of torque at 5900rpm, and 870hp at 6700. The team said typical racing fuel consumption was 3mpg. The magazine listed noise level in decibels as "one hundred and plenty."

To me, the acceleration felt like "a 1969 NASA moon shot."

joy that auto racing was an exciting exploration into the technological unknown.

I do grant that today's competition machinery is exquisitely made, each individual computer-crafted component far more elegant than most of the handmade stuff we saw in the "old" days. And it is true that current cars have fantastic performance capabilities, giving acceleration and braking and cornering g-loads we never dreamed of twenty years ago. They're more reliable, too, a lot more. And vastly safer.

Abruptly your world's axis tilts, and you're lying on your shoulder blades looking up the launch track. Things that just a moment before were all around you—people, trees—just sort of vanish. Your only cosmos now is the textured asphalt between the pair of big white fender-domes coming at you in long streaks, like when the starship Enterprise goes to warp velocity.

You may feel unnervingly exposed. You may sense a lot of air bathing your upper body, and find your mind dwelling on how light are the structures that embrace only your lower parts. You may become aware that the faster you go, the more darty and wandery the car behaves on the high-crowned road, while the grassy edges edge closer and closer. You may find yourself deciding that 5000 in fifth is rpm enough. Well, maybe you'll give it one more stab to see 5500. That's 145mph. That is enough.

Perhaps because you had backed off, showing just a touch of sense, you are allowed to make the 5-mile drive to the skid pad. On normal roadways, the car's ride is harsh, and the worst bumps cause violent shakes in the suede steering wheel and painful scraping noises underneath. This is no streetable dual-purpose sports car. Every stop sign means a rededication of mind to clutch. Every face within the range that faces can be distinguished is turned your way. Every yank on that lanyard is a fresh thrill.

On the friendly acres of smooth blacktop the big car happily slides around like a kart. The Beauteous Beast cannot boast the lateral grip of today's coldly scientific groundsuckers, but neither does it beat up your body so badly. As a driving instrument it turns out to be most straightforward, manageable, and rewarding. Ample sensual messages come in about what it's doing—although they come in very rapidly, and you have to answer as quickly. Steering and throttle responses are so sweet that any steady-state cornering attitude can be maintained at will, but the merest twitch of toe snaps the long, heavy tail away into a wild spinout.

I realize my two short stints at the wheels of historic vehicles hardly scratch the surface of the Can-Am driving experience.

But the experiences I did have fully lived up to my expectations—and then some.

Wow!

Still, there's something about them that fails to fully satisfy me. I was raised when racers ranged wild and free. I look at today's cars, and all I can see are the barbed-wire rules fences that hold them back from where they want to go.

We have come to a time when F1 cars, supposed pacesetters of modern motorsports technology, are waddling around with wooden surfboards strapped to their bellies.

The intervening years have brought me a small extra measure of maturity, in that I better recognize the need of discipline, yet I retain sympathy for the feelings I expressed in my *Autosport* report of the 1972 Riverside Can-Am. We had lost the Chaparrals and all they stood for two years earlier; now, already, we were hearing calls to ban the Panzer. I wrote:

I have a personal bias, in that I abhor rules. Over the past few Can-Am seasons more and more rules have come down, stifling the technology-for-technology's-sake spirit that had, in my eyes, excused many of Group 7's faults. The racing itself might not always be exciting (though sometimes it *was*), but there was sure to be something interesting about the cars. The reason for more and more regulations was that more equal cars might stage more competitive races.

I don't think it ever worked out that way. No simple car was ever really competitive with the deceptively simple McLarens. I think racing is more than rules. I think perhaps racing should have more to do with the independence-of-thought that so marks successful racing people. Formulae that aim at developing the next crop of drivers is one thing, but I think a *premier* series must offer a grander spectacle. The public should be able to see the best expression of *all* the varied skills and talents embodied by the people in the sport. In a genuinely top rank series there should be no holds barred.

Biased as I am, it's particularly gratifying to me that the Porsche engineers in developing their highly

Bonneville 1970-something: The author pauses to pose on The Salt during a cross-continent dash to the next race. His "Can-Van-Am" served as wheels, office, kitchen, motorcycle transporter, horse hauler, hunting lodge, and paddock palace for over 200 nights and at least 40,000 miles a year during some great years.
Ray Hutton

competitive car have concentrated their efforts on the two areas left unfettered: engine concept and chassis weight. I applaud their success, and I decry any movement to 'ban turbocharged aircooled engines and introduce weight limits.' Expensive? Sure it's expensive, but point out to me a cheap racing formula that offers any spectacle. Racing in the modern way is Show Biz. The people behind the fences pay our way, and they pay for a show. We must give them the most grandiose show we can devise, or they'll take up some other weekend diversion.

Two years later, when the Can-Am died, I took no comfort in seeing I'd been right.

Today, I admit racing has progressed beyond any stage I ever foresaw. But, for me, something has been lost on the way.

Could the Can-Am happen again? Is there any realistic prospect of bringing back wild, free, no-holds-barred race cars? Frankly, it's hard to credit. Let's be honest: free-formula sports car racing had several chances, and failed them all. Britain's Big Bangers faded to black in 1966. The USRRC of 1963–1968 suffered by the relative strength of its successor, the Can-Am. But the original, minimally-limited Can-Am only made it to the age of nine. Europe's Interserie died younger.

Later, IMSA launched a spiritual successor with its Grand Touring Prototypes. These high-powered, high-technology GTP coupes—and those of a European parallel called Group C—labored under many more regulations than did the roadsters of the old Group 7. However, GTP's big plus was strong automaker representation, something the Can-Am received only rarely. GTP cars raced thirteen seasons, from 1981 to 1993, before dwindling cash flow choked them to silence. IMSA has replaced them with World Sports Cars, open-cockpit two-seaters intended to recall the old Can-Am days, but the heavily regulated resemblance is mainly on the surface. In fact, the carefully controlled WSC engines aren't far from meeting the 5.0-liter formula the economy-minded SCCA proposed for the aborted 1975 Can-Am.

It does comes down to economics. Motor racing is perhaps the most commercial of arts. The Can-Am died partly because its appetite for money grew too ravenous. There's much more money in motorsport today, but it's there because motorsport became a bet-

ter marketing vehicle. A vehicle driven by people who prefer their horses nicely broken to harness. Wild-and-free is out.

Can-Am competitors complained about costs, but subsequent racers have found many more ways to spend their sponsors' money. The Can-Am didn't have the on-board electronics available today, nor the CAD/CAM construction techniques, nor the multitude of other expensive, if effective, aids. And so much time today is spent testing, testing, testing that not even the old McLaren and Porsche Can-Am teams could have imagined it. A reborn Can-Am series would rival a military weapons program for expense.

There is also the argument that, were all of today's available automotive technology to be unleashed, the resulting cars would overwhelm the drivers, not to mention the race tracks. It takes no great leap of imagination to foresee horsepower well beyond 2000, and given free aerodynamics, suspensions, and tires, the cars might be able to generate forces the drivers could not endure. It could reach the situation in modern fighter-jets, which must be performance-limited by their flight-control computers. The airframes are aerodynamically capable of generating g-loadings in turns that the pilots physically cannot stand. The soft human flesh inside the fighter is the weakest link.

A possible counter to that argument is an historical observation: during the relatively short Can-Am era, power grew from less than 500, then considered a heady value, to more than 1000, yet drivers and designers learned to cope just fine. Mark Donohue's 1100hp Porsche 917/30 was often described as one of the best-behaved racing machines ever seen.

Would the experience be the same with 2200hp? In chassis featuring all those techno-tricks banned in so-called premier forms of the sport today? Tricks such as fan- or flipper-created ground effects, and computer-governed active suspensions, and brake- and traction-control, and all-wheel-drive, plus perhaps all-wheel-steer with anti-yaw electronics, and possibly even some form of automatic course guidance?

Well, it would be fun to find out. But don't send cash money away for tickets. The times aren't right.

Maybe they'll never be right again. Maybe, like shining Camelot and Woodstock, the Can-Am could only have happened when it did.

I'm so glad I was there.

Grids and Results: 1966 – 1974

1. St. Jovite 9/11/66

5 Amon	4 McLaren	3 Surtees
McLaren M1B	McLaren M1B	Lola T70
1:38.8	1:38.5	1:38.4, 96.95 mph *

198 Jones	96 Motschenbacher
Lola T70	McLaren M1B
1:40.7	1:40.6

6 Morley	16 Donohue	62 Cannon
McLaren M1B	Lola T70	McLaren M1B
1:42.3	1:42.2	1:41.4

116 Follmer	30 Gurney
Lola T70	Lola T70
1:42.9	1:42.5 (non-starter)

8 Grant	55 J. Adams	10 Parsons
Lola T70	McLaren M1A	McLaren M1B
1:44.8	1:44.2	1:44.1

39 Heimrath	91 Scott
McLaren M1A	McLaren M1B
1:45.8	1:44.9

98 Hayes	22 Posey	37 Bucknum
McLaren M1B	McLaren M1B	Lola T70
1:46.3	1:46.0	1:45.9

52 Eve	88 Gregory
Genie Mk10	McLaren M1B
1:48.1	1:46.7

38 D. Brown	95 Harris	18 Lerch
McLaren M1B	Genie Mk10	McLaren M1A
1:48.3	1:48.2	1:48.2

41 Hansen	23 Alderman
Wolverine	Lola T70
1:49.9	1:49.5

33 Fejer	94 Wietzes	123 D. Revson
Chinook Mk1	Ford GT40	Porsche 906
1:53.2	1:51.0	1:50.7

44 Christianson	36 Ryan
Merlyn Mk8	Genie Mk10
1:55.7	1:54.3

73 Gates	169 N. Adams	70 Crawford
McLaren M1A	Cooper	Lola T70
1:57.4, 81.26 mph *	1:57.2	1:56.2

72 Seitz
Lotus 23
No Time

Results
1. John Surtees (Lola T70-Chevrolet), 75 laps of 2.65 mi. = 198.75 mi. in 2.06:51.0, 94.014 mph *
2. Bruce McLaren (McLaren M1B-Chevrolet), 75 laps
3. Chris Amon (McLaren M1B-Chevrolet), 74
4. John Cannon (McLaren M1B-Chevrolet), 73
5. George Follmer (Lola T70-Ford), 73
6. Chuck Parsons (McLaren M1B-Chevrolet), 73
7. Jerry Grant (Lola T70-Chevrolet), 71
8. Lothar Motschenbacher (McLaren M1B-Olds), 71
9. Bud Morley (McLaren M1A-Ford), 70
10. Dick Brown (McLaren M1B-Ford), 69
11. George Alderman (Lola T70-Ford), 69
12. Ludwig Heimrath (McLaren-Ford), 69
13. Eppie Wietzes (Ford GT40), 69
14. Doug Revson (Porsche 906), 69
15. Bob Harris (Genie Mk10-Olds), 65
16. Jim Adams (McLaren M1A-Ford), 65
17. Bud Gates (McLaren M1A-Chevrolet), 65
18. Jerry Crawford (Lola T70-Chrysler), 63
19. Nick Adams (Cooper-Ford), 62
20. Jerry Hansen (Wolverine-Chevrolet), 59
21. Sam Posey (McLaren M1B-Ford)
Retirements: 22-Ron Bucknum (Lola-Ford), overheating; 23-Peter Lerch (McLaren-Ford), blown engine; 24-Parnelli Jones (Lola T70-Ford), clutch, 21; 25-George Fejer (Chinook Mk1-Chevrolet), fuel leak; 26-Bill Eve (Genie Mk10-Ford), suspension; 27-Skip Scott (McLaren M1B-Ford) broken gear linkage, 14; 28-Charlie Hayes (McLaren-Chevrolet), blown engine, 7 laps; 29-Jack Ryan (Genie Mk10-Chevrolet), suspension; 30-Paul Christianson (Merlyn Mk8 -Chevrolet); 31-Phil Seitz (Lotus 23-Climax); 32-Masten Gregory (McLaren M1B-Chevrolet), radiator, 1; 33-Mark Donohue (Lola T70-Chevrolet), fire, broken steering, 1.
Fastest Lap: Amon, 1:37.3, 98.05 mph *

Did Not Start:
11 Hugh P.K. Dibley (Lola-Chevrolet)
9 Paul Hawkins (Lola Chevrolet)
83 Marius Amiot (McKee Mk6-Ford)
Dave Greenblatt (Ferrari 275 LM)
Max Biemler (Lotus 23)
Mike Goth (McLaren-Goth Spl-Chevrolet/Modified M1A)
Tom Payne (Cobra-Ford)
Alternate: Jim Roe (McLaren M1B)

* MPH calculated based on 2.65-mi. track length.

2. Bridgehampton 9/18/66

4 McLaren	7 Surtees	30 Gurney
McLaren M1B	Lola T70	Lola T70
1:33.4	1:33.4	1:33.2, 110.09 mph

65 P. Hill	5 Amon
Chaparral 2E	McLaren M1B
1:34.4	1:33.4

16 Follmer	86 Goth	6 Donohue
Lola T70	McLaren-Goth Spl	Lola T70

10 Parsons	19 Scott
McLaren M1B	McLaren M1B

88 Gregory	96 Motschenbacher	8 Grant
McLaren M1B	McLaren M1B	Lola T70

98 Jones *	62 Cannon
Lola T70	McLaren M1B

23 Alderman	97 Hayes	33 Posey
Lola T70	McLaren M1B	McLaren M1B

61 Morley	38 D. Brown
McLaren M1B	McKee

25 Hawkins	3 Rodriguez	00 B. Brown
Lola T70	Ferrari Dino	Lola T70

17 Buzzetta	12 D. Revson
Porsche 906	Porsche 906

52 Eve	60 Hamill	95 Harris
Genie Mk10	Hamill SR3	McLaren M1A

15 Wetanson	1 Kolb
Porsche 906	Ferrari Dino

70 Crawford +	41 Denner	77 Stanton
Lola T70	Porsche	Stanton Spl

36 Ryan	2 Wonder +
Genie	

28 Gammino +	29 Bucher
Lamborghini P538	Lola T70

* #98 (Parnelli Jones' car) raced by Al Unser.

+ Not listed in results. Presumed non-starter.

Note: Fastest qualifier was Jim Hall (Chaparral 2E) at 1:32.9 (110.44 mph), but he withdrew so the car could be taken over by teammate Phil Hill.

Results
1. Dan Gurney (Lola T70-Ford), 70 laps of 2.85 mi. = 199.5 mi. in 1.53:22.42 *, 105.58 mph (record)
2. Chris Amon (McLaren M1B-Chevrolet), 70 laps
3. Bruce McLaren (McLaren M1B-Chevrolet), 70
4. Phil Hill (Chaparral 2E-Chevrolet), 70
5. Mark Donohue (Lola T70-Chevrolet), 69
6. Chuck Parsons (McLaren M1B-Chevrolet), 67
7. Jerry Grant (Lola T70-Chevrolet), 66
8. Sam Posey (McLaren M1B-Ford), 66
9. Dick Brown (McKee-Ford), 65
10. Bill Eve (Genie Mk10-Ford), 64
11. Joe Buzzetta (Porsche 906), 64
12. Doug Revson (Porsche 906), 64
13. Bob Brown (Lola T70), 64
14. Bob Bucher (Lola T70-Ford), 63
15. Paul Hawkins (Lola T70-Chevrolet), 60
16. Jack Ryan (Genie-Chevrolet), 59
17. Herb Wetanson (Porsche 906), 59
18. Gene Stanton (Stanton Spl), 55
Retirements: 19-Skip Scott (McLaren M1B-Ford) dead battery, 62 laps; 20-John Cannon (McLaren M1B-Chevrolet), lost brakes, 59; 21-Masten Gregory (McLaren M1B-Chevrolet), spin, 58; 22-Charlie Kolb (Ferrari Dino), engine, 43; 23-Pedro Rodriguez (Ferrari Dino), lost wheel, 39; 24-Mike Goth (McLaren-Goth Spl-Chevrolet), lost wheel, 36; 25-John Denner (Porsche-Denmacher Mk2), ring and pinion, 31; 26-George Follmer (Lola T70-Ford), oil pressure, 29; 27-John Surtees (Lola T70-Chevrolet), losing oil, electrics, 17; 28-Lothar Motschenbacher (McLaren M1B-Olds), ignition, 12; 29-Bud Morley (McLaren M1B-Ford), gearbox and engine, 10; 30-Al Unser (Lola T70-Ford), accident, 7; 31-Ed Hamill (Hamill Spl), exhaust system, 1.
Disqualified: George Alderman (Lola T70-Ford), entered paddock, reentered race.
Fastest Lap: Gurney, 1:34.28, 108.88 mph (record)

* Total time of race not available in official results. Calculated from given information.

3. Mosport 9/25/66

4 McLaren	5 Amon	30 Gurney
McLaren M1B	McLaren M1B	Lola T70
1:53.5 +	1:53.0 +	1:50.7 +

33 Posey	81 Hulme
McLaren M1B	Lola T70
1:54.0 +	1:53.6 +

62 Cannon	16 Follmer	6 Donohue
McLaren M1B	Lola T70	Lola T70
1:56.3 +	1:56.1 +	1:55.7 +
	(non-starter)	

66 Hall	96 Motschenbacher
Chaparral 2E	Genie-Vinegaroon
1:22.9, 106.78 mph	1:58.3 +

19 Scott	65 P. Hill	7 Surtees
McLaren M1B	Chaparral 2E	Lola T70
1:26.5	1:24.5	1:24.5

10 Parsons	86 Goth
McLaren M1B	McLaren-Goth Spl
1:27.0	1:26.8

77 Kronn	39 Heimrath	61 Morley
McKee	McLaren M1B	McLaren M1B
1:28.6	1:28.4	1:27.0

88 Gregory	97 Hayes
McLaren M1B	McLaren M1B
1:29.7	1:28.8

38 D. Brown	60 Hamill	11 Hawkins
McLaren M1B	Hamill SR3	Lola T70
1:30.2	1:29.9	1:29.8

99 E. Jones	23 Lunger
McLaren M1B	Lola T70
++	1:30.5

52 Eve	94 Wietzes	57 Cordts
Genie Mk10	Ford GT40	McLaren M1A

53 Dibley	29 Bucher
Lola T70	Lola T70
++	++

00 B. Brown
Lola T70
++

+ Time set in Thursday qualifying which took precedence over times set Friday even if the Friday times were faster.

++ Position Determined by qualifying race.

Results
1. Mark Donohue (Lola T70-Chevrolet), 85 laps of 2.459 mi. = 209.15 mi. in 1.54:51.89, 109.25 mph (record)
2. Phil Hill (Chaparral 2E-Chevrolet), 83 laps
3. Chuck Parsons (McLaren M1B-Chevrolet), 82
4. Earl Jones (McLaren M1B-Chevrolet), 80
5. Paul Hawkins (Lola T70-Chevrolet), 79
6. Eppie Wietzes (Ford GT40), 78
7. Hugh Dibley (Lola T70-Chevrolet), 77
8. Bob Brown (Lola T70-Chevrolet), 74
9. Bill Eve (Genie Mk10-Ford), 70
10. Masten Gregory (McLaren M1B-Chevrolet), 68
11. Mike Goth (McLaren-Goth Spl-Chevrolet), 65
Retirements: 12-Dan Gurney (Lola T70-Ford), ignition; 13-Chris Amon (McLaren M1B-Chevrolet), suspension; 14-Bud Morley (McLaren M1B-Ford), engine; 15-Dick Brown (McLaren M1B-Ford); 16-Denny Hulme (Lola T70-Chevrolet), transmission; 17-Ludwig Heimrath (McLaren M1B-Ford), suspension; 18-Bruce McLaren (McLaren M1B-Chevrolet), suspension; 19-Mak Kronn (McKee-Chevrolet); 20-Sam Posey (McLaren M1B-Ford); 21-Jim Hall (Chaparral 2E-Chevrolet), engine; 22-Bob Bucher (Lola T70-Ford), transmission; 23-Charlie Hayes (McLaren M1B-Chevrolet), accident; 24-Ed Hamill (Hamill SR3-Chevrolet); 25-John Cannon (McLaren M1B-Chevrolet), gas tank leak; 26-John Cordts (McLaren M1A-Chevrolet); 27-Lothar Motschenbacher (Genie-Vinegaroon-Olds), accident; 28-John Surtees (Lola T70-Chevrolet), accident; 29-Skip Scott (McLaren M1B-Ford), accident; 30-Brett Lunger (Lola T70-Ford), accident.
Fastest Lap: Gurney, 1:23.1, 106.53 mph (record) *

* MPH calculated from lap time and track length of 2.459-miles. Does not agree with the 106.41 mph which appears on official results.

4. Laguna Seca 10/16/66

Heat One:

66 Hall	65 P. Hill
Chaparral 2E	Chaparral 2E
1:05.31	1:05.40

4 McLaren	30 Gurney
McLaren M1B	Lola T70
1:05.48	1:05.83

5 Amon	8 Hulme
McLaren M1B	Lola T70
1:06.11	1:06.47

7 Surtees	61 Donohue
Lola T70	Lola T70
1:06.72	1:07.66

Parsons McLaren M1B 1:08.01	Scott McLaren M1B 1:08.11
88 Gregory McLaren M1B 1:08.94	62 Cannon McLaren M1B 1:09.16
Adams McLaren M1B 1:09.43	10 Hayes McLaren M1B 1:09.53
Kronn McKee 1:09.60	16 Follmer Lola T70 1:09.79
Hawkins Lola T70 1:10.14	Amick McLaren 1:10.51
Reinhart Genie Mk8 1:10.77	Dibley Lola T70 1:10.80
98 P. Jones * Lola T70	86 Goth * McLaren-Goth Spl
E. Jones * McLaren	Jordan * Lola T70
Burnett * Burnett Spl	Lunger * Lola T70
Eve Genie Mk10	Heimrath * McLaren
Rodriguez * Ferrari Dino	D. Revson * Porsche 906
Tinglestad * McLaren M1B	Smith * Lola T70

* From the consolation race. This race was run prior to the heat races and served as a qualifying run. All 16 cars in the consolation race ran in either the first heat (top 12) or the second heat (remaining 4).

Heat One Results
1. Phil Hill (Chaparral 2E-Chevrolet), 53 laps of 1.9 mi. = 98.3 mi. in 1.01:29.9, 100.7 mph
2. Jim Hall (Chaparral 2E-Chevrolet), 53 laps
3. Bruce McLaren (McLaren M1B-Chevrolet), 53
4. John Surtees (Lola T70-Chevrolet), 53
5. Denny Hulme (Lola T70-Chevrolet), 53
6. Mark Donohue (Lola T70-Chevrolet), 52
7. John Cannon (McLaren M1B-Chevrolet), 51
8. Masten Gregory (McLaren M1B-Chevrolet), 51
9. Chuck Parsons (McLaren M1B-Chevrolet), 51
10. Earl Jones (McLaren-Chevrolet), 50
11. Jim Adams (McLaren M1B-Ford), 50
12. Bill Eve (Genie Mk10-Ford), 50
13. Hugh Dibley (Lola T70-Chevrolet), 49
14. Pedro Rodriguez (Ferrari Dino), 48
15. Ludwig Heimrath (McLaren-Ford), 48
16. Stan Burnett (Burnett Spl-Chevrolet), 48
17. Doug Revson (Porsche 906), 48
18. Norman Smith (Lola T70-Chevrolet), 46
19. George Follmer (Lola Mk2-Chevrolet), 44

Retirements: 20-Paul Hawkins (Lola T70-Chevrolet), 43; 21-Skip Scott (McLaren M1B-Ford), 38; 22-Dave Jordan (Lola T70-Ford), 31; 23-Mike Goth (McLaren-Goth Spl-Chevrolet), 30; 24-Mac Kronn (McKee-Chevrolet), 28; 25-Brett Lunger (Lola T70-Ford), 24; 26-Bud Tinglestad (McLaren M1A), 17; 27-Paul Reinhart (Genie Mk8-Chevrolet), 16; 28-Chris Amon (McLaren M1B-Chevrolet), 12; 29-Scooter Patrick (Mirage-Olds), 8; 30-Charlie Hayes (McLaren-Chevrolet), 8; 31-Parnelli Jones (Lola T70-Chevrolet), 8; 32-Dan Gurney (Lola T70-Ford), 5.

Fastest Lap: Hall, 1:05.31, 104.73+ mph

Heat Two Grid:

P. Hill	Hall
McLaren	Surtees
Hulme	Donohue

Cannon	Gregory
Parsons	Jones
Adams	Eve
Dibley	Rodriguez
Heimrath	D. Revson
Smith	Follmer
Hawkins	Kron
Amon	Motschenbacher McLaren 1:09.76
Posey McLaren M1B 1:10.19	Kumnick * Hamill SR3
Morley * McLaren 1:11.33	Challman * Lotus 30 Cherokee 1:16.46

Guldstrand *
PAM 1:20.47
(built from wrecked Lotus 30)

* From the consolation race.

Heat Two Results
1-Parnelli Jones (Lola T70-Chevrolet), 53 laps of 1.9 mi. = 100.7 mi. in 1.01:22.2, 98.9 mph; 2-Hill, 53; 3-Hall, 53; 4-Donohue, 53; 5-McLaren, 53; 6-Gregory, 52; 7-Cannon, 52; 8-Eve, 51; 9-Adams, 51; 10-Earl Jones, 51; 11-Motschenbacher, 50; 12-Dibley, 50; 13-Heimrath, 49; 14-Hawkins, 49; 15-Hamill, 49; 16-Smith, 49; 17-Guldstrand, 44; 18-Lunger, 42; 19-D. Revson, 40; **Retirements:** 20-Morley, 41; 21-Follmer, 39; 22-Surtees, 39; 23-Parsons, 34; 24-Amon, 24; 25-Rodriguez, 20; 26-Hulme, 11; 27-Challman, 12; 28-Posey, 3.

Fastest Lap: Jim Hall, 1:06.36, 103.07+ mph

Overall Positions
1-Hill, 106 laps; 2-Hall, 106; 3-McLaren, 106; 4-Donohue, 105; 5-Gregory, 103; 6-Cannon, 103; 7-Jones, 101; 8-Eve, 101; 9-Adams, 101; 10-Dibley, 99; 11-Heimrath, 97; 12-Surtees, 92; 13-Hawkins, 92; 14-Smith, 92; 15-D. Revson, 88; 16-Parsons, 85; 17-Follmer, 83; 18-Rodriguez, 68; 19-Lunger, 66; 20-Hulme, 63; 21-Jones, 61; 22-Motschenbacher, 50; 23-Hamill, 49; 24-Burnett, 48; 25-Guldstrand, 44; 26-Morley, 41; 27-Scott, 38; 28-Amon, 36; 29-Jordan, 36; 30-Goth, 30; 31-Kronn, 28; 32-Tinglestad, 16; 33-Reinhart, 16; 34-Hayes, 8; 35-Patrick, 8; 36-Gurney, 3; 37-Challman, 5; 38-Posey, 3.

+ Not shown on available results. Calculated from given information.

---

5. Riverside 10/30/66

4 McLaren McLaren M1B 1:44.7, 112.607 mph	7 Surtees Lola T70 1:45.0
66 Hall Chaparral 2E 1:45.2	43 Stewart Lola T70 1:46.1
3 G. Hill Lola T70 1:46.6	30 Gurney Lola T70 1:46.7
5 Amon McLaren M1B 1:46.9	65 P. Hill Chaparral 2E 1:47.4
16 Follmer Lola Mk2 1:48.1	91 Scott McLaren M1B 1:48.3
8 Hulme Lola T70 1:48.3	61 Donohue Lola T70 1:48.6
M. Andretti Lola T70 1:49.2	Motschenbacher McLaren 1:50.0

Parsons McLaren M1A 1:50.0	Posey McLaren M1B 1:50.1
81 Grant Lola T70 1:50.2	62 Cannon McLaren M1B 1:50.4
86 Goth McLaren-Goth Spl 1:50.5	10 Hayes McLaren 1:50.8
88 Gregory McLaren M1B 1st in consol	99 Earl Jones McLaren 2nd in consol
76 Leslie Webster 3rd in consol	Patrick Lola T70 4th in consol
Morley McLaren 5th in consol	Hudson Lola T70 6th in consol
Hawkins Lola T70 7th in consol	Hamill Hamill SR3 8th in consol
Lunger Lola T70 9th in consol	R. Brown McLaren 10th in consol
P. Revson McLaren 11th in consol	D. Revson Porsche 906 12th in consol
Amick McLaren 13th in consol	Eve Genie Mk10 16th in consol
Shelton Lola T70 18th in consol	(Grid Position Left Empty)
Foyt Lola T70 DNF in consol	98 P. Jones Lola T70 DNF in consol
Heimrath McLaren DNF in consol	

Results
1. John Surtees (Lola T70-Chevrolet), 62 laps of 3.275 mi. = 203.05 mi. in 1.53:59.5, 106.864 mph
2. Jim Hall (Chaparral 2E-Chevrolet), 62 laps
3. Graham Hill (Lola-Chevrolet), 62
4. Mark Donohue (Lola T70-Chevrolet), 62
5. George Follmer (Lola Mk2-Chevrolet), 61
6. Peter Revson (McLaren-Ford), 61
7. Paul Hawkins (Lola T70-Chevrolet), 60
8. Chuck Parsons (McLaren M1A-Chevrolet), 60
9. Lothar Motschenbacher (McLaren-Chevrolet), 60
10. Mike Goth (McLaren-Goth Spl-Chevrolet), 60
11. Earl Jones (McLaren-Chevrolet), 59
12. Ed Hamill (Hamill SR3-Chevrolet), 59
13. Jerry Grant (Lola T70-Chevrolet), 58
14. Doug Revson (Porsche 906), 57
15. Richard Brown (McLaren-Ford), 57
16. Bill Eve (Genie Mk10-Ford), 57
17. Skip Scott & Denny Hulme in relief (McLaren M1B-Chevrolet), 56
18. Sam Posey (McLaren M1B-Ford), 55
19. Skip Hudson (Lola T70-Chevrolet), 54

Retirements*: Scooter Patrick (Lola T70-Chevrolet), broken ring and pinion, 53; Bud Morley (McLaren-Ford), dead battery, 50; Chris Amon (McLaren M1B-Chevrolet), dead battery, 50; Jackie Stewart (Lola-Chevrolet), broken gear lever, 43; Mario Andretti (Lola T70-Ford), blown engine, 37; Monte Shelton (Lola T70-Chevrolet), overheating, 34; Bruce McLaren (McLaren M1B-Chevrolet), misfiring plugs, 29; Denny Hulme (Lola T70-Chevrolet), blown engine, 24; Ed Leslie (Webster-Olds), broken gear train, 22; Bill Amick (McLaren-Merc), undetermined, 20; Masten Gregory (McLaren M1B-Chevrolet), unable to maintain competitive speed, 20; Ludwig Heimrath (McLaren-Ford), overheating, 10; Brett Lunger (Lola T70-Ford), undetermined, 9; Charlie Hayes (McLaren-Chevrolet), oil spray in cockpit, 9; Phil Hill (Chaparral 2E-Chevrolet), no fuel pressure, 7; A.J. Foyt (Lola T70-Ford), overheating, 7; John Cannon (McLaren M1B-Chevrolet), overheating, 6; Parnelli Jones (Lola-Ford), overheating, 2; Dan Gurney (Lola T70-Ford), clutch, 1 lap.

Fastest Lap: Hall, 1:47.5, 109.67 mph

* These retirements are listed here in order of the number of laps completed, most to least. This is not the way they appeared in published race results. Publications showed them generally from least laps to most laps completed, but not entirely in order even then. For purposes of consistency in reporting results, they have been sorted here.

6. Las Vegas 11/13/66

65 P. Hill Chaparral 2E 1:35.4	66 Hall Chaparral 2E 1:34.5, 114.29 mph
7 Surtees Lola T70 1:36.1	5 Amon McLaren M1B 1:35.5
4 McLaren McLaren M1B 1:36.5	43 Stewart Lola T70 1:36.3
98 P. Jones Lola T70 1:36.6	16 Follmer Lola Mk2 1:36.6
P. Revson McLaren 1:38.2	30 Gurney Lola T70 1:38.0
88 Gregory McLaren M1B 1:38.7	8 Hulme Lola T70 1:38.4
61 Donohue Lola T70 1:39.1	Scott McLaren M1B 1:38.8
10 Hayes McLaren 1:39.2	86 Goth McLaren-Goth Spl 1:39.2
Parsons McLaren M1B 1:40.9	Posey McLaren M1B 1:40.0
M. Andretti Lola T70 1st in consol.	Motschenbacher McLaren 1:41.6
Titus Webster 3rd in consol.	Hawkins Lola T70 2nd in consol.
Dibley Lola T70 5th in consol.	Eve Genie Mk10 4th in consol.
Patrick Mirage 7th in consol.	Hamill Hamill SR3 6th in consol.
Smith Lola T70 9th in consol.	Diulo Lotus 19B 8th in consol.
D. Revson Porsche 906 11th in consol.	Harris Genie 10th in consol.
Jensen Burnett 13th in consol.	Tobin Brabham 12th in consol.
	Morley McLaren 1st alternate

Results

1. John Surtees (Lola T70-Chevrolet), 70 laps of 3.0 mi. = 210 mi. in 1:55:27.5, 109.25 mph
2. Bruce McLaren (McLaren M1B-Chevrolet), 70 laps
3. Mark Donohue (Lola T70-Chevrolet), 69
4. Peter Revson (McLaren-Ford), 68
5. Lothar Motschenbacher (McLaren-Chevrolet), 68
6. Jerry Titus (Webster-Olds), 67
7. Phil Hill (Chaparral 2E-Chevrolet), 67
8. Paul Hawkins (Lola T70-Chevrolet), 65
9. Parnelli Jones (Lola-Chevrolet), 65
10. Doug Revson (Porsche 906), 64
11. Bob Harris (Genie-Olds), 62
12. Masten Gregory (McLaren M1B-Chevrolet)

Retirements* Norm Smith (Lola T70-Chevrolet), accident, 66; Bill Eve (Genie Mk10-Ford), blown engine, 55; Mike Goth (McLaren-Goth Spl-Chevrolet), blown engine, 52; George Follmer (Lola Mk2-Chevrolet), no oil pressure, 51; Chuck Parsons (McLaren M1B-Chevrolet), suspension, 43; Scooter Patrick (Mirage-Olds), spin, 40; Dan Gurney (Lola T70-Ford), fuel tank breakage, 37; Don Jensen (Burnett-Chevrolet), blown engine, 36; Sam Posey (McLaren M1B-Ford), threw rod, 34; Charlie Hayes (McLaren-Chevrolet), lost wheel, 33; Denny Hulme (Lola T70-Chevrolet), gearbox, 22; Chris Amon (McLaren M1B-Chevrolet), broken left A-arm, 21; Jackie Stewart (Lola Chevrolet), fuel line, 14; Hugh Dibley (Lola T70-Chevrolet), broken left wishbone, 11; Tom Tobin (Brabham-Olds), misfiring, 10; Jim Hall (Chaparral 2E-Chevrolet), airfoil, 4; Steve Diulo (Lotus 19B-Ford), gearbox, 3; Bud Morley (McLaren-Ford), clutch, 3; Skip Scott (McLaren M1B-Chevrolet), ring & pinion, 1; Mario Andretti (Lola T70-Ford), gearbox, 1; Ed Hamill (Hamill SR3-Chevrolet), broken lug bolt, 0.

Fastest Lap: Sutees, 1:35.7, 112.84 mph

* These retirements are listed here in order of the number of laps completed, most to least. This is not the way they appeared in published race results. Publications showed them generally from least laps to most laps completed. For purposes of consistency in reporting results, they have been sorted here.

Also, _Autoweek_ reports at the end of the DNFs, "Retirement laps official but do not agree with CP&A [Competition Press & Autoweek] staff consensus." No explanation of this statement given.

Final Point Standings 1966

1	John Surtees	27
2	Mark Donohue	21
3	Bruce McLaren	20
4	Phil Hill	18
5	Jim Hall	12
6	Chris Amon	10
7	Dan Gurney	9
8	Chuck Parsons	6
9	Graham Hill *	4
10	John Cannon	4
	George Follmer	4
	Peter Revson	4
13	Earl Jones	3
14	Masten Gregory	2
	Paul Hawkins	2
	Lothar Motschenbacher	2
17	Eppie Wietzes	1
	Jerry Titus	1

* Ties for position resolved by driver's finishing record throughout the season.

1967

1. Elkhart Lake 9/3/67

5 Hulme McLaren M6A 2:12.7	4 McLaren McLaren M6A 2:12.6, 108.597 mph
16 Follmer Lola T70 2:15.7	36 Gurney Lola T70 Mk3B 2:14.4
26 Parsons McLaren M1C 2:16.6	6 Donohue Lola T70 2:15.8
52 P. Revson Lola T70 2:17.2	7 Surtees Lola T70 2:16.9
11 Motschenbacher Lola T70 2:18.6	66 Hall Chaparral 2G 2:17.4
25 Hayes McKee Mk7 2:19.8	91 Scott McLaren M1C 2:18.9
37 Morin McLaren M1C 2:21.0	Hansen McLaren M1C 2:20.0
14 Barber McLaren M1B 2:21.3	1 Posey Caldwell D7 2:21.0
87 Matich Matich SR3R 2:22.1	33 Cannon McLaren M1B 2:21.4
12 McCluskey Lola T70 2:23.7	76 Eve Lola T70 2:22.2
39 Heimrath McLaren M1B 2:25.2	57 Cordts McLaren M1C 2:24.6
2 Lunger McLaren M1B 2:25.7	31 Doran McLaren M1B 2:25.3
13 Morley McLaren M1B 2:26.6	78 Grant McLaren M1B 2:26.3
24 Nagel McKee Mk7 2:26.8	15 Entin McLaren M1B 2:26.6
28 Brown McLaren M1B 2:27.5	19 Wilson McLaren M1B 2:27.3
Courtney McLaren M1B 2:29.9, 96.06 mph	79 Greenville Lola T70 2:29.8

Did Not Start: Hugh Powell (Lola T70 Mk2-Chevrolet), broken oil line; Fred Pipen (McKee Mk6-Chevrolet), cracked drive shaft.

Results

1. Denny Hulme (McLaren M6A-Chevrolet) 50 laps of 4.0 mi. = 200 mi. in 1:54:53.0, 104.454 mph
2. Mark Donohue (Lola T70 Mk3B-Chevrolet), 50
3. John Surtees (Lola T70 Mk3B-Chevrolet), 50
4. Jim Hall (Chaparral 2G-Chevrolet), 49
5. Skip Scott (McLaren M1C-Chevrolet), 49
6. Jerry Hansen (McLaren M1B-Chevrolet), 48
7. Skip Barber (McLaren M1B-Chevrolet), 48
8. Bud Morley (McLaren M1B-Chevrolet), 48
9. Lothar Motschenbacher (Lola T70-Chevrolet), 47
10. Charlie Hayes (McKee Mk7-Olds), 47
11. Jerry Entin (McLaren M1B-Chevrolet), 47
12. Brooke Doran (McLaren M1B-Chevrolet), 46
13. Bob Nagel (McKee Mk7-Chevrolet), 46
14. Brett Lunger (McLaren M1B-Chevrolet), 46
15. Ross Greenville (Lola T70-Chevrolet), 46
16. Dick Brown (McLaren M1B-Ford), 46
17. Roger McCluskey (Lola T70-Chevrolet), 45
18. George Follmer (Lola T70 Mk3-Chevrolet), 44
19. Jerry Grant (Lola T70 Mk2-Chevrolet), 43
20. Ron Courtney (McLaren M1B-Chevrolet), 42
21. Ludwig Heimrath (McLaren M1B-Chevrolet), 38

Retirements: 22-John Cannon (McLaren M1B-Chevrolet), blown engine, 43; 23-John Cordts (McLaren M1B-Chevrolet), blown engine, 42; 24-Gary Wilson (McLaren M1B-Chevrolet), blown engine, 38; 25-Chuck Parsons (McLaren M1C-Chevrolet), gearbox failure, 31; 26-Dan Gurney (Lola T70 Mk3B-Ford), gearbox failure, 26; 27-Frank Matich (Matich SR3R Repco Brabham), stone in radiator, 15; 28-Bill Eve (Webster Lola T70 Mk3B-Chevrolet), broken oil line, 7; 29-Bruce McLaren (McLaren M6A-Chevrolet), oil leak, 6; 30-Don Morin (McLaren M1C-Chevrolet), reason unknown, 5; 31-Peter Revson (Lola T70 Mk3B-Chevrolet), rear suspension, 3; 32-Sam Posey (Caldwell D7-Chevrolet), broken half shaft, 2.

Fastest Lap: Hulme, 2:14.9, 106.746 mph

2. Bridgehampton 9/17/67

36 Gurney Lola T70 Mk3B 1:30.85	4 McLaren McLaren M6A 1:30.17	5 Hulme McLaren M6A 1:29.85, 114.14 mph
16 Follmer Lola T70 1:31.17		66 Hall Chaparral 2G 1:31.02
7 Surtees Lola T70 1:32.08	6 Donohue Lola T70 1:31.50	26 Parsons McLaren M1C 1:31.46
91 Scott McLaren M1C 1:32.30		11 Motschenbacher Lola T70 1:32.13
52 P. Revson Lola T70 1:33.13	78 Grant Lola T70 1:33.05	25 Hayes McKee Mk7 1:32.85
87 Matich Matich SR3R 1:33.49		22 Spence McLaren M1C 1:33.23
13 Morley McLaren M1B 1:34.80	37 Morin McLaren M1C 1:34.64	32 Scarfiotti Ferrari P3/4 1:34.48
76 Eve Lola T70 1:35.32		14 Barber McLaren M1B 1:35.11
17 Andretti Honker II 1:36.16	12 McCluskey Lola T70 1:35.99	1 Posey Caldwell D7 1:35.55
39 Heimrath McLaren M1B 1:36.90		2 Lunger McLaren M1B 1:36.70
28 Brown McLaren M1B 1:38.75	10 Patrick Mirage 1:37.81	24 Nagel McKee Mk7 1:37.36
Alderman McLaren M1B 1:39.26, 103.38 mph		57 Cordts McLaren M1C 1:39.08
		Hugh Powell Lola T70 Mk2 1:46.34 (non-starter)

Results

1. Denny Hulme (McLaren M6A-Chevrolet) 70 laps of 2.85 mi. = 200 mi. in 1:50:07.6, 109.73 mph
2. Bruce McLaren (McLaren M6A-Chevrolet), 70
3. George Follmer (Lola T70 Mk3-Chevrolet), 69
4. John Surtees (Lola T70 Mk3B-Chevrolet), 69
5. Lothar Motschenbacher (Lola T70-Chevrolet), 68
6. Chuck Parsons (McLaren M1C-Chevrolet), 68
7. Lodovico Scarfiotti (Ferrari P3/4), 68
8. Mario Andretti (Honker II-Ford), 68
9. Skip Barber (McLaren M1B-Chevrolet), 67
10. Bill Eve (Lola T70 Mk3B-Chevrolet), 66
11. Bob Nagel (McKee Mk7-Chevrolet), 63
12. Dick Brown (McLaren M1B-Ford), 58
13. Ludwig Heimrath (McLaren M1B-Chevrolet), 55

Retirements: 14-Scooter Patrick (Mirage-Chevrolet), fuel starvation, 52; 15-Skip Scott (McLaren M1C-Chevrolet), broken sway bar, 51; 16-Mike Spence (McLaren M1C-Chevrolet), frozen gearbox, 47; 17-Frank Matich (Matich SR3R Repco Brabham), fuel starvation, 45; 18-Mark Donohue (Lola T70 Mk3B-Chevrolet), blown engine, 38; 19-Jim Hall (Chaparral 2G-Chevrolet), broken chassis, 38; 20-George Alderman (McLaren M1B-Chevrolet), unknown, 36; 21-Roger McCluskey (Lola T70-Chevrolet), oil pressure, 27; 22-John Cordts (McLaren M1C-Chevrolet), gearbox, 19; 23-Bud Morley (McLaren M1B-Chevrolet), suspension, 17; 24-Sam Posey (Caldwell D7-Chevrolet), steering, 17; 25-Jerry Grant (Lola T70 Mk3-Chevrolet), fuel pump drive, 6; 26-Dan Gurney (Lola T70 Mk3B-Ford), fuel injection, 5; 27-Brett Lunger (McLaren M1C-Chevrolet), oil pressure, 4; 28-Peter Revson (Lola T70 Mk3B-Chevrolet), suspension, 3; 29-Don Morin (McLaren M1C-Chevrolet), gearbox, 3; 30-Charlie Hayes (McKee Mk7-Olds), broken valve, 1.

Fastest Lap: Hulme, 1:32.0, 111.52 mph

3. Mosport 9/23/67

4 McLaren McLaren M6A 1:21.1 (started late)	5 Hulme McLaren M6A 1:20.8, 109.615 mph
22 Spence McLaren M1B 1:21.9	36 Gurney Lola T70 Mk3B 1:21.1
52 P. Revson Lola T70 1:23.0	7 Surtees Lola T70 1:22.4
11 Motschenbacher Lola T70 1:24.1	16 Follmer Lola T70 1:24.0
12 McCluskey Lola T70 1:24.5	39 Heimrath McLaren M1B 1:24.4
Scarfiotti Ferrari P3/4 1:25.2	33 Cannon McLaren M1B 1:25.0
57 Cordts McLaren M1C 1:25.5	26 Parsons McLaren M1C 1:25.4
91 Scott McLaren M1C 1:25.7	1 Posey Caldwell D7 1:25.6
37 Morin McLaren M1C 1:26.6	6 Donohue Lola T70 1:25.9
Wietzes Ford GT40 1:28.9	14 Barber McLaren M1B 1:26.7
28 Brown McLaren M1B 1:29.0	2 Lunger McLaren M1B 1:29.0
76 Eve Lola T70 1:29.2	Causey McLaren M1C 1:29.2
Pipin McKee Mk6 1:31.0	Laton McLaren 1:29.4
Adams Chinook 1:38.0, 90.331 mph	Courtney McLaren M1B 1:32.6
	17 Andretti Honker II 1:39.9 (non-starter)

Results

1. Denny Hulme (McLaren M6A-Chevrolet) 80 laps of 2.46 mi. = 196.720 mi. in 1:51:25.7, 109.93 mph
2. Bruce McLaren (McLaren M6A-Chevrolet), 80

3. Mike Spence (McLaren M1B-Chevrolet), 79
4. Peter Revson (Lola T70 Mk3B-Chevrolet), 79
5. Roger McCluskey (Lola T70-Chevrolet), 79
6. George Follmer (Lola T70 Mk3-Chevrolet), 79
7. Skip Scott (McLaren M1C-Chevrolet), 78
8. John Cordts (McLaren M1C-Chevrolet), 75
9. Lothar Motschenbacher (LolaT70-Chevrolet), 75
10. Dick Brown (McLaren M1B-Ford), 74
11. Eppie Wietzes (Ford GT40), 74
12. Sam Posey (Caldwell D7-Chevrolet), 73
13. George Eaton (McLaren M1C-Ford), 72
14. Nate Adams (Chinook-Chevrolet), 69
15. Skip Barber (McLaren M1B-Chevrolet), 66
Retirements: 16-Dan Gurney (Lola T70 Mk3B-Ford), clutch, 70; 17-Bill Eve (Lola T70 Mk3B-Chevrolet), blown engine, 56; 18-Fred Pipin (McKee Mk6-Chevrolet), broken wheel, 55; 19-Mark Donohue (Lola T70 Mk3B-Chevrolet), blown engine, 52; 20-Chuck Parsons (McLaren M1C-Chevrolet), oil pressure, 47; 21-Lodovico Scarfiotti (Ferrari P3/4), crash, 44; 22-Brett Lunger (McLaren M1B-Chevrolet), crash, 43; 23-Ludwig Heimrath (McLaren M1B-Chevrolet), broken rocker arm, 38; 24-Ron Courtney (McLaren M1C-Chevrolet), blown engine; 25-John Surtees (Lola T70 Mk3B-Chevrolet), broken oil seal on valve guide, 17; 26-John Cannon (McLaren M1B-Chevrolet), gearbox, 13.
Fastest Lap: Hulme, 1:20.7, 109.695 mph

4. Laguna Seca 10/15/67

4 McLaren McLaren M6A 1:02.69, 108.74 mph	36 Gurney Lola T70 Mk3B 1:03.10
5 Hulme McLaren M6A 1:03.20	21 P. Jones Lola T70 1:03.72
66 Hall Chaparral 2G 1:03.93	22 Spence McLaren M1B 1:04.00
11 Motschenbacher Lola T70 1:04.26	25 Hayes McKee Mk7 1:04.30
6 Donohue Lola T70 1:04.35	52 P. Revson Lola T70 1:04.51
16 Follmer Lola T70 1:04.77	26 Parsons McLaren M1C 1:04.80
Matich Matich SR3R 1:05.07	7 Surtees Lola T70 1:05.17
91 Scott McLaren M1C 1:05.40	23 Amon Ferrari P4 1:05.77
37 Morin McLaren M1C 1:06.15	14 Morley Lola T70 1:06.24
1 Posey Caldwell D7 1:06.43	27 Williams Ferrari P4 1:07.35
33 Cannon McLaren M1B 1:07.42	Amick McLaren M1C 1:07.72
76 Eve Lola T70 1:07.76	Entin McLaren M1B 1:09.02
Settember Lola T70 1:09.87	Gupton Platypus 1:10.48
17 Brennan Genie Mk10 1:10.52	2 Lunger McLaren M1B 1:10.52

Grant Lola T70 1:11.59	Powell Lola T70 1:12.26
Greenville Lola T70 1:19.52, 86.01 mph	

Did Not Start: Scooter Patrick (Mirage-Chevrolet), no brakes; Tony Settember * (Matich SR3), distributor drive, oil pump; Roger McCluskey (Lola T70-Chevrolet), accident; Bobby Unser (Lotus 19G-Ford), blew engine; Jim Adams (McLaren M1B-Chevrolet), unknown; Tom Tobin (Brabham BT8), unknown.

* For the race, Settember transferred to the Lola scheduled to be driven by Ed Leslie.

Results

1. Bruce McLaren (McLaren M6A-Chevrolet), 106 laps of 1.9 mi. = 201.4 mi. in 1:58:55.33, 101.613 mph
2. Jim Hall (Chaparral 2G-Chevrolet), 105 laps
3. George Follmer (Lola T70 Mk3-Chevrolet), 104
4. Bud Morley (Lola T70-Chevrolet), 103
5. Chris Amon (Ferrari P4), 102
6. Bill Eve (Lola T70 Mk3B-Chevrolet), 101
7. John Cannon (McLaren M1B-Chevrolet), 101
8. Jonathan Williams (Ferrari P4), 99
9. Merle Brennan (Genie Mk10-Chevrolet), 94
Retirements: 10-Peter Revson (Lola T70 Mk3B-Chevrolet), crash, 86; 11-Miles Gupton (Platypus-Olds), 86; 12-Denny Hulme (McLaren M6A-Chevrolet), blew, 80; 13-Mark Donohue (Lola T70 Mk3B-Chevrolet), blew, 74; 14-Chuck Parsons (McLaren M1C-Chevrolet), gearbox, 61; 15-Lothar Motschenbacher (LolaT70-Chevrolet), oil pressure, 51; 16-Frank Matich (Matich SR3R), oil leak, overheating, 44; 17-Don Morin (McLaren M1C-Chevrolet), 44; 18-John Surtees (Lola T70 Mk3B-Chevrolet), accident, 31; 19-Brett Lunger (McLaren M1B-Chevrolet), oil pressure, 26; 20-Mike Spence (McLaren M1B-Chevrolet), brakes, 26; 21-Skip Scott (McLaren M1C-Chevrolet), overheating, 24; 22-Hugh Powell (Lola T70-Chevrolet), unknown, 23-Tony Settember (Lola T70-Chevrolet), gearbox, 18; 24-Parnelli Jones (Lola T70-Ford), vapor lock, 14; 25-Ross Greenville (Lola T70-Chevrolet), brakes, 13; 26-Dan Gurney (Lola T70 Mk3B-Ford), overheating, 12; 27-Jerry Entin (McLaren M1B-Chevrolet), accident, 11; 28-Bill Amick (McLaren M1C-Chevrolet), 6; 29-Sam Posey (Caldwell D7-Chevrolet), overheating, 5; 30-Charlie Hayes (McKee Mk7-Chevrolet), accident, 3; 31-Jerry Grant (Lola T70-Chevrolet), head gasket, 2.
Fastest Lap: McLaren, 1:04.75, 105.75 mph

5. Riverside 10/29/67

36 Gurney Lola T70 Mk3B 1:39.3, 118.731 mph	4 McLaren McLaren M6A 1:39.6
5 Hulme McLaren M6A 1:40.6	66 Hall Chaparral 2G 1:40.9
17 Andretti Honker II 1:41.6	21 P. Jones Lola T70 1:41.6
52 P. Revson Lola T70 1:41.8	11 Motschenbacher Lola T70 1:41.8
7 Surtees Lola T70 1:42.4	6 Donohue Lola T70 1:42.6
22 Spence McLaren M1B 1:43.0	16 Follmer Lola T70 1:43.5

55 Titus King Cobra 1:44.0	26 Parsons McLaren M1C 1:44.2
23 Amon Ferrari P4 1:44.4	91 Scott McLaren M1C 1:44.6
25 Hayes McKee Mk7 1:45.2	76 Eve Lola T70 1:45.2
31 Posey Caldwell D7 1:45.4	15 Matich Matich SR3 1:45.6
27 Williams Ferrari P4 1:45.7	81 Hills McLaren M1C 1:47.0
78 Grant Lola T70 1:47.0	39 Adams McLaren 1:47.6
12 McCluskey Lola T70 1:47.7	37 Morin McLaren M1C 1:47.8
45 Entin McLaren 1:48.6	14 Morley Lola T70 1:48.7
46 Muther Lola T70 1:49.0	19 Amick McLaren M1C 1:49.3
29 Paul McLaren M1C 1:49.4	77 Settember Matich SR3 1:49.5
33 Cannon McLaren M1B 1:49.5	10 Patrick Mirage 1:50.4
24 Powell Lola T70 1:52.8	43 Greenville Lola T70 1:54.2
79 Hooper Genie 1:54.5	62 Kumnick Hamill 1:54.8
9 Herrera McLaren M1C 1:55.1, 102.432 mph	

Results

1. Bruce McLaren (McLaren M6A-Chevrolet), 62 laps of 3.275 mi. = 201.4 mi. in 1:46:28.7, 114.406 mph
2. Jim Hall (Chaparral 2G-Chevrolet), 62 laps
3. Mark Donohue (Lola T70 Mk3B-Chevrolet), 61
4. Parnelli Jones (Lola T70-Ford), 61
5. Mike Spence (McLaren M1B-Chevrolet), 61
6. George Follmer (Lola T70 Mk3-Chevrolet), 60
7. Charlie Hayes (McKee-Chevrolet), 60
8. Chris Amon (Ferrari P4), 59
9. Bill Eve (Lola T70 Mk3B-Chevrolet), 59
10. Don Morin (McLaren M1C-Chevrolet), 59
11. John Cannon (McLaren M1B-Chevrolet), 58
12. Chuck Parsons (McLaren M1C-Chevrolet), 58
13. Sam Posey (Caldwell D7-Chevrolet), 58
14. Skip Scott (McLaren M1C-Chevrolet), 57
15. Lothar Motschenbacher (LolaT70-Chevrolet), 57
16. Jerry Entin (McLaren M1C-Chevrolet), 57
Retirements: 17-Roger McCluskey (Lola T70-Chevrolet), overheating, 49; 18-John Surtees (Lola T70 Mk3B-Chevrolet), rear end, 45; 19-Hugh Powell (Lola T70-Chevrolet), nose section dragging, 45; 20-Bill Amick (McLaren M1C-Chevrolet), rear end, 39; 21-Jay Hills (McLaren M1C-Chevrolet), transmission, 38; 22-Jim Paul (McLaren M1C-Chevrolet), shift linkage, 33; 23-Frank Matich (Matich SR3R Brabham), crash 30; 24-Tony Settember (Matich SR3-Olds), broken oil line, 27; 25-Ron Herrera (McLaren M1C-Chevrolet), shift linkage, 25; 26-Rick Muther (Lola T70-Chevrolet), gearbox, 19; 27-Doug Hooper (Genie-Chevrolet), crash,

18; 28-Peter Revson (Lola T70 Mk3B-Chevrolet), crash, 16; 29-Jerry Grant (Lola T70-Chevrolet), shift linkage, 16; 30-Jonathan Williams (Ferrari P4), crash, 13; 31-Ross Greenville (Lola T70-Chevrolet), crash, 13; 32-Mario Andretti (Honker II-Ford), gearbox, 10; 33-Bud Morley (Lola T70-Chevrolet), broken A-arm, 5; 34-Dan Gurney (Lola T70 Mk3B-Ford), overheating, 4; 35-Jerry Titus (King Cobra-Ford), fuel pump, 3; 36-Denny Hulme (McLaren M6A-Chevrolet), crash, 2.
Fastest Lap: McLaren, 1:40.4, 117.301 mph

6. Las Vegas 11/12/67

66 Hall Chaparral 2G 1:31.1	4 McLaren McLaren M6A 1:30.8, 118.94 mph
21 P. Jones Lola T70 1:31.3	36 Gurney Lola T70 Mk3B 1:31.2
52 P. Revson Lola T70 1:32.3	5 Hulme McLaren M6A 1:31.4
22 Spence McLaren M1B 1:32.6	6 Donohue Lola T70 1:32.6
11 Motschenbacher Lola T70 1:33.2	7 Surtees Lola T70 1:32.8
16 Follmer Lola T70 1:34.6	25 Hayes McKee Mk7 1:34.3
26 Parsons McLaren M1C 1:35.4	23 Amon Ferrari P4 1:35.0
12 McCluskey Lola T70 1:35.6	46 Muther Lola T70 1:35.6
27 Williams Ferrari P4 1:36.3	91 Scott McLaren M1C 1:36.1
14 Morley Lola T70 1:37.5	33 Cannon McLaren M1B 1:37.0
77 Settember Matich 1:39.3	37 Morin McLaren M1C 1:37.5
59 Wilson McLaren 1:42.7	45 Entin McLaren 1:39.7
24 Powell Lola T70 1:43.9	38 Herrera McLaren M1C 1:43.6
	29 Paul McLaren 1:46.7, 101.32 mph

Started Late: 43 Ross Greenville (Lola-Chevrolet), 1:39.0
Did Not Start: 17 Mario Andretti (Honker II-Ford), 1:33.2, bearings; 55 Jerry Titus (King Cobra-Ford), suspension failure; 78 Jerry Grant (Lola-Chevrolet), 1:36.1; 1 Sam Posey (Caldwell-Chevrolet), 1:36.4, fire in practice; 89 Bill Eve (Lotus-Ford), 1:44.8; 49 Denny Harrison (Platypus-Olds), 1:46.3, ring and pinion.

Results

1. John Surtees (Lola T70 Mk3B-Chevrolet), 70 laps of 3.0 mi. = 210 mi. in 1:52:05.5, 112.41 mph
2. Mark Donohue (Lola T70 Mk3B-Chevrolet), 70
3. Mike Spence (McLaren M1B-Chevrolet), 70
4. Charlie Hayes (McKee-Olds), 69
5. Bud Morley (Lola T70-Chevrolet), 66
6. Rick Muther (Lola T70-Chevrolet), 65

7. Jerry Entin (McLaren M1C-Chevrolet), 64
8. John Cannon (McLaren-Chevrolet), 55
9. Ross Greenville (Lola T70-Chevrolet), 54
10. Chuck Parsons (McLaren M1C-Chevrolet), 54
Retirements: 11-Chris Amon (Ferrari P4), crashed, 66; 12-Skip Scott (McLaren M1C-Chevrolet), spun and retired on course, 56; 13-Denny Hulme (McLaren M6A-Chevrolet), blown engine, 51; 14-Ron Herrera (McLaren M1C-Chevrolet), running at finish, 51; 15-George Follmer (Lola T70-Chevy), broken shifting fork, 44; 16-Lothar Motschenbacher (Lola T70-Chevrolet), spun after blowout, 39; 17-Gary Wilson (McLaren-Chevrolet), body damage after spinout, 24; 18-Jim Paul (McLaren M1C-Chevrolet), oil leak, 19; 19-Jim Hall (Chaparral 2G-Chevrolet), oil and water leak, 15; 20-Dan Gurney (Lola T70-Ford), vibration problems, 14; 21-Bruce McLaren (McLaren M6A-Chevrolet), blown engine, 7; 22-Parnelli Jones (Lola T70-Ford), shifting problems, 5; 23-Roger McCluskey (Lola T70-Chevrolet), body damage after crash, 1; 24-Tony Settember (Matich SR3-Olds), body damage after crash, 1; 25-Jonathan Williams (Ferrari P4), throttle stuck after ingesting stone in first-lap shunt, 0; 26-Don Morin (McLaren M1C-Chevrolet), crashed, first lap, 0; 27-Hugh Powell (McLaren-Chevrolet), crashed, first lap shunt, 0.
Disqualified: Peter Revson (Lola T70 Mk3B-Chevrolet), placed fifth in provisional standings, but was disqualified for a push start in the pits.
Fastest Lap: Hulme, 1:32.5, 116.75 mph

Final Point Standings 1967

1	Bruce McLaren	30
2	Denny Hulme	27
3	John Surtees	16
4	Mark Donohue	16
5	Jim Hall	15
6	George Follmer	10
	Mike Spence	10
8	Bud Morley	5
9	Charlie Hayes	3
	Parnelli Jones	3
	Peter Revson	3
12	Skip Scott	2
	Lothar Motschenbacher	2
	Chris Amon	2
15	Bill Eve	1
	Chuck Parsons	1
	Jerry Hansen	1
	Rick Muther	1

1968

1. Elkhart Lake 9/1/68

5 Hulme McLaren M8A 2:09.9	4 McLaren McLaren M8A 2:09.8, 110.940 mph
6 Donohue McLaren M6B 2:11.0	66 Hall Chaparral 2G 2:10.8
10 Parsons Lola T160 2:13.4	11 Motschenbacher McLaren M6B 2:13.4
21 Andretti Lola T70 Mk3B 2:13.9	52 P. Revson McLaren M6B 2:13.7
22 Rodriguez Ferrari P4 2:15.8	25 Hayes McKee Mark 7 2:15.2
44 Hansen McLaren M6A 2:17.7	32 Bucknum Lola T70 Mk3B 2:16.7
98 Eaton McLaren M1C 2:18.6	39 Heimrath McLaren M1C 2:18.0
9 Bonnier McLaren M6B 2:19.6	1 Posey Caldwell D7C 2:18.8
61 Pipin Lola T70 Mk3B 2:21.1	63 Kumnick Lola T70 Mk3B 2:21.0
2 Lunger Lola T160 2:21.7	57 Cordts McLaren M1C 2:21.2
18 Courtney McLaren M1C 2:22.6	34 Ralph Lola T70 2:21.8
15 O'Neil Lola T70 Mk3B 2:24.4	28 Brown McLaren M6B 2:24.0
26 Scott Lola T70 Mk3B 2:26.5	56 Trieschmann McLaren M1C 2:26.0
19 Wilson McLaren M1B 2:28.5	77 Janke McLaren M1C 2:27.4
	42 DaMota McLaren M1C 2:29.2, 96.515 mph

Results
1. Denny Hulme (McLaren M8A-Chevrolet), 50 laps of 4.0 mi. = 200 mi. in 2.06:55.8, 94.540 mph
2. Bruce McLaren (McLaren M8A-Chevrolet), 50
3. Mark Donohue (McLaren M6B-Chevrolet), 50
4. Peter Revson (McLaren M6B-Ford), 50
5. Jim Hall (Chaparral 2G-Chevrolet), 49
6. Lothar Motschenbacher (McLaren M6B-Ford), 48
7. Charlie Hayes (McKee Mark 7-Olds), 48
8. George Eaton (McLaren M1C-Ford), 48
9. John Cordts (McLaren M1C-Chevrolet), 48
10. Sam Posey (Caldwell D7C-Chevrolet), 47
11. George Ralph Jr. (Lola T70 Mk2B-Chevrolet), 46
12. Brett Lunger (Lola T160-Chevrolet), 45
13. Pedro Rodriguez (Ferrari P4), 45
14. Roy Kumnick (Lola T70 Mk3B-Chevrolet), 45
15. Candido DaMota (McLaren M1C-Chevrolet), 44
16. Fred Pipin (Lola T70 Mk3B-Chevrolet), 43
17. Ronnie Bucknum (Lola T70 Mk3B-Ford), 42
18. Jo Bonnier (McLaren M6B-Chevrolet), 42
19. Skip Scott (Lola T70 Mk3B-Chevrolet), 41
20. Ronald Courtney (McLaren M1C-Chevrolet), 39
Retirements: 21-Mario Andretti (Lola T70 Mk3B-Ford), lost oil and blew engine, 48; 22-Ludwig Heimrath (McLaren M1C-Chevrolet), engine problems, 43; 23-Leonard Janke (McLaren M1C-Chevrolet), gearbox, 38; 24-Jerry Hansen (McLaren M6A-Chevrolet), blown head gasket, 30; 25-Richard Brown (McLaren M6B-Chevrolet), engine failure, 28; 26-Gary Wilson (McLaren M1B-Chevrolet), engine problems, 27; 27-Chuck Parsons Lola T160-Chevrolet), blown engine, 26; 28-Ralph Trieschmann (McLaren M1C-Chevrolet), blown head gasket, 16.
Disqualified: Brian O'Neil (Lola T70 Mk3B-Chevrolet), for push start.
Fastest Lap: Motschenbacher, 2:16, 105.882 mph

2. Bridgehampton 9/15/68

4 McLaren McLaren M8A 1:27.77	5 Hulme McLaren M8A 1:27.69, 117.47 mph
6 Donohue McLaren M6B 1:28.53	52 P. Revson McLaren M6B 1:28.33
48 Gurney McLeagle * 1:29.27	66 Hall Chaparral 2G 1:28.85
21 Andretti Lola T70 Mk3B 1:30.95	11 Motschenbacher McLaren M6B 1:30.42
7 Surtees + Lola TS 1:31.79	26 Scott Lola T160 1:31.77
44 Hansen McLaren M6A 1:32.69 (non-starter)	22 Rodriguez Ferrari P4 1:32.10
2 Posey Lola T160 1:32.83	10 Parsons Lola T160 1:32.71
1 Lunger Caldwell D7C 1:34.41	98 Eaton McLaren M1C 1:33.20
28 Brown McLaren M6B 1:35.49	36 Savage Lola T160 1:34.49
24 Nagel Lola T70 1:38.79	37 Ralph Lola T70 Mk2B 1:36.93
15 O'Neil Lola T70 Mk3B 1:41.13	18 Courtney McLaren M1C 1:42.77
31 Bucknum Lola T70 Mk3B 1:44.06	9 Bonnier McLaren M6B 1:44.52
42 DaMota McLaren M1C 1:46.08, 97.17 mph	43 Pipin Lola T170 Mk3B/2B No Time

* Modified McLaren M6B-Ford
+ Modified Lola T160-Chevrolet

Results
1. Mark Donohue (McLaren M6B-Chevrolet), 70 laps of 2.85 mi. = 200 mi. in 1.47:34.30, 111.32 mph
2. Jim Hall (Chaparral 2G-Chevrolet), 70 laps
3. Lothar Motschenbacher (McLaren M6B-Ford), 68
4. Swede Savage (Lola T160-Ford), 65
5. Richard Brown (McLaren M6B-Chevrolet), 63
6. Dan Gurney (McLeagle-Ford), 61
7. Brian O'Neil (Lola T70-Chevrolet), 61
8. Sam Posey (Lola T160-Chevrolet), 58
Retirements: 9-Bruce McLaren (McLaren M8A-Chevrolet), main bearing, 62; 10-Denny Hulme (McLaren M8A-Chevrolet), broken rod, 53; 11-Ron Courtney (McLaren M1C-Chevrolet), crash, 51; 12-Brett Lunger (Caldwell D7C-Chevrolet), flat tire, 48; 13-Peter Revson (McLaren M6B-Ford), rear suspension, 48; 14-Bob Nagel (Lola T70-Chevrolet), gearbox, 35; 15-Fred Pipin (Lola T70 Mk3B-Chevrolet), electrical wiring, 33; 16-Jo Bonnier (McLaren M6B-Chevrolet), no oil pressure, tires, 30; 17-Ron Bucknum (Lola T70 Mk3B-Ford), overheating, pushrod, 27; 18-George Ralph Jr. (Lola T70 Mk2B-Chevrolet), broken shift lever, 23; 19-Skip Scott (Lola T160 Mk3B-Chevrolet), overheating, 23; 20-Chuck Parsons (Lola T160-Chevrolet), engine, 21; 21-George Eaton (McLaren M1C-Ford), half shaft, 17; 22-Candido DaMota (McLaren M1C-Chevrolet), black flag, 16; 23-John Surtees (Lola TS-Chevrolet), pushrod, 12; 24-Pedro Rodriguez (Ferrari P4), off course, 8; 25-Mario Andretti (Lola T70 Mk3B-Ford), oil pressure, 4.
Fastest Lap: McLaren, 1:28.88, 115.93 mph

3. Edmonton 9/29/68

5 Hulme McLaren M8A 1:26.0, 105.78 mph	4 McLaren McLaren M8A 1:26.0
66 Hall Chaparral 2G 1:26.4	6 Donohue McLaren M6B 1:26.5

52 P. Revson McLaren M6B 1:27.1	48 Gurney McLeagle 1:27.5
11 Motschenbacher McLaren M6B 1:29.8	2 Posey Lola T160 1:29.5
26 Scott Lola T160 1:30.1	10 Parsons Lola T160 1:30.3
17 Titus McLaren M6B 1:30.5	31 Bucknum Lola T70 Mk3B 1:31.2
36 Savage Lola T160 1:31.8	98 Eaton McLaren M1C 1:32.0
7 Surtees Lola TS 1:33.1	1 Lunger Caldwell D7C 1:33.9
19 Wilson McLaren M1B 1:34.1	57 Cordts McLaren 1:34.5
55 McCaig McLaren M6B 1:35.0	9 Bonnier McLaren M6B 1:38.3
99 Young Lola T70 1:38.5	45 Stevens Lola T70 1:39.3
25 Hayes McKee Mark 7 1:43.1, 88.2 mph	15 O'Neil Lola T160 No Time

Results
1. Denny Hulme (McLaren M8A-Chevrolet), 80 laps of 2.527 mi. = 202.16 mi. in 1.57:37.7, 103.15 mph
2. Bruce McLaren (McLaren M8A-Chevrolet), 80
3. Mark Donohue (McLaren M6B-Chevrolet), 80
4. Sam Posey (Lola T160-Chevrolet), 76
5. Chuck Parsons (Lola T160-Chevrolet), 74
6. Charlie Hayes (McKee Mark 7-Olds), 74
7. Gary Wilson (McLaren M1B-Chevrolet), 73
8. Skip Scott (Lola T160-Chevrolet), 72
9. Brian O'Neil (Lola T160-Chevrolet), 71
10. George Eaton (McLaren M1C-Ford), 69
11. Jim Hall (Chaparral 2G-Chevrolet), 66
12. John Cordts (McLaren M1C-Chevrolet), 63
Retirements: 13-Brett Lunger (Caldwell D7C-Chevrolet), broken chassis, 68; 14-Roger McCaig (McLaren M6B-Chevrolet), blown head gasket, 66; 15-Lothar Motschenbacher (McLaren M6B-Ford), radius rod ball joint failure, crashed, 63; 16-Peter Revson (McLaren M6B-Ford), main bearing, 56; 17-Jerry Titus (McLaren M6B-Chevrolet), broken rocker arm, 53; 18-Jo Bonnier (McLaren M6B-Chevrolet), clutch, oil leak, 47; 19-Jeff Stevens (Lola T70-Chevrolet), blew tire, crashed, 26; 20-Ron Bucknum (Lola T70 Mk3B-Ford), broken suspension, 18; 21-Bill Young (Lola T70-Chevrolet), blown pan gasket, 18; 22-Dan Gurney (McLeagle-Ford), oil leak, 15; 23-Swede Savage (Lola T160-Ford), stuck throttle, crash, 11; 24-John Surtees (Lola TS-Chevrolet), blown head gasket, 2.
Fastest Lap: Hall and McLaren, 1:25.3, 106.65 mph (MPH not given in results. Computed.)

4. Laguna Seca 10/13/68

4 McLaren McLaren M8A 1:01.44, 111.328 mph	66 Hall Chaparral 2G 1:01.53 (non-starter)
5 Hulme McLaren M8A 1:01.98	52 P. Revson McLaren M6B 1:02.44
6 Donohue McLaren M6B 1:02.69	10 Parsons Lola T160 1:03.50

34 Follmer
Lola T70
1:03.89

26 Scott
Lola T160
1:04.24

6 Donohue
McLaren M6B
1:39.20

66 Hall
Chaparral 2G
1:39.31

17 Titus
McLaren M6B
1:04.45

36 Savage
Lola T160
1:05.02

52 P. Revson
McLaren M6B
1:41.30

48 Gurney
Lola T160
1:41.54

44 Hansen
McLaren M6A
1:05.67

25 Hayes
McKee Mark 7
1:06.87 (non-starter)

10 Parsons
Lola T160
1:42.14

7 Surtees
Lola TS
1:42.61

76 Settember
Lola T70
1:07.11

2 Posey
Lola T160
1:07.32

2 Posey
Lola T160
1:42.64

17 Titus
McLaren M6B
1:43.73

62 Cannon
McLaren M1B
1:07.33

64 Burnett
Burnett Mk3
1:07.57

26 Scott
Lola T160
1:44.18

44 Hansen
McLaren M6A
1:44.35

11 Motschenbacher
McLaren M6B
1:07.60

98 Eaton
McLaren M1C
1:07.68

25 Hayes
McKee Mark 7
1:44.82

36 Savage
McLeagle
1:45.32

21 Paul
McLaren M1C
1:08.42

0 Jensen
Burnett Mk2
1:08.43

62 Cannon
McLaren M1B
1:45.74

98 Eaton
McLaren M1C
1:45.86

31 Brennan
Genie
1:08.53

15 O'Neil
Lola T160
1:09.13

9 Bonnier
McLaren M6B
1:46.57

76 Settember
Lola T70
1:47.03

48 Gurney
McLeagle
1:09.42

12 Entin
Lola T70
1:09.47

99 Young
Lola T70
1:47.50

43 Galloway
Lola T70
1:47.99

43 Galloway
Lola T70
1:09.65

57 Shelton
Porsche 906
1:10.97

11 Motschenbacher
McLaren M6B
1:49.11

34 Follmer
Lola T70
1:49.73

18 Leslie
Lola T70 Coupe
1:10.22

77 Millikan
Lola T70
1:12.07

15 O'Neil
Lola T160
1:50.16

2 Lunger
Caldwell D7C
1:50.67

41 LaPeer
Genie Mk10
1:11.14

1 Lunger
Caldwell D7C
1:12.30, 94.605 mph

28 Brown
McLaren M6B
1:50.77

12 Entin
Lola T70
1:50.78

18 Leslie
Lola T70 Coupe
1:51.07

0 Jensen
Burnett Mk2
1:51.18

64 Burnett
Burnett Mk3
1:51.34

41 Hills
McLaren M1B
1:51.67

71 Herrera
McLaren M1B
1:51.89

55 McCaig
McLaren M6B
1:52.55

22 Paul
McLaren M1C
1:53.51

77 Millikan
Lola T70
1:53.74

37 Barbour/Hollinger
Lola T70
1:54.50, 102.969 mph

Results
1. John Cannon (McLaren M1B-Chevrolet), 80 laps of 1.9 mi. = 152 mi. in 1.46:24.6, 85.6 mph
2. Denny Hulme (McLaren M8A-Chevrolet), 79 laps
3. George Eaton (McLaren M1C-Ford), 79
4. Lothar Motschenbacher (McLaren M6B-Ford), 79
5. Bruce McLaren (McLaren M8A-Chevrolet), 79
6. Jerry Titus (McLaren M6B-Chevrolet), 79
7. Skip Scott (Lola T160-Chevrolet), 79
8. Mark Donohue (McLaren M6B-Chevrolet), 79
9. Sam Posey (Lola T160-Chevrolet), 78
10. Stan Burnett (Burnett Mk3-Chevrolet), 77
11. Merle Brennan (Genie-Chevrolet), 77
12. Peter Revson (McLaren M6B-Ford), 76
13. Don Jensen (Burnett Mk2-Chevrolet), 75
14. Tony Settember (Lola T70-Chevrolet), 74
15. Brian O'Neil (Lola T160-Chevrolet), 73
16. Brett Lunger (Caldwell D7C-Chevrolet), 72
17. Rich Galloway (McLaren M6B-Chevrolet), 72
18. Jerry Entin (Lola T70-Chevrolet), 71
19. Monte Shelton (Porsche 906), 68
20. Jack Millikan (Lola T70-Chevrolet), 65
Retirements: 21-Chuck Parsons (Lola T160-Chevrolet), lost wheel, 60; 22-George Follmer (Lola T70-Ford), crash, 54; 23-Dan Gurney (McLeagle-Ford), loose fuel line, 44; 24-Ed Leslie (Lola T70 Coupe-Chevrolet), blown engine, 42; 25-Jim Paul (McLaren M1C-Chevrolet), holed radiator, 24; 26-Ron LaPeer (Genie Mk10-Chevrolet), broken cylinder, 20; 27-Jerry Hansen (McLaren M6A-Chevrolet), drowned ignition, 5; 28-Swede Savage (Lola T160-Ford), crash, 2.
Fastest Lap: Cannon, 1:14.4, 92.0 mph

5. Riverside 10/27/68

4 McLaren
McLaren M8A
1:38.51, 119.683 mph

5 Hulme
McLaren M8A
1:38.72

41; 18-George Follmer (Lola T70-Ford), no oil pressure, bearings, 40; 19-Bill Young (Lola T70-Chevrolet), running at finish, insufficient laps, broken fan pulley; 40; 20-Tony Settember (Lola T70-Chevrolet), broken wheel, 37; 21-Sam Posey (Lola T160-Chevrolet), swallowed injector screen, 33; 22-Jerry Entin (Lola T70-Chevrolet), running at finish, insufficient laps, overheating, 33; 23-Ron Herrera (McLaren M1B-Chevrolet), broken shift linkage, 32; 24-John Surtees (Lola TS-Chevrolet), broken water pump pulley, 31; 25-Skip Scott (Lola T160-Chevrolet), fuel pressure, 31; 26-Brian O'Neil (Lola T160-Chevrolet), hit guardrail, broken wheel, 31; 27-Roger McCaig (McLaren M6B-Chevrolet), engine failure, 25; 28-Jim Paul (McLaren M1C-Chevrolet), suspension, 22; 29-Stan Burnett (Burnett Mk3-Chevrolet), blown head gasket, overheating, 16; 30-Charlie Hayes (McKee Mark 7-Olds), boiling fuel, 10; 31-Rich Galloway (Lola T70-Chevrolet), loose wiring, 9; 32-Jay Hills (McLaren M1B-Chevrolet), brake failure, 8; 33-Dan Gurney (Lola T160-Ford), oil leak, 7; 34-Peter Revson (McLaren M6B-Ford), no oil pressure, 1; 35-Don Jensen (Burnett Mk2-Chevrolet), rear end failure, 0.
Fastest Lap: N/A

6. Las Vegas 11/10/68

5 Hulme
McLaren M8A
1:29.98

4 McLaren
McLaren M8A
1:29.63, 120.495 mph

6 Donohue
McLaren M6B
1:30.91 (non-starter)

66 Hall
Chaparral 2G
1:30.80

3 Andretti
Lola T160
1:31.60

1 Posey
Lola T160
1:31.47

52 P. Revson
McLaren M6B
1:31.69

48 Gurney
Lola T160
1:31.67

17 Titus
McLaren M6B
1:32.67

23 Amon
Ferrari 612
1:32.20

10 Parsons
Lola T160
1:33.06

11 Motschenbacher
McLaren M6B
1:32.81

25 Hayes
McKee Mark 7
1:33.88

16 Follmer
Lola T70
1:33.42

36 Savage
McLeagle
1:35.00

44 Hansen
McLaren M6A
1:34.97

76 Settember
Lola T70
1:37.34

62 Cannon
McLaren M1B
1:37.09

18 Leslie
Lola T70 Coupe
1:38.16

9 Bonnier
McLaren M6B
1:37.73

19 Wilson
Lola T70
1:40.22

98 Eaton
McLaren M1C
1:41.34

28 Brown
McLaren M6B
1:41.05

37 Barbour
Lola T70
1:42.49

72 Janke
McLaren M1C
1:42.38

55 McCaig
McLaren M6B
1:42.37

99 Young
Lola T70 Mk3B
1:42.62

77 Millikan
Lola T70
1:43.42

24 Nagel
Lola T70
1:43.13

41 Hills
McLaren M1B
1:45.60

22 Paul
McLaren M1C
1:43.58, 104.267 mph

Results
1. Denny Hulme (McLaren M8A-Chevrolet), 70 laps of 3.0 mi. = 210 mi. in 1.52:15.38, 113.1 mph (record)
2. George Follmer (Lola T70-Ford), 70 laps
3. Jerry Titus (McLaren M6B-Chevrolet), 70
4. Chuck Parsons (Lola T160-Chevrolet), 69
5. Sam Posey (Lola T160-Chevrolet), 69
6. Bruce McLaren (McLaren M8A-Chevrolet), 69
7. George Eaton (McLaren M1C-Ford), 66
8. Jo Bonnier (McLaren M6B-Chevrolet), 65
9. Dick Brown (McLaren M6B-Chevrolet), 63
10. Gary Wilson (Lola T70-Chevrolet), 63
11. Leonard Janke (McLaren M1C-Chevrolet), 63
12. Mario Andretti (Lola T160-Ford), 63
13. Bob Nagel (Lola T70-Ford), 61
14. Jay Hills (McLaren M1B-Chevrolet), 60
Retirements: 15-Lothar Motschenbacher (McLaren M6B-Ford), accident, 59; 16-Jim Hall (Chaparral 2G-Chevrolet), accident, 58; 17-Peter Revson (McLaren M6B-Ford), rear suspension, 55; 18-Roger McCaig (McLaren M6B-Chevrolet), running at finish, 47; 19-John Cannon (McLaren M1B-Chevrolet), running at finish, 45; 20-Tony Settember (Lola T70-Chevrolet), blown engine, 44; 21-Dick Barbour (Lola T70-Chevrolet), broken gear lever, 34; 22-Bill Young (Lola T70 Mk3B-Chevrolet), gearbox, 30; 23-Ed Leslie (Lola T70 Coupe-Chevrolet), oil pressure, 28; 24-Jack Millikan (Lola T70-Chevrolet), holed pan, 20; 25-Swede Savage (McLeagle-Ford), fuel pressure, 18; 26-Dan Gurney (Lola T160-Ford), broken half shaft, 15; 27-Jerry Hansen (McLaren M6A-Chevrolet), broken wheel, 5; 28-Jim Paul (McLaren M1C-Chevrolet), broken fuel tank, suspension damage, 5; 29-Chris Amon (Ferrari 612), dirt in injectors, 0; 30-Charlie Hayes (McKee Mark 7-Olds), accident, 0.
Fastest Lap: McLaren, 1:30.95, 118.75 mph (record)

Final Point Standings 1968

1	Denny Hulme	35
2	Bruce McLaren	24
3	Mark Donohue	23
4	Jim Hall	12
5	Lothar Motschenbacher	11
6	John Cannon	10
7	George Follmer	6
8	Jerry Titus+	5
9	Sam Posey	5
	Chuck Parsons	5
11	George Eaton	4
12	Peter Revson	3
	Swede Savage	3
14	Dick Brown	2
15	Dan Gurney	1
	Charlie Hayes	1

+ Titus awarded eighth place because of his third place finish at Las Vegas.

1969

1. Mosport 6/1/69

5 Hulme
McLaren M8B
1:18.8

4 McLaren
McLaren M8B
1:18.2, 113.2 mph

10 Parsons
Lola T163
1:21.0

7 Surtees
McLaren M12
1:20.0

48 Gurney
McLeagle
1:23.9

11 Motschenbacher
McLaren M12
1:21.0

86 Couture McLaren M1B 1:26.0	57 Cordts McLaren M1C 1:24.2
96 Faustina Lola T70 1:31.8	54 Koveleski McLaren M6B 1:31.3
24 Nagel Lola T70 1:32.5	34 Drolsom Lola T70 1:32.5
8 Crawford McLaren Pussycat 1:33.6	27 Galloway McLaren M6B 1:32.9
15 Terrell Lola T70 1:37.4	79 Dutton Lola T70 Mk3B 1:34.2
77 Janke McLaren M1C 1:41.9	55 McCaig McLaren M6B 1:41.5 (non-starter)
28 Brown McLaren M6B 1:45.6, 83.86 mph	99 Cannon McLaren M6B 1:43.8
15 Revson Ford G7A 3:17.3 (non starter)	98 Eaton McLaren M12 no time
	39 Kahlick* McLaren M1C 1:42.1

Results
1. Bruce McLaren (McLaren M8B-Chevrolet), 80 laps of 2.46 mi. = 197 mi. in 1.51:27.3, 105.90 mph
2. Denny Hulme (McLaren M8B-Chevrolet), 1:51.282, 80 laps
3. John Surtees (McLaren M12-Chevrolet), 1:52.23, 80
4. John Cordts (McLaren M1C-Chevrolet),76
5. Chuck Parsons (Lola-Chevrolet), 76
6. Jacques Couture (McLaren M1B-Chevrolet), 73
7. Oscar Koveleski (McLaren M6B-Chevrolet), 73
8. Rich Galloway (McLaren M6B-Chevrolet), 72
9. George Eaton (McLaren M1B-Chevrolet), 72
10. Leonard Janke (McLaren M1C-Chevrolet), 68
11. Tom Dutton (Lola T70 Mk3-Chevrolet), 67

Retirements: 12-George Drolsom (Lola T70 Mk3-Chevrolet), running at finish-insufficient laps, 59; 13-Dan Gurney (McLeagle-Ford), broken suspension, 49; 14-Dick Brown (McLaren M6B-Chevrolet), running at finish, 43; 15-Lothar Motschenbacher (McLaren M12-Chevrolet), clutch, oil pressure, 41; 16-Len Faustina (Lola T70 Mk2-Chevrolet), transaxle, 41; 17-Tom Terrell (Lola T70 Mk3-Chevrolet), broken rod, 26; 18-Jerry Crawford (McLaren-Chevrolet), lost airfoil, 11; 19-Frank Kahlich (McLaren M1C-Chevrolet), valve train, 5; 20-Bob Nagel (Lola T70 Mk3-Chevrolet), blown engine, 3; 21-John Cannon (McLaren M6B-Ford), engine failure, 1.

Fastest Lap: McLaren, 1:19.5, 111.25 mph (record).

* Kahlick appears at end of grid on all official documents, despite setting time better than slowest. No explanation given.

2. St. Jovite 6/15/69

5 Hulme McLaren M8B 1:32.2	4 McLaren McLaren M8B 1:31.7, 104.03 mph
7 Surtees McLaren M12 1:35.2	11 Motschenbacher McLaren M12 1:34.6
98 Eaton McLaren M12 1:37.9	10 Parsons Lola T163 1:36.4
17 Titus McLaren M1C 1:39.1	29 Baker McLaren M6B 1:38.5
55 Cordts McLaren M6B 1:39.8	25 Leonard McKee Mk7 1:39.3
24 Nagel Lola T70 1:43.7	54 Koveleski McLaren M6B 1:42.9
28 Brown McLaren M6B 1:45.1	86 Couture McLaren M1C 1:44.6
84 Drolsom Lola T70 1:51.7	27 Galloway McLaren M6B 1:47.0
12 Powell Lola T160 1:52.3	79 Dutton Lola T70 Mk3B 1:52.1
96 Faustina Lola T70 1:56.3, 82.03 mph	50 Terrell Lola T70 1:53.4

Results
1. Denny Hulme (McLaren M8B-Chevrolet), 60 laps of 2.65 mi. = 159 mi. in 1.37:52.0, 97.55 mph
2. Bruce McLaren (McLaren M8B-Chevrolet), 1:39.56, 60 laps
3. Chuck Parsons (Lola T163-Chevrolet) 59
4. Lothar Motschenbacher (McLaren M12-Chevrolet), 58
5. John Cordts (McLaren M6B-Chevrolet), 58
6. Fred Baker (McLaren M6B-Chevrolet), 58
7. George Eaton (McLaren M12-Chevrolet), 57
8. Joe Leonard (McKee Mk7-Olds turbo), 57
9. Jacques Couture (McLaren M1C-Chevrolet), 56
10. Tom Dutton (Lola T70 Mk3B-Chevrolet), 54
11. Hugh Powell (Lola T160-Chevrolet), 52
12. Tom Terrell (Lola T70-Chevrolet), 47

Retirements: 13-John Surtees (McLaren M12-Chevrolet), bodywork, 41 laps; 14-Bob Nagel (Lola T70 Mk3-Chevrolet), magneto, 33; 15-Jerry Titus (McLaren M1C-Ford), engine, 18; 16-Dick Brown (McLaren M6B-Chevrolet), oil leak, 18; 17-Len Faustina (Lola T70 Mk2-Chevrolet), off track, 17; 18-Rich Galloway (McLaren M6B-Chevrolet), puncture, 10; 19-George Drolsom (Lola T70 Mk3-Chevrolet), fire, 2; 20-Oscar Koveleski (McLaren M6B-Chevrolet), broken suspension.

Fastest Lap: Hulme and McLaren, 1:33.8, 101.7 mph (record).

3. Watkins Glen 7/13/69

5 Hulme McLaren M8B 1:02.54	4 McLaren McLaren M8B 1:02.21, 133.092 mph
7 Surtees McLaren M12 1:04.40	16 Amon Ferrari 612P 1:03.73
98 Eaton McLaren M12 1:06.21	11 Motschenbacher McLaren M12 1:05.69
29 Baker McLaren M6B 1:07.42	10 Parsons Lola T163 1:06.76
1 Siffert Porsche 908 1:08.54	19 Bonnier Lola T70 coupe 1:08.08
55 Cordts McLaren M6B 1:08.94	2 Redman Porsche 908 1:08.74
31 Bucknum Lola T163 1:09.25	14 Dean Porsche 908 1:08.95
75 Dini Lola T162 1:10.48	9 Servoz-Gavin Matra 650 1:10.46
54 Koveleski McLaren M6B 1:10.98	40 Rodriguez Matra 650 1:10.95
24 Nagel Lola T70 1:11.60	28 Brown McLaren M6B 1:11.38
22 Heuer Lola T70 1:13.14	79 Dutton Lola T70 Mk3B 1:12.17
77 Janke Lola T160 1:13.96	43 Doran Lola T160 1:13.84
	27 Galloway McLaren M6B 1:15.17, 110.124 mph

Results
1. Bruce McLaren (McLaren M8B-Chevrolet), 87 laps of 2.3 mi. = 200.1 mi. in 1.35:17.6, 125.99 mph
2. Denny Hulme (McLaren M8B-Chevrolet), 1.35:18.4, 87 laps
3. Chris Amon (Ferrari 612P), 1.35:48.0, 87 laps
4. George Eaton (McLaren M12-Chevrolet), 84
5. Chuck Parsons (Lola T163-Chevrolet) 83
6. Jo Siffert (Porsche 908 Spyder), 82
7. Jo Bonnier (Lola T70 coupe-Chevrolet), 81
8. Johnny Servoz-Gavin (Matra 650 V12), 81
9. Tony Dean (Porsche 908 Spyder), 81
10. Pedro Rodriguez (Matra 650 V12), 79
11. Oscar Koveleski (McLaren M6B-Chevrolet), 78
12. John Surtees (McLaren M12-Chevrolet), 78
13. Bob Nagel (Lola T70 Mk3-Chevrolet), 77
14. Harry Heuer (Lola T70 Mk3-Chevrolet), 67

Retirements: 15-Lothar Motschenbacher (McLaren M12-Chevrolet), timing, 72; 16-Brian Redman (Porsche 908 Spyder), misfiring, 71; 17-Fred Baker (McLaren M6B-Chevrolet), fuel starvation, 58; 18-Tom Dutton (Lola T70 Mk3B-Chevrolet), not classified, 46; 19-John Cordts (McLaren M6B-Chevrolet), tire and accident, 43; 20-Rich Galloway (McLaren M6B-Chevrolet), accident, 37; 21-Dick Brown (McLaren M6B-Chevrolet), radiator cap off - burnt driver, 32; 22-Ronnie Bucknum (Lola T163-Chevrolet), no power, 25; 23-Rob Dini (Lola T162-Chevrolet), clutch, 7; 24-Leonard Janke (Lola T160-Chevrolet), handling, 7; 25-Marshall Doran (Lola T160-Chevrolet), broken wheel, 7.

Fastest Lap: Hulme, 1:02.6, 132.27 mph.

4. Edmonton 7/27/69

5 Hulme McLaren M8B 1:22.9, 109.737 mph	4 McLaren McLaren M8B 1:22.9
16 Amon Ferrari 612P 1:24.9	98 Eaton McLaren M12 1:27.8
7 Surtees Chaparral 2H 1:28.1	11 Motschenbacher McLaren M12 1:30.2
10 Parsons Lola T163 1:31.9	15 Cannon Ford G7A 1:32.5
68 Grable Lola T70 1:33.4	64 Frederick McKee Mk6B 1:33.7
55 McCaig McLaren M6B 1:35.1	14 Williamson McLaren M1C 1:35.6
79 Dutton Lola T70 Mk3B 1:35.8	71 Burnett Burnett Mk3 1:36.0
77 Janke Lola T160 1:36.1	18 Harrison McLaren M1C 1:37.0
27 Galloway McLaren M6B 1:37.3, 93.496 mph	

Results
1. Denny Hulme (McLaren-Chevrolet M8B), 80 laps of 2.527 mi. = 202.16 mi. in 1.56:34.8, 104.35 mph
2. Chris Amon (Ferrari 612P), 1.56:39.7, 80 laps
3. George Eaton (McLaren M12-Chevrolet), 77
4. John Surtees (Chaparral 2H-Chevrolet), 76
5. Tom Dutton (Lola T70 Mk3B-Chevrolet), 73
6. Kris Harrison (McLaren M1C-Chevrolet), 70
7. Leonard Janke (Lola T160-Chevrolet), 60

Retirements: 8-Ron Grable (Lola T70-Chevrolet), blown clutch, 60; 9-Roger McCaig (McLaren M6B-Chevrolet), accident, 55; 10-Bruce McLaren (McLaren M8B-Chevrolet), broken piston, 36; 11-Duane Williamson (McLaren M1C-Chevrolet), rock through pan, 36; 12-Chuck Parsons (Lola T163-Chevrolet) water leak & fire, 34; 13-Rich Galloway (McLaren M6B-Chevrolet), engine failure, 24; 14-Stan Burnett (Burnett Mk3 Chevy), blown head gasket, 11; 15-Lothar Motschenbacher (McLaren M12-Chevrolet), engine failure, 9; 16-C.E. Frederick (McKee Mk6B), engine lost oil, 9; 17-John Cannon (Ford G7A), injector malfunction, 5.

Fastest Lap: Hulme, 1:23.7, 107.524 mph.

5. Mid-Ohio 8/17/69

5 Hulme McLaren M8B 1:25.9, 100.38 mph	4 McLaren McLaren M8B 1:26.2
6 Donohue Lola T163 1:29.5	10 Parsons Lola T163 1:30.0
7 Surtees Chaparral 2H 1:30.2	98 Eaton McLaren M12 1:30.8
0 Siffert Porsche 917PA 1:30.9	31 Revson Lola T163 1:31.1
11 Motschenbacher McLaren M12 1:31.6	99 Cannon McLaren M6B 1:33.3
9 Dean Porsche 908 1:34.9	16 Amon Ferrari 612P 1:36.0
28 Brown McLaren M6B 1:37.5	79 Dutton Lola T70 Mk3 1:37.6
54 Koveleski McLaren M6B 1:38.0	43 Doran Lola T162 1:38.8
18 Harrison McLaren M1C 1:39.1	19 Wilson Lola T163 1:39.1
14 Williamson McLaren M1C 1:39.9	24 Nagel Lola T70 Mk3 1:39.9
37 Apel McLaren M1C 1:45.7, 81.74 mph	

Results
1. Denny Hulme (McLaren M8B-Chevrolet), 80 laps of 2.4 mi. = 192 mi. in 2.02:16.6, 94.212 mph,
2. Bruce McLaren (McLaren M8B-Chevrolet), 80
3. Chris Amon (Ferrari 612P), 79
4. Jo Siffert (Porsche 917PA), 79
5. John Surtees (Chaparral 2H-Chevrolet), 78
6. George Eaton (McLaren M12-Chevrolet), 77
7. Peter Revson (Lola T163-Chevrolet), 76
8. Tony Dean (Porsche 908), 76
9. Dick Brown (McLaren M6B-Chevrolet), 74
10. Gary Wilson (Lola T162-Chevrolet), 72
11. Duane Williamson (McLaren M1C-Chevrolet), 71
12. Oscar Koveleski (McLaren M6B-Chevrolet), 71
13. Kris Harrison (McLaren M1C-Chevrolet), 70
14. Tom Dutton (Lola T70 Mk3B-Chevrolet), 66
15. Cliff Apel (McLaren M1C-Chevrolet), 66
16. Bob Nagel (Lola T70 Mk3-Ford), 65

Retirements: 17-Chuck Parsons (Lola T163-Chevrolet), broken rocker arm, 18; 18-Brooke Doran (Lola T162-Chevrolet), heat prostration, 42; 19-Lothar Motschenbacher (McLaren M12-Chevrolet), wheel bearings, 15; 20-Mark Donohue (Lola T163-Chevrolet), broken half shaft, 8; 21-John Cannon (McLaren M6B-Ford), broken oil, gas lines, 7.

Fastest Lap: Amon, 1:26.4, 100.0 mph.

6. Elkhart Lake 8/31/69

4 McLaren McLaren M8B 2:07.4	5 Hulme McLaren M8B 2:06.3, 114.014 mph

31 Revson Lola T163 2:12.1	1 Andretti McLaren M6B 2:08.4 (non-starter)
98 Eaton McLaren M12 2:12.3	10 Parsons Lola T163 2:12.3
0 Siffert Porsche 917PA 2:13.2	16 Amon Ferrari 612P 2:13.0
7 Surtees Chaparral 2H 2:15.6	15 Follmer Ford G7A 2:13.7
19 Wilson Lola T163 2:19.0	11 Motschenbacher McLaren M12 2:17.8
9 Dean Porsche 908 2:20.1	99 Hobbs McLaren M6B 2:19.2
43 Doran Lola T160 2:20.9	75 Dini Lola T162 2:20.4
28 Brown McLaren M6B 2:21.1	24 Nagel Lola T70 Mk3 2:21.0
51 Causey McLaren M6B 2:22.0	71 Burnett Burnett Mk3 2:21.8
79 Dutton Lola T70 Mk3B 2:24.3	54 Koveleski McLaren M6B 2:22.9
97 Kantrud Lola T70 Mk3B 2:25.4	77 Janke Lola T160 2:25.0
27 Galloway McLaren M6B 2:25.8	14 Williamson McLaren M1C 2:25.5
64 Frederick McKee Mk6B 2:27.7	49 Baker Lola T160 2:26.2
23 Lasiter McLaren M1B 2:27.9	34 Drolsom Lola T70 Mk3 2:27.8
37 Apel McLaren M1C 2:28.0	81 Stoddard McLaren M1C 2:28.0
18 Harrison McLaren M1C 2:35.0, 92.903 mph	91 Hooper Lola T70 Mk3B 2:29.7
25 Leonard McKee Olds 4WD 2:25.2 (non starter)	

Results

1. Bruce McLaren (McLaren M8B-Chevrolet), 50 laps of 4.0 mi. = 200 mi. in 1.51:39, 107.479 mph
2. Denny Hulme (McLaren M8B-Chevrolet), 50
3. Chuck Parsons (Lola T163-Chevrolet), 49
4. Peter Revson (Lola T163-Chevrolet), 49
5. Tony Dean (Porsche 908), 47
6. Lothar Motschenbacher (McLaren M12-Chevrolet), 47
7. Dick Brown (McLaren M6B-Chevrolet), 47
8. Oscar Koveleski (McLaren M6B-Chevrolet), 47
9. Brooke Doran (Lola T160-Chevrolet), 46
10. Kris Harrison (McLaren M1C-Chevrolet), 44
11. Cliff Apel (McLaren M1C-Chevrolet), 43
12. Dave Causey (McLaren M6B-Chevrolet), 42
13. Dick Kantrud (Lola T70 Mk3B-Chevrolet), 38

Retirements: 14-Chris Amon (Ferrari 612P), fuel pump, 43; 15-Harvey Lasiter (McLaren M1B-Chevrolet), out of gas, 29; 16-Spence Stoddard (McLaren M1C-Chevrolet), mechanical, 29; 17-David Hobbs (McLaren M6B-Ford), overheating, 29; 18-Rich Galloway (McLaren M6B-Chevrolet), broken rocker arm, 27; 19-Leonard Janke (Lola T160-Chevrolet), broken suspension, 26; 20-Bob Nagel (Lola T70 Mk3B-Ford), gearbox, 26; 21-Tom Dutton (Lola T70 MK3B-Chevrolet), fuel starvation, 18; 22-Robert Dini (Lola T162-Chevrolet), clutch, 15; 23-Chuck Frederick (McKee Mk6B-Chevrolet), broken axle, 15; 24-Fred Baker (Lola T160-Chevrolet), blown engine, 14; 25-Duane Williamson (McLaren M1C-Chevrolet), crash, 13; 26-Stan Burnett (Burnett Mk3-Chevrolet), crash, 8; 27-George Drolsom (Lola T70-Chevrolet), shift linkage, 8; 28-George Eaton (McLaren M12-Chevrolet), overheating, 7; 29-Jo Siffert (Porsche 917PA), blown engine, 6; 30-Doug Hooper (Lola T70 Mk3B-Chevrolet), overheating, 6; 31-Gary Wilson (Lola T163-Chevrolet), gearbox, 5; 32-John Surtees (Chaparral 2H-Chevrolet), flat tire, 3; 33-George Follmer (Ford G7A-Ford), transmission, 2; 34-Mario Andretti (McLaren M6B-Ford), broken U-joint, 0.

Fastest Lap: Hulme, 2:08.4, 122.150 mph.

7. Bridgehampton 9/14/69

5 Hulme McLaren M8B 1:24.94	4 McLaren McLaren M8B 1:24.62, 121.76 mph
7 Surtees McLaren M12 1:26.53	16 Amon Ferrari 612P 1:26.31
98 Eaton McLaren M12 1:28.85	31 Revson Lola T163 1:28.65
10 Parsons Lola T163 1:29.24	0 Siffert Porsche 917PA 1:29.19
75 Dini Lola T162 1:34.35	11 Motschenbacher McLaren M12 1:29.98
9 Dean Porsche 908 1:35.51	12 Rodriguez Ferrari 312P 1:34.42
79 Dutton Lola T70 Mk3B 1:38.75	28 Brown McLaren M6B 1:36.96
18 Harrison McLaren M1C 1:42.53	8 Wonder McLaren M1C 1:41.31
29 Stevens Lola T70 1:43.31	77 Janke McLaren M1C 1:42.89
24 Nagel Lola T70 Mk3 No Time	97 Goldleaf Lola T70 1:47.49, 95.450 mph

Results

1. Denny Hulme (McLaren M8B-Chevrolet), 70 laps of 2.85 mi. = 199.5 mi. in 1.45:40.58, 118.949 mph (record)
2. Bruce McLaren (McLaren M8B-Chevrolet), 70
3. Jo Siffert (Porsche 917PA), 70
4. Lothar Motschenbacher (McLaren M12-Chevrolet), 67
5. Pedro Rodriguez(Ferrari 312P), 66
6. Tony Dean (Porsche 908), 66
7. Chuck Parsons (Lola T163-Chevrolet), 65
8. Dick Brown (McLaren M6B-Chevrolet), 63
9. Leonard Janke (McLaren M1C-Chevrolet), 62
10. Kris Harrison (McLaren M1C-Chevrolet), 62
11. Tom Dutton (Lola T70-Chevrolet), 61
12. Bill Wonder (McLaren M1C-Ford), 60
13. Ron Goldleaf (Lola T70-Chevrolet), 57

Retirements: 14-John Surtees (McLaren M12-Chevrolet), blown engine, 56; 15-George Eaton (McLaren M12-Chevrolet), blown engine, 56; 16-Bob Dini (Lola T162-Chevrolet), engine failure, 28; 17-Peter Revson (Lola T163-Chevrolet), broken spindle, 10; 18-Chris Amon (Ferrari 612P), broken oil pump shaft, 3; 19-Jeff Stevens (Lola T70-Chevrolet), blown engine, 20; 20-Bob Nagle (Lola T70 3B-Ford), water pump belt, 2.

Fastest Lap: Hulme, 1:26.64, 118.949 mph (record).

8. Michigan 9/28/69

4 McLaren McLaren M8B 1:32.9	5 Hulme McLaren M8B 1:32.5, 116.756 mph
31 Revson Lola T163 1:36.8	0 Siffert Porsche 917PA 1:35.9
7 de Adamich McLaren M12 1:38.2	98 Eaton McLaren M12 1:37.2
8 Dean Porsche 908 1:42.0	10 Parsons Lola T163 1:39.6
15 Brabham Ford G7A 1:42.3	11 Motschenbacher McLaren M12 1:42.2
99 Hobbs McLaren M6B 1:44.8	19 Wilson Lola T163 1:43.2
51 Causey McLaren M6B 1:47.0	28 Brown McLaren M6B 1:46.0
24 Nagel Lola T70 1:48.8	75 Dini Lola T162 1:47.6
55 McCaig McLaren M6B 1:50.6	27 Galloway McLaren M6B 1:49.0
34 Drolsom Lola T70 1:51.0	18 Harrison McLaren M1C 1:50.8
43 Doran Lola T160 1:52.4	79 Janke McLaren M1C 1:51.1
37 Apel McLaren M1C 1:53.7	39 Kahlick McLaren M1C 1:52.5
97 Goldleaf Lola T70 No Time	8 Wonder McLaren M1C 1:53.94, 94.903 mph
	1 Gurney McLaren M8B No Time

Results

1. Bruce McLaren (McLaren M8B-Chevrolet), 65 laps of 3.0 mi. = 195 mi. in 1.48:14.09, 109.098 mph
2. Denny Hulme (McLaren M8B-Chevrolet), 65 laps
3. Dan Gurney (McLaren M8B-Chevrolet), 65
4. Jo Siffert (Porsche 917PA), 64
5. Andrea de Adamich (McLaren M12-Chevrolet), 63
6. Chuck Parsons (Lola T163-Chevrolet), 63
7. Tony Dean (Porsche 908), 62
8. George Eaton (McLaren M12-Chevrolet), 62
9. Dave Causey (McLaren M6B-Chevrolet), 59
10. David Hobbs (McLaren M6B-Ford), 59
11. Robert Dini (Lola T162-Chevrolet) 59
12. Dick Brown (McLaren M6B-Chevrolet), 58
13. Kris Harrison (McLaren M1C-Chevrolet), 56
14. Brooke Doran (Lola T160-Chevrolet), 55
15. Rich Galloway (McLaren M6B-Chevrolet), 54
16. Frank Kahlich (McLaren M1C-Chevrolet), 54
17. William Wonder (McLaren M1C-Ford), 53
18. Leonard Janke (McLaren M1C-Chevrolet), 53

Retirements: 19-Jack Brabham (Ford G7A), lost wheel, 46; 20-Bob Nagel (Lola T70 Mk3B-Ford), broken intake manifold, 37; 21-Ron Goldleaf (Lola T70-Chevrolet), handling, 36; 22-Cliff Apel (McLaren M1C-Chevrolet), crashed, 30; 23-Gary Wilson (Lola T163-Chevrolet), oil leak, 22; 24-Peter Revson (Lola T163-Chevrolet), cracked halfshaft, 17; 25-Lothar Motschenbacher (McLaren M12-Chevrolet), blown headgasket, 11; 26-George Drolsom (Lola T70 Mk3-Chevrolet), broken front suspension; 2; 27-Roger McCaig (McLaren M6B-Chevrolet), accident, broken suspension, 0.

Fastest Lap: Hulme, 1:36.1, 112.382 mph (record).

9. Laguna Seca 10/12/69

4 McLaren McLaren M8B :59.3, 114.898 mph	5 Hulme McLaren M8B :59.75
31 Revson Lola T163 1:36.8	48 Gurney McLeagle 1:35.9
98 Eaton McLaren M12 1:03.32	0 Siffert Porsche 917PA 1:03.47
10 Parsons Lola T163 1:42.0	1 Andretti McLaren M6B 1:03.81
11 Motschenbacher McLaren M12 1:04.56	7 Surtees Chaparral 2H 1:04.90 (non-starter)
99 Cordts McLaren M6B 1:07.54	88 Dykes Lola T162 1:07.97
19 Wilson Lola T163 1:08.03	75 Dini Lola T162 1:08.65
8 Dean Porsche 908 1:08.86	60 Jensen Burnett Mk2 1:09.45
57 Shelton McLaren M1B 1:09.91	28 Brown McLaren M6B 1:09.92
55 McCaig McLaren M6B 1:09.98	32 Nelli Lola T70 1:11.05
81 Stoddard McLaren M1C 1:11.10	24 Nagel Lola T70 1:12.07
23 Lasiter McLaren M1B 1:12.13	74 Hooper Lola T70 1:12.30
73 Williamson Lola T70 1:12.37	64 Frederick McKee Mk6B 1:12.40
20 Haga McLaren M1C 1:12.41	18 Harrison McLaren M1C 1:13.76, 92.732 mph
22 Oliver Ti22 No Time	3 Amon McLaren M8B No Time
27 Galloway McLaren M6B No Time	

Results

1. Bruce McLaren (McLaren M8B-Chevrolet), 80 laps of 1.9 mi. = 152 mi. in 1.27:29.77, 104.8 mph
2. Denny Hulme (McLaren M8B-Chevrolet), 80 laps
3. Chuck Parsons (Lola T163-Chevrolet), 80
4. Mario Andretti (McLaren M6B-Ford), 80
5. Jo Siffert (Porsche 917PA), 79
6. John Cordts (McLaren M6B-Ford), 76
7. Tony Dean (Porsche 908), 76
8. Lothar Motschenbacher (McLaren M12-Chevrolet), 75
9. Rich Galloway (McLaren M6B-Chevrolet), 73
10. Dick Brown (McLaren M6B-Chevrolet), 72
11. Roger McCaig (McLaren M6B-Chevrolet), 72
12. Doug Hooper (Lola T70-Chevrolet), 72
13. Jackie Oliver (Ti22-Chevrolet), 71
14. Kris Harrison (McLaren M1C-Chevrolet), 71
15. Harvey Lassiter (McLaren M1B-Chevrolet), 70
16. Don Jensen (Burnett Mk2-Chevrolet), 66

Retirements: 17-Chris Amon (McLaren M8B-Chevrolet), broken differential, 71*; 18-Vic Nelli (Lola T70-Chevrolet), running at fnish-insuf-

ficient laps, 55; 19-Spencer Stoddard (McLaren M1C-Chevrolet), running at finish, insufficient laps, 44; 20-George Eaton (McLaren M12-Chevrolet), no brakes, crashed, 35; 21-Dan Gurney (McLeagle-Chevrolet), blown piston, 24; 22-Peter Revson (Lola T163-Chevrolet), engine failure, 22; 23-Chuck Frederick (McKee Mk6B-Olds), broken lower A-arm, 20; 24-John Williamson (Lola T70-Chevrolet), blackflagged, too slow, 19; 25-Monte Shelton (McLaren M1B-Chevrolet), fire, 9; 26-Robert Dini (Lola T162-Chevrolet), mechanical, 8; 27-Gary Wilson (Lola T163-Chevrolet), blown engine, 5; 28-Ron Dykes (Lola T162-Chrysler Hemi), oil pressure, 2; 29-Eric Haga (McLaren M1C-Chevrolet), mechanical, 0; 30-Bob Nagel (Lola T70 Mk3B-Ford), mechanical, 0.

Did Not Start: John Surtees (Chaparral 2H-Chevrolet), oil pressure.

Fastest Lap: Hulme, 1:02.19, 109.980 mph.

*Amon is credited with 71 laps, but was not running at the finish. The official results put him behind Don Jensen with only 66 laps, but who was running at the finish.

---

10. Riverside 10/26/69

5 Hulme	4 McLaren
McLaren M8B	McLaren M8B
1:34.03, 126.342 mph	1:34.43
3 Amon	22 Oliver
Ferrari 712P	Ti22
1:35.09	1:36.23
1 Gurney	1 Andretti
McLeagle	McLaren M6B
1:36.72	1:36.84
31 Revson	98 Eaton
Lola T163	McLaren M12
1:37.36	1:37.76
10 Parsons	2 Gardner
Lola T163	Open Sports Ford
1:37.80	1:38.68
0 Siffert	11 Motschenbacher
Porsche 917PA	McLaren M12
1:38.90	1:39.78
19 Wilson	7 Surtees
Lola T163	Chaparral 2H
1:42.55	1:43.42
99 Cordts	27 Galloway
McLaren M6B	McLaren M6B
1:44.74	1:45.88
8 Dean	28 Brown
Porsche 908	McLaren M6B
1:46.93	1:47.97
57 Shelton	9 Campbell
McLaren M1B	BVC Mk1
1:48.63	1:48.87
20 Haga	88 Dykes
McLaren M1C	Lola T160
1:49.26	1:49.67
81 Stoddard	32 Nelli
McLaren M1C	Lola T70
1:50.36	1:50.66
55 McCaig	24 Nagel
McLaren M6B	Lola T70
1:50.66	1:51.17
79 Janke	64 Frederick
McLaren M1C	McKee Mk6B
1:51.41	1:52.13
18 Harrison	60 Jensen
McLaren M1C	Burnett Mk2
1:52.24	1:52.25
97 Goldleaf	77 Millikan
Lola T70	Lola T70
1:52.56	1:54.33

---

11. Texas 11/9/69

5 Hulme	1 Andretti
McLaren M8B	McLaren M6B
1:31.6, 117.904 mph	1:32.6
4 McLaren	3 Amon
McLaren M8B	Ferrari 612P
1:34.3	1:34.5
31 Revson	22 Oliver
Lola T163	Ti22
1:37.0	1:37.1
2 Brabham	10 Parsons
Open Sports Ford	Lola T163
1:37.6	1:37.8
0 Siffert	98 Eaton
Porsche 917PA	McLaren M12
1:38.2	1:38.8
11 Motschenbacher	8 Dean
McLaren M12	Porsche 908
1:40.3	1:42.2
19 Wilson	99 Cordts
Lola T163	McLaren M6B
1:43.4	1:43.9
51 Causey	27 Galloway
McLaren M6B	McLaren M6B
1:45.3	1:47.0

74 Hauser	92 Hurley
Lola T70	McLaren M1B
1:54.66	1:55.47
73 Pavesi	
Lola T70	
1:55.75, 102.634 mph	

Results
1. Denny Hulme (McLaren M8B-Chevrolet), 61 laps of 3.3 mi. = 201.3 mi. in 1:40.05, 120.08 mph
2. Chuck Parsons (Lola T163-Chevrolet), 60
3. Mario Andretti (McLaren M6B-Ford), 60
4. Dan Gurney (McLeagle-Chevrolet), 60
5. Peter Revson (Lola T163-Chevrolet), 58
6. Gary Wilson (Lola T163-Chevrolet), 57
7. Tony Dean (Porsche 908), 55
8. Dick Brown (McLaren M6B-Chevrolet), 54
9. Roger McCaig (McLaren M6B-Chevrolet), 54
10. Spencer Stoddard (McLaren M1C-Chevrolet), 53
11. Chuck Frederick (McKee Mk6B-Olds 425), 52
12. Ron Goldleaf (Lola T70-Chevrolet), 51
13. Monte Shelton (McLaren M1C-Chevrolet), 50
14. Jack Millikan (Lola T70-Chevrolet), 50
15. Bruce Campbell (BVC Mk1-Chevrolet), 47
16. Lothar Motschenbacher (McLaren M12-Chevrolet), 46

Retirements: 17-Eric Haga (McLaren M1C-Chevrolet), suspension failure, 47; 18-Bob Nagel (Lola T70 Mk3B-Ford), running at finish, 44; 19-David Hurley (McLaren M1B-Chevrolet), running at finish, 38; 20-Frank Gardner (Open Sports Ford) broken half shaft, 35; 21-Bruce McLaren (McLaren M8B-Chevrolet), crash, 34; 22-Rich Galloway (McLaren M6B-Chevrolet), transmission, 31; 23-Kris Harrison (McLaren M1C-Chevrolet), running at finish, 28; 24-George Eaton (McLaren M12-Chevrolet), engine failure, 28; 25-Jackie Oliver (Ti22-Chevrolet), differential, 26; 26-Leonard Janke (McLaren M1C-Chevrolet), transmission, 26; 27-Vic Nelli (Lola T70-Chevrolet), transmission, 24; 28-Jo Siffert (Porsche 917PA), oil leak, 17; 29-Eric Hauser (Lola T70-Chevrolet), transmission, 12; 30-John Cordts (McLaren M6B-Ford), suspension failure, 11; 31-Lou Pavesi (Lola T70-Chevrolet), steering failure, 7; 32-Don Jensen (Burnett Mk2-Chevrolet), steering failure, 6; 33-Chris Amon (Ferrari 712P), retired after blackflagged for push start; 5; 34-Ron Dykes (Lola T160-Chrysler Hemi), engine failure, 5;35- John Surtees (Chaparral 2H-Chevrolet), engine failure, 4.

Fastest Lap: Hulme, 1:35.23, 124.75 mph.

28 Brown	64 Frederick
McLaren M6B	McKee Mk6B
1:47.4	1:48.9
55 McCaig	97 Goldleaf
McLaren M6B	Lola T70
1:49.1	1:49.4
79 Janke	18 Harrison
McLaren M1C	McLaren M1C
1:50.2	1:51.0
9 Campbell	37 Apel
BVC Mk1	McLaren M1C
1:52.6	1:53.6, 96.070 mph

Results
1. Bruce McLaren (McLaren M8B-Chevrolet), 70 laps of 3.0 mi. = 210.0 mi. in 1:54:42.4, 109.845 mph
2. George Eaton (McLaren M12-Chevrolet), 70
3. Jack Brabham (Open Sports Ford), 69
4. Jo Siffert (Porsche 917PA), 69
5. Chuck Parsons (Lola T163-Chevrolet), 67
6. Lothar Motschenbacher (McLaren M12-Chevrolet), 65
7. David Causey (McLaren M6B-Chevrolet), 65
8. Tony Dean (Porsche 908), 64
9. Leonard Janke (McLaren M1C-Chevrolet), 63
10. Roger McCaig (McLaren M6B-Chevrolet), 63
11. Kris Harrison (McLaren M1C-Chevrolet), 62
12. Gary Wilson (Lola T163-Chevrolet), 60

Retirements: 13-Peter Revson (Lola T163-Chevrolet), engine failure, 65; 14-Denny Hulme (McLaren M8B-Chevrolet), engine failure, 59; 15-Dick Brown (McLaren M6B-Chevrolet), overheating, 51; 16-Chuck Frederick (McKee Mk6B-Olds), running at finish, 49; 17-Cliff Apel (McLaren M1C-Chevrolet), running at finish, 49; 18-John Cordts (McLaren M6B-Ford), engine failure, 45; 19-Bruce Campbell (BVC Mk1-Chevrolet), running at finish, 44; 20-Ron Goldleaf (Lola T70-Chevrolet), running at finish, 44; 21-Jackie Oliver (Ti22-Chevrolet), engine failure, 22; 22-Mario Andretti (McLaren M6B-Ford), engine failure, 10; 23-Chris Amon (Ferrari 612P), engine failure, 10; 24-Rich Galloway (McLaren M6B-Chevrolet), crashed, 2.

Fastest Lap: Hulme, 1:33.9, 115.016 mph.

Final Point Standings 1969

1	Bruce McLaren	165
2	Denny Hulme	160
3	Chuck Parsons	81
4	Jo Siffert	56
5.	George Eaton	50
6.	Chris Amon	39
7.	Lothar Motschenbacher	35
8.	Tony Dean	31
9.	John Surtees	30
10.	John Cordts	24
11.	Peter Revson	22
	Dan Gurney	22
	Mario Andretti	22
14.	Dick Brown	13
15.	Jack Brabham	12
16.	Leonard Janke	9
	Tom Dutton	9
	Pedro Rodriguez	9
19.	Jacques Couture	8
	Kris Harrison	8
	Andrea de Adamich	8
22.	Oscar Koveleski	7
	Gary Wilson	7
24.	Fred Baker	6
	Dave Causey	6
26.	Rich Galloway	5
27.	Jo Bonnier	4
28.	Joe Leonard	3
	Johnny Servoz-Gavin	3
	Roger McCaig	3
31.	Brooke Doran	2
32.	David Hobbs	1
	Spence Stoddard	1

Note: Split scoring system in Can-Am. Best four finishes in first five races are counted and the best five finishes are counted in the last six races.

1970

1. Mosport 6/14/70

5 Hulme	48 Gurney
McLaren M8D	McLaren M8D
1:17.6	1:16.8, 115.31 mph
26 Revson	22 Oliver
Lola T220	Ti22
1:18.6	1:18.1
16 Follmer	11 Motschenbacher
AVS Shadow	McLaren M8B
1:19.7	1:19.2
3 Brown	98 Eaton
McLeagle *	BRM P154
1:23.2	1:22.8
14 Lawrence	55 McCaig
McLaren M12	McLaren M8C
1:26.3	1:22.3
8 Dean	19 Wilson
Porsche 908	Lola T163
1:26.8	1:26.5
51 Causey	54 Koveleski
Lola T163	McLaren M8B
1:28.3	1:27.0
43 Doran	13 Titus
Lola T163	McLaren M12
1:29.7	1:28.5
81 Durant	57 Cordts
Lola T163	McLaren M8C
1:31.3	1:31.1
24 Nagel	21 Smith
Lola T70	Lola T163
1:33.9	1:32.1
39 Brezinka	75 Dini
McLaren M1C	Lola T163
1:36.2	1:34.4
84 Wonder	47 Dewar
McLaren M1C	McLaren M6A
1:39.6	1:36.2
17 Goldleaf	92 Hurley
McLaren M6B	McLaren M1C
1:43.6	1:42.4
77 Janke	67 De Pasquale
McLaren M1C	Lola T163
2:09.4, 68.44 mph	1:45.8

* McLeagle is the ex-Gurney modified McLaren M6B

Results
1. Dan Gurney (McLaren M8D-Chevrolet), 80 laps of 2.46 mi. = 196.72 mi. in 1:47:05.6, 110.214 mph (record)
2. Jackie Oliver (Ti22-Chevrolet), 80 laps
3. Denny Hulme (McLaren M8D-Chevrolet), 78
4. Tony Dean (Porsche 908), 73
5. Roger McCaig (McLaren M8C-Chevrolet), 73
6. Gordon Dewar (McLaren M6A-Chevrolet), 72
7. Dave Causey (Lola T163-Chevrolet), 70
8. Dick Durant (Lola T163-Chevrolet), 70
9. Brooke Doran (Lola T163-Chevrolet), 68
10. Rainer Brezinka (McLaren M1C-Chevrolet), 67
11. Lothar Motschenbacher (McLaren M8B-Chevrolet), not running at finish, accident, 64
12. Gary Wilson (Lola T162-Chevrolet), 56

Retirements: 13-Bob Brown (McLeagle-Chevrolet) valve spring, 52; 14-Bob Dini (Lola T163-Chevrolet), suspension failure, 49; 15-John Cordts (McLaren M8C-Chevrolet), distributor shaft, 45;

16-George Eaton (BRM P154-Chevrolet), oil and transmission, 33; 17-Ron Goldleaf (McLaren M6B-Chevrolet), running at finish, 28; 18-Peter Revson (Lola T220-Chevrolet), oil leak, 27; 19-Oscar Koveleski (McLaren M8B-Chevrolet), fuel feed and clutch, 25; 20-George Follmer (AVS Shadow-Chevrolet), engine overheating, 24; 21-David Hurley (McLaren M1C-Chevrolet), running at finish, 22; 22-Bob Nagel (Lola T70-Ford), overheating, 21; 23-Graeme Lawrence (McLaren M12-Chevrolet), oil pressure, 18; 24-Eno De Pasquale (Lola T163-Chevrolet), black flagged, 12; 25-Bill Wonder (McLaren M1C-Chevrolet), black flagged, 12; 26-Jerry Titus (McLaren M12-Chevrolet), oil leak, 8; 27-Jerry Smith (Lola T160-Chevrolet), black flagged, 8; 28-Leonard Janke (McLaren M1C-Chevrolet), black flagged, 8

Fastest Lap: Gurney, 1:18.0, 113.492 mph (record).

Dick Brown, M6B-Chevrolet, fatal accident in practice. Ceremonies honoring both Bruce McLaren and Dick Brown before start of race.

2. St. Jovite 6/28/70

5 Hulme		48 Gurney	
McLaren M8D		McLaren M8D	
1:33.3		1:33.0, 102.58 mph	
11 Motschenbacher		22 Oliver	
McLaren M8B		Ti22	
1:34.6		1:33.8	
3 Brown		57 Cordts	
McLeagle		McLaren M8C	
1:36.3		1:35.4	
13 Titus		26 Revson	
McLaren M12		Lola T220	
1:37.6		1:37.0	
16 Follmer		98 Eaton	
AVS Shadow		BRM P154	
1:38.4		1:38.0	
47 Dewar		55 McCaig	
McLaren M6A		McLaren M8C	
1:40.7		1:40.7	
54 Koveleski		14 Lawrence	
McLaren M8B		McLaren M12A	
1:41.9		1:40.9	
75 Dini		19 Parsons	
Lola T163		Lola T163	
1:42.0		1:42.0	
24 Nagel		21 Bondurant	
Lola T70		Lola T163	
1:46.1		1:43.3	
39 Peterman		51 Causey	
McLaren M1C		Lola T163	
1:48.3		1:47.8	
37 Apel		17 Goldleaf	
McLaren M6B		McLaren M6B	
1:53.0, 84.42 mph		1:48.7	

Results
1. Dan Gurney (McLaren M8D-Chevrolet), 75 laps of 2.65 mi. = 198.77 mi. in 2.01:45.7, 97.95 mph
2. Lothar Motschenbacher (McLaren M8B-Chevrolet), 75 laps
3. George Eaton (BRM P154-Chevrolet), 73
4. Bob Brown (McLeagle-Chevrolet), 71
5. Roger McCaig (McLaren M8C-Chevrolet), 70
6. Oscar Koveleski (McLaren M8B-Chevrolet), 69
7. Jerry Titus/Peter Revson (McLaren M12A-Chevrolet), 68
8. Chuck Parsons (Lola T163-Chevrolet), 67
9. Dave Causey (Lola T163-Chevrolet), not running at finish, engine failure, 63*
10. Clif Apel (McLaren M6B-Chevrolet), 63*
11. Horst Peterman (McLaren M1C-Chevrolet), 62*
Retirements: 12-Bob Nagel (Lola T70-Ford), en-

gine failure, 51; 13-Denny Hulme (McLaren M8D-Chevrolet), engine failure, 50; 14-Bob Bundurant (Lola T160-Chevrolet), engine failure, 29; 15-John Cordts (McLaren M8C-Chevrolet), transmission, 24; 16-Gordon Dewar (McLaren M6A-Chevrolet), accident, 20; 17-George Follmer (AVS Shadow-Chevrolet), overheating, 13; 18-Peter Revson (Lola T220-Chevrolet), engine failure, 7; 19-Ron Goldleaf (McLaren M6B-Chevrolet), engine failure, 1; 20-Jackie Oliver (Ti22-Chevrolet), accident, 0; 21-Graeme Lawrence (McLaren M12A-Chevrolet), accident, 0; 22-Bob Dini (Lola T163-Chevrolet), accident, 0.

Fastest Lap: Hulme, 1:34.3, 101.17 mph

* Reflects changes made by officials to results the week following event. Causey was not running at finish, but he did 63 laps in less time than Apel, moving Causey ahead of Apel in the final results. Peterman moved down to 11th.

3. Watkins Glen 7/12/70

48 Gurney		5 Hulme	
McLaren M8D		McLaren M8D	
1:03.22		1:02.76, 131.85 mph	
26 Revson		66 Stewart	
Lola T220		Chaparral 2J	
1:04.53		1:03.9	
11 Motschenbacher		92 Andretti	
McLaren M8B		Ferrari 512S	
1:05.11		1:04.71	
91 Ickx		3 Brown	
Ferrari 512S		McLeagle	
1:06.14		1:05.96	
2 Rodriguez		31 Elford	
Porsche 917		Porsche 917	
1:06.4		1:06.37	
1 Siffert		6 Redman	
Porsche 917		Porsche 917	
1:06.50		1:06.46	
57 Cordts		98 Eaton	
McLaren M8C		BRM P154	
1:07.16		1:06.63	
19 Wilson		32 Attwood	
Lola T163		Porsche 917	
1:07.77		1:07.17	
76 Adams		35 van Lennep	
Ferrari 512S		Porsche 917	
1:08.45		1:08.18	
15 Cannon		21 Bondurant	
Ford G7A		Lola T160	
1:09.03		1:08.66	
54 Koveleski		50 Bonnier	
McLaren M8B		Lola T70 coupe	
1:09.98		1:09.77	
36 Marko		55 McCaig	
Porsche 908		McLaren M8C	
1:11.22		1:11.18	
51 Causey		14 Lawrence	
Lola T163		McLaren M12A	
1:12.66		1:12.42	
24 Nagel		67 De Pasquale	
Lola T70		Lola T163	
1:13.12		1:13.06	
17 Goldleaf		8 Dean	
McLaren M6B		Porsche 908	
1:13.74		1:13.60	
33 Loos		37 Apel	
Ferrari 512S		McLaren M6B	
1:22.49, 100.37 mph		1:15.23	
		43 Doran	
		Lola T163	
		1:19.94	

Results
1. Denny Hulme (McLaren M8D-Chevrolet), 87 laps of 2.3 mi. = 200.1 mi. in 1.41:16, 118.56 mph
2. Jo Siffert (Porsche 917), 87 laps
3. Richard Attwood (Porsche 917), 85
4. Vic Elford (Porsche 917), 85
5. Mario Andretti (Ferrari 512S), 85
6. Gijs van Lennep (Porsche 917), 83
7. Brian Redman (Porsche 917), 82
8. Bob Brown (McLeagle-Chevrolet), 82
9. Dan Gurney (McLaren M8D-Chevrolet), 81
10. Gerard Larrousse (Porsche 908), 81
11. Joakim Bonnier (Lola T70 coupe-Chevrolet), 80
12. Oscar Koveleski (McLaren M8B-Chevrolet), 79
13. Dave Causey (Lola T163-Chevrolet), 79
14. Bob Bondurant (Lola T160-Chevrolet), 76
15. Gary Wilson (Lola T163-Chevrolet), 76
16. Tony Dean (Porsche 908), 75
17. Bob Nagel (Lola T70-Ford), 74
18. Roger McCaig (McLaren M8C-Chevrolet), 73
19. Peter Revson (Lola T220-Chevrolet), 72
20. Jim Adams (Ferrari 512S), 67
21. Eno de Pasquale (Lola T163-Chevrolet), 67
Retirements: 22-John Cordts (McLaren M8C-Chevrolet), overheating, 55; 23-George Eaton (BRM P154-Chevrolet), brake failure, 47; 24-John Cannon (Ford G7A-Ford), overheating, 46; 25-Pedro Rodriquez (Porsche 917), transmission failure, 31; 26-Georg Loos (Ferrari 512S), fuel pump failure, 31; 27-Lothar Motschenbacher (McLaren M8B-Chevrolet), broken half shaft, 25; 28-Graeme Lawrence (McLaren M12-Chevrolet), engine failure, 23; 29-Jackie Stewart (Chaparral 2J-Chevrolet), brake failure, 22; 30-Clif Apel (McLaren M6B-Chevrolet), unknown, 21; 31-Ron Goldleaf (McLaren M6B-Chevrolet), broken distributor shaft, 11; 32-Jackie Ickx (Ferrari 512S), unknown, 10; 33-Brooke Doran (Lola T163-Chevrolet), unknown, 5.

Fastest Lap: Stewart, 1:05.8, 125.84 mph

4. Edmonton 7/26/70

5 Hulme		48 Gethin	
McLaren M8D		McLaren M8D	
1:23.6, 108.818 mph		1:24.0	
11 Motschenbacher		3 Brown	
McLaren M8B		McLeagle	
1:24.1		1:25.6	
57 Cordts		98 Eaton	
McLaren M8C		BRM P154	
1:26.2		1:26.7	
19 Wilson		21 Bondurant	
Lola T163		Lola T160	
1:27.4		1:27.5	
26 Revson		76 Adams	
Lola T220		Ferrari 512S	
1:28.7		1:28.8	
15 Hobbs		51 Causey	
Ford G7A		Lola T163	
1:29.8		1:29.9	
14 Lawrence		55 McCaig	
McLaren M12A		McLaren M8C	
1:30.0		1:31.4	
47 Dewar		77 Janke	
McLaren M6A		McLaren M1C	
1:32.7		1:35.7	
33 Frederick		7 Shelton	
McKee Mk6		McLaren M1B	
1:36.6		1:38.0	
20 Losk		6 Moore	
McLaren M1C		Moore Mk2	
1:38.2		1:44.8	
70 Barbour		8 Dean	
Rattenbury Mk4B		Porsche 908	
1:52.8, 80.649 mph		No Time	

Results
1. Denny Hulme (McLaren M8D-Chevrolet), 80 laps of 2.4 mi. = 199.2 mi. in 2.01:03.3, 95.163 mph

Results
1. Denny Hulme (McLaren M8D-Chevrolet), 80 laps of 2.527 mi. = 202.16 mi. in 1.54:05.5, 106.4 mph
2. Peter Gethin (McLaren M8D-Chevrolet), 80 laps
3. Lothar Motschenbacher (McLaren M8B-Chevrolet), 79
4. Bob Brown (McLeagle-Chevrolet), 78
5. Dave Causey (Lola T163-Chevrolet), 76
6. Gary Wilson (Lola T163-Chevrolet), 76
7. Jim Adams (Ferrari 512S), 75
8. Roger McCaig (McLaren M8C-Chevrolet), 74
9. Leonard Janke (McLaren M1C-Chevrolet), 70
10. Chuck Frederick (McKee Mk6-Olds), 69
11. Tony Dean (Porsche 908), 68
12. Bob Bondurant (Lola T160-Chevrolet), not running at finish, blown engine, 60
13. Mike Barbour (Rattenbury Mk4B-Olds), 57
14. Dick Losk (McLaren M1C-Chevrolet), 57
15. Ric Moore (Moore Mk2-Chevrolet), 51
Retirements: 16-Peter Revson (Lola T220-Chevrolet), oil leak, 31; 17-Gordon Dewar (McLaren M6A-Chevrolet), coil, 25; 18-George Eaton (BRM P154-Chevrolet), wheel bearing, 24; 19-Monte Shelton ((McLaren M1B-Chevrolet), blown engine, 20; 20-John Cordts (McLaren M8C-Chevrolet), transmission, 18; 21-Graeme Lawrence (McLaren M12-Chevrolet), broken piston, 17; 22-David Hobbs (Ford G7A), lost water, 1.
Fastest Lap: Hulme, 1:23.9, 108.429 mph.

5. Mid-Ohio 8/23/70

5 Hulme		11 Motschenbacher	
McLaren M8D		McLaren M8B	
1:27.6, 98.63 mph		1:28.5	
26 Revson		7 Gethin	
Lola T220		McLaren M8D	
1:28.6		1:29.7	
20 Rodriguez		76 Adams	
Ferrari 512S		Ferrari 512S	
1:30.4		1:30.7	
1 Elford		10 Parsons	
AVS Shadow		Lola T163	
1:31.4		1:32.4	
79 Dutton		54 Koveleski	
McLaren M6B		McLaren M8B	
1:32.7		1:33.0	
51 Causey		19 Wilson	
Lola T163		Lola T163	
1:33.0		1:33.1	
55 McCaig		8 Dean	
McLaren M8C		Porsche 908	
1:34.4		1:34.4	
14 Lawrence		81 Durant	
McLaren M12A		Lola T163	
1:34.8		1:35.5	
77 Janke		47 Dewar	
McLaren M1C		McLaren M6A	
1:36.2		1:38.2	
24 Nagel		21 Bondurant	
Lola T70 Mk3B		Lola T160	
1:38.8		1:41.1	
71 Swindell		91 Thornsjo	
Lola T70 Mk3		Lola T160	
1:42.7		1:42.8	
17 Goldleaf		39 Brezinka	
McLaren M6B		McLaren M1C	
1:46.2		1:46.7, 80.97 mph	
98 Eaton		27 Kahlich	
BRM P154		McLaren M6B	
No Time		No Time	

Results
1. Denny Hulme (McLaren M8D-Chevrolet), 80 laps of 2.4 mi. = 199.2 mi. in 2.01:03.3, 95.163 mph

2. Peter Revson (Lola T220-Chevrolet), 80 laps
3. Lothar Motschenbacher (McLaren M8B-Chevrolet), 79
4. Chuck Parsons (Lola T163-Chevrolet), 77
5. Gary Wilson (Lola T163-Chevrolet), 76
6. Roger McCaig (McLaren M8C-Chevrolet), 75
7. Dick Durant (Lola T163-Chevrolet), 74
8. Jim Adams/Bob Bondurant (Ferrari 512S), not running at finish, out of gas, 72
9. Peter Gethin (McLaren M8D-Chevrolet), not running at finish, engine failure, 71
10. Bob Nagel (Lola T70 Mk3B-Ford), 70
11. Pedro Rodriguez (Ferrari 512S), 70
12. Graeme Lawrence (McLaren M12A-Chevrolet), 68
13. Tom Swindell (Lola T70 Mk3-Chevrolet), 68
14. Rainer Brezinka (McLaren M1C-Chevrolet), 67
15. Tom Dutton (McLaren M6B-Chevrolet), not running at finish, broken wheel, 66
16. Orly Thornsjo (Lola T160-Chevrolet), 64
17. Gordon Dewar (McLaren M6A-Chevrolet), 55
18. Ron Goldleaf (McLaren M6B-Chevrolet), 55
19. Dave Causey (Lola T163-Chevrolet), 47
Retirements: 20-Leonard Janke (McLaren M1C-Chevrolet), accident, 25; 21-Bob Bondurant (Lola T160-Chevrolet) ignition failure, 18; 22-Oscar Koveleski (McLaren M8B-Chevrolet), broken shift linkage, 12; 23-Vic Elford (AVS Shadow-Chevrolet), unbalanced wheel, 9; 24-George Eaton (BRM P154-Chevrolet), no fuel pressure, 8; 25-Tony Dean (Porsche 908), broken front wishbone, 7; 26-Frank Kahlich (McLaren M6B-Ford), no oil pressure, 3.
Fastest Lap: Hulme, 1:28.8, 97.30 mph

6. Elkhart Lake, 8/30/70

26 Revson Lola T220 2:11.4	5 Hulme McLaren M8D 2:10.6, 110.261 mph
73 Hobbs McLaren M12 2:15.8	11 Motschenbacher McLaren M8B 2:12.3
7 Gethin McLaren M8D 2:17.9	21 Bondurant Lola T160 2:17.9
8 Dean Porsche 908 2:20.0	19 Wilson Lola T163 2:18.1
32 Elford Lola T70 Mk3B 2:20.6	10 Parsons Lola T160 2:20.6
3 Brown McLeagle 2:21.2	81 Durant Lola T163 2:21.0
55 McCaig McLaren M8C 2:24.9	54 Koveleski McLaren M8B 2:22.3
51 Causey Lola T163 2:27.7	44 Hansen Lola T160 2:24.0
79 Dutton McLaren M6B 2:28.7	91 Thornsjo Lola T160 2:26.2
20 Rodriguez Ferrari 512S 2:31.4	14 Lawrence McLaren M12A 2:27.9
24 Nagel Lola T70 Mk3B 2:35.0	97 Kantrud Lola T70 Mk3B 2:33.3
34 Drolsom Lola T70 Mk3 2:44.1	33 Frederick McKee M6B 2:35.8
17 Goldleaf McLaren M6B 2:49.3	37 Apel McLaren M6B 2:39.1
70 Barbour Rattenbury Mk4B 2:56.0	71 Swindell Lola T70 Mk3 2:47.8
27 Kahlich McLaren M6B 3:04.2, 78.176 mph	15 Cannon Ford G7A 2:49.6
	18 Rosbach Lola T70 No Time

Results
1. Peter Gethin (McLaren M8D-Chevrolet), 50 laps of 4.0 mi. = 200 mi. in 1.54:16.1, 105.016 mph
2. Bob Bondurant (Lola T160-Chevrolet) 49
3. Dave Causey (Lola T163-Chevrolet), 48
4. Gary Wilson (Lola T163-Chevrolet), 48
5. Tony Dean (Porsche 908), 48
6. Bob Brown (McLeagle-Chevrolet), not running at finish, flat tire, 47
7. Pedro Rodriguez (Ferrari 512S), 47
8. Graeme Lawrence (McLaren M12A-Chevrolet), 47
9. Dick Durant (Lola T163-Chevrolet), 46
10. Ron Goldleaf (McLaren M6B-Chevrolet), 46
11. Clif Apel (McLaren M6B-Chevrolet), 45
12. Orly Thornsjo (Lola T160-Chevrolet), 41
Retirements: 13-Roger McCaig (McLaren M8C-Chevrolet), engine failure, 40; 14-Richard Kantrud (Lola T70 Mk3B-Chevrolet), engine failure, 38; 15-Denny Hulme (McLaren M8D-Chevrolet), illegal push start, 37; 16-Chuck Parsons (Lola T160-Chevrolet), overheating, 37; 17-Mike Barbour (Rattenbury Mk4B-Olds), running at finish, 37; 18-Jerry Rosbach (Lola T70-Chevrolet), running at finish, 36; 19-Lothar Motschenbacher (McLaren M8B-Chevrolet), broken suspension, 25; 20-Bob Nagel (Lola T70 Mk3B-Ford), clutch failure, 25; 21-Vic Elford (Lola T70-Chevrolet), broken water hose, 23; 22-George Drolsom (Lola T70-Chevrolet), broken fan belt, 21; 23-Oscar Koveleski (McLaren M8B-Chevrolet), gearbox, 19; 24-John Cannon (Ford G7A-Ford), overheating, 19; 25-David Hobbs (McLaren M12-Chevrolet), overheating, 19; 26-Peter Revson (Lola T220-Chevrolet), broken half shaft, 14; 27-Jerry Hansen (Lola T160-Chevrolet), flat tire, 12; 28-Tom Dutton (McLaren M6B-Chevrolet), oil pump failure, 11; 29-Frank Kahlich (McLaren M6B-Ford) engine failure, 9; 30-Chuck Frederick (McKee M6B-Olds), engine failure, 8; 31-Tom Swindell (Lola T70 Mk3-Chevrolet), engine failure, 2.
Fastest Lap: Hulme, 2:12.4, 108.762 mph

7. Road Atlanta, 9/13/70

5 Hulme McLaren M8D 1:18.68	66 Elford Chaparral 2J 1:17.42, 117.35 mph
26 Revson Lola T220 1:20.02	7 Gethin McLaren M8D 1:19.67
3 Brown McLeagle 1:21.92	98 Eaton BRM P154 1:21.04
10 Parsons Lola T163 1:24.09	21 Bondurant Lola T160 1:23.83
8 Dean Porsche 908 1:25.50	11 Motschenbacher McLaren M12 1:24.10
51 Causey Lola T163 1:27.39	15 Yarbrough Ford G7A 1:27.12
47 Dewar McLaren M6A 1:28.76	14 Lawrence McLaren M12A 1:28.27
54 Koveleski McLaren M8B 1:28.99	79 Dutton McLaren M6B 1:28.78
55 McCaig McLaren M8C 1:29.92	19 Wilson Lola T163 1:29.20
81 Durant Lola T163 1:30.47	32 Adamowicz Lola T70 Mk3B 1:30.10
37 Apel McLaren M6B 1:32.24	67 De Pasquale Lola T163 1:32.18
39 Brezinka McLaren M1C 1:35.89	17 Goldleaf McLaren M6B 1:32.71
74 Smith McLaren M12 1:45.81	34 Drolsom Lola T70 Mk3 1:35.95
70 Barbour Rattenbury Mk4B 1:48.09, 84.02 mph	

Results
1. Tony Dean (Porsche 908), 75 laps of 2.52 mi. = 190 mi. in 1.40:45, 103.45 mph
2. Dave Causey (Lola T163-Chevrolet), 75 laps
3. Lothar Motschenbacher (McLaren M12-Chevrolet), 72
4. Oscar Koveleski (McLaren M8B-Chevrolet), 72
5. Roger McCaig (McLaren M8C-Chevrolet), 72
6. Vic Elford (Chaparral 2J-Chevrolet), 69
7. Peter Gethin (McLaren M8D-Chevrolet), not running at finish, gearbox failure, 68
8. Dick Durant (Lola T163-Chevrolet), 66
9. Graeme Lawrence (McLaren M12-Chevrolet), 63
10. George Drolsom (Lola T70 Mk3-Chevrolet), 54
11. Rainer Brezinka (McLaren M1C-Chevrolet), 51
12. Chuck Parsons (Lola T163-Chevrolet), 50
Retirements: 13-George Eaton (BRM P154-Chevrolet), blown engine, 49; 14-Peter Revson (Lola T220-Chevrolet), suspension failure, accident, 29; 15-Bob Brown (McLeagle-Chevrolet), accident, 29; 16-Lee Roy Yarbrough (Ford G7A-Ford), fuel feed problems, 22; 17-Gordon Dewar (McLaren M6A-Chevrolet), oil leak, 20; 18-Bob Bondurant (Lola T160-Chevrolet), body damage, overheating, 18; 19-Tom Dutton (McLaren M6B-Chevrolet), accident, 16; 20-Clif Apel (McLaren M6B-Chevrolet), accident, 16; 21-Eno De Pasquale (Lola T163-Chevrolet), clutch failure, 11; 22-Denny Hulme (McLaren M8D-Chevrolet), body damage, 10; 23-Gary Wilson (Lola T163-Chevrolet), accident, 9; 24-Dick Smith (McLaren M12-Ford), oil leak, 2; 25-Mike Barbour (Rattenbury Mk4B-Olds), broken connecting rod, 1; 26-Ron Goldleaf (McLaren M6B-Chevrolet), accident, 1; 27-Tony Adamowicz (Lola T70 Mk3B-Chevrolet), fuel starvation, 0.
Fastest Lap: Gethin and Revson, 1:18.05, 116.40 mph (record)

8. Donnybrooke, 9/27/70

5 Hulme McLaren M8D 1:30.9	26 Revson Lola T220 1:30.8, 118.943 mph
7 Gethin McLaren M8D 1:31.7	77 Amon March 707 1:30.9
76 Adams Ferrari 512P * 1:33.1	98 Eaton BRM P154 1:32.2
11 Motschenbacher McLaren M12 1:34.0	1 Rodriguez BRM P154 1:33.2
8 Dean Porsche 908 1:34.7	10 Parsons Lola T163 1:34.4
19 Wilson Lola T163 1:35.8	21 Cordts Lola T160 1:34.9
59 Gregg Lola T165 1:36.3	51 Causey Lola T163 1:35.9
55 McCaig McLaren M8C 1:37.8	3 Brown Lola T163 1:37.0
54 Koveleski McLaren M8B 1:39.0	14 Lawrence McLaren M12A 1:38.1
18 Rosbach Lola T70 1:41.1	97 Kantrud Lola T70 1:40.6
81 Durant Lola T163 1:43.7	12 Roe McKee 1:43.0
47 Dewar McLaren M6A 1:44.3	33 Frederick McKee Mk6B 1:43.8
27 Elford McLaren M6B No Time	39 Brezinka McLaren M1C 1:45.8, 102.079 mph

* Car 76 is the ex-Amon 612P refitted with a 5.0 engine

Results
1. Denny Hulme (McLaren M8D-Chevrolet), 70 laps of 3.0 mi. = 210 mi. in 1.47:10.2, 117.57 mph
2. Peter Gethin (McLaren M8D-Chevrolet), 70
3. Peter Revson (Lola T220-Chevrolet), 69
4. Jim Adams (Ferrari 512P), 68
5. Chris Amon (March 707-Chevrolet), not running at finish, fuel pickup, 67
6. Lothar Motschenbacher (McLaren M12-Chevrolet), 66
7. Tony Dean (Porsche 908), 66
8. Dave Causey (Lola T163-Chevrolet), 66
9. Pedro Rodriguez (BRM P154-Chevrolet), 66
10. Peter Gregg (Lola T165-Chevrolet), 66
11. Graeme Lawrence (McLaren M12-Chevrolet), 65
12. Oscar Koveleski (McLaren M8B-Chevrolet), 64
13. Gordon Dewar (McLaren M6A-Chevrolet), 63
14. Dick Kantrud (Lola T70-Chevrolet), 63
15. Roger McCaig (McLaren M8C-Chevrolet), not running at finish, crash, 62
16. John Cordts (Lola T160-Chevrolet), 62
17. Chuck Frederick (McKee M6B-Olds), 60
18. Rainer Brezinka (McLaren M1C-Chevrolet), 59
19. Jerry Rosbach (Lola T70-Chevrolet), 59
20. Dick Roe (McKee-Chevrolet), 51
Retirements: 21-Dick Durant (Lola T163-Chevrolet), no oil pressure, 24; 22-Vic Elford (McLaren M6B-Ford), black flagged for push start, 22; 23-Chuck Parsons (Lola T163-Chevrolet), blown clutch, 12; 24-George Eaton (BRM P154-Chevrolet), broken rocker arm, 2; 25-Bob Brown (Lola T163-Chevrolet), suspension failure, crash, 2; 26-Gary Wilson (Lola T163-Chevrolet), suspension failure, crash, 2.
Fastest Lap: Hulme, 1:29.5, 120.67 mph (record)

9. Laguna Seca 10/18/70

5 Hulme McLaren M8D 1:00.6, 112.871 mph	7 Gethin McLaren M8D 1:00.6
26 Revson Lola T220 1:01.2	22 Oliver Ti22 Mk II 1:01.2
77 Amon March 707 1:01.8	21 Bondurant Lola T160 1:02.4
10 Parsons Lola T163 1:03.0	98 Eaton BRM P154 1:03.0

1 Rodriguez
BRM P154
1:03.0

76 Adams
Ferrari 512P
1:04.2

19 Wilson
Lola T163
1:04.2

73 Hobbs
McLaren M12
1:06.0

92 Leslie
McLaren Special
1:06.0

55 McCaig
McLaren M8C
1:06.0

59 Gregg
Lola T165
1:07.2

27 Brennan
Genie Mk10
1:07.8

32 Guldstrand
Lola T70
1:08.4

70 Selway
McLaren M1C
1:09.0

33 Frederick
McKee Mk6B
1:10.2

20 Losk
McLaren M1C
1:10.2

11 Motschenbacher
McLaren M8C
1:03.6

12 Adamowicz
McLaren M12
1:04.2

15 Cannon
Ford G7A
1:04.8

14 Lawrence
McLaren M12A
1:06.0

3 Brown
McLeagle
1:06.0

51 Causey
Lola T163
1:06.0

9 Woods
Lola T160/3
1:35.9

30 Jensen
Burnett Mk2
1:08.4

81 Durant
Lola T163
1:08.4

74 Smith
McLaren M12
1:09.6

42 Lassiter
Lola T70
1:10.2

6 Cupp
McLaren M1C
1:10.8, 96.610 mph

Results
1. Denny Hulme (McLaren M8D-Chevrolet), 80 laps of 1.9 mi. = 200 mi. in 1.25:58.8, 106.071 mph
2. Jackie Oliver (Ti22 Mk II-Chevrolet), 80 laps
3. Peter Revson (Lola T220-Chevrolet), 79
4. Chris Amon (March 707-Chevrolet), 78
5. Pedro Rodriguez (BRM P154-Chevrolet), 78
6. Chuck Parsons (Lola T163-Chevrolet), 78
7. Tony Adamowicz (McLaren M12-Chevrolet), 77
8. Gary Wilson (Lola T163-Chevrolet), 77
9. Dave Causey (Lola T163-Chevrolet), 76
10. Graeme Lawrence (McLaren M12-Chevrolet), 76
11. Roger McCaig (McLaren M8C-Chevrolet), 76
12. Peter Gregg (Lola T165-Chevrolet), 76
13. Merle Brennan (Genie Mk10-Chevrolet), 73
14. Ed Leslie (McLaren Special-Chevrolet), 72
15. Dick Durant (Lola T163-Chevrolet), 72
16. Don Jensen (Burnett Mk2-Chevrolet), 72
17. Dick Guldstrand (Lola T70-Chevrolet), 56
Retirements: 18-Lothar Motschenbacher (McLaren M8C-Chevrolet), loose axle, trans, 53; 19-David Hobbs (McLaren M12-Chevrolet), clutch, 50; 20-John Cannon (Ford G7A-Ford), overheating, 50; 21-Roy Woods (Lola T160/3-Dodge), running at finish, 50; 22-Bob Bondurant (Lola T160-Chevrolet), clutch, 49; 23-Dick Smith (McLaren M12-Ford), gearbox, 47; 24-Peter Gethin (McLaren M8D-Chevrolet), dead battery, 37; 25-Chuck Frederick (McKee Mk6B-Olds), engine, 37; 26-Harvey Lasiter (Lola T70-Ford), gearbox, 30; 27-Jim Adams (Ferrari 512P), linkage, 27; 28-Dick Losk (McLaren M1C-Chevrolet), overheating, 27; 29-Dave Selway (McLaren M1C-Chevrolet), crash, 22; 30-Bob Brown (McLeagle-Chevrolet), gearbox, 14; 31-George Eaton (BRM P154-Chevrolet), crash, 11; 32-Bill Cupp (McLaren M1C-Chevrolet), linkage, 3.
Did Not Start: Dean (Porsche), 1:04.2, warm-up crash
Fastest Lap: Oliver, 1:02.4, 109.615 mph

10. Riverside 11/1/70

66 Elford
Chaparral 2J
1:32.49, 128.446 mph

26 Revson
Lola T220
1:35.1

77 Amon
March 707
1:35.92

1 Rodriguez
BRM P154
1:38.57

11 Motschenbacher
McLaren M8C
1:38.78

76 Adams
Ferrari 512P
1:39.78

10 Parsons
Lola T163
1:40.47

15 Cannon
Ford G7A
1:41.89

54 Koveleski
McLaren M8B
1:44.82

55 McCaig
McLaren M8C
1:46.29

14 Lawrence
McLaren M12A
1:47.07

74 Smith
McLaren M12
1:47.69

24 Nagel
Lola T70 Mk3B
1:48.04

31 Hills
McLaren M6B
1:49.01

5 Hulme
McLaren M8D
1:34.69

22 Oliver
Ti22 Mk II
1:35.52

7 Gethin
McLaren M8D
1:36.28

12 Adamowicz
McLaren M12
1:38.59

3 Brown
McLeagle
1:39.68

21 Bondurant
Lola T160
1:40.05

59 Gregg
Lola T165
1:41.84

51 Causey
Lola T163
1:42.94

8 Dean
Porsche 908
1:45.04

32 Guldstrand
Lola T70
1:45.78

42 Sell
Lola T70
1:46.73

58 Shelton
McLaren M1B
1:47.52

9 Woods
Lola T160
1:47.75

45 McKitterick *
Terry T10
1:48.69

18 Rosbach
Lola T70 Mk3B
1:50.92, 107.104 mph

* Car 45 is a sister to the King Cobra of 1967.

Results
1. Denny Hulme (McLaren M8D-Chevrolet), 61 laps of 3.3 mi. = 201.3 mi. in 1.40:27.4, 120.284 mph
2. Jackie Oliver (Ti22 Mk II-Chevrolet), 61 laps
3. Pedro Rodriguez (BRM P154-Chevrolet), 59
4. Chris Amon (March 707-Chevrolet), 59
5. Lothar Motschenbacher (McLaren M8C-Chevrolet), 59
6. Bob Brown (McLeagle-Chevrolet), 57
7. Tony Adamowicz (McLaren M12-Chevrolet), 57
8. Dave Causey (Lola T163-Chevrolet), 56
9. Tony Dean (Porsche 908), 56
10. Roger McCaig (McLaren M8C-Chevrolet), 56
11. Jay Hills (McLaren M6B-Chevrolet), 55
12. Dick Guldstrand (Lola T70-Chevrolet), 55
13. Peter Gregg (Lola T165-Chevrolet), 54
14. Skeeter McKitterick (Terry T10-Chevrolet), 54
15. Monte Shelton (McLaren M1B-Chevrolet), 53
Retirements: 16-Roy Woods (Lola T70-Dodge, water leak, 43; 17-Bob Nagel (Lola T70-Ford), overheating, 23; 18-Lou Sell (Lola T70-Ford), mechanical, 22; 19-Peter Gethin (McLaren M8D-Chevrolet), blown engine, 21; 20-Oscar Koveleski (McLaren M8B-Chevrolet), engine failure, 18; 21-Jim Adams (Ferrari 512P), accident, 15; 22-John

Cannon (Ford G7A-Ford), accident, 14; 23-Dick Smith (McLaren M12-Ford), accident, 13; 24-Chuck Parsons (Lola T163-Chevrolet), clutch failure, 10; 25-Graeme Lawrence (McLaren M12A-Chevrolet), accident, 10; 26-Peter Revson (Lola T220-Chevrolet), overheating, 8; 27-Jerry Rosbach (Lola T70-Chevrolet), suspension failure, 7; 28-Bob Bondurant (Lola T160-Chevrolet), clutch failure, 6; 29-Vic Elford (Chaparral 2J-Chevrolet), engine failure, 5.
Fastest Lap: N/A

Final Point Standings 1970

1	Denny Hulme	132
2	Lothar Motschenbacher	65
3	Peter Gethin *	56
4	Dave Causey	56
5.	Jackie Oliver	45
6.	Tony Dean	44
7.	Dan Gurney	42
8.	Peter Revson	39
9.	Bob Brown	35
10.	Roger McCaig	34
11.	Chris Amon	28
12.	Gary Wilson	27
13.	Pedro Rodriguez	26
14.	Chuck Parsons	19
15.	Vic Elford	16
	Oscar Koveleski	16
17.	Jo Siffert	15
	Bob Bondurant	15
19.	Jim Adams	14
20.	George Eaton	12
	Richard Attwood	12
22.	Dick Durant *	12
23.	Mario Andretti	8
	Tony Adamowicz	8
25.	Gijs van Lennep	6
	Gordon Dewar	6
27.	Graeme Lawrence *	6
28.	Brian Redman	4
29.	Leonard Janke	2
	Brooke Doran	2
31.	Clif Apel	1
	Ranier Brezinka	1
	Gerard Larrousse	1
	Chuck Frederick	1
	Bob Nagel	1
	Ron Goldleaf	1
	George Drolsom	1
	Peter Gregg	1

* Ties for position resolved by driver's finishing record throughout the season.

Note: Split scoring system in Can-Am. Best four finishes in first five races are counted and the best four finishes are counted in the last five races.

1971

1. Mosport 6/13/71

5 Hulme
McLaren M8F
1:18.0

57 Cordts
McLaren M8C
1:20.4

12 Bondurant
McLaren M8E/D
1:20.8

76 Adams
Ferrari 512P
1:22.0

0 Minter
Porsche 917 PA
1:23.2 (non-starter)

55 McCaig
McLaren M8E
1:25.8

1 Stewart
Lola T260
1:17.3, 114.522 mph

7 Revson
McLaren M8F
1:18.1

11 Motschenbacher
McLaren M8D
1:20.8

3 Brown
McLeagle
1:21.4

88 Kazato
Lola T222
1:22.4

79 Dutton
McLaren M6B
1:25.0

47 Dewar
March 707
1:26.5

27 Kahlich
McLaren M8B
1:27.2

28 Matchett
Porsche 908
1:29.7

35 Hopkins
Lola T160
1:32.0

15 Wonder
McLaren M8C
1:34.0

24 Barbour
Porsche 908
1:34.3

81 Durant
Lola T163
1:59.9, 73.835 mph

Parsons
McLaren M8D
(non-starter)

54 Koveleski
McLaren M8B
1:26.3

51 Causey
Lola T222
1:26.7

39 Brezinka
McLaren M6B
1:29.6

168 Bartling
McLaren M1B
1:31.1

23 Kemp
McLaren M8C
1:33.9

77 Hodges
Lola T70 Mk3B
1:34.3

66 Szarkowicz
McLaren M12
1:35.5

74 Nagel
Lola T222
No Time

Results
1. Denny Hulme (McLaren M8F-Chevrolet), 80 laps of 2.46 mi. = 196.72 mi. in 1.48:15.2, 109.033 mph
2. Peter Revson (McLaren M8F-Chevrolet), 80 laps
3. Lothar Motschenbacher (McLaren M8D-Chevrolet), 79
4. Bob Bondurant (McLaren M8E/D-Chevrolet), 79
5. John Cordts (McLaren M8C-Chevrolet), 78
6. Bob Brown (McLeagle-Chevrolet), 78
7. Dave Causey (Lola T222-Chevrolet), 75
8. Jim Adams (Ferrari 512P), 75
9. Hiroshi Kazato (Lola T222-Chevrolet), 75
10. Roger McCaig (McLaren M8E-Chevrolet), 74
11. Tom Dutton (McLaren M6B-Chevrolet), 71
12. Dan Hopkins (Lola T160-Chevrolet), 70
13. Stanley Szarkowicz (McLaren M12-Chevrolet), 66
14. Frank Kahlich (McLaren M6B-Ford), not running at finish, blown engine, 62
15. Rainer Brezinka (McLaren M6B-Chevrolet), not running at finish, battery failure, 57
16. Bill Wonder (McLaren M8C-Chevrolet), 46
17. Dick Barbour (Porsche 908), 39
Retirements: 18-Gregory Hodges (Lola T70 Mk3B-Chevrolet), dead battery, 38; 19-Dick Durant (Lola T163-Chevrolet), unknown, 36; 20-Steve Matchett (Porsche 908), accident, 26; 21-Oscar Koveleski (McLaren M8B-Chevrolet), broken piston, 28; 22-Jackie Stewart (Lola T260-Chevrolet), broken crown wheel and pinion, 18; 23-Charlie Kemp (McLaren M8C-Chevrolet), blown engine, 16; 24-Gordon Dewar (March 707-Chevrolet), fuel pump failure, 15; 25-Bob Nagel (Lola T222-Chevrolet), clutch failure, 10; 26-Rudi Bartling (McLaren M1B-Chevrolet) front pinion, 9.
Fastest Lap: Hulme, 1:18.8, 112.343 mph

2. St. Jovite 6/27/71

1 Stewart
Lola T260
1:33.2

101 Oliver
Shadow Mk2
1:35.4

57 Cordts
McLaren M8C
1:36.2

0 Minter
Porsche 917 PA
1:38.5

79 Dutton
McLaren M6B
1:38.8

51 Causey
Lola T222
1:39.8

88 Kazato
Lola T222
1:42.0

5 Hulme
McLaren M8F
1:32.9, 102.692 mph

7 Revson
McLaren M8F
1:35.0

3 Brown
McLeagle
1:35.7

8 Parsons
McLaren M8D
1:35.7

12 Bondurant
McLaren M8E/D
1:38.6

47 Dewar
March 707
1:39.3

55 McCaig
McLaren M8E
1:40.2

85 Matchett Porsche 908 1:44.1	81 Durant Lola T163 1:43.6
18 Goldleaf McLaren M12 1:45.9	16 Nagel Lola T222 1:45.5
35 Hopkins Lola T160 1:47.7	39 Brezinka McLaren M6B 1:47.2
34 Drolsom McLaren M8C 1:50.9, 86.004 mph	15 Wonder McLaren M8C 1:50.8
	11 Motschenbacher* McLaren M8D 1:35.3

Results

1. Jackie Stewart (Lola T260-Chevrolet), 75 laps of 2.65 mi. = 200.75 mi. in 1.59:29.1, 100.95 mph
2. Denny Hulme (McLaren M8F-Chevrolet), 75 laps
3. Peter Revson (McLaren M8F-Chevrolet), 74
4. Chuck Parsons (McLaren M8D-Chevrolet), 73
5. Lothar Motschenbacher (McLaren M8D-Chevrolet), 73
6. Hiroshi Kazato (Lola T222-Chevrolet), 71
7. Dave Causey (Lola T222-Chevrolet), 70
8. Milt Minter (Porsche 917 PA), 70
9. Tom Dutton (McLaren M6B-Chevrolet), 69
10. Dick Durant (Lola T163-Chevrolet), 68
11. Bob Nagel (Lola T222-Chevrolet), 65
12. Rainer Brezinka (McLaren M6B-Chevrolet), 65
13. Dan Hopkins (Lola T160-Chevrolet), 59
14. Bill Wonder (McLaren M8C-Chevrolet), 57
15. George Drolsom (McLaren M8C-Chevrolet), 49

Retirements: 16-Bob Bondurant (McLaren M8E/D-Chevrolet), dead battery, 49; 17-Bob Brown (McLeagle-Chevrolet), no oil pressure, 47; 18-John Cordts (McLaren M8C-Chevrolet), blown engine, 40; 19-Roger McCaig (McLaren M8E-Chevrolet), bodywork damage, 33; 20-Steve Matchett (Porsche 908), overheating, 32; 21-Gordon Dewar (March 707-Chevrolet), transmission failure, 28; 22-Jackie Oliver (Shadow-Chevrolet), fuel starvation, 24; 23-Ron Goldleaf (McLaren M12-Chevrolet), overheating, 20.

Fastest Lap: Hulme, 1:33.6, 101.93 mph

* Due to illness, Lothar asked permission to start at the back of the grid. He was afraid he might be a danger to other drivers on the start. He actually qualified fourth fastest.

3. Road Atlanta 7/11/71

7 Revson McLaren M8F 1:18.0	5 Hulme McLaren M8F 1:17.7, 116.90 mph
101 Oliver Shadow Mk2 1:20.7	1 Stewart Lola T260 1:18.7
12 Bondurant McLaren M8E/D 1:21.4	11 Motschenbacher McLaren M8D 1:21.0
88 Kazato Lola T222 1:22.1	54 Adamowicz McLaren M8B 1:21.6
76 Adams Ferrari 512P 1:22.2	29 Elford McLaren M8E 1:22.3
8 Hobbs McLaren M8D 1:24.0	0 Minter Porsche 917 PA 1:22.8
47 Dewar March 707 1:24.4	51 Causey Lola T222 1:24.2
79 Dutton McLaren M6B 1:25.1	55 McCaig McLaren M8E 1:24.7
81 Durant Lola T163 1:26.7	16 Nagel Lola T222 1:25.8
23 Kemp McLaren M8C 1:31.8	27 Kahlich McLaren M6B 1:30.0
15 Wonder McLaren M8C 1:32.5	34 Drolsom McLaren M8C 1:32.0
35 Hopkins Lola T160 1:33.2	24 Barbour Porsche 908 1:32.8
	21 Weaver Lola T160 1:36.3, 94.32 mph

Results

1. Peter Revson (McLaren M8F-Chevrolet), 75 laps of 2.52 mi. = 189 mi. in 1.42:09, 111.17 mph
2. Denny Hulme (McLaren M8F-Chevrolet), 75 laps
3. Lothar Motschenbacher (McLaren M8D-Chevrolet), 74
4. Tony Adamowicz (McLaren M8B-Chevrolet), 72
5. Milt Minter (Porsche 917 PA), 71
6. Dick Durant (Lola T163-Chevrolet), 68
7. Roger McCaig (McLaren M8E-Chevrolet), 68
8. Tom Dutton (McLaren M6B-Chevrolet), 67
9. Charlie Kemp (McLaren M8C-Chevrolet), 64
10. Jim Adams (Ferrari 512P), not running at finish, broken connecting rod, 64
11. Jackie Stewart (Lola T260-Chevrolet), not running at finish, suspension failure, 62
12. Dick Barbour (Porsche 908), 60

Retirements: 13-Hiroshi Kazato (Lola T222-Chevrolet), heat prostration, 55; 14-Bob Nagel (Lola T222-Chevrolet), overheating, 54; 15-Jackie Oliver (Shadow-Chevrolet), fuel feed, 45; 16-George Drolsom (McLaren M8C-Chevrolet), vapor lock, 42; 17-Vic Elford (McLaren M8E-Chevrolet), clutch failure, 35; 18-Dave Causey (Lola T222-Chevrolet), accident, 33; 19-David Hobbs (McLaren M8D-Chevrolet), blown engine, 31; 20-Bill Wonder (McLaren M8C-Chevrolet), oil leak, 27; 21-Bob Bondurant (McLaren M8E/D-Chevrolet), oil pressure, 20; 22-Dan Hopkins (Lola T160-Chevrolet), dropped valve, 18; 23-Frank Kahlich (McLaren M6B-Chevrolet), overheating, 12; 24-Steve Weaver (Lola T160-Chevrolet), oil pressure, 4; 25-Gordon Dewar (March 707-Chevrolet), differential, 1.

Fastest Lap: Stewart, 1:17.42, 117.18 mph

4. Watkins Glen 7/25/71

7 Revson McLaren M8F 1:05.23	1 Stewart Lola T260 1:05.11, 134.244 mph
8 Hobbs McLaren M8D 1:06.56	5 Hulme McLaren M8F 1:05.47
6 Donohue Ferrari 512M 1:08.32	50 Andretti Ferrari 712M 1:07.66
92 van Lennep Porsche 917K 1:08.58	11 Motschenbacher McLaren M8D 1:08.41
14 Posey Ferrari 512M 1:08.91	20 Siffert Porsche 917/10 1:08.64
54 Adamowicz McLaren M8B 1:09.12	91 Attwood Porsche 917K 1:09.08
29 Elford McLaren M8E 1:09.83	12 Bondurant McLaren M8E/D 1:09.52
88 Kazato Lola T222 1:09.94	93 Bell Porsche 917K 1:09.87
101 Oliver Shadow Mk2 1:10.10	30 de Adamich Alfa Romeo T333 1:09.95
79 Dutton McLaren M6B 1:11.52	3 Brown McLeagle 1:11.32
57 Cordts McLaren M8C 1:12.43	55 McCaig McLaren M8E 1:12.29
43 de Cabral Porsche 917 1:16.51	23 Kemp McLaren M8C 1:16.16
87 Matchett Porsche 908 1:17.33	63 De Cadenet Ferrari 512M 1:17.12
	27 Apel McLaren M6B 1:21.26, 107.532 mph

Results

1. Peter Revson (McLaren M8F-Chevrolet), 82 laps of 2.428 mi.* = 199.096 mi. in 1.32:54.137, 128.58 mph
2. Denny Hulme (McLaren M8F-Chevrolet), 82 laps
3. Jo Siffert (Porsche 917/10), 80
4. Mario Andretti (Ferrari 712M), 80
5. Tony Adamowicz (McLaren M8B-Chevrolet), 79
6. Sam Posey (Ferrari 512M), 79
7. Andrea de Adamich (Alfa Romeo T333), 78
8. Vic Elford (McLaren M8E-Chevrolet), 78
9. Gijs van Lennep (Porsche 917K), 78
10. Hiroshi Kazato (Lola T222-Chevrolet), 78
11. Derek Bell (Porsche 917K), 77
12. John Cordts (McLaren M8C-Chevrolet), 77
13. Richard Attwood (Porsche 917K), 77
14. Bob Brown (McLeagle-Chevrolet), 77
15. Tom Dutton (McLaren M6B-Chevrolet), 73
16. Bob Bondurant (McLaren M8E/D-Chevrolet), 73
17. Mario de Cabral (Porsche 917), 71
18. Alain De Cadenet (Ferrari 512M), 69
19. Charlie Kemp (McLaren M8C-Chevrolet), 67

Retirements: 20-Jackie Oliver (Shadow Mk2-Chevrolet), broken tie rod, 65; 21-Mark Donohue (Ferrari 512M), holed piston, 57; 22-Jackie Stewart (Lola T260-Chevrolet), transmission failure, 56; 23-Clif Apel (McLaren M6B-Chevrolet), black flagged, suspension, 49; 24-Steve Matchett (Porsche 908), valve gear, 32; 25-Roger McCaig (McLaren M8E-Chevrolet), suspension failure, 18; 26-David Hobbs (McLaren M8D-Chevrolet), blown engine, 10; 27-Lothar Motschenbacher (McLaren M8D-Chevrolet), accident, 7.

Fastest Lap: Hulme, 1:06.083, 132.276 mph

*Revamped, widened Watkins Glen circuit.

5. Mid-Ohio 8/22/71

5 Hulme McLaren M8F 1:26.091, 100.36 mph	7 Revson McLaren M8F 1:26.576
1 Stewart Lola T260 1:26.985	20 Siffert Porsche 917/10 1:29.000
11 Motschenbacher McLaren M8D 1:29.083	51 Causey Lola T222 1:30.298
54 Adamowicz McLaren M8B 1:30.966	88 Kazato Lola T222 1:31.167
9 Parsons Lola T160 1:31.708	3 Brown McLaren M8E 1:31.754
48 Mueller Ferrari 512M 1:31.828	0 Minter Porsche 917 PA 1:31.863
81 Durant Lola T163 1:32.628	55 McCaig McLaren M8E 1:32.695
47 Dewar March 707 1:32.925	29 Elford McLaren M8E 1:33.668
79 Dutton McLaren M6B 1:35.107	18 Nagel McLaren M12 1:35.328
35 Hopkins Lola T160 1:38.260	34 Drolsom McLaren M8E 1:40.291
41 Butcher Lola T163 1:40.597	77 Klempel McLaren M1C 1:42.426
66 Szarkowicz McLaren M12 1:42.47	25 Hodges Hodges McKee 1:42.675, 84.15 mph
87 Matchett Porsche 908 No Time	91 Devine Lola T70 No Time
23 Kemp McLaren M8C No Time	

Results

1. Jackie Stewart (Lola T260-Chevrolet), 80 laps of 2.4 mi. = 192 mi. in 2.00:16.763, 95.777 mph
2. Jo Siffert (Porsche 917/10), 78 laps
3. Tony Adamowicz (McLaren M8B-Chevrolet), 77
4. Herbert Mueller (Ferrari 512M), 76
5. Chuck Parsons (Lola T160-Chevrolet), 75
6. Milt Minter (Porsche 917 PA), 75
7. Peter Revson (McLaren M8F-Chevrolet), not running at finish, broken half shaft, 72
8. Tom Dutton (McLaren M6B-Chevrolet), 70
9. Steve Matchett (Porsche 908), 70
10. Jim Butcher (Lola T163-Chevrolet), 69
11. Stan Szarkowicz (McLaren M12-Chervrolet), 68
12. Dick Durant (Lola T163-Chevrolet), 66

Retirements: 13-Roger McCaig (McLaren M8E-Chevrolet), blown engine, 64; 14-Danny Hopkins (Lola T160-Chevrolet), blown engine, 63; 15-Charlie Kemp (McLaren M8C-Chevrolet), running at finish, 52; 16-Lothar Motschenbacher (McLaren M8D-Chevrolet), transmission, 60; 17-George Drolsom (McLaren M8E-Chevrolet), engine-suspension, 56; 18-Vic Elford (McLaren M8E-Chevrolet), heat exhaustion, 27; 19-Jerry Hodges (McKee-Chevrolet), overheating, 21; 20-Hiroshi Kazato (Lola T222-Chevrolet), engine failure, 20; 21-Gordon Dewar (March 707-Chevrolet), broken half shaft, 19; 22-Don Devine (Lola T70-Chevrolet), bent wheel, 16; 23-Bob Brown (McLaren M8E-Chevrolet), fuel leak fire, 11; 24-Bob Nagel (McLaren M12-Chevrolet), engine faillure, 6; 25-Denny Hulme (McLaren M8F-Chevrolet), broken half shaft, 0; 26-Dave Causey (Lola T222-Chevrolet), accident, 0; 27-Bob Klempel (McLaren M1C-Chevrolet), blown engine, 0.

Fastest Lap: Revson, 1:27.975, 98.210 mph

6. Elkhart Lake 8/29/71

101 Oliver Shadow Mk2 2:08.952	5 Hulme McLaren M8F 2:06.662, 113.688 mph
11 Motschenbacher McLaren M8D 2:09.422	1 Stewart Lola T260 2:09.077
20 Siffert Porsche 917/10 2:12.242	29 Elford McLaren M8E 2:10.687
54 Adamowicz McLaren M8B 2:12.722	88 Kazato Lola T222 2:12.498
3 Brown McLaren M8E 2:13.966 (non-starter)	12 Young McLaren M8E/D 2:13.278
51 Causey Lola T222 2:17.435	48 Mueller Ferrari 512M 2:15.996
47 Dewar March 707 2:19.718	79 Dutton McLaren M6B 2:18.562
9 Parsons Lola T160/3 2:24.796	87 Matchett Porsche 908 2:23.868
91 Devine Lola T70 2:27.984	34 Drolsom McLaren M8C 2:26.756
66 Szarkowicz McLaren M12 2:28.879	27 Kahlich McLaren M6B 2:28.531
13 Place Lola T160 2:33.283, 93.944 mph	41 Butcher Lola T163 2:29.013
	7 Revson McLaren M8F No Time

Results

1. Peter Revson (McLaren M8F-Chevrolet), 50 laps of 4.0 mi. = 200 mi. in 1.50:04.758, 109.012 mph
2. Jo Siffert (Porsche 917), 49 laps
3. Vic Elford (McLaren M8E-Chevrolet), 49
4. Lothar Motschenbacher (McLaren M8D-

Chevrolet), 49
5. Hiroshi Kazato (Lola T222-Chevrolet), 47
6. Dave Causey (Lola T222-Chevrolet), 47
7. Tom Dutton (McLaren M6B-Chevrolet), 46
8. Steve Matchett (Porsche 908), 45
9. George Drolsom (McLaren M8C-Chevrolet), 44
10. Herbert Mueller (Ferrari 512M), 41
11. Jim Butcher (Lola T163-Chevrolet), 41
12. Jackie Oliver (Shadow Mk2-Chevrolet), 39
Retirements: 13-Stan Szarkowicz (McLaren M12-Chervrolet), accident, 34; 14-Chuck Parsons (Lola T160/3-Chevrolet), oil leak, 21; 15-Gordon Dewar (March 707-Chevrolet), driver ill, 21; 16-Denny Hulme (McLaren M8F-Chevrolet), broken crank shaft, 17; 17-Don Devine (Lola T70-Chevrolet), oil leak, 16; 18-Jackie Stewart (Lola T260-Chevrolet), overheating, 10; 19-Tony Adamowicz (McLaren M8B-Chevrolet), engine failure, 7; 20-Frank Kahlich (McLaren M6B-Ford), oil leak, 6; 21-Gregg Young (McLaren M8E/D-Chevrolet), broken gearbox, 3; 22-James Place (Lola T160-Chevrolet), suspension failure, 3.
Fastest Lap: Hulme, 2:08.137, 112.377 mph

---

7. Donnybrooke 9/12/71

5 Hulme	7 Revson
McLaren M8F	McLaren M8F
1:26.959	1:26.510, 124.957 mph
11 Motschenbacher	1 Stewart
McLaren M8D	Lola T260
1:29.677	1:29.144
29 Elford	101 Oliver
McLaren M8E	Shadow Mk2
1:30.123	1:29.864
20 Siffert	44 Hansen
Porsche 917/10	Lola T220
1:30.787	1:30.736
0 Minter	12 Young
Porsche 917 PA	McLaren M8E/D
1:32.659	1:31.664
88 Kazato	3 Brown
Lola T222	McLaren M8E
1:34.059	1:33.363
55 McCaig	48 Mueller
McLaren M8E	Ferrari 512M
1:36.785	1:35.493
17 Nagel	79 Dutton
Lola T222	McLaren M6B
1:38.300	1:37.298
34 Drolsom	87 Matchett
McLaren M8C	Porsche 908
1:39.960	1:39.733
89 Parkhill	66 Szarkowicz
McLaren M8E	McLaren M12
1:46.235	1:40.379
41 Butcher	18 Wilson
Lola T163	McLaren M12
1:48.441, 99.593 mph	1:48.386

Results
1. Peter Revson (McLaren M8F-Chevrolet), 70 laps of 3.0 mi. = 210 mi. in 1.45:45.643, 119.137 mph
2. Denny Hulme (McLaren M8F-Chevrolet), 70 laps
3. Gregg Young (McLaren M8E/D-Chevrolet), 69
4. Vic Elford (McLaren M8E-Chevrolet), 69
5. Jo Siffert (Porsche 917/10), 69
6. Jackie Stewart (Lola T260-Chevrolet), 68
7. Milt Minter (Porsche 917 PA), 67
8. Bob Brown (McLaren M8E-Chevrolet), 65
9. Hiroshi Kazato (Lola T222-Chevrolet), 64
10. Bob Nagel (Lola T222-Chevrolet), 64
11. Steve Matchett (Porsche 908), 62
12. Tom Dutton (McLaren M6B-Chevrolet), 62
13. Stan Szarkowicz (McLaren M12-Chevrolet), 62
14. George Drolsom (McLaren M8C-Chevrolet), 59
15. Fred Parkhill (McLaren M8E-Chevrolet), 56
Retirements: 16-Jerry Hansen (Lola T220-Chevrolet), gearbox failure, 53; 17-Herbert Mueller

(Ferrari 512M), broken shift linkage, 49; 18-Jim Butcher (Lola T163-Chevrolet), oil leak, 48; 19-Gary Wilson (McLaren M12-Chevrolet), blown engine, 6; 20-Roger McCaig (McLaren M8E-Chevrolet), broken rim, 31; 21-Lothar Motschenbacher (McLaren M8D-Chevrolet), spun bearing, 28; 22-Jackie Oliver (Shadow Mk2-Chevrolet), front brake CV joint, 28.
Fastest Lap: Hulme, 1:27.860, 122.923 mph

---

8. Edmonton 9/26/71

7 Revson	5 Hulme
McLaren M8F	McLaren M8F
1:20.3, 113.290 mph	1:21.4
(started late)	
1 Stewart	11 Motschenbacher
Lola T260	McLaren M8D
1:22.2	1:23.9
101 Oliver	76 Adams
Shadow Mk2	Ferrari 512P
1:24.1	1:25.1
20 Siffert	12 Parsons
Porsche 917/10	McLaren M8E/D
1:25.2	1:25.4
3 Brown	88 Kazato
McLaren M8E	Lola T222
1:25.7	1:25.8
0 Minter	55 McCaig
Porsche 917 PA	McLaren M8E
1:26.7	1:27.3
18 Wilson	57 Cordts
McLaren M12	McLaren M8C
1:29.0	1:29.6
79 Dutton	9 Brennan
McLaren M6B	Lola T160
1:29.9	1:31.0
6 Cupp	87 Matchett
Lola T163	Porsche 908
1:35.1	1:35.2
34 Drolsom	80 Dick Losk
McLaren M8C	McLaren M1C
1:35.8	1:36.4
41 Butcher	
Lola T163	
1:37.5, 93.305 mph	

Results
1. Denny Hulme (McLaren M8F-Chevrolet), 80 laps of 2.527 mi. = 202.16 mi. in 2.07:47.1, 94.922 mph
2. Jackie Stewart (Lola T260-Chevrolet), 80 laps
3. Jackie Oliver (Shadow Mk2-Chevrolet), 78
4. Jo Siffert (Porsche 917/10), 78
5. Milt Minter (Porsche 917 PA), 77
6. John Cordts (McLaren M8C-Chevrolet), 74
7. Lothar Motschenbacher (McLaren M8D-Chevrolet), 73
8. Chuck Parsons (McLaren M8E/D-Chevrolet), 73
9. George Drolsom (McLaren M8C-Chevrolet), 70
10. Gary Wilson (McLaren M12-Chevrolet), not running at finish, fuel pressure relief valve, 68
11. Steve Matchett (Porsche 908), 68
12. Peter Revson (McLaren M8F-Chevrolet), 67
13. Dick Losk (McLaren M1C-Chevrolet), 64
14. Jim Butcher (Lola T163-Chevrolet), 58
Retirements: 15-Tom Dutton (McLaren M6B-Chevrolet), suspension failure, 50; 16-Bill Cupp (Lola T163-Chevrolet), engine failure, 42; 17-Hiroshi Kazato (Lola T222-Chevrolet), gearbox failure, 41; 18-Merle Brennan (Lola T160-Chevrolet), overheating, 33; 19-Bob Brown (McLaren M8E-Chevrolet), disqualified for push start, 29; 20-Jim Adams (Ferrari 512P), broken ring and pinion gear, 16; 21-Roger McCaig (McLaren

M8E-Chevrolet), spun, unable to restart, 0.
Fastest Lap: Hulme, 1:26.3, 105.414 mph

---

9. Laguna Seca 10/17/71

7 Revson	5 Hulme
McLaren M8F	McLaren M8F
:58.78, 116.366 mph	:58.82
49 Hobbs	1 Stewart
Ti22 Mk II	Lola T260
59.45	59.75
101 Oliver	38 Redman
Shadow Mk2	BRM P167
1:00.50	1:00.73
20 Siffert	11 Motschenbacher
Porsche 917/10	McLaren M8D
1:01.49	1:01.59
2 Elford	76 Adams
McLaren M8E/D	Ferrari 512P
1:02.63	1:02.45
3 Brown	88 Kazato
McLaren M8E	Lola T222
1:02.46	1:02.80
12 Parsons	0 Minter
McLaren M8E/D	Porsche 917 PA
1:02.92	1:03.22
57 Cordts	55 McCaig
Lola T160	McLaren M8E
1:04.76	1:04.88
18 Wilson	51 Causey
McLaren M12	Lola T222
1:05.15	1:06.45
79 Dutton	24 Jordan
McLaren M6B	Porsche 908
1:06.97	1:08.38
87 Matchett	34 Drolsom
Porsche 908	McLaren M8C
1:08.52	1:09.51
16 Cupp	81 Hills
Lola T163	McLaren M6B
1:09.59	1:09.69
33 McConnell	84 Burke
McLaren M6B	McLaren M1B
1:10.14	1:10.59
25 Hodges	42 Jones
Hodges LSR	Lola T160
1:10.90	1:11.74
93 Stafford	54 Adamowicz
McLaren M1B	McLaren M8B
1:12.45, 94.410 mph	No Time

Results
1. Peter Revson (McLaren M8F-Chevrolet), 90 laps of 1.9 mi. = 171 mi. in 1.33:56.86, 109.210 mph
2. Jackie Stewart (Lola T260-Chevrolet), 90 laps
3. Denny Hulme (McLaren M8F-Chevrolet), 90
4. Brian Redman (BRM P167-Chevrolet), 89
5. Jo Siffert (Porsche 917/10), 88
6. Lothar Motschenbacher (McLaren M8D-Chevrolet), 87
7. Tony Adamowicz (McLaren M8B-Chevrolet), 87
8. Jim Adams (Ferrari 512P), 87
9. Milt Minter (Porsche 917 PA), 86
10. Chuck Parsons (McLaren M8E/D-Chevrolet), 84
11. John Cordts (Lola T160-Chevrolet), 84
12. Tom Dutton (McLaren M6B-Chevrolet), 80
13. Steve Matchett (Porsche 908), 78
14. Jay Hills (McLaren M6B-Chevrolet), 78
15. Gary Wilson (McLaren M12-Chevrolet), 77
16. George Drolsom (McLaren M8C-Chevrolet), 77
Retirements: 17-Bob Brown (McLaren M8E-Chevrolet), not running at finish, blown engine, 68; 18-Vic Elford (McLaren M8E/D-Chevrolet), starter motor, 68; 19-Bill Cupp (Lola T163-Chevrolet), running at finish, 64; 20-Dave Jordan

(Porsche 908), running at finish, 57; 21-Hiroshi Kazato (Lola T222-Chevrolet), suspension failure, 57; 22-Roger McCaig (McLaren M8E-Chevrolet), broken starter, 54; 23-Oliver Jones (Lola T160-Chevrolet), oil leak, 52; 24-Ron Stafford (McLaren M1B-Chevrolet), running at finish, 46; 25-Gary Burke (McLaren M1B-Chevrolet), loose radiator, 44; 26-David Hobbs (Ti22 Mk II-Chevrolet), starter, 26; 27-Dave Causey (Lola T222-Chevrolet), accident, 24; 28-Jackie Oliver (Shadow Mk2-Chevrolet), throttle linkage, 23; 29-Jerry Hodges (Hodges LSR Special-Chevrolet), broken ring and pinion gear, 14; 30-Chuck McConnell (McLaren M6B-Chevrolet), accident, 10.
Fastest Lap: Revson, 1:00.66, 112.759 mph

---

10. Riverside 10/31/71

5 Hulme	7 Revson
McLaren M8F	McLaren M8F
1:31.96, 129.186 mph	1:32.95
1 Stewart	2 Follmer
Lola T260	McLaren M8E/D
1:33.18	1:34.19
101 Oliver	11 Motschenbacher
Shadow Mk2	McLaren M8D
1:34.78	1:35.46
8 Posey	54 Adamowicz
McLaren M8E	McLaren M8B
1:35.59	1:35.64
38 Ganley	12 Parsons
BRM P167	McLaren M8E/D
1:35.69	1:35.94
88 Kazato	0 Minter
Lola T222	Porsche 917 PA
1:36.95	1:38.21
76 Adams	55 McCaig
Ferrari 512P	McLaren M8E
1:39.26	1:40.92
18 Wilson	57 Cordts
McLaren M12	Lola T160
1:41.46	1:42.59
23 Kemp	81 Hills
McLaren M8C	McLaren M6B
1:45.78	1:46.64
16 Cupp	79 Dutton
Lola T163	McLaren M6B
1:47.56	1:47.79
87 Dean	66 Szarkowicz
Porsche 908	McLaren M12
1:48.09	1:48.47
24 Jordan	42 Pfeifer
Porsche 908	Lola T160
1:48.75	1:51.52
35 Hopkins	32 Nelli
Lola T160	Lola T70
1:51.61	1:54.80
41 Butcher	49 Hobbs
Lola T163	Ti22 Mk II
1:58.25, 100.465 mph	No Time

Results
1. Denny Hulme (McLaren M8F-Chevrolet), 61 laps of 3.3 mi. = 201.3 mi. in 1.37:36, 123.727 mph
2. Peter Revson (McLaren M8F-Chevrolet), 61 laps
3. Howden Ganley (BRM P167-Chevrolet), 60
4. Sam Posey (McLaren M8E-Chevrolet), 60
5. Chuck Parsons (McLaren M8E/D-Chevrolet), 59
6. Milt Minter (Porsche 917 PA), 59
7. Roger McCaig (McLaren M8E-Chevrolet), 57
8. Gary Wilson (McLaren M12-Chevrolet), 57
9. George Follmer (McLaren M8E/D-Chevrolet), not running at finish, out of gas, 56
10. Charlie Kemp (McLaren M8C-Chevrolet), 55
11. Tom Dutton (McLaren M6B-Chevrolet), 54
12. Stan Szarkowicz (McLaren M12-Chevrolet), 54

13. Dave Jordan (Porsche 908), 54
14. Tony Dean (Porsche 908), 54
Retirements: 15-John Cordts (Lola T160-Chevrolet), engine failure, 46; 16-Steve Pfeifer (Lola T160-Chevrolet), engine failure, 40; 17-Bill Cupp (Lola T163-Chevrolet), running at finish, 40; 18-Jackie Stewart (Lola T260-Chevrolet), water in oil, 37; 19-Tony Adamowicz (McLaren M8B-Chevrolet), blown head gasket, 29; 20-Jay Hills (McLaren M6B-Chevrolet), overheating, 23; 21-David Hobbs (Ti22 Mk II-Chevrolet), body damage, 22; 22-Lothar Motschenbacher (McLaren M8D-Chevrolet), broken oil cooler, 19; 23-Jim Adams (Ferrari 512P), no brakes, 17; 24-Danny Hopkins (Lola T160-Chevrolet), spun, 17; 25-Jackie Oliver (Shadow Mk2-Chevrolet), broken constant velocity joint, 13; 26-Hiroshi Kazato (Lola T222-Chevrolet), overheating, 9; 27-Jim Butcher (Lola T163-Chevrolet), rear end failure, 8; 28-Vic Nelli (Lola T70-Chevrolet), too slow, 4.
Fastest Lap: Hulme, 1:34.33, 125.940 mph

Final Point Standings 1971

1. Peter Revson 142
2. Denny Hulme 132
3. Jackie Stewart 76
4. Jo Siffert 68
5. Lothar Motschenbacher 52
6. Milt Minter 37
7. Tony Adamowicz 34
8. Chuck Parsons 30
9. Vic Elford 25
10. Hiroshi Kazato 19
11. Sam Posey 16
12. John Cordts * 14
13. Dave Causey 14
14. Jackie Oliver 12
    Gregg Young 12
    Howden Ganley 12
17. Tom Dutton * 12
18. Herbert Mueller 11
19. Mario Andretti 10
    Bob Bondurant............................10
    Brian Redman 10
22. Roger McCaig * 10
23. Bob Brown 9
24. Dick Durant * 7
25. Jim Adams 7
26. Steve Matchett..............................5
27. Andrea de Adamich * 4
28. Gary Wilson * 4
29. George Drolsom 4
30. Charlie Kemp................................3
31. Gijs van Lennep 2
    George Follmer.............................2
33. Bob Nagel....................................1
    Jim Butcher..................................1

* Ties for position resolved by driver's finishing record throughout the season.

Note: Split scoring system in Can-Am. Best four finishes in first five races are counted and the best four finishes are counted in the last five races.

1972

Note: Beginning this year, all Lolas, McLarens and Shadows are understood to be Chevrolet-powered unless otherwise noted.

1. Mosport 6/11/72

4 Revson McLaren M20 1:15.0	6 Donohue Porsche 917/10K 1:14.2, 119.307 mph
1 Oliver Shadow Mk3 1:15.6	5 Hulme McLaren M20 1:15.2

55 McCaig McLaren M8FP 1:20.4	0 Minter Porsche 917/10 1:18.6
59 Gregg Porsche 917/10 1:21.8	11 Motschenbacher McLaren M8D 1:21.0
57 Cordts Lola T163 1:23.9	2 Young McLaren M8F 1:22.7
50 Dewar McLaren M8C 1:26.3	23 Kemp Lola T222 1:24.6
17 Nagel Lola T222 1:26.8	96 Durst McLaren M8E/D 1:26.7
77 Klempel McLaren M1C 1:32.2	81 Durant Lola T163 1:27.2
15 Wonder McLaren 8C 1:33.4, 94.783 mph	41 Butcher Lola T163/165 1:33.0

Results
1. Denny Hulme (McLaren M20), 80 laps of 2.46 mi. = 196.8 mi. in 1:46:40.0, 110.665 mph
2. Mark Donohue (Porsche 917/10K), 80 laps
3. Peter Revson (McLaren M20), not running at finish, broken crankshaft, 78
4. Milt Minter (Porsche 917/10), 78
5. Peter Gregg (Porsche 917/10), 78
6. Lothar Motschenbacher (McLaren M8D), 76
7. Steve Durst (McLaren M8E/D), 76
8. Gordon Dewar (McLaren M8C), 74
9. Charlie Kemp (Lola T222), 74
10. Bob Nagel (Lola T222), 67
11. William Wonder (McLaren M8C), 65
12. Jim Butcher (Lola T163/165), 65
13. Bob Klempel (McLaren M1C), 56
14. Dick Durant (Lola T163), 52
Retirements: 15-John Cordts (Lola T163), broken suspension, 14; 16-Jackie Oliver (Shadow Mk3), transmission, 14; 17-Gregg Young (McLaren M8F), blown piston, 2; 18-Roger McCaig (McLaren M8FP), broken steering, 1.
Fastest Lap: Revson, 1:15.2, 117.766 mph (record)

2. Road Atlanta 7/9/72

6 Follmer Porsche 917/10K 1:14.163	5 Hulme McLaren M20 1:14.134, 122.57 mph
22 Cevert McLaren M8F 1:15.260	4 Revson McLaren M20 1:14.465
59 Gregg Porsche 917/10 1:17.779	0 Minter Porsche 917/10 1:17.246
1 Hobbs Lola T310 1:18.655	2 Young McLaren M8F 1:18.091
96 Durst McLaren M8E/D 1:20.052	11 Motschenbacher McLaren M8D 1:20.031
55 McCaig McLaren M8FP 1:21.606	23 Kemp Lola T222 1:21.263
101 Oliver Shadow Mk3 1:22.294	33 Patrick Alfa Romeo T33/4 1:22.038
50 Dewar McLaren M8C 1:23.536	79 Parsons Lola T160/163 1:22.597
17 Nagel Lola T222 1:24.138	61 Heyser Lola T260 1:23.612

34 Drolsom McLaren M8C 1:29.199	99 Devine McLaren M12 1:27.013
77 Klempel McLaren M1C 1:30.049	15 Wonder McLaren M8C 1:29.711
35 Hopkins Lola T160 1:32.285, 98.41 mph	

Did Not Start: John Cordts, McLaren M8D; Dick Durant, Lola T163; Jerry Hodges, Hodges LSR

Results
1. George Follmer (Porsche 917/10K), 75 laps of 2.52 mi. = 189 mi. in 1:39:36.2, 113.96 mph
2. Gregg Young (McLaren M8F), 74 laps
3. Milt Minter (Porsche 917/10), 74
4. Charlie Kemp (Lola T222), 73
5. Peter Gregg (Porsche 917/10), not running at finish, out of fuel, 72
6. Lothar Motschenbacher (McLaren M8D), 71
7. David Hobbs (Lola T310), 71
8. Chuck Parsons (Lola T160/163), 69
9. Scooter Patrick (Alfa Romeo T33/4), 69
10. Roger McCaig (McLaren M8FP), 68
11. Tom Heyser (Lola T260), 66
12. Gordon Dewar (McLaren M8C), 65
13. Bob Nagel (Lola T222), 63
14. George Drolsom (McLaren M8C), not running at finish, blown engine, 58
15. William Wonder (McLaren M8C), 57
16. Don Devine (McLaren M12), 49
Retirements: 17-Bob Klempel (McLaren M1C), oil leak, 42; 18-Steve Durst (McLaren M8E/D), blown engine, 33; 19-Francois Cevert (McLaren M8F), cam shaft, 20; 20-Jackie Oliver (Shadow Mk3), blown engine, 20; 21-Danny Hopkins (Lola T160), stopped on course, 13; 22-Peter Revson (McLaren M20), ignition, 13; 23-Denny Hulme (McLaren M20), crash, 4
Fastest Lap: Revson, 1:16.281, 119.04 mph (record)

3. Watkins Glen 7/23/72

5 Hulme McLaren M20 1:40.472	4 Revson McLaren M20 1:39.187, 122.565 mph
22 Cevert McLaren M8F 1:41.222	6 Follmer Porsche 917/10K 1:40.515
101 Oliver Shadow Mk3 1:42.449	1 Hobbs Lola T310 1:42.414
0 Minter Porsche 917/10 1:43.417	2 Young McLaren M8F 1:42.923
61 Wisell Lola T260 1:46.195	59 Gregg Porsche 917/10K 1:44.571
96 Durst McLaren M8E/D 1:48.947	11 Motschenbacher McLaren M8D 1:46.433
55 McCaig McLaren M8FP 1:49.464	23 Kemp Lola T222 1:48.506
17 Nagel Lola T222 1:51.468	Patrick Alfa Romeo T33/4 1:51.241 (non-starter)
34 Dutton McLaren M8C 1:52.921	31 Agor McLaren M8B 1:51.843
42 Jost Porsche 908 1:55.007	57 Cordts Lola T160/3 1:53.001
40 Jarier Ferrari 712M No Time	68 Dean Porsche 908 2:01.198, 100.307 mph
	28 de Cadenet Duckham No Time

Results
1. Denny Hulme (McLaren M20), 60 laps of 3.377 mi. * = 202.62 mi. in 1:46:14.044, 114.44 mph
2. Peter Revson (McLaren M20), 60 laps
3. Francois Cevert (McLaren M8F), 60
4. David Hobbs (Lola T310), 59
5. George Follmer (Porsche 917/10K), 58
6. Milt Minter (Porsche 917/10), 57
7. Lothar Motschenbacher (McLaren M8D), 57
8. Bob Nagel (Lola T222), 54
9. Tony Dean (Porsche 908), 52
10. Jean-Pierre Jarier (Ferrari 712M), 48
11. Peter Gregg (Porsche 917/10), 42
12. Reinhold Jost (Porsche 908), 36
13. Tom Dutton (McLaren M8C), 33
14. Warren Agor (McLaren M8B), 30
Retirements: 15-Charlie Kemp (Lola T222), transmission, 22; 16-Steve Durst (McLaren M8E/D), oil pressure, 19; 17-Jackie Oliver (Shadow Mk3), brakes/crash, 18; 18-John Cordts (Lola T160/3), flat tire, 14; 19-Reine Wissell (Lola T260), engine, 13; 20-Gregg Young (McLaren M8F), engine, 8; 21-Roger McCaig (McLaren M8FP), crash, 3; 22-Alain de Cadenet (Duckham), engine problems, 2.
Fastest Lap: Revson, 1:44.300, 116.560 mph

* Circuit Lengthened.

4. Mid-Ohio 8/6/72

6 Follmer Porsche 917/10K 1:24.010, 102.845 mph	5 Hulme McLaren M20 1:24.113
4 Revson McLaren M20 1:24.588	101 Oliver Shadow Mk3 1:25.906
1 Hobbs Lola T310 1:26.557	0 Minter Porsche 917/10 1:26.724
59 Gregg Porsche 917/10K 1:27.347	11 Motschenbacher McLaren M8D 1:29.803
2 Young McLaren M8F 1:30.218	22 Cevert McLaren M8F 1:30.551
55 McCaig McLaren M8FP 1:31.007	57 Cordts McLaren M8D 1:31.534
19 Wilson McLaren M8E 1:32.505	23 Kemp Lola T222 1:32.790
17 Nagel Lola T222 1:32.895	81 Durant Lola T162 1:33.628
61 Heyser Lola T260 1:34.035	50 Dewar McLaren M8C 1:34.341
18 Johnson McLaren M8E 1:34.389	96 Durst McLaren M8E/D 1:34.513
30 Kahlich McLaren M12 1:34.767	31 Agor McLaren M8B 1:34.221
41 Butcher Lola T162 1:38.449	68 Dean Porsche 908/1 1:38.840
34 Drolsom McLaren M8C 1:39.249	77 Klempel McLaren M1C 1:39.936, 86.455 mph

Results
1. George Follmer (Porsche 917/10K), 80 laps of 2.4 mi. = 192 mi. in 2:04:2:18, 92.876 mph
2. Jackie Oliver (Shadow Mk3), 80 laps
3. Milt Minter (Porsche 917/10), 77
4. Denny Hulme (McLaren M20), 76

5. Charlie Kemp (Lola T222), 75
6. David Hobbs (Lola T310), 75
7. Gordon Dewar (McLaren M8C), 75
8. Gary Wilson (McLaren M8E), 75
9. Warren Agor (McLaren M8B), 72
10. Bob Nagel (Lola T222), 72
11. Francois Cevert (McLaren M8F), not running at finish, engine, 71
12. Frank Kahlich (McLaren M12), 71
13. Alan Johnson (McLaren M8E), 70
14. Tony Dean (Porsche 908/1), 69
15. Jim Butcher (Lola T163), 68
16. Roger McCaig (McLaren M8FP), 67
17. Bob Klempel (McLaren M1C), 66
18. Tom Heyser (Lola T260), not running at finish, locker/ring and pinion, 64
19. Steve Durst (McLaren M8E/D), 63
20. George Drolsom (McLaren M8C), 46
Retirements: 21-Gregg Young (McLaren M8F), accident, 36; 22-Peter Revson (McLaren M20), transmission, 31; 23-Lothar Motschenbacher (McLaren M8D), water bleed off line/vapor lock, 30; 24-Dick Durant (Lola T163), clutch, 21; 25-Peter Gregg (Porsche 917/10), fuel injector, 10; 26-John Cordts (McLaren M8D), blown engine, 0.
Fastest Lap: Hulme, 1:24.4, 102.37 mph

5. Elkhart Lake 8/27/72

22 Cevert McLaren M8F 2:07.552	5 Hulme McLaren M20 2:04.562, 115.605 mph
59 Gregg Porsche 917/10K 2:08.121	0 Minter Porsche 917/10 2:07.651
1 Hobbs Lola T310 2:10.574	102 Oliver Shadow Mk3 2:10.465
96 Durst McLaren M8E/D 2:11.626	2 Young McLaren M8F 2:10.928
40 Jarier Ferrari 712M 2:13.860	50 Dewar McLaren M8C 2:12.761
23 Kemp Lola T222 2:15.626	57 Cordts McLaren M8D 2:14.369
61 Heyser Lola T260 2:16.941	6 Follmer Porsche 917/10K 2:16.655
55 McCaig McLaren M8FP 2:19.602	91 Causey McLeagle 2:18.087
17 Nagel Lola T222 2:20.897	31 Agor McLaren M8B 2:20.393
34 Drolsom McLaren M8C 2:24.057	30 Kahlich McLaren M12 2:21.412
51 Sherman McLaren M12 2:26.202	35 Hopkins Lola T160 2:24.238
20 Cluxton Ferrari 512S 2:29.191 (non starter)	15 Wonder McLaren M8C 2:27.731
81 Durant Lola T163 2:33.861	4 Revson McLaren M20 2:31.046
36 Frederick Lola 160/163 2:34.832	11 Lunger McLaren M8D 2:31.255
101 Pace Shadow Mk3 2:36.283	13 Place Lola T160 2:35.821
19 Wilson McLaren M8E 2:46.621	77 Klempel McLaren M1C 2:37.050
47 Felter McLaren M8E 2:55.929, 81.851 mph	41 Butcher Lola T163 2:54.934

Results
1. George Follmer (Porsche 917/10K), 50 laps of 4.0 mi. = 200 mi. in 1:48:40.2, 110.426 mph
2. Francois Cevert (McLaren M8F), 49 laps
3. Peter Gregg (Porsche 917/10K), 49
4. Jean Pierre Jarier (Ferrari 712M), 48
5. Gregg Young (McLaren M8F), 48
6. Gary Wilson (McLaren M8E), 47
7. Milt Minter (Porsche 917/10), 47
8. Bob Nagel (Lola T222), 46
9. Warren Agor (McLaren M8B), 46
10. Roger McCaig (McLaren M8FP), 46
11. John Cordts (McLaren M8D), 45
12. Brett Lunger (McLaren M8D), 44
13. George Drolsom (McLaren M8C), 43
14. Charlie Kemp (Lola T222), 42
15. William Wonder (McLaren M8C), 42
16. Steve Durst (McLaren M8E/D), not running at finish, overheating, 40
17. Pete Sherman (McLaren M12), 37
18. Dave Causey (McLeagle), 36
19. James Place (Lola T160), 28
20. Bob Klempel (McLaren M1C), 27
Retirements: 21-Jackie Oliver (Shadow Mk3), broken exhaust, 26; 22-Gordon Dewar (McLaren M8C), overheating, 25; 23-Dick Durant (Lola T163), throttle stuck, 24; 24-Peter Revson (McLaren M20), clutch out, 21; 25-Frank Kahlich (McLaren M12), excluded after illegal fueling procedure, 21; 26-David Hobbs (Lola T310), fuel pickup, 16; 27-Jim Butcher (Lola T163), shift linkage, 16; 28-Denny Hulme (McLaren M20), lost magneto, 11; 29-Ed Felter (McLaren M8E), reared out, 10; 30-Chuck Frederick (Lola 160/163) ignition, 10; 31-Danny Hopkins (Lola T160), oil filter broken, 9; 32-Carlos Pace (Shadow Mk3), electrical failure, 4; 33-Tom Heyser (Lola T260),gearbox, 3.
Fastest Lap: Follmer, 2:07.264, 113.151 mph

6. Donnybrooke 9/17/72

7 Follmer Porsche 917/10K 1:25.647	6 Donohue Porsche 917/10K 1:25.208, 126.749 mph
4 Revson McLaren M20 1:26.864	5 Hulme McLaren M20 1:25.782
22 Cevert McLaren M8F 1:27.925	0 Minter Porsche 917/10 1:27.238
1 Hobbs Lola T310 1:28.121	101 Oliver Shadow Mk3 1:27.931
102 Pace Shadow Mk3 1:29.753	2 Young McLaren M8F 1:28.364
23 Kemp Lola T222 1:30.890	44 Hansen Lola T260 1:29.795
11 Motschenbacher McLaren M8D 1:31.529	8 Grant McLaren M8F 1:31.173
57 Cordts McLaren M8D 1:31.985	96 Durst McLaren M8E/D 1:31.693
34 Dutton McLaren M8C 1:34.092	19 Wilson McLaren M8E 1:32.447
17 Nagel Lola T222 1:35.056	37 Agor McLaren M8F 1:34.999
47 Felter McLaren M8E 1:35.481	30 Kahlich McLaren M12 1:35.259
31 Fellows McLaren M8F 1:36.811	91 Causey McLeagle 1:35.941
61 Heyser Lola T260 1:37.497	28 Rosbach McLaren M8E 1:37.163
41 Butcher Lola T163 1:40.866	51 Sherman McLaren M12 1:38.571
12 Wiedmer McLaren M8F No Time	99 Thornsjo McLaren M12 1:42.288, 105.584 mph

Did Not Start: Peter Gregg, Porsche 917/10K; Gordon Dewar, McLaren M8C; Danny Hopkins, Lola T160; Leigh Gardner, Lola T70.

Results
1. Francois Cevert (McLaren M8F), 70 laps of 3.0 mi. = 210 mi. in 1:46:43.269, 118.065 mph
2. Milt Minter (Porsche 917/10), 70 laps
3. Jackie Oliver (Shadow Mk3), 70
4. George Follmer (Porsche 917/10K), not running at finish, out of gas, 69
5. John Cordts (McLaren M8D), 68
6. Lothar Motschenbacher (McLaren M8D), 66
7. Ed Felter (McLaren M8E), 65
8. Bob Nagel (Lola T222), 65
9. Pete Sherman (McLaren M12), 61
10. Tom Heyser (Lola T260), 60
11. Charlie Kemp (Lola T222), not running at finish, out of gas, 59
12. Jerry Rosbach (McLaren M8E), 58
13. Orly Thornsjo (McLaren M12), 58
14. Kent Fellows (McLaren M8D), 57
15. Warren Agor (McLaren M8F), 55
16. Dave Causey (McLeagle), 52
17. Mark Donohue (Porsche 917/10K), not running at finish, blown tire, 43
18. Tom Dutton (McLaren M8C), 36
19. Hans Wiedmer (McLaren M8F), 28
Retirements: 20-Gregg Young (McLaren M8F), no oil pressure, 26; 21-Peter Revson (McLaren M20), smoking engine, 24; 22-Jerry Hansen (Lola T260), tire, body damage, 24; 23-Jim Butcher (Lola T163), losing oil, 21; 24-Steve Durst (McLaren M8E/D), smoking, 19; 25-Gary Wilson (McLaren M8E), spun off, 19; 26-Jerry Grant (McLaren M8F), oil pressure, 18; 27-Denny Hulme (McLaren M20), cracked block, 12; 28-Frank Kahlich (McLaren M12), engine seal, 12; 29-David Hobbs (Lola T310), front tire/axle, 10; 30-Carlos Pace (Shadow Mk3), magneto, 2.
Fastest Lap: Follmer, 1:28.308, 122.299 mph

7. Edmonton 10/1/72

7 Follmer Porsche 917/10K 1:19.549, 114.36 mph	6 Donohue Porsche 917/10K 1:19.595
5 Hulme McLaren M20 1:20.557	4 Revson McLaren M20 1:20.663
22 Cevert McLaren M8F 1:20.847	0 Minter Porsche 917/10 1:21.049
102 Pace Shadow Mk3 1:22.707	1 Hobbs Lola T310 1:22.869
102 Oliver Shadow Mk3 1:22.954	11 Motschenbacher McLaren M8D 1:25.282
23 Kemp Lola T222 1:25.768	9 Cordts McLaren M8D 1:26.514
19 Wilson McLaren M8E 1:27.162	72 Morris McLaren M12B 1:28.283
34 Dutton McLaren M8C 1:28.606	61 Heyser Lola T260 1:29.369
30 Kahlich McLaren M12 1:29.404	37 Agor McLaren M8F 1:29.416
57 Shelton Lola T163 1:32.487	41 Butcher Lola T163 1:35.099, 95.66 mph
12 Wiedmer McLaren M8F No Time	

Did Not Start: Gregg Young, McLaren M8F, crash in practice

Results
1. Mark Donohue (Porsche 917/10K), 80 laps of 2.527 mi. = 202.16 mi. in 1:50:26.091, 109.870 mph
2. Denny Hulme (McLaren M20), 80 laps
3. George Follmer (Porsche 917/10K), 80
4. Carlos Pace (Shadow Mk3), 78
5. David Hobbs (Lola T310), 78
6. Peter Revson (McLaren M20), 77
7. Lothar Motschenbacher (McLaren M8D), 76
8. Hans Wiedmer (McLaren M8F), 72
9. Tom Heyser (Lola T260), 71
10. Charlie Kemp (Lola T222), 67
11. Tom Dutton (McLaren M8C), 66
12. John Cordts (McLaren M8D), not running at finish, unknown, 52
13. Warren Agor (McLaren M8F), 49
14. Jim Butcher (Lola T163), 41
Retirements: 15-Francois Cevert (McLaren M8F), half shaft, 39; 16-Monte Shelton (Lola T163), rear sway bar, 36; 17-Gary Wilson (McLaren M8E), broken crank, 20; 18-Dave Morris (McLaren M12B), accident-broken upright, 15; 19-Jackie Oliver (Shadow Mk3), drive failure, 12; 20-Frank Kahlich (McLaren M12), unknown, 11; 21-Milt Minter (Porsche 917/10), cooling fan exploded, 0.
Fastest Lap: Follmer, 1:20.594, 112.877 mph

8. Laguna Seca 10/15/72

6 Donohue Porsche 917/10K :58.66, 116.604 mph	7 Follmer Porsche 917/10K :58.66
4 Revson McLaren M20 :59.40	101 Oliver Shadow Mk3 1:00.15
5 Hulme McLaren M20 1:00.57	0 Minter Porsche 917/10 1:00.76
8 Hiss * McLaren M8F 1:01.76	18 Kauhsen Porsche 917/10K 1:02.64
9 Cordts McLaren M8D 1:03.07	59 Gregg * Porsche 917/10 1:03.36
96 Durst * McLaren M8E/D 1:03.68	11 Motschenbacher McLaren M8D 1:03.71
20 Posey Porsche 917 PA 1:04.26	23 Kemp Lola T222 1:04.66
33 Patrick Alfa Romeo T33/3 1:04.66	34 Dutton McLaren M8C 1:04.84

55 Parsons
McLaren M8FP
1:04.92

47 Felter
McLaren M8E
1:05.21

61 Heyser
Lola T260
1:05.86

17 Nagel
Lola T222
1:06.34

10 Grable
Lola T163
1:06.71

1 Hobbs
Lola T310
1:08.03

57 Shelton
Lola T163
1:08.52

19 Wilson
McLaren M8E
1:11.25

12 Wiedmer
McLaren M8F
1:04.94

65 Dioguardi *
Ti22 Mk II
1:05.46

64 Peckham
McLaren M6B
1:05.91

3 Cuddy
McLaren M8D
1:06.42

31 Waco
McLaren M8B
1:07.22

30 Kahlich
McLaren M12
1:08.28

37 Agor
McLaren M8FP
1:09.44

22 Cevert
McLaren M8F
No Time

* Does not appear in official results.
Presumed non-starter.

Results
1. George Follmer (Porsche 917/10K), 90 laps of 1.9 mi. = 118 mi. in 1.34:18.39, 108.793 mph
2. Mark Donohue (Porsche 917/10K), 90 laps
3. Francois Cevert (McLaren M8F), 88
4. Milt Minter (Porsche 917/10), 86
5. Sam Posey (Porsche 917 PA), 85
6. Charlie Kemp (Lola T222), 85
7. Scooter Patrick (Alfa Romeo T33/3), 84
8. David Hobbs (Lola T310), 84
9. Tom Heyser (Lola T260), 83
10. Gary Wilson (McLaren M8E), 83
11. Lothar Motschenbacher (McLaren M8D), 82
12. Bill Cuddy (McLaren M8D), 82
13. Bob Peckham (McLaren M6B), 81
14. Bob Nagel (Lola T222), 81
15. Mark Waco (McLaren M8B), 80
16. Monte Shelton (Lola T163), 78
17. Hans Wiedmer (McLaren M8F), 77
18. Chuck Parsons (McLaren M8FP), not running at finish, engine, 74
19. Peter Revson (McLaren M20), not running at finish, gearbox, 52
20. Warren Agor (McLaren M8FP), 46
Retirements: 21-Ron Grable (Lola T163), halfshaft, 35; 22-Jackie Oliver (Shadow Mk3), oil leak, 25; 23-John Cordts (McLaren M8D), engine, 22; 24-Tom Dutton (McLaren M8C), gearbox, 17; 25-Denny Hulme (McLaren M20), timing chain, 16; 26-Frank Kahlich (McLaren M12), engine, 13; 27-Willi Kauhsen (Porsche 917/10K), turbocharger, 3; 28-Ed Felter (McLaren M8E), engine, 0.
Fastest Lap: Donohue, :59.80, 114.38 mph

9. Riverside 10/29/72

7 Follmer
Porsche 917/10K
1:31.70, 129.553 mph

5 Hulme
McLaren M20
1:32.00

6 Donohue
Porsche 917/10K
1:32.32

4 Revson
McLaren M20
1:32.41

102 Oliver
Shadow Mk3
1:34.25

0 Minter
Porsche 917/10K
1:34.22

22 Cevert
McLaren M8F
1:35.05

1 Hobbs
Lola T310
1:35.45

18 Kauhsen
Porsche 917/10K
1:36.44

11 Motschenbacher
McLaren M8D
1:37.58

9 Cordts
McLaren M8D
1:38.30

12 Wiedmer
McLaren M8D
1:39.40

23 Kemp
Lola T222
1:39.78

13 Parkes
Ferrari 512M
1:40.26

65 Dioguardi
Ti22 Mk II
1:40.59

20 Posey
Porsche 917 PA/K
1:41.28

30 Kahlich
McLaren M12
1:42.11

34 Dutton
McLaren M8D
1:42.95

37 Waco
McLaren M8F
1:43.17

31 Fellows
McLaren M8B
1:47.31

83 Hayes
Porsche 908
1:48.56, 109.433 mph

Did Not Start: Bobby Allison, Shadow Mk3; Tony Adamowicz, Porsche 908.

Results
1. George Follmer (Porsche 917/10K), 61 laps of 3.3 mi. = 201.3 mi. in 1.38:31.65, 122.585 mph
2. Peter Revson (McLaren M20), 61 laps
3. Mark Donohue (Porsche 917/10K), 61
4. Jackie Oliver (Shadow Mk3), not running at finish, gearbox, 59
5. David Hobbs (Lola T310), 59
6. Peter Gregg (Porsche 917/10K), 59
7. Mike Hiss (McLaren M8F), 59
8. Willi Kauhsen (Porsche 917/10K), 59
9. Scooter Patrick (Alfa Romeo T33/4), 57
10. Robert Peckham (McLaren M8C), 56
11. Frank Kahlich (McLaren M12), 55
12. Tom Dutton (McLaren M8D), 55
13. Nick Dioguardi (Ti22 Mk II), not running at finish, flat tire, 54
14. Kent Fellows (McLaren M8B), 53
15. Danny Hopkins (Lola T160), 53
16. Dick Hayes (Porsche 908), not running at finish, crash, 47
17. Hans Wiedmer (McLaren M8D), not running at finish, engine, 46
18. Tom Heyser (Lola T260), 46
19. Denny Hulme (McLaren M20), not running at finish, engine, 45
20. Bob Nagel (Lola T222), not running at finish, engine, 43
21. Gary Wilson (McLaren M8E), 43
Retirements: 22-Francois Cevert (McLaren M8F), transmission, 38; 23-Charlie Kemp (Lola T222), engine, 34; 24-Sam Posey (Porsche 917 PA/K), gearbox, 31; 25-Lothar Motschenbacher (McLaren M8D), head gasket, 26; 26-

59 Gregg
Porsche 917/10K
1:36.69

8 Hiss
McLaren M8F
1:38.07

17 Nagel
Lola T222
1:39.09

55 Parsons
McLaren M8FP
1:39.41

33 Patrick
Alfa Romeo T33/4
1:40.00

64 Peckham
McLaren M8C
1:40.35

47 Felter
McLaren M8E
1:41.27

61 Heyser
Lola T260
1:41.48

19 Wilson
McLaren M8E
1:42.49

10 Grable
Lola T163
1:43.09

57 Shelton
Lola T162
1:46.46

35 Hopkins
Lola T160
1:48.04

Ed Felter (McLaren M8E), running at finish, 20; 27-Milt Minter (Porsche 917/10), blown engine, 18; 28-Monte Shelton (Lola T162), transmission, 18; 29-Ron Grable (Lola T163), spin, 15; 30-Chuck Parsons (McLaren M8FP), suspension, 10; 31-John Cordts (McLaren M8D), mechanical, 8; 32-Mark Waco (McLaren M8F), overheating, 8.
Disqualified: Michael Parkes (Ferrari 512M) for violation of insurance rules by car owner.
Fastest Lap: N/A

Final Point Standings 1972
1. George Follmer 130
2. Denny Hulme * 65
3. Milt Minter 65
4. Mark Donohue 62
5. Francois Cevert 59
6. Peter Revson 48
7. David Hobbs 39
8. Jackie Oliver 37
9. Peter Gregg 34
10. Charlie Kemp 27
11. Lothar Motschenbacher 26
12. Gregg Young 23
13. Jean-Pierre Jarier * 11
14. Bob Nagel 11
15. Carlos Pace * 10
16. Gary Wilson 10
17. John Cordts 8
     Sam Posey 8
19. Scooter Patrick * 8
20. Gordon Dewar 7
21. Tom Heyser 5
22. Steve Durst 4
     Ed Felter 4
     Mike Hiss 4
25. Warren Agor * 4
26. Chuck Parsons 3
     Hans Wiedmer 3
     Willi Kauhsen 3
29. Tony Dean 2
     Pete Sherman 2
31. Roger McCaig * 2
32. Bob Peckham 1

* Ties for position resolved by driver's finishing record throughout the season.

Note: Split scoring system in Can-Am. Best four finishes in first five races are counted and all four finishes are counted in the remaining races.

1973

1. Mosport 6/10/73

0 Scheckter
Porsche 917/10K
1:15.8

6 Donohue
Porsche 917/30KL
1:14.1, 119.468 mph

23 Kemp
Porsche 917/10K
1:17.2

16 Follmer
Porsche 917/10K
1:15.9

9 Cordts
McLaren M8D
1:19.7

59 Haywood
Porsche 917/10K
1:19.4

4 Wiedmer
Porsche 917/10K
1:21.5

11 Cannon
McLaren M8F
1:20.2

17 Nagel
Lola T260
1:23.1

8 Patrick
McLaren M8F
1:23.0

13 Agor
McLaren M8FP
1:23.6

101 Oliver
Shadow DN2
1:23.2

3 Durst
Porsche 917/10
1:24.1

47 Felter
McLaren M8E
1:23.8

34 Dutton
McLaren M8B
1:24.6

15 Wonder
McLaren M8C
1:30.0

41 Butcher
McLaren M8C
1:30.9, 97.389 mph

51 Sherman
McLaren M8F
1:24.5

81 Durant
Lola T163
1:26.6

45 Saville-Peck
Costello SP7
1:30.8

Results
1. Charlie Kemp (Porsche 917/10K), 80 laps of 2.46 mi. = 196.80 mi. in 1.48:38.4, 108.654 mph
2. Hans Wiedmer (Porsche 917/10K), 78 laps
3. Bob Nagel (Lola T260), 77
4. Scooter Patrick (McLaren M8F), 77
5. Steve Durst (Porsche 917/10), 77
6. John Cannon (McLaren M8F), 77
7. Mark Donohue (Porsche 917/30KL), 73
8. Ed Felter (McLaren M8E), 71
9. John Cordts (McLaren M8D), not running at finish, out of fuel, 68
10. Pete Sherman (McLaren M8F), 67
11. William Wonder (McLaren M8C), 67
12. Tom Dutton (McLaren M8B), 64
Retirements: 13-George Follmer (Porsche 917/10K), countershaft failure, 53; 14-Jim Butcher (McLaren M8C), handling, 37; 15-Hurley Haywood (Porsche 917/10K), countershaft failure, 30; 16-Jody Scheckter (Porsche 917/10K), blown tire, accident, 29; 17-Dick Durant (Lola T163), oil leak, 22; 18-David O. Saville Peck (Costello SP7-Olds), overheating, 8; 19-Warren Agor (McLaren M8FP), seized oil pump, 3; 20-Jackie Oliver (Shadow DN2), gearbox failure, 2.
Fastest Lap: Donohue, 1:18.0, 113.492 mph

2. Road Atlanta 7/7/73
Heat I*

16 Follmer
Porsche 917/10K
1:14.725

6 Donohue
Porsche 917/30KL
1:12.95, 124.42 mph

59 Haywood
Porsche 917/10K
1:16.811

0 Scheckter
Porsche 917/10K
1:15.885

96 Andretti
McLaren M20
1:17.114 (non-starter)

101 Oliver
Shadow DN2
1:17.007

8 Patrick
McLaren M8F
1:17.739

73 Hobbs
McLaren M20
1:17.207

17 Nagel
Lola T260
1:19.548

11 Motschenbacher
McLaren M8D
1:19.110

4 Wiedmer
Porsche 917/10K
1:21.106

97 Minter
McLaren M8F
1:19.768

96 Hopkins
McLaren M8F
1:22.106

34 Dutton
McLaren M8B
1:22.749

14 Heyser
Lola T260
1:23.469

3 Durst
Porsche 917/10
1:22.175

9 Cordts
McLaren M8D
1:24.186

47 Felter
McLaren M8F
1:23.507

51 Sherman
McLaren M8F
1:28.349

13 Agor
McLaren M8FP
1:24.528

18 Fisher
Lola T222
1:29.736, 101.26 mph

• Beginning with this event, each Can-Am was split into two separate heats or races, scored

as if it were one event with a compulsory lone pit stop in the middle. The two heats' grids are shown here to underscore this new program, but for future events only the initial grid and the final results will be shown.

Heat II 7/8/73

16 Follmer Porsche 917/10K 40 laps	6 Donohue Porsche 917/30KL 40 laps
73 Hobbs McLaren M20 39 laps	0 Scheckter Porsche 917/10K 39 laps
17 Nagel Lola T260 38 laps	59 Haywood Porsche 917/10K 38 laps
3 Durst Porsche 917/10 37 laps	11 Motschenbacher McLaren M8D 38 laps
47 Felter McLaren M8F 36 laps	98 Hopkins McLaren M8F 37 laps
14 Heyser Lola T260 35 laps	13 Agor McLaren M8FP 35 laps
97 Minter McLaren M8F 19 laps	51 Sherman McLaren M8F 33 laps
4 Wiedmer Porsche 917/10K 18 laps	34 Dutton McLaren M8B 19 laps
101 Oliver Shadow DN2 11 laps	8 Patrick McLaren M8F 14 laps
18 Fisher Lola T222 2 laps	9 Cordts McLaren M8E 7 laps

Results
1. George Follmer (Porsche 917/10K), 90 laps of 2.46 mi. = 226 mi. in 1:55:45.4, 117.05 mph
2. Mark Donohue (Porsche 917/30KL), 90 laps
3. Jody Scheckter (Porsche 917/10K), 89
4. David Hobbs (McLaren M20), 87
5. Hurley Haywood (Porsche 917/10K), 85
6. Bob Nagel (Lola T260), 84
7. Steve Durst (Porsche 917/10), 83
8. Tom Heyser (Lola T260), 78
9. Pete Sherman (McLaren M8F), 74
10. Ed Felter (McLaren M8F), not running at finish, off course, 71
11. Tom Dutton (McLaren M8B), 65
12. John Cordts (McLaren M8D), not running at finish, oil temp, 49
13. Danny Hopkins (McLaren M8F), 47
14. Warren Agor (McLaren M8FP), not running at finish, ring gear, 41
15. Lothar Motschenbacher (McLaren M8D), 38

Retirements: 16-Hans Wiedmer (Porsche 917/10K), driver ill, 28; 17-Milt Minter (McLaren M8F), engine bearing, 19; 18-Scooter Patrick (McLaren M8F), accident, 14; 19-Jackie Oliver (Shadow DN2), front suspension, 11; 20-Gene Fisher (Lola T222), unknown, 2.

Fastest Lap: Donohue, 1:14.0, 119.68 * mph

* MPH not available. Computed.

3. Watkins Glen 7/22/73

16 Follmer Porsche 917/10K 1:39.891	6 Donohue Porsche 917/30KL 1:38.848, 122.989 mph
73 Hobbs McLaren M20 1:43.501	0 Scheckter Porsche 917/10K 1:41.950
23 Kemp Porsche 917/10K 1:44.873	59 Haywood Porsche 917/10K 1:44.160
11 Cannon McLaren M8F 1:47.373	101 Oliver Shadow DN2 1:47.057
17 Nagel Lola T260 1:48.698	4 Wiedmer Porsche 917/10K 1:48.653
8 Patrick McLaren M8F 1:49.164	9 Cordts McLaren M8D 1:49.129
98 Hopkins McLaren M8F 1:51.851	97 Brown McLaren M8F 1:50.466
34 Dutton McLaren M8B 1:53.324	14 Heyser Lola T260 1:53.233
47 Felter McLaren M8E 1:56.936	3 Durst Porsche 917/10 1:53.954
51 Sherman McLaren M8F 1:58.168, 102.881 mph	58 Gregg Porsche Carrera Prototype 1:58.026
	13 Agor McLaren M8FP No Time

Results
1. Mark Donohue (Porsche 917/30KL), 60 laps of 3.377 mi. = 202.62 mi. in 1:43:14.405, 117.757 mph
2. David Hobbs (McLaren M20), 60 laps
3. Jody Scheckter (Porsche 917/10K), 59
4. Charlie Kemp (Porsche 917/10K), 59
5. John Cannon (McLaren M8F), 57
6. Tom Dutton (McLaren M8B), 55
7. Steve Durst (Porsche 917/10), 55
8. Tom Heyser (Lola T260), 53
9. Peter Gregg (Porsche Carrera Prototype), 53
10. Scooter Patrick (McLaren M8F), 51
11. Bob Nagel (Lola T260), not running at finish, ring and pinion, 49
12. Warren Agor (McLaren M8F), 47
13. Danny Hopkins (McLaren M8F), 47
14. Pete Sherman (McLaren M8F), 45

Retirements: 15-Hans Wiedmer (Porsche 917/10K), turbo failure, 34; 16-Bob Brown (McLaren M8F), engine failure, 34; 17-Jackie Oliver (Shadow DN2), running, 34; 18-Ed Felter (McLaren M8E), accident, 27; 19-John Cordts (McLaren M8D), engine failure, 24; 20-George Follmer (Porsche 917/10K), turbo failure, 21; 21-Hurley Haywood (Porsche 917/10K), transmission, 18.

Fastest Lap: Donohue, 1:40.0, 122.74 mph (record)

4. Mid-Ohio 8/12/73

6 Donohue Porsche 917/30KL 1:20.335, 107.550 mph	0 Scheckter Porsche 917/10K 1:22.868
16 Follmer Porsche 917/10K 1:23.764	73 Hobbs McLaren M20 1:24.542
5 Kauhsen Porsche 917/10K 1:25.897	23 Kemp Porsche 917/10K 1:27.127 (non-starter)
59 Haywood Porsche 917/10K 1:27.202	101 Oliver Shadow DN2 1:27.920
11 Bell McLaren M8F 1:28.570	9 Cordts McLaren M8D 1:29.428
8 Patrick McLaren M8F 1:29.529	34 Dutton McLaren M8E 1:29.930
97 Brown McLaren M8F 1:29.973	13 Agor McLaren M8FP 1:30.632
98 Hopkins McLaren M8F 1:32.171	2 Wilson McLaren M8E 1:31.501
4 Wiedmer Porsche 917/10K 1:32.018	64 Peckham McLaren M8C 1:32.311
3 Durst Porsche 917/10 1:32.578	14 Heyser Lola T260 1:32.789
47 Felter McLaren M8E 1:33.030	51 Sherman McLaren M8F 1:34.603
45 Saville-Peck Costello SP7 1:38.253, 87.936 mph	17 Nagel Lola T260 No Time

Results
1. Mark Donohue (Porsche 917/30KL), 84 laps of 2.4 mi. = 209.6 mi. in 1:58:16.762, 101.409 mph
2. George Follmer (Porsche 917/10K), 84 laps
3. Hurley Haywood (Porsche 917/10K), 80
4. Derek Bell (McLaren M8F), 80
5. Bobby Brown (McLaren M8F), 79
6. Danny Hopkins (McLaren M8F), 79
7. Tom Dutton (McLaren M8E), 79
8. Jackie Oliver (Shadow DN2), 78
9. Gary Wilson (McLaren M8D), 78
10. Steve Durst (Porsche 917/10), 77
11. Bob Peckham (McLaren M8C), 77
12. Ed Felter (McLaren M8E), 77
13. Bob Nagel (Lola T260), 75
14. John Cordts (McLaren M8D), not running at finish, suspension, 73
15. Warren Agor (McLaren M8FP), 71
16. Tom Heyser (Lola T260), not running at finish, clutch, 65
17. Pete Sherman (McLaren M8F), 64

Retirements: 18-Scooter Patrick (McLaren M8F), gearbox, 56; 19-David Hobbs (McLaren M20), halfshaft, 49; 20-Jody Scheckter (Porsche 917/10K), spun/handling, 31; 21-David Saville-Peck (Costello SP7-Olds), oil pressure, 26; 22-Willi Kauhsen (Porsche 917/10K), gearbox, 9; 23-Hans Wiedmer (Porsche 917/10K), hit guardrail, 4.

Fastest Lap: Donohue, 1:22.804, 104.343 mph

5. Elkhart Lake 8/26/73

0 Scheckter Porsche 917/10K 2:00.799	6 Donohue Porsche 917/30KL 1:57.518, 122.534 mph
23 Kemp Porsche 917/10K 2:04.298	16 Follmer Porsche 917/10K 2:01.102
8 Patrick McLaren M8F 2:08.750	59 Haywood Porsche 917/10K 2:06.327
11 Bell McLaren M8F 2:10.919	97 Brown McLaren M8F 2:09.360
98 Hopkins McLaren M8F 2:12.609	11 Durst McLaren M8F 2:12.578
47 Felter McLaren M8E 2:13.765	2 Wilson McLaren M8E 2:13.615
101 Hunt Shadow DN2 2:14.190	34 Dutton McLaren M8E 2:13.851
64 Peckham McLaren M8C 2:15.266 (non-starter)	17 Nagel Lola T260 2:14.417
57 Causey McLaren M6A 2:17.807	14 Heyser Lola T260 2:15.715
13 Agor McLaren M8FP 2:19.871	41 Durant McLaren M8C 2:18.045
73 Hobbs McLaren M20 No Time (non-starter)	102 Oliver Shadow DN2 No Time
91 Sirois McLeagle No Time (non-starter)	9 Cordts McLaren M8D No Time (non-starter)
45 Saville-Peck Costello SP7 No Time (started race, not sprint)	74 Kampo Lola T222 No Time

As of this event, the two heats forming one Can-Am race are now two separate events, a heat and a race, each paying its own purse. Championship points are all awarded according to finishing positions in the race. The heat is known as the Can-Am Sprint, and the race is known as the Can-Am Cup.

Can-Am Sprint Results
1. Mark Donohue (Porsche 917/30KL), 25 laps or 100 miles
2. Jody Scheckter (Porsche 917/10K), 25 laps
3. George Follmer (Porsche 917/10K), 25
4. Hurley Haywood (Porsche 917/10K), 24
5. Charlie Kemp (Porsche 917/10K), 24
6. Scooter Patrick (McLaren M8F), 24
7. James Hunt (Shadow DN2), 24
8. Bobby Brown (McLaren M8F), 24
9. Bob Nagel (Lola T260), 24
10. Danny Hopkins (McLaren M8F), 23
11. Tom Dutton (McLaren M8E), 23
12. Tom Heyser (Lola T260), 23
13. Gary Wilson (McLaren M8E), 23
14. Warren Agor (McLaren M8FP), 23
15. Jigger Sirois (McLeagle), heat exhaust, 16
16. David Saville-Peck (Costello SP7-Olds), 15
17. Ed Felter (McLaren M8E), oil pressure, 13
18. Dick Durant (McLaren M8C), accident, 8
19. Derek Bell (McLaren M20), engine failure, 5
20. Steve Durst (McLaren M8F), oil pressure, 4
21. Jackie Oliver (Shadow DN2), engine failure, 3
22. Dave Causey (McLaren M6A), no clutch, 3
23. Dan Kampo (Lola T222), fuel pump, 2.

Can-Am Cup Results
1. Mark Donohue (Porsche 917/30KL), 25 laps of 4.0 mi. = 100 mi. in 52:37.2, 114.021 mph
2. Jody Scheckter (Porsche 917/ 10K), 25 laps
3. George Follmer (Porsche 917/10K), 25
4. Scooter Patrick (McLaren M8F), 24
5. Bobby Brown (McLaren M8F), 24
6. Bob Nagel (Lola T260), 23
7. Gary Wilson (McLaren M8E), 23
8. Warren Agor (McLaren M8FP), 23
9. Danny Hopkins (McLaren M8F), 22
10. Tom Heyser (Lola T260), 22
11. David Saville-Peck (Costello SP7-Olds), 21

Retirements: 12-Charlie Kemp (Porsche 917/10K), broken wheel, 20; 13-Jigger Sirois (McLeagle), flat tire, 10; 14-Hurley Haywood (Porsche 917/10K), blown tire, 9; 15-Tom Dutton (McLaren M8E), rear suspension, 7; 16-Ed Felter (McLaren M8E), engine, 0.

Did Not Start Cup: Steve Durst (McLaren M8F), Dick Durant (McLaren M8C), Derek Bell (McLaren M20), Dan Kampo (Lola T222), James Hunt (Shadow DN2), Jackie Oliver (Shadow DN2).

Fastest Lap: Donohue, 2:04.374, 115.780 mph

6. Edmonton 9/16/73

Grid for Can-Am Sprint 9/15/73

6 Donohue
Porsche 917/30KL
1:17.475, 117.421 mph

16 Follmer
Porsche 917/10K
1:18.327

0 Scheckter
Porsche 917/10K
1:20.418

23 Kemp
Porsche 917/10K
1:20.922

59 Haywood
Porsche 917/10K
1:21.469

73 Hobbs
McLaren M20
1:22.044

101 Oliver
Shadow DN2
1:22.080

39 Gunn
Lola T260
1:24.001

8 Patrick
McLaren M8F
1:24.950

97 Brown
McLaren M8F
1:25.937

98 Hopkins
McLaren M8F
1:26.541

9 Cordts
McLaren M8D
1:26.635

17 Nagel
Lola T260
1:27.213

34 Dutton
McLaren M8E
1:29.112

3 Durst
McLaren M8F
1:30.839

57 Shelton
Lola T162
1:34.238, 96.534 mph

45 Saville-Peck
Costello SP7 (non-starter)
No Time

Can-Am Sprint Results

1. Mark Donohue (Porsche 917/30KL), 30 laps
2. Jody Scheckter (Porsche 917/ 10K), 30
3. Jackie Oliver (Shadow DN2), 30
4. Charlie Kemp (Porsche 917/10K), 30
5. Steve Durst (McLaren M8F), 29
6. Bobby Brown (McLaren M8F), 29
7. Danny Hopkins (McLaren M8F), 28
8. John Gunn (Lola T260), 28
9. Tom Dutton (McLaren M8E), 24
10. Bob Nagel (Lola T260), 22
11. David Hobbs (McLaren M20), 19
12. Scooter Patrick (McLaren M8F), blown piston, 14
13. George Follmer (Porsche 917/10K), punctured tire, 9
14. John Cordts (McLaren M8D), 3
15. Hurley Haywood (Porsche 917/10K), crash, 2
Fastest lap: Follmer, 1:20.542, 112.950 mph

Can-Am Cup Results 9/16/73

1. Mark Donohue (Porsche 917/30KL), 50 laps of 2.527 mi. = 126.4 mi. in 1.09:22.746, 110.867 mph
2. George Follmer (Porsche 917/10K), 50 laps
3. Jackie Oliver (Shadow DN2), 48
4. David Hobbs (McLaren M20), 48
5. Steve Durst (McLaren M8F), 48
6. Scooter Patrick (McLaren M8F), 47
7. Bob Nagel (Lola T260), 47
8. Charlie Kemp (Porsche 917/10K), 45
Retirements: 9-John Cordts (McLaren M8D), blown engine, 35; 10-Tom Dutton (McLaren M8E), blown engine, 19; 11-Bobby Brown (McLaren M8F), blown engine, 18; 12-Jody Scheckter (Porsche 917/ 10K), blown engine, 11; 13-John Gunn (Lola T260), ring & pinion, 4; 14-David Saville-Peck (Costello SP7-Olds), broken oil pan, 2; 15-Danny Hopkins (McLaren M8F), accident, 1.

7. Laguna Seca 10/14/73

Grid for Sprint

6 Donohue
Porsche 917/30KL
:57.374, 119.217 mph

0 Scheckter
Porsche 917/10K
:59.404

---

16 Follmer
Porsche 917/10K
:59.478

3 Redman
Porsche 917/10K
:59.833

101 Oliver
Shadow DN2
1:00.932

59 Haywood
Porsche 917/10K
1:01.224

23 Kemp
Porsche 917/10K
1:01.811

98 Cannon
McLaren M8F
1:01.927

73 Hobbs
McLaren M20
1:02.625

8 Patrick
McLaren M8F
1:03.019

64 Peckham
McLaren M8C
1:03.027

39 Gunn
Lola T260
1:03.060

96 Andretti *
McLaren M20
1:03.303

3 Durst
McLaren M8F
1:03.433

33 Minter
Alfa Romeo T33/3
1:03.602

4 Cuddy
McLaren M8E
1:03.957

97 Brown
McLaren M8E
1:04.005

102 Elford
Shadow DN2
1:04.480

47 Felter
McLaren M8E
1:05.220

17 Nagel
Lola T260
1:05.368

45 Saville-Peck
Costello SP7
1:05.962

27 Settember
Lola T163
1:06.576

9 Cordts
McLaren M8D
1:08.906

34 Dutton
McLaren M8E
1:07.343

CanAm Cup Results

1. Mark Donohue (Porsche 917/30KL), 66 laps of 1.9 mi. = 125.04 mi. in 1.13:05.496, 102.190 mph
2. Jackie Oliver (Shadow DN2), 65 laps
3. Hurley Haywood (Porsche 917/10K), 65
4. Bobby Brown (McLaren M8F), 64
5. Milt Minter (Alfa Romeo T33/3), 64
6. Bob Nagel (Lola T260), 63
7. Bob Peckham (McLaren M8C), 63
8. Scooter Patrick (McLaren M8F), 62
9. David Hobbs (McLaren M20), 56
Retirements: 10-Steve Durst (McLaren M8F), brakes, 49; 11-George Follmer (Porsche 917/10K), turbocharger, 44; 12-Brian Redman (Porsche 917/10K), blown engine, 30; 13-Charlie Kemp (Porsche 917/10K), rear susp. arm, 27; 14-John Cordts (McLaren M8D), oil pressure, 26; 15-Vic Elford (Shadow DN2), brakes, 22; 16-Jody Scheckter (Porsche 917/10K), clutch, 11; 17-John Cannon (McLaren M20), accident, 3; 18-Bill Cuddy (McLaren M8E), accident, 2; 19-Tony Settember (Lola T163), engine, 2; 20-Ed Felter (McLaren M8E), accident, 2; 21-Tom Dutton (McLaren M8E), accident, 2; 22-David Saville-Peck (Costello SP7-Olds), accident, 2; 23-John Gunn (Lola T260), broken injector.
Fastest Lap: N/A

*John Cannon took over from Andretti for the final race. He finished 17th.

8. Riverside 10/28/73

Grid for Sprint

6 Donohue
Porsche 917/30KL
1:10.290, 130.089 mph

16 Follmer
Porsche 917/10K
1:11.600

0 Scheckter
Porsche 917/10K
1:11.809

3 Redman
Porsche 917/10K
1:13.706

---

73 Hobbs
McLaren M20
1:13.868

59 Haywood
Porsche 917/10K
1:14.097

23 Kemp
Porsche 917/10K
1:15.022

96 Andretti *
McLaren M20
1:15.191

101 Oliver
Shadow DN2
1:15.336

98 Cannon
McLaren M8F
1:15.393
(car non-starter)

8 Patrick
McLaren M8F
1:16.700

17 Nagel
Lola T260
1:17.099

97 Brown
McLaren M8F
1:17.352

102 Elford
Shadow DN2
1:17.651

13 Posey
Ferrari 512M
1:17.800

9 Cordts
McLaren M8D
1:17.900

33 Minter
Alfa Romeo T33/3
1:18.126

64 Peckham
McLaren M8C
1:18.178

39 Gunn
Lola T260
1:18.189 (non-starter)

11 Durst
McLaren M8F
1:18.231

30 Kahlich
McLaren M8F
1:18.461

34 Dutton
McLaren M8E
1:19.842

22 Muller-Perschl
Porsche SP20
1:34.781

2 Wilson
McLaren M8F
1:55.100, 96.151 mph
(non-starter)

CanAm Cup Results

1. Mark Donohue (Porsche 917/30KL), 49 laps of 2.54 mi. = 124.46 mi. in 1.02:04.182, 120.311 mph
2. Hurley Haywood (Porsche 917/10K), 49 laps
3. Charlie Kemp (Porsche 917/10K), 48
4. Bob Nagel (Lola T260), 47
5. Milt Minter (Alfa Romeo T33/3), 46
6. Bob Peckham (McLaren M8C), 46
7. Tom Dutton (McLaren M8E), 45
8. Steve Durst (McLaren M8F), not running at finish, piston, 44
9. Hanns Muller-Perschl (Porsche SP20), 41
Retirements: 10-Scooter Patrick (McLaren M8F), transmission, 34; 11-Brian Redman (Porsche 917/10K), suspension, 31; 12-Frank Kahlich (McLaren M8F), head gasket, 31; 13-Jody Scheckter (Porsche 917/10K), body loose, 17; 14-John Cordts (McLaren M8D), head gasket, 14; 15-John Cannon (McLaren M20), oil pressure, 12; 16-Sam Posey (Ferrari 512M), electrical, 12; 17-Jackie Oliver (Shadow DN2), body damage, 3; 18-David Hobbs (McLaren M20), overheating, 3; 19-Bobby Brown (McLaren M8F), broken wheel, 2; 20-George Follmer (Porsche 917/10K), accident-body, 1; 21-Vic Elford (Shadow DN2), throttle linkage, 1.
Fastest Lap: N/A

*John Cannon took over from Andretti for the final race. He finished 15th.

Final Point Standings 1973

1. Mark Donohue 139
2. George Follmer 62
3. Hurley Haywood 47
4. Charlie Kemp 45
5. Bob Nagel 44
6. Jody Scheckter 39
7. David Hobbs 37
8. Scooter Patrick 31
9. Jackie Oliver 30
10. Steve Durst 29
11. Bobby Brown 26
12. Milt Minter 16

---

13. Hans Wiedmer * 15
14. Tom Dutton 15
15. John Cannon 14
16. Derek Bell * 10
17. Robert Peckham 10
18. Danny Hopkins 8
19. Tom Heyser 7
20. Gary Wilson 6
21. Ed Felter * 4
22. John Cordts 4
23. Warren Agor * 3
24. Peter Sherman 3
25. Peter Gregg * 2
26. Hanns Muller-Perschl 2

*Ties for position resolved by driver's finishing record throughout the season.

1974

1. Mosport 6/16/74 *

1 Follmer
Shadow DN4
1:15.1

101 Oliver
Shadow DN4
1:14.5, 118.82 mph

6 Cordts
McLaren M8F
1:18.6

8 Patrick
McLaren M20
1:17.8

17 Nagel
Lola T260
1:20.8

11 Motschenbacher
McLaren M8F
1:20.0

12 Lazier
McLaren M8E
1:21.3 (non-starter)

7 Wietzes
Ferrari 512M
1:21.2

5 Durant
McLaren M8R
1:27.2

39 Gunn
Lola T260
1:25.4

41 Butcher
McLaren M8C
1:28.4

18 Fisher
Lola T222
1:28.2

9 Overhauser
McLaren M8D
1:29.5

139 Bytzek
Porsche 908
1:29.5

45 Saville-Peck
Costello SP8
1:31.3

77 Klempel
Lola T163
1:29.8

14 Forbes-Robinson
McLaren M8C
No Time

98 Butz
McLaren M8F
1:32.9, 95.29 mph

Did Not Start: 6 Janke (McLaren M8D), fire

Results

1. Jackie Oliver (Shadow DN4), 50 laps of 2.46 mi. = 122.95 mi. in 1:05.52.2, 112.00 mph
2. George Follmer (Shadow DN4), 50 laps
3. Scooter Patrick (McLaren M20), 49
4. Bob Nagel (Lola T260), 48
5. Lothar Motschenbacher (McLaren M8F), 48
6. Gene Fisher (Lola T222), 44
7. Dick Durant (McLaren M8R), 44
8. Harry Bytzek (Porsche 908), 43
9. David O. Saville-Peck (Costello SP8-Olds), 43
10. Tom Butz (McLaren M8F), 42
11. Eppie Wietzes (Ferrari 512M), not running at finish, fuel feed, 41
12. Bill Overhauser (McLaren M8D), 38
13. Bob Klempel (Lola T163), 35
14. Jim Butcher (McLaren M8C), 32
Retirements: 15-John Gunn (Lola T260), blown engine, 24; 16-Bob Lazier (McLaren M8E), spark shortage, 14; 17-Elliott Forbes-Robinson (McLaren M8C), burned valve, 13; 18-John Cordts (McLaren M8F), fuel injection malfunction, 1.
Fastest Lap: Follmer, 1:14.6, 118.66 mph (record)

*As in 1973, the 1974 events were run as two races, a sprint race followed by a feature event. Shown here are the grids for the sprints, while results are for the final races.

2. Road Atlanta 7/7/74

101 Oliver	1 Follmer
Shadow DN4	Shadow DN4
1:16.0	1:14.9, 121.27 mph
6 Cordts	8 Patrick
McLaren M8F	McLaren M8F
1:19.4	1:18.0 (non-starter)
17 Nagel	7 Mueller
Lola T260	Ferrari 512M
1:22.8	1:19.4
16 Aase	5 Durant
Porsche 908	McLaren M8R
1:26.7	1:25.9
45 Saville-Peck	12 Lazier
Costello SP8	McLaren M8E
1:29.2	1:27.3
14 Mull	77 Klempel
McLaren M8C	Lola T163
1:36.6	1:31.2
41 Butcher +	55 McNay
McLaren M8C	McLaren M12
1:38.9	1:38.3
75 Janke	9 Overhauser
McLaren M8D	McLaren M8D
No Time	1:40.1, 90.74 mph
11 Motschenbacher	10 Morrow
McLaren M8F	Lola T163
No Time	No Time
39 Gunn	3 Cuddy
Lola T260	McLaren M8F
No Time	No Time (non-starter)

Results
1. Jackie Oliver (Shadow DN4), 44 laps of 2.52 mi. = 110.88 mi. in :57:7.8, 116.90 mph
2. George Follmer (Shadow DN4), 44 laps
3. Lothar Motschenbacher (McLaren M8F), 42
4. Herbert Mueller (Ferrari 512M), 42
5. John Gunn (Lola T260), 41
6. Dick Durant (McLaren M8R), 39
7. Dennis Aase (Porsche 908), 39
8. David O. Saville-Peck (Costello SP8-Olds), 38
9. Mike Brockman (McLaren M8C), 38 +

Retirements: 10-William Morrow (Lola T163), engine, 24; 11-Bill Overhauser (McLaren M8D), overheating, 18; 12-Bob Nagel (Lola T260), accident, 13; 13-Bob Lazier (McLaren M8E), fuel injection, 12; 14-Leonard Janke (McLaren M8D), oil pressure, 9; 15-Bob Klempel (Lola T163), gear shift linkage, 6; 16-John Cordts (McLaren M8F), oil pressure, 4; 17-Jerry Mull (McLaren M8C), oil pressure, 2.

Fastest Lap: Oliver, 1:16.1, 119.35 mph

+ Butcher qualified the car, but did not race it. The car was raced by Mike Brockman, who placed tenth in the sprint race and ninth overall after the feature race.

3. Watkins Glen 7/14/74

101 Oliver	1 Follmer
Shadow DN4	Shadow DN4
1:41.223	1:39.969, 121.61 mph
6 Cordts #	8 Patrick
McLaren M8F	McLaren M20
1:45.779	1:42.520
7 Mueller #	11 Motschenbacher #
Ferrari 512M	McLaren M8F
1:48.207	Time Unknown
33 Minter *	39 Gunn
Alfa Romeo T33/4	Lola T260
1:49.115	1:47.977
5 Durant	41 Brockman
McLaren M8R	McLaren M8C
1:54.578	1:52.732
45 Saville-Peck	3 Cuddy
Costello SP8	McLaren M8F
1:56.806	1:54.794
18 Fisher	72 Jones
Lola T222	McLaren M1C
No Time	1:59.522, 101.72 mph
38 Peterman	16 Aase
Porsche 908	Porsche 908
No Time	No Time
17 Nagel	14 Hill
Lola T260	McLaren M8C
No Time	No Time
	10 Redman
	Ferrari 712M
	No Time

Results
1. Jackie Oliver (Shadow DN4), 33 laps of 3.377 mi. = 111.441 mi. in :57:15.448, 116.78 mph
2. George Follmer (Shadow DN4), 33 laps
3. Scooter Patrick (McLaren M20), 32
4. Bob Nagel (Lola T260), 31
5. Dick Durant (McLaren M8R), 29
6. Dennis Aase (Porsche 908), 29
7. Horst Peterman (Porsche 908), 29
8. Arturo Merzario (Alfa Romeo T33/4), 26 +
9. John Gunn (Lola T260), not running at finish, blown engine, 25
10. Bill Cuddy (McLaren M8F), not running at finish, engine, 20

Retirements: 11-Brian Redman (Ferrari 712M), rear suspension broke, off course, 14; 12-Jerry Mull (McLaren M8C), running at finish, 11; 13-Gene Fisher (Lola T222), engine failure, 3; 14-Mike Brockman (McLaren M8C), burned piston, 3; 15-David O. Saville-Peck (Costello SP8-Olds), off course, 1; 16-Jeff Jones (McLaren M1C), blown engine, 1; 17-Milt Minter (Alfa Romeo T33/4), accident, 0.

Fastest Lap: Oliver, 1:16.1, 119.35 mph

Started the sprint, but not the final.

* Minter qualified for the grid of the sprint, but did not start it. He started the feature event from the back of that grid.

+ Merzario did not start the sprint race, but did start the feature.

4. Mid-Ohio 8/11/74

66 Redman	1 Follmer
Porsche 917/30KL	Shadow DN4
1:21.093, 106.544 mph	1:22.285
101 Oliver	59 Haywood
Shadow DN4	Porsche 917/10
1:22.772	1:24.068
8 Patrick	6 Cordts
McLaren M20	McLaren M8F
1:24.451	1:26.124
17 Nagel	39 Gunn
Lola T260	Lola T260
1:27.160	1:28.482
11 Motschenbacher	7 Mueller
McLaren M8F	Ferrari 512M
1:28.893	1:28.918
57 Shelton	41 Brockman
McLaren M8F	McLaren M8C
1:29.183	1:29.678
2 Wilson	5 Durant
Sting GW1	McLaren M8R
1:29.744	1:31.124 (non-starter)
12 Lazier	3 Cuddy
McLaren M12	McLaren M8F
1:31.474	1:32.666
9 Woods	16 Aase
McLaren M8D	Porsche 908
1:33.427	1:34.065

5. Elkhart Lake 8/25/74

101 Oliver	1 Follmer
Shadow DN4	Shadow DN4
2:02.594	2:01.460, 118.558 mph
6 Cordts	8 Patrick
McLaren M8F	McLaren M20
2:08.449	2:06.168
59 Haywood	39 Gunn
Porsche 917/10K	Lola T260
2:09.021	2:08.666
41 Brockman	11 Motschenbacher
McLaren M8C	McLaren M8F
2:11.421	2:10.065
17 Nagel	7 Mueller
Lola T260	Ferrari 512M
2:13.694	2:13.033
57 Shelton	2 Wilson
McLaren M8F	Sting GW1
2:14.446	2:14.292
18 Fisher	5 Durant
Lola T222	McLaren M8R
2:18.224	2:17.676
45 Saville-Peck	59 Al Holbert +
Costello SP8	McLaren
2:20.276	2:18.569
25 Helferich	14 Mull
	McLaren M8C
2:20.624 (non-starter)	2:20.408
3 Cuddy	75 Janke
McLaren M8F	McLaren M8F
2:21.395	2:21.350
77 Klempel	9 Overhauser
Lola T163	McLaren M8D
2:22.792	2:21.733
95 Fairbanks	16 Aase
Lola T70	Porsche 908/2
2:26.793	2:25.557

18 Fisher	72 Jones
Lola T222	McLaren M1C
1:35.239	1:36.848
51 Lockhart	31 Bartlebaugh
McLaren M8F	McLaren M1C
1:39.192	1:39.74, 86.621 mph
45 Saville-Peck	
Costello SP8	
No Time	

Results
1. Jackie Oliver (Shadow DN4), 47 laps of 2.4 mi. = 112.8 mi. in 1.06:17.356, 102.085 mph
2. Brian Redman (Porsche 917/30KL), 47 laps
3. Hurley Haywood (Porsche 917/10), 46
4. Bob Nagel (Lola T260), 44
5. Monte Shelton (McLaren M8F), 44
6. Roy Woods (McLaren M8D), 42
7. Dennis Aase (Porsche 908), 40
8. Bob Lazier (McLaren M8C), 38
9. David O. Saville-Peck (Costello SP8-Olds), 38
10. John Gunn (Lola T260), not running at finish, flat tire, 32
11. Scooter Patrick (McLaren M20), 30

Retirements: 12-Mike Brockman (McLaren M8C), spun, 28; 13-George Follmer (Shadow DN4), driver quit, 27; 14-Bill Cuddy (McLaren M8F), valve, 20; 15-Jeff Jones (McLaren M1C), broken hub, 19; 16-Jim Lockhart (McLaren M8F), transaxle, 14; 17-John Cordts (McLaren M8F), clutch, 11; 18-Herbert Mueller (Ferrari 512M), engine, 11; 19-Gene Fisher (Lola T222), gearbox, 4; 20-Charles Bartlebaugh (McLaren M1C), tires, 4; 21-Lothar Motschenbacher (McLaren M8F), electrical, 2.

Fastest Lap: Follmer, 1:22.470, 104.765 mph (record)

Bartlebaugh +	McNay +
Lola	McLaren M12
2:30.761	2:28.304
Lockhart +	Morrow +
McLaren	McLaren
2:33.230, 95.52 mph	2:31.543
	12 Forbes-Robinson *
	McLaren M8E
	2:13.152

* Car #12 qualified 10th fastest, row 5, by Bob Lazier who broke his ankle in a preliminary race (Super Vee Gold Cup) on Sunday morning. Forbes-Robinson stepped in and started the car from the back of the grid.

+ Presumed non-starter since did not appear on results of sprint race.

Results
1. Scooter Patrick (McLaren M20), 28 laps of 4.0 mi. = 112 mi. in 1:01.14, 109.344 mph
2. John Cordts (McLaren M8F), 28
3. John Gunn (Lola T260), 28
4. Bob Nagel (Lola T260), 27
5. Gary Wilson (Sting GW1), 27
6. Herbert Mueller (Ferrari 512M), 27
7. Bill Cuddy (McLaren M8F), 25
8. Dennis Aase (Porsche 908/2), 25
9. Jackie Oliver (Shadow DN4), not running at finish, blown engine, 23
10. Lothar Motschenbacher (McLaren M8F), not running at finish, water pump, 23
11. Howie Fairbanks (Lola T70), 23
12. Bob Klempel (Lola T163), not running at finish, engine failure, 21
13. David O. Saville-Peck (Costello SP8-Olds), not running at finish, engine failure, 20
14. Dick Durant (McLaren M8R), 20
15. Hurley Haywood (Porsche 917/10K), not running at finish, body damage, 18
16. Bill Overhauser (McLaren M8D), not running at finish, gear box, 18
17. Monte Shelton (McLaren M8F), 11

Retirements: 18-Leonard Janke (McLaren M8F), manifold, 10; 19-Jerry Mull (McLaren M8C), spun, 2; 20-Elliott Forbes-Robinson (McLaren M8E), rear end, 1; 21-George Follmer (Shadow DN4), half shaft, 0; 22-Gene Fisher (Lola T222), gearbox, 0; 23-Mike Brockman (McLaren M8C), engine failure, 0

Fastest Lap: Oliver, 2:07.698, 112.766 mph
In sprint: Oliver, 2:04.894, 115.298 mph

Final Point Standings 1974

Drivers' Time Line
Points Scored By Year, Listed Top to Bottom, Most Points to Least

(☐ means championship year)

Driver/Year	66	67	68	69	70	71	72	73	74	TOT
Denny Hulme		27	[35]	160	[132]	132	65			551
Peter Revson	4	3	3	22	39	[142]	48			261
Mark Donohue	21	16	23				62	[139]		261
George Follmer	4	10	6			2	[130]	62	45	259
Bruce McLaren	20	[30]	24	[165]						239
Motschenbacher	2	2	11	35	65	52	26		21	214
Jackie Oliver					45	12	37	30	[82]	206
Chuck Parsons	6	1	5	81	19	30	3			145
Jo Siffert				56	15	68				139
Milt Minter						37	65	16		118
Bob Nagel					1	1	11	44	40	97
Scooter Patrick							8	31	44	83
Chris Amon	10	2		39	28					79
Tony Dean				31	44		2			77
David Hobbs				1			39	37		77
Jackie Stewart						76				76
Charlie Kemp						3	27	45		75
Dan Gurney	9		1	22	42					74
John Surtees	[27]	16		30						73
Bob Brown					35	9		26		70
Dave Causey				6	49	14				69
George Eaton			4	50	12					66
John Cordts				24		14	8	4	15	65
Gary Wilson				7	27	4	10	6	8	62
Francois Cevert							59			59
Hurley Haywood								47	12	59
Peter Gethin					56					56
Roger McCaig				3	34	10	2			49
Tony Adamowicz					8	34				42
Vic Elford					16	25				41
Mario Andretti				22	8	10				40
Jim Hall	12	15	12							39
Jody Scheckter								39		39
Dick Durant						12	7		18	37
Peter Gregg					1		34	2		37
Tom Dutton				9		12		15		36
Pedro Rodriguez				9	26					35
Gregg Young						12	23			35
Steve Durst							4	29		33
Sam Posey		5				16	8			29
Brian Redman				4	10				15	29
John Cannon	4		10						14	28
Herbert Mueller						11			16	27
Bob Bondurant				15	10					25
Oscar Koveleski			7	16						23
John Gunn								23		23
Jim Adams				14	7					21
Hiroshi Kazato				19						19
Phil Hill	18									18
Hans Wiedmer							3	15		18
Dennis Aase									17	17
Dick Brown		2	13							15
Gordon Dewar				6		7				13
Jack Brabham				12						12
Andrea de Adamich			8		4					12
Richard Attwood				12						12
Howden Ganley					12					12
Tom Heyser							5	7		12
Leonard Janke			9	2						11
Jean-Pierre Jarier						11				11
Robert Peckham								10	1	11
Mike Spence		10								10
Carlos Pace							10			10
Derek Bell								10		10
Jacques Couture			8							8
Kris Harrison			8							8
Gijs van Lennep				6	2					8
Ed Felter							4	4		8
Danny Hopkins								8		8
Monte Shelton									8	8
Warren Agor							4	3		7
David Saville-Peck								7		7
Fred Baker			6							6
Graeme Lawrence				6						6
Gene Fisher									6	6
Roy Woods									6	6

Driver/Year	66	67	68	69	70	71	72	73	74	TOT
Jerry Titus	1		5							6
Bud Morely		5								5
Rich Galloway				5						5
Steve Matchett						5				5
Bill Cuddy									5	5
George Drolsom					1	4				5
Pete Sherman							2	3		5
Graham Hill	4									4
Jo Bonnier			4							4
Mike Hiss							4			4
Horst Petermann									4	4
Charlie Hayes		3	1							4
Brooke Doran					2	2				4
Earl Jones	3									3
Parnelli Jones		3								3
Swede Savage			3							3
Joe Leonard					3					3
Johnny Servoz-Gavin					3					3
Willi Kauhsen							3			3
Harry Bytzek									3	3
Arturo Merzario									3	3
Bob Lazier									3	3
Masten Gregory	2									2
Paul Hawkins	2									2
Skip Scott		2								2
Hanns Muller-Perschl									2	2
Mike Brockman									2	2
Eppie Wietzes	1									1
Bill Eve		1								1
Jerry Hansen		1								1
Rick Muther		1								1
Spence Stoddard					1					1
Clif Apel						1				1
Ranier Brezinka						1				1
Gerard Larrousse						1				1
Chuck Frederick						1				1
Ron Goldleaf						1				1
Jim Butcher							1			1
Tom Butz									1	1
William Morrow									1	1

Can-Am Winners at a Glance

Year	Track	Winner	Marque	Model	Engine
1966	St. Jovite	Surtees	Lola	T70	Chevrolet SB
1966	Bridgehampton	Gurney	Lola	T70	Ford SB
1966	Mosport	Donohue	Lola	T70	Chevrolet SB
1966	Laguna Seca	P. Hill	Chaparral	2E	Chevrolet SBA
1966	Riverside	Surtees	Lola	T70	Chevrolet SB
1966	Las Vegas	Surtees	Lola	T70	Chevrolet SB
1967	Elkhart Lake	Hulme	McLaren	M6A	Chevrolet SB
1967	Bridgehampton	Hulme	McLaren	M6A	Chevrolet SB
1967	Mosport	Hulme	McLaren	M6A	Chevrolet SB
1967	Laguna Seca	McLaren	McLaren	M6A	Chevrolet SB
1967	Riverside	McLaren	McLaren	M6A	Chevrolet SB
1967	Las Vegas	Surtees	Lola	T70	Chevrolet SB
1968	Elkhart Lake	Hulme	McLaren	M8A	Chevrolet BBA
1968	Bridgehampton	Donohue	McLaren	M6B	Chevrolet BBA
1968	Edmonton	Hulme	McLaren	M8A	Chevrolet BBA
1968	Laguna Seca	Cannon	McLaren	M1B	Chevrolet SB
1968	Riverside	McLaren	McLaren	M8A	Chevrolet BBA
1968	Las Vegas	Hulme	McLaren	M8A	Chevrolet BBA
1969	Mosport	McLaren	McLaren	M8B	Chevrolet BBA
1969	St. Jovite	Hulme	McLaren	M8B	Chevrolet BBA
1969	Watkins Glen	McLaren	McLaren	M8B	Chevrolet BBA
1969	Edmonton	Hulme	McLaren	M8B	Chevrolet BBA
1969	Mid-Ohio	Hulme	McLaren	M8B	Chevrolet BBA
1969	Elkhart Lake	McLaren	McLaren	M8B	Chevrolet BBA
1969	Bridgehampton	Hulme	McLaren	M8B	Chevrolet BBA
1969	Michigan	McLaren	McLaren	M8B	Chevrolet BBA
1969	Laguna Seca	McLaren	McLaren	M8B	Chevrolet BBA
1969	Riverside	Hulme	McLaren	M8B	Chevrolet BBA
1969	Texas	McLaren	McLaren	M8B	Chevrolet BBA
1970	Mosport	Gurney	McLaren	M8D	Chevrolet BBA
1970	St. Jovite	Gurney	McLaren	M8D	Chevrolet BBA
1970	Watkins Glen	Hulme	McLaren	M8D	Chevrolet BBA
1970	Edmonton	Hulme	McLaren	M8D	Chevrolet BBA
1970	Mid-Ohio	Hulme	McLaren	M8D	Chevrolet BBA
1970	Elkhart Lake	Gethin	McLaren	M8D	Chevrolet BBA
1970	Road Atlanta	Dean	Porsche	908	Porsche 8
1970	Donnybrooke	Hulme	McLaren	M8D	Chevrolet BBA
1970	Laguna Seca	Hulme	McLaren	M8D	Chevrolet BBA
1970	Riverside	Hulme	McLaren	M8D	Chevrolet BBA
1971	Mosport	Hulme	McLaren	M8F	Chevrolet BBA
1971	St. Jovite	Stewart	Lola	T260	Chevrolet BBA
1971	Road Atlanta	Revson	McLaren	M8F	Chevrolet BBA
1971	Watkins Glen	Revson	McLaren	M8F	Chevrolet BBA
1971	Mid-Ohio	Stewart	Lola	T260	Chevrolet BBA
1971	Elkhart Lake	Revson	McLaren	M8F	Chevrolet BBA
1971	Donnybrooke	Revson	McLaren	M8F	Chevrolet BBA
1971	Edmonton	Hulme	McLaren	M8F	Chevrolet BBA
1971	Laguna Seca	Revson	McLaren	M8F	Chevrolet BBA
1971	Riverside	Hulme	McLaren	M8F	Chevrolet BBA
1972	Mosport	Hulme	McLaren	M20	Chevrolet BBA
1972	Road Atlanta	Follmer	Porsche	917/10K	Porsche 12T
1972	Watkins Glen	Hulme	McLaren	M20	Chevrolet BBA
1972	Mid-Ohio	Follmer	Porsche	917/10K	Porsche 12T
1972	Elkhart Lake	Follmer	Porsche	917/10K	Porsche 12T
1972	Donnybrooke	Cevert	McLaren	M8F	Chevrolet BBA
1972	Edmonton	Donohue	Porsche	917/10K	Porsche 12T
1972	Laguna Seca	Follmer	Porsche	917/10K	Porsche 12T
1972	Riverside	Follmer	Porsche	917/10K	Porsche 12T
1973	Mosport	Kemp	Porsche	917/10K	Porsche 12T
1973	Road Atlanta	Follmer	Porsche	917/10K	Porsche 12T
1973	Watkins Glen	Donohue	Porsche	917/30	Porsche 12T
1973	Mid-Ohio	Donohue	Porsche	917/30	Porsche 12T
1973	Elkhart Lake	Donohue	Porsche	917/30	Porsche 12T
1973	Edmonton	Donohue	Porsche	917/30	Porsche 12T
1973	Laguna Seca	Donohue	Porsche	917/30	Porsche 12T
1973	Riverside	Donohue	Porsche	917/30	Porsche 12T
1974	Mosport	Oliver	Shadow	DN4	Chevrolet BBA
1974	Road Atlanta	Oliver	Shadow	DN4	Chevrolet BBA
1974	Watkins Glen	Oliver	Shadow	DN4	Chevrolet BBA
1974	Mid-Ohio	Oliver	Shadow	DN4	Chevrolet BBA
1974	Elkhart Lake	Patrick	McLaren	M20	Chevrolet BBA

Engine Legend: SB = Small Block, BB = Big Block, A = Aluminum, T = Turbocharged